HANDBOOK OF PREVENTIVE INTERVENTIONS FOR CHILDREN AND ADOLESCENTS

HANDBOOK OF PREVENTIVE INTERVENTIONS FOR CHILDREN AND ADOLESCENTS

Lisa A. Rapp-Paglicci

Catherine N. Dulmus

John S. Wodarski

WILEY

John Wiley & Sons, Inc.

This book is printed on acid-free paper. ∞

Library of Congress Cataloging-in-Publication Data:

Handbook of preventive interventions for children and adolescents / Lisa A. Rapp-Paglicci,
   Catherine N. Dulmus, and John S. Wodarski.
      p.   cm.
   ISBN 0-471-27433-X (cloth)
   1. Child health services—Handbooks, manuals, etc.   2. Child mental health
services—Handbooks, manuals, etc.   3. Teenagers—Medical care—Handbooks, manuals, etc.
4. Medicine, Preventive—Handbooks, manuals, etc.   5. Preventive health
services—Handbooks, manuals, etc.   6. Social work with children—Handbooks, manuals,
etc.   7. Social work with teenagers—Handbooks, manuals, etc.   I. Title: Preventive
interventions for children and adolescents.   II. Rapp-Paglicci, Lisa A.   III. Dulmus,
Catherine N.   IV. Wodarski, John S.
   RJ101.H16 2004
   362.198′92—dc22   2003059502

Printed in the United States of America.

10 9 8 7 6 5 4 3 2 1

Contents —————————————————————

Part III   Preventive Interventions for Children's and Adolescents' Health Problems

Part IV   Preventive Interventions for Children's and Adolescents' Social Problems

Part V   Conclusion

Preface ────────────────────────────────────

Children's and adolescents' emotional, health, and social problems have become pervasive in our society and often have devastating effects on children, families, and communities. For example, more than 80% of American youth experiment with drugs before graduating from high school, 11% to 80% of adolescent females report at least one symptom of an eating disorder, close to 581,000 children are currently in foster care, approximately 50,000 babies are born with some degree of alcohol-related birth defects each year, and 12.9% of children have a reported mental or emotional problem. These problems have long-term ramifications for juveniles and cost the United States billions of dollars each year.

Consequently, preventive interventions have begun to be developed to prevent serious problems in youth. Such problems encompass emotional, health, and social problems and, specifically, can include unresolved grief, aggression, school failure, birth defects, obesity, teenage pregnancy, dating violence, and foster care failure, to name just a few. These preventive interventions have shown promise in deterring problems.

Despite these advances in research and the devastating effects of social problems, very few books are devoted solely to prevention, and no prevention books thoroughly cover the various types of preventive interventions available for children and adolescent problems until now. The intent of this book is to provide the most effective and current preventive interventions and programs available on child and adolescent emotional, health, and social problems. Each chapter provides an introduction summary of the problem; trends; incidence; risk factors; interventions available on a universal, selective, and indicated level; and future directions.

As this handbook indicates, in many instances it is no longer necessary for youth, families, and communities to endure an array of physical, emotional, and social problems because we now have the ability to prevent many. Policymakers, administrators, and practitioners must increase their awareness of effective preventive interventions for children and adolescents and make available these tactics instead of waiting for problems to occur.

LISA A. RAPP-PAGLICCI
CATHERINE N. DULMUS
JOHN S. WODARSKI

Acknowledgments ———————————————

We thank all of the expert contributors for their hard work and enthusiasm in providing us with outstanding chapters. We also acknowledge the diligence and support from Peggy, Tracey, and Isabel at Wiley and Sons.

Finally, we thank our families for their patience and endurance of the many long hours spent in preparing this book. Thank you, David, Emily, Guy, Josh, Abby, and Lois Ann.

L. A. R-P.
C. N. D
J. S. W.

About the Editors

Lisa A. Rapp-Paglicci, PhD, MSW, is an associate professor at the University of South Florida, Lakeland, School of Social Work. Her research focuses on juvenile violence, prevention, and at-risk youth. Dr. Rapp-Paglicci serves on the editorial boards of the *Journal of Human Behavior in the Social Environment* and *Journal of Evidence-Based Social Work: Advances in Practice, Programming, Research and Policy.* She received the 1999/2000 Outstanding Teaching Award from the Greenspun College of Urban Affairs.

Catherine N. Dulmus, PhD, ACSW, is an assistant professor in the College of Social Work at the University of Tennessee. Her research focuses on child mental health, prevention, and violence. Dr. Dulmus is founding coeditor of *Journal of Evidence-Based Social Work Practice: Advances in Practice, Programming, Research and Policy* and associate editor of *Stress, Trauma, and Crisis: An International Journal.* In 2002, she was awarded an excellence in teaching citation from the University of Tennessee. Before obtaining the PhD, her social work practice background encompassed almost a decade of experience in the fields of mental health and school social work.

John S. Wodarski, PhD, MSSW, is the director of research at the University of Tennessee College of Social Work. Dr. Wodarski is the founding coeditor of *Journal of Human Behavior in the Social Environment* and *Journal of Evidence-Based Social Work,* as well as editor of *Stress, Trauma, and Crisis: An International Journal.* He has written more than 400 published articles; authored, edited, or coedited more than 38 books; and contributed to more than 300 professional publications.

Contributors

Rebecca K. Andrews
Arizona State University
Department of Psychology
Tempe, Arizona

Lisa Armistead, PhD
Georgia State University
Department of Psychology
Atlanta, Georgia

Gary L. Bowen, ACSW, PhD
University of North Carolina–
    Chapel Hill
School of Social Work
Chapel Hill, North Carolina

Natasha K. Bowen, MSW, PhD
University of North Carolina–
    Chapel Hill
School of Social Work
Chapel Hill, North Carolina

Kathleen H. Darby, MSSW
University of Tennessee
College of Social Work
Knoxville, Tennessee

Beth Doll, PhD
University of Nebraska–Lincoln
School Psychology Program
Lincoln, Nebraska

Catherine N. Dulmus, PhD, ACSW
University of Tennessee–Knoxville
College of Social Work
Knoxville, Tennessee

Adrienne Ekas, MSW
University of Nevada, Las Vegas
School of Social Work
Las Vegas, Nevada

John P. Elder, MPH, PhD
San Diego State University
Graduate School of Public Health
San Diego, California

Rodney A. Ellis, PhD, MSW
University of Tennessee
College of Social Work
Nashville, Tennessee

Gretchen E. Ely, MSW, PhD
University of Tennessee–Chattanooga
Department of Social Work
College of Education and Applied
    Professional Services
Chattanooga, Tennessee

Rex Forehand, PhD
University of Vermont
Department of Psychology
Burlington, Vermont

Mark W. Fraser, MSW, PhD
University of North Carolina–
   Chapel Hill
School of Social Work
Chapel Hill, North Carolina

Sarah L. Herald
Arizona State University
Department of Psychology
Tempe, Arizona

Robyn Hess, PhD
University of Northern Colorado
Division of Professional Psychology
Greeley, Colorado

Carolyn Hilarski, ACSW, CSW, PhD
Rochester Institute of Technology
Social Work Department
Rochester, New York

Esmeralda M. Iniguez, MPH
San Diego State University
Graduate School of Public Health
San Diego, California

Dorota Iwaniec, MA, PhD
Queen's University of Belfast
Institute of Childcare Research
Northern Ireland, United Kingdom

Debra Keelean, MS, CGC
East Carolina University
Brody School of Medicine
Greenville, North Carolina

Susan Klein-Rothschild, MSW
Clark County Family Services Department
Las Vegas, Nevada

Beth A. Kotchick, PhD
Loyola College–Maryland
Baltimore, Maryland

Gary W. Ladd, EdD
Arizona State University
Department of Psychology and
   Department of Family and Human
   Development
Tempe, Arizona

Sandra Larios, BA
San Diego State University
Department of Psychology
San Diego, California

Craig Winston LeCroy, MSW, PhD
Arizona State University
School of Social Work
Tucson, Arizona

Joyce Elizabeth Mann, MA, MSW
Mirasol, Inc.
Tucson, Arizona

Andrea K. McCarter, MSSW
University of Tennessee
College of Social Work
Knoxville, Tennessee

Kaye McGinty, MD
Brody School of Medicine
Child and Adolescent Psychiatry
   Residency Program
Greenville, North Carolina

Gail McVey, PhD, C. Psych
Hospital for Sick Children and
   University of Toronto
Toronto, Ontario, Canada

John H. Pierpont, PhD
East Carolina University
School of Social Work & Criminal
   Justice Studies
Greenville, North Carolina

Joelle D. Powers, MSW
University of North Carolina–
   Chapel Hill
School of Social Work
Chapel Hill, North Carolina

Lisa A. Rapp-Paglicci, PhD, MSW
University of South Florida–Lakeland
School of Social Work
Lakeland, Florida

Dominique E. Roe-Sepowitz, MSW
Florida State University
School of Social Work
Tallahassee, Florida

Carly B. Slutzky
Arizona State University
Department of Family and Human
   Development
Tempe, Arizona

Helga Sneddon, C. Psychol., PhD
Institute of Childcare Research
Queen's University of Belfast
Northern Ireland, United Kingdom

Karen M. Sowers, PhD, MSW
University of Tennessee
College of Social Work
Knoxville, Tennessee

Barbara Thomlison, PhD
Florida International University
School of Social Work
Miami, Florida

Bruce A. Thyer, PhD, LCSW
Florida State University
School of Social Work
Tallahassee, Florida

John Wiley, PhD
East Carolina University
Brody School of Medicine
Greenville, North Carolina

Sheara A. Williams, MSW
University of North Carolina–
   Chapel Hill
School of Social Work
Chapel Hill, North Carolina

John S. Wodarski, PhD, MSSW
University of Tennessee–Knoxville
College of Social Work
Knoxville, Tennessee

Lois Ann Wodarski, PhD, RD
Knoxville, Tennessee

Michael E. Woolley, MSW, DCSW
University of North Carolina–
   Chapel Hill
School of Social Work
Chapel Hill, North Carolina

PART I

Introduction

Chapter 1

PREVENTION AND RESILIENCE

CATHERINE N. DULMUS AND LISA A. RAPP-PAGLICCI

Children and adolescents are being diagnosed earlier and more often with an array of serious and debilitating disorders ranging from mental illness to obesity and diabetes. Add to this teen pregnancy, substance abuse, and school violence, and it becomes clear that our youth are at risk for numerous emotional, health, and social problems.

The personal consequences of these problems can include developmental delays, school dropout, future unemployment and poverty, imprisonment, and even premature death. On a societal level, financial costs, loss of competent citizens, ineffective parents, and a future cycle of more problems may be the aftereffects of childhood and adolescent disorders and problems (Dulmus & Rapp-Paglicci, 2000).

The case can easily be made for a preventative approach to such disorders and problems that would be far more fruitful financially and personally than treating the problems once they occur. In the United States during the latter half of the twentieth century, the dominant approach to prevention was the public health model (Institute of Medicine, 1994). The original classification system of disease was proposed by the Commission on Chronic Illness (1957) and consisted of three types of prevention intervention: primary, secondary, and tertiary. The primary level seeks to prevent a disorder or problem. The secondary level addresses treatment of the disorder or problem once it occurs, and the tertiary level focuses on rehabilitation. This approach to prevention started out as an effort to prevent infectious disease. Because of its success, it was later extended for use with noninfectious diseases and physical illnesses (Institute of Medicine, 1994). The public health model of prevention, although a good beginning, does not focus all efforts on preventing a disorder or problem (Dulmus & Wodarski, 1997).

PREVENTION RECONSTRUCTION

The Institute of Medicine (1994) defines *prevention* as those interventions that occur before the initial onset of the disorder, with preventive research and interventions being limited to the processes that occur before there is a diagnosable disorder or problem. The treatment of such disorders is defined as *maintenance*. We support this approach because, unlike the public health model, this approach focuses on interventions to prevent the onset of a disorder or problem. Gordon's model addresses prevention from this perspective (Gordon, 1983, 1987). Its interventions are broken down into three areas: universal, selective, and indicated:

1. *Universal preventive interventions* are defined as interventions for disorders or problems that are targeted to the general public or a whole population group that has not been identified on the basis of individual risk.

2. *Selective preventive interventions* are interventions that are targeted to individuals or a subgroup of the population at high risk of developing a specific disorder or problem at some point in their lifetime.

3. *Indicated preventive interventions* are defined as interventions that are targeted to high-risk individuals who do not meet the specific criteria for a mental or medical disorder, but who otherwise are identified as having minimal but detectable signs or symptoms of a specific disorder or who have a biological marker indicating predisposition for the disorder (Institute of Medicine, 1994).

Thus, a risk reduction model to prevention complements Gordon's approach to prevention.

RISK REDUCTION MODEL

A risk reduction model is a promising approach to prevention, whereby risk factors are identified and matched to empirically tested interventions (Institute of Medicine, 1994). Risk factors are characteristics, variables, or hazards that, if present for a given individual, make it more likely that this individual, rather than someone selected from the general population, will develop a particular disorder (Werner & Smith, 1982). Risk groups could be identified on the basis of biological, psychological, or social risk factors that are known to be associated with the onset of a specific disorder. Once identified, individuals or subgroups of the population at risk for developing a particular disorder could be targeted with selective preventive interventions (Institute of Medicine, 1994).

It is likely that both biogenetic factors and social conditions jointly operate to heighten the risk status of children (Garmezy, 1993). The manifestations of problematic development in vulnerable children are as varied as the risk factors to which they are exposed (Hauser, Vieyra, Jacobson, & Wertlieb, 1985). Psychosocial development from early childhood through adolescence and into adulthood is shaped by myriad specific events, ongoing circumstances, and inherent strengths and vulnerabilities of the individual (Hauser et al., 1985). Certain events and circumstances are especially likely to adversely affect this development. Cowen and Work (1988, p. 591) state: "Negative psychological effects of multiple stressful life events and circumstances cumulate like lead poisoning." These situations vary widely, but if risk factors can be decreased or in some way altered and/or if protective factors can be enhanced, the likelihood of at-risk individuals eventually developing a specific disorder or problem would decrease (Dulmus & Rapp-Paglicci, 2000).

RESILIENT CHILDREN

Of interest to researchers are children who are exposed to risk factors associated with development of particular disorders, yet maintain their mental and/or physical health. These children are referred to in the literature as "resilient," "invulnerable," or "ego-resistant" children. *Resilience* is defined as "the tendency to rebound or recoil," "to return to a prior state," "to spring back," and "the power of recovery." Garmezy (1993) defines a *competence item* as one that measures successes and achievement in meeting the major adaptational expectations or requirements of people of the age of the subject. Rutter (1981, p. 323) defines *resilience* as a phenomenon, "as shown by the young people who 'do well' in some sense in spite of having experienced a form of 'stress', which in the population as a whole is known to carry a substantial risk of an adverse outcome."

Arnold (1990) reports that the way children respond to stress may either promote growth and a sense of efficacy or cause behavioral, social, academic, or psychosomatic problems. Children exposed to stress that increases the risk of an adverse outcome are said to be "vulnerable" to that outcome; therefore, their resilience is defined in terms of two concepts—vulnerability and competence: Children who are vulnerable to an adverse outcome yet achieve competence are "resilient." Cowen and Work (1988) state:

> Knowledge about the effects of multiple, chronic stressful life events and circumstances on children and in vivo factors that shield them against serious psychological problems are key building blocks that undergird efforts to understand

the nature and determinants of invulnerability and develop preventive interventions to promote wellness in profoundly stressed children. (p. 596)

Fortunately, the majority of children exposed to various forms of adversity grow up to enjoy productive, normal lives (Hauser et al., 1985). Only a minority of children at risk experience serious difficulties in their personality and physical development (Garmezy, 1981).

Resilient children may hold the key that can change a professional's present focus on pathology to one of health and wellness. Cowen and Work (1988) report the primary goal of intervention is to provide the adjustment-enhancing skills and conditions that many profoundly stressed children fail to acquire in their natural life experiences and, thus, to disrupt the inevitable maladaptive spiral in which they are caught. Garmezy (1993) states:

> Once we have identified the biological, psychological, and sociocultural mechanisms that activate resilient behavior and the developmental processes that are integral to the operation of these mechanisms, we will then be in a better position to generate scientifically sturdy programs for intervention that may enable us to develop methods for enhancing resilient behavior in children disadvantaged by status and stress. (p. 133)

These intervention programs would need to use empirical measures so outcomes could be tracked for evaluation purposes.

PROMOTING RESILIENCY

Garmezy (1993, p. 129) states: "The central element in the study of resilience lies in the power of recovery and in the ability to return once again to those patterns of adaptation and competence that characterized the individual prior to the pre-stress period." Practitioners, policymakers, and researchers must look for protective factors that promote health and resiliency and presumably compensate for risk elements that are inherent in the lives and in the environments of many underprivileged children. Focus on those elements in person, family, and community that may be conducive in the development of adaptive or maladaptive behaviors.

How then do we promote resilient outcomes? There is no comprehensive intervention at a single time that accomplishes comprehensive goals of prevention for a lifetime. The ultimate goal to achieve optimal prevention should be to build the principles of prevention that enhance development into the ordinary activities of everyday life and into the community structures over the entire life span. Risk factors that occur in multiple domains—home, school, peer group, neighborhood, or work site—require interventions in all of these domains. Children benefit from a variety of different programs, including those that focus directly on the child and those that provide parent education and support (Bradley et al., 1994).

The more that is known about etiology, the more it becomes possible to target preventive interventions that intervene in causal chains. The Institute of Medicine (1994) reports:

> Because it appears that most risk and protective factors are not specific to a single disorder, the most fruitful approach for preventive interventions at this time may be to use a risk reduction model that includes the enhancement of protective factors and to aim at clusters or constellations of populations, but the interventions will be aimed at those causal and malleable risk factors that appear to have a role in the expression of several mental disorders. Identification of relative and attributable risks associated with various clusters could greatly facilitate prevention intervention research. (p. 128)

FURTHER RESEARCH

Further research on the process of adaptation will lead to a better understanding of normal and pathological development and will have direct relevance for refining existing intervention and prevention programs. Understanding the processes by which some individuals remain confident and develop supportive relationships in the midst of adversity is crucial to the development of effective prevention and intervention strategies (Rutter, 1990).

As researchers, it is imperative that we continue to build on the literature. Cicchetti and Garmezy (1993) state:

> Currently the popularity of resilience as a construct has exceeded the research output associated with it. As such, resilience is at risk for being viewed as a popularized trend that has not been verified through research and thereby in danger of losing credibility within the scientific community. To prevent this it is imperative that theorists in the area of resilience devote equal effort to advancing the construct empirically. (p. 499)

There is an urgent need to develop standardized and validated measures of resiliency. Researchers must continue to do empirical research in the area of childhood resiliency and assist practitioners in the development and implementation of resiliency enhancement programs for both children and families.

The need for preventative strategies is imperative. For example, in relation to mental disorders, preventive interventions to assist families in developing strategies that over time will prevent the emergence of a mental disorder in their youngsters and substantially enhance their resiliency are essential (Beardslee & MacMillan, 1993). Although there has been progress in treating childhood depression, few programs focus on the prevention of this disorder in youngsters (Beardslee & MacMillan, 1993). Cognitive therapy principles can be applied as a form of prevention because cognitive skills and styles are consistently reported as associated with stress-resistant outcomes (Hauser et al., 1985). Shure and Spivack (1978) suggest that primary prevention intervention with children be based on interpersonal cognitive problem-solving training. Dubow and Tisak (1989) found that social support and social problem-solving skills enhanced children's functioning by buffering the negative effects of stressful life events. Behavioral strategies can be taught to patients who have anxieties associated with life crises, and stress management can help the patient gain a sense of mastery and thereby increase self-esteem (Kiely & McPherson, 1986; Teare-Skinner, 1984).

Osborn (1990) states:

> The most powerful explanation for resilience in children might be resilience in parents who successfully cope with life's problems despite economic hardships, inadequate housing and other stressors. Although the inner character of resilient children is of much interest, it is the enabling external and environmental factors which foster and support resilience that are of special consequence since this is the domain in which intervention is potentially feasible. (p. 41)

PREVENTION INTERVENTION

A more rewarding approach to prevention, given current knowledge of etiology, lies in the identification of risk factors and the design of interventions aimed at reducing these risks in vulnerable individuals (Fraser & Galinsky, 1997). The economic as well as the clinical and sociomedical arguments for primary mental health care prevention are growing (Murray, 1992). The lack of educational campaigns aimed at prevention from the mental health sector reflects the absence of consensus on etiology of the more prevalent minor affective disorders and the wide range of biological, personality, educational, social, and behavioral factors that influence susceptibility (Murray, 1992).

In relation to prevention of mental disorders in children, the Institute of Medicine's Committee on Prevention of Mental Disorders (1994, p. 467) strongly recommended that the nation mount a significant program to prevent mental disorders, stating: "Much greater effort than ever before needs to be directed to prevention. Opportunities now exist to effectively exploit existing knowledge to launch a promising research agenda on the prevention of mental disorders." The committee found the need for prevention of mental disorders so compelling and the current opportunities for success so abundant that it recommended an increased investment across all federal agencies over a five-year period (1995 to 1999) to facilitate the development of the following three major areas of the research agenda:

1. Building the infrastructure to coordinate research and service programs and to train and support new investigators
2. Expanding the knowledge base for preventive intervention
3. Conducting well-evaluated preventive interventions

The committee viewed research training as an immediate and critical need in preventive intervention research to develop researchers' expertise in preventative research techniques so that expansion of the knowledge base for preventive interventions would and could continue.

Although these recommendations are timely and critical, it is imperative to formulate preventive interventions not only for the individual and the family, but also for the community. Social issues such as poverty, inadequate housing and health care, and violence negatively affect children and their families. Rappaport (1992) states:

We find it more attractive to blame people, rather than social institutions for problems in living. . . . In the United States, the National Institute of Mental Health has been forced to deal with the government's individual responsibility social agenda that since 1980 has forced prevention policies to become less concerned with social conditions and more focused on specific disorders." (p. 97) This is because prevention defined as interventions to prevent diagnosable mental disorders by searching for causal agents in individuals will always be supported by governments.

It is crucial to have preventionists who also have an interest in preventive social change and a focus on a community mental health perspective that addresses the social factors putatively underlying individuals' emotional distress (Baker, 1982). Albee (1982) states: "Efforts at prevention require the ideological decision to line up with the humanists who believe in social change, in the effectiveness of consultation, in education, in the primary prevention of human physical and emotional misery and in the maximization of individual competence."

OVERVIEW OF BOOK

It is time to promote a purely preventative approach to children's physical and mental health. The *Handbook of Preventive Interventions for Children and Adolescents* brings together outstanding scholars to summarize the empirical literature related to a variety of disorders and to provide guidelines for preventive interventions relative to each level of Gordon's model. This handbook assists practitioners and policymakers in best meeting the preventive needs of our youth.

REFERENCES

Albee, G. W. (1982). Preventing psychopathology and promoting human potential. *American Psychologist, 37,* 143–150.

Arnold, E. L. (1990). *Childhood stress.* New York: Wiley.

Baker, F. (1982). Effects of value systems on service delivery. In H. C. Schulberg & M. Killilea (Eds.), *The modern practice of community mental health.* San Francisco: Jossey-Bass.

Beardslee, W. R., & MacMillan, H. (1993). Preventive intervention with the children of depressed parents. *Psychoanalytic Study of the Child, 48,* 249–276.

Bradley, R. H., Whiteside, L., Mundfrom, D. J., Case, P. H., Kelleher, K. J., & Pope, S. K. (1994). Early indications of resilience and their relation to experiences in the home environments of low birth weight, premature children living in poverty. *Child Development, 65,* 240–260.

Cicchetti, D., & Garmezy, N. (1993). Milestones in the development of resilience. *Development and Psychopathology, 5*(4), 497–502.

Commission on Chronic Illness. (1957). *Chronic illness in the United States* (Vol. 1) [Published for the Commonwealth Fund]. Cambridge, MA: Harvard University Press.

Cowen, E. L., & Work, W. C. (1988). Resilient children, psychological wellness, and primary prevention. *American Journal of Community Psychology, 16*(4), 591–607.

Dubow, E. F., & Tisak, J. (1989). The relation between stressful life events and adjustment in elementary school children: The role of social support and social problem-solving skills. *Child Development, 60,* 1412–1423.

Dulmus, C. N., & Rapp-Paglicci, L. A. (2000). The prevention of mental disorders in children and adolescents: Future research and public policy recommendations. *Families in Society, 81*(3), 294–303.

Dulmus, C. N., & Wodarski, J. S. (1997). Prevention of childhood mental disorders: A literature review reflecting hope and a vision for the future. *Child and Adolescent Social Work Journal, 14*(3), 181–197.

Fraser, M. W., & Galinsky, M. J. (1997). Toward a resilience-based model of practice. In M. W. Fraser (Ed.), *Risk and resilience in childhood* (pp. 195–215). Washington, DC: National Association of Social Workers Press.

Garmezy, N. (1981). Children under stress: Perspectives on antecedents and correlates of vulnerability and resistance to psychopathology. In A. I. Rabin, J. Aronoff, A. Barclay, & R. A. Zucker (Eds.), *Further explorations in personality* (pp. 196–270). New York: Wiley.

Garmezy, N. (1993). Children in poverty: Resilience despite risk. *Psychiatry Interpersonal and Biological Processes, 56*(1), 127–136.

Gordon, R. (1983). An operational classification of disease prevention. *Public Health Reports, 98,* 107–109.

Gordon, R. (1987). An operational classification of disease prevention. In J. A. Steinberg & M. M. Silverman (Eds.), *Preventing mental disorders: A research perspective* (pp. 20–26). Rockville, MD: Department of Health and Human Services.

Hauser, S. T., Vieyra, M. B., Jacobson, A. M., & Wertlieb, D. (1985). Vulnerability and resilience in adolescence: Views from the family. *Journal of Early Adolescence, 5*(1), 81–100.

Institute of Medicine. (1994). *Reducing risks for mental disorders: Frontiers for preventative intervention research.* Washington, DC: National Academy Press.

Kiely, B. G., & McPherson, I. G. (1986). Stress self-help packages in primary care: A controlled trial evaluation. *Journal of the Royal College of General Practitioners, 36,* 307–309.

Murray, J. (1992). Prevention and the identification of high risk groups. *International Review of Psychiatry, 4,* 281–286.

Osborn, A. F. (1990). Resilient children: A longitudinal study of high achieving socially disadvantaged children. *Early Child Development and Care, 62,* 23–47.

Rappaport, J. (1992). The dilemma of primary prevention in mental health services: Rationalize the status quo or bite the hand that feeds you. *Journal of Community and Applied Social Psychology, 2,* 95–99.

Rutter, M. (1981). Stress, coping and development: Some issues and some questions. *Journal of Child Psychology and Psychiatry, 22,* 323–356.

Rutter, M. (1990). Psychosocial resilience and protective mechanisms. In A. Rolf, A. S. Masten, D. Cicchetti, K. H. Nuechterlein, & S. Weintraub (Eds.), *Risk and protective factors in the development of psychopathology* (pp. 181–214). New York: Cambridge University Press.

Shure, M. B., & Spivack, G. (1978). *Problem-solving techniques in child-rearing.* San Francisco: Jossey-Bass.

Teare-Skinner, P. (1984). Skills not pills: Learning to cope with anxiety symptoms. *Journal of the Royal College of General Practitioners, 34,* 258–260.

Werner, E. E., & Smith, R. S. (1982). *Vulnerable but invincible: A longitudinal study of resilient children and youth.* New York: McGraw-Hill.

PART II

Preventive Interventions for Children's and Adolescents' Emotional Problems

Chapter 2 ———————————————————

PEER GROUP REJECTION

GARY W. LADD, SARAH L. HERALD, CARLY B. SLUTZKY, AND REBECCA K. ANDREWS

THE CONSTRUCT OF PEER REJECTION

Peer rejection has come to be understood as a type of social role or relational status that is conferred on children by persons in their peer group. Thus, unlike the concept of friendship, which implies a voluntary, dyadic relationship, the construct of peer rejection refers to a social position that is seldom under the child's control but rather imposed by members of the child's peer *group* (e.g., a child's classmates). Most researchers define the construct of *peer group rejection* in terms of group members' sentiments toward specific children in the group (Bukowski & Hoza, 1989; Ladd, 1999). To say that a child is rejected means that evidence indicates that he or she is disliked by a majority of the children in his or her peer group. The meaning of this concept is also understood in relation to its opposite—that is, the construct of *peer group acceptance*. A child can be seen as accepted when evidence indicates that he or she is liked by a majority of peers. Later in this section, we see that, depending on the degree to which children are liked versus disliked by peers, it is also possible to designate other types of social roles or statuses within peer groups.

Measurement of the Peer Rejection Construct

Sociometry has been the principal approach used to measure the constructs of peer group acceptance and rejection. Beginning in the 1930s (see Moreno, 1932) and over the course of the past several decades, researchers have devised and

Preparation of this chapter was supported in part by grants from the National Institutes of Health (1-RO1MH-49223, 2-RO1MH-49223, and RO1HD-045906 to Gary W. Ladd).

evaluated many types of sociometric measures as a means of indexing children's social standing in peer groups (for a review, see Bagwell, Coie, Terry, & Lochman, 2000; Cillessen & Bukowski, 2000; Ladd & Coleman, 1993). Advances in sociometry have evolved to the point that it is now standard practice for researchers to use one of two types of sociometric tools—either a ratings-based procedure or a nominations method—to determine how well liked (accepted) or disliked (rejected) children are within their peer groups.

Rating-scale sociometrics, when used in classroom contexts, are administered by asking peers to think about individual classmates and rate each person in terms of the degree to which they do versus do not like to associate with him or her (e.g., play with, work with in school). Ratings are made on a continuous, bipolar, Likert-type scale. Typically, a 1 to 5 scale is used with older children and a 1 to 3 scale is used with younger children (e.g., 1 = "I don't like to play with this person very much"; 3 = "I like to play with this person a lot"). Once ratings are obtained from all group members, they are averaged over classmates. These averaged or mean scores are then standardized (e.g., converted to Z-scores) to permit statistical comparisons across classrooms or peer groups of different sizes. Within a given peer group, children who received high average ratings are considered to be well-liked or accepted by their peers, and those with low average ratings are viewed as less accepted or rejected.

Nomination sociometric measures, when used in classrooms, are administered in much the same way except that peers are asked to designate classmates that they most and least like to associate with (e.g., play with or work with) in school. The most widely used nomination sociometric in modern-day peer relations research was created by Coie and colleagues (Coie & Dodge, 1983; Coie, Dodge, & Coppotelli, 1982), although alternative approaches exist and are used (see Asher & Dodge, 1986; Newcomb & Bukowski, 1983). In this scheme, peers nominate members of their group that they most and least like to associate with, and the number of positive (liked) and negative (disliked) nominations that each child receives from group members are summed and then standardized to create distributions of *liked most* and *liked least* scores, respectively. The resulting standardized *liked most* and *liked least* scores are added to create *social impact* scores and then subtracted from each other to create *social preference* scores. The resulting social preference and impact scores are then standardized within classrooms or peer groups and used to classify children into one of five peer status categories, labeled *rejected, neglected, controversial, average,* and *popular.* Children identified as *rejected* by peers are those who receive low social preference scores (greater than 1 standard deviation below the group's average social preference score), very few positive nominations (i.e., a "like most" score below the group's average like most scores), and a large number of negative nominations (i.e., a "like least" score above the group's average like-least scores). Thus, children who are classified as rejected tend to receive few positive nominations and many negative nominations from peers. Instead of specifying the exact algorithms, the other status classifications can be summarized as follows:

1. *Neglected*—Children who receive few positive or negative nominations (overlooked by peers)
2. *Controversial*—Children who receive many positive *and* many negative nominations
3. *Average*—Children who receive modest numbers of positive and negative nominations (i.e., not strongly liked or disliked by peers)
4. *Popular*—Children who receive a large number of positive nominations and few negative nominations

Peer Rejection as Target for Preventive Interventions

It has long been argued that children's relationships with peers influence the course of their development and that early exposure to problematic peer relationships can lead to later maladjustment (e.g., see Berndt & Ladd, 1989; Kupersmidt, Coie, & Dodge, 1990; Parker, Rubin, Price, & DeRosier, 1995). To address these premises, researchers have attempted to differentiate among the types of relationships children form with peers and identify the processes that occur in these relationships that might influence children's psychosocial adaptation and maladjustment. To date, the forms of peer relationships that have received the most empirical attention are friendship, bully-victim relations, and peer group rejection (Ladd, 1999, 2003). Of these three forms of relationship, the construct of peer group rejection has received the most empirical attention and, with few exceptions, extant evidence suggests that peer rejection is a risk factor for a host of life-course adjustment problems (MacDougall, Hymel, Vaillancourt, & Mercer, 2001; Parker & Asher, 1987).

Early attempts to elucidate the role of peer group rejection in the development of adjustment problems and psychopathology were conducted primarily with males in school or clinic populations (see Kupersmidt et al., 1990; Parker & Asher, 1987). Evidence obtained from early follow-back studies (for a more extensive review, see Parker & Asher, 1987), most of which were based on retrospective analyses of school and clinic records, suggested that many psychologically impaired men had poor peer group relations as children, including histories of peer rejection. Collectively, results from early longitudinal investigations indicated that peer rejection in childhood was linked with a range of adjustment problems in adolescence and adulthood, including suicide, alcoholism, juvenile delinquency, conduct problems, criminality, and dishonorable discharges from the military service (see Kupersmidt et al., 1990; Parker & Asher, 1987).

Recent data from controlled, prospective longitudinal studies tend to corroborate earlier evidence indicating that early peer rejection is a relatively stable form of peer group status that predicts children's internalizing and externalizing problems later in childhood and adolescence (for reviews, see Ladd, 2003; MacDougall et al., 2001; Parker et al., 1995). For example, Ollendick, Weist, Borden, and Green (1992) followed children belonging to different peer acceptance groups (i.e., popular, rejected, average, neglected, and controversial) from ages 9 through 14 and found that rejected children were more likely than popular children to exhibit externalizing problems such as misconduct, delinquency, and substance abuse.

Another important discovery that emerged from longitudinal studies was that the severity of children's internalizing and externalizing problems increased as a function of the chronicity of their peer rejection. That is, children who were rejected by peers over longer rather than shorter time periods were found to be at greater risk for internalizing and externalizing forms of dysfunction (e.g., DeRosier, Kupersmidt, & Patterson, 1994; Ladd & Burgess, 2001; Ladd & Troop-Gordon, 2003). In addition to internalizing and externalizing problems, researchers have found that early peer rejection predicts loneliness during both early (Cassidy & Asher, 1992) and middle childhood (Asher, Hymel, & Renshaw, 1984; Crick & Ladd, 1993).

There is also a growing body of evidence that attests to a link between children's peer group rejection and indicators of their school adjustment and educational progress. Early research findings, summarized by Parker and Asher (1987), showed that low peer acceptance was a significant correlate of later school maladjustment, particularly dropping out of high school. More recently, investigators have discovered that early peer rejection—at school entry—predicts negative school attitudes, school avoidance, and underachievement during the first year of grade school (Buhs & Ladd, 2001; Ladd, 1990; Ladd, Birch, & Buhs, 1999). Later, in the elementary years, peer rejection has been linked with loneliness, peer interaction difficulties, lower emotional well-being, and academic deficits (Ladd & Burgess, 2001; Ladd, Kochenderfer, & Coleman, 1997; Parker & Asher, 1993; Vandell & Hembree, 1994). Evidence from other longitudinal studies suggests that peer rejection predicts absenteeism during the grade school years (e.g., DeRosier et al., 1994; Hymel, Rubin, Rowden, & LeMare, 1990) and grade retention and adjustment difficulties during the transition to middle school (Coie, Lochman, Terry, & Hyman, 1992).

In other studies, researchers have attempted to distinguish the contributions of peer group acceptance and rejection from those attributable to other potential risk factors such as deviant child behavior (e.g., aggression, shyness, social with-drawal) and other forms of relationship (e.g., peer friendship, bully victim rela-tions, teacher-child relationships). Coie and colleagues (e.g., Coie et al., 1992) and Hymel and colleagues (e.g., Hymel, Rubin, et al., 1990) have shown that both aggression and peer rejection during grade school make separate contribu-tions to the prediction of later maladjustment. Further, Ladd and colleagues (Ladd & Burgess, 2001; Ladd et al., 1999) discovered that, even after controlling for children's behaviors and participation in other peer and teacher-child rela-tionships, peer group rejection was one of the strongest predictors of children's classroom participation. In addition, Buhs and Ladd (2001) found that children's peer acceptance at school entry predicted changes in classroom participation that, in turn, forecasted later features of their academic and emotional adjust-ment. These findings are consistent with the hypothesis that, even in the context of other risk factors, peer group rejection is an important antecedent of chil-dren's interpersonal, psychological, and scholastic adjustment.

In view of the accumulated evidence, it seems appropriate to consider peer group rejection as a suitable target for the development and dissemination of pre-ventive interventions. First, not only has peer group rejection been implicated in the etiology of multiple disorders, but substantial evidence has also shown that peer group rejection during childhood antecedes both early- and later emerging forms of maladjustment. Second, there is growing support for the contention that peer group rejection is itself a cause of children's adjustment problems and not simply a marker for other types of underlying risk factors (e.g., behavioral disorders, such as aggression and shyness/withdrawal; see Ladd, 1999, 2003; MacDougall et al., 2001). Finally, after decades of research on peer rejection, a substantial number of researchers and policymakers have concluded that peer group rejection is a legitimate target for prevention research and practice. This assertion is substantiated by the fact that peer group rejection has achieved a prominent position in agendas for prevention science (see Coie et al., 1993).

In the sections that follow, we consider some of the factors that have guided investigators' efforts to devise and empirically evaluate preventive interventions for peer group rejection. We review evidence that serves to identify: (1) the per-vasiveness of the target population (e.g., empirical estimates of the prevalence of peer group rejection among school-age children) and (2) the precursors of peer group rejection (i.e., empirically identified child and environmental risk factors). We then survey existing interventions for peer group rejection and identify exemplary methods that have been implemented as universal, selective, or indicated prevention programs. The effectiveness of these approaches for the prevention of peer group rejection is also considered. For purposes of this chapter, the terms *universal, selective,* and *indicated* preventive interventions, respectively, are used to designate interventions that are intended to prevent all children from experiencing peer group rejection (universal), avert exposure to peer group rejection among children who are at risk for it (selective), and alleviate rejection among children who are currently experiencing it (indicated).

PREVALENCE AND INCIDENCE OF PEER REJECTION

From an epidemiological perspective, *prevalence* is defined as "instances of a given disease or other condition, in a given population at a designated time . . ." (Last, 2001, p. 140). In contrast, the term *incidence* refers to "the number of instances of illness commencing, or of persons falling ill, during a given period in a specified population" (p. 91). The former metric (typically a proportion) conveys information about how widespread a disease is within a population, and the latter provides an approximation of how rapidly the disease is spreading. Because peer group rejection is an interpersonal problem and not a disease, the aim in this chapter is to consider the prevalence of this problem rather than approximate its incidence.

Research on the prevalence of peer group rejection can be of value to prevention researchers and practitioners in numerous ways. First, prevalence estimates provide an empirical basis from which professionals can gauge the scope of peer group rejection as a social problem and make judgments about whether its occurrence is above or below established benchmarks (e.g., differentiate whether peer group rejection is rare versus at epidemic levels within a community). Such information may be useful for professionals who are charged with the responsibility of making sure that adequate resources and services exist and are available for the prevention and treatment of social or public health concerns. Likewise, it is not uncommon for policymakers to use information about a disorder's prevalence to raise community or public awareness about the significance of specific health problems. When gathered longitudinally on equivalent samples, prevalence estimates can be useful for detecting temporal patterns or secular trends, such as increases or decreases in the proportion of school-age children who experience peer group rejection. The usefulness of prevalence estimates depends on their accuracy, which is enhanced by deriving them from samples that are sufficiently large to suppress sampling error and by ensuring that sample participants are representative of the target population (in this case, school-age children). The use of stratified samples for this purpose can be particularly valuable because, when it is possible to estimate prevalence by subgroups, there is a greater probability that attention will be focused on those children who are most likely to encounter peer group rejection (e.g., boys versus girls, children from differing demographic or ethnic backgrounds).

The data that investigators have gathered to estimate the prevalence of peer group rejection during childhood predominately come from research on the psychometric properties of sociometric measures and from studies of children's peer acceptance and status group membership in classroom settings. Classrooms have been a favored location for studies of peer rejection because more than 90% of the nation's children attend school (Coie et al., 1993), and it is in this context that children are required to negotiate the dynamics of sizable, diverse peer groups.

Historical and contemporary estimates of the prevalence of peer group rejection, expressed as the percentage of children in investigators' samples that met this criterion, are shown in Tables 2.1 and 2.2. The values are rough estimators of prevalence because it has been rare for investigators in this discipline to use

Table 2.1   Estimated Prevalence of Peer Group Rejection and Other Types of Social Status by Grade Levels

Study	Sample Size	Grade	Peer Status Measure	Percent Classified				
				Rej	Neg	Con	Pop	Ave
Bagwell, Coie, Terry, & Lochman (2000)	824	4	CD	16	15	07	14	48
Brendgen, Little, & Krappmann (2000)	746	2–5	CDC	12	04	03	15	45
O'Neil, Welsh, Parke, Wang & Strand (1997)	345	K	CDC	19	10	06	19	28
Crick & Grotpeter (1995)	491	3–6	CD	11	14	05	13	31
Volling, Mackinnon-Lewis, Rabiner, & Baradaran (1993)	1,318	1–4	CDC	14	07	06	14	59
Terry & Coie (1991)	1,119	3–5	CDC	13	07	07	13	60
			AD	15	15	05	13	52
			NB (adj)	13	08	07	13	58
Kupersmidt & Coie (1990)	112	5	CDC	17	10	04	13	56
Coie & Dodge (1983)	96	3	CD	22	20	05	22	31
	122	5	CD	20	19	08	24	29

Note: Percentage values shown have been rounded. Prevalence estimates for average peer status vary substantially across studies because some investigators classify all children who do not qualify for the other four status groups into this category and others do not. AD = Asher and Dodge (1986) measure; Ave = Average peer status; CD = Coie and Dodge (1983) measure; CDC = Coie, Dodge, and Coppotelli (1982) measure; Con = Controversial peer status; NB (adj) = Adjusted Newcomb and Bukowski (1983) measure; Neg = Neglected peer status; Pop = Popular peer status; Rej = Rejected peer status.

Table 2.2   Estimated Prevalence of Peer Group Rejection by Gender and Ethnicity

Status Group (Sample $N = 824$)	Males n (%)	Females n (%)	Males + Females n (%)
A. Sample Breakdown by Status Groups			
Average	205 (25%)	191 (23%)	396 (48%)
Popular	39 (5%)	76 (9%)	115 (14%)
Neglected	50 (6%)	72 (9%)	122 (15%)
Controversial	39 (5%)	23 (3%)	62 (8%)
Rejected	81 (10%)	48 (6%)	129 (16%)
B. Breakdown of Rejected Children by Behavior			
Aggressive	19 (15%)	14 (11%)	33 (26%)
Nonaggressive	62 (48%)	34 (26%)	96 (74%)
C. Breakdown of Rejected Children by Ethnicity			
Caucasian			61 (47%)
African American			68 (53%)

Note: From "Peer Clique Participation and Social Status in Preadolescence," by C. L. Bagwell, J. D. Coie, R. A. Terry, and J. E. Lochman, 2000, *Merrill-Palmer Quarterly, 46,* pp. 280–305.

sampling designs that are as rigorous as those typically found in epidemiological research. Moreover, the studies and samples included in this table are by no means exhaustive of the body of evidence that is relevant to this objective. Tables 2.1 and 2.2 feature exemplary findings that were obtained with larger (for the most part) community samples and that permit comparisons of prevalence estimates across age groups. Estimates from one of these investigations (i.e., Bagwell et al., 2000) are further profiled in Table 2.2 because they are among the most recently published and permit comparisons by both gender and ethnicity.

An inspection of the prevalence estimates in Table 2.1 suggests that approximately 11% to 22% of children in normative, community samples can be considered rejected by peers, using one of the several classification criteria that investigators have established for this purpose. This range of prevalence estimates becomes slightly less disparate—12% to 16%—if they are gauged from the largest of the samples shown in Table 2.1 (i.e., those with n's > 500). An examination of the peer status classifications reveals that most samples contain about as many rejected children as they do popular children and that actively disliked children sometimes, but not always, outnumber those who are neglected (overlooked) by peers.

Even though the prevalence estimates reported in Table 2.2 (obtained by Bagwell et al., 2000) are based on a single sample and age group (fourth graders), they offer some insight into the question of whether prevalence rates differ by child gender, aggressiveness, and ethnicity. As shown in the A section of Table 2.2, the percentage of rejected children in the entire sample ($n = 824$) was approximately 16% ($n = 129$), and the percentage of rejected boys in the sample was nearly double that of rejected girls (10% versus 6%, respectively). Of the 129 children who were classified as rejected, peers perceived 26% as aggressive, and 74% were seen as nonaggressive (see B section of Table 2.2). The group of children who were identified as rejected and aggressive ($n = 33$) contained a similar percentage of males and females (15% versus 11%, respectively). Approximately 47% of the 129 rejected children were Caucasian and 53% were African American. The finding that more boys than girls were identified as rejected by peers is consistent with prior evidence (e.g., Coie et al., 1982; O'Neil, Welsh, Parke, Wang, & Strand, 1997; Volling, MacKinnon-Lewis, Rabiner, & Baradaran, 1993) and implies that boys may be at greater risk for peer rejection than are girls. Although fewer girls than boys were identified as actively disliked by peers, it appears that rejected females are just as likely as rejected males to have reputations as aggressors (French, 1990). Assuming that the children sampled in this study were representative of their ethnic groups, the results imply that the prevalence of peer rejection in the Caucasian and African American subsamples was not highly disproportionate.

Although not reported in the tables, evidence from longitudinal studies indicates that children's status as rejected members of their peer groups remains moderately stable over time (Coie & Dodge, 1983; Newcomb & Bukowski, 1984; see also Cillessen & Bukowski, 2000). In a five-year longitudinal study conducted by Coie and Dodge, 30% to 45% of rejected children retained their membership in this status group over a four-year period. Similar results were found by gender and ethnicity. However, rejected status was found to be less stable in a younger as compared to an older cohort of children (e.g., those initially identified as rejected in grade 3 versus grade 5).

RISK FACTORS

The question "Why do some children become rejected or disliked by members of their peer group whereas others become accepted or well liked?" has been an enduring challenge for investigators who have explored children's peer group relations (see Ladd, 1999). To address this question, many investigators have attempted to identify *risk factors* that are associated with peer group rejection. The concept of a *risk factor* originated in the discipline of epidemiology (see Pellegrini, 1990) and refers to characteristics of the person (i.e., the child), the environment (e.g., the peer group, school, family, or other element of the child's ecology), and changing or dynamic combinations of these attributes (e.g., the interface between child and environmental attributes; child by environment interactions) that impair adaptation and increase the likelihood of later disorder (Coie et al., 1993; Ladd, 2003). In contrast, protective factors have been construed as attributes of the individual, the environment, or both, that increase resistance to disease or dysfunction (see Coie et al., 1993; Pellegrini, 1990).

Much of the early work on risk factors for peer group rejection was carried out with cross-sectional designs and, as a result, more was learned about the concomitants than antecedents of this social problem (Ladd, 1999). However, with the advent of longitudinal studies, important strides were made toward the discovery of actual risk factors—that is, preexisting attributes of the child, the child's rearing environment, or both, that *forecasted* the emergence of peer group rejection. Some of these discoveries—primarily those relevant to the purposes of this chapter—are considered in the remaining paragraphs of this section.

In the sections that follow, exemplars of risks for peer group rejection are considered within four categories of risk factors, and evidence from longitudinal studies is emphasized. Moreover, the purview of this taxonomy has been limited to risk factors that have had an important bearing on the development of preventive interventions for school-age children. More exhaustive reviews of factors that may increase versus decrease children's risk for peer group rejection can be found in other publications (see Ladd, in press; MacDougall et al., 2001).

Child Factors

A number of different child attributes have been investigated as potential antecedents, or risk factors for peer group rejection. Included among these are the behaviors children direct toward peers, the cognitions they formulate to define and interpret social situations, and the emotions they exhibit and respond to during peer interactions.

Children's Behavior with Peers

Findings from research on children's behavior in new peer groups (e.g., newly formed playgroups, classrooms) suggest that the types of behaviors they use with peers may affect their social status in these contexts. Longitudinal studies conducted with preschool and grade school samples reveal that children who act aggressively are more likely to be rejected (e.g., Coie & Kupersmidt, 1983; Dodge, 1983; Ladd, Price, & Hart, 1988). For example, in a study of emerging peer status in boys' playgroups, Dodge found that boys who frequently aggressed toward peers were seen as disruptive and were eventually rejected by members of their playgroups. In contrast, boys who were more prosocial in their interactions with peers tended to become well liked or popular among members of their playgroups. Other investigators have found that peer group rejection is predicted by not only the frequency of children's aggressive interactions, but also the number of group members they attempt to coerce (Ladd & Price, 1987). Studies indicate that several forms of aggression, including direct and indirect or covert expressions (Cairns & Cairns, 1994; Crick & Grotpeter, 1995), are linked with peer group acceptance and that some aggressive acts, particularly instrumental aggression in boys, predict peer rejection better than others (Coie, Dodge, Terry, & Wright, 1991).

There is also evidence to indicate that withdrawn behavior leads to peer rejection, although this link appears to be age-dependent. With preschool samples, investigators tend to find that withdrawn children are not rejected by peers (e.g., Ladd & Burgess, 1999). By middle childhood, it is more common for investigators to find that asocial behavior is linked with peer rejection, possibly because older classmates tend to judge such behavior as deviant (e.g., Rubin, LeMare, & Lollis, 1990). Other findings suggest that withdrawn children are prone to peer neglect (i.e., receive few liking or disliking nominations from peers) rather than peer rejection (e.g., Dodge, 1983), and early peer isolation has been associated with low peer acceptance in both early and later grade levels (Hymel, Rubin, et al., 1990).

In contrast, prosocial behaviors have been shown to antecede peer-group acceptance (Coie & Kupersmidt, 1983; Dodge, 1983; Ladd et al., 1988). Coie and Kupersmidt found that boys who asked questions and made positive comments were better liked by peers, and Ladd et al. (1988) found that preschoolers who played cooperatively with peers gained in peer acceptance over a school year.

In summary, substantial evidence corroborates the premise that children's interpersonal behaviors have a bearing on the status they achieve in peer groups. In general, findings support the inference that children's behaviors play an important role in shaping relationship formation but may have less of an effect on peers' sentiments once such reputations are formed (see Hymel, Wagner, & Butler, 1990).

Children's Social Cognitions

There is also evidence indicating that children's ideas, beliefs, and inferences about peers and the way they define their own goals, strategies, and expectations in social encounters are associated with their acceptance and rejection in peer groups. Findings from a number of investigations reveal that rejected or unpopular children are prone to have atypical ideas about how to interact successfully with peers, interpret peer interactions in defensive ways, and construe their own and peers' motives in ways that interfere with relationship formation and conflict resolution (see Crick & Dodge, 1994). For example, findings from research on social problem-solving tasks show that, compared to well-accepted children, rejected or low-accepted children are more likely to have unfriendly goals, interpret peers' intentions as hostile, devise antisocial or self-centered ways to resolve peer conflicts, and believe that aggression is an effective means of achieving their ends in peer situations (e.g., Crick & Ladd, 1990; Dodge, Murphy, & Buchsbaum, 1984).

Children's Emotions and Emotional Regulation

To successfully interact with others, children must not only know how to regulate their own emotions, but also be able to identify and adjust to peers' emotions. Several researchers have examined the relationship between emotion understanding and social competence. Results suggest that children who have difficulty regulating their emotions and interpreting peers' emotions are prone to be disliked or rejected by peers (Bierman & Wargo, 1995; Cassidy, Parke, Butkovsky, & Braungart, 1992; Dodge et al., 1984; Eisenberg et al., 1993; Fabes et al., 1999). It appears that children who are able to recognize emotions in others and respond accordingly are more likely to interact with peers in socially appropriate ways, thus reducing their risk for rejection.

Socialization/Environmental Factors

Differences in the way children are socialized, and features of their social environments have also been linked with peer group rejection. Within these domains, dimensions of children's family life and parent-child relationships, and differences in school and classroom contexts have received the most empirical attention.

Family Relationships and Processes

Numerous aspects of family life and parent-child relations have been identified as factors that may increase or decrease children's risk for peer group rejection (for a review, see Ladd & Pettit, 2002). Included among these are parents' behaviors and socialization practices, such as child-rearing styles, methods of discipline, and management of children's informal play contacts with peers. Additionally, relationships in the family context, especially those that children form with caregivers, have been linked with their social competence and success in the peer culture. Evidence suggests that children who are exposed to coercive parenting styles have stronger propensities toward aggressive and antisocial behaviors in peer groups (Patterson, Reid, & Dishion, 1992), and those who are exposed to harsh, punitive disciplinary styles are more likely to experience social problems, including peer group rejection (Pettit, Bates, & Dodge, 1997; Pettit, Dodge, & Brown, 1988). Conversely, children whose parents value peer relationships, teach relevant interpersonal competencies, and encourage them to participate in informal playgroups appear better prepared to form friendships and establish positive reputations in contexts such as classrooms (e.g., Clark & Ladd, 2000; Ladd & Hart, 1992; Mize, Pettit, & Brown, 1995).

Schooling and Peer Group Factors

There is also evidence to suggest that features of the school and the nature of children's peer groups are associated with the status they achieve in these contexts. Illustrations include Hallinan's (1976) finding that patterns of interpersonal liking and disliking in peer groups were more evenly distributed in open classrooms (where peer interaction is permitted, students choose their own seats, etc.) than in traditional classrooms. Open classrooms, as compared to those with more traditional arrangements, tended to have fewer social isolates and fewer highly popular children.

The fit between the child and the social dynamics of his or her peer groups—sometimes referred to as *person-group similarity* (see Stormshak, Bierman, Bruschi, Dodge, & Coie, 1999)—may also have a bearing on the extent to which individuals experience peer acceptance or rejection (see Ladd, Buhs, & Troop, 2002). For example, there is evidence to suggest that, in peer groups where aggressive behavior is common, children who act aggressively are not as likely to be ostracized or rejected by their groupmates (see Wright, Giammarino, & Parad, 1986). Similarly, Stormshak et al. (1999) found that children's tolerance of specific behaviors, such as aggression and withdrawal, varied according to the norms of their peer group.

EXEMPLARY PREVENTIVE INTERVENTIONS

In the sections that follow, existing prevention programs for peer group rejection are classified into three categories: universal, selective, and indicated preventive interventions. The purpose of this taxonomy is to distinguish among interventions that, in retrospect, appear to have been designed to accomplish the objectives of these three different approaches to prevention.

Most of the interventions developed for these purposes have been based on the hypotheses that children are either deficient in social skills that promote peer group acceptance or possess an overabundance of one or more attributes that contribute to relationship difficulties or peer group rejection (i.e., the *skill deficit* and *behavioral excess* hypotheses; see Ladd, 1999). Thus, researchers have tended to devise treatment methods designed to help children:

1. Acquire competence at skills that are conducive to peer group acceptance (e.g., learn prosocial perspectives and corresponding behavioral skills) and/or

2. Eliminate or reduce propensities that foster peer group rejection (e.g., antisocial perspectives and behaviors; see Bierman & Montminy, 1993; Ladd et al., 2002).

In large part, the treatment methods and curricula devised to address these objectives have been formulated on basic social learning principles that have been organized and implemented in different ways (see Ladd & Mize, 1983).

It has become commonplace for researchers to use the terms *modeling, shaping,* and *coaching* to distinguish among interventions that are based on one or more social learning principles and that expose children to different treatment experiences and program content. In general, *modeling* refers to interventions in which children are encouraged to imitate others who serve as exemplars of effective skills and/or are shown examples of how to inhibit or refrain from negative thoughts and behaviors. *Shaping* has been used to describe programs in which the principle treatment strategy is the provision of rewards to children for performing targeted skills or successive approximations of targeted social skills or behaviors. In some cases, this strategy may be augmented with procedures designed to eliminate reinforcement for negative or antisocial behaviors (e.g., via ignoring or extinction trials). The term *coaching* has been reserved for programs in which children learn to become proficient at performing social skills by participating in training sequences that integrate performance-based instruction, rehearsals, and ongoing critiques of skill applications.

Effective Universal Preventive Interventions

Universal preventive interventions are typically applied to entire populations of children with the intent of lowering the incidence of peer group rejection in that population. Of the interventions that have been designed to alter peer group rejection, only a limited number can be considered exemplars of universal preventive interventions. Moreover, of the universal interventions that have included measures of children's peer acceptance or rejection, only a few have been found to yield improvements in this domain.

In one study, Rotheram, Armstrong, and Booraem (1982) randomly assigned all of the fourth- and fifth-grade classrooms (and some sixth-grade classrooms) in one school to one of three conditions: assertiveness training, intervention control, or nontreatment control. Assertiveness training consisted of instruction in self-management and problem-solving skills for social situations, followed by opportunities for rehearsal and use of shaping techniques to enhance assertive responses. In the control intervention, teacher ratings were used to group children by levels of social responsiveness, and those participating within more or less responsive groups played competitive games that encouraged social participation. Children who received assertiveness training, unlike those in the control conditions, improved in assertiveness and exhibited posttreatment gains in peer popularity. However, the reliability of the latter finding appears uncertain because the changes observed in children's peer status were found on a teacher-report measure but not a peer-report sociometric measure (the latter source is more reliable).

In a study conducted by Hepler (1994), two classrooms of fifth graders were selected, and one was randomly assigned to receive a social skills training program whereas the other served as a nontreatment control group. Evaluation of this program produced somewhat equivocal results, perhaps in part because all participants (i.e., children, teachers, and parents) were informed of their experimental status before treatment. Included among the findings was a nonsignificant trend indicating that the sociometric ratings of children in the skills training classroom, as compared to those in the control classroom, were somewhat higher at posttest. Analysis by subtypes of children (i.e., those who differed in peer status in each classroom) showed that improvements in peer acceptance as measured by positive peer nominations occurred for average-status children in the skills training classroom and for low-status children in the control classroom. Reductions in negative peer nominations were found for children in both the skills training and control classrooms.

Using a similar, two-classroom design, Choi and Hechenlaible-Gotto (1998) evaluated the effects of a classroom-based social skills intervention on second-grade children's peer acceptance ratings. In the skills training classroom, children were taught prosocial skills through modeling, behavioral role playing, and social support (praise for skill performance). Analysis of adjusted posttest scores (peer rating scores for classrooms were nonequivalent at pretest) failed to detect significant differences in two types of peer acceptance ratings that were measured in each classroom (i.e., the ratings children received from peers as preferred playmates versus workmates in school). However, comparisons of pre- to posttest scores within classrooms showed an improvement in "work with" but not "play with" ratings for children in the skills training but not the control classroom.

Hepler and Rose (1998) designed a skills training intervention to promote children's competence in three interpersonal domains (e.g., conversational skills, group entry, peer inclusion) and implemented it in one of two fifth-grade classrooms. Comparisons of the two classrooms across pre-, post-, and follow-up assessments showed that children in the skills training classroom, relative to those in the control classroom, manifested gains in peer acceptance from posttest to follow-up. Secondary analyses were used to examine changes in peer acceptance for a subgroup of children in each classroom that was low in peer status at the investigation's inception. It was found that, over time, low-status children in the intervention classroom, more than their counterparts in the control classroom, received fewer negative nominations or became less disliked by classmates.

In summary, evidence to support the effectiveness of universal interventions for preventing peer group rejection is limited. Often, the conclusions that investigators have drawn from their findings have been based on changes in individual children in single treatment and control classrooms and rarely, if ever, has it been possible to evaluate intervention effectiveness when [original is correct—this is a statistical expression and "a" should not be used in front of the word classroom] classroom is used as the level of analysis. Perhaps more definitive inferences about the effectiveness of universal peer relations interventions can be drawn as investigators begin to implement universal prevention trials with much larger samples of children.

Although there is movement toward this objective (see the Conduct Problems Prevention Research Group, 1999a, 1999b), early findings from large-scale universal interventions are not particularly encouraging. For example, a universal intervention containing classroom-level instruction in social and emotional skills was included as a component of the Fast Track prevention trial (Conduct Problems Prevention Research Group, 1999b). Fast Track is an ongoing, multi-site prevention program aimed at behaviorally disordered children and their families. Children were identified in kindergarten and began receiving the intervention in first grade. Although the intervention proved to be effective at reducing aggressive behavior and improving classroom atmosphere by the end of first grade, no significant changes were found in children's classroom peer relations at that time or in a third-grade follow-up (Conduct Problems Prevention Research Group, 2002).

Effective Selective Preventive Interventions

Selective preventive interventions are targeted to individuals or subgroups of children who are not currently experiencing peer group rejection but appear to be at risk for developing this social problem. Children recruited for selective preventive interventions include those who manifest risk factors that are prognostic of peer group rejection (e.g., children whose aggressive behavior greatly exceeds the norm).

Many of the risk factors linked to peer group rejection have also been implicated in development of other, broader forms of psychopathology (e.g., internalizing, externalizing problems). Most of the interventions implemented to address these risks have been evaluated in terms of their ability to attenuate specific risk factors or to deflect children from trajectories toward psychopathology, rather than to prevent peer group rejection per se. That is, in the evaluation of these prevention programs, assessment has been focused on changes in children's risk status rather than on alterations in their peer acceptance.

Examples of preventive interventions that target risk factors for peer group rejection include those designed to:

1. Reduce children's aggressive and oppositional behaviors (e.g., Kellam, Ling, Merisca, Brown, & Ialongo, 1998; Webster-Stratton & Hammond, 1997)
2. Modify children's social cognitive biases (e.g., Hudley & Graham, 1993)
3. Increase children's control over negative affect (e.g., Lochman, Burch, Curry, & Lampron, 1984)
4. Improve family functioning (see Lochman, 2000)

Three of these interventions are summarized. Webster-Stratton and Hammond assigned young children (ages 4 to 7) with conduct problems to child, parent, or child-and-parent training conditions. Whereas child training was designed to promote problem solving, social skills, and affect regulation, the focus of parent training was to build positive parenting skills and attenuate coercive discipline. Compared to wait-list controls, children in all three training conditions showed significant posttest gains in conflict management in laboratory peer-play sessions (see also Webster-Stratton, Reid, & Hammond, 2001). Hudley and Graham (1993) implemented a social cognitive intervention in which aggressive children learned concepts such as intention and ambiguity. They then practiced skills such as identifying peers' intentions, distinguishing intended from unintended outcomes, and using decision rules to respond to ambiguous situations. Program participants, as compared to those in attention-control and control conditions, were rated as significantly less aggressive by their teachers and showed a reduction of hostile bias in both hypothetical and laboratory simulated ambiguous situations. In the Lochman et al. Anger Coping Program (Lochman & Lenhart, 1993; Lochman et al., 1984), aggressive boys were trained in perspective-taking skills, anger recognition, social problem-solving skills, and impulse inhibition. Postintervention results (as cited in Lochman, Dunn, & Klimes-Dougan, 1993) demonstrated that the program effectively reduced aggressive behavior and increased on-task classroom behavior. However, follow-up data gathered seven months later with a subsample of treatment group participants indicated that postintervention reductions in disruptive off-task behavior were not maintained (Lochman & Lenhart, 1993).

Beyond the probative value of these findings, new evidence suggests that interventions implemented at the selective level may protect children from peer group rejection. Initial findings from the Fast Track prevention trial (Conduct Problems Prevention Research Group, 1999a) imply that a combination of universal and selective treatment for behaviorally disruptive kindergartners subsequently reduced their exposure to peer group rejection. During first grade, approximately half of the at-risk sample of children participated in a universal intervention (e.g., classroom-level curriculum on emotional, self-control, friendship, and social problem-solving skills) that was supplemented with selective interventions (e.g., skills-training friendship group for children, parenting skills groups for parents). The other half of the sample served as controls (for procedural details, see Conduct Problems Prevention Research Group, 1999a, pp. 635–636). Assessment data gathered at the end of first grade showed that children in the intervention group were more accepted among their first-grade classmates than were children in the control group. Moreover, it was also found that children in the intervention condition had fewer conduct problems and engaged in higher levels of positive interaction with their first-grade classmates. However, because the effects of the multiple manipulations that were included in this program were not dismantled, it was not possible to distinguish the relative contributions of the universal versus selective intervention components.

Effective Indicated Preventive Interventions

The aim of indicated prevention programs is to intervene on behalf of children who are currently experiencing some degree of peer group rejection and either eliminate or reduce the severity of this social problem. Investigators first experimented with interventions for peer group rejection in the 1930s and, since that time, have devised many programs that have contributed to this objective (for reviews, see Asher, Parker, & Walker, 1996; Ladd & Mize, 1983; Ladd et al., 2002; Schneider, 1992). Because of the longevity of researchers' efforts, the number of interventions developed for this purpose far outnumbers those created to address universal or selective prevention objectives. Greater priority was placed on this form of intervention because researchers wished to know whether peer group rejection was responsive to treatment before they began to address other types of prevention objectives.

One feature that these intervention studies have in common is that they were conducted with children who were known to be unpopular or mildly to severely disliked by members of their classroom peer groups. With few exceptions, the interventions implemented in these studies were deemed *social skills training programs* because the treatment methods and content were based on the premise that peer group rejection is caused by social skill deficits and that training in peer-oriented social skills (e.g., promoting skills used by well-liked peers; see competence-correlates rationale, Ladd, 1999) would improve children's peer acceptance.

Coaching

Results from a number of investigations suggest that coaching interventions can benefit children who are unpopular or rejected by members of their peer group. In one of the first interventions of this type, Gottman, Gonso, and Schuler (1976) trained two unpopular third graders to engage in positive peer interaction using a coaching strategy that included videotaped instructions, role playing, and participation in tasks that emphasized listening skills. Results showed that, compared to unpopular children in an attention control group, the trained children evidenced significant gains in peer acceptance that were maintained over a nine-week interval. In a much larger investigation, Oden and Asher (1977) used coaching to train low-accepted third and fourth graders to perform skills that corresponded to four domains of interpersonal interaction: communication, cooperation, participation, and validation support. The coached children, unlike controls, participated in a series of training sessions in which they received instruction in the targeted social skills, skill-rehearsal opportunities with peer partners, and feedback about how to improve their skill performance. Children in the coaching condition, as compared to controls, exhibited significant improvements in classroom peer acceptance immediately after the intervention and in a one-year follow-up assessment.

Ladd (1981) extended the Oden and Asher (1977) investigation by comparing the progress of low-accepted third graders who were coached or assigned to two types of control groups (i.e., attention controls and no-treatment controls). In addition, modifications were made to the coaching procedure so that low-accepted children were trained in specific peer-interaction skills (asking questions of peers, leading peers, making supportive statements to peers) and given greater opportunities to rehearse and improve their skill performance (e.g., rehearsal sessions were graduated to approximate the classroom peer context; performance feedback was individualized to minimize skill failures). Changes in social skills and peer acceptance were evaluated at posttest and a four-week follow-up, and results showed that coached children, unlike their counterparts in the two control conditions, made significant gains in two of the three trained skills and in classroom peer acceptance.

In subsequent studies, researchers examined further variants of the coaching procedure, used coaching to train other types of social skills, intervened with different age groups, and contrasted the effects of coaching against other treatment manipulations. For example, Csapo (1983) adapted Ladd's (1981) coaching procedures for use with severely withdrawn children and trained participants until they achieved a skill-mastery criterion. Results showed that the target children gained in both social skills and peer acceptance, suggesting that the benefits of this form of intervention may extend to populations of children who are severely withdrawn.

Coaching interventions have also been adapted for young children. Mize and Ladd (1990) coached unpopular preschoolers in four social skills (i.e., leading, asking questions, supporting, and making comments) and found that, relative to an attention control group, these children gained significantly in social knowledge and in two of the four trained skills. Gains in the trained children's peer acceptance were not apparent immediately after the intervention, but evidence to this effect was found two weeks later in a follow-up assessment.

Instead of intervening with younger grade-school children, Bierman and Furman (1984) identified a sample of low-accepted preadolescents (i.e., fifth and sixth graders) and assigned them to one of four experimental conditions: coaching in conversational skills, positive peer experience, coaching plus positive peer experience, or control. Coaching was administered using procedures based on Oden and Asher (1977) and Ladd (1981), and the peer experience condition was administered by having low-accepted children participate in a film-making activity with other, high-accepted children. Children in the combined condition received training in conversational skills and the peer experience component (i.e., which likely provided children with opportunities to rehearse their skills and receive peer feedback). Analysis of the posttest and follow-up assessments showed differential effects by condition. Whereas participants in the coaching condition gained significantly in conversational skills, those in the peer experience condition exhibited temporary gains in peer acceptance. Children in the combined coaching and peer pairing condition posted gains not only in their conversational skills, but also in their peer acceptance. In a reanalysis of these data, Bierman (1986) examined the relation between children's skill improvement and their gains in peer acceptance. These analyses revealed that only the children in the combined condition showed gains in conversational skills that were accompanied by positive peer support. Further, only in this group were children's improvements in conversational skills found to predict gains in peer group acceptance.

It should be recognized, however, that not all of the evidence yielded by social skills training studies attests to the effectiveness of coaching as an intervention strategy. The reality is that, although many investigators have obtained corroborative findings, some have failed to detect intervention-related improvements in children's peer status, and others have reported unequivocal results. Hymel and Asher (1977), for example, compared unpopular third through fifth graders who received group versus individualized coaching conditions or a peer-play activity (control condition) and did not find significant posttest changes in children's peer acceptance. La Greca and Santogrossi (1980) administered an intervention that resembled coaching with low-accepted grade schoolers and found that trained children, more than controls, made significant gains in skill knowledge and performance, but not peer acceptance. A failure to detect coaching effects was also reported by Tiffen and Spence (1986) for children who were identified as isolated from peers versus rejected by peers. Unfortunately, failures to replicate are difficult to explain because of a host of factors that may be responsible for null findings (e.g., samples, statistical power, measurement sensitivity, treatment fidelity, specious hypotheses; see Hymel & Asher, 1977; Ladd, 1985; Tiffen & Spence, 1986).

Coaching and Modeling

In addition to coaching, a number of studies were conducted to assess the efficacy of interventions based on modeling and variations on this observational learning principle (e.g., showing films of peers using specific social skills, having a narrator describe skilled behavior; see O'Connor, 1969, 1972). Evaluations of modeling as a treatment methodology indicated that, when used alone, it rarely fostered lasting changes in children's social skills (see Ladd & Mize, 1983). Moreover, investigators who initially researched modeling strategies as an intervention tended to evaluate its impact on children's behavior and seldom studied its effects on children's peer relations. In later years, however, the value of modeling was reexamined in relation to other forms of intervention, such as coaching.

To assess the efficacy of coaching versus modeling interventions, Gresham and Nagle (1980) assigned low-accepted third and fourth graders to one of four experimental conditions: coaching, modeling, a combination of coaching and modeling, or control. Children in the coaching condition received a treatment similar to that provided by Oden and Asher (1977), and those in the modeling condition saw a narrated film in which the same social skills were depicted (but not rehearsed or refined). Participants assigned to the combined conditions received an abbreviated form of both treatments. Posttreatment assessments showed that, compared to controls, children in all three treatment conditions improved in peer acceptance and had higher levels of positive interactions with classmates. However, of the three treatments, only coaching was found to have an ameliorative effect on children's negative peer interactions.

Coaching and Training in Academic Skills

Coie and Krehbiel (1984) proposed that, in addition to deficits in social skills, peers might reject some grade-school children because they exhibit academic difficulties in their classrooms, such as poor reading skills. To test this hypothesis, these researchers randomly assigned fourth graders who had underdeveloped social and reading skills to one of three intervention conditions (i.e., social skills coaching, academic skills training, combined social and academic skills training) or a nontreatment control group. Children in the coaching condition were taught prosocial skills using the procedures developed by Oden and Asher (1977). Their counterparts in the academic skills condition were tutored in reading skills, and children in the combined condition received both forms of treatment. It was discovered that children in the academic skills group made sustained improvements not only in reading and math, but also in classroom peer acceptance. In contrast, children who were coached in social skills evidenced gains in reading comprehension only—a result that the investigators attributed to the brevity of the training period that was used to administer this form of treatment. Nonetheless, these findings corroborated the investigator's initial premise and implied that interventions for peer group rejection are most likely to be effective when they are designed to address the specific deficits that may be responsible for children's social difficulties. Findings from subsequent investigations buttress this conclusion (see Ladd et al., 2002).

Coaching and Shaping

Evidence linking aggressive behavior with peer group rejection encouraged investigators to develop interventions that could not only promote prosocial skills, but also inhibit children's use of aggression and antisocial behavior in peer contexts. Bierman, Miller, and Stabb (1987) investigated the relative efficacy of coaching and/or shaping interventions. These investigators identified first- through third-grade children who evidenced higher levels of peer rejection and negative classroom behaviors (e.g., aggression, noncompliance) and assigned them to one of the following treatment conditions: coaching, rules for negative behavior (prohibitions), coaching and prohibitions, and no-treatment control. Children in the first condition were coached on prosocial interaction skills such as sharing and helping peers and then participated in play sessions where they rehearsed their skills, received feedback about their performance, and were given tokens (rewards) after using the skills. Participants in the prohibitions condition were not coached, but instead received rules that forbade antisocial behaviors such as fighting, arguing, and yelling. After the rules were presented, these children took part in the same types of play sessions that were used in the coaching condition and were precluded from earning tokens each time they exhibited negative behaviors. Children in the combined condition received both types of treatment. Coaching was found to increase children's use of prosocial skills, and these gains were maintained over a six-week period. Prohibitions brought about stable decrements in negative behaviors but only temporary increases in prosocial skills. Improvements in peer acceptance were found only for the children who had participated in the combined treatment program and were limited in the sense that the gains were evident only in the presence of children's training partners (the peers who participated in the play sessions) and did not generalize to the classroom.

Coaching Combined with Social Problem Solving and Emotion Regulation

Following Bierman et al.'s (1987) lead, other investigators began to develop complex, multicomponent interventions for children who were both aggressive and rejected within their peer groups. Lochman, Coie, Underwood, and Terry (1993) developed one such program by combining treatments that were designed to help children:

1. Think of adaptive responses to social problems (social problem-solving component)
2. Develop effective skills for forming relationships with peers and entering peer group activities (coaching and skill acquisition components)
3. Cope with aggression-promoting emotions (anger reduction component)

To test the intervention's effects, two types of children—those who were rejected and aggressive (RA) and those who were rejected but not aggressive (RONLY)—were randomly assigned to intervention or control conditions. Analyses performed on posttest and follow-up assessments revealed that RA children, relative to controls, declined significantly in peer group rejection and aggressive behavior. Moreover, this intervention benefited rejected aggressive children more than it did rejected nonaggressive children. This finding was attributed to the fact that the intervention's components were designed to address the needs of children who are rejected *because* they are aggressive with peers.

Deficit-Specific Social Skills Training Interventions

The movement toward tailoring the content of interventions to the needs of the child is further exemplified in an investigation conducted by Bienert and Schneider (1995). The preadolescents that participated in this intervention were initially identified because they had low scores on a measure of classroom peer acceptance. Of these children, those who also had high scores on a peer aggression or a peer isolation measure were assigned to either a treatment or control group. Specifically, children who scored low on peer acceptance and high on aggression (but not isolation) were assigned to either an aggression-specific training condition or a wait-list control group, whereas those who scored low on acceptance and high on isolation (but not aggression) were assigned to either an isolation-specific training condition or wait-list control group. A smaller number of children who fit each of these designations were assigned to crossover training conditions—that is, low-accepted aggressive children were given the isolation-specific intervention, and low-accepted isolated children received the aggression-specific training. Children's behavior and peer acceptance were assessed before and after the intervention (pretest, posttest) and 6 to 10 months after posttest (follow-up). At posttest, significant reductions in aggression were found for aggressive children who participated in aggression-specific training, but not for aggressive children who received the isolation-specific training. Likewise, isolated children became significantly less isolated only when they received isolation-specific training. These pre- to posttest changes in behavior were maintained from posttest to follow-up. More importantly, children who were matched to appropriate treatments also increased significantly in peer group acceptance from pretest to post-test. However, additional findings revealed that only the aggressive children in the aggression-specific condition maintained gains in peer acceptance until follow-up. Further, there was evidence to indicate that aggressive children achieved greater peer acceptance even when they received isolation-specific training. Thus, although these findings provide some support for dysfunction-specific interventions, they also highlight conceptual issues that require further investigation. For example, Bienert and Schneider's findings do not make it clear whether the interventions deployed for different types of children were differentially effective (i.e., powerful at instituting change) or whether the characteristics of the identified children were differentially malleable (i.e., responsive to treatment).

Practice and Policy Implications

Data attesting to the prevalence of peer group rejection and evidence linking this problem with early and later emerging mental health and school adjustment difficulties suggest that greater emphasis be placed on the prevention of peer group rejection, especially in the context of America's schools. At present, research on the prevention of peer group rejection provides a stronger empirical foundation for the design and implementation of indicated interventions than for universal or selected prevention programs. Essentially, more is known about how to help children escape from peer group rejection once they have experienced it than about how to prevent them from encountering it. Accordingly, the implications for practice are clear. Practitioners have more tools at their disposal for accomplishing the former objective than for achieving the latter aim.

Unfortunately, there is little systematic research to address the question of whether the protective functions of preventive interventions are best accomplished by intervening earlier versus later in children's development or schooling. Policies that favor early intervention are supported by evidence indicating that children experience peer group rejection at early ages (e.g., for a review, see Ladd & Coleman, 1993) and profit from early childhood prevention programs (e.g., Conduct Problems Prevention Research Group, 1999a; Mize & Ladd, 1990). Additionally, it appears that young children may be both more amenable and responsive to intervention than are older children and adolescents. Lochman (1990), for example, contends that young children are more willing to participate in interventions, less concerned about why they have been selected, and more facile at changing their behavior patterns. Further, fewer of the factors that often diminish prevention effects with older children and adolescents (e.g., peer crowds' support for deviance, peers' subversion of behavioral or reputational change) are present during early childhood (Forehand & Long, 1991). However, policies that advocate early intervention exclusively have limitations. For example, the skills that children acquire from early interventions may not endure or generalize to later developmental and social challenges (Bierman & Montminy, 1993), and some proven prevention procedures are not feasible with young children (Weisz, 1997). All things considered, the most effective prevention programs may be those implemented early in children's development and then extended over time with regularly scheduled, developmentally appropriate "booster treatments" (see Lochman, 1990).

FUTURE DIRECTIONS

Peer group rejection has been an enduring concern within the research community, and past and recent prevalence estimates indicate that this concern has not been misplaced. Historically, the interventions developed to improve children's peer relations have evolved from relatively simple social learning strategies (e.g., showing children skilled models or shaping their social behaviors) to more complex, multicomponent methods (i.e., intervention packages) that are based on diverse theoretical models (e.g., principles from social cognitive, motivational, emotional, behavioral, ecological, and reinforcement theories; see Ladd & Mize, 1983; Ladd et al., 2002) and that address the specific needs of the child (e.g., particular skill deficits). Another emergent trend is that investigators have progressively adjusted the focus of interventions to keep pace with evolving theory and evidence that has implicated multiple risk factors as causes for peer group rejection. For example, consistent with evidence implicating both skill deficits and behavioral excesses as causes of peer group rejection (see Ladd, 1999), there has been a significant shift in treatment curricula toward multicomponent programs aimed at facilitating both skill acquisition and the elimination of antisocial behavior.

The research initiatives needed to guide future research are numerous and varied. Of the universal preventive interventions developed thus far, few have been designed specifically to prevent peer group rejection, and of those that have, most have produced equivocal findings. Consequently, insight into the value of this form of prevention is limited, and a much higher level of research investment is needed before firm conclusions can be drawn about the effectiveness of universal preventive interventions for problems such as peer group rejection. Similarly, it has been rare for researchers to deploy prevention trials for peer group rejection at the selective level. There is growing evidence, however, to suggest that some risk factors for peer group rejection are responsive to treatment (e.g., aggressive behavior, deviant social cognitions), suggesting that it may be possible to prevent this malady by reducing or eliminating some of the conditions that antecede it. Although speculative, this conclusion receives some support from evidence obtained by the Conduct Problems Prevention Research Group (1999a). It is conceivable, therefore, that knowledge about the prevention of peer group rejection might be advanced by implementing interventions that have proven effective for reducing other forms of psychopathology, particularly dysfunctions that are known to be risk factors for peer group rejection. Alternatively, this could also be accomplished if measures of peer group rejection were routinely incorporated into a broader spectrum of prevention trials.

In contrast, a variety of *indicated* preventive interventions have proven effective for children who have been exposed to or are currently experiencing peer group rejection. On balance, evidence suggests that interventions based on variations of the coaching paradigm, which have been designed to promote skill acquisition and behavior change, have produced some of the most promising results. Asher et al. (1996) found that 9 of 13 coaching programs produced gains in peer acceptance at posttest and/or follow-up. Yet, further research is needed to clarify why some coaching programs have produced gains in skill acquisition and peer acceptance (e.g., Bierman, 1986; Bierman et al., 1987; Csapo, 1983; Gresham & Nagle, 1980; Ladd, 1981) whereas others produced improvements in either social skills or peer acceptance but not both (see Coie & Koeppl, 1990).

These findings underscore the need for research on the mediators of skill acquisition and the processes that bring about relational changes, such as peer group acceptance. Implicit in this approach to prevention is the premise that changes in the individual child (e.g., the acquisition of specific social skills, the elimination of antisocial behaviors) are instrumental in changing peers' sentiments toward that child (i.e., feelings of liking or disliking), which ultimately determine the child's social status among peers (e.g., peer acceptance, rejection). However, with the exception of Bierman (1986), few have examined this premise, and much remains to be learned about how peers perceive changes in children's behavioral competencies and how children's existing reputations among peers are altered (see Hymel, Wagner, et al., 1990). It is also unclear whether the efficacy and efficiency of existing indicated interventions could be improved by adding components that are designed to alter features of children's peer groups (e.g., building tolerance/respect for individual differences).

In summary, peer group rejection is a serious problem that affects the lives of children throughout their formative years. Although progress toward the prevention of peer group rejection is evident, more is known about how to reduce this problem's severity than about how to inoculate children against it or reduce their risk of exposure. Studies of preventive interventions at the indicated level suggest that coaching procedures can be effective for helping children recover from peer group rejection (i.e., gain acceptance in their peer groups). This is an important achievement, and a widespread implementation of these tools could greatly reduce the population of children who are likely to remain rejected and develop associated mental heath problems.

REFERENCES

Asher, S. R., & Dodge, K. A. (1986). Identifying children who are rejected by their peers. *Developmental Psychology, 22,* 442–449.

Asher, S. R., Hymel, S., & Renshaw, P. D. (1984). Loneliness in children. *Child Development, 55,* 1456–1464.

Asher, S. R., Parker, J. G., & Walker, D. L. (1996). Distinguishing friendship from acceptance: Implications for intervention and assessment. In W. M. Bukowski & A. F. Newcomb (Eds.), *The company they keep: Friendship in childhood and adolescence* (pp. 366–405). New York: Cambridge University Press.

Bagwell, C. L., Coie, J. D., Terry, R. A., & Lochman, J. E. (2000). Peer clique participation and social status in preadolescence. *Merrill-Palmer Quarterly, 46,* 280–305.

Berndt, T. J., & Ladd, G. W. (1989). *Peer relationships in child development.* New York: Wiley.

Bienert, H., & Schneider, B. H. (1995). Deficit-specific social skills training with peer-nominated aggressive-disruptive and sensitive-isolated preadolescents. *Journal of Clinical Child Psychology, 24,* 287–299.

Bierman, K. L. (1986). Process of change during social skills training with preadolescents and its relation to treatment outcome. *Child Development, 57,* 230–240.

Bierman, K. L., & Furman, W. (1984). The effects of social skills training and peer involvement on the social adjustment of preadolescents. *Child Development, 55,* 151–162.

Bierman, K. L., Miller, C. L., & Stabb, S. D. (1987). Improving the social behavior and peer acceptance of rejected boys: Effects of social skill training with instructions and prohibitions. *Journal of Consulting and Clinical Psychology, 55,* 194–200.

Bierman, K. L., & Montminy, H. P. (1993). Developmental issues in social-skills assessment and intervention with children and adolescents. *Behavior Modification, 17,* 229–254.

Bierman, K. L., & Wargo, J. B. (1995). Predicting the longitudinal course associated with aggressive-rejected, aggressive (nonrejected), and rejected (nonaggressive) status. *Development and Psychopathology, 7,* 669–682.

Brendgen, M., Little, T. D., & Krapmann, L. (2000). Rejected children and their friends: A shared evaluation of friendship quality? *Merrill-Palmer Quarterly, 46,* 45–70.

Buhs, E., & Ladd, G. W. (2001). Peer rejection in kindergarten: Relational processes mediating academic and emotional outcomes. *Developmental Psychology, 37,* 550–560.

Bukowski, W. M., & Hoza, B. (1989). Popularity and friendship: Issues in theory, measurement, and outcome. In T. J. Berndt & G. W. Ladd (Eds.), *Peer relationships in child development* (pp. 15–45). New York: Wiley.

Cairns, R. B., & Cairns, B. D. (1994). *Lifelines and risks: Pathways of youth in our time.* New York: Cambridge University Press.

Cassidy, J., & Asher, S. R. (1992). Loneliness and peer relations in young children. *Child Development, 63,* 350–365.

Cassidy, J., Parke, R. D., Butkovsky, L., & Braungart, J. M. (1992). Family-peer connections: The roles of emotional expressiveness within the family and children's understanding of emotions. *Child Development, 55,* 1486–1492.

Choi, H., & Hechenlaible-Gotto, M. J. (1998). Classroom based social skills training: Impact on peer acceptance of first-grade students. *Journal of Educational Research, 91,* 209–214.

Cillessen, A. H., & Bukowski, W. M. (2000). *Recent advances in the measurement of acceptance and rejection in the peer system* [New Directions for Child Development, No. 88]. San Francisco: Jossey-Bass.

Clark, K. E., & Ladd, G. W. (2000). Connectedness and autonomy support in parent-child relationships: Links to children's socioemotional orientation and peer relationships. *Developmental Psychology, 36,* 485–498.

Coie, J. D., & Dodge, K. A. (1983). Continuities and changes in children's social status: A five-year longitudinal study. *Merrill-Palmer Quarterly, 29,* 261–282.

Coie, J. D., Dodge, K. A., & Coppotelli, H. (1982). Dimensions and types of social status: A cross-age perspective. *Developmental Psychology, 18,* 557–570.

Coie, J. D., Dodge, K. A., Terry, R., & Wright, V. (1991). The role of aggression in peer relations: An analysis of aggression episodes in boys' play groups. *Child Development, 62,* 812–826.

Coie, J. D., & Koeppl, G. K. (1990). Adapting intervention to the problems of aggressive and disruptive rejected children. In S. R. Asher & J. D. Coie (Eds.), *Peer rejection in childhood* (pp. 309–337). New York: Cambridge University Press.

Coie, J. D., & Krehbiel, G. (1984). Effects of academic tutoring on the social status of low-achieving, socially rejected children. *Child Development, 55,* 1465–1478.

Coie, J. D., & Kupersmidt, J. B. (1983). A behavioral analysis of emerging social status in boys' groups. *Child Development, 54,* 1400–1416.

Coie, J. D., Lochman, J. E., Terry, R., & Hyman, C. (1992). Predicting early adolescent disorder from childhood aggression and peer rejection. *Journal of Consulting and Clinical Psychology, 60,* 783–792.

Coie, J. D., Watt, N. F., West, S. G., Hawkins, J. D., Asarnow, J. R., Markman, H. J., et al. (1993). The science of prevention: A conceptual framework and some directions for a national research program. *American Psychologist, 48,* 1013–1022.

Conduct Problems Prevention Research Group. (1999a). Initial impact of the Fast Track prevention trial for conduct problems: I. The high-risk sample. *Journal of Consulting and Clinical Psychology, 67*(5), 631–647.

Conduct Problems Prevention Research Group. (1999b). Initial impact of the Fast Track prevention trial for conduct problems: II. Classroom effects. *Journal of Consulting and Clinical Psychology, 67*(5), 648–657.

Conduct Problems Prevention Research Group. (2002). Evaluation of the first 3 years of the Fast Track prevention trial with children at high risk for adolescent conduct problems. *Journal of Abnormal Child Psychology, 30,* 19–35.

Crick, N. R., & Dodge, K. A. (1994). A review and reformulation of social information-processing mechanisms in children's social adjustment. *Psychological Bulletin, 115,* 74–101.

Crick, N. R., & Grotpeter, J. K. (1995). Relational aggression, gender, and social-psychological adjustment. *Child Development, 66,* 710–722.

Crick, N. R., & Ladd, G. W. (1990). Children's perceptions of the consequences of aggressive strategies: Do the ends justify being mean? *Developmental Psychology, 26,* 612–620.

Crick, N. R., & Ladd, G. W. (1993). Children's perceptions of their peer experiences: Attributions, social anxiety, and social avoidance. *Developmental Psychology, 29,* 244–254.

Csapo, M. (1983). Effectiveness of coaching socially withdrawn/isolated children in specific social skills. *Educational Psychology, 3,* 31–42.

DeRosier, M. E., Kupersmidt, J. B., & Patterson, C. J. (1994). Children's academic and behavioral adjustment as a function of the chronicity and proximity of peer rejection. *Child Development, 65,* 1799–1813.

Dodge, K. A. (1983). Behavioral antecedents of peer social status. *Child Development, 54,* 1386–1399.

Dodge, K. A., Murphy, R. M., & Buchsbaum, K. (1984). The assessment of intention-cue detection skills in children: Implications for developmental psychopathology. *Child Development, 55,* 163–173.

Eisenberg, N., Fabes, R., Bernzweig, J., Karbon, M., Poulin, R., & Hanish, L. (1993). The relations of emotionality and regulation to preschooler's social skills and sociometric status. *Child Development, 64,* 1418–1438.

Fabes, R., Eisenberg, N., Jones, S., Smith, M., Guthrie, I., Poulin, R., et al. (1999). Regulation, emotionality, and preschooler's socially competent peer interactions. *Child Development, 70,* 432–442.

Forehand, R., & Long, N. (1991). Prevention of aggression and other behavior problems in the early adolescent years. In D. J. Pepler & K. H. Rubin (Eds.), *The development and treatment of childhood aggression* (pp. 317–330). Hillsdale, NJ: Erlbaum.

French, D. C. (1990). Heterogeneity of peer-rejected girls. *Child Development, 61,* 2028–2031.

Gottman, J. M., Gonso, J., & Schuler, P. (1976). Teaching social skills to isolated children. *Journal of Abnormal Child Psychology, 4,* 179–197.

Gresham, F. M., & Nagle, R. J. (1980). Social skills training with children: Responsiveness to modeling and coaching as a function of peer orientation. *Journal of Consulting and Clinical Psychology, 48,* 718–729.

Hallinan, M. T. (1976). Friendship patterns in open and traditional classrooms. *Sociology of Education, 49,* 245–265.

Hepler, J. B. (1994). Evaluating the effectiveness of a social skills program for preadolescents. *Research on Social Work Practice, 4,* 411–435.

Hepler, J. B., & Rose, S. F. (1998). Evaluation of a multicomponent group approach for improving the social skills of elementary school children. *Journal of Social Service Research, 11,* 18.

Hudley, C., & Graham, S. (1993). An attributional intervention to reduce peer-directed aggression among African American boys. *Child Development, 64,* 124–138.

Hymel, S., & Asher, S. R. (1977, April). *Assessment and training of isolated children's social skills.* Paper presented at the biennial meeting of the Society for Research in Child Development, New Orleans, LA.

Hymel, S., Rubin, K. H., Rowden, L., & LeMare, L. (1990). Children's peer relationships: Longitudinal prediction of internalizing and externalizing problems from middle to late childhood. *Child Development, 61,* 2004–2021.

Hymel, S., Wagner, E., & Butler, L. J. (1990). Reputational bias: View from the peer group. In S. R. Asher & J. D. Coie (Eds.), *Peer rejection in childhood: Cambridge studies in social and emotional development* (pp. 156–186). New York: Cambridge University Press.

Kellam, S. G., Ling, X., Merisca, R., Brown, C. H., & Ialongo, N. (1998). The effect of the level of aggression in the first grade classroom on the course and malleability of aggressive behavior into middle school. *Development and Psychopathology, 10,* 165–185.

Kupersmidt, J. B., & Coie, J. D. (1990). Preadolescent peer status, aggression, and school adjustment as predictors of externalizing problems in adolescence. *Child Development, 61,* 1350–1362.

Kupersmidt, J. B., Coie, J. D., & Dodge, K. A. (1990). The role of poor peer relationships in the development of disorder. In S. R. Asher & J. D. Coie (Eds.), *Peer rejection in childhood* (pp. 274–305). New York: Cambridge University Press.

Ladd, G. W. (1981). Effectiveness of a social learning method for enhancing children's social interaction and peer acceptance. *Child Development, 52,* 171–178.

Ladd, G. W. (1985). Documenting the effects of social skill training with children: Process and outcome assessment. In B. Schneider, K. Rubin, & J. Ledingham (Eds.), *Children's peer relations: Issues in assessment and intervention* (pp. 243–269). New York: Springer-Verlag.

Ladd, G. W. (1990). Having friends, keeping friends, making friends, and being liked by peers in the classroom: Predictors of children's early school adjustment? *Child Development, 61,* 1081–1100.

Ladd, G. W. (1999). Peer relationships and social competence during early and middle childhood. *Annual Review of Psychology, 50,* 333–359.

Ladd, G. W. (2003). Probing the adaptive significance of children's behavior and relationships in the school context: A child by environment perspective. In R. Kail (Ed.), Advances in Child Behavior and Development (pp. 43–104). New York: Wiley.

Ladd, G. W., Birch, S. H., & Buhs, E. S. (1999). Children's social and scholastic lives in kindergarten: Related spheres of influence? *Child Development, 70,* 1373–1400.

Ladd, G. W., Buhs, E., & Troop, W. (2002). Children's interpersonal skills and relationships in school settings: Adaptive significance and implications for school-based prevention and intervention programs. In P. K. Smith & C. H. Hart (Eds.), *Blackwell's Handbook of Childhood Social Development* (pp. 394–415). London: Blackwell Publishers.

Ladd, G. W., & Burgess, K. B. (1999). Charting the relationship trajectories of aggressive, withdrawn, and aggressive/withdrawn children during early grade school. *Child Development, 70,* 910–929.

Ladd, G. W., & Burgess, K. B. (2001). Do relational risks and protective factors moderate the linkages between childhood aggression and early psychological and school adjustment? *Child Development, 72,* 1579–1601.

Ladd, G. W., & Coleman, C. (1993). Young children's peer relationships: Forms, features, and functions. In B. Spodek (Ed.), *Handbook of research on the education of young children* (pp. 57–76). New York: Macmillan.

Ladd, G. W., & Hart, C. H. (1992). Creating informal play opportunities: Are parents and preschooler's initiations related to children's competence with peers? *Developmental Psychology, 28,* 1179–1187.

Ladd, G. W., Kochenderfer, B. J., & Coleman, C. C. (1997). Classroom peer acceptance, friendship, and victimization: Distinct relational systems that contribute uniquely to children's school adjustment? *Child Development, 68,* 1181–1197.

Ladd, G. W., & Mize, J. (1983). A cognitive-social learning model of social-skill training. *Psychological Review, 90,* 127–157.

Ladd, G. W., & Pettit, G. S. (2002). Parents and children's peer relationships. In M. Bornstein (Ed.), *Handbook of parenting* (2nd ed., Vol. 4, pp. 377–409). Hillsdale, NJ: Erlbaum.

Ladd, G. W., & Price, J. M. (1987). Predicting children's social and school adjustment following the transition from preschool to kindergarten. *Child Development, 58,* 1168–1189.

Ladd, G. W., Price, J. M., & Hart, C. H. (1988). Predicting preschoolers' peer status from their playground behaviors. *Child Development, 59,* 986–992.

Ladd, G. W., & Troop-Gordon, W. (2003). The role of chronic peer adversity in the development of children's psychological adjustment problems. Child Development, 74, 1325–1348.

La Greca, A. M., & Santogrossi, D. A. (1980). Social skills training with elementary school students: A behavioral group approach. *Journal of Consulting and Clinical Psychology, 48,* 220–227.

Last, J. M. (2001). *A dictionary of epidemiology.* New York: Oxford University Press.

Lochman, J. E. (1990). Modification of childhood aggression. In M. Hersen, R. M. Eisler, & P. M. Miller (Eds.), *Progress in behavior modification* (pp. 47–85). Newbury Park, CA: Sage.

Lochman, J. E. (2000). Parent and family skills training in targeted prevention programs for at-risk youth. *Journal of Primary Prevention, 21,* 253–265.

Lochman, J. E., Burch, P. R., Curry, J. F., & Lampron, L. B. (1984). Treatment and generalization effects of cognitive-behavioral and goal-setting interventions with aggressive boys. *Journal of Consulting and Clinical Psychology, 52,* 915–916.

Lochman, J. E., Coie, J. D., Underwood, M. K., & Terry, R. (1993). Effectiveness of a social relations intervention program for aggressive and nonaggressive, rejected children. *Journal of Consulting and Clinical Psychology, 61*(6), 1053–1058.

Lochman, J. E., Dunn, S. E., & Klimes-Dougan, B. (1993). An intervention and consultation model from a social-cognitive perspective: A description of the Anger Coping Program. *School Psychology Review, 22,* 456–469.

Lochman, J. E., & Lenhart, L. A. (1993). Anger coping intervention for aggressive children: Conceptual models and outcome effects. *Clinical Psychology Review, 13,* 785–805.

MacDougall, P., Hymel, S., Vaillancourt, T., & Mercer, L. (2001). The consequences of childhood peer rejection. In M. R. Leary (Ed.), *Interpersonal rejection* (pp. 213–247). Oxford, England: Oxford University Press.

Mize, J., & Ladd, G. W. (1990). A cognitive-social learning approach to social skill training with low-status preschool children. *Developmental Psychology, 26,* 388–397.

Mize, J., Pettit, G., & Brown, G. (1995). Mother's supervision of their children's peer play: Relations with beliefs, perceptions, and knowledge. *Developmental Psychology, 31,* 311–321.

Moreno, J. L. (1932). *Applications of the group method to classification.* New York: National Committee on Prisons and Prison Labor.

Newcomb, A. F., & Bukowski, W. M. (1983). Social impact and social preference as determinants of children's peer group status. *Developmental Psychology, 19,* 856–867.

Newcomb, A. F., & Bukowski, W. M. (1984). A longitudinal study of the utility of social preference and social impact sociometric classification schemes. *Child Development, 55,* 1434–1447.

O'Connor, R. D. (1969). Modification of social withdrawal through symbolic modeling. *Journal of Applied Behavior Analysis, 2,* 15–22.

O'Connor, R. D. (1972). Relative efficacy of modeling, shaping, and the combined procedures for modification of social withdrawal. *Journal of Abnormal Psychology, 79,* 327–334.

Oden, S., & Asher, S. R. (1977). Coaching children in social skills for friendship making. *Child Development, 48,* 495–506.

Ollendick, T. H., Weist, M. D., Borden, M. G., & Green, R. W. (1992). Sociometric status and academic, behavioral, and psychological adjustment: A five-year longitudinal study. *Journal of Consulting and Clinical Psychology, 60,* 80–87.

O'Neil, R., Welsh, M., Parke, R. D., Wang, S., & Strand, C. (1997). A longitudinal assessment of the academic correlates of early peer acceptance and rejection. *Journal of Clinical Child Psychology, 26,* 290–303.

Parker, J. G., & Asher, S. R. (1987). Peer relations and later personal adjustment: Are low-accepted children at risk? *Psychological Bulletin, 102,* 357–389.

Parker, J. G., & Asher, S. R. (1993). Friendship and friendship quality in middle childhood: Links with peer group acceptance and feelings of loneliness and social dissatisfaction. *Developmental Psychology, 29,* 611–621.

Parker, J. G., Rubin, K. H., Price, J. M., & DeRosier, M. E. (1995). Peer relationships, child development, and adjustment: A developmental psychopathology perspective. In D. Cicchetti & D. J. Cohen (Eds.), *Developmental psychopathology: Risk, disorder, and adaptation* (Vol. 2, pp. 96–161). New York: Wiley.

Patterson, G. R., Reid, J. B., & Dishion, T. J. (1992). *Antisocial boys.* Eugene, OR: Castalia.

Pellegrini, D. S. (1990). Psychosocial risk and protective factors in childhood. *Developmental and Behavioral Pediatrics, 11,* 201–209.

Pettit, G. S., Bates, J. E., & Dodge, K. A. (1997). Supportive parenting, ecological context, and children's adjustment: A seven-year longitudinal study. *Child Development, 68,* 908–923.

Pettit, G. S., Dodge, K. A., & Brown, M. (1988). Early family experience, social problem-solving patterns, and children's social competence. *Child Development, 59,* 107–120.

Rotheram, M. J., Armstrong, M., & Booraem, C. (1982). Assertiveness training in fourth- and fifth-grade children. *American Journal of Community Psychology, 10,* 567–582.

Rubin, K. H., LeMare, L., & Lollis, S. (1990). Social withdrawal in childhood: Developmental pathways to peer rejection. In S. R. Asher & J. D. Coie (Eds.), *Peer rejection in childhood* (pp. 217–252). New York: Cambridge University Press.

Schneider, B. H. (1992). Didactic methods for enhancing children's peer relations: A quantitative review. *Clinical Psychology Review, 12,* 363–382.

Stormshak, E. A., Bierman, K. A., Bruschi, C., Dodge, K. A., & Coie, J. D. (1999). The relation between behavior problems and peer preference in different classroom contexts. Child Development, 70, 169–182.

Terry, R., & Coie, J. D. (1991). A comparison method for defining sociometric status among children. *Developmental Psychology, 27,* 867–890.

Tiffen, K., & Spence, S. H. (1986). Responsiveness of isolated versus rejected children to social skills training. *Journal of Child Psychology and Psychiatry and Allied Disciplines, 27,* 343–355.

Vandell, D. L., & Hembree, S. E. (1994). Peer social status and friendship: Independent contributors to children's social and academic adjustment. *Merrill-Palmer Quarterly, 40,* 461–477.

Volling, B. V., MacKinnon-Lewis, C., Rabiner, D., & Baradaran, L. P. (1993). Children's social competence and sociometric status: Further exploration of aggression, social withdrawal, and peer rejection. *Development and Psychopathology, 5,* 459–483.

Webster-Stratton, C., & Hammond, M. (1997). Treating children with early onset conduct problems: A comparison of child and parent training interventions. *Journal of Consulting and Clinical Psychology, 65*(1), 93–109.

Webster-Stratton, C., Reid, M. J., & Hammond, M. (2001). Social problem solving training for children with early onset conduct problems: Who benefits? *Journal of Child Psychology and Psychiatry, 42,* 943–952.

Weisz, J. R. (1997). Effects of interventions for child and adolescent psychological dysfunction: Relevance of context, developmental factors, and individual differences. In S. S. Luthar, J. A. Burack, D. Cicchetti, & J. R. Weisz (Eds.), *Developmental psychopathology: Perspectives on adjustment, risk, and disorder* (pp. 3–22). New York: Cambridge University Press.

Wright, J. C., Giammarino, M., & Parad, H. W. (1986). Social status in small groups: Individual-group similarity and the social "misfit." *Journal of Personality and Social Psychology, 50,* 523–536.

Chapter 3

UNRESOLVED GRIEF

CAROLYN HILARSKI

An overwhelming number of youth are exposed to loss in the United States. In the year 2000, 750,000 American youth experienced the death of one parent (Grieve, 2000). Three of every 100 children annually suffer the loss of a significant other family member (Kmietowicz, 2000). Further, more than 40,000 youths die each year. This loss influences a minimum of four individuals. A subgroup of bereaved youth, more often males than females, perceive their loss as traumatic (Selekman, Busch, & Kimble, 2001). This subgroup, experiencing complicated bereavement, is at risk for anxiety, depression, and conduct disorder behavior (Black, 1996; Sanchez, Fristad, Weller, Weller, & Moye, 1994; Weller, Weller, Fristad, & Bowes, 1991). These maladaptive responses become entrenched if the trauma reaction is not resolved (Bentovim, 1986).

Prevention services for bereaved children are lacking (Black, 1996; Dowdney et al., 1999). For example, parentally bereaved children under 5 years tend not to receive services. Parentally bereaved children over 5 years do not receive services unless they began them before their parent's expected death (often through hospice) or their parent committed suicide. In addition, there is often no relationship between the service provided and the child's response to loss (Dowdney et al., 1999) because of incorrect parent/professional assessment resulting from a self-limiting behavioral response in the child (Bentovim, 1986). In addition, parent and professional ambiguity about the child's ability to mourn contributes to this lack of relationship (Black, 1998; Cohen, Mannarino, Greenberg, Padlo, & Shipley, 2002; Norris-Shortle, Young, & Williams, 1993). This ambiguity restrains intervention activity and increases the likelihood of youth experiencing unresolved grief (Norris-Shortle et al., 1993).

Prevention efforts to reduce unresolved grief in bereaved youth are available (Selekman et al., 2001). Children experience loss and need to be aware of the bereavement experience (Black, 1996), which includes an understanding that life changes after loss and talking about the change helps to promote reconciliation (Black, 1996; Cohen et al., 2002). Families need support during the mourning process. This support may include bereavement counseling or education for all family members (Bentovim, 1986; Black & Urbanowicz, 1987). A bereaved child living with a bereaved parent (usually female) who is experiencing complicated bereavement or unresolved grief is at risk for unresolved grief and its long-term ramifications (Dowdney et al., 1999). Indeed, therapeutic intervention after bereavement is a successful preventive tool for unresolved grief in adults and is expected to be equally so for youth (Black, 1996).

DEFINITIONS

Loss is a universal human experience and children are not exempt (Breslau, Chilcoat, Kessler, & Davis, 1999). The human response to loss is complicated and relates to the individual's stage of development, prior experiences, and social supports (Cohen et al., 2002; Selekman et al., 2001). When an individual experiences loss, certain processes occur. The following definitions delineate these processes:

- *Bereavement* is the *objective state of being* due to loss (Charkow, 1998). Often the context is in the loss of a loved person although it could be the loss of a loved thing (Foster, 1981; Marwit & Carusa, 1998).
- *Mourning* is the culturally influenced emotional process of dealing with loss (Foster, 1981). It is the working through or the reframing of the loss with the help of cultural dogma and rituals so that homeostasis remains (Neimeyer, Prigerson, & Davies, 2002).
- *Grief* is the emotional and psychological reaction to the individual's perception of the loss (Marwit & Carusa, 1998). This condition is a subjective response influenced by the nature of the relationship with the loved thing or person, the reactions of others to the loss, in addition to early childhood attachment experience (Neimeyer et al., 2002).
- *Unresolved grief* is a more chronic state and is associated with health consequences that often require intervention. The nature, duration, and severity of physiological and emotional symptoms distinguish unresolved grief from mourning (Marwit, 1996). Circumstances where mourning is interrupted or there is a history of depression and the relationship with the deceased was characterized by a hostile interaction may predict an unresolved grief reaction.

TRENDS AND INCIDENCE OF UNRESOLVED
GRIEF IN YOUTH

There are no published prevalence rates for unresolved grief in youth because of the general understanding that children do not have the developmental capacity to mourn (Miller, 1971; Rosen, 1985; Wolfenstein, 1966). Decathexis (the emotional withdrawal of psychic energy) is an essential factor in the mourning process (Christ, 2000; Sekaer, 1987). Children are considered incapable of completing decathexis because of their inability to fully understand the concept of death or manage their emotional responses (Christ, 2000; Miller, 1971; Rosen, 1985; Wolfenstein, 1966, 1969). If a child does not understand that death is permanent or does understand but chooses to engage in denial because of overwhelming emotions, the work of letting go of the loved object (decathexis) is not begun.

Bowlby (1984) and Furman (1983), on the other hand, assert that children do mourn. Moreover, children understand when separated from a loved object and emotionally respond to this circumstance. The process of mourning for bereaved children can be healthy or unhealthy, as it is with adults (Bowlby, 1984; Furman, 1983). However, because of developmental issues (e.g., language development), children do not exhibit their emotions as adults do. For example, bereaved youth may initially respond to loss with cheerfulness or disinterest (termed *absence of mourning*; Cheifetz, Stavrakakis, & Lester, 1989). The condition of absence of mourning is seen, but it is not to be expected (Vida & Grizenko, 1989). If the behavior is exhibited, it is a stage-related coping response (Cheifetz et al., 1989).

Similar to adults, bereaved children and adolescents report feeling shock, anger, fear, confusion, guilt, responsibility, and hopelessness. Additionally, like adults, bereaved youth experience depression, anxiety, posttraumatic stress disorder (PTSD), conduct disorders, phobic reactions, hallucinations, suicidal ideation and attempts, and reduced psychosocial functioning (Black, 1996, 1998; Dowdney et al., 1999). Finally, bereaved children use defense mechanisms, as adults, to reduce seemingly unmanageable emotions in response to loss. Thus, it is reasonable to assume that children share unresolved grief prevalence rates comparable to adults.

The published prevalence rates for adult individuals suffering from unresolved grief range from 14% to 64% (Horowitz et al., 1997; Kim & Jacobs, 1991; McDermott et al., 1997; Middleton, Burnett, Raphael, & Martinek, 1996; Prigerson et al., 1997; Zisook & DeVaul, 1984). The wide range of estimates results from the diverse sample selection criteria and the lack of standardized criteria for unresolved grief. Standardized criteria for unresolved grief is difficult to obtain because the mourning process is individual and developmentally and contextually influenced.

The time line for uncomplicated mourning is believed to be somewhere between four and six months (Clayton, 1990; Jacobs & Ostfeld, 1980; Parkes, 1972). The presence of symptoms (or responsive behaviors) after six months puts the bereaved person in an unresolved grieving pattern (Prigerson & Jacobs, 2001). In this pattern, the individual is at increased risk for psychological, physical, and social impairment because unattended, unresolved grief symptoms do not appear to change over time (Prigerson et al., 1997; Prigerson, Shear, et al., 1999; Prigerson & Jacobs, 2001; Zisook & DeVaul, 1983). The intensity of unresolved grief response peaks six months after a loss and tends to remain high 25 months and beyond (Prigerson, Shear, et al., 1999).

RISK FACTORS FOR UNRESOLVED GRIEF IN YOUTH

Unresolved grief reaction in youth is not fully understood because of the debate over the child's ability to mourn. However, the underlying emotional processes of mourning in adults and children are similar (both populations experience similar feelings of anger, detachment, despair, and protest), but presenting behaviors of these emotions differ (Christ, 2000). There is also a significant difference in the context of mourning for these populations. Specifically, the absence of a supportive parenting figure complicates successful mourning for youth (Cohen et al., 2002). Indeed, the absence of the parenting figure during the mourning process is a greater threat to the child's sense of security and health than the loss itself (Neimeyer et al., 2002).

Furthermore, children at certain ages are developmentally unable to understand the concepts of finality and causality of loss (Norris-Shortle et al., 1993). For example, up to the age of 3 years, the child's concept of death is related to separation. Death is *magically reversible* at the age of 4 or 5 and *absolute* by age 9 (Selekman et al., 2001). *School-age youth* begin to understand that loss is permanent but lack the ability and skills to integrate the intense emotions they experience. Parentally bereaved *adolescents* find their work of differentiating from a primary caregiver unattainable (Worden & Silverman, 1996), especially in early teen years, when the youth is home more with a bereaved parent in complicated mourning.

Age and Gender Risk Factors for Unresolved Grief

Dysphoria, withdrawn behavior, and deterioration in school performance present similarly across age and gender categories (Van Eerdewegh, Clayton, & Van Eerdewegh, 1985). Depression, sleep and appetite difficulties, loss of interest in activities, bedwetting, and temper tantrums differ by age and gender. Specifically, depression, sleep, and appetite difficulties are more prevalent in female adolescents. Younger youth are more likely to present with conduct problems, bedwetting, and withdrawn behavior.

Bereaved middle childhood and adolescent males are more likely to experience an unresolved grief response (e.g., withdrawal) to a same-gender parent's death. Females, on the other hand, are more likely to respond behaviorally to the death of a same-gender sibling. Behaviorally, adolescent females present with attention and anger issues whereas middle childhood females are more likely to display depressive and anxious behavior (Worden, Davies, & McCown, 1999).

The explanation for this female same-gender sibling reaction is clarified by the work of Buhrmester (1990). Females report that siblings provide important social and emotional supports beginning in middle childhood. Additionally, adolescent females are more likely to share intimate details with other females and with a same-gender sibling than with a parent. Thus, a same-gender sibling's death is a significant loss of an intimate partner, especially when the sibling is an older sister (Worden et al., 1999).

Males, on the other hand, may share intimate interactions with their fathers well into their teen years because they do not report sharing confidences with others until high school (Worden et al., 1999). Thus, the death of a father, perceived as an intimate comrade, is a significant loss for a male youth.

Family Functioning Risk Factors for Unresolved Grief

When a parental death occurs, the surviving parent's reaction to the death is central to the surviving child's perception (Cicchetti, Rogosch, & Toth, 1998) and integration of the loss (Davies, 1998; Kranzler, Shaffer, Wasserman, & Davies, 1990). Families that do not permit and/or support honest interaction, productive problem solving, member individuality, structural change, and resource input are not able to nourish a child's integration of loss (Davies, 1998).

Bereaved youth with a family history of psychiatric disorders (e.g., depression, somatic disorder) are at risk for unresolved grief in addition to comorbid disorders (Sood, Weller, Weller, Fristad, & Bowes, 1992; Weller et al., 1991). Further, bereaved youth whose parent or sibling died of suicide are at risk for suicide (Cerel, Fristad, Weller, & Weller, 2000).

Life Experiences That Are Risk Factors for Unresolved Grief

Bereaved youth with experiences such as troubled family environments, marital discord, long-term separation from a parent, financial hardships, and previous losses are at high risk for unresolved grief in addition to comorbid disorders (Elizur & Kaffman, 1983).

Youth Characteristics That Are Risk Factors for Unresolved Grief

Bereaved children with poor impulse control, emotional lability, and those responding with rage to frustrations are at risk for unresolved grief (Elizur & Kaffman, 1983). Further, bereaved youth with aggressive/independent and passive/dependent personality styles are at higher risk for depression (a disorder highly associated with unresolved grief; Gray, 1987).

Summary

The process of mourning a loss is generally self-limiting and lasts from four to six months. After six months, mourning may become a more chronic state, termed *unresolved grief.* There is no actual understanding of the prevalence of unresolved grief in adults or in youth. Terms used for chronic mourning are *pathological, atypical, abnormal, complicated, unresolved,* or *traumatic* grief. These diverse terms describe the struggle to understand the forces that influence the path an individual may take in the mourning process.

Complete understanding of the consequence of loss among children and adolescents is illusive. Although it is suggested that children mourn, experience similar emotions and health disorders as adults, and are capable of integrating the loss, *loss integration work* needs to be revisited at each new developmental stage (Furman, 1983, 1985, 1986). This reworking is needed, not because the effort was not completed in the previous stage, but because reconciliation is an ongoing process as life experience, language, and cognitive ability develops (Christ, 2000; Furman, 1983, 1985; Silverman & Worden, 1992).

Bereaved children appear to be most at risk for unresolved grief under the age of 5 and in early adolescence (Elizur & Kaffman, 1983; Fristad, Jedel, Weller, & Weller, 1993; Gray, 1987; Kranzler et al., 1990). These two groups appear to experience high levels of depression when compared with other age groups (Gray, 1987; Kranzler et al., 1990).

Surviving parental influence is essential in the child's reconciliation of his or her loss (Bifulco, Harris, & Brown, 1992; Breier, Kelsoe, Kirwin, Wolkowitz, & Pickar, 1988; Elizur & Kaffman, 1983; Gray, 1987; Harris, 1991; Hurd, 1999; Saler & Skolnick, 1992; Van Eerdewegh et al., 1985). Helpful parenting characteristics are an ability to listen, problem solve, openly communicate, and maintain a positive worldview (Bifulco et al., 1992; Black & Urbanowicz, 1987; Breier et al., 1988; Hurd, 1999).

UNIVERSAL PREVENTIVE INTERVENTIONS

There are no formal universal prevention programs for youth with unresolved grief. However, schools are an appropriate place to begin such an effort (Charkow, 1998; Findlay, 1999; Milton, 1999a, 1999b). Death education and group sharing is appropriate in the health or personal development portion of a school curriculum and most helpful if begun in kindergarten (Findlay, 1999; Milton, 1999a). Moreover, parents need to be included in this prevention effort because they are a primary influencing factor in the child's response to loss (Charkow, 1998; Cohen et al., 2002; Findlay, 1999; Milton, 1999a). *System* prevention is far superior to individual intervention (Black, 1991; Cohen et al., 2002).

Age-appropriate death education in the school curriculum helps to inoculate children for future loss exposure (Milton, 1999b). Further, it helps to identify bereaved children that may not be presenting with identifiable symptoms and thwart further escalation of any complicated mourning issues. Additionally, it encourages a dialogue between children; parents and children; and parents, children, and *others* about this very difficult subject (Cohen et al., 2002). Open communication about death and the accompanying emotions and thoughts are helpful in the mourning process by offering the child the opportunity to ask questions and diffuse incorrect fantasies about child, parent, or *other's* feelings about loss (Charkow, 1998). Finally, it offers parents the chance to observe helpful age-appropriate communication and interaction by other parents, teachers, or group leaders. If honest communication in the family system begins before a loss exposure or anytime during the mourning continuum, reconciliation is more likely (Charkow, 1998).

The parent and child's group needs to feel safe during the school-based death education component (Findlay, 1999; Milton, 1999a). To promote group member well-being, the teacher or group leader might share that tears and emotions are normal and natural when talking about loss and death. Questions to explore include: "What is death?" "What happens at a funeral?" "What is it like to lose a pet?" (Milton, 1999a). Some kind of group relaxation technique is helpful at termination of the educational and sharing session (Milton, 1999b).

An early middle-school intervention effort is Kaleidoscope Kids. Although the intervention is for bereaved youth, this intervention is likely a helpful universal prevention tool. The intervention, which includes a puppet show based on a bereaved aardvark, is presented in classrooms followed by a discussion of thoughts, feelings, and an invitation to share personal experiences (Charkow, 1998).

Books are a helpful way for parents and children to explore thoughts and feelings about loss (Milton, 1999b). Moreover, books are safe because the person experiencing the loss and the negative emotions surrounding that loss is in the book, not the child or parent (Milton, 1999a). Parents need to discuss loss with their children whenever the opportunity presents itself.

SELECTIVE PREVENTIVE INTERVENTIONS

The mourning process for bereaved children includes a series of tasks accomplished over time. The early task involves understanding the loss. If the child does not know about the nature of the loss, he or she is inclined to use fantasy to fill in the gaps. Moreover, a fear that he or she or a family member will die could emerge, leading the child to resort to psychological defenses such as denial or regression. The middle phase of grief is characterized by three tasks: accepting and emotionally acknowledging the reality of the loss, exploring and reevaluating the relationship to the loss, and facing and bearing the psychological pain that accompanies the realization of the loss. The mourning process will be incomplete if this undertaking is not accomplished, and the bereaved child will stay clinging to the lost object. The final work involves the reorganization of the child's sense of identity and of significant relationships. Over- and underidentification can be problematic in this phase where the bereaved child either overly identifies with the lost person out of a sense of loyalty or counter-identifies based on the fear of dying like the dead person (Cohen et al., 2002; Neimeyer et al., 2002; Norris-Shortle et al., 1993; Sekaer, 1987). This response to bereavement evolves over time and can often extend into adulthood.

Bereaved children are able to mourn successfully under facilitative circumstances such as psychotherapy or in an environment in which other family members and/or professionals encourage emotional expression (Charkow, 1998; Furman, 1985). Family member support is paramount and may include educating the primary caregivers about developmentally influenced responses to prevent misunderstandings and promote open communication and acceptance. For example, children under 5 years consider death reversible and may ask repeatedly when the deceased person is coming back. Children older than 6 often understand death as a punishment rather than an inevitable event and may withdraw because of guilt over causing the loss. The following sections describe how children generally respond to bereavement according to their developmental age and how parents might promote a healthy mourning process for the child.

Infants to 2 Years

Bereaved children at this age experience separation (Cohen et al., 2002). Their mourning response includes sleep and eating issues and an inability to be comforted (Black, 1998; Emswiler & Emswiler, 2000). Homeostasis is maintained by the infant's cathexis (transfer of emotional energy) to a new *love object* (i.e., a reliable, empathic, and loving caregiver; Sekaer, 1987). Reestablishing routine as soon as possible encourages this process and relieves the infant of the agonizing work of decathexis (disconnection of emotional energy to the lost love object).

Ages 3 to 5 years

Bereaved children at this age may withdraw in the presence of a strong adult bereavement response. In addition, the child may confuse and/or anger adults with verbal expressions that allude to understanding the loss or death, then declare, "I know Mommy will buy me that doll when she gets back."

Children in this stage of development often express their bereavement response through regressive behavior. They share their thoughts and feelings through play and drawings rather than language. Indeed, the death event is best described through doll role play that recreates concrete scenarios (Cohen et al., 2002).

Parents must be available to the child (Milton, 1999a). This includes showing respect and acceptance of the child's thoughts and feelings. Understanding the fundamental concepts of play therapy is helpful in this endeavor (Kottman, 1994). Additionally, the mourning process moves forward when both parent(s) and child are willing and able to talk about the deceased person or loss through sharing of memories and ritual behaviors (Milton, 1999a). Parents must understand that children in this stage of development may not understand the permanence of the death or loss for many months. Moreover, these children may exhibit their bereavement response through irritable and regressive behavior, which may precipitate negative feelings in the parent. Bereavement skills training is helpful for parents (Hare & Skinner, 1988). Discussion topics include children's understanding of loss, parents' fears of loss, factors that affect children's response to loss, and common behaviors that children display in response to loss (Charkow, 1998).

Ages 6 to 8 Years

Bereaved children in this age group generally understand irreversibility; however, they may *pretend in play* that the deceased person is still with them or the loss did not happen to reduce any overwhelming emotional response to the loss. These children are able to express only brief moments of sadness, anger, anxiety, and fear because of their inability to reframe the cognitions that precipitate these feelings. They may also express a desire, with no general plan, to die so they can be with the deceased person (Cohen et al., 2002). At this stage of development, there is a common belief that a bad circumstance can cause death (Charkow, 1998). For example, the *thought* "I want daddy to stop hurting" may cause daddy's death. There is also a need in this group to form a positive memory of the deceased person or loss that is comforting and lasting.

School is an additional support for this age group, although the support from home remains primary. Honest communication remains a key issue, especially when it pertains to any kind of change that might trigger abandonment thoughts and feelings. Additionally, thoughts and deeds can cause death, so communication is essential for reframing any kind of irrational beliefs. Finally, talking about the deceased person allows the child to integrate memories into a memory figure that will provide comfort (Charkow, 1998).

Ages 9 to 11 Years

Bereaved children in this age group need a great deal of information about the death or loss (Christ, 2000). They believe "Knowledge is power over the circumstance." The more information the child has, the less out of control he or she feels. Control is the mode of behavior because these youth wish to control not only their own negative feelings but also others' negative feelings, which causes problems in the family social system. Rarely communicating their feelings, these youth choose to express themselves in behaviors (e.g., aggressive, depressive, or obsessive; Cohen et al., 2002). Items that belonged to the deceased person bring comfort and an opportunity to talk about feelings.

The difficult issue with this age group is respecting the child's need to control and defend against perceived fear and promoting health through communication. Communication can be encouraged through engaging in family art projects (for example, quilt making) or a memory book that includes the participation of the entire family (Charkow, 1998; Dalke, 1994).

Ages 12 to 14 Years

Bereaved early adolescents choose not to know any details about the death or loss, unlike their younger counterparts (Christ, 2000). Their emotions are stifled except for displays of anger and hostility fueled by thoughts such as "Why me?" or "Why is life so unfair?" (Christ, 2000; Cohen et al., 2002). However, they are able to talk openly about dreams, wishes, and thoughts relating to the loss. Moreover, they seem willing to openly share conversations with the deceased person. These youth fear what others will think of them, so control remains an issue. Mourning behaviors such as going to the cemetery are declined because they do not want to be seen as a freak. However, wearing something that belonged to the deceased person or relates to the loss is permissible (Christ, 2000).

An essential skill with these children is the parent's understanding and practice of conflict resolution. Using such skills promotes communication and healthy movement through the mourning process. Further, parents need to be appropriate boundary setters while respecting the child's need for peer support and differentiation (Cohen et al., 2002). Private and formal mourning rituals may offer an opportunity for the youth to express emotions. In addition, support groups are helpful. *Rainbows,* a family/child support program designed to aid youth and families with loss (Schroeder, 1998), is present in schools across the nation and freely facilitates age-appropriate games and interactions that send a message of hope and recovery.

INDICATED PREVENTIVE INTERVENTIONS

Complete resolution of a loss is the exception rather than the rule (Zisook & DeVaul, 1985), likely because of the lack of bereavement prevention efforts for the majority of bereaved youth and the presence of trauma symptomatology (Eth, 2001). A youth presenting with unresolved grief needs trauma symptom assessment because the presence of trauma symptoms is likely and will impede the work of mourning (Cohen et al., 2002). The initial prevention work will be trauma symptom reduction should distress be found. Reducing the distress symptoms increases the youth's ability to extend his or her energy for the work of decathexis. Trauma symptom reduction is accomplished through the telling of the story of loss with the attached responsive emotions and thoughts. In the course of the telling, the story is changed, as new cognitions are integrated with the subjective emotional response (Eth, 1990). Prevention efforts for unresolved grief must include trauma and bereavement components. Relieving trauma symptoms may increase bereavement symptomatology, which may take many sessions to reconcile (Cohen et al., 2002).

Studies that address prevention efforts for youth experiencing unresolved grief are lacking. However, two school-based trauma and grief-focused intervention models have been empirically evaluated for *adolescents* experiencing trauma response and unresolved grief symptoms. One was a trauma- and grief-focused group intervention for adolescents exposed to war (Layne et al., 2001); the other was a trauma- and grief-focused group for adolescents exposed to community violence (Saltzman, Pynoos, Layne, Steinberg, & Aisenberg, 2001).

Both Saltzman et al. (2001) and Layne et al. (2001) developed similar 20-week school-based interventions focused on reducing the trauma and grief symptoms and increasing academic and personal functioning in *adolescents* exposed to loss. The manualized psychoeducational programs included cognitive restructuring for the trauma response and trauma reminders, issues related to complicated bereavement, stress management, and problem-solving methods. The posttreatment outcome evaluations showed significant reduction in trauma and unresolved grief symptoms and improved academic and personal performance.

In the Saltzman et al. (2001) study, the entire student body engaged in a self-report questionnaire on their degree of violence exposure and posttrauma symptoms. The questionnaires identified 40 students with both trauma exposure and symptoms previously unidentified, suggesting that universal assessment is essential for unresolved grief prevention.

Trauma cues are significant relapse triggers for children attempting to reconcile a traumatic response to loss. Thus, an initial component of the two aforementioned programs engaged children in discovering what their trauma triggers were and how they might reduce the influence of these triggers (Layne et al., 2001; Saltzman et al., 2001).

There is only one evaluation of a model attempting to help bereaved children and adolescents (ages 6 to 15 years; Pfeffer, Jiang, Kakuma, Hwang, & Metsch, 2002). The intervention consisted of ten 90-minute psychoeducational group sessions on problem solving, dealing with emotions, suicide, and relationship building (Pfeffer, 2002). The outcome showed significant improvement in feelings of anxiety and depression.

PRACTICE AND POLICY IMPLICATIONS

Children, as human beings, are influenced by life experiences, including their exposures to loss. We know that adults experience health-related disorders associated with unresolved response to loss (Geis, Whittlesey, McDonald, Smith, & Pfefferbaum, 1998). Moreover, the adult's unresolved grief is often the outcome of a childhood experience (e.g., complicated mourning, attachment issue, or trauma) that went undetected. It is economically and socially profitable for professionals to engage in prevention of unresolved grief because the consequences of not doing so are devastating (Charkow, 1998; Geis et al., 1998). This means that physicians, school employees, nurses, and mental health professionals need to be educated about effective prevention efforts for youth experiencing unresolved grief (Charkow, 1998; Cohen et al., 2002). Moreover, professionals need to recognize that all youth require prevention intervention before a loss, if possible, and certainly during an expected loss or recent loss (Charkow, 1998).

Professionals need to educate and assist parents in bereavement prevention efforts for their children and the family in general. Family members who understand the importance of open communication and mourning rituals within the developmental constraints of the evolving family and the youth members are likely to follow an uncomplicated mourning path (Norris-Shortle et al., 1993).

Governmental agencies need to comprehensively support unresolved grief prevention efforts. This prevention endeavor needs to focus on children as well as families (Dowdney et al., 1999). General screening for unresolved grief symptoms in a group of school-age children showed previously unidentified trauma symptoms (March, Amaya-Jackson, Terry, & Costanzo, 1997). Trauma symptoms in youth have long-term academic and health-related consequences (Black, 1998). Thus, periodic governmentally funded screening for unresolved grief symptoms is essential. This universal screening will help to identify bereaved children who very likely have bereaved family members in need of help. Early assessment and appropriate intervention is the key to preventing further health-related issues in bereaved families (Black, 1998; Cohen et al., 2002).

FUTURE DIRECTIONS

Bereaved children experiencing unresolved grief do not get better without prevention efforts (Goenjian et al., 1997). It is a myth that "time is healing"; studies show that early prevention efforts reduce traumatic response to bereavement. Cognitive-behavioral group therapy prevention efforts show promising outcomes; however, the studies are few and the samples are small (Cohen et al., 2002). There is no argument that a paucity of empirically driven research concerning prevention of unresolved grief in children exists. Family education and support for bereavement offer the child and his or her family members opportunities to obtain skills for future or current loss experiences. Research should specify subgroup of youth, type of prevention effort, types of family intervention helpful with particular family structures, dynamics, and developmental stages. Longitudinal studies will discern the long-term effects of a universal family involved in bereavement prevention efforts in addition to cognitive-behavioral efforts with bereaved youth.

REFERENCES

Bentovim, A. (1986). Bereaved children. *British Medical Journal, 292*(6534), 1482.

Bifulco, A., Harris, T., & Brown, G. (1992). Mourning or inadequate care? Reexamining the relationship of maternal loss in childhood with adult depression and anxiety. *Developmental Psychopathology, 4,* 433–449.

Black, D. (1991). Family intervention with families bereaved or about to be bereaved. In D. Papadatou & C. Papadatos (Eds.), *Children and death*. New York: Hemisphere Publishing.

Black, D. (1996). Childhood bereavement. *British Medical Journal, 312*(7045), 1496.

Black, D. (1998). Coping with loss: Bereavement in childhood. *British Medical Journal, 316*(7135), 931–933.

Black, D., & Urbanowicz, M. A. (1987). Family intervention with bereaved children. *Journal of Child Psychology and Psychiatry, 28*(3), 467–476.

Bowlby, J. (1984). Violence in the family as a disorder of the attachment and caregiving systems. *American Journal of Psychoanalysis, 44*(1), 9–27, 29–31.

Breier, A., Kelsoe, J., Kirwin, P., Wolkowitz, O., & Pickar, D. (1988). Early parental loss and development of adult psychopathology. *Archives of General Psychiatry, 45,* 987–993.

Breslau, N., Chilcoat, H. D., Kessler, R. C., & Davis, G. C. (1999). Previous exposure to trauma and PTSD effects of subsequent trauma: Results from the Detroit Area Survey of Trauma. *American Journal of Psychiatry, 156*(6), 902–907.

Buhrmester, D. (1990). Intimacy of friendship, interpersonal competence, and adjustment during preadolescence and adolescence. *Child Development, 61*(4), 1101–1111.

Cerel, J., Fristad, M. A., Weller, E. B., & Weller, R. A. (2000). Suicide-bereaved children and adolescents: II. Parental and family functioning. *Journal of the American Academy of Child and Adolescent Psychiatry, 39*(4), 437–444.

Charkow, W. B. (1998). Inviting children to grieve. *Professional School Counseling, 2*(2), 117–123.

Cheifetz, P. N., Stavrakakis, G., & Lester, E. P. (1989). Studies of the affective state in bereaved children. *Canadian Journal of Psychiatry, 34*(7), 688–692.

Christ, G. H. (2000). Impact of development on children's mourning. *Cancer Practice, 8*(2), 72–81.

Cicchetti, D., Rogosch, F. A., & Toth, S. L. (1998). Maternal depressive disorder and contextual risk: Contributions to the development of attachment insecurity and behavior problems in toddlerhood. *Developmental Psychopathology, 10*(2), 283–300.

Clayton, P. J. (1990). Bereavement and depression. *Journal of Clinical Psychiatry, 51*(Suppl., July), 34–40.

Cohen, J. A., Mannarino, A. P., Greenberg, T., Padlo, S., & Shipley, C. (2002). Childhood traumatic grief: Concepts and controversies. *Trauma, Violence, & Abuse, 3*(4), 307–327.

Dalke, D. (1994). Therapy-assisted growth after parental suicide: From a personal and professional perspective. *Omega Journal of Death and Dying, 29*(2), 113–151.

Davies, B. (1998). *Shadows in the sun: The experience of sibling bereavement in childhood.* Philadelphia: Brunner/Mazel.

Dowdney, L., Wilson, R., Maughan, B., Allerton, M., Schofield, P., & Skuse, D. (1999). Psychological disturbance and service provision in parentally bereaved children: Prospective case-control study. *British Medical Journal, 319*(7206), 354–357.

Elizur, E., & Kaffman, M. (1983). Factors influencing the severity of childhood bereavement reactions. *American Journal of Orthopsychiatry, 53*(4), 668–676.

Emswiler, M. A., & Emswiler, J. P. (2000). *Guiding your child through grief.* New York: Bantam Books.

Eth, S. (1990). Posttraumatic stress disorder in childhood. In M. Hersen & C. G. Last (Ed.), *Handbook of child and adult psychopathology: A longitudinal perspective* (pp. 263–274): New York: Pergamon Press.

Eth, S. (2001). *PTSD in children and adolescents: A developmental-interactional model of child abuse.* Washington, DC: American Psychiatric Association.

Findlay, B. (1999). Using the text "Lucy Bay" to explore loss and grief: Unit overview. *Primary Educator, 5*(3), 17–19.

Foster, S. (1981). Explaining death to children. *British Medical Journal, 282*(6263), 540–542.

Fristad, M. A., Jedel, R., Weller, R. A., & Weller, E. B. (1993). Psychosocial functioning in children after the death of a parent. *American Journal of Psychiatry, 150*(3), 511–513.

Furman, E. (1983). Studies in childhood bereavement. *Canadian Journal of Psychiatry, 28*(4), 241–247.

Furman, E. (1985). Children's patterns in mourning the death of a loved one. *Issues in Comprehensive Pediatric Nursing, 8*(1–6), 185–203.

Furman, E. (1986). On trauma: When is the death of a parent traumatic? *Psychoanalytic Study of the Child, 41,* 191–208.

Geis, H. K., Whittlesey, S. W., McDonald, N. B., Smith, K. L., & Pfefferbaum, B. (1998). Bereavement and loss in childhood. *Child and Adolescent Psychiatric Clinics of North America, 7*(1), viii, 73–85.

Goenjian, A. K., Karayan, I., Pynoos, R. S., Minassian, D., Najarian, L. M., Steinberg, A. M., et al. (1997). Outcome of psychotherapy among early adolescents after trauma. *American Journal of Psychiatry, 154*(4), 536–542.

Gray, R. E. (1987). Adolescent response to the death of a parent. *Journal of Youth and Adolescence, 16*(6), 511–525.

Grieve, H. S. (2000). Helping students grieve. *National Education Association Today, 18*(6), 22.

Hare, J., & Skinner, D. (1988). A child bereavement training program for parents. *Early Child Development and Care, 36,* 31–48.

Harris, E. S. (1991). Adolescent bereavement following the death of a parent: An exploratory study. *Child Psychiatry and Human Development, 21*(4), 267–281.

Horowitz, M. J., Siegel, B., Holen, A., Bonanno, G. A., Milbrath, C., & Stinson, C. H. (1997). Diagnostic criteria for complicated grief disorder. *American Journal of Psychiatry, 154*(7), 904–910.

Hurd, R. (1999). Adults view their childhood bereavement experiences. *Death Studies, 23*(1), 17–41.

Jacobs, S., & Ostfeld, A. (1980). The clinical management of grief. *Journal of the American Geriatrics Society, 28*(7), 331–335.

Kim, K., & Jacobs, S. (1991). Pathologic grief and its relationship to their psychiatric disorders. *Journal of Affective Disorders, 21*(4), 257–263.

Kmietowicz, Z. (2000). More services needed for bereaved children. *British Medical Journal, 320*(7239), 893.

Kottman, T. (1994). Adlerian play therapy. In C. E. Schaefer & K. J. O'Connor (Ed.), *Handbook of play therapy: Advances and innovations* (Vol. 2, pp. 3–26). New York: Wiley.

Kranzler, E. M., Shaffer, D., Wasserman, G., & Davies, M. (1990). Early childhood bereavement. *Journal of the American Academy of Child and Adolescent Psychiatry, 29*(4), 513–520.

Layne, C. M., Pynoos, R. S., Saltzman, W. S., Arslanagic, B., Black, M., Savjak, N., et al. (2001). Trauma/grief-focused group psychotherapy: School based postwar intervention with traumatized Bosnian adolescents. *Group Dynamics: Theory, Research, and Practice, 5*(4), 277–290.

March, J. S., Amaya-Jackson, L., Terry, R., & Costanzo, P. (1997). Posttraumatic symptomatology in children and adolescents after an industrial fire. *Journal of the American Academy of Child and Adolescent Psychiatry, 36*(8), 1080–1088.

Marwit, S. J. (1996). Reliability of diagnosing complicated grief: A preliminary investigation. *Journal of Consulting and Clinical Psychology, 64*(3), 563–568.

Marwit, S. J., & Carusa, S. S. (1998). Communicated support following loss: Examining the experiences of parental death and parental divorce in adolescence. *Death Studies, 22*(3), 237–255.

McDermott, O. D., Prigerson, H. G., Reynolds, C. F., III, Houck, P. R., Dew, M. A., Hall, M., et al. (1997). Sleep in the wake of complicated grief symptoms: An exploratory study. *Biological Psychiatry, 41*(6), 710–716.

Middleton, W., Burnett, P., Raphael, B., & Martinek, N. (1996). The bereavement response: A cluster analysis. *British Journal of Psychiatry, 169*(2), 167–171.

Miller, J. B. (1971). Children's reactions to the death of a parent: A review of the psychoanalytic literature. *Journal of American Psychoanalytic Association, 19*(4), 697–719.

Milton, J. (1999a). Loss and grief. *Primary Educator, 5*(3), 10–13.

Milton, J. (1999b). Providing anticipatory guidance for our children: Loss and grief education. *Primary Educator, 5*(3), 13–17.

Neimeyer, R. A., Prigerson, H. G., & Davies, B. M. (2002). Mourning and meaning. *American Behavioral Scientist, 46*(2), 235–251.

Norris-Shortle, C., Young, P. A., & Williams, M. A. (1993). Understanding death and grief for children three and younger. *Social Work, 38*(6), 736–742.

Parkes, C. M. (1972). *Bereavement: Studies of grief in adult life.* New York: International Universities Press.

Pfeffer, C. R. (2002). Suicide in mood disordered children and adolescents. *Child and Adolescent Psychiatric Clinics of North America, 11*(3), x, 639–647.

Pfeffer, C. R., Jiang, H., Kakuma, T., Hwang, J., & Metsch, M. (2002). Group intervention for children bereaved by the suicide of a relative. *Journal of the American Academy of Child and Adolescent Psychiatry, 41*(5), 505–513.

Prigerson, H. G., Bierhals, A. J., Kasl, S. V., Reynolds, C. F., III, Shear, M. K., Day, N., et al. (1997). Traumatic grief as a risk factor for mental and physical morbidity. *American Journal of Psychiatry, 154*(5), 616–623.

Prigerson, H. G., Bridge, J., Maciejewski, P. K., Beery, L. C., Rosenheck, R. A., Jacobs, S. C., et al. (1999). Influence of traumatic grief on suicidal ideation among young adults. *American Journal of Psychiatry, 156*(12), 1994–1995.

Prigerson, H. G., & Jacobs, S. C. (Eds.). (2001). *Traumatic grief as a distinct disorder: A rationale, consensus criteria, and a preliminary empirical test.* Washington, DC: American Psychological Association.

Prigerson, H. G., Shear, M. K., Jacobs, S. C., Reynolds, C. F., III, Maciejewski, P. K., & Davidson, J. R. T. (1999, January). Consensus criteria for traumatic grief: A preliminary empirical test. *British Journal of Psychiatry, 174,* 67–73.

Rosen, H. (1985). Prohibitions against mourning in childhood sibling loss. *Omega Journal of Death and Dying 15*(4), 307–316.

Saler, L., & Skolnick, N. (1992). Childhood parental death and depression in adulthood: Roles of surviving parent and family environment. *American Journal of Orthopsychiatry, 62*(4), 504–516.

Saltzman, W. R., Pynoos, R. S., Layne, C. M., Steinberg, A. M., & Aisenberg, E. (2001). Trauma/grief-focused intervention for adolescents exposed to community violence: Results of a school-based screening and group treatment protocol. *Group Dynamics: Theory, Research, and Practice, 5*(4), 291–303.

Sanchez, L., Fristad, M. A., Weller, R. A., Weller, E. B., & Moye, J. (1994). Anxiety in acutely bereaved prepubertal children. *Annals of Clinical Psychiatry, 6*(1), 39–43.

Schroeder, K. (1998). Grief support group. *Education Digest, 64*(1), 75.

Sekaer, C. (1987). Toward a definition of "childhood mourning." *American Journal of Psychotherapy, 41*(2), 201–219.

Selekman, J., Busch, T., & Kimble, C. J. (2001). Grieving children: Are we meeting the challenge? *Pediatric Nursing, 27*(4), 414–419.

Silverman, P. R., & Worden, J. W. (1992). Children's reactions in the early months after the death of a parent. *American Journal of Orthopsychiatry, 62*(1), 93–104.

Sood, B., Weller, E. B., Weller, R. A., Fristad, M. A., & Bowes, J. (1992). Somatic complaints in grieving children. *Mental Health Care, 2*(1), 17–25.

Van Eerdewegh, M. M., Clayton, P., & Van Eerdewegh, P. (1985, August). The bereaved child: Variables influencing early psychopathology. *British Journal of Psychiatry, 147,* 188–194.

Vida, S., & Grizenko, N. (1989). *DSM-III-R* and the phenomenology of childhood bereavement: A review. *Canadian Journal of Psychiatry, 34*(2), 148–155.

Weller, R. A., Weller, E. B., Fristad, M. A., & Bowes, J. M. (1991). Depression in recently bereaved prepubertal children. *American Journal of Psychiatry, 148*(11), 1536–1540.

Wolfenstein, M. (1966). How is mourning possible? *Psychoanalytic Study of the Child, 21,* 93–123.

Wolfenstein, M. (1969). Loss, rage, and repetition. *Psychoanalytic Study of the Child, 24,* 432–460.

Worden, J. W., Davies, B., & McCown, D. (1999). Comparing parent loss with sibling loss. *Death Studies, 23*(1), 1–15.

Worden, J. W., & Silverman, P. R. (1996). Parental death and the adjustment of school-age children. *Omega: Journal of Death and Dying, 35*(2), 91–102.

Zisook, S., & DeVaul, R. A. (1983). Grief, unresolved grief, and depression. *Psychosomatics, 24*(3), 247–256.

Zisook, S., & DeVaul, R. A. (1984). Measuring acute grief. *Psychiatric Medicine, 2*(2), 169–176.

Zisook, S., & DeVaul, R. A. (1985). Unresolved grief. *American Journal of Psychoanalysis, 45*(4), 370–379.

Chapter 4

ADOLESCENT MENTAL HEALTH

DOMINIQUE E. ROE-SEPOWITZ AND BRUCE A. THYER

The years of adolescence can be a difficult time for both parents and teens. The forces that influence the behavior of an adolescent include wanting to be liked by peers, attempting to be comfortable with changes in their bodies and their physical appearance, the school environment, family characteristics, and having to make decisions about their future (SAMHSA, 2002). For the purposes of this chapter, we define *adolescence* as a period of change and growth that begins between 10 and 12 years old and ends around 18 or 19 years old.

Adolescence is a time filled with change. The human body creates increasing hormones, physical growth accelerates, energy levels fluctuate, there is an increased demand for sleep, moods can change rapidly, and relationships with peers become paramount. The risk of developing a mental health problem during adolescence is real and can be severe and painful for both the teens and their families. Mental health problems come in many shapes and forms, but all influence the ability of an adolescent to adapt and cope with the challenges of life.

Mental health has been defined by the Surgeon General of the United States as the "successful performance of mental function, resulting in productive activities, fulfilling relationships with other people, and the ability to adapt to change, and cope with adversity" (Surgeon General's Report on Mental Health, 1999, p. vii). Mental health is also a source of how people function in society, including the way that they think, react, learn, and grow emotionally with positive self-esteem and resiliency (Surgeon General's Report on Mental Health, 1999). The prevention of mental health problems during adolescence really means the prevention of the onset of mental illness. Mental illness or mental health problems embody alterations in thinking, behavior, and mood with concomitant impairments in social, educational, and psychological functioning. Mental health problems during adolescence are important to target because they can lead to school failure, disintegration of friendships and family relationships, and, the most extreme result, suicide or homicide. The diagnosis of mental health problems during childhood and adolescence began in the mid-1990s with the intention of targeting those children and adolescents for early intervention services to help combat the life-altering effects of mental health problems.

The number of mental health problem prevention programs developed and implemented has steadily increased since the Institute of Medicine's (1994) publication titled *Reducing Risks for Mental Disorders: Frontiers for Preventive Intervention Research* created a new agenda for preventive research specifically focused on mental health and children (Dulmus & Wodarski, 1997). Mental health problem prevention has received greater attention with the perceived increase in school violence, the disintegration of the family, and the rising numbers of children being diagnosed with mental health problems. The goals of mental health problem prevention programs are to improve child and adolescent social and emotional development and to reduce the impact of risk factors (e.g., abuse and neglect or poverty) in an effort to forestall the onset of mental disorders or to minimize their impact.

Although mental health problem prevention programs have steadily grown in numbers, relatively few have been empirically supported. Three types of prevention programs are discussed in this chapter: universal, selective, and indicated. Programs aimed toward preventing an entire population from developing mental disorders are labeled *universal* preventive interventions. Programs aimed toward a population that is known to be at risk for mental health problems such as children and adolescents whose parents are divorced, have witnessed violence at home and in the community, and children and adolescents who have lost a person in their lives to death are called *selective* prevention programs. Preventive interventions aimed at children and adolescents who are already showing the signs and symptoms of mental health problems such as depression, attention deficit/hyperactivity disorder (ADHD), conduct disorder, eating disorders, anxiety, and posttraumatic stress disorder are called *indicated* prevention programs. Because of space limitations, this chapter presents only evidence-based indicated prevention programs for depression, anxiety, and eating disorders. Although we follow the diagnostic nomenclature found in the *Diagnostic and Statistical Manual of Mental Disorders* (*DSM,* American Psychiatric Association [APA], 1994), our use of this language does not imply that we uncritically embrace the concepts of *mental* disorders. The etiology of the conditions enumerated in the *DSM* remains largely undetermined, and it is an unwarranted assumption to define them as *mental* disorders at all. It would be much more parsimonious to label the system the *Diagnostic Manual of Behavioral, Affective, and Intellectual Disorders* and to do away with the language that implies that the causal factors for these conditions resides in the individual's *mind.* To the extent that so-called mental disorders have etiologies related to environ*mental,* biological, familial, or peer factors, they are not justifiably construed as mental disorders at all. Using the term *mental disorder* or our references to mental health problems is simply a convenient convention of contemporary language and does not imply our necessary agreement that these are *mental* problems at all.

TRENDS AND INCIDENCE

Statistics show that mental health problems during adolescence have increased in the past decade. The reasons for this growth may be better reporting measures or increases in risk factors for adolescents such as homelessness or parental drug and alcohol problems. In addition, a growing number of American children and adolescents are at extremely high risk for developing a mental disorder because of high rates of child abuse and neglect (Dulmus & Wodarski, 1997). Approximately 1.5 million children are reported abused and neglected, and 14.6 million children under the age of 18 live in poverty (American Academy of Child and Adolescent Psychiatry, 1990).

The National Health Interview Survey on Disability (1994–1995) found that 12.9% (529,000) of children in the civilian, noninstitutionalized population of the United States have a reported mental/emotional problem. The statistics are overwhelming. Approximately one of every five children under the age of 18 demonstrates the signs and symptoms of a diagnosable mental, emotional, or behavioral disorder specified in the *DSM-IV* (SAMHSA, para. 6). Up to 1 in 10 youths may suffer from a serious emotional disturbance although 70% do not receive mental health services (Surgeon General's Report on Mental Health, 1999). As many as 1 in every 8 adolescents may have depression (Center for Mental Health Services [CMHS], 1998), and teenage girls are more likely to have depression than boys (National Institute of Mental Health [NIMH], 2000).

GENERALIZED RISK FACTORS

The U.S. Surgeon General wrote that children from all socioeconomic and background types are vulnerable to mental disorders and mental health problems, but some factors are known to increase the risk of problems—factors such as physical problems, low birth weight, intellectual disabilities, family history of mental illness or substance abuse, multigenerational poverty, homelessness, separation from the primary caregiver, and neglect and abuse of all types (Surgeon General's Report on Mental Health, 1999, p. xv).

Rutter (1979) found that a number of factors contribute to an elevated risk of psychiatric disorders in children, including:

1. The placement of children into foster care
2. Low socioeconomic status
3. Severe marital discord
4. Overcrowding or large family size
5. Paternal criminality

Each of these factors contributes stress to the life of an adolescent and has been found to accumulate and lead to the risk of educational, behavioral, and psychological problems.

SAMSHA's Children's and Adolescents' Mental Health web site lists risk factors for adolescent mental health problems, such as exposure to environmental toxins (e.g., high levels of asbestos or lead); exposure to violence, such as witnessing or being the victim of domestic violence; emotional, physical, or sexual abuse; drive-by shootings, terrorism, muggings, or other disasters; stress related to chronic poverty, discrimination, or other serious hardships; and the loss of important people in the lives of young people through death, divorce, or broken relationships. Kazdin (1993) also identifies biological factors that place children and adolescents at risk for mental health problems such as having a parental history of mental health problems and/or drug and alcohol problems, drug use, and unprotected sexual intercourse because these affect their physical, psychological, and social development.

If risk factors can be decreased, prevented, or in someway altered, the likelihood of an adolescent's developing mental health problems may be lowered. Some of these risk factors may be diminished by universal public health initiatives such as lead paint abatement programs and the promotion of safer sex or sexual abstinence. But few of these risks can be completely eradicated. The recognition of the risks present in the life of an adolescent can be addressed by social workers and school systems through the provision of specific prevention programs created to combat the deleterious mental health effects of the risk factors. The adolescents can be identified within risk groups constructed of factors that are known to be associated with the likeliness of mental health problems (Dulmus & Wodarski, 1997). Entire populations can be identified as risk groups as well as adolescents exposed to specific risk factors. Adolescent mental health problem prevention programs are created for entire populations, specific risk groups, and groups of adolescents who are beginning to show signs and symptoms of mental health problems.

HOW MUCH EVIDENCE IS ENOUGH?

The American Psychological Association's Division 12 (Clinical Psychology) Task Force (Division 12 Task Force, 1995) on Promotion and Dissemination of Psychological Procedures has developed preliminary evidentiary guidelines for making judgments as to whether a given intervention can be viewed as well established in terms of effectiveness. These writers suggest the following minimal standards:

1. The intervention in question is supported by at least two well-designed between-group experiments demonstrating efficacy in one or more of the following ways:
   a. The experimental treatment is superior to a credible pill or psychological placebo treatment.
   b. The experimental treatment is equivalent to an already-established treatment in experiments with adequate statistical power (e.g., at least 30 persons per group).
2. Experiments must be conducted following treatment manuals to aid in replicating interventions and in disseminating the treatment to practitioners.
3. The characteristics of the clients sampled must be clearly described.
4. Positive effects must have been obtained by at least two different investigators or investigatory teams.

A simplified answer to the question "How much evidence is enough evidence for us to claim that a mental health problem prevention program can be considered well established and effective?" is "Two well-designed, randomized controlled clinical trials." Although this seems like a rather minimalist standard, very few mental health problem preventive interventions can be found to meet this criterion. We conducted our review of the literature on adolescent mental health problem preventive interventions with these guidelines in mind and found the programs discussed in the following sections meet these criteria, with the exception of the eating disorder prevention programs and one of the two anxiety prevention programs. These latter programs were included because of their outstanding original research design and our desire to present what appear to be some promising leads.

EFFECTIVE UNIVERSAL PREVENTION PROGRAMS

Universal prevention programs for mental disorders are programs created for the general population or a specific group within a population that has been selected based on risk for mental disorders. Populations that may benefit from the universal type of prevention programs include children at risk for witnessing or perpetrating violence, children from single-parent families, children with few role models, and children with poor social skills. The focus of universal prevention programs is to enhance protective factors that may guard against risk factors associated with mental health problems. The development of protective factors such as learning to be assertive or how to express anger may be desirable for the entire population of adolescents.

Universal prevention programs are provided to large groups of adolescents, thus removing the stigma of attending a mental health group and providing a proactive and positive motivation. Two types of universal prevention programs are discussed in this chapter: violence/victimization and anger prevention and social-cognitive skill-building programs. Only two programs for adolescents were found to meet the Task Force's criteria for determining whether an intervention should be considered well established: the Bullying Prevention Program and Responding in Peaceful and Positive Ways.

The Bullying Prevention Program was first implemented in Norway in the 1984 to 1985 school year. The program, based on a formal intervention manual and provided in elementary and middle schools, included classroom interventions to establish and enforce specific rules to stop and prevent bullying activities. Individual interventions included discussions with bullies, victims, and their parents. The purpose of the Bullying Prevention Program is the reduction and prevention of bullying activity and victimization in elementary, middle, and junior high schools. The program is implemented by school staff and provided to all students in a school.

Olweus (1989) conducted a study that reported a significant reduction (more than 50%) in bullying and victimization rates four months after the Bullying Prevention Program was implemented. The participants also reported dramatic reductions in behaviors such as truancy, drunkenness, theft, fighting, and vandalism. Effects of the prevention program were noted to increase after two years. A report by the Center for the Study and Prevention of Violence (1997) indicated that participants in the Bullying Prevention Program reported improved social climates in their classrooms and schools. Participants also reported they had more positive attitudes toward schoolwork and school, had more positive relationships, and were more orderly and disciplined in the school environment.

Responding in Peaceful and Positive Ways (RIPP), created by Meyer and Northup (1995), is a 25-session program based on learning theory, with a focus on social and cognitive skill building to encourage the nonviolent resolution of conflict and enhance positive communication (Greenberg, Domitrovich, & Bumbarger, 2001). The RIPP program is a manual-based program and includes activities such as role playing, identifying feelings, peer mediation, dealing with prejudices, team building, small groups, and relaxation techniques. Students learn a specific set of anger management skills and self-evaluation techniques that they repeat and use daily. The steps include to stop, calm down, identify the problem and feelings about it, decide among nonviolent options (resolve, avoid, ignore, or defuse), do it, look back, and evaluate (Farrell, Meyer, & White, 2001).

Meyer (1997) found that the RIPP program produced fewer violence-related injuries, fewer incidents of bringing a weapon to school, positive changes in self-esteem, and increased use of peer mediation for conflict resolution. The experimental students also had fewer behavioral problems and a far lower rate of suspension than the control group. Farrell et al. (2001) evaluated the RIPP program in a randomized trial with more than 600 middle school students from Virginia. They found that the participants had fewer disciplinary violations for violent activity and fewer in-school suspensions after the RIPP program compared with the control group. Participants also reported an increase in use of peer mediation to resolve conflicts and fewer fight-related injuries.

EFFECTIVE SELECTIVE PREVENTIVE INTERVENTIONS

Selective prevention intervention programs are interventions targeted at individuals or a subgroup of a population who are at high risk for developing a mental health problem because of biological or environmental contributing factors. Those factors can include observing violence, divorce, and death of a parent or loved one. Risk groups may be identified on the basis of biological, psychological, or social risk factors that are known to be associated with the onset of a mental health problem or disorder. Programs are designed to enhance coping skills and mobilization of support to prevent the onset of one or multiple mental health problems.

In a national survey, Furstenberg, Morgan, and Allison (1987) found that children of divorce, for example, demonstrated greater problems with academic performance, problem behaviors, and psychological distress than children from intact families. Programs specific for children of divorced parents include a nationwide ongoing prevention program called Big Brothers/Big Sisters (BBBS) and the Children of Divorce Intervention Program (CODIP).

Big Brothers/Big Sisters was created by the United Way to prevent the negative effects of divorce on children, including high levels of boredom and loneliness (Zill, 1983) and social, academic, and psychological adjustment problems (Kelly, 1988). The program matches children from single-parent homes with a screened adult volunteer of the same gender. The adult volunteer and the child are expected to spend between three and five hours a week together filled with friendship, understanding, and role modeling.

Turner and Scherman (1996), in their study of 45 boys ages 7 to 13, found that the children involved in the BBBS had fewer complaints of boredom and loneliness, reported higher levels of self-concept and lower levels of anxiety, were more inclined to approve of their physical appearance, and reported feeling more popular with their peers. Rhodes, Haight, and Briggs (1999) conducted a study on the impact of the BBBS program with foster children. The foster children were found to have improved social skills and greater ease interacting and trusting their peers. The foster children also were reported to have improved prosocial and self-esteem-enhancing support. Grossman and Tierney (1998) found that after 18 months, the 571 youths between the ages of 10 and 16 involved in the BBBS program were significantly less likely to skip school, hit somebody, and start using drugs or alcohol. The subjects also displayed increased confidence in their schoolwork and had better relationships with their families.

The Children of Divorce Intervention Project (CODIP) is a school-based prevention program created by Pedro-Carroll and Cowen (1985) for children of parents who are separated or divorced. The program was designed to prevent or mitigate the behavioral and emotional problems that some children may experience after their parents separate or divorce (Cowen et al., 1996). The program also aims to provide support and assist in communication skill development to assist with problem solving. The program is provided in a supportive group format designed to provide children with an outlet to discuss their parents' divorce. Pedro-Carroll, Sutton, and Wyman (1999) and Pedro-Carroll, Alpert-Gilles, and Cowen (1992) found that, overall, the participants showed improved adjustment at home with better parent-child communication and at school with peer relationships and classroom behavior. Results also showed that participants' levels of anxiety significantly decreased.

Exposure to violence or victimization has been linked to the development of mental health problems during adolescence (SAMHSA, para. 8) with the inclusion of primary victims (being the victim) and secondary victims (observing or knowing the victim). Aggression, social adjustment, and conflict resolution are addressed in the following prevention program.

Positive Adolescent Choices Training (PACT) was developed by Yung (1991) to prevent aggression in children by enhancing their social adjustment, developing

Adolescent Mental Health   75

and improving communication skills, and learning anger management skills. The PACT prevention program was designed for at-risk students in 6th to 12th grades to reduce the chance that they may be victimized or perpetrate violence. The program was specifically designed for African American youth but has been used with multiethnic groups. Participants are selected by teachers who identify them as having poor social skills, displaying aggressive behaviors, and/or having a history of violent behavior. The program, which follows a manual, is provided to groups with no greater than 10 members to teach students social and negotiation skills to use during situations involving conflict. Yung (1991) and Hammond and Yung (1993) in separate quasi-experimental studies found that participants reported improved social and anger management skills and fewer incidents of aggressive or violent behavior. Participants also demonstrated an increase in problem-solving and communication skills, negotiation skills, and decreased aggressive behavior.

EFFECTIVE INDICATED PREVENTIVE INTERVENTIONS

Indicated preventive interventions are programs focused on high-risk individuals who do not meet the *DSM* criteria for a mental disorder, but who otherwise are identified as having detectable signs or symptoms of a mental disorder or mental health problem or who have a biological marker indicating predisposition for the mental disorder (Institute of Medicine, 1994). Indicated prevention programs are for adolescents who may eventually meet the *DSM* criteria but have not yet reached that level of pathology.

The mental health problems covered by the following evidence-based indicated prevention programs are depression, anxiety problems, and eating disorders. This limited coverage of specific disorders and indicated prevention programs results from the limited amount of solid empirically supported prevention programs described in the literature.

Depression

Childhood and adolescent depression differs from adult forms of depression. Depressed children and adolescents rarely have psychotic features, and if there are psychotic features, they are most often auditory rather than delusional (Surgeon General's Report on Mental Health, 1999). Depressed children and adolescents complain more of anxiety symptoms such as separation anxiety, reluctance to meet people, and somatic symptoms of headaches and stomachaches than do depressed adults. Depression in children and adolescents is a diagnosis that is a concern for clinicians because of its link to an increase in risk for suicide, which is the third-leading cause of death during the teen years (Centers for Disease Control and Prevention [CDC], 1999). Also categorized as mood disorders are dysthymic disorder and bipolar disorder.

The Institute of Medicine (1994) identified five risk factors that may influence the probability of the three types of adolescent depression:

1. Having a parent or other close biological relative with a mood disorder

2. Having a severe stressor such as a loss, divorce, marital separation, unemployment, job dissatisfaction, a physical disorder such as a chronic medical condition, a traumatic experience, or, in children, a learning disability

3. Having low self-esteem, a sense of low self-efficacy, and a sense of helplessness and hopelessness

4. Being female

5. Living in poverty

Two adolescent depression prevention programs have met the Task Force's criteria for evidence-based practice: the Coping with Stress (CWS) course (Clarke et al., 1995) and the Penn Prevention Program (PPP). These programs serve adolescents who have elevated self-reported depressive symptoms and risks, including marital conflict, low family cohesion, and conduct problems.

The CWS prevention program was developed by Clarke, Lewinsohn, and Hops (1990) for adolescents with elevated self-reported depressive symptomatology. CWS is a manualized program using cartoons, group activities, and role plays to teach adolescents techniques including cognitive-restructuring skills to identify and reorganize negative or irrational thoughts. Coping with Stress is focused on developing adaptive coping skills and consists of 15 group sessions of 45 minutes each usually conducted after school. The group leaders are specially trained school psychologists and counselors. Clarke et al. (1995) conducted a randomized controlled trial of the CWS course and found that although there were no differences between experimental and control groups immediately at the end of the program, assessments conducted 12 months later found a highly significant difference between the incidence of major depressive disorder or dysthymia in the control group versus the treatment group (Beardslee & Gladstone, 2001; Clarke et al., 1995; Greenberg et al., 2001), favoring those receiving the CWS program.

The Penn Prevention Program was developed by Martin Seligman and his research team at Penn State University (Jaycox, Reivich, Gillham, & Seligman, 1994) with the purpose of altering cognitive distortions and improving coping skills for adolescents who are at risk for depression. Participants had elevated depressive symptomatology and high levels of perceived family conflict. The PPP, which consists of twelve 90-minute group sessions, is a manualized program using instruction and homework techniques to teach problem interpretation and problem solving/coping skills. A quasi-experimental evaluation study using a randomized, mixed method, nested design found that the program resulted in clinically significant decreases in depressive symptoms at the end of the program and at six-month follow-up posttreatment (Gillham, Reivich, Jaycox, & Seligman, 1995; Jaycox et al., 1994), again favoring the PPP group.

Eating Disorders

Eating disorders generally fall into three diagnoses—anorexia nervosa, bulimia nervosa, or binge eating disorder—with about 3% of young women meeting the *DSM* criteria for the diagnosis of an eating disorder diagnosis (Becker, Grinspoon, Klibanski, & Herzog, 1999). Risk factors and causes of eating disorders are not known but are thought to be a combination of genetic, neurochemical, psychodevelopmental, and sociocultural factors (Becker et al., 1999). Eating disorders are the third-leading cause of illness in adolescent females and can be life threatening (Rosen & Neumark-Sztainer, 1998). The number of adolescents being diagnosed and treated for eating disorders appears to be increasing (Rosen & Neumark-Sztainer, 1998). Much has been written about the prevention of the teenage onset of eating disorders, but few prevention programs have been tested, replicated, and empirically supported. The following indicated preventive eating disorder programs are supported by only a single quasi-experimental study, but we include them as examples of the most promising directions in the field.

Everybody's Different (ED) is a manualized, school-based eating disorder prevention program focused on the improvement of body image and eating attitudes and eating behaviors of adolescents (O'Dea, 1995). The program is designed for nine consecutive weeks of 50- to 80-minute sessions to middle and high school students. Everybody's Different can be provided by any teacher and includes activities using group and teamwork, games, and drama. O'Dea and Abraham (2000) studied males and females between the ages of 11 and 14 years old and found that the experimental group had higher posttest scores of body satisfaction and positive changes in self-esteem. They also found that the participants had a lower drive for thinness and greater body satisfaction after 12 months.

The Weight to Eat Program (WEP) is a school-based eating disorder prevention program created to improve knowledge, attitudes, and behaviors related to weight management and nutrition; to enhance adolescents' body image; and to facilitate improved self-efficacy for food and weight issues (Neumark-Sztainer, Butler, & Palti, 1995). The program is provided by a nutritionist or health educator for one hour a week for 10 weeks. The WEP targets adolescents with unhealthy dieting or binge-eating behaviors. The program includes activities such as poster creating and discussing movies and issues. Neumark-Sztainer et al. found in their quasi-experimental study of 10th-grade girls that the program had good effects on adolescents' knowledge of nutrition and eating patterns as well as preventing the onset of problematic eating behaviors.

Anxiety Disorders

The term *anxiety disorders* subsumes a number of so-called mental health problems including separation anxiety, agoraphobia, panic disorder, generalized anxiety, social phobia, and obsessive-compulsive disorder, among others. The combined prevalence of these conditions is the highest of all mental disorders of childhood and adolescents (Costello et al., 1996). Anxiety disorders can severely impair the cognitive and social functioning of an adolescent. Risk factors specific to adolescent anxiety disorders are early childhood temperament, negative life events, parents' behavior, and adolescents' coping style (Spence & Dadds, 1996). Each of these risk factors can be used to target the adolescent for specific intervention programs.

Stress Inoculation Training (SIT) is a preventive school-based program created to reduce "negative emotional arousal" and other stress-related problems (Hains, 1992). The program consists of 13 sessions of training on cognitive restructuring, anxiety management, and problem-solving skills. Program features include a stress diary, relaxation techniques, and assertiveness training. Hains found in his small study of adolescent males ages 15 to 17 that the participants displayed decreased anxiety symptoms after SIT. Karpe, Kumaraiah, Mishra, and Sheshadri (1994) found in their small single group study that SIT with boys ages 13 to 16 resulted in a significant reduction in angry outbursts and stress; and Kiselica, Baker, Thomas, and Reedy (1994) found that their participants showed significantly greater improvements on anxiety and stress symptoms four weeks post-SIT, relative to a control group.

Although the Queensland Early Intervention and Prevention of Anxiety Project (QEIPAP) has only one empirically valid study, it was well constructed. This program was a manualized school-based program for 7- to 14-year-old children and adolescents found to have high levels of anxiety (Dadds, Spence, Holland, Barrett, & Laurens, 1997). The QEIPAP combined child and family groups and psychoeducational training. Its purpose was to reduce the rate of existing anxiety and prevent the onset of additional anxiety problems. The program taught students how to use cognitive, behavioral, and physiological coping strategies while being exposed to stressful or anxiety-causing situations (Dadds et al., 1997). In a controlled trial, Dadds et al. found that after six months, the prevention program participants demonstrated lower rates of anxiety, and fewer new anxiety symptoms were noted. Dadds et al. (1999) found that after two years, the participants continued to display lower rates of anxiety than the control group.

PRACTICE AND POLICY IMPLICATIONS AND FUTURE IMPLICATIONS

The risk factors for adolescent mental health problems are vast and appear to be easier to react to than to prevent. Nevertheless, contemporary scientific research is beginning to reveal the foundations for evidence-based psychosocial prevention programs. From a strictly scientific perspective, there are few policy applications that may be drawn from the existing evidence-based research literature. There are also few (or none) psychosocial preventive interventions that meet strict contemporary standards for being anointed with the label of *evidence-based* or *established* in terms of effectiveness. But evidence-based practice does not require practitioners to base their choice of interventions solely on approaches well and convincingly supported by multiple, independent, and well-designed randomized controlled clinical trials. Rather, evidence-based practice suggests the more modest standard: All things equal, human service practitioners should base their interventive and prevention program choices on the *best available* research findings. It may be that, for a given area of practice, the findings consist of only one randomized controlled trial or solely a series of quasi-experiments or even replicated single-system research studies. Evidence-based practice suggests that such studies provide valuable clues on what may work best in selected areas of adolescent mental health prevention services, and we have reviewed several of these services in this chapter. Practitioners involved in selecting and providing adolescent mental health prevention services should become familiar with those we have briefly described (see Table 4.1), acquaint themselves with other similarly supported psychosocial prevention programs, and keep abreast of the emerging empirical literature as newly researched prevention programs are developed. Testing the prevention programs that have already shown positive results and applying them makes sense. It is an ethical and more justifiable approach to prevention practice than relying primarily on theory, anecdote, tradition, and authority to justify the selection and delivery of services.

Table 4.1   References for Selected Adolescent Mental Health Prevention Programs

Big Brothers/Big Sisters
      National web site: http://www.bbbsa.org

Bullying Prevention Program: Grades K-8

Contact: Susan Limber
              Institute on Family and Neighborhood Life
              Clemson University
              158 Poole Agricultural Center
              Clemson, SC 29634
              Phone: (864) 656-6320
              Fax: (864) 656-6281

Children of Divorce Intervention Program

Contact: JoAnne Pedro-Carroll, PhD
              Primary Mental Health Project
              University of Rochester
              575 Mt. Hope Avenue
              Rochester, NY 14620
              Phone: (716) 275-2547
              Web site: www.prevention.psu.edu/COPID.htm

Coping with Stress Course
      Manual is available at: http://www.kpchr.org/public/acwd/acwd.html

Everybody's Different

Contact: Dr. J. O'Dea
              University of Sydney
              Building A35, NSW 2006
              Australia
              E-mail: odeaj@edfac.usyd.edu.au

Penn Prevention Program
      Web site: http://www.prevention.psu.edu/PPP.htm

Positive Adolescent Choice Training Program (PACT)

Contact: Dr. Betty Yung
              Program Developer
              PACT School of Professional Psychology
              Wright State University
              9 North Edwin C. Moses Blvd.
              Dayton, OH 45407
              Phone: (937) 775-4300
              Fax: (937) 775-4323
              E-mail: Byung@wright.edu

Table 4.1   *Continued*

To purchase: Mr. Dennis Wiziecki
Research Press
P.O. Box 9177
Champaign, IL 61826
Phone: (800) 519-2707
E-mail: rp@researchpress.com

Responding in Peaceful and Positive Ways (RIPP)

Contact: Melanie McCarthy
Youth Violence Prevention Project
Virginia Commonwealth University
808 West Franklin St.
Box 2018
Richmond, VA 23284-2018
Phone: (804) 828-8793
Fax: (804) 827-1511

The Weight to Eat

Contact: Diane Neumark-Sztainer, PhD
Associate Professor
Division of Epidemiology
School of Public Health
University of Minnesota
300 W B O B
1300 S. 2nd St.
Minneapolis, MN 55454
E-mail: neuma011@umn.edu

REFERENCES

American Academy of Child and Adolescent Psychiatry. (1999). Retrieved September 12, 2002, from http://www.aacap.org/about/q&a.htm.

American Psychiatric Association. (1994). *Diagnostic and statistical manual of mental disorders* (4th ed.). Washington, DC: Author.

Beardslee, W. R., & Gladstone, T. R. G. (2001). Prevention of childhood depression: Recent findings and future prospects. *Biological Psychiatry, 49,* 1101–1110.

Becker, A. E., Grinspoon, S. K., Klibanski, A., & Herzog, D. B. (1999). Eating disorders. *New England Journal of Medicine, 340,* 1092–1098.

Center for Mental Health Services. (1998). *Children's and adolescent's mental health.* Retrieved September 12, 2002, from http://www.mentalhealth.org/publications /allpubs/CA-0004/default.asp.

Center for the Study and Prevention of Violence. (1997). *Big Brothers/Big Sisters of America.* Retrieved September 12, 2002, from http://www.colorado.edu/cspv /publications/factsheets /blueprints/pdf/ FS-BPM02.pdf.

Centers for Disease Control and Prevention. (1999). *Suicide deaths and rates per 100,000.* Retrieved September 15, 2002, from http://www.cdc.gov/ncipc/data /us9794/suic.htm.

Clarke, G. N., Hawkins, W., Murphy, M., Sheeber, L. B., Lewinsohn, P. M., & Seeley, J. S. (1995). Targeted prevention of unipolar depressive disorder in an at-risk sample of high school adolescents: A randomized trial of a group cognitive intervention. *Journal of the American Academy of Child and Adolescent Psychiatry, 34,* 312–321.

Clarke, G. N., Lewinsohn, P. M., & Hops, H. (1990). *Instructor's manual for the adolescent coping with depression course.* Portland, OR: Kaiser Permanente Center for Health Research.

Costello, E. J., Angold, A., Burns, B. J., Stangl, D. K., Tweed, D. L., Erkanli, A., et al. (1996). The great smoky mountains study of youth: Goals, design, methods, and the prevalence of *DSM-III-R* disorders. *Archives of General Psychiatry, 53,* 1129–1136.

Cowen, E. L., Hightower, A. D., Pedro-Carroll, J. L., Work, W. C., Wyman, P. A., & Haffey, W. G. (1996). *School based prevention for children at risk: The primary mental health project.* Washington, DC: American Psychological Association.

Dadds, M. R., Holland, D. E., Laurens, K. R., Mullins, M., Barrett, P. M., & Spence, S. H. (1999). Early intervention and prevention of anxiety disorders in children: Results at 2-year follow up. *Journal of Consulting and Clinical Psychology, 67,* 145–150.

Dadds, M. R., Spence, S. H., Holland, D. E., Barrett, P. M., & Laurens, K. R. (1997). Prevention and early intervention for anxiety disorders: A controlled trial. *Journal of Consulting and Clinical Psychology, 65,* 627–635.

Division 12 Task Force. (1995). Training in and dissemination of empirically validated psychological treatments: Report and recommendations. *Clinical Psychologist, 16,* 319–324.

Dulmus, C. N., & Wodarski, J. S. (1997). Prevention of childhood mental disorders: A literature review reflecting hope and a vision for the future. *Child and Adolescent Social Work Journal, 14*(3), 181–198.

Farrell, A. D., Meyer, A. L., & White, K. S. (2001). Evaluation of Responding in Peaceful and Positive Ways (RIPP): A school-based prevention program for reducing violence among urban adolescents. *Journal of Clinical Child and Adolescent Psychology, 30,* 451–463.

Furstenberg, F. F., Jr., Morgan, S. P., & Allison, P. D. (1987). Parental participation and children's well-being after marital dissolution. *American Sociological Review, 52,* 695–701.

Gillham, J. E., Reivich, K. J., Jaycox, L. H., & Seligman, M. E. P. (1995). Prevention of depressive symptoms in schoolchildren: Two-year follow up. *Psychological Science, 6,* 343–351.

Greenberg, M. T., Domitrovich, C., & Bumbarger, B. (2001). The prevention of mental disorders in school-aged children: Current state of the field. *Prevention and*

Treatment, 4, 1–62. Retrieved August 1, 2002, from http://journals.apa.org /prevention/volume4/pre0040001a.html.

Grossman, J. B., & Tierney, J. P. (1998). Does mentoring work? An impact study of the Big Brothers/Big Sisters program. *Evaluation Report, 22,* 403–426.

Hains, A. A. (1992). Comparison of cognitive-behavioral stress management techniques with adolescent boys. *Journal of Counseling and Development, 70,* 600–605.

Hammond, R., & Yung, B. (1993). Psychology's role in the public health response to assaultive violence among young African American men. *American Psychologist, 48,* 142–154.

Institute of Medicine. (1994). *Reducing risks for mental disorders: Frontiers for preventative intervention research.* Washington, DC: National Academy Press.

Jaycox, L. H., Reivich, K. J., Gillham, J., & Seligman, M. E. P. (1994). Prevention of depressive symptoms in school children. *Behavior Research and Therapy, 32,* 801–816.

Karpe, S., Kumaraiah, V., Mishra, H., & Sheshadri, S. (1994). Behavioral interventions of anger outbursts in adolescents. *National Institute of Mental Health and Neuro Sciences Journal, 12,* 163–167.

Kazdin, A. E. (1993). Adolescent mental health: Prevention and treatment programs. *American Psychologist, 48,* 121–141.

Kelly, J. (1988). Long-term adjustment in children of divorce: Converging findings and implications for practice. *Journal of Family Psychology, 2,* 119–140.

Kiselica, M. S., Baker, S. B., Thomas, R. N., & Reedy, S. (1994). Effects of stress inoculation training on anxiety, stress, and academic performance among adolescents. *Journal of Counseling Psychology, 41,* 335–342.

Meyer, A. L. (1997). What is violence prevention, anyway? *Educational Leadership, 54*(8), 31–34.

Meyer, A. L., & Northup, W. (1995). *Responding in peaceful and positive ways: A violence prevention curriculum for the sixth grade.* Unpublished manuscript.

National Health Interview Survey on Disability. (1994–1995). Retrieved September 12, 2002, from http://www.cdc.gov/nchs/about/major/nhis_dis/nhis_dis.htm.

National Institute of Mental Health. (2000). *Adolescent depression.* Retrieved September 12, 2002, from http://www.nimh.nih.gov/.

Neumark-Sztainer, D., Butler, R., & Palti, H. (1995). Eating disturbances among adolescent girls: Evaluation of a school-based primary prevention program. *Journal of Nutrition Education, 27,* 24–22.

O'Dea, J. A. (1995). *Everybody's different: A self esteem program for young adolescents.* Sydney, Australia: University of Sydney Press.

O'Dea, J. A., & Abraham, S. (2000). Improving the body image, eating attitudes, and behaviors of young male and female adolescents: A new educational approach that focuses on self-esteem. *International Journal of Eating Disorders, 28,* 43–57.

Olweus, D. (1989). Bully/victim problems among schoolchildren: Basic facts and effects of a school-based intervention program. In K. Rubin & D. Heppler (Eds.), *The development and treatment of childhood aggression* (pp. 411–448). Hillsdale, NJ: Erlbaum.

Pedro-Carroll, J. L., Alpert-Gilles, L. J., & Cowen, E. L. (1992). An evaluation of the efficacy of a preventative intervention for 4th–6th grade urban children of divorce. *Journal of Primary Prevention, 13,* 115–130.

Pedro-Carroll, J. L., & Cowen, E. L. (1985). The children of divorce intervention program: An investigation of the efficacy of a school-based prevention program. *Journal of Consulting and Clinical Psychology, 53,* 603–611.

Pedro-Carroll, J. L., Sutton, J. L., & Wyman, P. A. (1999). A two-year follow-up evaluation of a preventive intervention for young children of divorce. *School Psychology Review, 28,* 467–476.

Rhodes, J. E., Haight, W. L., & Briggs, E. C. (1999). The influence of mentoring on the peer relationships of foster youth in relative and nonrelative care. *Journal of Research on Adolescence, 9,* 185–201.

Rosen, D. S., & Neumark-Sztainer, D. (1998). Review of options for primary prevention of eating disturbances among adolescents. *Journal of Adolescent Health, 23,* 354–363.

Rutter, M. (1979). Protective factors in children's response to stress and disadvantage. In M. W. Kent & J. E. Rolf (Eds.), *Primary prevention of psychopathology.* Hanover, NH: University Press of New England.

Spence, S. H., & Dadds, M. R. (1996). Preventing childhood anxiety disorders. *Journal of Behaviour Change, 13,* 241–249.

Substance Abuse and Mental Health Services Administration. (2002). *Children's and adolescents' mental health.* Retrieved August 3, 2002, from http://www .mentalhealth.org/publications/allpubs/ca-0004/.

Surgeon General's Report on Mental Health. (1999). *Mental health: A report of the Surgeon General-Executive Summary.* Rockville, MD: U.S. Department of Health and Human Services.

Turner, S., & Scherman, A. (1996). Big brothers: Impact on little brothers' self-concepts and behaviors. *Adolescence, 31,* 875–883.

Yung, B. (1991). Preventing violence in at-risk African American youth. *Journal of Health Care for the Poor and Underserved, 2,* 359–373.

Zill, N. (1983). *Happy, healthy and insecure.* New York: Doubleday.

Chapter 5

ADOLESCENT SUICIDE PREVENTION

ANDREA K. McCARTER, KAREN M. SOWERS, AND
CATHERINE N. DULMUS

Statistics provide evidence that teenage depression and suicide are two of the most pressing problems that afflict adolescents today (Wodarski, Wodarski, & Dulmus, 2003). Currently, 20% of children and adolescents suffer from a mental disorder such as clinical depression (National Plan for Research on Child and Adolescent Mental Health, 1990), and often these youth are not diagnosed until it is too late. Adolescent suicide is a problem that has been growing for the past three decades. Currently, data show that suicides are the third highest cause of death for people ages 15 to 19 (National Center for Health Statistics, 2000; U.S. Public Health Service, 1999). Although this is triple the number of youth suicides over the past three decades (Peters, Kochanek, & Murphy, 1998), it is possibly still a low estimate because of "a tendency to under report suicide because of religious implications, concern for the family and financial considerations regarding insurance payment restrictions" (Garland & Zigler, 1993, p. 169). In addition to the completed suicides are suicide attempts, which are estimated to be 50 to 100 for each completion (Kalafat, 1990). Griffiths, Farley, and Fraser (1986) suggest that becoming a more technical society leads to an increased insensitivity to human emotion, causing more feelings of hopelessness, which leads to increased suicides. These numbers are distributed "across class lines, educational lines and localities" (DenHouter, 1981, p. 3). Other authors cite an emphasis on increased stress (Hemming, 1977) and alienation or powerlessness (Ferguson, 1983) in society. Because of the increasing number of tragic deaths among the youths of the United States, there is also a developing emphasis on prevention and intervention (Silverman & Felner, 1995). Intervention and prevention programs range from telephone crisis hotlines to outpatient therapy to hospitalization, although school systems have been found to have the most access to youths for implementing prevention programs.

This chapter first provides information on the trends and incidents related to adolescent suicide as well as the suicide literature. Second, we provide a literature review pertaining to the suicide risk factors of adolescents and suggested assessment instruments for depression. Treatment methods for dealing with suicidal ideation and attempts are discussed in the third section where information on universal, selective, and indicated preventive interventions is presented. Last, implications for policy and practice in the social work field are discussed, including some potential directions for future research.

TRENDS AND INCIDENCE

Suicide is a growing problem in society among the adolescent population. In the 1960s, youth suicide was a rare event (Maris, 1985). During that decade, there were 5.6 male youth suicides per 100,000 people and 1.6 female suicides per 100,000 people (Kalafat & Neigher, 1991). Between the 1960s and the 1980s, the suicide rates increased dramatically to 13.8 per 100,000 for male youths and 3 per 100,000 for female youths. Male suicides continued to increase to 21 per 100,000 in 1984 (Kalafat & Neigher, 1991). In 1988, there were an estimated 2,059 suicides: 11.3 per 100,000 for males and females combined (Garland & Zigler, 1993). The Centers for Disease Control (2001) reports that persons younger than 25 accounted for 15% of all suicides in 1998. From 1952 to 1995, the incidence of suicide among adolescents and young adults nearly tripled, with the rate of suicide among persons ages 15 to 19 years increasing by 11% and among persons ages 10 to 14 years by 109% between 1980 and 1997. Such statistics speak to the epidemic of child and adolescent suicide and the need for a better empirical understanding of the problem and a preventive approach. A review of the literature indicates a dearth of information on adolescent suicide and prevention programs (Kalafat, 1990), although there is literature pertaining to adult suicide. Most of the available literature and research was disseminated in the late 1980s and early 1990s. There are a number of articles discussing the evaluation of the effectiveness of available programs (Ciffone, 1993; Lester, 1997; Streiner & Adam, 1987). Numerous articles also discuss the risk factors of suicide (Crespi, 1990; Evans, Marte, Betts, & Silliman, 2001; Griffiths et al., 1986; Maris, 1985; Wetzler et al., 1996). Risk factors include individual, familial, community, and societal issues.

RISK FACTORS

Many articles have been written about the risk factors of suicide for adolescents. Some authors refer to the factors as a *continuum* or stages that develop over time. The literature offers multiple risk factors for suicide, alluding to a need to focus on multiple facets of an adolescent's life rather than looking just at a specific factor.

There are different levels of threat to consider when looking at the risk factors for suicide with adolescents. James and Wherry (1991) describe these levels as a "hierarchy of behavior" (p. 23). This continuum includes a progression of suicidal thought and action ranging from "suicidal tendency [a statement made], suicidal gesture [attention getting action], suicidal threat [serious threat statement], suicidal attempt [dangerous attempt] and suicide [actual death]" (p. 23).

On a community and society level, several risk factors may play a role in the number of suicides that are attempted or completed. Kachur, Potter, Powell, and Rosenberg (1992) and Kellermann et al. (1992) offer three indicators of higher suicide rates in a community: people who live in communities with limited opportunities economically, high levels of unemployment, and instability in residency.

Individual and family indicators of suicide potential range from family dysfunction (DenHouter, 1981; Faber, 1978) to individual substance abuse (Evans et al., 2001; Lewinsohn, Rohde, & Seeley, 1993). One of the most discussed factors of suicide risk is depression or other psychopathology. Lewinsohn et al. (1993), Harris and Lenings (1993), Crespi (1990), and Wetzler et al. (1996) all consider depression a key risk factor. Other factors include previous attempts or ideation (Crespi, 1990; DenHouter, 1981) and gender (Lewinsohn et al., 1993). Research has shown that females are more likely to attempt suicide whereas males have higher completion rates.

In addition to individual, family, and community or society factors, several authors have placed indicators into stages or continuums that develop over time (Calhoun, 1972; Ciffone, 1990; Hipple, 1987; James & Wherry, 1991; Kalafat & Neigher, 1991; Lester & Leenaars, 1996). Calhoun looks at presuicide thinking indicating a suicidal person as catalogic, logical, contaminated, or paleologic. A person who is classified as catalogic is one who cannot think rationally whereas the logical category includes people who think through their decision to commit suicide. A third category is people who believe that they should commit suicide for spiritual or religious reasons. Finally, a person who commits suicide based on hallucinations is considered paleologic according to Calhoun's model.

Ciffone (1990) also adheres to the idea that there is no single explanation for adolescent suicide. He considers three sets of factors: predisposing, precipitating, and poor coping skills. Predisposing factors of suicide risk are not necessarily specific events that occur, but rather characteristics that exist and include issues such as parental dysfunction (Blumenthal & Kupfer, 1988), relationship (Wodarski & Harris, 1987) or interaction (Pfeffer, 1986) dysfunction in the family, physical anomalies (Goffman, 1963) and hormonal changes (Blumenthal & Kupfer, 1988) that occur during adolescence, and personality traits. On the other hand, precipitating events are those that happen in the life of an adolescent such as an interpersonal conflict or loss, perceived disapproval, external stressors (Brent et al., 1988), or sexual development (Hirschfeld & Blumenthal, 1986). The final category of risk factors is poor coping skills. Many adolescents choose to deal with problems on their own without help, potentially leading to substance abuse (Brent et al., 1988), distorted views of the world (Wodarski & Harris, 1987), and skewed beliefs about death (Pfeffer, 1986). Adolescents also have limited problem-solving abilities (Elkind, 1984).

Lester and Leenaars (1996) classify suicide risks in two categories. The intrapsychic category includes risk factors such as psychological pain (Schneidman, 1985) and inability to adjust (Leenaars, 1988). More external factors are considered in the interpersonal category, including relationships and rejection. Similar to the categories of thought presented by Calhoun (1972), Kalafat and Neigher (1991) discuss five risk domains, which is a model created by Blumenthal and Kupfer (1987). Biology, psychosocial events, personality, family history including genetics, and psychiatric disorder are all areas that need to be assessed when working with a potentially suicidal adolescent.

Another way of looking at the risk factors of suicide is as behavior developing over time. Hipple (1987) notes the first stage of suicidal behavior as a stressful situation in the life of an adolescent. Second, the stress of that event intensifies and the adolescent begins to feel helpless. Helplessness leads to the third stage, which is a crisis point where the person potentially becomes a threat to himself or herself.

Although there are a number of ways to view the risk factors of an adolescent suicide, an important overriding concept remains: Adolescent suicide is a growing problem, and there are potential warning signs that can be assessed and subsequent intervention provided to prevent it.

ASSESSMENT OF DEPRESSION AND SUICIDAL BEHAVIOR IN ADOLESCENTS

Beginning in the 1980s, researchers have become interested in treating depression in adolescents (Marcotte, 1997) because frequently depression precipitates suicide. It is estimated that 20% to 25% of boys and 25% to 40% of girls report having depressed moods (Peterson et al., 1993), and 4% to 12% fit the *DSM-IV* criteria as exhibiting clinical depression (Reynolds, 1992). Identification of those youth with clinical depression is essential for treatment and thus prevention of suicide. Research findings indicate that major depression presents clinically different in children and adolescent compared with adults (Puig-Antich et al., 1989), though all are diagnosed using the same *DSM-IV-TR* (American Psychological Association [APA], 2000) criteria. A focus on empirical assessment is essential. Adequate assessment using measures with good reliability and validity is recommended to evaluate depression in youth (Wodarski et al., 2003). A variety of such measures are now available for clinical use, for example:

- *The Children's Depression Inventory* (Kovacs, 1981) is one of the most widely used measures of depression to date, with high internal consistency and good test-retest reliability (Kazdin, 1990). This 27-item measure can be used with children and adolescents between 8 and 17 years of age.
- The *Diagnostic Interview for Children and Adolescents* (DICA; Robins, Helzer, Croughan, & Ratcliff, 1981) is a highly structured instrument with multiple items covering diverse symptoms. It is easily administered and is available in computerized format.
- The *Reynolds Adolescent Depression Scale* (RADS; Reynolds, 1992) is a 30-item, self-report inventory developed specifically for measuring depression in adolescents ages 13 to 18. It takes 5 to 10 minutes to complete, and items are worded at a third-grade reading level. There is high internal consistency and test-retest reliability.
- The *Center for Epidemiological Studies Depression Scale* (Radloff, 1991), a 20-item inventory covering a range of depressive symptoms, has been highly used with both adults and adolescents.

TREATMENTS

"Despite the seriousness of adolescent suicide, no comprehensive empirically validated treatment exists for this population" (Rathus & Miller, 2002, p. 146). Although there haven't been empirically based treatments to this point, "prevention has become a central goal among those concerned with a wide array of human conditions" (Cowen, 1985; Felner, Jason, Moritsugu, & Farber, 1983; Silverman & Felner, 1995). Although prevention is a new topic of conversation in many fields, it has been a central focus of practice in social work (Lurie & Monahan, 2001).

"Prevention is a proactive rather than reactive process which is concerned on a case-by-case basis with assisting to build adaptive strengths, resilient characteristics, and internal and external resources to ward off psychosocial dysfunction" (Lurie & Monahan, 2001). According to Silverman and Felner (1995), three critical factors should be considered when developing preventive programs:

1. Whether the program will be designed to address suicide reduction before the fact for those contemplating suicide or for those who have previously attempted suicide

2. Screening mechanisms and analysis most appropriate for the participants of the program

3. Careful delineation of factors targeted through the program (p. 95)

Treatment for risks of suicide in the adolescent population begins with prevention. Prevention takes place on a number of levels (Parad & Parad, 1990). In primary prevention, the goal is to avoid negative behaviors, often through use of consultation and education. Secondary prevention requires the offering of treatment during the early signs of suicide risks. Limiting further increase in dysfunction is the third level of prevention. Lurie and Monahan (2001) offer eight principles considered important in working with families and individuals, including offering opportunities, promptly helping with problems, counseling, raising awareness, and increasing support levels.

One characteristic of working with a suicidal person is communication. Suicidal people often need a social worker/counselor/helper who is patient, listens carefully, does not judge or belittle their words or actions, asks questions, and shows empathy (James & Wherry, 1991). It is important that states create written policies on prevention of adolescent suicides (Malley, Kush, & Bogo, 1994). Preventing adolescent suicide is a team or community effort, and this collaborative effort is considered crucial to reducing the number of suicides among adolescents (Ward, 1995).

Several authors have summarized key characteristics of prevention programs (Dryfoos, 1990; Felner, Silverman, & Adix, 1991). Assumptions that are thought to create an effective program include:

- There is no one solution to a problem.
- High-risk behaviors are interrelated.
- An integrative package of services and programs is required in each community.
- Preventive interventions should be aimed at changing institutions.
- The timing of interventions is critical and should start early.
- Continuity of efforts must be maintained (Silverman & Felner, 1995).

Garfinkel (1989) notes that suicide prevention approaches in school-based programs must include early identification, evaluation, crisis intervention, programs to be instituted immediately, education, monitoring and follow-up, community linkage, research, and advocacy. Similarly, Malley et al. (1994) compiled a number of components that should be included in prevention in school-based programs. Most programs reviewed by Malley et al. were created between 1979 and 1994, with the majority of states developing programs in the 1980s after the Youth Suicide Prevention Act of 1985 (Garland, Shaffer, & Whittle, 1989; Metha, Weber, & Webb, 1998). Programs are divided generally into three categories as defined by the Gordon model: universal prevention interventions, selective prevention interventions, and indicated prevention interventions.

Universal Preventive Interventions

Universal preventive interventions are targeted to the general public or a whole population group. This group has not been identified for a particular problem. The whole population we consider in this chapter is the general public of children and adolescents who are in school. Many of the interventions that fall into this category as to adolescent suicide are services that are available to anyone in the community who desires to use or learn about them. One such intervention is crisis hotlines. Hotlines are a popular type of prevention program (Garland & Zigler, 1993), evidenced by the more than 1,000 hotlines in the United States (Garland et al., 1989). Another type of prevention is the education of media workers about adolescent suicide (Garland & Zigler, 1993). This also entails informing media workers of the data about the potential for suicide imitations following a suicide in a community to promote communitywide education and prevention. Universal prevention can also be employed through passage of legislation. For example, because possession of firearms is believed to be correlated with increased adolescent suicides (Boyd, 1983; Boyd & Moscicki, 1986; Garland & Zigler, 1989), prevention could be accomplished by restricting access to weapons, for example, through stricter gun controls (Boor, 1981; Lester & Murrell, 1980). Another example is reduction in carbon monoxide in gasoline (Brown, 1979). An additional method of universal prevention intervention for adolescent suicide is a crisis intervention committee (Ward, 1995). This committee, composed of community members such as law enforcement, ministerial, public and mental health workers, and educators (Ward, 1995), would be responsible for suicide prevention program development. Finally, there is a need to educate people to be able to identify those who are at risk to commit suicide (Shaffer & Craft, 1999). Informing and educating community members in all these methods are key components for effective prevention of adolescent suicides.

Selective Preventive Interventions

Selective preventive interventions are targeted to a subgroup of the population who are at a risk of developing the specified problem. In the case of children and adolescents, the most common selective prevention intervention is school-based programs. The goals of these programs, as defined by Garland and Zigler (1993), are to increase awareness, train people to identify risk factors, and educate people about the resources in the community. Schools provide a good setting for this type of program because of their ability to reach great numbers of the population. In addition, school personnel interact with students on a daily basis and have the opportunity to identify changes in behavior (Ward, 1995). Ward offers a description of potential duties for every employee in a school system from the administrators' creating policy to support staff's taking note of student interactions. School-based programs may include "social competence building problem-solving skill training and basic mental health education" (Garland & Zigler, 1993). Programs that are at least one-year long are more effective than those that are shorter (Botvin, Schinke, Epstein, Diaz, & Botvin, 1995; Eggert, Thompson, Herting, & Nicholas, 1995). A comprehensive program that includes suicide prevention, intervention, and postvention or interventions to be conducted after a suicide has occurred is crucial for schools to address the increase in youth suicide (Ward, 1995).

Use of educators and community leaders to identify students with behavior considered to be high risk for suicide may also be a useful community approach to suicide prevention. Referred to as *gatekeepers,* these natural community helpers who are in regular contact with adolescents can, with appropriate training, provide important early identification of children at risk (Gould & Kramer, 2001, p. 15). Gatekeepers may be teachers, coaches, pediatricians, clergy, or police. Gatekeeper training entails the development of "knowledge, attitudes, and skills to identify students at risk" (Gould & Kramer, 2001, p. 15).

Indicated Preventive Interventions

Indicated preventive interventions are targeted to individuals who do not currently meet the criteria or risk factors of a specific problem, but who have been identified as having some signs and symptoms. This group consists of adolescents who have been diagnosed with depression or other psychopathology that increases risk of suicide and adolescents who are at risk to drop out of high school. Interventions used with adolescents who exhibit suicidal behaviors and verbalizations include medication (Ciffone, 1990), inpatient and outpatient therapy (Ciffone, 1990; Stiles & Kottman, 1990), and home visitation by a counselor (DenHouter, 1981). More specific are prevention programs that have been created for implementation with adolescents identified to be at risk. Two programs designed for use with adolescents at risk of dropping out of high school are Counselors CARE (C-CARE) and Coping and Support Training (CAST; Randall, Eggert, & Pike, 2001). Another program is for adolescents diagnosed with borderline personality disorder. The participants receive dialectical behavior therapy (DBT) as a preventative measure to suicide (Rathus & Miller, 2002).

Although predisposing factors (internal or family factors) and events precipitating (external stressors) suicide can't be predicted, there are methods of treating the negative effects (Ciffone, 1990). Medication is one way of alleviating the negative effects of depression, which possibly may also reduce the risk of suicide in adolescents. Historically, the recommended treatment for suicidal behavior has been hospitalization (Pfeffer, 1984). As many as 25,000 children are hospitalized annually in the United States because they express suicidal thoughts (Hipple, 1987; Stiles & Kottman, 1990). Outpatient therapy has increased for treatment of suicidal ideation and suicidal attempts (Robinson, 1984). This type of treatment is most effective when used on a long-term basis (Stiles & Kottman, 1990). Specific types of family therapy approaches (DenHouter, 1981) and home visitations (Schlachter, 1975) also show promise in intervening with suicidal adolescents. Family treatment and home visits allow the worker to assess the adolescent in his or her environment while alleviating the stress of visiting a professional's office or getting to appointments on time.

More recently, research has been conducted with adolescents who have potential risk of dropping out of high school. Eggert et al. (1995) state that approximately 40% of students in this group also screen at risk for suicidal behavior. One study compared the use of two programs with potential for reducing suicide risks with this population of adolescents (Randall et al., 2001). The first program, C-CARE, is a "comprehensive, computer-assisted assessment of risk and protective factors that [is] followed by a brief intervention designed to enhance a youth's personal resources and social network connections" (Randall et al., 2001, p. 42). It allows the youths to explore alternatives to their situations, provides emphasis to strengths, and interrupts risk behaviors. The second program, CAST, an intervention offered to some students in addition to C-CARE, is a "brief, peer-group, life skills training program" (p. 42). The life skills training consists of topics such as "self-esteem, mood management, drug-use control, and [seeking] support and help from parents and friends" (p. 42). The results indicate that the risk of suicidal behaviors of youth in all three groups (C-CARE only, C-CARE with the additional CAST program and the control groups) decreased; however, depression scores decreased primarily for the C-CARE group. Personal control was demonstrated to increase over time for the youth participating in the C-CARE plus

CAST group. The results of this study show early support for the effectiveness of these two interventions.

Dialectical behavior therapy (DBT), an evidence-based psychotherapy, has been used primarily with adults who are suicidal as well as having a diagnosis of borderline personality disorder (Rathus & Miller, 2002). Research compared youths who received the therapy and youths who received the usual treatment. DBT was thought to be an appropriate intervention for adolescents because it targets the reduction of life-threatening behaviors, decreases therapy-interfering behaviors, and decreases quality-of-life interfering behaviors (p. 147). Adolescents receiving DBT had significantly fewer hospitalizations and a greater treatment completion rate. A third outcome, however, was that there was not a difference between the groups in suicide attempts during the time in which they were receiving treatment. This preliminary data suggest that DBT may be appropriately adapted for an adolescent population and appears to offer a promising treatment for suicidal adolescents with borderline personality disorder (p. 156).

PRACTICE AND POLICY IMPLICATIONS AND FUTURE DIRECTIONS

The first federal attention given to adolescent suicide was the Youth Suicide Prevention Act of 1985 (Metha et al., 1998). Passage of this act allowed support for prevention programs in schools. In 1990, the Public Health Services Act provided funds for the National Institute of Mental Health (NIMH) grants for demonstration projects (p. 151). Most recently, an objective related to adolescent suicide was added to the Healthy People 2000: National Health Promotion and Disease Prevention Objectives (Metha et al., 1998); The goal was set to reduce youth suicides to 8.2 per 100,000 by the year 2000.

Social workers can do a number of things to support preventive interventions on both a policy and a practice level. Social workers can gain an awareness and understanding of the issue (Dudley, 2000). There is a need for continued research and evaluation of existing policies and programs in an attempt to reduce adolescent suicide. Policies that support and strengthen prevention programs need to be developed, and social workers and educators must proactively lobby and advocate for passage of legislation and policies that promote adolescent mental health. Further, development of national guidelines to support adolescent mental health practice could be extremely useful in nationally targeting adolescent suicide prevention (Bracht, 2000; Lurie & Monahan, 2001).

CONCLUSION

Suicide is an ever-growing problem in our society, especially for adolescents. Although there is some promising evidence of effective methods to prevent and treat adolescent suicide, much more work needs to be done. Given the scope of the problem and the vast and devastating consequences associated with adolescent suicide, professionals must renew efforts to identify and test preventive and interventive programs for efficacy with this population. Simultaneously, we must strengthen our efforts to educate our communities, schools, and families about adolescent suicide.

REFERENCES

American Psychological Association. (2000). Quick reference to the diagnostic criteria from *DSM-IV-TR*. Washington, DC: Author.

Blumenthal, S., & Kupfer, D. (1987). Overview of early detection and treatment strategies for suicidal behavior in young people. *Journal of Youth and Adolescence, 17,* 1–23.

Boor, M. (1981). Methods of suicide and implications for suicide prevention. *Journal of Clinical Psychology, 37,* 70–75.

Botvin, G. J., Schinke, S. P., Epstein, J. A., Diaz, T., & Botvin, E. M. (1995). Effectiveness of culturally focused and generic skills training approaches to alcohol and drug abuse prevention among minority adolescents: Two-year follow up results. *Psychology of Addictive Behaviors, 9,* 183–194.

Boyd, J. H. (1983). The increasing rate of suicide by firearms. *New England Journal of Medicine, 308,* 872–874.

Boyd, J. H., & Moscicki, E. K. (1986). Firearms and youth suicide. *American Journal of Public Health, 76,* 1240–1242.

Bracht, N. (2000). Prevention: Additional thoughts. *Social Work in Health Care, 30*(4), 1–6.

Brent, D., Perper, C., Goldstein, D., Kolko, M., Allan, C., & Zelenak, J. (1988). Risk factors for adolescent suicide. *Archives of General Psychiatry, 45,* 582–587.

Brown, J. H. (1979). Suicide in Britain. *Archives of General Psychiatry, 36,* 1119–1124.

Calhoun, J. F. (1972). *Abnormal psychology.* New York: Random House.

Centers for Disease Control and Prevention. (2001). *Suicide prevention fact sheet.* Atlanta, GA: Author. Available from http//www.cdc.gov/ncipc/factsheets/suifacts.htm.

Ciffone, J. (1990). Adolescents suicide: A review of possible causal factors and implications for prevention. *School Social Work Journal, 14*(2), 7–17.

Ciffone, J. (1993). Suicide prevention: A classroom presentation to adolescents. *Social Work Journal, 38*(2), 197–203.

Cowen, E. L. (1985). Person centered approaches to primary prevention in mental health: Situation-focused and competence-enhancement. *American Journal of Community Psychology, 13,* 31–48.

Crespi, T. (1990). Approaching adolescent suicide: Queries and signposts. *School Counselor, 37,* 256–259.

DenHouter, K. V. (1981). To silence one's self: A brief analysis of the literature on adolescent suicide. *Child Welfare, 60*(1), 2–10.

Dryfoos, J. G. (1990). *Adolescents at risk: Prevalence and prevention.* New York: Oxford University Press.

Dudley, J. R. (2000). Confronting stigma within the services system. *Social Work, 45*(5), 449–455.

Eggert, L. L., Thompson, E. A., Herting, J. R., & Nicholas, L. J. (1995). Reducing suicide potential among high-risk youth: Tests of a school-based prevention program. *Suicide and Life-Threatening Behavior, 25,* 276–296.

Elkind, D. (1984). *All grown up and no place to go: Teenagers in crisis.* Menlo Park, CA: Addison-Wesley.

Evans, W. P., Marte, R. M., Betts, S., & Silliman, B. (2001). Adolescent suicide risk and peer-related violent behaviors and victimization. *Journal of Interpersonal Violence, 16*(12), 1330–1348.

Faber, M. (1978, February 7). *Issues in adolescent health* [Lecture]. Lansing: University of Michigan.

Felner, R. D., Jason, L. A., Moritsugu, J. M., & Farber, S. S. (1983). *Preventive psychology: Theory, research, and practice.* New York: Pergamon Press.

Felner, R. D., Silverman, M. M., & Adix, R. (1991). Prevention of substance abuse and related disorders in children and adolescence: A developmentally based, comprehensive ecological approach. *Family and Community Health: Journal of Health Promotion and Maintenance, 14*(3), 12–22.

Ferguson, W. F. (1983). *Stress as a precursor of depression, psychosomatic illness, and suicidal ideation among White middle class adolescents.* Doctoral Dissertation, Bryn Mawr College, Bryn Mawr, PA.

Garfinkel, B. D. (1989). The Components of School-Based Suicide Prevention. In *Adolescent Suicide: Recognition, Treatment, and Prevention.* Binghamton, NY: Haworth Press.

Garland, A. F., Shaffer, D., & Whittle, B. A. (1989). A national survey of school-based, adolescent suicide prevention programs. *Journal of the American Academy of Child and Adolescent Psychiatry, 28,* 931–934.

Garland, A. F., & Zigler, E. (1993). Adolescent suicide prevention: Current research and social policy implications. *American Psychologist, 48*(2), 169–182.

Goffman, E. (1963). *Stigma.* Englewood Cliffs, NJ: Prentice-Hall.

Gould, M. S., & Kramer, R. A. (2001). Youth suicide prevention. *National Suicide Prevention Conference Background Papers, 31,* 6–31.

Griffiths, J. K., Farley, O. W., & Fraser, M. W. (1986). Indices of adolescent suicide. *Journal of Independent Social Work, 1*(1), 49–63.

Harris, T., & Lenings, J. (1993). Suicide and adolescence. *International Journal of Offender Therapy and Comparative Criminology, 37*(3), 263–270.

Healthy People 2000: National health promotion and disease prevention objectives (1990). Washington, DC: U.S. Public Health Service, U.S. Department of Health and Human Services publication (PHS) 91-50212.

Hemming, J. (1977). Saving teenage suicide. *Journal of Psychosomatic Research, 22,* 291–296.

Hipple, J. (1987, November). *Suicide in children and adolescents.* Paper presented at the meeting of the North Central Texas Association for Counseling and Development, Dallas, TX.

Hirschfeld, R., & Blumenthal, S. (1986). Personality, life events and other psychosocial factors in adolescent depression and suicide: A review. In G. Klerman (Ed.), *Suicide among adolescents and young adults.* Washington, DC: American Psychiatric Press.

James, L., & Wherry, J. N. (1991). Suicide in residential treatment: Causes, assessment, and treatment issues. *Residential Treatment for Children and Youth, 9*(2), 23–36.

Kachur, S. P., Potter, L. B., Powell, K. E., & Rosenberg, M. L. (1992). Suicide: Epidemiology, prevention, and treatment. *Adolescent Medicine, 6,* 171–182.

Kalafat, J. (1990). Adolescent suicide and the implications for school response programs. *School Counselor, 37,* 359–360.

Kalafat, J., & Neigher, W. D. (1991). Experimental and pragmatic approaches to the incidence of adolescent suicide. *Evaluation and Program Planning, 14,* 377–383.

Kazdin, A. E. (1990). Psychotherapy for children and adolescents. *Annual Review of Psychology, 41,* 21–54.

Kellermann, A. L., Rivera, R. P., Somes, G., Reary, D. T., Francisco, J., Gillentine Banton, J., et al. (1992). Suicide in the home in relation to gun ownership *New England Journal of Medicine, 327,* 467–472.

Kovacs, M. (1981). Rating scales to assess depression in school aged children. *Acta Paedopsychiatrica, 46*(5/6), 305–315.

Leenaars, A. (1988). *Suicide notes.* New York: Human Sciences Press.

Lester, D. (1997). The effectiveness of suicide prevention centers: A review. *Suicide and Life-Threatening Behavior, 27*(3), 304–310.

Lester, D., & Leenaars, A. (1996). The ethics of suicide and suicide prevention. *Death Studies, 20,* 163–184.

Lester, D., & Murrell, M. E. (1980). The influence of gun control laws on suicidal behavior. *American Journal of Psychiatry, 137,* 121–122.

Lewinsohn, P. M., Rohde, P., & Seeley, J. R. (1993). Psychosocial characteristics of adolescents with a history of suicide attempt. *Journal of American Academy of Child Adolescent Psychiatry, 31*(1), 60–68.

Lurie, A., & Monahan, K. (2001). Prevention principles for practitioners: A solution or an illusion? *Social Work in Health Care, 33*(1), 69–86.

Malley, P. B., Kush, F., & Bogo, R. J. (1994). School-based adolescent suicide prevention and intervention programs: A survey. *School Counselor, 42,* 130–136.

Marcotte, D. (1997). Treating depression in adolescence: A review of the effectiveness of cognitive-behavioral treatments. *Journal of Youth and Adolescence, 26*(3), 273–284.

Maris, R. (1985). The adolescent suicide problem. *Suicide and Life-Threatening Behavior, 15*(2), 91–109.

Metha, A., Weber, B., & Webb, L. D. (1998). Youth suicide prevention: A survey and analysis of policies and efforts in the 50 states. *Suicide and Life-Threatening Behavior, 28*(2), 150–164.

National Center for Health Statistics. (2000). Suicide Rates per 100,000 living population (all ages) 1998 [GMWK 291], http://www.cdc.gov/nchs/data/gm291_1.pdf, U.S. Department of Health and Human Services.

National Plan for Research on Child and Adolescent Mental Disorder. (1990). Department of Health and Human Services publication No. 90-1683. Washington, DC: National Institute of Mental Health.

Parad, H., & Parad, L. (1990). *The practitioner's sourcebook for brief therapy* [Crisis intervention, Book 2]. Milwaukee, WI: Family Service America.

Peters, K. D., Kochanek, K. D., & Murphy, S. L. (1998). *Deaths: Final data for 1996* [Center for Disease Control National Vital Statistics Report No. 47-9]. Hyattsville, MD: National Center for Health Statistics.

Peterson, A. C., Compas, B. E., Brooks-Gunn, J., Stemmler, M., Ey, S., & Grant, K. E. (1993). Depression in adolescence. *American Psychology, 48,* 155–168.

Pfeffer, C. R. (1984). Modalities of treatment for suicidal children: An overview of the literature on current practice. *American Journal of Psychotherapy, 38,* 364–372.

Pfeffer, C. R. (1986). *The suicidal child.* New York: Guilford Press.

Puig-Antich, J., Goetz, D., Davis, M., Kaplan, T., Davies, S., Ostrow, L., et al. (1989). A controlled family history study of prepubertal major depressive disorder. *Archives of General Psychiatry, 46,* 406–418.

Radloff, L. S. (1991). The use of the Center for Epidemiological Studies depression scale in adolescents and young adults. *Journal of Youth and Adolescents, 20,* 149–166.

Randall, B. P., Eggert, L. L., & Pike, K. C. (2001). Immediate postintervention effects of two brief youth suicide preventive interventions. *Suicide and Life-Threatening Behavior, 31*(1), 41–61.

Rathus, J. H., & Miller, A. L. (2002). Dialectical behavior therapy adapted for suicidal adolescents. *Suicide and Life-Threatening Behavior, 32*(2), 146–157.

Reynolds, W. M. (1992). Depression in children and adolescents. In W. M. Reynolds (Ed.), *Internalizing disorders in children and adolescents.* New York: Wiley.

Robins, L. N., Helzer, J. E., Croughan, J. L., & Ratcliff, K. S. (1981). National Institute of Mental Health Diagnostic Interview Schedule: Its history, characteristics, and validity. *Archives of General Psychiatry, 38*(4), 381–389.

Robinson, L. (1984). Outpatient management of the suicidal child. *American Journal of Psychotherapy, 38,* 399–412.

Schlachter, T. H. (1975). Notes for practice. *Social Work, 20*(6), 427–481.

Schneidman, E. (1985). *Last wish.* New York: Wiley.

Shaffer, D., & Craft, L. (1999). Methods of adolescent suicide prevention. *Journal of Clinical Psychiatry, 60*(2), 70–74.

Silverman, M. M., & Felner, R. D. (1995). Suicide prevention programs: Issues of design, implementation, feasibility, and developmental appropriateness. *Suicide and Life-Threatening Behavior, 25*(1), 92–104.

Stiles, K., & Kottman, T. (1990). Mutual storytelling: An intervention for depressed and suicidal children. *The School Counselor, 37,* 337–342.

Streiner, D. L., & Adam, K. S. (1987). Evaluation of the effectiveness of suicide prevention programs: A methodological perspective. *Suicide and Life-Threatening Behavior, 17*(2), 93–106.

U.S. Public Health Service. (1999). *The Surgeon General's call to action to prevent suicide.* Washington, DC: Department of Health and Human Services.

Ward, B. R. (1995). The school's role in the prevention of youth suicide. *Social Work in Education, 17*(2), 92–100.

Wetzler, S., Asnis, G. M., Hyman, R. B., Virtue, C., Zimmerman, J., & Rathus, J. H. (1996). Characteristics of suicidality among adolescents. *Suicide and Life-Threatening Behavior, 26*(1), 37–45.

Wodarski, J., & Harris, P. (1987). Adolescent suicide: Review of influences and the means for prevention. *Social Work, 32,* 480–481.

Wodarski, J. S., Wodarski, L. S., & Dulmus, C. N. (2003). *Adolescent depression and suicide: A comprehensive empirical intervention for prevention and treatment.* Springfield, IL: Charles C Thomas.

Chapter 6 ————————————————————

AGGRESSIVE BEHAVIOR

MARK W. FRASER AND SHEARA A. WILLIAMS

Aggressive behavior in childhood is a risk factor for a variety of social and health problems. Beginning in early childhood, conduct problems such as frequent opposition, arguing, tantrums, inattention, and disobedience are associated with rejection by peers, poor adjustment in school, and a variety of other adaptational failures (Farmer, Bierman, & the Conduct Problems Prevention Research Group [CPPRG], 2002). From school entry through elementary school, aggressive behavior, peer rejection, and low academic achievement are highly correlated, and they predict more serious conduct problems in adolescence (Reid, Patterson, & Snyder, 2002).

As a keystone feature of conduct problems in childhood and early adolescence, *aggressive behavior* is defined as a pattern of conduct that causes or threatens to cause harm to people or animals. Because harm can occur when a child disrupts the classroom, intimidates peers, destroys property, sets fires, or steals from others, the term *aggressive behavior* includes frequent fighting, intimidation with a weapon (such as a stick or knife), cruelty to animals, lying or cheating, stealing from parents and others, and other violations of age-appropriate rules and norms. This definition implies that aggressive behavior is antisocial in nature and not based solely on overt, physical aggression. It can have covert or indirect elements. For example, it can involve relational aggression, a concept that includes harming others by manipulating peer relationships (Crick, Grotpeter, & Bigbee, 2002). Relational aggression is characterized by purposive attempts to harm the social status of another child ("You can't come to my birthday party unless . . ."), spreading false rumors ("Her mother is a drunk . . ."), and starting damaging gossip ("Mary failed her end-of-grade exams and has to attend summer school . . ."; Crick &

This chapter was prepared with support from the National Institute on Drug Abuse grant R21-DA13874.

Bigbee, 1998). A defining feature of aggressive behavior is harm. Whether overtly or covertly, children who engage in aggressive behavior use aggression to meet social and instrumental goals. They garner social dominance over others through force, and they obtain instrumental control—for example, control of a bus seat or a particular toy—by causing or threatening to cause harm to others.

If not disrupted, this pattern of behavior has serious developmental consequences. For both boys and girls, aggressive behavior appears to be relatively stable over time when it develops at an early age (Moffitt, 1997; Moffitt, Caspi, Rutter, & Silva, 2001; Patterson, Forgatch, Yoerger, & Stoolmiller, 1998). It has a strong relationship to negative developmental outcomes, including school dropout, adolescent pregnancy, delinquency, drug abuse, early sex, and—in young adulthood—criminal offending (Miller-Johnson, Coie, Maumary-Gremaud, Bierman, & CPPRG, 2002; Nagin & Farrington, 1992; Patterson & Yoerger, 2002). A report by the Surgeon General found that aggressive behavior, substance use, and court or police involvement between ages 6 and 11 were the principal individual level predictors for violence at ages 15 to 18 (U.S. Department of Health and Human Services [USDHHS], 2001, p. 60). To prevent school failure, drug abuse, delinquency, and youth violence, strategies to interrupt the linkages between early aggressive behavior and later offending are needed and, if effective, could produce significant social and health benefits (USDHHS, 2001).

The purpose of this chapter is to describe:

1. The prevalence of aggressive behavior in childhood and adolescence
2. The risk factors related to aggressive behavior
3. Promising universal and selective prevention programs

In the past 20 years, important advances have been made in charting the developmental trajectories that lead from early aggressive behavior to later offending. At the same time, a variety of prevention programs have been developed, and the research on these programs is promising. We describe recent progress both in understanding the etiology of aggressive behavior and in developing practice strategies to disrupt the developmental sequences that lead from aggressive behavior in childhood to serious conduct problems in adolescence and young adulthood.

PREVALENCE OF AGGRESSIVE BEHAVIOR IN CHILDHOOD AND ADOLESCENCE

Juvenile arrests are, perhaps, the most common means of assessing the prevalence of aggressive behavior and other conduct problems in childhood and adolescence.

Juveniles under the age of 18 comprise about 26% of the population (Federal Interagency Forum on Child and Family Statistics [FCFS], 2002), and they account for about 17% of all arrests, about 16% of all violent crime arrests, and about 32% of all property crime arrests (Office of Juvenile Justice and Delinquency Prevention [OJJDP], 2002a). The juvenile arrest rate for all offenses peaked in 1996 and declined through the beginning of the century (OJJDP, 2002b).

The increases observed up to the mid-1990s were proportionally greater for girls, and declines at the turn of century were proportionally greater for boys (OJJDP, 2002c). By the year 2001, overall arrest rates for males had returned to 1983 levels, but for girls they remained some 42% above 1983 levels (OJJDP, 2002c). Thus, increases in antisocial behavior among girls contributed disproportionately to the increase in arrest rates observed in the 1980s and 1990s. Unlike boys, the level of antisocial behavior among girls has not regressed to early 1980s levels.

Ethnically and racially, the largest declines since the mid-1990s have been observed for African American youths. Their arrest rates fell in 2001 to pre-1980s levels. In contrast, arrest rates for other racial and ethnic groups remained at early 1980s levels (OJJDP, 2002d).

Overall, changes in arrest rates present a complicated picture. Rates have not declined as steeply for girls as for boys, and there are some indicators that the true level of aggression has declined little, if at all, over the years. For example, arrest rates for aggravated assault remain today some 42% higher than they were in the early 1980s (OJJDP, 2002e). This suggests that fighting and other forms of conflict among youths may be at least as prevalent now as they were before the early 1990s when most indicators increased dramatically. In part, serious injuries and deaths because of fighting among adolescents may have declined in the later part of the 1990s because of advances in trauma medicine, a widespread decline in weapons-carrying among youth, and the emergence of less violent forms of dispute resolution among factions within urban drug cultures (Blumstein & Wallman, 2000; USDHHS, 2001).

Every two years, the Centers for Disease Control and Prevention (CDC) conducts a Youth Risk Behavior Surveillance (YRBS) survey, and data from this survey provide an alternative means to assess the prevalence of conduct problems among youth. Collected in public and private high schools (grades 9 to 12), the data describe a variety of behaviors related to injury and other health-focused outcomes. The survey relies on self-report—as opposed to official reports such as police contacts and arrests. Therefore, it may provide a better estimate of the prevalence of problems because it includes behaviors that do not necessarily rise to the attention of public officials, but nonetheless affect the character of social relationships in childhood and adolescence. On balance, the percentage of students who carried a gun, knife, club, or other weapon at school (Centers for Disease Control and Prevention [CDC], 2002a) and the percentage of students involved in physical fights (CDC, 2002f, 2002g) declined from the early 1990s through 2001. But these data also suggest that the percentage of students who do not go to school because they feel unsafe (CDC, 2002b), who have been threatened with or injured by a weapon at school (CDC, 2002c), and who carry a gun (CDC, 2002e) declined throughout the 1990s—only to rise ominously in 2001.

Yet another source of information on levels of aggression among children and youths is an annual survey of students called Monitoring the Future (MTF). Supported by the National Institute on Drug Abuse, MTF focuses on substance use and abuse. While substance abuse is highly correlated with serious health problems, it can be considered an indicator of aggressive behavior because it is associated with a subculture that relies on violent dispute resolution, illicit gun marketeering, and the development of gangs. Recent data from the MTF project suggest that the use of cocaine, methamphetamines, ecstasy, and unprescribed anabolic steroids is increasing (CDC, 2002d; Johnston, O'Malley, & Bachman, 2002). On the other hand, the use of heroin, cigarettes, LSD, and inhalants appears to be declining (Johnston et al., 2002). Therefore, putting it all together, self-report studies such as the YRBS and the MTF corroborate the patterns observed in juvenile arrest data. On balance, levels of antisocial behavior appear to have declined since peaking in the mid-1990s. However, recent increases in gun-carrying, the use of some drugs, and continued high levels of conflict—indicated by arrests for aggravated assault—suggest that aggressive behavior remains a major social and health problem.

A DEVELOPMENTAL AND ECOLOGICAL PERSPECTIVE

The risk factors for aggressive behavior and other conduct problems in childhood can be sequenced into a developmental trajectory (see Figure 6.1). From the first moments of life, both biological and environmental factors potentiate a child's growth and adaptation. When these factors include maternal substance abuse or smoking or when early development is complicated by poor prenatal care, the odds of developmental difficulties increase. Similarly, when constitutional problems such as neurological impairments make a child more difficult to nurture and raise, the chances for neglect and poor parenting increase. It is a sequence of events or conditions that leads to a cumulation of risk. As risk increases, it produces ever-higher odds for poor developmental outcomes. This cumulative risk sequence is sometimes called the *early start* model. From this perspective, individual, family,

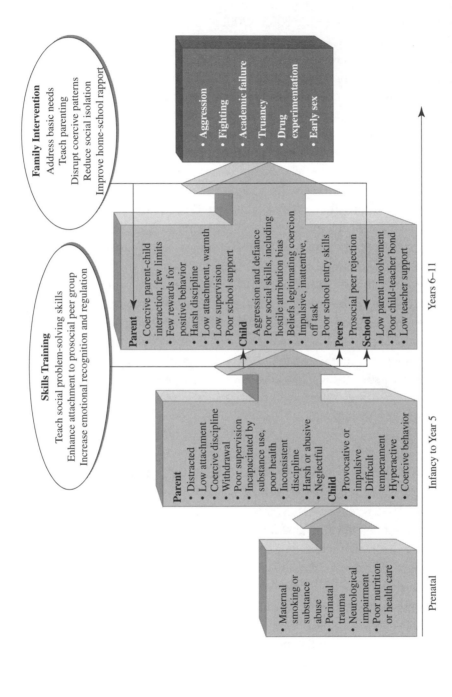

Figure 6.1 Ecological, Developmental Perspective: Risk Sequences and Intervention. Adapted from "Interventions for Antisocial Behavior: Overview" (pp. 195–201), by J. B. Reid and J. M. Eddy, in *Antisocial Behavior in Children and Adolescents*, by J. B. Reid, G. R. Patterson, and J. Snyder (Eds.), 2002, Washington DC: American Psychological Association.

school, and peer factors are thought to influence developmental outcomes such as frequent fighting, academic failure/success, early sex, and experimentation with drugs (Patterson, Dishion, & Yoerger, 2000). As you might suspect, the early start model is counterbalanced by a *late start* or adolescence limited model (Moffitt, 1997). We focus on the early start model in this chapter.

Ecological theory and a multisystems perspective on child development (Bronfenbrenner, 1979, 1986; Henggeler, Schoenwald, Borduin, Rowland, & Cunningham, 1998) suggest that aggressive behavior develops in the context of macrosocial and microsocial processes. Based on the interplay among genetic predisposition, physiological influences (e.g., exposure to lead, exposure to fetal alcohol), and conflicting forces in the social environment (e.g., the forces of racism and poverty, the influence of a supportive extended family), behavior is thought to be transactional and subject to the dynamics of social exchange. In the context of biological influences, a developmental and ecological perspective posits that children grow and adapt through transactions with parents, siblings, peers, teachers, coaches, neighbors, religious leaders, and a variety of others who people their lives. This person-in-environment perspective, where transactions between organism and environment are thought to produce behavior, lies at the heart of social work, psychology, social medicine, and other helping professions (see, e.g., Council on Social Work Education, 2001).

For this chapter, we focus on microsocial processes in the family, at school, and among peers. Higher order macrosocial processes such as the flourishing of international drug cartels, growing disparities between rich and poor, and the spread of weapons of mass destruction clearly affect the social and physical environments that condition opportunities for children and youth. Indirectly and directly, they affect local labor markets; the relative allocation of public funds to social, educational, and health services; the roles available to young adults, especially women (and, consequently, the role models presented to girls); and the character of public discourse and exchange.

These forces are important, but they are largely beyond the influence of individual practitioners. Therefore, we discuss them from the perspective of the influence they have on families. That is, we portray them as factors that affect maternal and child health, increase family stress, and disrupt effective parenting. This is, however, only one way to construct these influences, and dealing with them in practice is only one way to address macrosocial forces that affect child development. Although they are beyond the scope of this chapter, global actions to repudiate terror and torture; to promote rule by laws made by the people or freely elected representatives of the people; to expand religious, racial, and ethnic tolerance and understanding; and to rapidly accelerate the growth of middle classes are urgently needed.

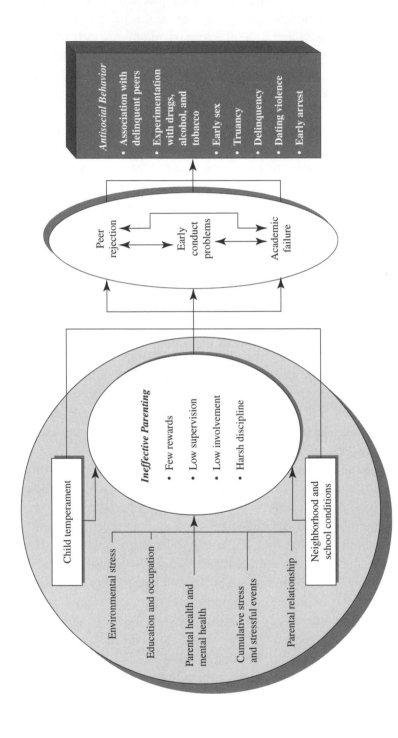

Figure 6.2 Mediational Model of Parenting: Relationship between Family Contextual Factors, Peer Rejection, Early Conduct Problems, Academic Failure, and Antisocial Behavior. Adapted from "Contextual Risk across the Early Life Span and Association with Antisocial Behavior" (pp. 123–145), by D. Capaldi, D. DeGarmo, G. R. Paterson, and M. Forgatch, in *Antisocial Behavior in Children and Adolescents*, by J. B. Reid, G. R. Patterson, and J. Snyder (Eds.), 2002, Washington, DC: American Psychological Association.

In conceptualizing the influence of macrosocial risk factors vis-à-vis the design of interventions, we argue that risk processes affect child development through their influence on microsocial systems, principally the family and school. Broader social influences on developmental outcomes are mediated through the family and expressed principally in the effectiveness of parenting (see Figure 6.2). Ineffective parenting is multidimensional, as suggested in Figure 6.1. It consists of coercive discipline, low supervision and monitoring, failure to reward a child's prosocial behaviors, low support of school-related activities (e.g., homework completion), and an interpersonal style consisting of frequent nagging and nattering that leads to low parent-child attachment and warmth.

The figures also show that the effectiveness of parenting is transactional; it is affected by child characteristics. A child's temperament may be influenced by biological factors related to poor prenatal care and maternal substance abuse or smoking during pregnancy. In turn, a child with a difficult temperament is more difficult to parent. From an ecological perspective, parenting is affected by characteristics of the child (e.g., the child's temperament), the capacity of parents (as influenced, e.g., by parental health and mental health, the relationship between parents, and parental education and occupational status), and the relative amount of stress in the social environment. Many of these are malleable and present opportunities for intervention.

A RISK AND PROTECTIVE FACTOR PERSPECTIVE

Prevention intervention for conduct problems in childhood and early adolescence is based on a process of identifying malleable risk factors and targeting them with specific interventions (see Figure 6.1; arrows indicate risk factors that may be subject to skills training and family interventions). Early aggressive behavior is a key risk factor for conduct problems in adolescence. But because there is no single cause or pathway that produces conduct problems, assessment to identify relevant risk factors is essential.

Culture and Context

Although research suggests that the core risk structures may be similar across gender and race/ethnicity (e.g., academic failure is a risk factor for both boys and girls from different racial and ethnic backgrounds; see, e.g., Deater-Deckard, Dodge, Bates, & Pettit, 1998; Moffitt et al., 2001), the strength of specific risk factors and their developmental consequences is almost always intertwined with culture, language, religion, and socioeconomic conditions, especially poverty. Behavior considered adaptive and normative in one culture may not be similarly adaptive and normative in other cultures (Coll & Magnuson, 2000). This affects not only the scripts, roles, and schema presented as normative to children, but also the support available to families.

The influence of the neighborhood can be similarly conceptualized (see Figure 6.2). The collective efficacy of neighborhoods—defined in part as the degree of agreement on values and the relative capacity of neighbors to assist one another in child supervision and other activities—is often thought to have two effects (Sampson, 2001). First, it affects the effectiveness of parenting; second, it influences the behavior of children by exposing them to both prosocial and antisocial role models who differentially reinforce commitment to conventional activities (for a more comprehensive review of community risk factors and interventions, see Herrenkohl, Hawkins, Chung, Hill, & Battin-Pearson, 2001). Therefore, a risk assessment based on an understanding of culture, neighborhood conditions, and resources is required in devising contextually and culturally relevant prevention programs.

Protective Factors, Strengths, and Assets

The design of prevention programs is informed also by pioneering studies in mental health that in the 1970s and 1980s began to identify protective factors that seem to buffer some children against the effects of risk (e.g., Garmezy, 1971). The defining feature of protective mechanisms is a modification of the risk situation. This requires some form of "amelioration (protection) of the reaction to a factor that in ordinary circumstances leads to a maladaptive outcome" (Rutter, 1987, p. 317).

Whereas the related concepts of assets and strengths are widely accepted in social work (Saleebey, 1997, 2000), the nature of protective processes and their relationship to risk mechanisms is much debated in the social and health sciences (see, e.g., Masten, 2001). Terms such as *promotive effects* have been advanced for factors that seem to promote positive developmental outcomes regardless of risk level (Sameroff & Gutman, 2004), and, to date, there is little agreement on how to measure protective factors (for reviews, see Fraser, 2004; Stouthamer-Loeber, Loeber, Wei, Farrington, & Wikstrom, 2002). More work is needed in conceptualizing protective versus risk effects. For this chapter, we define *protective factors* as both *internal and external resources that modify risk*.

In spite of the conceptual and methodological challenges raised by the phenomenon of protection, we know that at all levels of risk, children have resources that buffer them from adversity. We also know, however, that at the highest levels of risk, these protective resources are often insufficient to offset adversity

(Pollard, Hawkins, & Arthur, 1999). Nevertheless, we cannot base interventions solely on an understanding of risk factors. During assessment, it is important to identify the protective factors—both constitutional and environmental—that might be bolstered in intervention. Although risk and protection are negatively correlated, most high-risk children have strengths or assets that can be leveraged in developing an intervention plan. From research on risk and protection, two crucial practice strategies emerge: *reduce risk* and *promote protection* based on an understanding of culture, gender, and socioeconomic conditions.

THREE PREVENTION STRATEGIES

As an outgrowth of the expansion of knowledge of the consequences of early aggressive behavior, scholars have argued that a principal goal of public policy should be to disrupt risk mechanisms (see Figures 6.1 and 6.2). Prevention, they say, has come of age (Reid & Eddy, 2002b). If provided with sufficient focus, fidelity, and intensity, developmentally sequenced programs should be capable of altering the developmental trajectories that produce youth violence, substance abuse, and a variety of other poor life course outcomes. Whether designed for young children or early adolescents, programs should be informed by the constellation of risk and protective factors whose net effect produces poor outcomes at particular points in development. Across stages of child development, three basic strategies have shown promise, and successful prevention programs often invoke these strategies concurrently: (1) behavioral parent training, (2) child-focused skill building, and (3) school-related academic enhancement.

Behavioral Parent Training

For most children, their first and, arguably, most important learning experiences occur in the home. Holmes, Slaughter, and Kashani (2001, p. 187) observed, "A child's family experience is one of the most influential environmental factors contributing to conduct disorder and antisocial personality disorder, beginning at birth and continuing throughout childhood and adolescence." Strategies to strengthen families are based on a key idea in behavior theory: Children's behaviors can be changed through interventions that focus on strengthening parental skills in problem solving, communication, and discipline.

The careful work of Patterson, Reid, Capaldi, Dishion, Eddy, Forgatch, Stoolmiller, and their colleagues at the Oregon Social Learning Center over the past three decades has been critical in advancing knowledge about parent training and family-related intervention. In their efforts to develop a theoretical basis for parenting interventions, they studied the interactions of children with their parents. Now widely known, coercion theory arose from this work (Patterson, 1982; Patterson, Reid, & Dishion, 1992). The theory posits that maladaptive parent-child interactions negatively influence the behaviors of both parents and children. Mutually coercive interactions reinforce behaviors associated with the development and maintenance of aggressive behavior in children (Reid et al., 2002). From a coercion perspective, the goals of parent-training interventions are to reduce family stress, to reestablish systematic parental monitoring of children's behavior, to create explicit contingencies (rewards and mild punishments) for children's behaviors, and to promote prosocial (noncoercive) parent-child exchanges. Parenting programs often begin by dealing with the concrete problems—transportation, child care, and health care—that disrupt family life, impede effective parenting, and make attending a parenting program difficult. In parenting programs, parents are taught to use proactive child management techniques (e.g., rewarding positive and desirable behaviors and consequating problematic behavior), and, in more recent preventive interventions, children are involved concomitantly in problem-solving skill-building groups (see, e.g., Reid, Eddy, Fetrow, & Stoolmiller, 1999; Webster-Stratton & Taylor, 2001).

Child-Focused Skills Training

Learned in the family, in the extended family, and in child care settings, a child's skills, beliefs, and attitudes begin to affect interactions with others as early as preschool. In particular, deficits in problem-solving and emotional regulation skills are associated with a variety of negative developmental outcomes, ranging from rejection by peers to poor adjustment in school (Werner & Kerig, 2000). They are implicated, too, in the early development of aggressive behavior (Farmer et al., 2002, p. 300). In a recent longitudinal study of 295 kindergarten children, poor social problem-solving skills predicted initiation of substance use by 12 years of age, controlling for age, gender, race, socioeconomic status, parental involvement, parental verbal reasoning skill, parental drug use, and a variety of child characteristics (e.g., thought problems and overactivity; Kaplow, Curran, Dodge, & CPPRG, 2002). From very early in childhood, social competence in resolving disputes without resorting to force affects developmental trajectories.

Interventions that focus on social competence have shown promise in preschool, elementary school, and middle school settings (Gottfredson, Jones, & Gore, 2002). Typically, these interventions involve teaching interpersonal problem-solving skills, training to alter cognitions (such as hostile attribution biases) that lead to aggressive behavior, exercises in developing emotional regulation skills (control of arousal and anger), and role play to strengthen skills in real-life scenarios. The effectiveness of these strategies appears to be related to the other strategies that are used in consort with them.

When used as a component of a larger, multifaceted intervention that focuses on parent- and school-related risk factors, problem-solving skills training appears to contribute to positive outcomes (August, Realmuto, Hektner, & Bloomquist, 2001; Ialongo et al., 1999; Taylor, Eddy, & Biglan, 1999). For example, Barrera et al. (2002) randomly assigned 284 kindergarten through third-grade children to a no-treatment control condition ($n = 143$) or a multielement intervention ($n = 141$) involving parenting training, supplemental reading instruction, social skills training, and an individualized classroom behavior management program. At one-year follow-up, children who received the program showed less coercive behavior and aggression in the home. Unfortunately, Barrera et al. do not separately estimate the effects of skills training. As in the findings from many other studies that involve social problem solving, we are not able to assess the relative contribution of problem-solving preventive interventions. This has led some to conclude that findings are equivocal (Reid & Eddy, 2002a). But, while more research is needed, a growing number of prevention studies using skills training alone or research designs that permit the estimation of the effect of skills training separately from other program components report that it contributes significantly to outcomes (Greenberg, Kusche, Cook, & Quamma, 1995; Grossman et al., 1997; Kazdin, Siegel, & Bass, 1992; Lochman, Coie, Underwood, & Terry, 1993; Smokowski, Fraser, Day, Galinsky, & Bacallao, 2002). On balance, however, the most common use of problem-solving skills programs is as one element of an overarching multi-element program designed to address delinquency, drug use, and youth violence. Indeed, leading to guarded optimism about skills training for children, it is an element of some of the most promising prevention intervention programs (see, e.g., Lonczak, Abbott, Hawkins, Kosterman, & Catalano, 2002; Reid et al., 1999; Webster-Stratton, 2000).

Academic Enhancement and School Reform

The third element of major prevention programs focuses on the school environment. The public elementary school system is the "only existing system of care with widespread contact with young children in the United States" (Reid & Eddy, 2002b, p. 222). Because academic performance and school bonding (i.e., involvement in and attachment or commitment to school) are predictors of developmental outcomes (for a detailed review, see Najaka, Gottfredson, & Wilson, 2002), school settings are favored for many preventive interventions. School-related strategies attempt to promote academic success by strengthening parental involvement in school, altering teachers' classroom behavior management systems, creating new opportunities for student participation and learning, and improving children's study and social skills. Teachers fill a critical role in school-based prevention strategies. They use innovative classroom management techniques and employ innovative curricula for teaching traditional content (e.g., math or language arts) as well as content on social skills, behavioral health (e.g., drug refusal techniques), peer relations, and other topics.

Programs that infuse academic or instructional interventions with behavioral interventions have been found effective in both improving academic outcomes and reducing problematic behaviors ranging from classroom disruptions to delinquency and drug use (Battistich, Schaps, Watson, Solomon, & Lewis, 2000; CPPRG, 1999a, 1999b; Ialongo et al., 1999). These programs often combine parenting interventions with academic enhancements such as interactive teaching, cooperative learning, specialized curricula, and tutoring (e.g., Slavin & Cooper, 1999). In the Success, Health, and Peace (SHAPe) program, for example, seventh graders received weekly homeroom-based lessons on study strategies, conflict resolution, and drug abstinence. Each week, students and their parents participated in homework assignments linked to classroom content. Assignments focused on school success, peer relationships, and rewards for prosocial behavior. The SHAPe intervention included a family resource center that, as a supplemental selective prevention intervention, provided supportive services to some 60 families that were identified as *at risk*. Compared to youths randomized to a control group, children in the SHAPe program had lower levels of drug initiation in the seventh, eighth, and ninth grades. Moreover, the program appeared to benefit students from both high- and low-risk backgrounds (Dishion, Kavanagh, Schneiger, Nelson, & Kaufman, 2002). Programs such as SHAPe foster stronger bonds of attachment between parents and the school by creating new structures to assist parents and new learning opportunities to prepare students for future academic and social challenges. Like earlier programs in school settings (see, e.g., Hawkins, Catalano, Kosterman, Abbott, & Hill, 1999; Knoff & Batsche, 1995), programs such as SHAPe show that the school is a fertile site for prevention.

EIGHT PROMISING PREVENTION PROGRAMS

We highlight eight exemplary preventive interventions that incorporate behavioral parent training, child-focused skills training, and/or school-related academic-enhancement strategies. These interventions have been identified through reviews of delinquency, youth violence, and substance abuse prevention programs. Between January and August 2002, a literature search was conducted to identify studies that reported results of prevention programs/trials targeting children from birth through 10 years of age. (Consequently, promising programs for older children, such as SHAPe, are not included in the review. Programs for adolescents are reviewed elsewhere; see, e.g., Elliott, 2002; Greenberg, Domitrovich, & Bumbarger, 2001.) The search was initiated by using the PsycINFO (WebSPIR) and Social Sciences Citation Index (ISI Web of Knowledge and Web of Science) databases. The following key words were used to guide the search of studies published since 1990: *prevention of conduct problems, childhood aggression, delinquency prevention, violence prevention,* and *substance abuse prevention.* In addition, the following resources were consulted to augment the identification of prevention programs: The Surgeon General's 2001 report on youth violence (USDHHS, 2001), the Center for Substance Abuse Prevention Model Programs web site (Center for Substance Abuse Prevention [CSAP], 2002), and the Office of Juvenile Justice and Delinquency Prevention (Office of Juvenile Justice and Delinquency Prevention [OJJDP], 2002f) web site.

Interventions included in this review were selected on the basis of:

- An explicit focus on risk factors associated with conduct problems
- Evidence of effectiveness from controlled studies with experimental or quasi-experimental designs
- Evidence of program fidelity and replicability (e.g., structured trainings and training materials, a program manual, and ongoing assessment of program delivery)

These programs are exemplary and are not the only programs that show promise. They and others are reviewed in more comprehensive reports supported by the OJJDP (Howell, Krisberg, Hawkins, & Wilson, 1995), the National Institute for Child Health and Human Development (Catalano, Berglund, Ryan, Lonczak, & Hawkins, 2002), the *Blueprints* book series (Elliott, 2002), and syntheses of prevention research (Greenberg et al., 2001; Loeber & Farrington, 1998, 2001; Taylor & Biglan, 1998). We highlight these programs because the evidence for their effectiveness is relatively strong, the theory behind the design of the interventions is clear (i.e., specific risk factors are targeted), and interventions were concretized in detailed treatment manuals or protocols. A more extensive description—in table form—that fully describes program elements and evaluative findings is available from the authors. See Appendix I for a directory containing contact information for each program.

Preventive Interventions: Prenatal through the Early Years

In this section, we highlight five preventive programs. Each focuses on the early childhood phases of development, ranging from the prenatal period through third grade. Long term evaluations of these comprehensive early interventions suggest that they are effective in reducing (or preventing) aggressive behavior and conduct problems in childhood.

Nurse Home Visitation

Through two separate large-scale randomized trials, Olds and his colleagues (Olds, Henderson, Cole, et al., 1998; Olds, Henderson, Hitzman, et al., 1998) have demonstrated the effectiveness of the Nurse Home Visitation (NHV) program, a selective intervention. The program is designed to interrupt risk processes associated with conduct problems in adolescence. Now implemented in many states across the country (Olds, 2002), the NHV program was designed in 1978. During home visits, nurses use parenting training strategies (including working with mothers to solve concrete health, housing, and other problems) to promote positive health behaviors during pregnancy and early childhood, competence in the care of infants, and the development of personal care or career plans (e.g., plans related to education, employment, and family planning; Olds, Henderson, Cole, et al., 1998).

In a 15-year follow-up study of the NHV program, Olds and colleagues collected data on children's court adjudications, disruptive behavior in school, school suspensions, sexual activity, pregnancies, number of sexual partners, and use of alcohol, cigarettes, and illegal drugs (Olds, Henderson, Cole, et al., 1998). At the time of the program's initiation, mothers and their children were randomized to a full ($n = 116$), partial ($n = 100$), or comparison group ($n = 184$) condition. Findings favored children in the full treatment condition. Compared to children from the comparison group, these children—adolescents at the time of follow-up—had fewer arrests, convictions, and probation violations; fewer sexual partners; fewer episodes of running away; and fewer behavioral problems related to drug and alcohol use (Olds, Henderson, Cole, et al., 1998; Olds, Henderson, Hitzman, et al. 1998). Moreover, significantly fewer adolescents from the full NHV condition reported tobacco and alcohol use (Olds, 2002).

Dare to Be You

Dare to Be You (DTBY) is a multifaceted, selective prevention program designed for high-risk children between 2 and 5 years of age (Miller-Heyl, MacPhee, & Fritz, 1998). Protective factors in seven specific domains and a risk assessment guide service delivery to families. The DTBY program has two elements:

1. A community development program for agencies that provide services to children and their families
2. A comprehensive parent-child intervention designed to improve parental self-efficacy, internal locus of control, decision-making skills, child-rearing

strategies, stress management, understanding of child development, and peer support (Miller-Heyl et al., 1998)

Implemented in four sites over a five-year period, the program recruited 797 families and randomly assigned them to control ($n = 301$) and experimental ($n = 496$) groups. In an analysis of cohorts in years two through four, 227 children and their families in the experimental group were compared to their control group counterparts ($n = 136$) at one- and two-year follow-up (Miller-Heyl et al., 1998). Parental self-esteem and self-efficacy increased in the experimental group over the two-year period, whereas no changes were observed among parents in the control group. Through the two-year follow-up, parents in the experimental group reported reductions in the use of harsh discipline and increased use of disciplinary techniques such as time out and limit-setting. In contrast, the disciplinary practices of parents in the control group remained unchanged over time. Changes in children's problem and oppositional behaviors favored the experimental group at both one- and two-year follow-up (p. 276).

Incredible Years

The Incredible Years (IY) intervention consists of multiple universal, selective, and indicated prevention programs for children ages 4 through 8, their parents, and their teachers (Webster-Stratton, 1990, 1994; Webster-Stratton & Hammond, 1997). The program is focused on preventing the development of oppositional defiant disorder (ODD) and conduct disorder (CD) in children. The child-focused elements of IY are designed to address the academic needs and social competencies of children. The parent-focused programs are designed to teach behavioral parenting skills, encourage parental involvement at school and collaboration with teachers, and improve parental interpersonal coping skills (Webster-Stratton, 1998; Webster-Stratton, Reid, & Hammond, 2001). Teachers are trained to use classroom behavior management techniques for reducing aggressive behaviors and promoting academic achievement. In addition, teachers are encouraged to develop explicit home-school collaborations (Webster-Stratton, 1998; Webster-Stratton et al., 2001).

In an evaluation of IY, 394 (experimental = 264; control = 130) families with children in nine Head Start centers were randomly assigned to experimental or control conditions (Webster-Stratton, 1998). Baseline, post-, and follow-up assessments were conducted. At postintervention assessment, effects favored the IY group. Compared to control group parents, parents in IY reported significantly greater use of consistent discipline and appropriate limit-setting. Moreover, they reported significantly less use of harsh, physical, and negative disciplinary techniques. The IY parents were significantly more involved in school. Intervention group children showed significant decreases in deviant and noncompliant behavior and increases in social competence. In contrast, the control group showed no changes. Of those IY mothers assessed as high risk at baseline, 69% showed at least a 30% decrease in high-risk behaviors at postintervention assessment. No comparable changes were observed for high-risk control group mothers. Likewise, among high-risk children who received the intervention, 73% showed at least a 30% decrease in negative behaviors. In contrast, some 55% of the high-risk children in the control group showed comparable declines (Webster-Stratton, 1998). Follow-up assessments conducted between 12 and 18 months later showed that treatment effects were maintained over time (Webster-Stratton, 1998).

Good Behavior Game

Designed to be infused into routine preschool and elementary school activities, the Good Behavior Game (GBG) is a universal preventive intervention that uses peer pressure to promote good or prosocial classroom behavior. The GBG requires students to function in teams for which membership is strategically determined by the teacher. Teams are composed of approximately the same percentages of children with prosocial and disruptive behavior. The teams are rewarded for complying with behavioral standards (e.g., Raise your hand before speaking.) clearly defined by the teacher. The game is designed to improve students' social adaptation to classroom rules and "to create an integrated classroom social system with little aggressive, disruptive behavior, [that is] supportive of all children being able to learn" (Kellam, Ling, Merisca, Brown, & Ialongo, 1998, p. 170). An extensive reading curriculum, Mastery Learning (ML), has also been used in conjunction with the GBG to promote academic achievement through reading enrichment.

Multiple evaluations of the GBG and the ML curriculum suggest that the programs reduce aggressive/disruptive behaviors, while improving academic achievement (Dolan et al., 1993; Ialongo et al., 1999; Kellam, Rebok, Ialongo, & Mayer, 1994; Kellam, Rebok, Mayer, Ialongo, & Kalodner, 1994; Kellam et al., 1998). For example, the GBG was evaluated in a study of 1,084 children who entered first grade in Baltimore public schools in 1985 (see Dolan et al., 1993; Kellam, Rebok, Ialongo, et al., 1994; Kellam, Rebok, Mayer, et al., 1994). Nineteen schools were randomly assigned as intervention or matched comparison schools. Within the intervention schools, internal controls (classrooms) were also established. Although the effects of the GBG varied as a function of baseline levels of aggression, significant behavioral changes were observed at posttest and, remarkably, at six-year follow-up. For GBG boys, steady reductions in aggression were observed from third through sixth grades, compared to their internal control counterparts, whose aggressive behavior rose. In a separate study, a modified version of the GBG has been found effective in reducing the initiation of smoking in GBG participants at six-year follow-up (see Kellam & Anthony, 1998; Storr, Ialongo,

Kellam, & Anthony, 2002). Children seem to enjoy GBG, and bringing peer influence to bear on classroom behavior appears to promote both social and academic adjustment.

Fast Track

Perhaps the largest prevention trial to date, Fast Track (FT) is a multicomponent intervention introduced during the first grade and continuing through elementary school (CPPRG, 1999a, 1999b). It incorporates universal, selective, and indicated prevention strategies by blending a variety of programs to address child, parent, and teacher-related risk factors for conduct problems. It is universal in the sense that it provides classroom-based skills training to teachers and children; and it is both selective and indicated through the provision of home visits for parents, parent training groups, tutoring services, peer-pairing, and social skills training for children (Webster-Stratton & Taylor, 2001). The goals of the child component include improvements in emotion regulation, social-cognitive skills, and academic achievement. The family component focuses on behavioral parenting skills and parental involvement in school. A classroom component is guided by a teacher-administered classroom curriculum focused on skills related to "understanding and communicating emotions," positive social behavior, and self-control (CPPRG, 1999b, p. 651).

In an evaluation that continues today, 891 children attending 54 schools were identified from a population of 9,000 kindergarten students in four regions across the nation. All children were regarded as high risk. Schools were randomly assigned to intervention or control conditions (CPPRG, 2002). Of the 891 participants, 445 received the intervention in 191 first-grade classrooms, and 446 children in 210 first-grade classrooms served as the control group. At the end of participants' third-grade year, significant effects were found in favor of the intervention condition. Compared to control group children, children in the intervention had significantly fewer conduct problems. Children in the control group were significantly more likely to have been placed in special education programs. Additionally, parents in the intervention group reported significantly lower rates of physical punishment and greater use of behavioral parenting techniques (e.g., time out) when compared to control group parents. In this continuing study, the researchers reported that 37% of the children in the experimental group remain free of "serious conduct-problem dysfunction, in contrast with 27% of the control group" (p. 19).

Preventive Interventions: Middle Childhood

The three preventive interventions are reviewed in this section. Each extends intervention efforts beyond early childhood into middle childhood. Although the primary setting of these preventive interventions is the school, each program contains components that focus on parents and parental involvement in school.

Seattle Social Development Project

Promising programs for children in the upper grades of elementary school have also used behavioral parenting, child skills training, and academic enhancement strategies. A universal prevention intervention, the Seattle Social Development Project (SSDP) was a nonrandomized trial of a multielement intervention with children in grades 1 through 6 in eight elementary schools in high-risk areas of Seattle, Washington (Hawkins et al., 1992). The intervention consisted of classroom, child-focused, and parental components. The classroom intervention trained teachers to use specific proactive classroom management techniques, including interactive teaching and cooperative learning. The child intervention included training in social problem-solving and (drug) refusal skills. It was intended to promote goal accomplishment without "resorting to problem behaviors" (O'Donnell, Hawkins, Catalano, Abbott, & Day, 1995, p. 91). The third and final component of the SSDP targeted parents. Behavioral parent training classes were offered on a voluntary basis. These classes focused on reducing inconsistent family management and family conflict. In addition, parents were encouraged to become involved in school activities, to assist their children in completing homework, to monitor their children's friends, and to oppose community norms favorable to substance use (O'Donnell et al., 1995, p. 92).

A longitudinal study of the SSDP showed significant effects (Hawkins et al., 1999). The study was based on comparison of a full intervention group ($n = 149$) that received the intervention package from grades 1 though 6, a late intervention group ($n = 243$) that received the intervention package in grades 5 and 6 only, and a control group ($n = 206$) that received routine school services only. Six years after the close of services, findings favored the full intervention condition on a variety of outcomes: commitment to school, attachment to school, self-reported achievement, grade completion, school misbehavior, heavy drinking, number of sex partners, pregnancy or causing pregnancy, and violent offenses (Hawkins et al., 1999). Ten years after the close of services, full intervention participants were found to have lower rates of adolescent pregnancy, birthing, and sexually transmitted diseases when compared to the comparison group (Lonczak et al., 2002). The results imply that early and continuous intervention that focuses on child, parent, and school-related risk factors can significantly affect developmental trajectories.

Child Development Project

Like the SSDP, the Child Development Project (CDP) is a universal, multi-faceted school reform program. It uses classroom, school-wide, and family-centered strategies simultaneously. The classroom component of the CDP involves cooperative learning, literature-based language arts, and developmental discipline. The purpose of the school-wide component is to build a "caring community of learners." It includes the involvement of "teachers, students, parents, and extended family members in a wide range of projects and activities that are noncompetitive and inclusive" (Battistich et al., 2000, p. 80). In addition to a family school involvement program, parents and caregivers are involved in other CDP activities. For example, each student and his or her family is assigned *homeside* activities, which are directly related to classroom learning.

In a four-year demonstration, CDP was implemented at 24 elementary schools (12 intervention, 12 comparison schools) across six urban, suburban, and rural school districts in the United States. A quasi-experimental, cohort sequential design was employed to assess outcomes of students in grades 3 through 6. One year before the implementation of the CDP, baseline measures were collected on 679 students attending comparison schools and 755 students attending intervention schools. Annual follow-up assessments were conducted over the next three years. The researchers observed considerable variability in program implementation among the 12 intervention schools. Comparing the five schools with high program fidelity (i.e., faithful implementation of CDP) to five matched control schools, significant effects were found in favor of CDP schools (Battistich et al., 2000). For example, rates of alcohol and marijuana use at baseline decreased over time for students attending the high fidelity schools; however, among the matched comparison schools, rates of alcohol and marijuana use increased. Weaker but significant effects were observed in favor of students attending the five high fidelity schools on measures of running away, taking a vehicle without the permission of the owner, and involvement in gang fights. The findings suggest that school-based interventions can be effective, but they also suggest that fidelity in implementing interventions is related to programmatic outcomes.

Linking the Interests of Families and Teachers

The Linking the Interests of Families and Teachers (LIFT) program in Oregon combined many of the best elements of SSDP, FT, GBG, and other promising programs. It blended classroom skills training with parenting training in a 10-week intervention for first- and fifth-grade students (Reid et al., 1999). A universal prevention program, LIFT consisted of a 6-session parenting training module, a 20-session classroom-based social skills training program, a playground version of the Good Behavior Game, and home-school communication. Over a three-year period, 671 students in 12 schools, which were randomized to LIFT or a control group, participated (intervention = 382; control = 289). Posttest comparisons across schools indicated that the program was effective at both grade levels in improving children's social skills. Observations of mother-child and child-child interactions suggested that the program also reduced maternal aversive behavior (e.g., nagging during mother-child interactions) and child physical aggression (Reid et al., 1999; Stoolmiller, Eddy, & Reid, 2000).

IMPLICATIONS FOR PRACTICE

As exemplified in these eight programs, preventive interventions that disrupt behavioral trajectories leading from aggressive behavior in very early childhood to serious conduct problems in adolescence focus on specific risk factors or risk mechanisms (e.g., coercive parent-child interactions). Although for adolescents there is substantial variation in interventions—ranging from multisystemic family treatment (Henggeler et al., 1998), to mentoring (e.g., McGill, Mihalic, & Grotpeter, 1997), to antibullying school mobilization (e.g., Olweus, Limber, & Mihalic, 1999), to educational incentive programs (e.g., Lattimore, Mihalic, Grotpeter, & Taggart, 1998), to treatment foster care (Chamberlain, Fisher, & Moore, 2002), and a host of different types of out-of-home placements—three core strategies appear to characterize preventive interventions in early childhood. On balance, promising preventive interventions for preschool and elementary-age children seek to strengthen parenting, improve children's social problem-solving skills, and alter conditions in schools to promote academic achievement and social involvement.

The eight programs reviewed in this chapter restructure environments so that children have successful experiences in the home, with their peers, and in school. In addition, some programs employ strategies to reduce family stress by providing concrete services to address health, nutrition, and other needs. Although health and nutrition are widely conceptualized as risks in the prenatal/infancy period (see Figure 6.1), there is strong evidence that they disrupt effective parenting whenever they occur (for reviews, see Capaldi, DeGarmo, Patterson, & Forgatch, 2002; Fraser, Kirby, & Smokowski, 2004). Moreover, because they interfere with learning and because many promising interventions rely on learning-related practice strategies, addressing concrete needs is an essential aspect of intervention, especially intervention that involves low-income parents or children.

When parents are targeted, services usually consist of efforts to reduce environmental risk, promote connectedness to school and other parents, and strengthen parenting, problem-solving, and communications skills. Parenting training attempts to break coercive parent-child interactions that produce alienation, low attachment, and—in the longer term—aggressive behavior (Reid et al., 2002). In addition, parent-focused strategies ensure that children are not exposed to harsh discipline and that an adequate child monitoring system is put into place.

School-based programs modify classroom content and change reward structures to focus the attention of both teachers and children on behaviors that promote academic success and social adjustment. In doing this, they introduce new curricular material, new methods of teaching, and new classroom management systems. These strategies range from discrete skills-training programs focused on social competence or behavioral health (e.g., Fraser, Nash, Galinsky, & Darwin, 2001; Grossman et al., 1997) to peer-based cooperative learning and behavioral management that are infused across regular education curricula (e.g., Ialongo et al., 1999; Slavin & Cooper, 1999). The GBG exemplifies efforts to infuse behavioral intervention into routine classroom activities.

Based on findings from these eight programs and from other studies describing preventive interventions that promote positive youth development (e.g., Lochman et al., 1993; Tremblay, Pagani-Kurtz, Masse, Vitaro, & Pihl, 1995), there is growing optimism as to delinquency and drug abuse prevention. Studies suggest that it is possible to disrupt risk mechanisms that lead from early aggressive behavior to later conduct problems. Given the poor developmental outcomes associated with early aggressive behavior and the promising findings from prevention studies, there is no compelling reason to delay the implementation of prevention programs in preschools and elementary schools. Although significant challenges remain in tailoring programs on the basis of culture, race/ethnicity, and gender, both universal and selective prevention strategies show promise. In the context of continued prevention research to further refine intervention strategies, a new conundrum is emerging: How can we induce schools and social service agencies to transform the roles of social workers, school counselors, psychologists, and teachers to enable them to implement promising parent training, skills training, and academic enhancement programs? In light of the continued commitment of many schools to programs such as Drug Abuse Resistance Education (DARE) that have marginal evidence of impact (see, e.g., Clayton, Cattarello, & Johnstone, 1996) and the differential outcomes observed when programs such as the CDP are implemented poorly, the challenge of taking to scale the knowledge from recent prevention trials should not be underestimated.

REFERENCES

August, G. J., Realmuto, G. M., Hektner, J. M., & Bloomquist, M. L. (2001). An integrated components preventive intervention for aggressive elementary school children: The early risers program. *Journal of Consulting and Clinical Psychology, 69*(4), 614–626.

Barrera, M., Jr., Biglan, A., Taylor, T. K., Gunn, B. K., Smolkowski, K., Black, C., et al. (2002). Early elementary school intervention to reduce conduct problems: A randomized trial with Hispanic and non-Hispanic children. *Prevention Science, 3*(2), 83–94.

Battistich, V., Schaps, E., Watson, M., Solomon, D., & Lewis, C. (2000). Effects of the child development project on students' drug use and other problem behaviors. *Journal of Primary Prevention, 21*(1), 75–99.

Blumstein, A., & Wallman, J. (2000). *The crime drop in America.* Cambridge, England: Cambridge University Press.

Bronfenbrenner, U. (1979). *The ecology of human development: Experiments by nature and design.* Cambridge, MA: Harvard University Press.

Bronfenbrenner, U. (1986). Ecology of the family as a context to human development: Research perspectives. *Development Psychology, 22,* 723–742.

Capaldi, D., DeGarmo, D., Paterson, G. R., & Forgatch, M. (2002). Contextual risk across the early life span and association with antisocial behavior. In J. B. Reid, G. R. Patterson, & J. Snyder (Eds.). *Antisocial behavior in children and adolescents* (pp. 123–145). Washington, DC: American Psychological Association.

Catalano, R. F., Berglund, M. L., Ryan, J. A. M., Lonczak, H. S., & Hawkins, J. D. (2002). Positive youth development in the United States: Research findings on evaluations of positive youth development programs. *Prevention and Treatment, 5.* Retrieved September 26, 2002, from http://journals.apa.org/prevention.

Centers for Disease Control and Prevention. (2002a). *Youth risk behavior surveillance survey: Percentage of youth who carried a gun, knife, or other weapon on school property.* Retrieved August 14, 2002, from http://apps.nccd.cdc.gov/YRBSS /TrendV.asp?Site=XX&Cat=1&Qnum=Q15.

Centers for Disease Control and Prevention. (2002b). *Youth risk behavior surveillance survey: Percentage of youth who feel unsafe at school.* Retrieved August 14, 2002, from http://apps.nccd.cdc.gov/YRBSS/TrendV.asp?Site=XX&Cat=1&Qnum=Q16.

Centers for Disease Control and Prevention. (2002c). *Youth risk behavior surveillance survey: Percentage of students who had been threatened or injured with a weapon on school property one or more times during the past 12 months.* Retrieved August 14, 2002, from http://apps.nccd.cdc.gov/YRBSS/TrendV.asp ?Site=XX&Cat=1&Qnum=Q17.

Centers for Disease Control and Prevention. (2002d). *Youth risk behavior surveillance survey: Alcohol and drug use.* Retrieved August 14, 2002, from http://apps .nccd.cdc.gov/YRBSS/ListV.asp?site1=XX&Cat=3.

Centers for Disease Control and Prevention. (2002e). *Youth risk behavior surveillance survey: Percentage of students who carried a gun on one or more of the past 30 days.* Retrieved August 14, 2002, from http://apps.nccd.cdc.gov/YRBSS /TrendV.asp?Site=XX&Cat=1&Qnum=Q14.

Centers for Disease Control and Prevention. (2002f). *Youth risk behavior surveillance survey: Percentage of students who were in a physical fight one or more times during the past 12 months.* Retrieved August 14, 2002, from http://apps.nccd.cdc .gov/YRBSS/TrendV.asp?Site=XX&Cat=1&Qnum=Q18.

Centers for Disease Control and Prevention. (2002g). *Youth risk behavior surveillance survey: Percentage of students who were in a physical fight on school property one or more times during the past 12 months.* Retrieved August 14, 2002, from http://apps.nccd.cdc.gov/YRBSS/TrendV.asp?Site=XX&Cat=1&Qnum=Q20.

Center for Substance Abuse Prevention. (2002). *SAMHSA Model Programs: Effective substance abuse and mental health programs for every community.* Retrieved August 30, 2002, from http://modelprograms.samhsa.gov/model_prog.cfm.

Chamberlain, P., Fisher, P. A., & Moore, K. (2002). Multidimensional treatment foster care: Applications of the OSLC intervention model to high-risk youth and their families. In J. B. Reid, G. R. Patterson, & J. Snyder (Eds.), *Antisocial behavior in children and adolescents* (pp. 203–218). Washington, DC: American Psychological Association.

Clayton, R. R., Cattarello, A. M., & Johnstone, B. M. (1996). The effectiveness of Drug Abuse Resistance Education (DARE), 5-year follow-up results. *Preventive Medicine, 25,* 307–318.

Coll, C. G., & Magnuson, K. (2000). Cultural differences as sources of developmental vulnerabilities and resources. In J. P. Shonkoff & S. J. Meisels (Eds.), *Handbook of early childhood intervention* (2nd ed., pp. 94–114). New York: Cambridge University Press.

Conduct Problems Prevention Research Group. (1999a). Initial impact of the Fast Track prevention trial for conduct problems: I. The high-risk sample. *Journal of Consulting and Clinical Psychology, 67*(5), 631–647.

Conduct Problems Prevention Research Group. (1999b). Initial impact of the Fast Track prevention trial for conduct problems: II. Classroom effects. *Journal of Consulting and Clinical Psychology, 67*(5), 648–657.

Conduct Problems Prevention Research Group. (2002). Evaluation of the first 3 years of the Fast Track prevention trial with children at high risk for adolescent conduct problems. *Journal of Abnormal Child Psychology, 30*(1), 19–35.

Council on Social Work Education. (2001). *Educational policy and accreditation standards.* Washington, DC: Author.

Crick, N. R., & Bigbee, M. A. (1998). Relational and overt forms of peer victimization: A multiinformant approach. *Journal of Consulting and Clinical Psychology, 66*(2), 337–347.

Crick, N. R., Grotpeter, J. K., & Bigbee, M. A. (2002). Relationally and physically aggressive children's intent attributions and feelings of distress for relational and instrumental peer provocation. *Child Development, 73*(4), 1134–1142.

Deater-Deckard, K., Dodge, K. A., Bates, J. E., & Pettit, G. E. (1998). Multiple risk factors in the development of externalizing behavior problems: Group and individual differences. *Development and Psychopathology, 10*(3), 469–493.

Dishion, T. J., Kavanagh, K., Schneiger, A., Nelson, S., & Kaufman, N. K. (2002). Preventing early adolescent substance use: A family centered strategy for the public middle school. *Prevention Science, 3*(3), 191–201.

Dolan, L. J., Kellam, S. G., Brown, C. H., Werthamer-Larsson, L., Rebok, G. W., Mayer, L. S., et al. (1993). The short-term impact of two classroom-based preventive interventions on aggressive and shy behaviors and poor achievement. *Journal of Applied Developmental Psychology, 14,* 317–345.

Elliott, D. S. (2002). *Blueprints for violence prevention.* Boulder: University of Colorado, Institute of Behavioral Science, Center for the Study and Prevention of Violence. Retrieved September 30, 2002, from http://www.colorado.edu/cspv/blueprints/.

Farmer, A. D., Bierman, K. L., & the Conduct Problems Prevention Research Group. (2002). Predictors and consequences of aggressive-withdrawn problem profiles in early grade school. *Journal of Clinical Child and Adolescent Psychology, 31*(3), 299–311.

Federal Interagency Forum on Child and Family Statistics. (2002). *America's children: Key national indicators of well-being, 2002.* Washington, DC: U.S. Government Printing Office.

Fraser, M. W. (Ed.). (2004). *Risk and resilience in childhood: An ecological perspective* (2nd ed.). Washington, DC: NASW Press.

Fraser, M. W., Kirby, L. D., & Smokowski, P. R. (2003). Risk and resilience in childhood. In M. W. Fraser (Ed.), *Risk and resilience in childhood: An ecological perspective* (2nd ed.). Washington, DC: NASW Press.

Fraser, M. W., Nash, J. K., Galinsky, M. J., & Darwin, K. E. (2001). *Making choices: Social problem-solving skills for children.* Washington, DC: NASW Press.

Garmezy, N. (1971). Vulnerability research and the issue of primary prevention. *American Journal of Orthopsychiatry, 41,* 101–116.

Gottfredson, G. D., Jones, E. M., & Gore, T. W. (2002). Implementation and evaluation of a cognitive-behavioral intervention to prevent problem behavior in a disorganized school. *Prevention Science, 3*(1), 43–56.

Greenberg, M. T., Domitrovich, C., & Bumbarger, B. (2001, March 30). The prevention of mental disorders in school-aged children: Current state of the field. *Prevention and Treatment, 4,* 1–62 [Online journal]. Retrieved September 26, 2002, from http://journals.apa.org/prevention/volume4/pre0040001a.html.

Greenberg, M. T., Kusche, C. A., Cook, E. T., & Quamma, J. P. (1995). Promoting emotional competence in school-aged children: The effects of the PATHS curriculum. *Development and Psychopathology, 7*(1), 117–136.

Grossman, D. C., Neckerman, H. J., Koepsell, T. D., Liu, P. Y., Asher, K. N., Beland, K., et al. (1997). Effectiveness of a violence prevention curriculum among children in elementary school. A randomized controlled trial. *Journal of the American Medical Association, 277,* 1605–1611.

Hawkins, J. D., Catalano, R. F., Kosterman, R., Abbott, R., & Hill, K. G. (1999). Preventing adolescent health-risk behaviors by strengthening protection during childhood. *Archives of Pediatric and Adolescent Medicine, 153,* 226–234.

Hawkins, J. D., Catalano, R. F., Morrison, D. M., O'Donnell, J., Abbott, R. D., & Day, L. E. (1992). The Seattle Social Development Project: Effects of the first four years on protective factors and problem behaviors. In J. McCord & R. E. Tremblay (Eds.), *Preventing antisocial behavior in children: Intervention from birth through adolescence* (pp. 139–161). New York: Guilford Press.

Henggeler, S. W., Schoenwald, S. K., Borduin, C. M., Rowland, M. D., & Cunningham, P. B. (1998). *Multisystemic treatment of antisocial behavior in children and adolescents.* New York: Guilford Press.

Herrenkohl, T. I., Hawkins, J. D., Chung, I., Hill, K. G., & Battin-Pearson, S. (2001). School and community risk factors and interventions. In R. Loeber & D. P. Farrington (Eds.), *Child delinquents: Development, intervention, and service needs* (pp. 211–246). Thousand Oaks, CA: Sage.

Holmes, S. E., Slaughter, J. R., & Kashani, J. (2001). Risk factors in childhood that lead to the development of conduct disorder and antisocial personality disorder. *Child Psychiatry and Human Development, 31*(3), 183–193.

Howell, J. C., Krisberg, B., Hawkins, J. D., & Wilson, J. J. (Eds.). (1995). *A sourcebook: Serious, violent, and chronic juvenile offenders.* Thousand Oaks, CA: Sage.

Ialongo, N. S., Werthamer, L., Kellam, S. G., Brown, C. H., Want, S., & Lin, Y. (1999). Proximal impact of two first-grade preventive interventions on the early risk behaviors for later substance abuse, depression, and antisocial behavior. *American Journal of Community Psychology, 27*(3), 599–641.

Johnston, L. D., O'Malley, P. M., & Bachman, J. G. (2002). *Monitoring the future: Overview of key findings, 2001* [NIH Publication No. 02–5105]. Bethesda, MD: National Institute on Drug Abuse.

Kaplow, J. B., Curran, P. J., Dodge, K. A., & the Conduct Problems Prevention Research Group. (2002). Child, parent, and peer predictors of early onset substance use: A multisite longitudinal study. *Journal of Abnormal Child Psychology, 30*(3), 199–216.

Kazdin, A. E., Siegel, T. C., & Bass, D. (1992). Cognitive problem-solving skills training and parent management training in the treatment of antisocial behavior in children. *Journal of Consulting and Clinical Psychology, 60*(5), 733–747.

Kellam, S. G., & Anthony, J. C. (1998). Targeting early antecedents to prevent tobacco smoking: Findings from an epidemiologically based randomized field trial. *American Journal of Public Health, 88*(10), 1490–1495.

Kellam, S. G., Ling, X., Merisca, R., Brown, C. H., & Ialongo, N. (1998). The effect of the level of aggression in the first grade classroom on the course and malleability of aggressive behavior into middle school. *Development and Psychopathology, 10,* 165–185.

Kellam, S. G., Rebok, G. W., Ialongo, N., & Mayer, L. S. (1994). The course and malleability of aggressive behavior from early first grade into middle school: Results of a developmental epidemiologically based preventive trial. *Journal of Child Psychology and Psychiatry and Allied Disciplines, 35*(2), 259–281.

Kellam, S. G., Rebok, G. W., Mayer, L. S., Ialongo, N., & Kalodner, C. R. (1994). Depressive symptoms over first grade and their response to a developmental epidemiological based preventive trial aimed at improving achievement. *Development and Psychopathology, 6,* 463–481.

Knoff, H. M., & Batsche, G. M. (1995). Project ACHIEVE: Analyzing a school reform process for at-risk and underachieving students. *School Psychology Review, 24*(4), 579–603.

Lattimore, C. B., Mihalic, S. F., Grotpeter, J. K., & Taggart, R. (1998). The Quantum Opportunities program. In D. S. Elliott (Series Ed.), *Blueprints for violence prevention* (Vol. 4). Golden, CO: Venture.

Lochman, J. E., Coie, J. D., Underwood, M. K., & Terry, R. (1993). Effectiveness of a social relations intervention program for aggressive and nonaggressive, rejected children. *Journal of Consulting and Clinical Psychology, 61*(6), 1053–1058.

Loeber, R., & Farrington, D. P. (Eds.). (1998). *Serious and violent juvenile offenders: Risk factors and successful interventions.* Thousand Oaks, CA: Sage.

Loeber, R., & Farrington, D. P. (Eds.). (2001). *Child delinquents: Development, intervention, and service needs.* Thousand Oaks, CA: Sage.

Lonczak, H. S., Abbott, R. D., Hawkins, J. D., Kosterman, R., & Catalano, R. F. (2002). Effects of the Seattle Social Development Project on sexual behavior, pregnancy, birth, and sexually transmitted disease outcomes by age 21 years. *Archives of Pediatric and Adolescent Medicine, 156,* 438–447.

Masten, A. (2001). Ordinary magic: Resilience processes in development. *American Psychologist, 56*(3), 227–238.

McGill, D. E., Mihalic, S. F., & Grotpeter, J. K. (1997). Big Brother, Big Sister of America. In D. S. Elliott (Series Ed.), *Blueprints for violence prevention* (Vol. 2). Golden, CO: Venture.

Miller-Heyl, J., MacPhee, D., & Fritz, J. J. (1998). DARE to be you: A family support, early prevention program. *Journal of Primary Prevention, 18*(3), 257–285.

Miller-Johnson, S., Coie, J. D., Maumary-Gremaud, A., Bierman, K., & the Conduct Problems Prevention Research Group. (2002). Peer rejection and aggression and early starter models of conduct disorder. *Journal of Abnormal Child Psychology, 30*(3), 217–230.

Moffitt, T. E. (1997). Adolescence-limited and life-course persistent offending: A complementary pair of developmental theories. In T. P. Thornberry (Ed.), *Developmental theories of crime and delinquency: Advances in criminological theory* (Vol. 7, pp. 11–54). New Brunswick, NJ: Transaction.

Moffitt, T. E., Caspi, A., Rutter, M., & Silva, P. A. (2001). *Sex differences in antisocial behavior.* New York: Cambridge University Press.

Nagin, D., & Farrington, D. P. (1992). The stability of criminal potential from childhood to adulthood. *Criminology, 30,* 235–260.

Najaka, S. S., Gottfredson, D. C., & Wilson, D. B. (2002). A meta-analytic inquiry into the relationship between selected risk factors and problem behavior. *Prevention Science, 2*(4), 257–271.

O'Donnell, J., Hawkins, J. D., Catalano, R. F., Abbott, R. D., & Day, L. E. (1995). Preventing school failure, drug use, and delinquency among low-income children: Long-term intervention in elementary schools. *American Journal of Orthopsychiatry, 65*(1), 87–100.

Office of Juvenile Justice and Delinquency Prevention. (2002a). *Juvenile arrests.* Retrieved August 14, 2002, from http://ojjdp.ncjrs.org/ojstatbb/html/qa251.html.

Office of Juvenile Justice and Delinquency Prevention. (2002b). *Juvenile arrests rates.* Retrieved August 14, 2002, from http://ojjdp.ncjrs.org/ojstatbb/asp/JAR_Display.asp?ID=qa2200012002.

Office of Juvenile Justice and Delinquency Prevention. (2002c). *Juvenile arrests rates by sex.* Retrieved August 14, 2002, from http://ojjdp.ncjrs.org/ojstatbb/asp/JAR_Display.asp?ID=qa2300031502.

Office of Juvenile Justice and Delinquency Prevention. (2002d). *Juvenile arrests rates by racial groups.* Retrieved August 14, 2002, from http://ojjdp.ncjrs.org/ojstatbb /asp/JAR_Display.asp?ID=qa2401031502.

Office of Juvenile Justice and Delinquency Prevention. (2002e). *Juvenile arrests rates for aggravated assault.* Retrieved August 14, 2002, from http://ojjdp.ncjrs .org/ojstatbb/asp/JAR_Display.asp?ID=qa2205012002

Office of Juvenile Justice and Delinquency Prevention. (2002f). *Programs.* Retrieved March 2, 2002, from http://ojjdp.ncjrs.org/programs/programs.html.

Olds, D. L. (2002). Prenatal and infancy home visiting by nurses: From randomized trials to community replication. *Prevention Science, 3*(3), 153–163.

Olds, D. L., Henderson, C. R., Cole, R., Eckenrode, J., Kitzman, H., Luckey, D., et al. (1998). Long-term effects of nurse home visitation on children's criminal and antisocial behavior: 15 year follow-up of a randomized controlled trial. *Journal of the American Medical Association, 280*(14), 1238–1244.

Olds, D. L., Henderson, C. R., Hitzman, H., Eckenrode, J., Cole, R., & Tatelbaum, R. (1998). The promise of home visitation: Results of two randomized trials. *Journal of Community Psychology, 26*(1), 5–21.

Olweus, D., Limber, S., & Mihalic, S. (1999). Bullying prevention program. In D. S. Elliott (Series Ed.), *Blueprints for violence prevention series* (Vol. 9). Golden, CO: Venture.

Patterson, G. R. (1982). *Coercive family process: A social learning approach.* Eugene, OR: Castalia.

Patterson, G. R., Dishion, T. J., & Yoerger, K. (2000). Adolescent growth in new forms of problem behavior: Macro- and micro-peer dynamics. *Prevention Science, 1*(1), 3–13.

Patterson, G. R., Forgatch, M. S., Yoerger, K., & Stoolmiller, M. (1998). Variables that initiate and maintain an early onset trajectory for juvenile offending. *Development and Psychopathology, 10,* 541–547.

Patterson, G. R., Reid, J. B., & Dishion, T. J. (1992). *Antisocial boys.* Eugene, OR: Castalia.

Patterson, G. R., & Yoerger, K. (2002). A developmental model for early- and late-onset delinquency. In J. B. Reid, G. R. Patterson, & J. Snyder (Eds.), *Antisocial behavior in children and adolescents: A developmental analysis and model for intervention* (pp. 147–172). Washington, DC: American Psychological Association.

Pollard, J. A., Hawkins, J. D., & Arthur, M. W. (1999). Risk and protection: Are both necessary to understand diverse behavioral outcomes in adolescence? *Social Work Research, 23*(3), 145–158.

Reid, J. B., & Eddy, J. M. (2002a). Interventions for antisocial behavior: Overview. In J. B. Reid, G. R. Patterson, & J. Snyder (Eds.), *Antisocial behavior in children and adolescents: A developmental analysis and model for intervention* (pp. 195–201). Washington, DC: American Psychological Association.

Reid, J. B., & Eddy, J. M. (2002b). Preventive efforts during the elementary schools years. In J. B. Reid, G. R. Patterson, & J. Snyder (Eds.), *Antisocial behavior in children and adolescents: A developmental analysis and model for intervention* (pp. 219–233). Washington, DC: American Psychological Association.

Reid, J. B., Eddy, J. M., Fetrow, R. A., & Stoolmiller, M. (1999). Description and immediate impacts of a preventive intervention for conduct problems. *American Journal of Community Psychology, 27*(4), 483–517.

Reid, J. B., Patterson, G. R., & Snyder, J. (Eds.). (2002). *Antisocial behavior in children and adolescents: A developmental analysis and model for intervention.* Washington, DC: American Psychological Association.

Rutter, M. (1987). Psychosocial resilience and protective mechanisms. *American Journal of Orthopsychiatry, 57,* 316–331.

Saleebey, D. (Ed.). (1997). *The strengths perspective in social work practice: Power in the people* (2nd ed.). White Plains, NY: Longman.

Saleebey, D. (2000). Power in the people: Strengths and hope. *Advances in Social Work, 1*(2), 127–136.

Sameroff, A. J., & Gutman, L. M. (2004). Contributions of risk research to the design of successful interventions. In P. A. Meares & M. W. Fraser (Eds.), *Intervention with children and adolescents: An interdisciplinary perspective* (pp. 9–26). Needham Heights, MA: Allyn & Bacon.

Sampson, R. J. (2001). How do communities undergird or undermine human development? What are the relevant contexts and what mechanisms are at work. In A. Booth & A. C. Crouter (Eds.), *Does it take a village?* (pp. 3–30). Mahwah, NJ: Erlbaum.

Slavin, R. E., & Cooper, R. (1999). Improving intergroup relations: Lesson learned from cooperative learning programs. *Journal of Social Issues, 55*(4), 647–663.

Smokowski, P. R., Fraser, M. W., Day, S. H., Galinsky, M. J., & Bacallao, M. L. (2002). *School-based skills training to prevent aggressive behavior and peer rejection in childhood: The effectiveness of the. Making Choices program.* Chapel Hill: University of North Carolina, School of Social Work. Manuscript submitted for publication.

Stoolmiller, M., Eddy, J. M., & Reid, J. B. (2000). Detecting and describing preventive intervention effects in a universal school-based randomized trial targeting delinquent and violent behavior. *Journal of Consulting and Clinical Psychology, 68*(2), 296–306.

Storr, C. L., Ialongo, N. S., Kellam, S. G., & Anthony, J. C. (2002). A randomized trial of two primary school intervention strategies to prevent early onset tobacco smoking. *Drug and Alcohol Dependence, 66,* 51–60.

Stouthamer-Loeber, M., Loeber, R., Wei, E., Farrington, D. P., & Wikstrom, P. (2002). Risk and promotive effects in the explanation of persistent serious delinquency in boys. *Journal of Consulting and Clinical Psychology, 70*(1), 111–123.

Taylor, T. K., & Biglan, A. (1998). Behavioral family interventions for improving child-rearing: A review of the literature for clinicians and policymakers. *Clinical Child and Family Psychology Review, 1*(1), 41–60.

Taylor, T. K., Eddy, J. M., & Biglan, A. (1999). Interpersonal skills training to reduce aggression and delinquent behavior: Limited evidence and the need for an evidence-based system of care. *Clinical Child and Family Psychology Review, 2,* 169–182.

Tremblay, R. E., Pagani-Kurtz, L., Masse, L. C., Vitaro, F., & Pihl, R. O. (1995). A bimodal preventive intervention for disruptive kindergarten boys: Its impact through mid-adolescence. *Journal of Consulting and Clinical Psychology, 63*(4), 560–568.

U.S. Department of Health and Human Services. (2001). *Youth violence: A report of the Surgeon General.* Rockville, MD: U.S. Department of Health and Human Services, Centers for Disease Control and Prevention, National Center for Injury Prevention and Control, Substance Abuse and Mental Health services Administration, Center for Mental Health Services, and National Institutes of Health, National Institute of Mental Health.

Webster-Stratton, C. (1990). Long-term follow-up of families with young conduct problem children: From preschool to grade school. *Journal of Clinical Child Psychology, 19*(2), 144–149.

Webster-Stratton, C. (1994). Advancing videotape parent training: A comparison study. *Journal of Consulting and Clinical Psychology, 62*(3), 583–593.

Webster-Stratton, C. (1998). Preventing conduct problems in Head Start children: Strengthening parenting competencies. *Journal of Consulting and Clinical Psychology, 66*(5), 715–730.

Webster-Stratton, C. (2000). *The Incredible Years training series.* Washington, DC: Office of Juvenile Justice and Delinquency Prevention.

Webster-Stratton, C., & Hammond, M. (1997). Treating children with early onset conduct problems: A comparison of child and parent training interventions. *Journal of Consulting and Clinical Psychology, 65*(1), 93–109.

Webster-Stratton, C., Reid, M. J., & Hammond, M. (2001). Preventing conduct problems, promoting social competence: A parent and teacher partnership in Head Start. *Journal of Clinical Child Psychology, 30*(3), 283–302.

Webster-Stratton, C., & Taylor, T. (2001). Nipping early risk factors in the bud: Preventing substance abuse, delinquency, and violence in adolescence through interventions targeted at young children (0–8 years). *Prevention Science, 2*(3), 165–192.

Werner, C., & Kerig, P. (2000). *Developmental psychopathology: From infancy through adolescence* (1th ed.). Boston: McGraw-Hill Companies

PART III

Preventive Interventions for Children's and Adolescents' Health Problems

Chapter 7 ————————————————————

BIRTH DEFECTS

DEBRA KEELEAN, JOHN H. PIERPONT, JOHN WILEY,
AND KAYE McGINTY

Any discussion about preventing human problems should be undertaken with humility and caution. When considering human behavior and interactions, an endless stream of factors may seem to contribute to a problem, and we must acknowledge the possibility that there are confounding factors, as yet unknown, that might account for an improvement in our outcome(s) of interest. Nevertheless, efforts to prevent human problems are critical; and although in recent years advances in genetics and medical technology have become increasingly important in birth defect prevention, prevention efforts that target human behaviors and environmental conditions continue to play a vital role. In this chapter, we apply Gordon's Operational Classification of Disease Prevention (Gordon, 1907) in a discussion of birth defects that have behavioral and, therefore, preventable, antecedents. We begin with an introduction to smoking and alcohol-related birth defects, followed by the application of Gordon's universal, selective, and indicated measures to the prevention of these birth defects. We conclude with remarks about the usefulness of Gordon's classification schema for effectively addressing the problem of birth defects.

BIRTH DEFECTS AND KNOWN
BEHAVIORAL ANTECEDENTS

Birth defects account for more than 20% of all infant deaths and not only constitute the leading cause of infant mortality in the United States, but also contribute to morbidity and long-term disability (Yoon et al., 2002). A *teratogen* is an agent that causes birth defects, that is, an agent that interferes with the normal development of a fetus. Although some biological teratogens, for example, the rubella virus and thalidomide, are known, the etiologies of more than 70% of birth defects are still unknown (Yoon et al., 2002). Epidemiologists find it difficult to study birth defects because

1. So many teratogens are unknown and
2. A fetus is exposed to many genetic and environmental factors that might affect its development.

This has led to the belief that a combination of genetic and environmental teratogens and their interaction may be important in the etiology of many birth defects (Yoon et al., 2002).

Two pervasive environmental factors known to contribute to birth defects are cigarette smoking and alcohol consumption. Women who smoke have an increased risk for infertility, ovulatory dysfunction, ectopic pregnancy, fetal loss, adverse pregnancy outcomes, and early menopause (American College of Obstetrics & Gynecology [ACOG], 1997; United States Department of Health and Human Services [USDHHS], 2002b). Health risks associated with cigarette smoking during pregnancy include a higher rate of placental complications such as placenta previa and placental abruption, giving birth to low birth-weight babies, premature rupture of membranes, preterm delivery, miscarriage, stillbirth, and SIDS (DiFranza & Lew, 1995; March of Dimes, 2000). It is estimated that a 10% reduction in infant deaths would occur if all pregnant women in the United States stopped smoking (March of Dimes, 2000).

Each year, more than 50,000 babies are born with some degree of alcohol-related birth defects, and as many as 12,000 may be born with fetal alcohol syndrome (FAS). Fetal alcohol syndrome is characterized by mental retardation, growth retardation, congenital heart defects, and characteristic facial features. Children born with FAS may also exhibit behavioral difficulties including short attention span, aggressiveness, destructiveness, and nervousness. Children without a diagnosis of FAS may still suffer from the effects of exposure to alcohol in utero, but not have all the clinical indicators of FAS. In the past, fetal alcohol effect (FAE) was the diagnosis usually given to these children. However, there is as yet no consensus on either the clinical definition or the term to be used for children who have some but not all of the clinical signs of FAS. As a result, two other terms, *alcohol-related neurodevelopmental disorder* (ARND) and *alcohol-related birth defects* (ARBD), are commonly used. The first, ARND, describes functional impairments and "cognitive abnormalities including learning difficulties, poor school performance, poor impulse control, and problems with mathematical skills, memory, attention, and/or judgment," whereas ARBD is used to describe "malformations of the skeletal system and major organ systems, such as defects of the heart, kidneys, bones, and/or auditory system" (Centers for Disease Control and Prevention [CDC], 2002b, pp. 8, 17). The prevalence of ARND and ARBD is believed to be approximately three times greater than for FAS (CDC, 2002b).

Universal Measures

Although Gordon's notions on prevention were originally applied to mental illness, his *operational classification* may be beneficial in conceptualizing the prevention of any number of conditions or problems in which human behavior plays a causative role. Here, we apply his approach in discussing universal, selective, and indicated measures in the prevention of birth defects associated with cigarette smoking and alcohol consumption. Universal measures to prevent smoking and alcohol-related birth defects include public education and regulatory policies that target the general population. Selective measures consist of programs that target women of childbearing age who may smoke or consume alcohol during pregnancy. Indicated measures are programs that serve women who have already given birth to a child with smoking- or alcohol-related birth defects in an attempt to prevent another such birth.

It is estimated that 66.5 million Americans 12 years or older use one or more tobacco products (Substance Abuse and Mental Health Services Administration [SAMHSA], 2002). In 1995, approximately 2 million individuals in developed countries died prematurely because of smoking, and tobacco use was responsible for nearly one in every five deaths in the United States. Since 1964, when the Surgeon General identified smoking as a significant health hazard, numerous government regulations have been implemented in an effort to reduce the health risks associated with cigarette smoking. These regulations include both indirect and direct approaches to providing information and altering behavior. Indirect approaches consist of public information campaigns, for example, requiring warning labels on cigarette packages that delineate the health risks associated with smoking and banning cigarette ads on television and radio. Direct approaches include policy changes at the national, state, and local levels. These policy changes include forbidding the sale of cigarettes to minors, creating and requiring nonsmoking public facilities, and banning smoking on domestic airline flights (Viscusi, 1992). More recently, the government's nationwide antismoking campaign has emphasized that health education combined with social, economic, and regulatory approaches is essential to counterbalance the tobacco industry's advertising and promotion and to foster nonsmoking environments (American Cancer Society, 2002).

Although studies have not conclusively demonstrated significant independent effects attributable to the antismoking campaign, statistics do indicate a reduction in the number of smokers. During the period from 1993 to 2000, substantial reductions in smoking prevalence were noted for all age groups except the 18 to 24 age group (CDC, 2002a). However, the 2002 annual survey conducted by the National Institute on Drug Abuse (NIDA, 2002) found a reduction in the number of teenagers who recalled smoking cigarettes in the past month. Of eighth graders polled in 2001, 12.2% reported using cigarettes in the past month versus 14.6% in 2000. Trends were similar for 10th graders (21.3% in 2001 versus 23.9% in 2000) and high school seniors (29.5% in 2001 versus 31.4% in 2000). The Substance Abuse and Mental Health Services Administration 2002 report (SAMHSA, 2002) found that the number of new cigarette users per year has fluctuated in the past decade, but has decreased in the past three years. It further indicates that the number of daily smokers rose to approximately 1.4 million per year in the late 1980s, peaked at 1.7 million per year in 1997, and later decreased to 1.4 million per year in 2000. In addition, the annual number of new daily smokers ages 12 to 17 decreased from 1.1 million per year in 1997 to 747,000 per year in 2000.

In addition to nationwide figures, more information from state programs is becoming available. In California and Massachusetts, statewide campaigns have resulted in increased cigarette excise taxes and the designation of a portion of the revenues for comprehensive tobacco control programs. Records from these states indicate that the excise tax on cigarettes is a cost-effective short-term strategy for reducing tobacco consumption among adults and preventing initiation of smoking in youths. In addition, the ability to sustain lower consumption improves when tax increases are combined with an antismoking campaign. Data from Florida show that past-month smoking decreased significantly among public middle and high school students following the implementation of a comprehensive program to prevent and reduce tobacco use among youths in that state (United States Department of Health and Human Services [USDHHS], 2002b).

The federal government continues to campaign for the implementation of additional smoking control measures. *Healthy People 2010* presents the USDHHS prevention agenda for the nation and delineates objectives for the nation's health, which identify and address significant preventable health threats (USDHHS, 2002a). Background and statistical information, goals and objectives, and future steps are set out in the two-volume online publication *Healthy People 2010* (USDHHS, 2002a). As to smoking, goals and objectives are varied but continue to focus on:

1. Public education through strategic use of the media and
2. Policy and regulatory strategies, especially those targeting prevention of smoking among minors.

It is hoped that universal prevention measures such as these will reduce the number of smokers in the population and result in a reduction of smoking-related birth defects.

Selective Measures

Selective measures to prevent smoking-related birth defects are appropriate for women who smoke and who are or may become pregnant. Women seem to be more knowledgeable about the detrimental effects of smoking during pregnancy than they are about certain other medical issues. Roth and Taylor (2001) found that whereas only 24% of women thought cigarette smoking is associated with cervical cancer and 22% of women thought it is associated with infertility, 91% were aware of the possible pregnancy complications associated with cigarette smoking. As a group, pregnant women are thought to be highly motivated to protect their health and the health of their unborn children (SAMHSA, 2001b). According to the Substance Abuse and Mental Health Services Administration, in 1999, 17% of pregnant women reported smoking cigarettes in the month before the survey compared to 31% of nonpregnant women, and 20% of pregnant smokers quit by the time of their first prenatal visit (SAMHSA, 2001b).

For women who have difficulty quitting smoking without assistance, some programs have been shown to be effective in helping them quit. In an analysis of 10 randomized trials (Dolan-Mullen, Ramirez, & Groff, 1994), an organized prenatal smoking intervention showed a 50% increase in smoking cessation between the sixth and ninth months of pregnancy. Interventions that influenced smoking cessation included personal visits to the patient, phone contact, a 10-minute counseling session, and personal letters. Self-help booklets alone did not result in significant change. However, in conjunction with other interventions, a self-help booklet specifically written for pregnant women was a useful tool. As might be expected, those programs demonstrating the greatest effect used more intensive intervention and multiple approaches. However, even a short counseling session was better than no intervention (Dolan-Mullen et al., 1994).

A program adapted from the U.S. Public Health Service has been shown to increase smoking cessation by 30% to 70% among women who smoke less than 20 cigarettes per day (ACOG, 2001; Melvin, Dolan-Mullen, Windsor, Whiteside, & Goldenberg, 2000). This program includes a few simple steps that may be integrated into a woman's prenatal care. The initial step is an assessment of the patient's smoking status, that is, whether she is or has ever been a smoker and, if so, has she stopped smoking since learning that she is pregnant. If she has never smoked or has been a smoker but has now quit, she is congratulated and encouraged to abstain from smoking during her pregnancy and after. If she is a smoker and has continued to smoke after becoming pregnant, the following steps are included in her prenatal care:

1. The patient is given straightforward, clear information about the impact of smoking on herself and the fetus, and she is strongly encouraged to quit smoking.
2. The patient's willingness to quit smoking within the next 30 days is assessed.
3. Those who are interested in quitting are assisted in doing so; that is, they receive pregnancy-specific smoking cessation self-help material, they are taught problem-solving techniques and are encouraged to use them, and they are referred to social supports in their environment.
4. Follow-up appointments, which include regular prenatal visits, are used to track the patient's progress and to offer further encouragement to quit smoking.

Many women who are pregnant and smoke need selective interventions to quit smoking. Short, brief interventions have been shown to increase a woman's smoking cessation rate. Such interventions might easily be incorporated into regularly scheduled prenatal visits, but could also be provided in coordination with any other program that provides regular contact with the patient.

Indicated Interventions

Women who have had a baby with smoking-related complications are the obvious target group for Gordon's indicated measures. However, successful intervention with these women has been problematic because they are more likely to be those who find it most difficult to quit. Because 91% of women are aware that cigarette smoking is associated with pregnancy complications (Roth & Taylor, 2001), universal measures may have already failed with many, if not most, women who deliver a child with smoking-related birth defects. In addition, premature delivery, low birth weight, SIDS, and other problems may be due to myriad factors or their interactions. Therefore, although medical research has demonstrated the increased risk for complications during pregnancy and for birth defects secondary to maternal cigarette smoking, it has not been possible to demonstrate conclusively that smoking is the reason for a neonate's complications. As a result, indicated measures, that is, smoking cessation interventions for women who have delivered a child with smoking-related birth defects, are still awaiting development and dissemination.

Universal Measures

In 2000, 47% of Americans ages 12 or older reported drinking alcohol in the previous month. In addition, 21% reported binge drinking and 6% reported heavy drinking in the previous month (SAMHSA, 2001a). Among current drinkers, 46% had been intoxicated at least once in the past year. Nearly 10% of current drinkers meet diagnostic criteria for alcohol dependence and 7% meet criteria for alcohol abuse (USDHHS, 2002a). This percentage represents nearly 14 million Americans, or 1 in every 13 adults, who abuse alcohol or who are alcoholics (National Institute on Alcohol Abuse & Alcoholism, 2001). The National Highway Transportation Safety Administration (2002) reports that 438,000 crashes in the United States involved a driver or pedestrian with a positive blood alcohol content. Furthermore, long-term heavy drinking has long been associated with an increased risk for hypertension, arrhythmias, cardiomyopathy, stroke, cirrhosis, and other liver diseases. In addition, heavy drinking is associated with cancer, particularly of the esophagus, mouth, throat, larynx, colon, rectum, and breast. Alcohol use has also been linked to a substantial portion of injuries and deaths from falls, fires, and drownings (USDHHS, 2002a).

Current strategies for reducing alcohol abuse, alcoholism, and alcohol-related problems include government regulatory and enforcement efforts as well as public education campaigns. Governmental regulatory efforts include controls such as minimum age restrictions, limits on the number and nature of sales outlets, excise taxes, licensing of liquor manufacturers, regulation of public drinking places, regulation of available alcohol, liability rules for bartenders, setting a legal blood alcohol content limit, enforcement visibility, stricter rules for penalties, and creation of the National Institute on Alcohol Abuse and Alcoholism (Moore & Gerstein, 1981).

Historically, the minimum age for drinking has fluctuated. In many states, the minimum age for alcohol consumption was lowered in the 1970s. However, research has shown that reductions in the legal drinking age correspond to increases in the rate of auto crashes and fatalities involving young drivers (Moore & Gerstein, 1981). As a result, many states have now raised the minimum age for alcohol consumption to 21 years. Raising taxes on alcoholic beverages is another regulatory policy shown to reduce consumption in light and moderate drinkers (Cook, 1981). Cook studied changes in states' alcohol taxes between 1960 and 1975 and found that as liquor taxes increase, per capita consumption, auto fatalities, and deaths due to cirrhosis decrease.

Public education is the primary means of distributing information and advice about alcohol use to pregnant women. Public education campaigns include television advertisements, public service announcements, pamphlets, and posters to encourage responsible drinking and to educate the public about the risks of alcohol abuse and the dangers of drinking during pregnancy (Stratton, Howe, & Battaglia, 1996). In 1981, the Surgeon General of the United States first advised all women to abstain from drinking alcohol during pregnancy (Hankin & Sokol, 1995). Additional public education measures have included placing warning labels on all alcoholic beverages and placing point of purchase signs in liquor stores and bars (Weiner, Morse, & Garrido, 1989).

In 1989, Public Law 100-690, requiring warning labels on all alcoholic beverage containers sold or distributed in the United States, was passed and signed. A study involving 3,572 women living in the Detroit inner city (Hankin, 1994) found that among women who drink in moderation, alcohol consumption decreased slightly following the implementation of Public Law 100-690, whereas women who reported being heavier drinkers did not change their rate of consumption. Hankin, McCaul, and Heussner (2000) reported on a study of pregnant African American and American Indian women living in California. Almost 95% believed beverage warning labels on the dangers of prenatal drinking were accurate. However, 28% continued to drink during their pregnancy.

The CDC is currently investigating strategies to make media campaigns more effective in delivering public service messages about alcohol use and pregnancy. Studies to evaluate the success of these public education campaigns are underway, including more recent efforts to assess their effectiveness among various ethnic groups (CDC, 2002b).

Selective Measures

Whereas universal measures target the general population, including pregnant women, selective measures are specifically intended to reduce alcohol use by women who are pregnant or who may become pregnant and/or to increase effective contraceptive use by women who drink during their childbearing years. Pregnant women who drink are at higher risk of miscarriage, stillbirth, neonatal death, having a low birth-weight baby, or having a baby with FAS or FAE (March of Dimes, 1998). In a 2001 survey conducted by the Substance Abuse and Mental Health Services Administration (SAMHSA, 2002), approximately 316,000 pregnant women (13%) reported drinking alcohol in the past month; 80,000 pregnant women (3%) reported binge alcohol use, defined as drinking five or more drinks of alcohol on the same occasion at least once in the past 30 days; and an estimated 6,000 pregnant women (0.23%) reported heavy drinking, defined as drinking five or more drinks of alcohol on the same occasion on each of five or more days in the past 30 days.

No level of alcohol consumption has been proven to be safe during pregnancy. In general, universal measures have proven effective in targeting women who are light to moderate drinkers, but do not effect change in the drinking habits of women who are heavy drinkers (Stratton et al., 1996). Therefore, additional efforts have been made to intervene with women of childbearing age who are at-risk drinkers. However, the range and availability of interventions beyond the level of universal measures are not consonant with the seriousness of the health problems caused by fetal exposure to alcohol, in part, because of the absence of a single clinical case definition of FAS and FAE. Currently, the National Task Force on Fetal Alcohol Syndrome and Fetal Alcohol Effect, established in 1998 by the Public Health Service Act (Pub. L. 105-392), is developing a clinical case definition and a uniform surveillance case definition to facilitate epidemiological and research studies (CDC, 2002b). Three programs providing selective measures to prevent alcohol-related birth defects are discussed next.

Arkansas Center for Addictions Research, Education, and Services

The Arkansas Center for Addictions Research, Education, and Services (AR-CARES) provides residential and outpatient services for women who are pregnant or who have had children. Services include substance abuse treatment, childcare, job training, transportation, and assistance with housing. A study comparing participants with nonparticipants found that 4% of women who participated in the program were using alcohol at the time of delivery, compared to 33.3% of women who did not participate. Similar results were achieved for other drug use. In addition, women who participated in the AR-CARES program had significantly less preterm labor and maternal infection, and their babies tended to be of greater gestational age. Finally, participants who remained in the program for a longer time period tended to have babies with a greater birth weight (Whiteside-Mansell, Crone, & Conners, 1999).

Project CHOICES

Over the past decade, the Centers for Disease Control has funded numerous programs aimed at identifying strategies to reduce and eliminate alcohol-related birth defects. Most prominent among these are Project CHOICES (Changing High Risk Alcohol Use and Increasing Contraception Effectiveness Study) and Project BALANCE (Birth Control and Alcohol Awareness: Negotiating Choices Effectively). Project CHOICES began in 1997 when the CDC funded grants and developed cooperative agreements with three universities: Nova Southeastern University in Ft. Lauderdale, Florida; the University of Texas Health Sciences Center in Houston, Texas; and the Medical College of Virginia at Virginia

Commonwealth University in Richmond, Virginia. This program was developed to prevent alcohol-exposed pregnancies among high-risk women in special community settings as diverse as primary care centers in the North Brossard Hospital District in Ft. Lauderdale to the Harris County Jail in Houston to the Gynecology Outpatient Unit of the Medical College of Virginia in Richmond. Project CHOICES identifies women at high risk for an alcohol-exposed pregnancy before conception and provides them with a brief educational intervention that focuses on both alcohol risk reduction and pregnancy postponement until alcohol issues are resolved (CDC 2002d). Initial results from this project are expected soon.

Project BALANCE

Project BALANCE (Birth Control and Alcohol Awareness: Negotiating Choices Effectively) is a variation of Project CHOICES and is underway at the same universities as Project CHOICES. Project BALANCE is intended to identify the prevalence of high-risk behaviors related to alcohol consumption and contraceptive use in a population of 18- to 24-year-olds and to test the efficacy of a brief intervention. In a randomized trial, the results achieved with a group of young women receiving an assessment and one face-to-face counseling session will be compared with results obtained with young women receiving an assessment only. Efforts are also underway to better characterize the at-risk population, to identify those eligible for the intervention, and to explore the effects of alcohol consumption on sexual behavior, including the use of contraception (CDC, 2002c). As with Project CHOICES, initial results from Project BALANCE are expected soon.

Indicated Measures

According to Gordon's operational classification, indicated measures target women who have already given birth to a child with alcohol-related birth defects to prevent another such birth. Unfortunately, as with selective measures, the absence of clinical and surveillance definitions, no doubt combined with the complications associated with special needs of the population, has stymied the development of indicated measures to prevent FAS and FAE. When queried about prevention programs designed for women who have delivered a child with FAS or FAE to prevent recurrence, a staff member from the CDC indicated that the CDC is not aware of any successful programs of this nature (E. Parra, personal communication, March 5, 2003). Although the epidemiologic and research efforts of the National Task Force will help, much work remains in this very difficult area of prevention.

Although there are no known FAS/FAE prevention programs meeting the criteria for Gordon's indicated measures, the Parent-Child Assistance Program (PCAP) in Seattle, Washington, is a selective measure program that also attempts to prevent recurrence among women who have already delivered a baby with FAS or FAE. According to PCAP director Therese Grant, "After we enroll these mothers, get a good history, and meet their children, we often refer a child (or children) to the FAS diagnostic clinic for evaluation and diagnosis. So, after the fact, we realize we're serving a woman who has given birth to a child with ARBD" (T. Grant, personal communication, March 11, 2003). PCAP receives far more referrals in the selective measures category, probably because so many of the children who are diagnosed with FAS do not live with their biologic mother and the mother's whereabouts are unknown (T. Grant, personal communication, March 11, 2003).

The PCAP (cf. Grant, Streissguth, & Ernst, 2002) was originally begun as the Seattle Birth to 3 Project and was designed to test the efficacy of a model of intensive, long-term paraprofessional advocacy with very high-risk mothers who abuse alcohol or drugs heavily during pregnancy and who are estranged from community service providers. Mothers are enrolled during pregnancy or within a month after delivery.

The primary goal of the PCAP is to prevent alcohol and drug exposure among the future children of these mothers. In the PCAP model, paraprofessional advocates provide the intervention. The model uses a case management approach to help mothers reduce the spectrum of risk behaviors associated with substance abuse and to increase protective factors to enhance the health and social well-being of the mothers and their children. PCAP does not provide substance abuse treatment or clinical services. Rather, paraprofessional home visitors link mothers and their families with community resources, with an emphasis on alcohol/drug treatment, family planning, housing, health care, parenting, and legal resources.

In a recently completed study of outcomes achieved by PCAP, Grant et al. (2002) found that of 146 program participants, the women who spent more time with their advocates (greater than or equal to 90 minutes per week on average) were more likely to achieve positive outcomes than those who spent less time (less than 30 minutes per week on average). These outcomes included:

- Completed inpatient substance abuse treatment (86% versus 39%)
- Abstinence from alcohol and drugs for at least one year at exit from PCAP (44% versus 36%)
- Use of a reliable form of birth control (53% versus 45%)

Thirty-eight women had a subsequent birth during the program. Babies born to women who spent more time with their advocates were less likely to be exposed to alcohol or drugs in utero (33% versus 55%). The PCAP is effective in reducing the risk factors associated with alcohol-related birth defects, that is, alcohol consumption and failure to use contraceptives by women of childbearing age, subsequently reducing the likelihood that babies will be exposed to alcohol in utero.

Summary

By far the greatest efforts to reduce the incidence of birth defects related to smoking tobacco and drinking alcohol consist of universal measures. Some public education campaigns have been in place for nearly a quarter of a century, and many governmental regulatory measures, including product warning labels and a ban on selling alcohol and tobacco products to minors, have been part of public policy for a decade or longer. Selective measures aimed at reducing risk factors among women in their childbearing years have been developed more recently. In the case of smoking, selective measures pertain largely to smoking cessation during pregnancy. To prevent birth defects related to alcohol, selective measures consist of efforts to help women abstain from drinking during pregnancy and to use effective forms of contraception. Indicated measures, interventions specifically for women who have already had a child with smoking- or drinking-related birth defects, have yet to be successfully developed and implemented, in part because the etiology of birth defects is so complex. Birth defects associated with smoking may be caused by other factors as well. The singular effect of alcohol on fetal development is clearer. However, identifying women who have given birth to a child with FAS or FAE can be difficult, and successful referral and service delivery is difficult. Programs that deliver selective measures may identify women who have previously given birth to a child with FAS or FAE and can effectively intervene to prevent a recurrence.

RECOMMENDATIONS

The universal measures now in effect should be continued. Public education programs, in particular those that reach young women, should be expanded. Warning labels on tobacco products and alcoholic beverages keep the dangers associated with them, including the danger of birth defects, in the public eye and enhance public awareness. Enacting policies that hold retailers accountable for selling alcohol or tobacco products to minors is a step in the right direction, and these policies should be vigorously enforced.

Treating extant problems carries its own sense of urgency and has always attracted more funding than has prevention. Nevertheless, preventing human problems is often more cost-effective and is certainly more humane. No doubt, many smoking cessation and substance abuse treatment programs reach and help women of childbearing age. However, many more programs that intentionally provide selective measures to prevent smoking- and drinking-related birth defects are needed. The selective measures described in this chapter are not unique, but similar programs are too few. As public spending on citizens' welfare decreases, more emphasis should be given to prevention, including selective measures that combine treatment with prevention. The Parent-Child Assistance Program in Seattle is a good example. The PCAP model addresses multiple issues, including substance abuse treatment, and reduces the likelihood of birth defects due to fetal exposure to alcohol. This program also identifies women who have already given birth to children with FAS or FAE and serves as a de facto indicated measure for these clients. Where resources permit, programs providing selective measures should make intensive efforts to offer indicated measures as well.

Although many interventions to prevent birth defects occur in medical settings using medical personnel, this is not always necessary. The PCAP is instructional in this regard; it uses well-trained paraprofessionals as home visitors and advocates. By using nonmedical paraprofessionals to provide services, prevention efforts may be implemented in areas where medical and other professionals are in short supply. Using paraprofessionals may also reduce costs, and by combining treatment with prevention, these programs may become more affordable and, therefore, more feasible.

Finally, continued research and training is critical to success in preventing birth defects. According to the Centers for Disease Control, birth defects associated with tobacco and alcohol are among the most preventable of all birth defects (CDC, 2002b). The National Task Force on fetal alcohol syndrome and fetal alcohol effects has recommended development of a clinical case definition and a uniform surveillance definition for FAS and for alcohol related neural defects—a crucial and necessary step. The Task Force has also recommended cataloging existing research on FAS and FAE as well as existing services available to persons who have these conditions. This will help clarify current research and service agendas. In response to a Congressional mandate, the CDC is coordinating efforts:

1. To survey practitioners in medicine and allied health fields on current training, knowledge, and attitudes toward FAS and other alcohol-related conditions
2. To develop guidelines for curricula to be used in the training of medical and allied health professionals
3. To disseminate these guidelines

The results from these efforts will be used to develop, implement, and evaluate future education and training of medical and allied health practitioners (CDC, 2002b). Similar activities are needed concerning smoking-related birth defects. Birth defects associated with smoking and drinking can be prevented. An expanded knowledge base, improved public education and professional training, and greater availability of effective interventions will be critical to success.

REFERENCES

American College of Obstetrics and Gynecology. (1997). Smoking and women's health. *International Journal of Gynecology and Obstetrics, 60,* 71–82.

American College of Obstetrics and Gynecology. (2001). Smoking cessation during pregnancy. *International Journal of Gynecology and Obstetrics, 75,* 345–348.

American Cancer Society. (2002). *Cancer facts & figures 2002.* Retrieved November 18, 2002, from http://www.cancer.org/.

Centers for Disease Control and Prevention. (2002a). *Cigarette smoking among adults— United States, 2000: MMWR highlights.* Retrieved November 13, 2002, from http://www.cdc.gov/tobacco/research_data/adults_prev/mmwr5129_highlights.htm.

Centers for Disease Control and Prevention. (2002b). *Fetal alcohol syndrome prevention: Increasing public awareness of the risks of alcohol use during pregnancy through targeted media campaigns.* Retrieved November 20, 2002, from http://www.cdc.gov/ncbddd/fas/.

Centers for Disease Control and Prevention. (2002c). *Fetal alcohol syndrome: Project BALANCE.* Retrieved September 3, 2002, from http://www.cdc.gov/ncbddd/fas/.

Centers for Disease Control and Prevention. (2002d). *Fetal alcohol syndrome: Project CHOICES.* Retrieved September 3, 2002, from http://www.cdc.gov/ncbddd/fas/.

Cook, P. J. (1981). The effect of liquor taxes on drinking, cirrhosis, and auto accidents. In M. H. Moore & D. R. Gerstein (Eds.), *From alcohol and public policy: Beyond the shadow of prohibition* (pp. 225–285). Washington, DC: National Academy Press.

DiFranza, J. R., & Lew, R. (1995). Effect of maternal cigarette smoking on pregnancy complications and sudden infant death syndrome. *Journal of Family Practice, 40,* 85–394.

Dolan-Mullen, P., Ramirez, G., & Groff, J. Y. (1994). A meta-analysis of randomized trials of prenatal smoking cessation interventions. *American Journal of Obstetrics and Gynecology, 171,* 1328–1334.

Gordon, R. (1987). An operational classification of disease prevention. In J. Steinberg & M. Silverman (Eds.), *Preventing mental disorders: A research perspective* (pp. 20–26). Rockville, MD: Department of Health and Human Services.

Grant, T., Streissguth, A., & Ernst, C. (2002). Benefits and challenges of paraprofessional advocacy with mothers who abuse alcohol and drugs and their children. *Zero to Three: Bulletin of the National Center for Clinical Infant Programs, 23*(2), 14–20.

Hankin, J. R. (1994). FAS prevention strategies. *Alcohol Health and Research World, 18,* 62–66.

Hankin, J. R., McCaul, M. E., & Heussner, J. (2000). Pregnant, alcohol-abusing women. *Alcoholism: Clinical and Experimental Research, 24,* 1276–1286.

Hankin, J. R., & Sokol, R. J. (1995). Identification and care of problems associated with alcohol ingestion in pregnancy. *Seminars in Perinatology, 19,* 286–292.

March of Dimes. (1998). *Drinking alcohol during pregnancy* [Brochure]. Wilkes-Barre, PA: Author.

March of Dimes. (2000). *Smoking during pregnancy* [Brochure]. Wilkes-Barre, PA: Author.

Melvin, C. L., Dolan-Mullen, P., Windsor, R. A., Whiteside, H. P., Jr., & Goldenberg, R. L. (2000). Recommended cessation counseling for pregnant women who smoke: A review of the evidence. *Tobacco Control, 9*(Suppl. III), iii80–iii84.

Moore, M. H., & Gerstein, D. R. (1981). *From alcohol and public policy: Beyond the shadow of prohibition.* Washington, DC: National Academy Press.

National Highway Transportation Safety Administration. (2002). *Impaired driving in the United States.* Retrieved November 26, 2002, from http://www.nhtsa.dot .gov/people/injury/alcohol/U.S.htm.

National Institute on Alcohol Abuse and Alcoholism. (2001). *Alcoholism: Getting the facts.* Retrieved November 26, 2002, from http://www.niaaa.nih.gov/publications/ booklet-text.htm.

National Institute on Drug Abuse. (2002). *Annual survey shows teen smoking down, rise in MDMA use slowing.* Retrieved November 14, 2002, from http://www.drugabuse .gov/NIDA_Notes/NNVol16N6/Tearoff.html.

Roth, L. K., & Taylor, H. S. (2001). Risks of smoking to reproductive health: Assessment of women's knowledge. *American Journal of Obstetrics and Gynecology, 184,* 934–939.

Stratton, K., Howe, C., & Battaglia, F. (1996). *Fetal alcohol syndrome: Diagnosis, epidemiology, prevention, and treatment.* Washington, DC: National Academy Press.

Substance Abuse and Mental Health Services Administration. (2001a). *The NHSDA report: Alcohol use.* Retrieved November 26, 2002, from http://www.samhsa.gov /oas/2k2/alcNS/alcNS.htm.

Substance Abuse and Mental Health Services Administration. (2001b). *The NHSDA report: Tobacco and alcohol use among pregnant women.* Retrieved November 14, 2002, from http://www.samhsa.gov/oas/2k2/PregAlcTob/PregAlcTob.cfm.

Substance Abuse and Mental Health Services Administration. (2002). *Results from the 2001 national household survey on drug abuse: Vol. I. Summary of national findings.* Retrieved November 14, 2002, from http://www.samhsa.gov/oas/nhsda /2k1nhsda/vol1/toc.htm.

United States Department of Health and Human Services. (2002a). *Healthy people 2010.* Retrieved November 25, 2002, from http://www.healthypeople.gov/.

United States Department of Health and Human Services. (2002b). *Women and smoking: A report of the Surgeon General—2001.* Retrieved November 14, 2002, from http://www.cdc.gov/tobacco/sgr/sgr_forwomen/ataglance.htm.

Viscusi, W. K. (1992). *Smoking: Making the risky decision.* New York: Oxford University Press.

Weiner, L., Morse, B. A., & Garrido, P. (1989). FAS/FAE: Focusing prevention on women at risk. *International Journal of Addictions, 24,* 385–395.

Whiteside-Mansell, L., Crone, C. C., & Conners, N. A. (1999). The development and evaluation of an alcohol and drug prevention and treatment program for women and children: The AR-CARES program. *Journal of Substance Abuse Treatment, 16,* 265–275.

Yoon, P. W., Rasmussen, S. A., Lynberg, M. C., Moore, C. A., Anderka, M., Carmichael, S. L., et al. (2002). National birth defects prevention study. *Public Health Reports, 116*(Suppl. 1), 32–40.

Chapter 8

FAILURE TO THRIVE

DOROTA IWANIEC AND HELGA SNEDDON

During the first year after birth, human growth is quicker than at any other period during childhood, decreasing rapidly until the end of the third year, then continuing at about one-third of its postnatal rate until puberty. However, some children do not grow at the same rate as others but instead lag behind. These children have been described as *failing to thrive,* and compared to their peers, they are significantly smaller and can be expected to have poorer outcomes (Iwaniec, Herbert, & McNeish, 1985a; Sneddon & Iwaniec, 2002). They can be found in all social classes and levels of society. Without help, their physical growth, cognitive progress, and emotional development can be negatively affected, with these children at high risk for development delays, personality problems, abuse, and death. If successful intervention does not occur at an early stage, failure to thrive (FTT) may lead to the distortion of the parent-child relationship, serious attachment disorders, disturbed behavior, and developmental impairment (Iwaniec, 1995).

Unfortunately, diagnosis and intervention in this area are not straightforward. There is much debate and confusion over how growth failure should be defined and diagnosed, what the consequences are for a child and his or her family, and how practitioners can successfully intervene and treat failure to thrive. This chapter contains information on trends and incidence of different types of growth failure, risk factors for nonorganic growth-faltering in families, different techniques for intervention, practice and policy implications, and future directions.

TRENDS AND INCIDENCE

The term *failure to thrive* is applied to infants whose weight, height, head circumference, and general psychosocial development are significantly below age-related norms and whose well-being causes concern (Iwaniec & Sneddon,

2002). In the United Kingdom, current practice is to further investigate children whose weight is below the second centile. Children who drop two or more percentile curves on the weight chart over a short time period are also likely be evaluated further to determine if there is a problem. In America, common practice is to use the fifth centile as a cutoff point for weight.

Although still identified primarily by physical growth measures, it is now recognized that failure to thrive goes beyond the physical: The term describes a condition rather than a specific disease, and, consequently, it has many causes, which may be organic or psychosocial or a mixture of both. It is conceived as a variable syndrome of severe growth retardation, delayed skeletal maturation, and problematic psychomotor development, which are often associated with illnesses, inadequate nutrition for normal growth, acute feeding difficulties, disturbed mother-child interaction and relationship, insecure or disorganized attachment, family dysfunctioning, and poverty (Iwaniec, 1995).

Failure to thrive is normally diagnosed within the first two years of life, although its effects and progress can be observed much later than this. Estimates of prevalence have varied from as many as 10% of children seen in outpatient clinics in both urban and rural areas to 1% of all pediatric hospitalizations. MacMillan (1984) estimated that failure to thrive probably affects 1% to 3% of the pediatric population at some time.

Some children may fail to thrive because of an *organic* or medical condition. Virtually all serious pediatric illnesses and minor recurrent or chronic ones can result in impeded growth. A direct predictable link can normally be observed between the course of the illness and the child's growth patterns; for example, after a successful course of treatment or an operation, the child's patterns gradually stabilize or return to normal. However, it is estimated that less than 5% of all FTT is due solely to organic reasons (Wynne, 1996).

Other children may have nothing physically wrong with them, but their environment may be inadequate or stressful and, therefore, detrimental to their growth; these are commonly termed as suffering from *nonorganic* failure to thrive. Some estimates suggest that nonorganic failure to thrive may account for around 50% of the growth-faltering observed in the pediatric population (Spinner & Siegel, 1987). Children failing to thrive for nonorganic reasons may show a number of characteristics, as described in Table 8.1, although there is a large variation between the presentation of different cases.

For many years, failure to thrive was dichotomized into two categories: organic and nonorganic. Diagnosis was seen as either one category or the other: The possibility of an interaction effect between physical factors and behavioral or psychosocial process was largely ignored. However, as more data was gathered, it

Table 8.1   Profile of Children with Nonorganic Failure to Thrive

Failure to Thrive
Child falls below expected norms for the chronological age in weight, often in height and head circumference.

Physical Appearance
Small, thin, wasted body; thin arms and legs; enlarged stomach; thin, wispy, dull, and falling hair; dark circles around the eyes

Characteristic Features
- Frequent eating problems
- Vomiting, heaving
- Refusal to chew and swallow
- Diarrhea
- Frequent colds and infections

Insecure or Avoidant Attachment
Tense when in the mother's company; does not show interest and pleasure when with the mother or caretaker; does not show distress when mother leaves or is too clingy.

Developmental Retardation
- Motor development
- Social development
- Emotional development
- Language development
- Intellectual development
- Cognitive development

Psychological Description and Behavior
- Sadness, withdrawal, and detachment
- General lethargy
- Tearful
- Minimal or no smiling
- Lack of cuddliness
- Extreme states such as passivity or overactivity
- Expressionless face
- Staring blankly at people or objects
- Frequent whining
- Diminished vocalizations
- Unresponsiveness

Problematic Behavior
- Whining and crying
- Irritability
- Anxiety
- Poor sleeping pattern
- Enuresis or encopresis
- Restlessness
- Apprehension
- Resistance to socialization
- Feeding and eating problems

Note: From Iwaniec, D. (1995). *The emotionally abused and neglected child: Identification, assessment, and intervention.* Chichester, England: Wiley.

was clear that this approach was inadequate. Many studies found that between 15% and 35% of the infants who were studied fell between the organic and nonorganic groups (Woolston, 1984). For example, Homer and Ludwig (1981) found that more than one-quarter of failure-to-thrive cases exhibited a combination of organic and nonorganic features. These children are generally classified as *combined* or mixed etiology growth-faltering. The interaction between the organic and nonorganic may help explain why some children with a physical problem such as moderately severe cardiac disease or cleft lip may fail to thrive whereas others with virtually the same degree of organic impairment will thrive. It may also shed light on why some children's growth-faltering persists after any organic problems are resolved.

Goldson (1987) suggested that this group of children with mixed etiology be divided roughly into three categories:

1. *Children with subtle neuromotor problems* may have difficulty eating because of oral-motor disturbances such as difficulties with sucking, chewing, swallowing, tongue thrusting, involuntary tonic biting of the spoon or nipple, excessive drooling, and an intolerance of the textures of developmentally appropriate food (Lewis, 1982).

2. *Children with aversive eating experiences* may have already had prior aversive experiences with eating because of allergic reactions or having gastroesophageal reflux. Other children may have required prolonged parental nutrition and never have had the normal experience of eating.

3. *Children with significant psychiatric disorders* may suffer from rumination or self-induced gagging resulting in vomiting; they may lose control over themselves and progress to a state of severe protein-energy malnutrition and profound growth failure.

A final group of older children, classified as *psychosocial short stature,* show unusual symptoms, thought to stem from inadequate nurturing in their home environments. These symptoms include voracious appetites, gorging and vomiting, polyphagia, and polydipsia. Frequently, there is no element of malnutrition associated with the growth failure: Even though these children eat large amounts of food, they still fail to grow normally. The primary etiology is thought to be a disturbance in growth hormone dynamics due to stress (Skuse, Pickles, Wolke, & Reilly, 1994). These children suffer from psychosocial dwarfism, which is much less common than the other forms of growth failure and generally diagnosed after the age of 2.

RISK FACTORS

The remainder of this chapter focuses on children whose growth-faltering has no organic cause. Several characteristics of families with children who fail to thrive for nonorganic reasons are summarized in Table 8.2 and are discussed in the following sections.

Poverty

Failure to thrive is associated with poverty. Almost all studies of growth-faltering have been done in low-income populations; little is known about failure to thrive in affluent ones (Dawson, 1992). Children from low-income families are lighter and shorter than their peers (Jones, Nesheim, & Habicht, 1985); minority children are smaller than White children (Centers for Disease Control and Prevention, 1987). However, classifying into social class can sometimes be misleading. For example, Skuse et al. (1994) suggested that the ability to manage money may be a better predictor of growth-faltering than actual levels of income in a household.

Family Stresses

Family stresses have been observed as more common in families with children who are failing to thrive. These include chronic illnesses in the parents, siblings, or extended family; prior divorce, current separation, or strain between parents; unmarried parents with young children; and financial and housing problems (Drotar, Malone, Negray, & Dennstedt, 1981). The stress that the mother is placed under while pregnant may also have an effect. For example, high levels of anxiety in the mother during pregnancy are linked to problems such as increased irritability in the baby, which may lead to more difficult interactions (Ferriera, 1969; Ottinger & Simmons, 1964).

Table 8.2   Characteristics Associated with Families with Children Who Fail to Thrive

• Poverty	• Increased levels of family stress
• Low maternal education	• Lack of knowledge about parenting
• Poor social support	• Dietary restraint in caretakers
• Maternal depression	• Low parental self-esteem
• Distorted parental perceptions and attitudes	• Poor quality interactions between parent and child

Low Maternal Education

Low maternal education may be a risk factor for growth-faltering (Drotar & Sturm, 1988). Skuse et al. (1994) found that mothers of children who began growth-faltering before 6 months of age had significantly higher IQs than mothers whose children began growth-faltering after 6 months of age.

Knowledge about Parenting

Knowledge about parenting is also important with respect to what, when, and how to feed the child. Sometimes, nonorganic failure to thrive can result from relatively simple, correctable feeding errors (Hathaway, 1989). For example, a caretaker may not understand the importance of formula preparation and, trying to save money, may overdilute the expensive formula so that it lasts longer, while not realizing that the child will be inadequately nourished. Alternatively, many parents offer drinks such as apple juice in preference to sugary or fizzy drinks to feed their children more healthy diets. These natural juices may be offered instead of milk, sweets, and other snacks, but parents may not realize that excess juice intake may result in an unbalanced diet and growth-faltering because it can affect the uptake of calories (Maggioni & Lifshitz, 1995).

Social Support

Parenting takes a great deal of time and emotional commitment, and it is useful to have good networks of social support to help cope with these demands. However, several studies have found that the mothers of nonorganic failure-to-thrive children are socially isolated and lack social support (Bithoney & Rathburn, 1983). In addition, family life is often seen as filled with conflict and tension, rather than as a source of emotional support (Hathaway, 1989). Mothers are thought to be less available to bond with a baby when their emotional resources are depleted. This isolation may result in fewer opportunities to escape caregiving, and clinicians should enlist the help of social workers and other outreach agencies such as visiting nurses, homemakers, and so on to alleviate the situation.

Maternal Depression

Maternal depression has been included in cumulative risk scores outside the context of failure to thrive (Hutcheson et al., 1997). Several researchers have found that mothers who have children with nonorganic failure to thrive are more likely to be depressed (Hathaway, 1989; Polan et al., 1991). However, others have found no differences (Wolke, Skuse, & Mathisen, 1990). Skuse et al. (1994) suggested that there may be variability among mothers depending on when their child's failure to thrive began. They found that mothers of early growth-faltering infants (i.e., children who began growth-faltering in the first six months after birth) were comparable in their depression scores to those in a normative sample of inner city pregnant women. However, mothers of late growth-faltering infants (i.e., children who began growth faltering after the first six months) showed higher depression scores, implying that more were suffering from some depressive symptoms. Because few of these studies are prospective, it is also difficult to ascertain whether the psychological problems *preceded* or were a *result* of the failure to thrive. Duniz et al. (1996) found that mothers who were very distressed at the time of the infant's referral showed a sudden and almost complete abatement of psychiatric symptoms coinciding with the infants' recovery after successful treatment. The mothers' complaints included sleep disturbances, mood disturbances, anxiety, exhaustion, panic attacks, fear, bad dreams, feelings of insufficiency, guilt, hopelessness, and suicidal fantasies.

Low Parental Self-Esteem

Failure to thrive is also associated with low parental self-esteem. It is not clear, however, whether the low esteem is a result or a precursor of the child's growth-faltering because parents often end up feeling blamed by health care professionals for their child's poor growth.

Distorted Perceptions and Expectations

Sometimes, parents of a growth-faltering child can exhibit distorted perceptions and expectations of the child. For example, some parents may see the child's growth as giving no cause for concern and maintain that the child is just small for his or her age. There may also be unrealistic expectations as to what children can be expected to accomplish or do for themselves at a particular age. For example, a parent may become frustrated by a child's repeated messy attempts to feed himself or herself, which results in food smeared in the hair, on the high-chair, dropped on the floor, and so on. The parent may mistakenly believe that the child is being deliberately naughty, rather than its being a natural way for children to learn about their world.

Poor Quality Interactions

On the whole, there may be poor quality interactions between the parent and child. In many cases, these problems may be focused on feeding interactions, with mealtimes being stressful and unpleasant events for all involved. When a parent is concerned about a child's growth and food intake, feeding time can soon deteriorate to a battle of wills, and, often, parents can become nearly obsessive about what the child is eating. This in turn brings increased pressure to the feeding process, which may make it less likely that the child will eat properly. Over time, the problems may spread throughout other interactions between parent and child. There may be physical and emotional distancing of the parent from the child, with limited interactions, and the parent may find the child difficult to manage and enjoy.

PLANNING INTERVENTION FOR FAILURE-TO-THRIVE CHILDREN AND THEIR FAMILIES

Helping failure-to-thrive children and their caregivers varies considerably from case to case and should be based on the outcomes of vigorous assessment. Failure to thrive seldom arises because of a single factor, but rather as a combination of amalgamated difficulties adversely affecting a child's physical growth and, often, psychosocial development. Failure to thrive tends to be multidimensional, and it is essential to examine each of these dimensions to plan appropriate and successful interventions. Intervention programs can take many forms, can follow different routes, and may require several methods and approaches to deal effectively and suitably with the presenting problems. It is now generally accepted that a combination of interventions and use of different therapeutic methods and services produces better results in the longer term than a single approach (Batchelor, 1999; Iwaniec, 1995; Iwaniec, Herbert, & McNeish, 1985b; Iwaniec & Sneddon, 2001; Wolfe & Wekerle, 1993).

Equally, full participation of caregivers in planning and decision making as to choices and the nature of intervention has proven to enhance successful outcomes (Iwaniec, 1997). For example, the use of a therapeutic program at home to resolve feeding problems might be enhanced and accelerated if a child attends a day nursery and is fed by people who do not show anxiety or put pressure on a child to eat. Additionally, the use of a family center can help the child with developmental deficit, help parents to acquire parenting skills, or provide group work for parents who are socially isolated, depressed, and generally disengaged.

Increasingly, it is being recognized that failure to thrive more often than not is the result of child-rearing difficulties mostly associated with eating problems combined with various personal and structural problems, rather than deliberate parental action, although maltreatment and neglect feature in some cases (Azar, Ferrare, & Breton, 1998). Helping parents in more effective child-rearing practices and raising their awareness about children's developmental needs and different problems that growing children might present should dominate intervention strategies. The available evidence suggests that support and monitoring of more serious cases alone is insufficient to produce long-lasting changes in children's and their parents' lives (Iwaniec, 2000; Wolfe, 1990). More proactive skill-teaching approaches and methods are advocated, where parents can be actively involved in problem recognition and problem solving, which would, in turn, generate a sense of achievement and competence (Herbert, 1993; Iwaniec, 1997). However, there is not a single or simple way to deal with the many and complex problems; neither is there an identified single approach or method that could claim an all-embracing success. Intervention strategies need to be tailored to the specific requirements of the individual families in their special circumstances. For example, if failure to thrive is due to child-rearing deficit, parent training including developmental counseling appears to be the most suitable approach to adopt. If FTT is due to acute feeding problems or oral motor dysfunction, modeling how to feed and interact with the child during the process of feeding is advocated. If, on the other hand, FTT is due to parental rejection, a step-by-step approach of reducing hostile feelings toward the child will be required using various methods of attachment work and modeling of fear-reducing interaction on the part of the child and hostility and anger on the part of the parent. Parents who have obsessive attitudes toward diet and weight might need cognitive restructuring or another type of psychotherapy to change their beliefs and behavior.

The following sections discuss first, the most common/universal intervention when dealing with failure-to-thrive problems; second, selective prevention/intervention, for example, dealing with feeding/eating problems and distorted relationship problems between child and the caregiver; and last, targeted prevention intervention, for example, children who have to be removed from home for safety.

EFFECTIVE UNIVERSAL PREVENTION INTERVENTION

In child welfare and protection, most countries have three levels of interventions to provide help for children and families: universal, selected, and targeted.

Universal prevention intervention is available to all people in the welfare states as required or requested. This includes community medical services, education, social services, and other local services open to all citizens. For failure-to-thrive children, advice and assistance are provided routinely at a basic level by the health visitor and early on by a midwife, baby clinic, community pediatrician, or general practice doctor. Advice is given on how to feed the baby, how often, what formula to use if the child is bottle fed, how to deal with sucking difficulties, frequent vomiting, and, later, how and when to introduce solids and how to deal with food refusal. The child's early growth and development is regularly monitored and measured by the health visitors as a matter of statutory duties. It is difficult to estimate how many children who present eating and growth problems are helped early. No data are available because such help is considered routine and available to all.

Children who present growth-faltering are seen by the health visitor at home, health center, or baby clinic on a regular basis to provide help on how to feed and care for the baby. The majority of infants who fail to thrive in the first few months of their life as a rule improve steadily once the mother becomes more relaxed, confident, and more skillful in her parenting role and when a baby adapts to a daily routine. First-time parents, single mothers, and those without extended family support seek advice and guidance often because they lack child-rearing experience.

Some of these children might need to be referred by the general practitioner to a pediatrician if progress is slow. Some fail to thrive because of illness and, therefore, need to be investigated medically to find out whether there is an organic reason for their poor growth and development. Such children will be seen in outpatient clinics or as inpatients if observation is required. It is immensely important to eliminate or confirm any medical reason for FTT as a matter of good practice to prevent distortion of parental perceptions about the child, interaction, and relationship. In many countries, such services are available, and presenting problems of early feeding difficulties and poor growth are seldom considered a result of parenting problems. However, repeated admissions into the hospital and lack of progress, if there is nothing wrong with the child, or repeated visits to the general practitioner require the next level of intervention.

EFFECTIVE SELECTIVE PREVENTION INTERVENTION

Selective intervention refers to specific, more intensive family support when a problem or problems cannot be resolved at a universal level. Selective intervention is voluntary, which aims to prevent further escalation of difficulties and to provide suitable services and/or treatments for parents and children who are in need of help.

The concept of *family support* (as a preventive measure) was introduced in the United Kingdom following the implementation of the Children Act (1989) in England and Wales and the equivalent in Scotland and Northern Ireland in 1995. It replaced and widened the early procedures of so-called preventive work, for example, provision of help and services to prevent children coming into care, which was in operation from the 1960s to the late 1980s. The Children Act philosophy and aims were to redirect child welfare work from focusing almost exclusively on child abuse and protection to more child-oriented care work within the family and community. Family support means allocation of services for children in need and the use of services and interventions with agreement and in partnership with parents.

The majority of children whose failure to thrive is more persistent and where there are concerns expressed by the professionals or parents come into a category of selective intervention using various family support services. This section discusses well-tested and rigorously evaluated intervention programs with more persistent cases of failure-to-thrive children (Iwaniec & Sneddon, 2001). Intervention and treatment strategies have been developed and modified over the past 25 years as the knowledge about failure to thrive increased and as evaluation of the effectiveness dictated. The first author has dealt with 297 cases from referral point to termination, and some of these cases were followed up for 20 years (Iwaniec, 1983, 1991, 1995, 2000; Iwaniec & Sneddon, 2001, 2002; Iwaniec et al., 1985a, 1985b).

Program of Interventions

Treatment of failure to thrive might involve several stages. This treatment entails a multielement package that depends for its final shape and extent on comprehensive assessment. Intervention for failure to thrive should be carried out by an interdisciplinary team to meet the multiple needs that a child with FTT and the family may present (Dawson, 1992; Hanks & Hobbs, 1993), with different professions being better suited to deal with different aspects of the syndrome. The physician, for example, should look for medical etiology if there are signs of an organic cause for failure to thrive; the nutritionist should evaluate the child's intake of food and feeding behavior; and the health visitor should measure and monitor the child's weight and development and observe feeding interaction during home visits. There might be a need for psychiatrist involvement if there are mental health problems or a psychologist if psychometric testing or specialized therapy for parents or a child is required. More often than not, social work involvement is necessary to assist when FTT is a result of neglect, abuse, poverty, or other environmental factors. Multidisciplinary teamwork has been described and positively evaluated by several writers, for example, McMillen's (1988) St. Elizabeth's Failure-to-Thrive Program in Covington, Kentucky, and Hobbs and Hanks (1996), a specialist clinic in Leeds, United Kingdom, to provide help for FTT children and their families. The results of treatment outcomes are very encouraging and indicate that team effort and opportunity to discuss and monitor cases on a regular basis produce quicker and better results.

Intervention with failure-to-thrive cases usually falls into two basic categories: immediate (crisis intervention) and longer term therapeutic work with more complex cases. During the assessment period, attention is paid to immediate and urgent needs. It is sometimes necessary to arrange a day nursery for a child if there are developmental delays because of the lack of stimulation or when a child is at risk of mismanagement or neglect. Provision of daycare services gives a child much needed social stimulation, safety, and the opportunity to reduce developmental deficit. Additionally, it gives the therapist and the parents the opportunity to explore in-depth issues and problems associated with child rearing, as well as their personal relationship and functioning problems.

Some families might need assistance with welfare rights, housing, health and addiction problems, employment, financial difficulties, family violence, marital frictions, and managing children's behavior and their activities. These issues should be dealt with early on to reduce stress and to create an atmosphere where further intervention can be conducted. Equally, in cases of substance or alcohol abuse or maternal depression, treatment should start in resolving parental problems before embarking on relationships and interactional issues. It is often observed that once the child is placed in the daycare services, the involvement with the family is reduced to minimum, yet this is where it should begin in earnest. Providing daycare for the child facilitates developmental enhancement and possibly physical growth, but it seldom resolves the child's problems at home. Newly learned skills and emotional stability have to be reinforced and nurtured at home by parents to produce sustainable positive change. Therefore, helping strategies for a child must go hand-in-hand in helping parents to be better equipped to parent the child satisfactorily. No amount of intervention will produce long-lasting, meaningful change to the child if an alcoholic mother is not helped to stop drinking or when a depressed one does not receive treatment.

Most parents, but most specifically mothers of failure-to-thrive children, are found to be very anxious, worried, helpless, or disillusioned about their ability to parent a child; they tend to lack confidence; and their self-esteem is at rock bottom. This learned helplessness, portrayed by depressive moods and apathy in some and high anxiety levels—expressed by outbursts of anger and frustration—in others, requires therapeutic help to prepare the ground and general emotional energy to help their FTT children. Some level of calmness may be achieved (before any formal treatment takes place) by doing relaxation exercises of maximum 20-minutes' duration. The relaxation tape (easy to follow) is rehearsed with the mother and then used by her at least twice a day to learn how to relax different parts of the body. Additionally, parents are taught how to control anger, frustration, and irrational thoughts. Anger control, stress management, and problem-solving techniques play an important part in helping parents to think and feel positively about their children (Iwaniec, 1995).

Child-Focused Intervention

The *therapeutic* part of the program (extensively tested and positively evaluated) is presented as an example of effective treatment of FTT children. The treatment intervention adopted a full partnership model with the parents from an assessment stage to the termination of the case. Joint planning and negotiation, as well as evaluation of each stage of the program, have been observed. The therapeutic part of the treatment, carried out with the parents and children together, normally involves five stages, which are discussed later.

Dealing with Inadequate Intake of Food

The primary objective of all failure-to-thrive cases is to increase nutritional intake by children and subsequent weight gain. Because many children present feeding difficulties, this situation is dealt with first to help the child to take more food and for the parents to manage better the process of feeding. Some children are simply not given a sufficient amount of food, or the feeding formula is wrong, so they are instructed and shown how to feed, when to feed, and how much food is required for the child's chronological age. Parent-education methods play an important role in problem solving in such cases, as well as frequent home visits and monitoring of the cases. It must be remembered that a small number of FTT cases are the result of deliberate withholding of food, which can be extremely harmful to a child. Intervention for such cases is discussed in the section on targeted intervention.

Stage 1.   Resolving Eating Difficulties

When a child is given sufficient food but refuses to eat or presents various eating problems, this is dealt with by gradual reduction of tension and anxiety during mealtimes and making the act of eating more enjoyable to the child. Much effort is put into making mealtimes more relaxed for everybody in the family, but in particular for the mother and child, because the mother is often the main person who feeds the child. Mealtime arrangements and appropriate feeding behavior are discussed and modeled by the therapist. By direct modeling (showing how to do it, what to do, and the manner of interaction), the mother or other caregiver can learn by observation how to create a relaxed atmosphere before and during the mealtime. To create calmness and harmony between the caregiver and the child, the child should be spoken to warmly, quietly, and encouragingly and should be taken to the kitchen to observe the caregiver preparing the food and assist in this task, for example, asking the child to hand over something or to hold something such as a carrot or potato. As food is prepared, the caregiver should tell the child what he or she is doing and thank the child for helping, which generates interest in food and eating. While doing this, the caregiver should occasionally kiss, hug, smile at the child, and stroke the child's hair, helping the child to relax and feel more at ease. Food should be arranged on a plate in a small quantity in an interesting and appetizing way, for example, in the shape of a smiling face, fish finger boy, a tree, or an animal. The caregiver should tell a story, referring to the arrangement on the plate to generate more interest and appetite, which tends to speed up eating (see Figure 8.1).

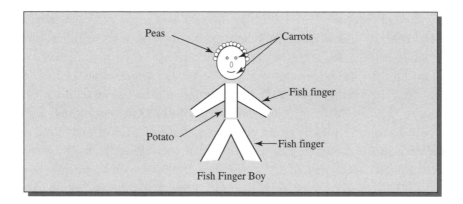

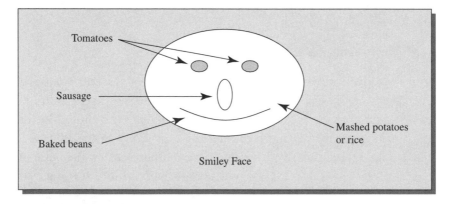

Figure 8.1   Techniques for Arranging Food in an Interesting and Appetizing Way: Fish Finger Boy and Smiley Face

A strong fish finger champion story:

Once upon a time, there was a little boy named (give the name of a child). He loved playing football, and he wanted to be a football player when he grew up, but he was very small and thin because he did not eat enough to grow strong and fast. One day, a fish finger champion appeared on his plate and said: "If you want to be a football player, you need to eat more and a lot of things to get strong and big. Show me how fast you can eat fish fingers, potatoes, carrots, and peas. You must eat everything that is on the plate so I will be a very happy fish finger champion— see you again. Tomorrow, smiley face will be on a plate to talk to you."

Most toddlers are fascinated by the character on the plate and a story, which needs to be devised to appeal to individual children. It takes two minutes to arrange food in an interesting shape, and most food is suitable for such displays. The benefits are extensive in terms of largely increased intake of food, variety of food consumed, speed of eating, a pleasant atmosphere during mealtime, and parental satisfaction of a job well done.

The therapist needs to be actively involved during the early stages of the feeding program to model the style and tone of feeding interactions. Advice and instructions alone—a didactic approach—do not seem to work in more difficult cases, especially when parents received a variety of advice and instructions earlier that did not work for them, when they did not get sufficient support and encouragement, or when methods of working were not evaluated and modified according to needs. Treatment seems to be more effective if it is based on very rigorous assessment, underpinned by sound theoretical knowledge and empirical evidence. Once a caregiver becomes more confident and relaxed (because of improvement in the child's intake and speed of eating), distance reassurance and rehearsal of what should be done and how (over the telephone) is often sufficient.

To maintain an already achieved positive change, further reinforcements can be used in the form of symbolic activity and verbal reward for toddlers and older children. A picture chart of characters or shapes, for example, fairytale figures, cars, airplanes, football players, and so on, can be used to reward the child for eating and at reasonable speed (20 to 25 minutes). The chart can be placed on the kitchen or refrigerator door for everyone to see, to make positive comments, and to give praise for good eating and good behavior at mealtimes. If the child meets the minimum requirements, he or she can choose a picture from the envelope and stick it on the chart with the help of the caregiver. Such events should be accompanied by much praise, hugs, and satisfaction, not only by the family but also by neighbors, extended family, and professionals involved.

Activity rewards are particularly beneficial for children who fail to thrive because their interaction with parents is often limited or of confrontational quality.

A child might be rewarded for good eating behavior by activities he or she likes, for example, going to the park and playing on the swings and slides, being read a favorite story, being played with, watching with parents a favorite television program, getting a little toy, and so on. Increased positive interaction tends to improve mutual attachment and relationship and decreases anxiety and apprehension when in each other's company. By being appreciated, and when achievements are acknowledged in different ways, the child's self-esteem and sense of achievement are naturally enhanced.

Some parents' anxiety level at the point of referral is so high and emotional energy is so low that it is in the child's and parents' best interest to place a child, either on a full- or part-time basis, into daycare. Resolving feeding/eating problems in daycare is similar to the situation at home but has the advantage of having *good eater* models at the table. The assumption is that watching other children eat stimulates appetite and prompts the child to eat as well. One nursery nurse should be trained to supervise the child during mealtimes and to take responsibility for effective implementation of the treatment program.

An important lesson was learned from the program of intervention when excessive attention was being given to some children in the form of frequent prompting or other forms of social reinforcement. Observation of the eating behavior showed that some children responded less favorably when a great deal of attention was directed at them. They tended to push the plate away, play with the food, store food in the mouth, or walk away from the table. When attention was redirected from a FTT child to other children who were eating well, the performance was much better. Comments such as: "What a great eater you are, Mark; you will be a football player soon and win all the matches" or "Jack is a champion; he has already eaten all his sausage—it was nice, wasn't it?" can help. Being approached in a matter-of-fact way and only occasionally being prompted in a low key increased the intake of food and speed of eating. Such children respond better to competition (e.g., "Who will empty the plate first, second, or third?") and when attention is switched from them to other children at the table. It appears that because of excessive pressure at home for FTT children to eat, they developed food avoidance behavior and strategies to cope with such pressure. By associating eating with excessive attention, which made them feel uncomfortable, they reverted to social reinforcement, at first negatively. Direct observation and experimentation can help to choose the appropriate approach to resolve the problems. Intervention must be tailor-made to suit a particular child and family in their special circumstances.

Stage 2.   Resolving Insecure Attachments

Some failure-to-thrive children (not all) are insecurely attached to their mothers, and there is a lack of maternal bonding to the child. Interaction between the mother and the target child is limited to the bare essentials of care and control and is negative in nature. The child's fear and apprehension when in the mother's company are observable, as are anxiety and hostility on the part of the mother. To bring them closer together and to reduce the negative feelings, structured interaction, increasing in time, is introduced. This stage of intervention may take different forms, for example:

1. Structured interaction increasing in time, using play to reduce negative feelings, brings the mother and child closer together, and they begin to enjoy each other's company.
2. Video recording and feedback increases awareness of parental responses.

Treatment to Strengthen Mother-Child Relationship

This phase is discussed in detail with parents: Rationale and methods are explained carefully and sometimes written down. In most cases, a contract is drawn up specifying the mutual obligations and rules for the family and therapist. What might happen in situations where parent-child interactions are highly (and sometimes mutually) aversive—a common finding—is that each day the mother is encouraged to play exclusively with her child for 10 to 15 minutes during the first week and for 15 to 20 minutes during the fourth and subsequent weeks. After the mother's session with the child, the rest of the family might join in for a family play session. The way the mother plays and the toys she uses may have to be demonstrated and rehearsed (some parents do not know how to play with their children). The mother is encouraged to talk to her child in a soft, reassuring manner and to encourage him or her to participate in the play.

Mothers are encouraged—as a general principle—to smile at their children, look at them, hold their hands, stroke their hair, and praise them for each response they give. This may require careful programming if their behavior is very timid. The mothers' approaches are shaped by a series of successive approximations; they are encouraged to initiate as well as react. After a few days or even weeks, mothers are guided to seek proximity by hugging their children briefly and holding them on their laps for increasing time intervals, eventually holding them closely but gently, while reading to them, looking at or describing pictures, and so on.

In our sample, there were several rejecting mothers, and they usually found this exercise very difficult and, at times, distasteful. This aversion gradually lessened when the children began to smile back, seek their mothers' presence, and in other ways respond to their overtures. This period of therapy requires a great deal of support for the mother and the whole family. Frequent visits and telephone calls were made to monitor the program (reinforcing the reinforcer is critical in this work). It could take three months of hard work to bring a parent and child closer together and to the point of beginning to enjoy (or stop disliking/ fearing) each other.

Video Recording and Feedback

A variety of techniques can be used to increase parents' or caregivers' awareness and understanding of what is happening and how to correct inappropriate responses to their children. Very effective work has been done videotaping the interaction of parents who persistently criticize, rebuke, ridicule, and react with hostility to their children as well as during aversive feeding of failure-to-thrive children (Hampton, 1996; Hobbs & Hanks, 1996; Iwaniec, 1995). Examples of aversive parental behavior are videotaped and then played back to parents so they can see and hear for themselves how they behaved and what they said. They are asked to pay particular attention to their tone of voice, eye contact, facial expression, and general body language when they speak and deal with the child. They are also asked to observe their child's anxious and fearful reaction to them and their apprehension when in the parents' company. The impact of parental emotionally abusive behavior on the child is discussed in terms of immediate pain and long-term consequences (such as prevention of developing strong self-esteem and self-confidence, a sense of belonging and security, and a general feeling of being loved and wanted).

Parents are asked to imagine how they would feel and how they would react if they were treated in the same way as they were treating their child. By asking them to reflect on their harsh and hostile behavior, it is hoped that they can get in touch with their own and the child's feelings, which in turn will help them to empathize and recognize pain and hurt inflicted by them on the child. Parents are asked to observe the role play conducted by a therapist demonstrating warm, encouraging, and caring behavior when doing things with the child. In turn, they are asked to play with the child, which is videotaped, played back, and discussed.

Stage 3.   Intensifying Interaction

The third stage is planned to include two weeks of deliberately intensified mother-child interaction. The mother is to take the child with her almost everywhere she goes and include the child in whatever she does—within reason. She is asked to chat with the child as much as possible, regardless of whether the child fully understands what she is doing or saying. She is told to make a lot of eye contact, smile, cuddle, and hug the infant as often as possible. These requirements of a tired mother—particularly a single parent—could be counterproductive if demanded insensitively. Discussions are important, as are child-minding arrangements that give the mother a break. During the period of intervention at the home, the children and their families should routinely attend outpatient clinics or health centers to monitor weight and other indexes.

Stage 4.   Reinforcing Good Behavior

Children still presenting behavioral problems at this stage of treatment can be helped by behavioral methods such as effective use of positive reinforcements: They are praised for good conduct or for even attempting to behave in a prosocial manner. They are rewarded by favorable activities, for example, story-reading, favorite foods, or special play. Parents are guided through the process to create a warm, anxiety-free atmosphere so children can begin to feel that they are liked and wanted (see Iwaniec, 1995, for further discussion).

Stage 5.   Helping the Parents

We have discussed therapeutic intervention mainly to help children. Stage 5 of the *selective intervention* was set up to help the parents. Because parents of failure-to-thrive children are socially isolated and suffer from low self-esteem, it was felt that organizing parents' groups would facilitate meeting some of these needs. There are many advantages for meeting in a group, such as a forum for peer support, the opportunity to exchange tips and ideas about parenting children and specifically dealing with eating problems, and coping with a child's poor growth and often difficult behavior.

In our sample, group work consisted of 10 sessions, each lasting two hours. After each session, there was a pleasant coffee break with cakes and snacks prepared by the group members to facilitate informal chats and getting to know one another. A playgroup for children was run by two students to free the mothers from looking after them while being engaged in the group work. Attending parents were consulted (before the start) about formulation of the group, content of the program, and ways of conducting group activities and running it. During the first meeting, group members decided to have two parts to each session: Part 1 was allocated for a more serious topic to be presented and discussed, and Part 2, a free discussion about individual problems and issues and small chats to learn about one another. The formal part included topics such as stress management, child development and difficulties associated with growing up, behavior management, anger control, learning to play and having fun with the child, dealing with sleeping problems, and learning about local resources and ways of accessing them. With minimum help, the members themselves ran the group. They invited speakers to facilitate the first part of the session and rotated running the second part of the session. They also recruited new members to the group by getting in touch with the Children's Hospital and inviting new mothers to join the group if they wished.

EFFECTIVE TARGETED PREVENTION INTERVENTION

The third level of intervention applies to children who are at risk of significant harm if no action is taken. They require, as a rule, removal from an abusive or dangerous environment as a matter of safety through the court system. The criteria for significant harm vary among countries and over time. In countries where child welfare and protection are legislated and observed, substantial services at all levels are available, whereas in less-developed countries, there are very few and they are difficult to access (Gough, 2002).

Some children who present persistent growth failure that is due to seriously inadequate or dangerous parenting come into this category of intervention. These cases might include persistent and severe physical and emotional neglect, rejection, deliberate withholding of food, and fictitious illnesses resulting in child starvation and psychosocial short-stature children. In most of these cases, the parent-child relationship is extremely poor, and attachment of children to parents is weak and insecure. There is also observable lack of parental emotional bond with the children and lack of commitment to their welfare and well-being. The reasons for this sad and dangerous state of parenting vary from immature, ill-informed parenting style associated with intergenerational deficit to psychological disturbances in cognitive functioning mental illness or learning disabilities. In such cases, application for a care order to the court is necessary to protect the child from harm or even death and to determine a care plan for the future. Most children are placed in foster homes on a short- or long-term basis, and some are considered for freeing for adoption if the possibility of rehabilitation at home is remote or impossible. Sometimes the child is placed with extended family if it is considered safe and the family is willing. Such kinship care can be arranged voluntarily without taking a case to court. Not all such placements are satisfactory and some are highly inappropriate (Lernihan, 2003). In the majority of cases, parents of children in care have a right of reasonable access to their children. They can see them periodically, and access may be supervised. The frequency and nature of access visits is usually determined by the court. Recent years have seen some changes and less rigid arrangements for adopted children. So-called open adoption is considered for each child, which gives a range of possibilities for contact with birth parents, for example, two to four face-to-face contacts a year and contact in exceptional circumstances and events as well as exchange of photographs, birthday cards, or letters. The nature of contact is determined by the best interest of the child in terms of security, stability, and social adjustment. Children who grow up away from home who are aware of their origin and, better still, who have ongoing contact with the natural parents have a better developed sense of identity and less unrealistic and disturbing fantasies about their parents. The 20-year follow-up study of children who failed to thrive as children (Iwaniec, 2000; Iwaniec & Sneddon, 2001, 2002) found that children who were adopted satisfactorily overcame acute adversity of childhood experiences and became well-adjusted individuals and parents in later life. Children in long-term undisrupted and well-selected foster homes have done equally well. Those, however, who had frequent admissions into care on a voluntary basis but remain at home have done less well in terms of stability, attachment with peers and romantic partners, educational attainments, employment, self-esteem, as well as physical growth.

It is important to emphasize that children in this category require intensive intervention when placed in substitute care in their own right to eliminate or minimize emotional disturbances and to make good developmental deficit. Provision of daycare services, play therapy, and systematic positive monitoring of behavior by various forms of reinforcement is essential to avoid break-up of the placements. Substitute caregivers require support and active help to guide them to understand and deal with children's difficult behavior. Some suitable intervention methods were discussed in the selective intervention section earlier in the chapter.

POLICY AND PRACTICE IMPLICATIONS

We suggest the following implications for policy and practice:

1. Early intervention is essential to prevent escalation of negative parent/ child interaction and relationship and to prevent poor growth and development. Failure to thrive when attended to early on appears to have less of a detrimental effect on children's growth, development, social adjustment, and educational attainments. Family support in terms of service provision and direct therapeutic input is required at an early stage of failure to thrive.

2. Regular monitoring of children's growth (weight, height, and head circumference) should be mandatory for all children. Many children may not be referred for assessment and treatment until they are between 3 and 6 years of age, despite health visiting records that indicate growth failure. A growth and development chart is a good instrument to identify problems early and respond to them quickly.

3. Parental concerns and complaints about poor feeding and inadequate weight gain should be taken seriously, dealt with, and monitored until satisfactory weight gain for the child's chronological age is established and maintained for at least six months. Repeated parental visits to the doctors concerning worries about the child's poor physical health should be investigated because, in some cases, the medical reason for failure to thrive may not be recognized, risking a presumption that the cause was inadequate or neglectful parenting.

4. Full psychosocial assessment is essential when failure to thrive is persistent. There are many reasons that children fail to thrive. The assessment of problems and needs must be done comprehensively so that intervention can be tailored to each family's needs and acted on promptly. A care plan addressing all aspects of identified difficulties should be devised on a multidisciplinary basis and tasks allocated to appropriate professions such as social workers, health visitors, general practitioners, pediatricians, and dieticians. Daycare services such as family centers, day nurseries, and community centers can help the child and parents.

5. The parents have to be committed to the intervention; otherwise, improvements are likely to be only short term. Clear goals for intervention work best when a contract of mutual obligations is written down and negotiated with both parties. Loosely defined support does not work.

6. Cases should be monitored and followed up to ensure that improvements and changes in family interaction are sustained, particularly in cases of neglect and abuse.

7. Most serious cases of failure to thrive, especially those where rejection and emotional maltreatment are present, need to be conferenced promptly and an appropriate care plan put into action urgently.

8. Children who are identified as severe psychosocial short stature should be removed from stressful and abusive environments. The prognosis of problem solving at home is extremely poor.

FUTURE DIRECTIONS

Early explanations of nonorganic failure to thrive drew on the extensive literature on the effects of institutionalization, hospitalism, and maternal deprivation in children. The ideas were influenced by a society that saw a child's upbringing as being primarily the responsibility of the mother. However, during the past decade, the focus has shifted to recognize the role that other people play in a child's upbringing. We need to look at both sides of the role of others such as the father, as well as investigate how subtle characteristics of infants (such as temperament) may stress relationships with others and result in disturbed interactions.

We also need to learn more about the interactions between different risk and protective factors in these cases, with the aim of taking a holistic approach to diagnosing and treating problems. Only by treating the individual child's and family's needs can we successfully enable these cases to reach their potential for physical and psychological growth and development.

REFERENCES

Azar, S. T., Ferrare, M. M., & Breton, S. J. (1998). Intraglamical child maltreatment. In T. H. Ollendick & M. Hersen (Eds.), *Handbook of child psychopathology* (3rd ed., pp. 483–504). New York: Plenum Press.

Batchelor, J. A. (1999). *Failure-to-thrive in young children: Research and practice evaluated.* London: The Children's Society.

Bithoney, W. G., & Rathburn, J. (1983). Failure-to-thrive. In M. Levine, W. Carey, A. Crocker, & R. Gross (Eds.), *Developmental-behavioral pediatrics* (pp. 557–572). Philadelphia: Saunders.

Centers for Disease Control and Prevention. (1987). Nutritional status of minority children—United States, 1986. *Morbidity and Mortality Weekly Report, 36,* 366–369.

Dawson, P. (1992, June). Should the field of early child and family intervention address failure-to-thrive? *Zero to Three: Bulletin of the National Center for Clinical Infant Programs,* 20–24.

Drotar, D., Malone, C. A., Negray, J., & Dennstedt, M. (1981). Psychosocial assessment and care for infants hospitalized for nonorganic failure-to-thrive. *Journal of Clinical Child Psychology, Winter 1981,* 63–66.

Drotar, D., & Sturm, L. (1988). Prediction of intellectual development in young children with early histories of nonorganic failure-to-thrive. *Journal of Pediatric Psychology, 13,* 281–296.

Duniz, M., Scheer, P. J., Trojovsky, A., Kaschnitz, W., Kvas, E., & Macari, S. (1996). Changes in psychopathology of parents of NOFT (nonorganic failure-to-thrive) infants during treatment. *European Child and Adolescent Psychiatry, 5,* 93–100.

Ferriera, A. J. (1969). *Prenatal environment.* Springfield, IL: Charles C Thomas.

Goldson, E. (1987). Failure-to-thrive: An old problem revisited. *Progress in Child Health and Nutrition Research, 7,* 83–99.

Gough, D. (2002). To or from whom: A social policy perspective on child abuse and child protection. In K. Browne, H. Hanks, P. Stratton, & C. Hamilton (Eds.), *Early prediction and prevention of child abuse: A handbook* (pp. 183–201). Chichester, England: Wiley.

Hampton, D. (1996). Resolving the feeding difficulties associated with nonorganic failure-to-thrive. *Child: Care, Health and Development, 22*(4), 261–271.

Hanks, H., & Hobbs, C. (1993, February). Failure-to-Thrive: A model for treatment. *Baillière's Clinical Pediatrics, 1*(1), 101–119.

Hathaway, P. (1989). Failure-to-thrive: Knowledge for social workers. *Health and Social Work, 14*(2), 122–126.

Herbert, M. (1993). *Working with children and the Children Act.* Leicester, England: British Psychological Society.

Hobbs, C., & Hanks, H. G. I. (1996). A multidisciplinary approach for the treatment of children with failure-to-thrive. *Child: Care, Health and Development, 22*(4), 273–284.

Homer, C., & Ludwig, S. (1981). Categorisation of etiology of failure-to-thrive. In C. H. Kempe & R. E. Helfer (Eds.), *The battered child* (3rd ed., pp. 163–182). Chicago: University of Chicago Press.

Hutcheson, J. J., Black, M. M., Talley, M., Dubowitz, H., Berenson-Howard, J., Starr, R. H., et al. (1997). Risk status and home intervention among children with failure-to-thrive: Follow-up at age 4. *Journal of Pediatric Psychology, 22*(5), 651–668.

Iwaniec, D. (1983). *Social and psychological factors in the aetiology and management of children who fail to thrive.* Unpublished doctoral dissertation, University of Leicester, Leicester, England.

Iwaniec, D. (1991). Treatment of children who fail to grow in the light of the new Children Act. *Association for Child Psychology and Psychiatry Newsletter, 13*(3), 21–27.

Iwaniec, D. (1995). *The emotionally abused and neglected child: Identification, assessment, and intervention.* Chichester, England: Wiley.

Iwaniec, D. (1997). An overview of emotional maltreatment and failure-to-thrive. *Child Abuse Review, 6,* 370–388.

Iwaniec, D. (2000). From childhood to adulthood: The outcomes of a 20-year follow-up of children who failed to thrive. In D. Iwaniec & M. Hill (Eds.), *Child welfare policy and practice: Current issues in child care research* (pp. 203–223). London: Jessica Kingsley.

Iwaniec, D., Herbert, M., & McNeish, A. S. (1985a). Social work with failure-to-thrive children and their families, Part I: Psychosocial factors. *British Journal of Social Work, 15,* 243–259.

Iwaniec, D., Herbert, M., & McNeish, A. S. (1985b). Social work with failure-to-thrive children and their families, Part II: Behavioral Social Work Intervention. *British Journal of Social Work, 15*(4), 375–389.

Iwaniec, D., & Sneddon, H. (2001). Attachment style in adults who failed to thrive as children: Outcomes of a 20-year follow up study of factors influencing maintenance or change in attachment style. *British Journal of Social Work, 31,* 179–195.

Iwaniec, D., & Sneddon, H. (2002). The quality of parenting of individuals who had failed-to-thrive as children. *British Journal of Social Work, 32,* 283–298.

Jones, D., Nesheim, M., & Habicht, J. (1985). Influences on child growth associated with poverty in the 1970s: An examination of HANES I and HANES II, cross-sectional, U.S. national surveys. *American Journal of Clinical Nutrition, 42,* 714–724.

Lernihan, U. (2003). *A study of kinship foster caregivers in Northern Ireland in relation to: 1. selected characteristics in the wider context of traditional foster caregivers; 2. the attitude of kinship foster caregivers to the involvement of Social Services in their lives.* Doctoral dissertation, Queen's University Belfast, Belfast, Northern Ireland.

Lewis, J. A. (1982). Oral motor assessment and treatment of feeding difficulties. In P. J. Accardo (Ed.), *Failure-to-thrive in infancy and early childhood, a multidisciplinary approach* (pp. 265–298). Baltimore: University Park Press.

MacMillan, A. B. (1984). Failure-to-thrive: A historical perspective. In *Failure-to-Thrive Symposium* (pp. 4–31). Ontario Ministry of Community and Social Services, Ontario Center for the Prevention of Child Abuse. Ontario: 1984.

Maggioni, A., & Lifshitz, F. (1995). Nutritional management of failure-to-thrive. *Pediatric Clinics of North America, 42*(4), 791–810.

McMillen, P. (1988, January/February). Infants thrive with Failure-to-Thrive Program. *Health Progress, 69*(1), 70–71.

Ottinger, D. R., & Simmons, J. E. (1964). Behavior of human neonates and prenatal maternal anxiety. *Psychological Reports, 14,* 391–394.

Polan, J. H., Kaplan, M. D., Kessler, D. B., Shindledecker, R., Newmark, M., Stern, D. N., et al. (1991). Psychopathology in mothers of children with failure-to-thrive. *Journal of Infant Mental Health, 12,* 55–64.

Skuse, D., Pickles, A., Wolke, D., & Reilly, S. (1994). Postnatal growth and mental development: Evidence for a sensitive period. *Journal of Child Psychology and Psychiatry, 35,* 521–546.

Sneddon, H., & Iwaniec, D. (2002). *Characteristics of failure-to-thrive cases* [Occasional paper]. Belfast, Northern Ireland: Institute of Child Care Research.

Spinner, M. R., & Siegel, I. (1987). Nonorganic failure-to-thrive. *Journal of Preventive Psychiatry, 3*(3), 279–297.

Wolfe, D. A. (1990). Preventing child abuse means enhancing family functioning. *Canada's Mental Health, 38,* 27–29.

Wolfe, D. A., & Wekerle, C. (1993). Treatment strategies for child physical abuse and neglect: A critical progress report. *Clinical Psychology Review, 13*(6), 473–500.

Wolke, D., Skuse, D., & Mathisen, B. (1990). Behavioral style in failure-to-thrive infants: A preliminary communication. *Journal of Pediatric Psychology, 15*(2), 237–254.

Woolston, J. (1984). Failure-to-thrive syndrome: The current challenge of diagnostic classification. In *Failure-to-Thrive Symposium* (pp. 70–85). Ontario Ministry of Community and Social Services, Ontario Center for the Prevention of Child Abuse.

Wynne, J. (1996). Failure-to-thrive: An introduction. *Child: Care, Health and Development, 22*(4), 219–221.

Chapter 9

CHEMICAL EXPOSURE

KATHLEEN H. DARBY, RODNEY A. ELLIS, KAREN M. SOWERS, AND
ANDREA K. McCARTER

This chapter provides an overview of issues concerning children's environmental health and its increasingly important role on the agendas of many governmental agencies and the general public. First, it examines the environmental health risks American children face today. Next, it reviews trends and prevention approaches that will help minimize the negative impact of chemical exposure on children's health and development. Finally, it considers future directions in policy and practice that can continue to protect children from environmental hazards and preventable childhood diseases.

Chemicals are a necessary evil in American society, being critical for health, the food supply, and general lifestyle. However, a cost is associated with their use. The average lifespan has been increased through the uses of synthetic chemicals (drugs). Yet the environment has become increasingly contaminated with toxic chemicals, resulting in increased frequency and quantity of exposure for most Americans. Hundreds of new chemicals are developed every year and released into the environment, in addition to the thousands already being released.

Individuals are exposed to chemicals by three methods: ingestion by the mouth, penetration through the skin, and inhalation into the lungs. The chemicals then move into the bloodstream and are distributed throughout the body. The body can metabolize the chemical and either store it or excrete it. The actual amount of chemical that enters the body determines the level of toxicity. Most often, the doses are low and do not pose a health risk, but the higher the dose and frequency, the greater the risk. Exposure to chemicals does not always result in toxic effects. The dose-response relationship is different for every chemical and for every individual. This variation takes into account the structure of the chemical, how it is metabolized, the rate it is absorbed into the body, and the amount that is excreted. An individual's susceptibility to a chemical exposure depends largely on age.

CHILDREN'S VULNERABILITY

The most vulnerable populations to chemical exposure are the very young and the very old. This chapter focuses on the former group, the very young. Infants are perhaps at greatest risk because they are particularly permeable and more readily absorb substances. A resting infant's air intake is double that of an adult per pound of body weight. Generally, children ingest more food, drink more water, and breathe more air relative to their weight and size than adults do and, as a result, may be exposed to more contaminants during important developmental stages. Because children are rapidly growing and developing, they are more vulnerable than adults to the adverse effects of environmental chemicals. Their biological systems, less developed than those of adults, are less able to repair damage caused by environmental toxicants and leave the organ dysfunctional. Children are also less efficient, especially in the first months after birth, at metabolizing and excreting hazardous chemicals, so smaller amounts of a potentially hazardous chemical can do irreversible health and developmental damage.

Behavioral characteristics of toddlers, such as hand-to-mouth activities and playing on the ground or crawling on carpets that have been treated with chemicals add yet another pathway through which children may be exposed to toxins. Their diets, which are less varied than those of adolescents or adults, may potentially expose them to concentrated pesticide residues. According to the U.S. Department of Agriculture (USDA), the average 1-year-old drinks 21 times more apple juice and eats two to seven times more grapes, bananas, pears, carrots, and broccoli than an adult. The simplest behavioral patterns of children put them at greater risk of exposure to environmental contaminants via the air, water, food, and soil.

Developmentally, children have several stages of rapid growth occurring from infancy to adolescence. Normal brain development begins in the uterus and continues throughout adolescence. A child's development is complex and has specific processes of physical growth. If this process is interrupted, the child is at high risk of suffering from a neurological disorder such as autism, aggression, dyslexia, and/or attention deficit/hyperactivity disorder. Because children have more future years of life than adults, they have more time to develop chronic diseases that may be triggered by early life exposures. Many diseases triggered by environmental toxicants require many years to develop. Toxic exposures early in life, such as in the prenatal and early postnatal periods, appear more likely to lead to disease than do exposures late in life. Children also spend as much as 50% more time outdoors than adults, often engaged in vigorous play. Because children take in more air per pound of body weight than adults and because their respiratory systems are still developing, they are increasing their risk of exposure to potential adverse effects from air pollutants.

SOCIAL VULNERABILITIES: CHILDREN LIVING IN POVERTY

All children risk chemical exposure through multiple media, but children living in poverty are at a disproportionate risk for exposure to environmental hazards. Seven percent of American children live in extreme poverty. African Americans and Hispanics are three times more likely to be in poverty (Young Children in Poverty Report [YCPR], 1999). This places the poor, particularly poor minorities, at substantially greater risk than children from homes of higher socioeconomic status. Children from impoverished homes have greater risk of acute illness, becoming sick twice as often as the general child population. They also get twice as many infections, suffer five times more intestinal problems, and have six times the number of speech impediments than other children (National Center on Family Homelessness, 1999). Given these conditions, the vulnerability that creates higher environmental risks for children is clear.

Children in poverty are subjected to a disproportionately large amount of pollution, pesticides, toxic metals, and other environmental stressors. Many subsidized housing facilities, where these children are most likely to live, were built before 1950 and almost certainly have lead paint on their walls or soil that is heavily contaminated with lead particles. Older houses and buildings also are more likely to have lead pipes that can contaminate drinking water. Experts have determined that many of the increases seen in childhood disease are linked to early contact with pesticides, poor indoor and outdoor air quality, lead, and contaminated water (Environment Protection Agency [EPA], 2003a). Nutritional deficiencies can also affect a child's risk from exposure to toxic substances. Malnutrition is a recognized consequence of poverty and affects children's immune systems, making them more vulnerable to pathogens in their environment (UNICEF, 1998).

Little research has been done on environmental stressors such as municipal solid waste facilities, hazardous waste landfills, and toxic waste dumps, chemical emissions from industrial parks, and on-the-job hazards in low-income communities. These neighborhoods are at higher risk than the general public because they lack the organizational and financial resources to successfully oppose the locations of facilities and industries that release toxic chemicals in or near their neighborhoods. It is possible that some of the multigenerational problems often seen in this population arc a result, at least in part, of ongoing exposure to environmental contamination.

ENVIRONMENTAL RACISM: MINORITY CHILDREN LIVING NEAR HAZARDOUS WASTE SITES

The literature makes it clear that children are at risk for harm from chemical exposure because of their unique growth and developmental patterns, small size, multiple pathways of exposure, and diet. The literature also makes it clear that poverty compounds these issues. In addition, research has identified a strong correlation among race, ethnicity, and geographical locations of toxic waste sites. Some experts have referred to this phenomenon as *environmental racism,* referring to the intentional placement of hazardous waste sites, landfills, incinerators, and polluting industries in communities inhabited predominantly by African Americans, Hispanics, Native Americans, Asians, migrant farm workers, and the working poor.

The Agency for Toxic Substances and Disease Registry (ATSDR) estimates three to four million American children live within one mile of at least one hazardous waste site. African Americans are significantly more likely than Whites to live within a mile of an uncontrolled hazardous waste site (74% versus 54%) or a polluting industrial facility (73% versus 50%). Minority children in low-income populations experience higher than average exposures to selected air pollutants, hazardous facilities, contaminated fish, and agricultural pesticides (ATSDR, 1997b).

ENVIRONMENTAL CONTAMINANTS

It is not possible in a single chapter to effectively discuss the tens of thousands of potentially toxic substances released in the environment or to evaluate their individual and combined effects on American children. It is possible to provide an overview of several contaminants that can be considered a twentieth-century environmental problem created by human activities and urban growth, which illustrates the nature of the danger of chemical poisoning faced by children in modern society.

As recently as 60 years ago, comparatively few environmental chemicals were known to have an adverse health effect on children. Knowledge about toxicity remains low. A National Academy of Sciences study found that 78% of frequently used commercial chemicals had never undergone minimal toxicity testing (Environmental Defense Fund, 1997). As human exposure to synthetic chemicals in the environment has risen, so has childhood cancer. The following examples make this reality clear.

Indoor/Outdoor Pollutants

Several pollutants are common in the immediate environments of many children, particularly for those from lower income and minority families. These pollutants include lead, various indoor and outdoor air pollutants, a variety of land contaminants, and toxins in municipal water.

Lead is the greatest environmental health risk to young children, especially under the age of 6. Lead levels accumulate in the body, and lead has reached toxic levels for 1.7 million children below the age of 5 (Centers for Disease Control and Prevention [CDC], 1991). High levels of lead in a child's blood have been linked to learning disabilities, reduced IQ, behavioral problems, and attention disorders. Lead poisoning is discussed in greater depth in a later section of this chapter.

Air pollutants are a second common source of contamination for children. Childhood illnesses associated with indoor and outdoor air pollution are increased bronchitis, pneumonia, and asthma; decreased lung functioning; and increased cases of chronic cough and ear infections. Air pollution is often thought of as an outdoor phenomenon, but the EPA estimates that indoor air pollution may be at least two to five times higher than levels found outdoors (EPA, 2003a).

Some of the most common indoor pollutants are carbon monoxide, formaldehydes (VOCs), pesticides, heavy metals, and tobacco smoke. Indoor pollutants are either generated by occupants or associated with building materials, appliances, tobacco smoke, and cleaning supplies. Poor ventilation can cause indoor pollutants to intensify through concentration. Over the past decade, the U.S. Environmental Protection Agency has consistently ranked indoor air pollution among the top five health care risks to children and the general public (EPA, 2003a).

Carbon monoxide (CO) is an odorless and colorless gas and is, therefore, difficult to detect. Exposure to carbon monoxide reduces the blood's capacity to carry oxygen, thereby decreasing oxygen to tissues and organs such as the heart. Prolonged exposure is lethal, even at very low levels. Health problems from nonlethal doses may include fatigue, frequent headaches, nausea, dizziness, and vomiting.

Volatile organic compounds (VOCs) are another form of dangerous air pollutant. Many VOCs, such as formaldehyde, are found in modern building materials and home furnishings, cleaning supplies, and paints. Formaldehyde is a reactive chemical and an irritant to eyes, nasal pathways, lungs, and skin and is classified as a potential carcinogen.

Several chemical products substances are regularly used in many homes with little regard to their potential toxicity. They may also exist in the home because of application in the surrounding environment. Pesticides are such a substance. Children are exposed to pesticides through use in the home, agricultural and commercial applications in areas surrounding the home, and through the ingestion of pesticide residue on foods or in water. Pesticides include herbicides, fungicides, insecticides, and rodenticides. A 1993 National Academy of Sciences report stated that pesticides may interfere with physiological processes of children, including the immune, respiratory, and neurological systems (National Research Council, 1993). Today, one of every six American children suffers from a neurological disorder such as autism, aggression, dyslexia, and attention deficit/hyperactivity disorder, and rates of diagnosis are rising at alarming rates (Mount Sinai School of Medicine, 2002).

The CDC estimates that 43% of children between the ages of 2 months and 11 years live in homes where at least one family member smokes. Environmental tobacco smoke (ETS), commonly known as *second-hand smoke,* is a complex mixture of carbon monoxide, nicotine tars, formaldehyde, and cyanide. Exposure to these toxins may cause illnesses such as bronchitis, pneumonia, and respiratory and ear infections. Exposed children are more susceptible to lung cancer, heart disease, and cataracts than are other children (American Academy of Pediatrics [AAP], 2002). Asthma is more prevalent in children who are exposed to frequent second-hand smoke, and respiratory illnesses increase by 50% in children under the age of 2 years old (Asthma and Allergy Foundation [AAFA], 2002).

Outdoor pollutants are a substantial risk to children because they spend 50% more time outdoors than adults. The six primary outdoor pollutants are ozone, particulate matter, carbon monoxide, lead, nitrogen dioxide, and sulfur dioxide (EPA, Office of Air and Radiation, 2001). Ozone, the most pervasive outdoor pollutant in the United States, is produced when hydrocarbons and nitrogen oxides are emitted from motor vehicles and VOCs react to the sun. Ozone levels are at their highest in the summer months, when children are out of school and playing outdoors for long time periods. Ozone levels are especially high downwind from coal-burning power plants and industries and around major traffic arteries and interchanges. From 1991 to 1993, ozone levels in more than 104 cities or counties exceeded the National Ambient Air Quality Standard on four or more occasions (AAFA, 2002). Minority children are disproportionately represented in the areas with excessive ozone levels (CDC, 1995). Exposure to ozone is associated with increased asthma rates in children, as well as a reduction in lung functioning in many others (CDC, 1995). Particulate matter originates from many sources, especially the burning of fossil fuels in vehicle engines, furnaces, electricity production, and incinerators. Studies have shown that chronic exposure to particulates results in reduced pulmonary function and increased respiratory diseases and symptoms in children with asthma. The same studies suggest that chronic exposure to particulate matter may be associated with mortality in infants (Woodruff, Grillo, & Schoendorf, 1997). There has been a significant reduction in the public's exposure to lead since the ban on lead in gasoline. Lead continues to be released into the environment via lead smelters, incineration of lead batteries, and burning lead-committed waste oil. Another outdoor pollutant is nitrogen dioxide, which is produced when fuel is burned, especially in power plants. Nitrogen dioxide and similar nitrogen oxides are major contributors to the formation of ozone levels that can lead to health problems.

Both sulfur dioxides and nitrogen dioxides are associated with a variety of children's health effects, including decreased lung functioning, increased respiratory symptoms for children with asthma, and aggravation of existing cardiovascular diseases. Nitrogen dioxide is a major contributor to the formation of ground-level ozone.

Land Contaminations

About one in four American children live within four miles of a hazardous waste site, according to the Agency for Toxic Substances and Disease Registry (ATSDR, 2003). Three of every five Black and Hispanic Americans lived in communities with one or more toxic waste sites (Weintraub, 1994). In 1996, the EPA listed approximately 15,000 waste sites in the United States. The National Priorities List (NPL) is the EPA's listing of sites that have undergone preliminary assessment and site inspection to determine locations that pose immediate threat to persons living or working near the release. These sites are most in need of cleanup. Each of the states has at least one NPL on the basis of a hazardous ranking system, and approximately three to four million children under the age of 17 years live within one mile of an NPL site (Agency for Toxic Substances and Disease Registry [ATSDR], 2003). The substances most commonly released into the environment from uncontrolled hazardous waste sites are heavy metals and organic solvents that contaminate the air and the ground water. Children who live near hazardous waste sites may have greater exposure and greater potential for health risk than adults. Exposure to these chemicals at a young age can cause growth and developmental problems, such as learning disabilities, mental retardation, cerebral palsy, and hyperactive airways, as well as cancer (ATSDR, 1997b).

Facts about toxic exposures from hazardous waste sites and impacts on children include:

- Children exposed to trichloroethylene (TCE) in drinking water contaminated by 15 different hazardous waste sites reported an increase in speech and hearing impairments (ATSDR, 1997b).

- Newborn babies whose parents were exposed to TCE in drinking water supplies contaminated by hazardous waste had an increased rate of congenital defects (ATSDR, 1997b).

- Children exposed to lead from a smelter in Idaho showed reduced neurobehavioral and peripheral nerve function when tested as young adults 15 to 20 years later (ATSDR, 1997a).

- Children living near a municipal waste incinerator had a threefold increase in risk of lower respiratory tract infection (ATSDR, 1997b).

- Race was the most significant variable associated with the location of hazardous waste sites (ATSDR, 1997a).

- The portion of minority children living in communities with existing incinerators is 89% higher than the national average (ATSDR, 1997a).

Many of these sites have been abandoned; they cover large geographical areas and harbor complex mixtures of waste. The majority (65% to 70%) of uncontrolled hazardous waste sites in the United States are waste storage/treatment facilities (including landfills) or former industrial properties (ATSDR, 1997b). Other groups of hazardous wastes sites are associated with the federal government, such as military facilities, nuclear energy complexes, and medical waste (medwaste) incinerators. Medwaste incinerators produce more dioxin than all paper mill boilers, industrial furnaces and boilers, cars and trucks, hazardous waste incinerators, and coal and oil burning power plants combined. Dioxin is one of the most toxic chemicals known. The U.S. EPA, in a September 1994 report, described dioxin as a serious public health threat, comparable to the impact DDT had on public health in the 1960s. The EPA further reported that there appears to be no safe level of exposure to dioxin, but dioxin and dioxin-like chemicals have been found in the general U.S. population. The EPA report also confirmed that dioxin is a cancer hazard to people and can cause severe immune system damage and developmental problems.

Toxins in Municipal Water

A main source of exposure to toxins for children is through the skin. An early study showed that an average of 64% of the total dose of waterborne contaminants is absorbed through the skin (Brown, Bishop, & Rowan, 1984). Children are particularly at risk for dermal absorption because of the increased time they may spend in a bath. Waterborne contaminants in tap water can include a range of chlorides to a multitude of chemicals, depending on the water source and chemicals added to the water during treatment (EPA, 2003a).

Millions of American children drink tap water that may be contaminated with toxic chemicals such as lead, arsenic, pesticides, VOCs, radioactive materials, and herbicides. Many of these toxins have been linked to the development of childhood cancers. Ground water becomes contaminated through industrial processes and discharges from manufacturing facilities, leaks from hazardous waste sites, and dumps. Nitrates are found in drinking water as a result of chemical fertilizers that leach into the ground water. Ingesting small amounts of nitrate is not harmful, but large amounts are toxic to infants and cause oxygen depletion in the body. Children are also exposed to waterborne contaminates by eating contaminated fish or swallowing water while swimming in contaminated water.

One of the most interesting and troubling issues in chemical exposure is the common practice of the fluoridation of drinking water. For more than 40 years, fluoride has been included in drinking water to help teeth resist decay. Before fluoridation, studies showed that a 12-year-old child would have eight permanent teeth affected by decay; by the 1990s, because of the added fluoride, this had dropped to fewer than two. Studies over the past 40 years have indicated that the practice of adding fluoride to public drinking water was safe, economical, and beneficial. Advocates of water fluoridation include health and science professionals nationwide. Other experts, however, are critical of the practice. Some studies have questioned the dental benefits of fluoridation and have cited already high levels of fluoride delivered through food, beverages, and the environment as detrimental to health. Opponents to fluoridation claim fluoride is linked to a host of health problems, among them bone fractures, cancer, neurological damage, learning disabilities, thyroid disease, and lower IQs in children.

BODY BURDENS

Body burdens are the amount of chemicals, both naturally occurring and manmade, that are present in our bodies at any given time. Unfortunately, few chemicals have received sufficient testing to determine their short- and long-term effect on humans. Body burdens are a measure of the levels of chemicals in the body but cannot determine the source(s) of exposure (Environmental Working Group [EWG], 2003).

Lead in the Blood

Lead as a toxic threat was introduced in an earlier section of this chapter. Its prominence as a body burden warrants further discussion here. Lead is found in the air, drinking water, rivers, lakes, oceans, dust, and soil. It is also found in the animals and plants we eat. Lead is accumulative, building up in the body over time. Inhaling or ingesting lead can be highly toxic to young children. Lead is the number one environmental health risk to children, especially for those under the age of 6. According to the CDC data, lead poisoning affects as many as 1.7 million children age 5 and under. Many children face multiple and repeated exposures through their developmental years. Exposure may begin in their mother's womb. Later, lead may be ingested through breast milk, foods, and contaminated water. The environmental conditions described earlier in this chapter provide further exposure.

Lead in drinking water is not the predominant source of lead poisoning, but it can increase total lead exposure, particularly the exposure of infants who drink baby formulas and juices mixed with water. On average, about 10% to 20% of a child's total exposure might come from drinking water. Infants who are fed formula could get 40% to 60% of their lead intake from water. CDC has released studies over the past 15 years that show levels of lead in children have been decreasing. This downward trend is partly due to bans on residential paints, gasoline, and solder used for food cans and water pipes. Still, about 900,000 American children between the ages of 1 and 5 years are believed to have blood levels equal to or greater than acceptable levels (CDC, 1999).

On entering the body, lead travels through the blood, to the soft tissues such as the liver, kidneys, lungs, brains, spleen, muscles, and heart. After several weeks, it enters the bones and teeth. Approximately 73% of the lead found in children is stored in their bones (ATSDR, 1997a). Lead may stay in the bones for decades, or it could reenter the bloodstream and affect organs. Most adults expel lead through waste within two to three weeks after exposure, but a child is capable of expelling only 32% of consumed lead. The primary target for lead is the nervous system for both adults and children.

High levels of lead in a child's blood have been linked to learning disabilities, reduced IQ, and behavioral and attention disorders. The United States Census Bureau estimated that one of six children in the United States will suffer from one or more developmental, learning, or behavioral problems because of lead exposure (Augustine-Reeves, 1995). As for other environmental toxins, the effects of exposure to lead are particularly prominent among minorities. Studies have linked lead poisoning and delinquent behavior (Augustine-Reeves, 1995). For example, a study of 987 African American youths (487 males and 500 females) concluded that lead poisoning in the male participants was the most significant predictor of disciplinary problems (Environmental Health Watch [EHW], 2002a). African American children are five times more likely to experience high blood lead levels (BLL) than Caucasian children. Even though the nation has seen a dramatic decline in children's average BLL, for poor and minority children living in deteriorated housing, the rates remain at epidemic levels (EHW, 2002a).

For many years, researchers knew that lead was poisonous at high dosages, but recent studies have shown that young children experience physical and mental developmental damage at lower levels than previously thought. As a result, the exposure levels once considered acceptable have been lowered. Whereas some effects of lead poisoning may diminish if exposure is reduced, others are irreversible.

Mercury in Blood

Mercury constitutes a second important body burden for many persons. Like lead, young children are more sensitive to mercury than adults. According to the EPA, more than 1.6 million women and children were at risk for mercury poisoning in 1999. Like lead, mercury can be highly toxic even in extremely small amounts. Mercury is a natural heavy metal found in the earth's crust. It is used in the medical field, which represents 20% of the mercury found in solid waste systems throughout America (EHW, 2003b). The U.S. EPA estimates that every year, the United States emits more than 150 tons of mercury into the air.

Methyl mercury and metallic mercury vapors are most harmful to children because they can cause permanent brain damage. Metallic mercury is used to produce batteries, chlorine gas, and thermometers and was formerly used to produce dental fillings. Thimerosal, an organic form of mercury, is a preservative in some vaccines, prescriptions, and over-the-counter medicines. Certain types of fish are known to be hazardous because of mercury contamination. The Food and Drug Administration (FDA) has advised that young children not eat shark, swordfish, king mackerel, and tilefish because they may contain high levels of methyl mercury. A child's nervous system is very sensitive to all forms of mercury, especially methyl mercury and metallic mercury. Exposure to high levels of metallic, inorganic, or organic mercury can permanently damage the brain, kidneys, and developing fetus.

Cotinine in Blood

Cotinine, a by-product of nicotine, is an important health risk for children who are exposed to environmental tobacco smoke. Nicotine and cotinine are almost never present in the metabolic systems of those who have not been exposed to tobacco smoke. In fact, smoking by parents is the predominant determinant of their child's cotinine levels (David & Lucie Packard Foundation, 1994). Levels in infants and young children tend to increase with the levels of parental smoking, particularly when the mother is a smoker.

Infants and children under the age of 6 years old are at higher risk for harm from environmental tobacco smoke than are older children or adults (EPA, 2003b). Cotinine can easily be measured in either the child's saliva or urine. A study conducted by the CDC (1991) found that children with high or moderate levels of cotinine are more likely to have moderate or severe asthma. Cotinine is also linked to respiratory infections, bronchitis, pneumonia, middle ear infections/disease, decreased lung function, and sudden infant death syndrome. Although involuntary tobacco smoke has not been linked directly to asthma, there is strong evidence that it worsens the symptoms associated with asthma.

In 1992, the U.S. EPA classified environmental tobacco smoke as a Class A carcinogen. The EPA estimates that involuntary tobacco smoke is responsible for 150,000 to 300,000 lower respiratory tract infections in infants and children under the age of 18 months (EPA, 2003a). These childhood infections result in approximately 7,500 to 15,000 hospitalizations annually (AAP, 2002). From 1988 to 1991, 85% of adults tested for cotinine had detectable levels compared to 1999 to 2000 where the detectable levels ranged from 50% to 75% (Mannino, Moorman, Kingsley, Rose, & Repace, 2001). The decrease is attributed to the ban on public smoking. Children showed far less improvement during the same period; in fact, children had twice the levels of cotinine than nonsmoking adults.

CHILDHOOD ILLNESSES

American children live in a complex environment where new technology is constantly developing and new synthetic chemicals are being produced. Currently, tens of thousands of chemicals are allowed in the United States, and little is known about their effects on children, much less the animal and human population as a whole. Exposure to many environmental toxins is now known to cause permanent damage to children's current and future health (Goldstein, 1992). Despite efforts to decrease hazardous chemicals through new regulations and standards, children continue to be exposed to large quantities of toxic substances. Trends in childhood illnesses indicate that environmental contaminants play a role in many of the illnesses (Goldstein, 1992).

Respiratory Disease

Air pollutants have an adverse effect on children's respiratory development and functioning. Respiratory diseases cause moderate to serious limitations in children's activities; missed school days; increased physician and emergency visits; and asthma, bronchitis, and upper respiratory infections. In 2001, 8.7%

(6.3 million) of all children in America had asthma. Asthma is increasing in the United States, and researchers look to genetic and environmental factors to explain the significant increase. Asthma is a chronic respiratory disease that is characterized by episodes of coughing, wheezing, breathlessness, and chest tightness. Researchers believe that common air pollutants, such as emissions from cars, incinerators, chemical plants and refineries, fine airborne particulates, and smog exacerbate or may contribute to causing asthma. Children suffering from asthma are particularly sensitive to outdoor air pollutants, such as ozone, particulate matter, and sulfur dioxide (Fauroux, Sampil, Quenel, & Lemoullec, 2000). Researchers have noted that asthma has become the leading cause of children's hospital admissions among children living in large urban areas such as New York and Los Angeles. In 1990 alone, asthma was estimated to cost the nation $6 billion in health care expenditures (Bogo, 2001). The percentage of children with asthma differs by race/ethnicity and family income. Children from lower income homes are more likely than others to experience asthma and to have asthma attacks (EPA, 2003b).

Childhood Cancers

Typical childhood cancers differ from those of adults. Adults experience more lung, colon, breast, prostate, and pancreas cancer. Children most often experience cancers that attack the white blood cells, brain, bone, kidneys, lymphatic system, and the nervous system. When children are first diagnosed with cancer, more than 80% are found to be in advanced stages as opposed to 20% for adults (National Childhood Cancer Foundation [NCCF], 2003). Childhood cancer causes more deaths than any factor, other than injuries and accidents, among children 1 to 19 years of age (Reis, Smith, Gurney, & Linet, 1999). The National Cancer Institute shows that cancer rates are highest among infants, decline until age 9, and then rise as a child ages.

There is strong evidence that paternal and, particularly, maternal exposure to environmental contaminants contributes to an increased frequency of some childhood cancers (Reis et al., 1999). Overall, childhood cancers were on the rise between 1973 and 1994 as humans were increasingly exposed to synthetic chemicals in the environment (Reis, 1997).

Neurodevelopmental Disorders

There is an epidemic of learning, developmental, and behavioral disabilities among children today. Certain environmental contaminants are known to contribute to overall rates of neurodevelopmental disorders in children by affecting the brain and nervous system. Childhood exposure to lead and PCBs has contributed to learning disabilities such as reduced intelligence and cognitive development, attention deficit/hyperactivity disorder, and increased risk of anti-social and delinquent behavior (Bellinger, Leviton, & Waternaux, 1987).

PREVENTION AND INTERVENTION

Effective prevention and intervention must involve a comprehensive approach that considers all three levels of the at-risk individual or family's environment: micro, mezzo, and macro. Particularly in lower socioeconomic communities where multiple risk exposures are likely to compound individual effects, prevention and intervention activities must incorporate a broad and thorough response.

The Micro Level: Promoting Strategies That Protect Children and Families

Several strategies can be employed to protect children and families from environmental chemical hazards. The nature of the strategies requires that they be used by individuals in their own homes. Because many persons at risk for exposure to these toxins are unaware of their presence and have little knowledge about how to deal with them, a three-step process is necessary to implement the intervention: (1) awareness, (2) education, and (3) preparation.

Awareness

The first step of the intervention involves making the at-risk persons aware that the problem exists. There is often little awareness among the general public about the problem of environmental toxins. There is even less awareness in the lower income communities in which the problem is worst. Successful intervention at the micro level requires the implementation of some macro strategies. A comprehensive approach designates a specific number or percentage of households to be reached and advertises awareness-raising presentations at a variety of readily accessible sites (such as recreational centers, churches, and schools) in the community. Fliers and educational brochures should be prepared and circulated. For homes with transportation or mobility issues, in-home educational meetings should be arranged. Block watches, parent-teacher associations, or similar organizations active in the community should be accessed, both as methods of advertising and as potential sites for awareness-raising presentations.

Education

Education involves informing community members about the dangers of specific chemicals and the techniques they can use to protect themselves and their families from exposure. In some situations, it may be preferable to combine awareness-raising with education. In others, separate meetings might be more effective. The education portion should include information about known or possible sources of contaminants as well as strategies for protecting against them. The EPA's Office of Children's Health Protection (OCHP, 2003) offers the following list of protective strategies:

Help Children Breathe Easier
- Don't smoke and don't let others smoke in your home or car.
- Keep your home as clean as possible. Dust, mold, certain household pests, secondhand smoke, and pet dander can trigger asthma attacks and allergies.
- Limit outdoor activity on ozone alert days when air pollution is especially harmful.
- Walk, use bicycles, join or form carpools, and take public transportation.
- Limit motor vehicle idling.
- Avoid open burning.

Protect Children from Lead Poisoning
- Get kids tested for lead by their doctor or health care provider.
- Test your home for lead paint hazards if it was built before 1978.
- Wash children's hands before they eat; wash bottles, pacifiers, and toys often.
- Wash floors and windowsills to protect kids from dust and peeling paint contaminated with lead, especially in older homes.
- Run the cold water for at least 30 seconds to flush lead from pipes.

Keep Pesticides and Other Toxic Chemicals Away from Children
- Store food and trash in closed containers to keep pests from coming into your home.
- Use baits and traps when you can; place baits and traps where kids can't get them.
- Read product labels and follow directions.
- Store pesticides and toxic chemicals where kids can't reach them. Never put them in other containers that kids can mistake for food or drink.

- Keep children, toys, and pets away when pesticides are applied; don't let them play in fields, orchards, and gardens after pesticides have been used for at least the time recommended on the pesticide label.
- Wash fruits and vegetables under running water before eating; peel them before eating, when possible.

Protect Children from Carbon Monoxide (CO) Poisoning

- Have fuel-burning appliances, furnace flues, and chimneys checked once a year.
- Never use gas ovens or burners for heat; never use barbecues or grills indoors or in the garage.
- Never sleep in rooms with unvented gas or kerosene space heaters.
- Don't run cars or lawnmowers in the garage.
- Install in sleeping areas a CO alarm that meets UL, IAS, or Canadian standards.

Protect Children from Contaminated Fish and Polluted Water

- Be alert for local fish advisories and beach closings. Contact your local health department for additional information.
- Take used motor oil to a recycling center; properly dispose of toxic household chemicals.
- Learn what's in your drinking water. Call your local public water supplier for annual drinking water quality reports; have private drinking water wells tested annually by a certified laboratory. Call (800) 426-4791 or contact www.epa.gov/safewater for help.

Keep Children and Mercury Apart

- Eat a balanced diet, but avoid fish with high levels of mercury.
- Replace mercury thermometers with digital thermometers.
- Don't let kids handle or play with mercury.
- Never heat or burn mercury.
- Contact your state or local health or environment department if mercury is spilled. Never vacuum a spill.

Preparation

Preparation involves helping community members obtain the resources necessary to implement in-home interventions. For example, some may need money to have fuel-burning appliances inspected. Others may need a locking cabinet in which to store chemicals or cleaning devices and supplies to remove toxic substances that are already present. A comprehensive intervention provides all the resources, expertise, and equipment needed by members of the community to facilitate the micro-level interventions in their own homes.

Mezzo and Macro Levels: Combating Toxic Exposure on a Broader Scale

Several initiatives to address chemical exposure at the mezzo and macro levels are already underway. At the federal, state, and local levels, a network of policy and agencies exist to monitor and intervene in environmental issues. Unfortunately, the agencies are a patchwork in which the members often communicate rarely or poorly. This fragmented system is void of the necessary collaboration to understand and react to local environmental health concerns. In an attempt to facilitate collaboration in April 1997, President Clinton signed an Executive Order, Protection of Children from Environmental Health Risks and Safety Risks, charging agencies to consider special environmental risks to children. His order, in part, was intended to improve communication and collaborative efforts within the system.

An exhaustive discussion of the agencies charged with protecting children from environmental toxins is not possible in a single chapter. The following examples are offered for illustrative purposes.

In August 1998, The National Institute of Environmental Health Sciences (NIEHS) and the U.S. EPA established Centers for Children's Environmental Health and Disease Prevention Research sites throughout the nation. These sites exist to conduct multidisciplinary basic and applied research in combination with community-based research projects on environmental threats to children's health. The research findings will be used to create local public policies and meet communities' specific needs to address environmental contributions to children's health. The goal of these local centers is to coordinate local programming by incorporating exposure assessments and health effects research to develop risk management and health prevention strategies. Specific areas of research include respiratory diseases, neurodevelopment and neurobehavior, childhood cancers, and birth defects.

The overarching aims of the Centers for Children's Environmental Health and Disease Prevention Research are:

- To provide for multidisciplinary interactions among basic, clinical, and behavioral scientists as a means of establishing outstanding, state-of-the-art research programs addressing environmental contributions to children's health and diseases

- To support a coordinated program of research/prevention centers pursuing high-quality research in environmental aspects of children's diseases, with the ultimate goal of facilitating and accelerating translation of basic science knowledge into clinical applications or intervention strategies that can be used to reduce the incidence of environmentally related childhood diseases

- To develop fully coordinated programs that incorporate exposure assessment and health effects research with development and validation of risk management and health prevention strategies

- To establish a national network that fosters communication, innovation, and research excellence, with the ultimate goal of reducing the burden of morbidity among children as a result of exposure to harmful environmental agents

In September 1998, centers were established at the following eight institutes:

1. The University of Southern California is developing a better understanding of how host susceptibility and environmental exposures contribute to children's respiratory disease. This research will provide health and environmental officials with a variety of useful intervention tools.

2. The University of California at Berkeley is quantifying exposure of children to pesticides in agricultural areas of California and will determine the impacts of these exposures on growth and development. They will work with the farm worker community to investigate approaches for reducing these exposures.

3. The University of Washington is investigating biochemical, molecular, and exposure mechanisms that define children's susceptibility to pesticides. This center will implement research and intervention projects among children of farm workers in the Yakima Valley of Washington State.

4. The University of Iowa is studying causes of airway disease in children from rural communities. They hope to gain a better understanding of such diseases and develop a multiple component intervention approach for reducing these diseases.

5. The University of Michigan is investigating childhood asthma and conducting assessments that will lead to neighborhood and household interventions to reduce risks. This research will fill critical gaps in our knowledge of environmental factors contributing to pediatric asthma.

6. Johns Hopkins University is examining how exposures to environmental pollutants and allergens relate to asthma and other lung diseases in children living in the inner city of Baltimore. They will search for new ways to reduce asthma in children exposed to environmental pollutants.

7. Mt. Sinai School of Medicine is studying risks in inner-city children to multiple known and potential neurodevelopmental toxicants. These exposures include pesticides and lead in their homes and dietary sources of polychlorinated biphenyls. The center will partner with community groups in East Harlem to study effects of integrated pesticide management and dietary modification on the health of children.

8. Columbia University is undertaking a comprehensive community-based assessment of environmental risks to African American and Latino infants and children. Researchers in the center will study the health consequences of residential sources of pollution and the ability of inadequate nutritional status to exacerbate impacts of environmental toxicants. Scientists work closely with community members to advance society's understanding of how environmental agents affect children's health. As the program grows and research findings lead to new and improved policies and practices, children's exposures to environmental pollutants and childhood illnesses and diseases will be reduced.

POLICY AND PRACTICE

This section provides a brief overview of policies and practices in the pediatric environmental health arena at the federal level. The federal government develops regulations and recommendations to protect public health. Regulations can be enforced by law when necessary. Federal agencies that develop regulations for toxic substances include the EPA, the Occupational Safety and Health Administration (OSHA), and the FDA. Federal agencies that develop recommendations for toxic substances include the Agency for Toxic Substance and Disease Registry (ATSDR) and the National Institute of Occupational Safety and Health (NIOSH).

In 1992, the National Institute of Environmental Health (NIEHS) helped to establish the first national network on this issue, the Children's Environmental Health Network (CEHN). The CEHN's mission is to promote a healthy environment and protect the fetus and the child from environmental hazards. The NIEHS and the CEHN collaborated in sponsoring the first national workshop on pediatric environmental health research in 1993. From this relationship came several reports that helped the CEHN to develop recommendations that could be used as a guide in reviewing existing policies. In March 1994, the following recommendations were made to the federal government:

1. Adopt a public health, preventive approach to environmental exposure, which protects the most vulnerable subsets of populations. Set standards regulating air, food, water, and homes.
2. Children must be incorporated into the risk assessment process.
3. Federal legislation, regulation, and agency mandate should undergo immediate review to identify where children are not taken into account.
4. A federal interagency workgroup should be convened to coordinate policies and activities concerning pediatric environmental health.
5. Community participation must be an essential part of policy development.
6. An international approach to pediatric environmental health should be adopted.

In 1970, the Clean Air Act was passed mandating that quality standards be set by federal regulatory agencies at levels that would protect "the most vulnerable members of society" (Landrigan & Carlson, 1995). Two other laws that specifically protect children against environmental hazards were enacted in 1996: the Food Quality Protection Act and the Safe Drinking Water Act. Other important initiatives taken to protect children during the 1990s were:

- The Executive Order issued by President Clinton focused on reducing environmental health and safety risks to children.
- The Agency for Toxic Substances and Disease Registry (ATSDR) launched a Child Health Initiative in April 1996 to emphasize policies and projects that promote the health of infants, children, and youth.
- In September 1996, the EPA issued a report, "Environmental Health Threats to Children," which included an ambitious national agenda to protect children's health from environmental threats. To assist in implementing this agenda, the agency has created an Office of Children's Health Protection (OCHP).
- The US Department of Health and Human Services (HHS) Environmental Health Policy Committee (EHPC), which coordinates HHS environmental health policy, created a Subcommittee on the Public Health Approach to Children and the Environment in December 1996.
- The National Center for Environmental Health (NCEH), part of the CDC, developed a healthy homes and communities project to address environmental

health problems such as childhood lead poisoning, hypothermia, infectious diseases, and injuries through a coordinated and comprehensive program.

The U.S. EPA's 2000 to 2005 strategic plan (2003a) outlines long-term goals over a five-year period proposing updated quality standards for clean air, clean and safe water, safe food, preventing pollution, and better waste management and emergency response. A number of the objectives in the 2000 to 2005 strategic plan are related to children's vulnerability to environmental health risks.

FUTURE DIRECTIONS

Federal agencies, researchers, scientists, and health care practitioners have repeatedly voiced concern about the absence of a system for collection and dissemination of national data on environmental toxins. Much of the data collection and monitoring is conducted at the state level, and many of these states do not adequately monitor environmental contaminants. The data that is being captured at the state level generally does not include settings where children spend a majority of their time: homes, schools, and playgrounds. The lack and inconsistency of data pertaining to childhood illnesses may prevent scientists from determining the role environmental contaminants may play in the prevalence of some childhood diseases. No national data is available for a number of childhood diseases. In The Pew Environmental Health Commission, third report (2001, January), the Commission charged that the nation faces an environmental health gap because fewer than nine states currently track developmental disabilities such as mental retardation and cerebral palsy, and more than half of the states have no ongoing tracking and monitoring of asthma. Although the country tracks more than 50 infectious diseases, the Commission found almost no national monitoring of chronic diseases.

The Commission proposes a Nationwide Health Tracking Network to identify and track environmental hazards to public health and the incidence of chronic diseases such as asthma, cancer, and various forms of birth defects. The Nationwide Health Tracking Network would involve a network of local, state, federal, and public health prevention programs based at community levels.

The five core components of the Network are:

1. Nationwide baseline tracking of priority diseases such as asthma, birth defects, cancers, and neurological disease such as Alzheimer's, multiple sclerosis, and Parkinson's disease, as well as priority exposure such as PCBs, dioxin, mercury, lead, pesticides, and water and air contaminations

2. Monitoring of immediate health crises such as heavy metal and pesticide poisonings to trigger early action against hazards

3. Establishing pilot programs to allow 20 different regional and state initiatives to investigate local environmental health priorities

4. Developing a federal, state, and local rapid response capability to investigate clusters, outbreaks, and emerging threats

5. Supporting community interests and scientific research to further health tracking efforts

The Nationwide Health Tracking Network will provide an early warning system to alert the public about potentially hazardous contaminants; identify populations at high risk; examine health concerns at the local, state, and federal levels; recognize environmental factors; begin to establish prevention strategies; and provide citizens with a right to know about the health status of their communities (Pew Environmental Health Commission, 2001).

CONCLUSION

The problem of the presence and proliferation of environmental toxins and their effect on children is alarming and compelling. This problem is particularly severe among minority populations and the poor. Interventions are both necessary and available for micro, mezzo, and macro levels. Indeed, both agencies and policies are in place to direct interventions, but lack of coordination and collaboration hinders their efforts. A coordinated response is needed that (1) provides awareness, education, and preparation at the individual and family level; (2) creates active, organized education, monitoring, and enforcement activities among agencies at the local, state, and federal levels; and (3) pursues proactive policy analysis, advocacy, and action.

REFERENCES

Agency for Toxic Substances and Disease Registry. (1997a, August). *Public Health Statement for Lead* [CAS #12709-98-7].

Agency for Toxic Substances and Disease Registry. (1997b). Healthy children—Toxic environments [Report of the Child Health Workgroup to the Board of Scientific Counselors]. Available from http://www.atsdr.cdc.gov/child/chw497.html.

Agency for Toxic Substances and Disease Registry. (2003). Final FY 2002 performance report for the Agency for Toxic Substances and Disease Registry. Available from http://www.atsdr.cdc.gov/performanceplan/performanceplan.html.

American Academy of Pediatrics. (2002). Just the facts: Environmental tobacco smoke. Available from http://www.aap.org/mrt/factsets.htm.

Asthma and Allergy Foundation. (2002). What is asthma? Available from http://www.aafa.org/templ/display.cfm?id=2&sub=25.

Augustine-Reeves, P. (1995, July). *Consumer reports: How to find out* (Vol. 60, p. 469). New Haven, CT: Yale University, Teachers Institute.

Bellinger, D. C., Leviton, A., & Waternaux, C. (1987). Longitudinal analyses of prenatal and postnatal lead exposure and early cognitive development. *New England Journal of Medicine, 316*(17), 1037–1043.

Bogo, J. (2001, October). Children at risk: Widespread chemical exposure threatens our most vulnerable population. *E Magazine.* Available from http://www.emagazine.com/september-october_2001/0901feat1.html.

Brown, H. S., Bishop, D. R., & Rowan, C. A. (1984). Wholly water, toxic hazards in the bath and shower. *American Journal of Public Health, 74*(5), 479–484.

Centers for Disease Control and Prevention. (1995). Populations at risk from air pollution in the United States. *Morbidity and Mortality Weekly Report, 44,* 309–312.

Centers for Disease Control and Prevention. (1999). *Report to Congress on worker's home contamination study.* (DHHS Publication No. 95-123). Available from http://www.cdc.gov/niosh/95-123.html.

David and Lucie Packard Foundation. (1994). *The future of children: Involuntary exposure to environmental tobacco smoke* (Vol. 4, no. 3). Los Altos, CA: Author.

Environmental Defense Fund. (1997). *Toxic ignorance: The continuing absence of basic health testing for top-selling chemicals in the United States.* Available from http://www.environmentaldefense.org/documents/243_toxicignorance%2Epdf.

Environmental Health Watch. (2002a). *Childhood lead poisoning, down but not out.* Available from http://www.ehw.org/Lead/LEAD_home3.htm.

Environmental Protection Agency. (2003a). *America's children and the environment: Measures of contaminants, body burdens, and illnesses* (2nd ed.). Washington, DC: Author.

Environmental Protection Agency. (2003b). *Tips to protect children from environmental risks.* Washington, DC: Author.

Environmental Working Group. (2003). *The power of information: What's in my body? What environmental contaminants are inside your or around you today?* Available from http://www.ewg.org/reports/bodyburden/usertest/index.php.

Fauroux, B. M., Sampil, P., Quenel, P., & Lemoullec, Y. (2000). Ozone: A trigger for hospital pediatric asthma emergency room visits. *Pediatric Pulmonology, 30*(1), 41–46.

Goldstein, G. W. (1992, June). Neurologic concepts of lead poisoning in children. *Pediatric Annals, 21*(6), 384–388.

Landrigan, P. J., & Carlson, J. (1995, Summer/Fall). The future of children: Critical issues for children and youths. *Environmental Policy and Children's Health, 5,* 43.

Mannino, D. M., Moorman, J. E., Kingsley, B., Rose, D., & Repace, J. (2001). Health effects related to environmental tobacco smoke exposure in children in the United

States: Data from the Third National Health and Nutrition Examination Survey. *Archives of Pediatrics and Adolescent Medicine, 155*(1), 36–41.

Mount Sinai School of Medicine. (2002). *Neurotoxins and the health of children.* New York: Center for Children's Health and the Environment.

National Center for Children in Poverty. (1999). Young children in poverty: A statistical update, 1999 edition. Available from http://www.nccp.org/media/fmc94-text.pdf.

National Childhood Cancer Foundation. (2003). *Childhood cancer is different.* Available from www.nccf.org http://www.nccf.org/ childhoodcancer/ different.asp.

National Research Council. (1993). *Pesticides in the diets of infants and children.* Washington, DC: National Academy Press.

Pew Environmental Health Commission. (2001, January). *Strengthening our public health defense against environmental threats* [Transition report to the new administration]. Baltimore: Johns Hopkins School of Public Health.

Reis, L. (1997). *SEER Cancer Statistics Review, 1973–1994* (NIH Publication No. 97-2789). Bethesda, MD: National Cancer Institute.

Reis, L. A., Smith, M. A., Gurney, J. G., & Linet, M. (1999). *Cancer incidence and survival among children and adolescents* (NIH Publication No. 99–4649). Bethesda, MD: National Institutes of Health.

UNICEF. (1998). *The state of the world's children: Summary.* Available from http://www.unicef.org/sowc03/.

Weintraub, I. (1994). *Fighting environmental racism: A selected annotated bibliography.* Available from http://www.mapcruzin.com/EI/ejigc.html.

Woodruff, T. J., Grillo, J., & Schoendorf, K. C. (1997). The relationship between selected cases of postneonatal infant mortality and particulate air pollution in the United States. *Environmental Health Perspective, 105*(6), 608–612.

Chapter 10

SUBSTANCE ABUSE

CRAIG WINSTON LeCROY AND JOYCE ELIZABETH MANN

In today's society, drugs and alcohol play an increasing role as young people transition into adulthood. Because the prevalence rate of drug and alcohol use is so high, many experts now consider alcohol and drug experimentation a normal part of growing up. Unfortunately, such experimentation and subsequent use can lead to potentially harmful results. Furthermore, drug and alcohol use has also been implicated in a variety of other risk behaviors such as unwanted pregnancy, automobile accidents, crime, and school dropout. Thus, the prevention of alcohol and drug use has become a major goal of parents, educators, health promoters, law enforcement officers, and society at large.

This chapter begins with an update on the prevalence, incidence, and frequency of substance use and is followed by a discussion of risk and protective factors that have become a primary conceptualization for planning substance abuse prevention programs. The bulk of the chapter presents information on effective programs targeted to three different populations: universal, selective, and indicated, and discusses research-based best practices for school, family, and community approaches to prevention. The chapter presents a broad sweep of what is known about effective work in the substance use field.

PREVALENCE AND INCIDENCE

Estimates of the prevalence and incidence of substance use among American youth are reported in annual surveys conducted by the University of Michigan and the National Institute on Drug Abuse (NIDA). The former summarizes patterns of lifetime, past month, and current use reported by 8th-, 10th-, and 12th-grade students, whereas the National Household Survey of Drug Abuse (NHSDA) assesses use, incidence, and age of initiation among youth ages 12 to 17. Despite the scope of these surveys, it is likely that they underestimate the severity of substance use among young people: They fail to assess drug use among students who are chronic absentees or dropouts; they fail to collect data on homeless, transient, or runaway youth; and they rely on youth self-report. In addition, though these surveys extensively assess drug use among youth ages 12 to 18, there is little study of use among younger children.

Still, what is known is cause for concern. Among American youth, more than 80% have experimented with drugs before graduating from high school. Most often, this drug use begins with alcohol, tobacco, or marijuana. Alarmingly, many youth try alcohol or cigarettes before the age of 12, and by the eighth grade, more than one-third have tried an illicit drug (Johnston, O'Malley, & Bachman, 2002). A summary of key findings from the most recent national surveys is presented in Table 10.1.

Table 10.1   Prevalence of Substance Use

Substance	Findings
Cigarettes	By high school graduation, 61% have smoked cigarettes.
	12% of 8th graders are current smokers; 20% of 10th graders are current smokers.
	Among youth ages 12 to 17, 24% smoked a pack or more daily.
Alcohol	By high school graduation, 80% have tried alcohol.
	Current use measured in the past 30 days is 20% of 8th graders, 39% for 10th graders, and 50% for 12th graders.
	Past 30 days having been drunk was 21% for 10th graders and 33% for 12th graders.
	Among youth 12 to 17, more than 10% are binge drinkers.
Illicit drug use	By high school graduation, 54% have used illicit drugs—mostly marijuana followed by ecstasy, cocaine, and LSD.
	Current use measured in the past 30 days is 12% of 8th graders, 23% of 10th graders, and 26% of 12th graders.
	Among youth who used cigarettes, past 30-day use was 43%; among youth who were heavy drinkers, past 30-day use was 66%.
	Inhalant use in the last 30 days was 4%; ecstasy was 2%.

Note: Based on *The Monitoring the Future National Survey Results on Adolescent Drug Use: Overview of Key Findings, 2001,* by L. D. Johnston, P. M. O'Malley, and J. G. Bachman, 2002, Bethesda, MD: National Institute on Drug Abuse and "Summary of findings from the 2000 National Household Survey of Drug Abuse " by Substance Abuse and Mental Health Services Administration, 2001, Rockville, MD: Author.

Despite the widespread use of drugs among youth, decreases are being observed in the incidence of substance use among youth. According to data from the Substance Abuse and Mental Health Services Administration (SAMSHA; 2001) between 1998 and 1999, rates of new use of marijuana and cigarettes decreased from 44 to 31 per 1,000 potential new users. The number of young people initiating cocaine, heroin, inhalant, and smokeless tobacco use remained unchanged from the previous year. Even so, reports indicate that youth are initiating drug use at younger ages. For example, in 1965, the age of first marijuana use was 20; in recent years, it has averaged 16 to 17 years of age.

Current trends in child and adolescent substance use are contradictory. Between 2000 and 2001, increases in the use of steroids at 12th grade and ecstasy at all grade levels were noted. In the same period, tobacco, heroin, and cocaine use showed evidence of decline. Use of alcohol and marijuana remained unchanged.

Viewed in the context of the past decade, these data support various trends in drug use among youth: Cigarette and tobacco use is declining; alcohol use is remaining steady with only binge drinking decreasing in frequency; marijuana use, after increasing, remains stable; ecstasy may be replacing cocaine. For example, teen use of ecstasy increased across all age groups in 2001, continuing a trend that began in 1998 with a sharp rise in use. In contrast, the use of heroin, which attained peak levels in the late 1990s, shows continued decline among 8th graders and initial decline among 10th and 12th graders. Also significant is the continued decrease in prevalence and frequency of cigarette smoking across age groups. In the 1990s, cigarette smoking steadily increased and peaked in 1996. Since then, cigarette smoking has diminished by 42%, 30%, and 19% among 8th, 10th, and 12th graders, respectively (Johnston et al., 2002). Unfortunately, trends in alcohol use have not demonstrated such dramatic improvement.

Survey data from the University of Michigan study (Johnston et al., 2002) highlight differences relative to several variables. In general, age differences in drug-use patterns indicate that prevalence increases with increasing age. Of concern is evidence that the age of initiating substance use is decreasing, particularly for marijuana and alcohol. Males are more likely than females to use illicit drugs frequently and engage in heavy drinking; however, females are as likely as males to smoke. The Northeast and West have the highest proportions of students using any illicit drug, whereas the South has the lowest; the South and the West continue to have slightly lower rates of drinking among youth. In addition, substance use is somewhat more prevalent in rural than metropolitan areas. Differences associated with ethnicity soundly dispute popular assumptions about youth drug use. Across all age groups, African American youth have substantially lower rates of substance use than Whites for alcohol, cigarettes, and any illicit drug. Hispanics' rates of use tend to fall between these two groups. Only for crack and ecstasy did Hispanics' use exceed that of Whites and African Americans; for heroin, Hispanic use is equivalent to rates of White teens (Johnston et al., 2002). Data on Native American substance abuse indicates alcohol use equivalent to Whites (SAMSHA, 2001). In addition, differences in use by socioeconomic status are small, with declines in use occurring among students from more educated families.

RISK FACTORS

Risk and protective factors have become a central feature in the design and planning of substance abuse prevention programs. Under what conditions is substance abuse most likely? This question points to critical risk factors that may inform the development of effective interventions. Under what conditions is substance use least likely? This question points to critical protective factors that may inform the development of effective interventions. Risk and protective factors are the individual factors or environmental conditions that research has found to be related to the development of substance use.

In the past, disappointing results emerged from efforts to inform youth about the legal and social consequences of substance use. Today, efforts are more focused by directing interventions to the risk factors associated with more likely substance use (Center for Substance Abuse Prevention [CSAP], 2002). The CSAP (1999) developed a framework referred to as the *web of influence* and includes five primary risk and protective factors related to substance use: society-related factors, family environment, community environment, school-related factors, and peer associations.

We have learned more about how to prevent substance use through the study of risk factors than protective factors. However, the notion that protective factors might help reduce and prevent substance use is an important concept. Indeed, the exclusive focus on risk factors led some to refer to the efforts as the "damage model" (Wolin & Wolin, 1995), directing increased efforts to examine both risk and protective factors. And although it is often stated that protective factors are not a mirror image of risk factors (e.g., dysfunctional family versus healthy family), the distinction is difficult to make (see Newcomb & Felix-Ortiz, 1992). The conclusion from a CSAP review (Brounstein & Zweig, 1999, p. 7) is noteworthy: "The literature on protective factors and resilience is more diffuse than that for risk factors, and there is less clarity about which factors are most important in the prevention of substance use." Nonetheless, most programs emphasize both risk and protective factors.

Researchers have studied numerous variables for their ability to predict adolescent substance use, and much agreement exists about the import of various factors in predicting both use and later abuse (Dryfoos, 1990). Generally, those variables associated with initiation of substance use are also those associated with abuse; however, some researchers contend that adolescent drug use is a normal developmental process (Kandel, 1980) highly associated with social influences whereas drug abuse is associated with psychological factors (Newcomb & Bentler, 1990).

The risk factors associated with drug use have been categorized and conceptualized in various ways. Two conceptual models often referred to are CSAP's internal and external variables (see Table 10.2) and Hawkins and colleagues' (Hawkins, Catalano, & Miller, 1992) contextual and interpersonal influences (see Table 10.3).

Research indicates that various combinations of the risk factors impact drug use in adolescents. Moreover, the risk of drug use is directly proportional to the number of risk factors present (Bry, McKeon, & Pandina, 1982). In addition, the

Table 10.2 External and Internal Risk and Protection

External Risk and Protection

Family supervision	Setting rules, monitoring whereabouts, parental concern about friends and activities
School prevention environment	Classroom environment is conducive to prevention messages, positive personal development
Community protection environment	Community activities, learning opportunities
Neighborhood risk	Neighborhood disorganization, public substance use, crimes

Internal Risk and Protection

Family bonding	Positive orientation toward home and family, pride, enjoyment in the family environment
School bonding	Connectedness to school
Self-efficacy	Confidence in engaging in meaningful tasks, belief in one's success
Self-control	Degree of control over one's actions and impulses
Self-confidence	Ability to get along with others, contribution to the social group, trust and respect by peers

Source: From *Understanding Risk, Protection, and Substance Use among High-Risk Youth* by the Center for Substance Abuse Prevention, 2002, Rockville, MD: U.S. Department of Health and Human Services.

Table 10.3   Contextual and Interpersonal Influences

Social and cultural risk factors	Laws and societal norms favorable to drug use, availability of drugs, economic deprivation, neighborhood disorganization
Family risk factors	Parent and sibling modeling of drug use, parent norms and attitudes accepting of drug use, lack of closeness in the family, conflict in the family
Peer risk factors	Early and persistent behavior problems, academic failure, low commitment to school, alienation and rebelliousness, favorable attitudes toward drug use, early onset of drug use, genetic predisposition to drug use, physiological susceptibility to the effects of drugs

Source: From "Risk and Protective Factors for Alcohol and Other Drug Problems in Adolescence and Early Adulthood: Implications for Substance Abuse Problems," by J. D. Hawkins, R. F. Catalano, and J. Y. Miller, 1992, *Psychological Bulletin, 112,* p. 64–105.

influence of the risk factors varies depending on the developmental stage of the child. For example, poor parental attachment and nurturing poses a greater risk in childhood than in adolescence.

PREVENTIVE INTERVENTIONS: UNIVERSAL, SELECTIVE, AND INDICATED

Although no single definition of prevention exists, *substance abuse prevention* generally refers to interventions whose goal is to delay, deter, or eliminate the onset of substance use or abuse. Prevention also refers to efforts that seek to reduce harm associated with drug use, a goal that has seen increased emphasis although it remains somewhat controversial (Marlatt, Baer, & Larimer, 1995). A variety of approaches reflecting different theoretical orientations have been used in the prevention of youth substance abuse, including knowledge-based, affective, social skills, family skills training, and peer refusal skills approaches, and a number of these have been identified as effective (Paglia & Room, 1998).

In 1994, a framework for classifying preventive interventions based on R. Gordon's (1987) model of disease prevention was proposed (Institute of Medicine, 1994). The Institute of Medicine framework categorized preventive interventions along a risk continuum according to the vulnerability of the target audience. Three types of prevention approaches reflecting increasing degrees of risk were defined. Universal prevention strategies are directed toward all youth, regardless of individual risk, and are designed to prevent precursors of drug use and initiation. Selective prevention strategies are directed toward youth who are at greater risk of substance use due to environmental or biological risks (i.e., low income, parents who abuse substances). Indicated prevention strategies are directed toward youth who are already using drugs or displaying precursors of drug use, such as thrill seeking, aggression, or conduct disorders.

The demand for effective, empirically supported prevention programs has driven considerable research to determine what works. Typically, much of the research has been conducted by recipients of federal grants. Effective preventive interventions have been identified through conducting a meta-analysis, critical literature reviews, as well as reports from federal agencies such as the Center for Substance Abuse Prevention (CSAP) and the National Institute on Drug Abuse (NIDA). From this research, general principles of effective prevention as well as guidelines for selecting and implementing effective programs have been gleaned (Gardner, & Brounstein, 2001; Gardner, Brounstein, & Stone, 2001a, 2001b; Hansen, 1997; Kumpfer, 1997).

A discussion of effective universal, selective, and indicated preventive interventions follows. The categories of intervention are defined in terms of population and risk factors targeted for selection. Features critical to the intervention are given, along with their advantages and disadvantages. Approaches typical to the particular intervention and examples of effective prevention programs are identified. For this chapter, *effective programs* are defined as research-based programs that demonstrate positive outcome in reducing risk factors for drug use or actual drug use. Programs were selected for inclusion based on a review of current research including meta-analyses (Foxcroft, Ireland, Lister-Sharp, Lowe, & Breen, 2002; Tobler, 1997; Tobler & Stratton, 1997; Tobler et al., 2000), critical literature reviews (Jansen, 1997; Norman, Turner, Zunz, & Stillson, 1997; Paglia & Room, 1998), as well as reports from the CSAP (Brounstein & Zweig, 1999; CSAP, 2000; Gardner et al., 2001b) and the NIDA (Kumpfer & Baxley, 1997; Kumpfer, Williams, & Baxley, 1997; NIDA, 1997; Sorenson, Phil, & Baxley, 1997). Programs identified as effective are by no means inclusive of all effective programs. This section concludes by discussing research relevant to all universal, selective, and indicated intervention efforts and by identifying general principles of program effectiveness.

Universal Preventive Interventions

Universal prevention is defined as an intervention delivered to general populations of youth and families to increase all members' resistance to drug use or abuse. Universal programs are delivered to large groups without any prior screening of individuals' risk for substance abuse based on the assumption that all members of the population are at risk for substance abuse and will benefit from the prevention program (Institute of Medicine, 1994). As to youth substance abuse prevention, populations targeted by universal prevention programs might include teenagers, elementary-age children, families, or communities. Identification of normal periods of stress and vulnerability can help universal prevention programs have more impact (LeCroy & Daley, 2001). For example, selecting a target population for substance abuse prevention programming is best directed at early adolescents before the likely onset of problem substance use occurs.

The purpose of universal prevention programs is to deter the onset of substance abuse by providing all individuals in the population with the information and skills necessary to prevent drug use. By increasing the drug-use resistance skills of everyone in the target population, universal programs benefit persons at risk even though their individual risk factors are not specifically addressed. In addition, because a general population is targeted for intervention, universal prevention programs avoid problems associated with labeling.

Rather than focus on individual risk factors, universal prevention programs target environmental risks such as community values, school support, and society norms. In doing so, some individual and subgroup risks may be addressed. For example, among junior high students who are recipients of a universal prevention effort targeting school values, some may be children of parents who use substances, some may come from stable homes, and some may have low self-esteem. Yet, regardless of their individual risk, they could all benefit from universal prevention efforts. Examples of universal preventive interventions for drug abuse include substance abuse education for all children in a school district, media and public awareness campaigns, and school policy changes on drug-free zones.

Typically, universal prevention programs use mass media, television, and advertising campaigns to help establish norms against drug use and increase awareness about the problems. Increasing efforts are being made to use norm-based interventions where part of the media campaign is to accurately identify the norms in the population. Too often, young people assume that everyone is using drugs when, in fact, a small portion of the population may be engaging in the behavior (Radecki & Jaccard, 1995). The goal is to educate youth and adults about the prevailing norm in the population because their behavior may be influenced by an inaccurate perception. Universal prevention programs have the greatest potential for success when they involve all factors that influence youth, including the school, family, and community.

One significant advantage of universal prevention strategies is that they are often less expensive per participant because costs are spread over a large group.

Schools provide an optimum delivery setting because they reach all students regardless of risk. Disadvantages of universal prevention strategies include the reality that at-risk youth frequently do not benefit from universal approaches because of high rates of absence or dropout. In addition, unless the program is designed with the population in mind, it may be too generic to meet the specific needs of the recipients or may not include enough dosage to have the intended effect.

Universal prevention programs tend to focus drug abuse prevention efforts in the school, the family, or the community. School-based prevention programs have included cognitive and affective approaches, social influence approaches, personal and social skills training, as well as school climate change approaches. Family-based prevention programs target parents and youth through parent education, parent involvement programs, and parent and family skills training. Public awareness campaigns, information clearinghouses, community coalitions, and health policy change represent community-based universal interventions. A NIDA publication provides discussion of efforts in each of these areas (Sorenson et al., 1997). A list of types of universal prevention programs with examples of each is presented in Table 10.4.

Findings from research on universal prevention approaches suggest that several factors should be considered in the design and implementation of universal prevention programs to be most effective. Included are the long-term effects of the prevention effort, the need for identification of appropriate targets for the intervention, the comprehensiveness of the approach, as well as the nature of risk factors targeted. Research suggests that universal prevention programs are most effective when they are comprehensive and target the school, family, and community simultaneously. Further, multicomponent efforts have the greatest chance of success when implemented in the broader community (Pentz, 1995). The success of universal prevention strategies is also maximized when programs focus on the broader influences on youth and when they are specific to the cultural, language, and demographic characteristics of the population being targeted. Unfortunately, the long-term effects of universal prevention programs are difficult to detect because their effectiveness hinges on delaying first-time substance use. In addition, few long-term evaluations of universal programs have been conducted (Foxcroft et al., 2002).

Selective Preventive Intervention

Selective preventive interventions are designed to target subgroups of the population that are at greater risk for substance use than the general population. These subgroups are identified as *at risk* based on the presence of risk factors known to be associated with substance abuse. With respect to youth substance abuse,

Table 10.4 Universal Preventive Interventions

Type	Approach	Effective Program
School-based	Social influence	All Stars Program (Hansen, 1996)
		Alcohol Misuse Prevention Study (AMPS; Dielman et al., 1989)
		ATLAS (Goldberg et al., 2000)
		DARE to be You (Center for Substance Abuse Prevention, 1999)
		Project SMART delivered in Project STAR & I-STAR (Pentz, 1995)
		Seattle Social Development Project (Hawkins, Catalano, Morrison, et al., 1992)
	Personal/social skills training	Life Skills Training (Botvin, 1996)
	School climate change	Child Development Project (Battistich et al., 1996)
		Aban Aya Project (Flay, 1987)
		Project PATHE (Gottfredson, 1986)
		Project HIPATHE (Kumpfer et al., 1991)
	Mentoring	SMART Moves (Schinke & Cole, 1995)
		Across Ages (LoSciuto et al., 1996)
Family-focused programs	Parent education/training	Preparing for the Drug Free Years (Catalano et al., 1998)
		Positive Action (Flay & Ordway, 1999)
	Parent involvement	Parent Drug Education and Homework Involvement (Pentz et al., 1989)
	Parent skills	Incredible Years (Webster-Stratton, 1990)
	Family skills	STARS for Families (Werch, et al., 2000)
		Iowa Strengthening Families Program (Kumpfer et al., 1996)
		Strengthening Families Program (Kumpfer et al., 1996)
		Project Family (Spoth & Redmond, 1996)
	Family involvement	Adolescent Transitions Program (Dishion et al., 1996)
Community-based programs	Legal	Community Trials Project (Holder et al., 1997)
	Policy change	Communities Mobilizing for Change on Alcohol (Wagenaar et al., 2000)
	Coalitions	Communities That Care (Hawkins et al., 2002)
	Multicomponent	Midwestern Prevention Program (Pentz et al., 1989)
		Project Northland (Perry et al., 1996)
		Say Yes First (Zavela et al., 1997)
		Woodrock Youth Development Project (LoSciuto et al., 1997)

groups identified as at risk may be defined on the basis of age, family circumstance, income, or physical/sexual abuse history. In addition, groups at greater risk than the general population include children of alcoholics, students who have dropped out of school, youth from low-income neighborhoods, students transferred from other schools, or families with high mobility. Although each member of the targeted subgroup may not show evidence of individual risks, the program is delivered to the entire subgroup because the group as a whole is deemed at greater risk than the larger population.

The purpose of selective prevention is to deter and/or delay the onset of substance abuse by directly targeting and reducing identified risk factors and increasing protective factors found in the group. Groups may be targeted for selected intervention programs on the basis of various demographic, biological, psychosocial, and environmental risks including age, gender, and socioeconomic status; genetic predisposition, fetal damage in utero, hyperactivity, and attention deficit disorder; family dysfunction, lack of school bonding, or parental emotional disturbance; or factors such as community disorganization or neighborhood climate that supports drug use. Because groups are identified for selective prevention on the basis of risk vulnerabilities, the programs must target the group's specific risk and protective factors to be most effective.

Various types of selective prevention programs have been used to prevent and/or delay the onset of substance use in groups at risk for developing the problem. These approaches include psychoeducational and skills training activities, tutoring or mentoring programs, youth leadership programs, rites of passage programs, family strengthening approaches, and cultural competency training activities. General examples of selective prevention programs include special clubs and groups for children of alcoholics, rites of passage programs for at-risk males, or skills training programs for children of substance-abusing parents. Table 10.5 lists effective selective intervention programs. Frequently, these programs are implemented as pullout programs in school whereby students are pulled out of regular classroom activities to participate in the prevention program or as after-school programs. These programs may also be implemented in low-income neighborhoods, public housing communities, or in community agencies.

Because selective prevention programs target groups at increased risk of substance use, to be effective, they must be of longer duration and more intensive than universal programs. In addition, they must directly target those risk and protective factors characteristic of the particular subgroup. For example, a group targeted for selective prevention on the basis of biological risk needs interventions different from a group targeted on the basis of low-income status. Additionally, it is likely that booster sessions are needed to review skills and maintain effectiveness over time because participants present with increased risk.

Table 10.5   Selective Preventive Interventions

Type	Approach	Effective Program
School-based	Social influence	All Stars (Hansen, 1996)
		ATLAS (Goldberg et al., 2000)
		DARE to be You (Center for Substance Abuse Prevention, 1999)
		Project ALERT (Ellickson & Bell, 1990)
		Project SUCCESS (Richards-Colocino et al., 1996)
	Skills training	Seattle Social Development Project (Hawkins, Catalano, Morrison, et al., 1992)
	Personal/social skills	Opening Doors (Addiction Research Foundation, 1995)
	High-risk youth	Reconnecting Youth Program (Eggert et al., 1994)
		Resiliency Skills Training (Richardson, 1996)
	Mentor	Across Ages (LoSciuto et al., 1996)
Family-focused programs	Parent education/training	DARE to be You (Center for Substance Abuse Prevention, 1999)
	Family skills training	Family Effectiveness Training (Szapocznik, Santisteban, et al., 1989)
		Family and Schools Together (FAST; McDonald et al., 1991)
		Positive Action (Flay & Ordway, 1999)
		Safe Haven Program (Atkan et al., 1996)
		Strengthening Families Program (Kumpfer et al., 1991)
	Parents who receive methadone treatment	Focus on Families (Catalano et al., 1997)
	Family involvement	Adolescent Transitions Program (Dishion et al., 1996)
		Family Advocacy Network (FAN Club; St. Pierre et al., 1997)
		SUPER STARS (Emshoff et al., 1996)
	Parent education/family therapy	La Familia Fuerte (Gardner et al., 2001b)
	Home visits	Perry Preschool Project (Berrueta-Cement et al., 1985)
Community-based programs	Community building	Greater Alliance of Prevention Systems (Brounstein & Zweig, 1999)
		Creating Lasting Connections (Johnson et al., 1996)
	Youth clubs/youth centers	Stay SMART (Tierney et al., 1995)
		SMART Leaders (Tierney et al., 1995)
		Hispanic Youth Leadership Institute Program (Stoil & Hill, 1996)
	Alternative programs	Amazing Alternatives (Murray & Perry, 1985)

Because selective prevention programs are targeted to at-risk groups who are likely in need of preventive intervention, selective programs may be more efficient in their use of resources. In addition, because content of programs is tied to the needs of the group, program effectiveness is generally increased. However, because the criteria for defining the group's risk status can be too vague, a potential for stereotyping exists. For instance, groups defined by minority status are not homogeneous in terms of risk vulnerabilities and cultural strengths (African American students present with different risks than Native American students), and programs implemented without regard for specific group characteristics may be less effective.

Research demonstrates the effectiveness of selective interventive efforts (Goplerud, 1991; Lorion & Ross, 1992). Selective prevention programs that focus on skills training do improve youth's school, family, and peer-group functioning and may also reduce depression and increase self-esteem if implemented for a sufficient time period. The limited long-term evaluations of selective prevention efforts do indicate positive gains of participants over time (Berrueta-Cement, Schweinhart, Barnett, Epstein, & Weikart, 1985; Casto & Mastrepieri, 1986). Furthermore, selective approaches that focus on both youth and parents demonstrate greater effectiveness than approaches that target either in isolation. Evaluation of selective interventions have shown promise in reducing risk factors, but it is less clear how such interventions have influenced long-term substance use.

Indicated Preventive Interventions

Indicated preventive interventions are targeted to youth who already are using substances or are displaying signs of substance misuse. Indicated interventions are also targeted to youth who may not be using substances but who show evidence of other problems or disorders that increase their chances of developing a substance abuse problem, for example, depression or being suicidal. Individuals identified for indicated prevention programs show only signs of drug use and misuse and do not meet the diagnostic criteria for an identifiable substance abuse disorder.

Because individuals targeted for the program are often already experimenting with substances, the goal of indicated interventions is not the reduction of use or the delay of use. Rather, their purpose is to prevent the progression of use to abuse and/or reduce the severity of substance use. This approach is more similar to a harm-reduction approach than a universal preventive approach because goals include giving information and skills to reduce harm associated with substance use and to seek help for substance abuse problems, in addition to abstaining from illegal drug use. Individuals may be referred for indicated preventive programs by teachers, parents, school counselors, or the court system.

Individuals targeted for indicated prevention efforts may or may not be using substances, but by definition, they are exhibiting individual and personal risk factors including school failure, interpersonal social problems, delinquency, antisocial behaviors, and psychological difficulties such as depression or other affective disorders. Indicated prevention programs address individual risk factors including low self-esteem, conduct disorder, poor bonding with parents, and peer-related difficulties. Unlike universal prevention programs, indicated prevention efforts focus little attention on environmental risk factors such as community norms and values.

Indicated preventive interventions include programs for preschool and elementary children identified as having conduct disorder and substance abuse programs for high school students experiencing problems such as truancy, academic failure, depression, or suicidal ideation. Student assistance programs designed for students exhibiting behavioral and emotional problems are also examples of indicated interventions. Table 10.6 lists examples of indicated preventive intervention programs with demonstrated effectiveness.

Advantages of indicated prevention programs are similar to those of selective interventions because they directly target the individual's risk factors through intensive efforts and, in doing so, have the potential to be more effective than universal preventive approaches for at-risk individuals. Their disadvantage is that because the programs are more intensive, they require well-trained staff to administer the program. Thus, they may be more expensive to implement than either universal or selective approaches.

For indicated intervention programs to be maximally effective, they must be comprehensive, including the youth and family in preventive efforts (Kumpfer & Baxley, 1997). Multicomponent programs, therefore, are more effective than single interventive approaches. Programs directed toward individuals determined to be at risk must appropriately identify, target, and match the intervention to the presenting risks to be effective (NIDA, 1997).

Research Evaluations: Universal, Selective, and Indicated Approaches

Although universal, selective, and indicated preventive interventions are distinguished by their intended targets, all universal, selective, and indicated preventive efforts may be categorized as school, family, or community focused. In fact, research evaluating program effectiveness has often centered on the program focus

Table 10.6   Indicated Preventive Interventions

Type	Approach	Effective Program
School-based	Social influence/skills training	Project SUCCESS (Richards-Colocino et al., 1996)
		Anger Coping Program (Lochman & Wells, 1996)
		Coping Power Program (Lochman & Wells, 1996)
		I Can Problem Solve Program (Shure, 1992)
		Social Skills Training in the Fast Track Program (Bierman et al., 1996)
		Problem Solving Social Skills Training Intervention (Kazdin, 1995)
	Life skills/dropout prevention	Reconnecting Youth Program (Eggert et al., 1994)
		Personal Growth Class (Eggert et al., 1994)
	School climate change	Project HIPATE (Kumpfer et al., 1991)
	Support groups	Treatment Aftercare Support Groups (Kumpfer et al., 1991)
Family-focused programs	Parent education/skills training	Strengthening Families Program (Kumpfer, et al., 1996)
		Family Effectiveness Training (Szapocznik, Santisteban, et al., 1989)
		Family and Schools Together (FAST; McDonald et al., 1991)
		Fast Track Program (McMahon, et al., 1996)
	Family involvement	Adolescent Transitions Program (Dishion et al., 1996)
	Family therapy	Structural Family Therapy (Szapocznik, Kurtines, et al., 1989)
		Home-Based Functional Family Therapy (D. A. Gordon, 1994)
Community-based programs	Community building	Creating Lasting Connections (Johnson et al., 1996)
	Residential programs	Residential Student Assistance Programs (Morehouse & Tobler, 2000)
	Alternative programs	Amazing Alternatives (Murray & Perry, 1995)

(i.e., school, family, or community) rather than the population target. Therefore, it is appropriate to discuss research findings relative to school-based, family-focused, or community-focused efforts because they are applicable to all universal, selective, and indicated interventions and, where pertinent, to note findings specific to particular approaches.

School-Based Interventions

School-based programs have been the most commonly developed programs among universal, selective, and indicated prevention approaches. Typically, school-based programs have reflected knowledge-only approaches, affective approaches that appeal to moral values and norms, social influence or skills training approaches, as well as school climate change or mentoring approaches. Meta-analysis of school-based programs indicates that not all approaches are equally effective (Tobler, 1997; Tobler & Stratton, 1997; Tobler et al., 2000). Knowledge-oriented approaches, which teach students about the negative consequences of substance use, do result in increased knowledge, but fail to impact student behavior. As such, they are considered the least effective preventive strategy. Sadly, knowledge-oriented approaches such as Drug Abuse Resistance Education (DARE) continue to be widely implemented in schools even though they have been found to be ineffective (Clayton, Cattarello, & Johnstone, 1996; Foxcroft et al., 2002; Tobler & Stratton, 1997). Affective programs have also shown poor results, with few effects on students' substance use (Tobler, 1992). The most effective prevention programs implemented in schools are those that involve intensive social or life skills training and use a psychosocial approach to teach skills to counter pressure to use substances (Tobler, 1997).

Tobler (1997) found that successful school-based programs are characterized by appropriate content, interactive process, and small group size. Content must be developmentally age appropriate for the recipients, neither using scare tactics nor exaggerating the effects of drug use. The content should be delivered in an interactive process, including all participants, allowing youth to practice skills, receive feedback, and engage in interactions with others. Programs that are delivered in a teacher-directed didactic manner are less successful than programs that rely on peers in conjunction with teachers in a more interactive manner. Additionally, small group size has been associated with increased effectiveness.

Research further suggests that to be effective, school-based programs should be ongoing from early grades to high school and should incorporate booster sessions to maintain gains. This is particularly appropriate for selective intervention programs that target groups at risk by virtue of their group status. In addition, because early identification of at-risk youth is possible, selective interventions can be implemented as early as preschool. Regardless of intervention type, effective programs are targeted to the recipients, considering factors such as age, developmental needs, demographics, culture, and language. Specific risks and protective factors must be addressed by selective and indicated intervention efforts.

Unlike universal preventive approaches that are directed toward all students, issues of labeling are concerns for both selective and indicated prevention efforts. Some research indicates that labeling associated with intensive indicated approaches increases the probability of further deviance (Mechanic, 1978). Youth may learn more deviant behaviors through association with other youth engaged in deviant behavior. In addition, because of the relationship between substance use and other adolescent health problems (Jessor & Jessor, 1977), indicated interventions often consider the problem cluster in establishing desired outcomes.

Family-Based Intervention Efforts

Family-focused efforts are important components of universal, selective, and indicated interventions because they target risk factors associated with individuals and their families. Typically, programs directed toward families include parent education and skills training, parent involvement, parent support groups, family case management, home visits, and structured therapy approaches.

Research indicates that effective family prevention programs emphasize the development of parenting skills rather than the acquisition of information; thus, effective programs provide opportunities for parent-child participation in learning and practicing skills. Further, effective family intervention efforts focus on developing family communication skills through interactive processes, by using modeling, coaching, rehearsal, and role play.

Family skills training, in which the family participates in activities to improve communication and interaction, is considered the most effective selective prevention approach. Parent and family skills training often includes instruction in parenting, communication, coping skills, decision making, and reduction of stress and family conflict. Both selective and indicated family-based prevention programs include skills training, family therapy, and in-home family support approaches. Unlike universal family-based approaches, the most effective indicated family approaches involve in-home support to provide parents with services that meet their needs and family therapy to assist families in reducing negative behaviors and increase skills that lead to healthy interactions (NIDA, 1997). In particular, structured family therapy approaches seem to be the most effective approaches with families (Kumpfer, 1997).

In general, research supports that universal, selective, and indicated family interventions are most effective when they address risk and protective factors in the family domain (Kumpfer, Molgaard, & Spoth, 1996), are culturally sensitive to the participants (Kumpfer & Alvarado, 1995), emphasize client strengths, and are age and developmentally appropriate (Hawkins, Catalano, Morrison, et al., 1992). For family interventions to be maximally effective, they must be of sufficient duration and intensity to achieve goals (Kumpfer et al., 1996) and incorporate booster sessions to maintain these effects (Botvin, Schnike, Epstein, Diaz, & Botvin, 1995). Indicated family-based interventions, for example, may require 15 sessions or longer to achieve positive outcomes (Kumpfer et al., 1996).

A significant problem in the implementation of family-based programs is the issue of recruitment and retention of parents. Effective recruitment may require the use of incentives (Bry, Catalano, Kumpfer, Lochman, & Szapocznik, 1998). Retention may be improved by developing programs that are culturally sensitive (Kumpfer & Alvarado, 1995) and, especially in indicated programs, strengthening the connection between program participants (Cohen & Linton, 1995). In addition, delivering family-focused interventions in churches and community centers rather than in schools may facilitate participation because schools may not be welcoming for some parents or may not be as accessible to working parents (Kumpfer et al., 1996).

Community-Focused Interventions

Universal, selective, and indicated community-focused interventions are applied through the community, targeting families, schools, governmental institutions, the media, and community organizations. Typically, community-based efforts include public awareness campaigns, information clearinghouses, social and legal policy change efforts, community mobilization, development of coalitions and partnerships, as well as mentoring programs, youth groups and clubs, and alternative activities. Each of these strategies has its place in effective community-focused intervention. Mass media as well as legal and policy approaches (Paglia & Room, 1998) are effective in influencing community awareness and community norms. Community mobilization efforts are also effective in raising awareness about the problem of substance abuse and coordinating intervention services (Phillips & Springer, 1997). Alternative programs, such as youth groups and clubs, may not impact substance use directly but can provide participants with opportunities to develop personal capabilities as well as opportunities for prosocial interactions. Though alternative programs by themselves may not prevent substance use, in combination with other efforts, they may have a positive impact (Norman et al., 1997). Effective selective and indicated community-based approaches include an integration of alternative programs, mentoring and rites of passage programs, as well as skills training programs.

Generally, effective community-based interventions are most effective when they target the school, family, and community simultaneously. However, implementation of such programs is difficult. These multicomponent programs have the greatest likelihood of success when implemented in the broader community setting (Pentz, 1995). Phillips and Springer (1997) identify guiding principles for the implementation of community interventions.

General Principles of Effective Interventions

General principles of effective preventive interventions applicable to all universal, selective, and indicated preventive efforts have been identified by the CSAP (Gardner & Brounstein, 2001). These principles are categorized according to domain of influence in keeping with the CSAP *web of influence* model. (See the Center for Substance Abuse reports; Gardner & Brounstein, 2001; Gardner et al., 2001b.)

Health Canada (2001) has identified principles of effective substance use programs based on the evidence culled from scientific literature. The more fully reflected these principles are in a program, the greater likelihood for effectiveness. The authors also suggest that when professionals are considering adoption of a program or curriculum, these principles may be used in an assessment of the program's potential effectiveness. The principles are summarized in Table 10.7.

Table 10.7   Principles of Effective Programs

Build a strong framework.	Address protective factors, risk factors, and resiliency.
	Seek comprehensiveness.
	Ensure sufficient program duration and intensity.
Strive for accountability.	Base program on accurate information.
	Set clear and realistic goals.
	Monitor and evaluate the program.
	Address program sustainability from the beginning.
Understand and involve young people.	Account for the implications of adolescent psychosocial development.
	Recognize youth perceptions of substance use.
	Involve youth in program design and implementation.
Create an effective process.	Develop credible messages.
	Combine knowledge and skill development.
	Use an interactive group process.
	Give attention to teacher and leader qualities and training.

Source: From *Preventing Substance Abuse Problems among Young People: a Compendium of Best Practices,* by Health Canada, 2001, Ottawa, Ontario: Minister of Public Works and Governmental Services.

IMPLICATIONS FOR PRACTICE

Despite the identification of effective preventive interventions through rigorous evaluation and program analysis and despite the synthesis of principles of effective prevention gleaned from this research data, programs with unsubstantiated results continue to be implemented. Worse, programs identified as effective are implemented in such a way as to undermine their effectiveness. Research-based programs are not often replicated as they were piloted and tested because of the process of tailoring them for specific community, school, or family needs. Significant responsibility lies with practitioners, community leaders, and school district personnel not only to select programs demonstrated to be effective, but also to implement them with fidelity.

Guidelines for choosing a prevention program based on empirical research have been offered by Kumpfer and Baxley (1997). Effective prevention models and programs must be identified through examination of relevant literature reviews and program evaluation studies. Local data concerning the substance abuse problem must be gathered such that appropriate targets of intervention may be identified along with risk factors and other correlates of use. Prevention leaders must determine where to focus prevention efforts and ultimately determine if the community is receptive to preventive intervention.

Proper program implementation is a critical issue that can affect outcomes. Kumpfer (1997) provides guidelines for successful program implementation. Successful implementation requires that practitioners first assess target group readiness for the program and their desire for the program and that the program be delivered by well-trained and effective leaders. Empowering leadership styles are most effective, and personal qualities such as warmth, empathy, and genuineness are critical. Sufficient training involves direct experience with interactive methods (Tobler & Stratton, 1997). Successful program implementation also requires that goals, mission, and objectives be clearly defined with activities logically tied to them and that sufficient resources exist to implement the program, including incentives for participation with high-risk youth and their families. Interactive techniques rather than didactic lectures are most effective delivery methods (Tobler & Stratton, 1997). Ultimately, successful program implementation requires that program evaluation rely on feedback, as well as quality process and outcome evaluations.

DIRECTIONS FOR FUTURE RESEARCH

In this section, we focus on aspects of future research that are directly related to the use of science-based or evidence-based programs. The first direction for future research concerns obtaining a better understanding of the implementation of programs. Implementation is the primary consideration in understanding how evidence-based programs can lead to better outcomes under large-scale dissemination. Second, future research must look at standards for assessing evidence, and more efforts are needed to examine the limitations inherent in adopting an evidence-based perspective.

More research needs to examine the implementation process of evidence-based programs. For example, how much variation in program design can local implementation accommodate and still expect similar outcomes found in the original study? This question is difficult to answer because most studies have failed to discover how variations in implementation affect outcomes. Especially when there are modest effects, more analysis needs to be done to assess how implementation variation may affect results to allow for local implementation to be flexible in ways that might not compromise results. And it is important to recognize that evidence-based programs come from well-funded research studies that may look different from local implementation of such programs.

Such local studies are rarely examined in reviewing evidence because they rarely meet the methodological standards required to be *evidence based*. However, although randomized trials are the source of evidence and are excellent on internal validity, they often lack external validity. The lack of external validity may indeed become a critical issue when programs are touted as having the necessary evidence to be disseminated on a large-scale basis. More attention needs to be placed on the smaller implementations of evidence-based programs that can offer important data on how well an evidence-based program is doing when implemented at a local level. For example, LeCroy and Milligan Associates (2002) evaluated outcomes from Botvin's (1996) life skills training conducted at a local level and found mixed results not consistent with the original evidence presented on the program. Examination of multiple efforts to implement evidence-based programs may reap important conclusions about the real-world value the program has to offer.

The surge in evidence-based practice has also resulted in a proliferation of guidelines and lists of what works. However, there are few standards for assessing a program as effective, which can lead to a confusing set of principles and a contradictory set of programs deemed effective. CSAP (2002) has promoted its *effective practice principles* based on its work with the national cross-site evaluation of demonstration projects, the Cochrane Library (Foxcroft et al., 2002) has issued recommendations based on a thorough but extremely conservative assessment of effectiveness, and independent reviewers (e.g., Tobler et al., 2000) have conducted meta-analyses to derive effectiveness conclusions. Although it is heartening to have such attention paid to effectiveness, more attention needs to address barriers in promoting the use of such guidelines. Factors that need to be considered include extent of awareness of effectiveness guidelines, processes for teaching practitioners about the guidelines, and procedures for sorting out the various and confusing lists of guidelines. Evidence-based programs may lead to better outcomes, but if they aren't being used, their value is diminished.

In the mania to push evidence-based guidelines, important limitations of the evidence may be overlooked. For example, Botvin's life skills training program is routinely touted as one of the best evidence-based programs. However, recent criticism (Brown, 2001; Cohn, 2001; Gorman, 1998) has pointed to several concerns: The studies supporting the program have been produced only by Botvin, who benefits financially from the promotion of the program; the decreases in substance use far exceed any results from similar programs, raising questions about likely replications; and results may have been overadvocated because it appears that outcomes for alcohol use (the number one substance used by youth) have produced mixed results. In spite of the widespread acceptance of this program as science-based, many potentially serious questions remain. Advocates of evidence-based programs need to undertake a serious critique of how evidence is weighted and develop better models for assessing the confidence that can be placed on the evidence. With continued pursuit of better evidence, we can increase the outcomes obtained from our programs and rest more comfortably knowing that some impact has been obtained.

REFERENCES

Addiction Research Foundation. (1995). *Opening doors: A personal and social skills program.* Toronto, Ontario, Canada: Author.

Atkan, G., Kumpfer, K. L., & Turner, C. (1996). Effectiveness of a family skills training program for substance abuse prevention with inner city African American families. *Substance Use and Misuse, 31,* 157–175.

Battistich, V., Schaps, E., Watson, M., & Solomon, D. (1996). Prevention effects of the Child Development Project: Early findings from an ongoing multisite demonstration trial. *Journal of Adolescent Research, 11,* 6–11.

Berrueta-Cement, J. R., Schweinhart, L. J., Barnett, W. S., Epstein, A. S., & Weikart, D. P. (1985). *Changed lives: The effects of the Perry Preschool Program for youths through age 19.* Ypsilanti, MI: High/Schop Press.

Bierman, K. L., Greenberg, M. T., & the Conduct Problems Prevention Research Group. (1996). Social skills training in the Fast Track Program. In R. DeV. Peters & R. J. McMahon (Eds.), *Preventing childhood disorders, substance abuse and delinquency* (pp. 65–89). Thousand Oaks, CA: Sage.

Botvin, G. J. (1996). Substance abuse prevention through Life Skills Training. In R. DeV. Peters & R. J. McMahon (Eds.), *Preventing childhood disorders, substance abuse, and delinquency* (pp. 215–240). Thousand Oaks, CA: Sage.

Botvin, G. J., Schnike, S. P., Epstein, J. A., Diaz, T., & Botvin, E. M. (1995). Effectiveness of culturally focused and generic skills training approaches to alcohol and drug abuse prevention among minority adolescents: Two-year follow-up results. *Psychology of Addictive Behaviors, 9,* 183–194.

Brounstein, P. J., & Zweig, J. (1999). *Understanding substance abuse prevention. Toward the twenty-first century: A primer on effective programs* (DHHS Publication No. SMA 99–3301). Rockville, MD: U.S. Department of Health and Human Services.

Brown, J. (2001). Youth, drugs, and resilience in education. *Journal of Drug Education, 31,* 83–122.

Bry, B. H., Catalano, R. F., Kumpfer, K. L., Lochman, J. E., & Szapocznik, J. (1998). Scientific findings from family preventive intervention research. In R. S. Ashery, E. B. Robertson, & K. L. Kumpfer (Eds.), *Drug abuse prevention through family interventions* (NIDA Research Monograph 177, pp. 103–129). Rockville, MD: National Institute on Drug Abuse.

Bry, B. H., McKeon, P., & Pandina, R. J. (1982). Extent of drug use as a function of number of risk factors. *Journal of Abnormal Psychology, 91,* 273–279.

Casto, G., & Mastrepieri, M. A. (1986). The efficacy of early childhood programs: A meta-analysis. *Exceptional Children, 5,* 417–424.

Catalano, R. F., Haggerty, K. P., Gainey, R. R., & Hoppe, M. J. (1997). Reducing parental risk factors for children's substance misuse: Preliminary outcomes with opiate-addicted parents. *Substance Use and Misuse, 32,* 699–721.

Catalano, R. F., Kosterman, R., Haggerty, J., Hawkins, J. D., & Spoth, R. L. (1998). A universal intervention for the prevention of substance abuse: Preparing for the drug free years. In R. S. Ashery, E. B. Robertson, & K. L. Kumpfer (Eds.), *Drug abuse prevention through family interventions* (NIDA Research Monograph 177, pp. 130–159). Rockville, MD: National Institute on Drug Abuse.

Center for Substance Abuse Prevention. (2000). *Prevention works through community partnerships: Findings from SAMHSA/CSAP's national evaluation.* Rockville, MD: U.S. Department of Health and Human Services.

Center for Substance Abuse Prevention. (2002). *Understanding risk, protection, and substance use among high-risk youth* (DHHS Publication No. SMA 00–3375). Rockville, MD: U.S. Department of Health and Human Services.

Clayton, R. R., Cattarello, A. M., & Johnstone, B. M. (1996). The effectiveness of Drug Abuse Resistance Education (Project DARE): Five year follow-up results. *Preventive Medicine, 25,* 307–318.

Cohen, D. A., & Linton, K. L. P. (1995). Parent participation in an adolescent drug abuse prevention program. *Journal of Drug Education, 25,* 159–169.

Cohn, J. (2001, May 24). Drug education: The triumph of bad science. *Rolling Stone,* 18–19.

Dielman, T. E., Shope, J. T., Leech, S. L., & Butchart, A. T. (1989). Differential effectiveness of an elementary school-based alcohol misuse prevention program. *Journal of School Health, 59,* 255–263.

Dishion, T. J., Andrews, D. W., Kavanagh, K., & Soberman, L. H. (1996). Preventive interventions for high risk youth: The Adolescent Transitions Program. In R. DeV. Peters & R. J. McMahon (Eds.), *Preventing childhood disorders, substance abuse and delinquency* (pp. 184–214). Thousand Oaks, CA: Sage.

Dryfoos, J. G. (1990). *Adolescents at risk: Prevalence and prevention.* New York: Oxford University Press.

Eggert, L. L., Thompson, E. A., Herting, J. R., Nicholas, L. J., & Garii Dicker, B. (1994). Preventing adolescent drug abuse and high school drop-out through an intensive school-based social network development program. *American Journal of Health Promotion, 8,* 202–215.

Ellickson, P. L., & Bell, R. M. (1990). Drug prevention in junior high: A multisite longitudinal test. *Science, 247,* 1299–1305.

Emshoff, J., Avery, E., Raduka, G., Anderson, D. J., & Calvert, C. (1996). Findings from SUPER STARS: A health promotion program for families to enhance multiple protective factors. *Journal of Adolescent Research, 11*(1), 68–96.

Flay, B. R. (1987). Social psychological approaches to smoking prevention: Review and recommendations. *Advances in Health Education and Promotion, 2,* 121–180.

Flay, B. R., & Ordway, N. (1999). *Positive Action Program studies and evaluations 1978–1999: Evaluation of an integrated comprehensive model for improving school performance and reducing disciplinary problems.* Chicago: Health Research and Policy Centers.

Foxcroft, D. R., Ireland, D., Lister-Sharp, D. J., Lowe, G., & Breen, R. (2002). Primary prevention for alcohol misuse in young people (Cochrane Review). In *Cochrane Library* (Vol. 3). Oxford, England: Update Software.

Gardner, S. E., & Brounstein, P. J. (2001). *Principles of substance abuse prevention.* Center for Substance Abuse Prevention (DHHS Publication No. SMA 01-3507). Rockville, MD: U.S. Department of Health and Human Services, Center for Substance Abuse Prevention.

Gardner, S. E., Brounstein, P. J., & Stone, D. B. (2001a). *Promising and proven substance abuse prevention programs* (DHHS Publication No. SMA 01–3506). Rockville, MD: U.S. Department of Health and Human Services, Center for Substance Abuse Prevention.

Gardner, S. E., Brounstein, P. J., & Stone, D. B. (2001b). *Science-based substance abuse prevention: A guide* (DHHS Publication No. SMA 01–3505). Rockville, MD: U.S. Department of Health and Human Services, Center for Substance Abuse Prevention.

Goldberg, L., MacKinnon, D. P., Elliot, D. L., Moe, E. L., Clarke, G., & Cheong, J. (2000). The Adolescents Training and Learning to Avoid Steroids Program. *Archives of Pediatric and Adolescent Medicine, 154,* 332–338.

Goplerud, E. N. (1991). *Breaking new ground for youth at risk: Program summaries* (OSAP Technical Report 1, DHHS Publication No. ADM 91–1658). Washington, DC: U.S. Government Printing Office.

Gordon, D. A. (1994). *Home-based behavioral systems family therapy.* Athens: Ohio University, Department of Psychology.

Gordon, R. (1987). An operational classification of disease prevention. In J. A. Steinberg & M. M. Silverman (Eds.), *Preventing mental disorders: A research perspective* (pp. 20–26). Washington, DC: U.S. Government Printing Office.

Gorman, D. M. (1998). The irrelevance of evidence in the development of school-based drug prevention policy, 1986–1996. *Evaluation Review, 22*(1), 118–146.

Gottfredson, G. D. (1986). An empirical test of school-based environmental and individual interventions to reduce the risk of delinquent behavior. *Criminology, 24,* 705–731.

Hansen, W. B. (1996). Pilot results comparing the All Stars program with seventh grade, D.A.R.E: Pilot test integrity and mediating variable analysis. *Substance Use and Misuse, 31,* 1359–1377.

Hansen, W. B. (1997). Prevention programs: Factors that individually focused programs must address. In *Secretary's youth substance abuse prevention initiative: Resource papers* (pp. 53–66). Rockville, MD: Substance Abuse and Mental Health Services Administration.

Hawkins, J. D., Catalano, R. F., & Arthur, M. W. (2002). Promoting science-based prevention in communities. *Addictive Behaviors, 27,* 951–976.

Hawkins, J. D., Catalano, R. F., & Miller, J. Y. (1992). Risk and protective factors for alcohol and other drug problems in adolescence and early adulthood: Implications for substance abuse problems. *Psychological Bulletin, 112,* 64–105.

Hawkins, J. D., Catalano, R. F., Morrison, D. M., O'Donnell, J., Abbott, R. D., & Day, L. E. (1992). The Seattle Social Development Project: Effects of the first four years on protective factors and problem behaviors. In J. McCord & R. E. Tremblay (Eds.), *Preventing antisocial behavior in children: Intervention from birth through adolescence* (pp. 139–161). New York: Guilford Press.

Health Canada. (2001). *Preventing substance abuse problems among young people: A compendium of best practices.* Ottawa, Ontario: Minister of Public Works and Governmental Services.

Holder, H. D., Saltz, R. F., Grube, J. W., Voas, R. B., Gruenewald, P. J., & Treno, A. J. (1997). A community prevention trial to reduce alcohol-involved accidental injury and death: Overview. *Addiction, 92*(Suppl. 2), S155–S171.

Institute of Medicine. (1994). New directions in definitions. In P. J. Mrazek & R. J. Haggerty (Eds.), *Reducing risks for mental disorders: Frontiers for preventive intervention research.* Washington, DC: National Academy Press.

Jansen, M. A. (1997). *Prevention: What works—From research to practice: Scientifically based models of prevention.* Paper presentation.

Jessor, R., & Jessor, S. L. (1977). *Problem behavior and psychosocial development: A longitudinal study of youth.* New York: Academic Press.

Johnson, K., Strader, T., Berbaum, M., Bryant, D., Bucholtz, G., Collins, D., et al. (1996). Reducing alcohol and other drug use by strengthening community, family, and youth resiliency: An evaluation of the Creating Lasting Connections program. *Journal of Adolescent Research, 11,* 36–67.

Johnston, L. D., O'Malley, P. M., & Bachman, J. G. (2002). *The monitoring the future national survey results on adolescent drug use: Overview of key findings, 2001* (NIH Publication No. 02–5105). Bethesda, MD: National Institute on Drug Abuse.

Kandel, D. B. (1980). Drug and drinking behavior among youth. *Annual Review of Sociology, 6,* 235–285.

Kazdin, A. E. (1995). *Conduct disorders in childhood and adolescence* (2nd ed.). Thousand Oaks, CA: Sage.

Kumpfer, K. L. (1997). What works in the prevention of drug abuse: Individual, school, and family approaches. In *Secretary's youth substance abuse prevention initiative: Resource papers* (pp. 69–106). Rockville, MD: Substance Abuse and Mental Health Services Administration.

Kumpfer, K. L., & Alvarado, R. (1995). Strengthening families to prevent drug use in multiethnic youth. In G. Botvin, S. Schnike, & M. Orlandi (Eds.), *Drug abuse prevention with multiethnic youth* (pp. 255–294). Thousand Oaks, CA: Sage.

Kumpfer, K. L., & Baxley, G. B. (1997). *Drug abuse prevention: What works?* (NIH Publication No. 97–4110). Rockville, MD: National Institute on Drug Abuse.

Kumpfer, K. L., Molgaard, V., & Spoth, R. (1996). The Strengthening Families program for the prevention of delinquency and drug use. In R. DeV. Peters & R. J. McMahon (Eds.), *Preventing childhood disorders, substance abuse and delinquency* (pp. 241–267). Thousand Oaks, CA: Sage.

Kumpfer, K. L., Turner, C., & Alvarado, R. (1991). A community change model for school health promotion. *Journal of Health Education, 22,* 94–110.

Kumpfer, K. L., Williams, M. K., & Baxley, G. B. (1997). *Drug abuse prevention for at-risk groups* (NIH Publication No. 97–4114). Rockville, MD: National Institute on Drug Abuse.

LeCroy, C. W., & Dalcy, J. (2001). *Empowering adolescent girls.* New York: Norton.

LeCroy, C. W., & Milligan Associates. (2002). *Community substance abuse council. Life Skills Training program evaluation.* Tucson, AZ: Author.

Lochman, J. E., & Wells, K. C. (1996). A social-cognitive intervention with aggressive children: Prevention effects and contextual implementation issues. In R. DeV. Peters & R. J. McMahon (Eds.), *Preventing childhood disorders, substance abuse and delinquency* (pp. 111–143). Thousand Oaks, CA: Sage.

LoSciuto, L., Freeman, M. A., Harrington, E., Altauan, B., & Lanphear, A. (1997). An outcome evaluation of the Woodrock Youth Development Project. *Journal of Early Adolescence, 17,* 51–66.

LoSciuto, L., Rajala, A. K., Townsend, T. N., & Taylor, A. S. (1996). An outcome evaluation of Across Ages: An intergenerational mentoring approach to drug prevention. *Journal of Adolescent Research, 11*(1), 116–129.

Lorion, R. P., & Ross, J. G. (1992). Programs for change: A realistic look at the nation's potential for preventing substance involvement among high-risk youth [Special issue: Programs for change: Office for Substance Abuse Prevention demonstration models]. *Journal of Community Psychology,* 3–9.

Marlatt, G. A., Baer, J. S., & Larimer, M. (1995). Preventing alcohol abuse in college students: A harm-reduction approach. In G. M. Boyd, J. Howard, & R. A. Zucker

(Eds.), *Alcohol problems among adolescents: Current directions in prevention research* (pp. 147–172). Hillsdale, NJ: Erlbaum.

McDonald, L., Coe-Braddish, D., & Billingham, S. (1991). Families and schools together: An innovative substance abuse prevention program. *Social Work in Education, 13,* 118–129.

McMahon, R. J., Slough, N. M., & the Conduct Problems Prevention Research Group. (1996). Family-based intervention in the FAST program. In R. DeV. Peters & R. J. McMahon (Eds.), *Preventing childhood disorders, substance abuse and delinquency* (pp. 90–110). Thousand Oaks, CA: Sage.

Mechanic, D. (1978). *Medical sociology* (2nd ed.). New York: Free Press.

Murray, D. M., & Perry, C. L. (1985). The prevention of adolescent drug abuse: Implications of etiological, developmental, behavioral, and environmental models. In C. L. Jones & R. J. Battjes (Eds.), *Etiology of drug abuse: Implications for prevention* (NIDA Research Monograph 56, pp. 236–256). Rockville, MD: National Institute on Drug Abuse.

National Institute on Drug Abuse. (1997). *Drug abuse prevention for at-risk individuals* (NIH Publication No. 97–4115). Rockville, MD: Author.

Newcomb, M. D., & Bentler, P. M. (1990). *Antecedents and consequences of cocaine use: An eight-year study from early adolescence to young adulthood* (pp. 158–181). New York: Cambridge Press.

Newcomb, M. D., & Felix-Ortiz, M. (1992). Multiple protective and risk factors for drug use and abuse: Cross-sectional and prospective findings. *Journal of Personality and Social Psychology, 63,* 280–296.

Norman, E., Turner, S., Zunz, S. J., & Stillson, K. (1997). Prevention programs reviewed: What works. In E. Norman (Ed.), *Drug-free youth: A compendium for prevention specialists* (pp. 22–45). New York: Garland Press.

Paglia, A., & Room, R. (1998). *Preventing substance abuse problems among youth: A literature review and recommendations* (ARF Document No. 142). Toronto, Ontario, Canada: Addiction Research Foundation.

Pentz, M. A. (1995). Local government and community organization strategies for drug abuse prevention: Theory and methods. In R. H. Coombs & D. Ziedonia (Eds.), *Handbook on drug abuse prevention: A comprehensive strategy to prevent the abuse of alcohol and other drugs* (pp. 62–92). Englewood Cliffs, NJ: Prentice-Hall.

Pentz, M. A., Dwyer, J. H., MacKinnon, D. P., Flay, B. R., Hansen, W. B., Wang, E. Y. I., et al. (1989). A multicommunity trial for primary prevention of adolescent drug abuse. *Journal of the American Medical Association, 261,* 3259–3266.

Perry, C. L., Williams, C. L., Veblen-Mortenson, S., Toomey, T. L., Komro, K. A., Anstine, P. S., et al. (1996). Project Northland: Outcomes of a community-wide alcohol use prevention program during early adolescence. *American Journal of Public Health, 86,* 956–965.

Phillips, J. L., & Springer, J. F. (1997). Implementation of community interventions: Lessons learned. In *Secretary's youth substance abuse prevention initiative: Resource papers* (pp. 69–106). Rockville, MD: Substance Abuse and Mental Health Services Administration.

Radecki, C. M., & Jaccard, J. (1995). Perceptions of knowledge, actual knowledge, and information search behavior. *Journal of Experimental Social Psychology, 31,* 107–118.

Richards-Colocino, N., McKenzie, P., & Newton, R. (1996). Project Success: Comprehensive intervention services for middle school high risk youth. *Journal of Adolescent Research, 2,* 12–35.

Richardson, G. (1996). *Resiliency in youth program.* Salt Lake City: University of Utah, Department of Health Education.

Schinke, S., & Cole, K. (1995). Prevention in community settings. In G. Botvin, S. Schnike, & M. A. Orlandi (Eds.), *Drug abuse prevention with multiethnic youth* (pp. 15–232). Thousand Oaks, CA: Sage.

Schure, M. B. (1992). *I can problem solve: An interpersonal cognitive problem solving program, intermediate elementary grades* (Vol 3). Champaign, IL: Research Press.

Sorenson, S. L., Phil, M., & Baxley, G. B. (1997). *Drug abuse prevention for the general population* (NIH Publication No. 97–4113). Rockville, MD: National Institute on Drug Abuse.

Spoth, R., & Redmond, C. (1996). Illustrating a framework for rural prevention research: Project Family studies of rural family participation and outcomes. In R. DeV. Peters & R. J. McMahon (Eds.), *Preventing childhood disorders, substance abuse, and delinquency* (pp. 299–328). Thousand Oaks, CA: Sage.

Stoil, M. J., & Hill, G. (1996). *Preventing substance abuse: Interventions that work.* New York: Plenum Press.

St. Pierre, T. L., Mark, M. M., Kaltreider, D. L., & Aikin, K. J. (1997). Involving parents of high-risk youth in drug prevention: A three year longitudinal study in Boys & Girls Clubs. *Journal of Early Adolescence, 17,* 21–50.

Substance Abuse and Mental Health Services Administration. (2001). *Summary of findings from the 2000 National Household Survey of Drug Abuse* (NHSDA Series H-13, DHHS Publication No. SMA 01–3549). Rockville, MD: Author.

Szapocznik, J., Kurtines, W. M., & Contributors. (1989). *Breakthroughs in family therapy with drug abusing and problem youth.* New York: Springer Verlag.

Szapocnik, J., Santisteban, D., Rio, A., Perez-Vidal, A., & Kurtines, W. M. (1989). Family effectiveness training: An intervention to prevent drug abuse and problem behaviors in Hispanic adolescents. *Hispanic Journal of Behavioral Sciences, 11*(1), 4–27.

Tierney, J. P., Grossman, J. B., & Resch, N. L. (1995). *Making a difference: An impact study of Big Brothers/Big Sisters.* Philadelphia: Public/Private Ventures.

Tobler, N. S. (1992). Drug prevention programs can work: Research findings. *Journal of Addictive Diseases, 11,* 1–28.

Tobler, N. S. (1997). Meta-analysis of adolescent drug prevention programs: Results of the 1993 meta-analysis. In W. J. Bukoski (Ed.), *Meta-analysis of drug abuse prevention programs* (NIDA Research Monograph No. 170, pp. 5–68). Rockville, MD: National Institute on Drug Abuse.

Tobler, N. S., Roona, M. R., Ochshorn, P., Marshall, D. G., Streke, A. V., & Stackpole, K. M. (2000). School-based adolescent drug prevention programs: 1998 meta-analysis. *Journal of Primary Prevention, 20,* 275–336.

Tobler, N. S., & Stratton, H. H. (1997). Effectiveness of school-based drug prevention programs: A meta-analysis of the research. *Journal of Primary Prevention, 20,* 71–128.

Wagenaar, A. C., Murray, D. M., Gehan, J. P., Wolfson, M., Forster, J. L., Toomey, T. L., et al. (2000). Communities mobilizing for change on alcohol: Outcomes from a randomized community trial. *Journal of Studies on Alcohol, 61,* 85–94.

Webster-Stratton, C. (1990). Enhancing the effectiveness of self-administered videotape parent training for families with conduct problem children. *Journal of Abnormal Psychology, 18,* 479–482.

Werch, C. E., Pappas, D. M., Carlson, J. M., Edgemon, P., Sinder, J. A., & DiClemente, C. C. (2000). Evaluation of a Brief Alcohol Prevention program for urban school youth. *American Journal of Health Behavior, 24,* 120–131.

Wolin, S., & Wolin, S. (1995). Resilience among youth growing up in substance-abusing families. *Pediatric Clinics of North America, 42,* 415–429.

Zavela, K. J., Battistich, V., Dean, B. J., Flores, R., Barton, R., & Delaney, R. J. (1997). Say yes first: A longitudinal, school-based alcohol and drug prevention project for rural youth and families. *Journal of Early Adolescence, 17,* 67–96.

Chapter 11

TEENAGE PREGNANCY, SEXUALLY TRANSMITTED DISEASES, AND HIV/AIDS

LISA ARMISTEAD, BETH A. KOTCHICK, AND REX FOREHAND

Adolescents are at high risk for many negative health outcomes related to sexual risk behavior, including HIV infection, other sexually transmitted diseases (STDs; e.g., syphilis, chlamydia), and pregnancy (Centers for Disease Control and Prevention [CDC], 2000). Unlike many other health problems, teenage pregnancy and the contraction of STDs, including HIV, are preventable and controllable through behavioral change. Thus, there is a critical need for researchers and practitioners to understand the psychosocial context in which sexual initiation and sexual risk-taking behavior occurs and to develop comprehensive prevention strategies designed to reduce sexual risk behavior among adolescents.

This chapter provides an overview of current trends in adolescent sexual risk behavior, its impact on adolescent health and well-being, and the factors identified in the clinical and public health literature as related to sexual risk-taking and risk-reduction practices. We then review empirically evaluated prevention programs designed to reduce adolescent sexual risk behavior and discuss implications for clinical practice and policy development. Finally, we offer some thoughts on what is still needed to enhance our understanding of adolescent sexual risk behavior and its effective prevention.

The writing of this chapter was supported, in part, by the Centers for Disease Control and Prevention, William T. Grant Foundation, and the University of Georgia's Institute for Behavioral Research.

ADOLESCENT SEXUAL RISK TAKING: TRENDS AND INCIDENCE

Consistent data across a number of national surveys indicate that many American adolescents are currently sexually active. According to the 2001 Youth Risk Behavior Survey (YRBS), more than 45% of students in grades 9 to 12 have engaged in sexual intercourse (Grunbaum et al., 2002). This figure represents a decline in youth reporting sexual activity from the last YRBS report when 49.9% of sampled students reported being sexually experienced (Kann et al., 1998). However, a substantial number of young persons in the United States still report having engaged in sexual intercourse at least once.

National survey data published during the past five years also reveal that a considerable number of teenagers are initiating sexual activity by early or middle adolescence. Estimates of teens reporting having experienced sexual intercourse by the age of 13 range from nearly 7% to 17% (Grunbaum et al., 2002; Resnick et al., 1997). Early sexual debut is related to multiple aspects of risky sexual behavior throughout adolescence, including inconsistent condom use and a greater number of sexual partners (Melcher & Burnett, 1990; Smith, 1997).

Considering the rate of sexual activity among adolescents, it is alarming that many sexually active teenagers engage in behaviors that are considered risky or unsafe and that may expose them to HIV/AIDS, other STDs, or pregnancy. For example, only half of sexually active adolescents report using a condom during their most recent sexual encounter (Grunbaum et al., 2002), and a smaller proportion (i.e., approximately 10% to 20%) report using condoms consistently (Kann et al., 1995; Seidman & Rieder, 1994). In addition, approximately 14% of high school students nationwide report having had at least four sexual partners in their lifetime (Grunbaum et al., 2002). Exposure to multiple sexual partners, especially in combination with inconsistent condom use, places adolescents at increased risk for HIV infection and other negative consequences of sexual risk-taking behavior (Overby & Kegeles, 1994).

Although sexual activities appear to vary by adolescent gender and race, adolescents of both genders and across all studied ethnic groups engage in some sexual practices that place them at risk for HIV, STDs, or pregnancy (Luster & Small, 1994; Tubman, Windle, & Windle, 1996). For example, boys report higher rates of sexual activity and more sexual partners than do girls (Grunbaum et al., 2002; Tubman et al., 1996), but girls tend to report less consistent use of condoms with their sexual partners than do boys (Romer et al., 1994; Shrier, Emans, Woods, & DuRant, 1996). National surveys have found higher rates of sexual activity and less consistent use of condoms among ethnic minority youth as compared to White adolescents (Airhihenbuwa, DiClemente, Wingood, & Lowe, 1992; Brown, DiClemente, & Park, 1992) however, more recent studies have found that both male and female Black high school students were more likely to report using a condom the last time they had sexual intercourse than were their White or Hispanic peers (Grunbaum et al., 2002). Studies examining racial and gender differences in sexual behavior and risk-reduction strategies yield inconsistent results, with the findings depending on the racial groups being compared and the sexual behaviors being considered.

Sexual risk-taking behaviors, such as inconsistent condom use and sex with multiple partners, have already had devastating effects on the health of American adolescents. Surveillance data indicate that more than 4,200 cases of AIDS have been diagnosed in the United States among persons between 13 and 19 years of age, with another 2,532 cases of HIV infection within this age bracket being reported from states with confidential HIV infection reporting (CDC, 2001). However, these figures likely represent an underestimate of the number of adolescents currently infected with HIV. The most recent surveillance data indicate that another 32,700 cases of HIV have been identified among adults ages 20 to 29. Because HIV has a median incubation period of approximately 10 years, a large proportion of adults diagnosed with AIDS in their 20s are thought to have become infected with HIV during their early adolescence (Chesney, 1994; Joseph, 1991). As such, many more adolescents are suspected to be unknowingly infected with HIV.

National data also reveal that 15- to 19-year-old adolescents have the highest rates of gonorrhea and chlamydia in the United States, with infections appearing to be on the rise (CDC, 2000). The United States also has one of the highest teenage pregnancy rates among Western industrialized countries (see Kirby, Barth, Leland, & Fetro, 1991; Kirby et al., 1994). Nearly 4 in 10 young women become pregnant at least once before they reach the age of 20, with 80% of these pregnancies being unintended and 79% among unmarried teens (Henshaw, 1998; Martin, Hamilton, Ventura, Menacher, & Park, 2002). The annual financial cost of teen pregnancy for the United States totals approximately $7 billion, and the social and economic price paid by the adolescent mother herself is great: Teen mothers are less likely to complete high school and more likely to end up on welfare (National Campaign to Prevent Teen Pregnancy, 2002).

CONTRIBUTING FACTORS: A MULTISYSTEMIC PERSPECTIVE

Statistics such as these underscore the fact that the consequences of adolescent sexual risk-taking behavior are of grave concern and are in immediate need of efforts to prevent their occurrence. To do so effectively, we need to have a thorough understanding of the psychosocial context surrounding the initiation of sexual activity, as well as the factors that influence adolescents' decisions to engage in behaviors (e.g., sex with multiple partners, unprotected sexual intercourse) considered to be sexually risky because of potential exposure to HIV/AIDS, other STDs, or pregnancy.

In this section of the chapter, we briefly summarize the literature on adolescent sexual risk behavior from a multisystemic perspective. Such an approach is guided by Bronfenbrenner's (1979, 1989) Ecological Systems Theory, which emphasizes the reciprocal relations among multiple systems of influence on a person's behavior. According to this perspective, an accurate and comprehensive understanding of adolescent sexual risk behavior must necessarily include some knowledge of both the personal and the environmental factors that may contribute to the decision to become sexually active and, subsequently, the decision to engage in risk-promoting or risk-reducing sexual behaviors. Our attention is focused on factors from three systems of influence believed to be the primary contributors to adolescent sexual behavior: the adolescent, the family, and the extrafamilial context.

Adolescent Factors

As noted earlier, adolescent age, gender, and race have all been correlated with various measures of sexual risk behavior. However, the findings are often inconsistent, with the results varying by the sexual risk behaviors being examined. Inconsistencies in rates of sexual risk behavior across age, gender, and racial groups may also be explained by the psychosocial factors that are so inherently tied with those categorical variables. For example, adolescent age is often confounded with physical development, which has an impact not only on the adolescent, but also on the way he or she is perceived by others. Likewise, both race and gender have multiple psychosocial correlates that may account for the differences found with respect to adolescent sexual behavior, including socioeconomic status (SES), education, access to health care and family planning services, experience of sexual coercion, and cultural expectations for male and female sexual behavior (e.g., Biglan, Noell, Ochs, Smolkowski, & Metzler, 1995). A review of all of the literature pertaining to adolescent age, gender, and race and their relation to sexual risk behavior is well beyond the scope of this chapter; see Kotchick, Shaffer, Forehand, and Miller (2000) for a more comprehensive examination of these issues.

As to psychological variables related to adolescent sexual behavior, several cognitive, emotional, and behavioral factors have been identified as important predictors of sexual risk. In terms of cognitive factors, better academic performance has been associated with decreased sexual risk in a number of studies. Adolescents who became pregnant tend to have lower GPAs (Hardy, Astone, Brooks-Gunn, Shapiro, & Miller, 1998; Scaramella, Conger, Simons, & Whitbeck, 1998), whereas higher GPAs have been associated with sexual abstinence, fewer sexual partners, and more condom use among youth (Luster & Small, 1994).

What teens know about sex and its risks has received considerable attention as a predictor of sexual risk behavior. However, there does not appear to be a clear association between knowledge of sexuality or sexual risk and adolescent sexual risk-taking practices. Some studies indicate that more knowledge about sexual risk practices and prevention was significantly associated with more consistent condom use (e.g., Reitman et al., 1996; Stanton et al., 1994; Stanton, Li, Galbraith, Feigelman, & Kaljee, 1996), contraception use in general (L. S. Jemmott & Jemmott, 1990; J. B. Jemmott, Jemmott, & Fong, 1998), or fewer sexual partners (Zimet et al., 1992), while others have found no association between knowledge and sexual risk practices (e.g., Brown et al., 1992; Romer et al., 1994). The lack of consensus concerning the relation between accurate knowledge of sexuality and sexual risk practices is consistent with the observation of many researchers in the area of sexual risk behavior prevention that knowledge alone does not necessarily translate to behavior or behavior change (e.g., Baldwin, Whitely, & Baldwin, 1990; St. Lawrence et al., 1995).

Other cognitive processes, such as perception of personal risk or attitudes toward sex in general, may provide the missing link between sexual knowledge and sexual behavior. Unfortunately, the findings pertaining to such factors have not been much clearer. Some studies have found that youth who perceived themselves to be more vulnerable to potential negative sexual health outcomes were more likely to engage in risk-reduction strategies such as condom use (Pendergrast, DuRant, Gaillard, 1992; Zimet et al., 1992) or to have fewer sexual partners (Miller, Forehand, & Kotchick, 1999), whereas others found that increased perception of risk was associated with greater levels of sexual risk-taking behavior (Langer & Tubman, 1997; Millstein & Moscicki, 1995). Still others found no association between risk perception and sexual risk behavior (Orr, Beiter, & Ingersoll, 1991; Shafer & Boyer, 1991).

Attitudinal factors relating to the morality of sex and toward risk reduction practices have been more consistently associated with sexual risk behaviors. For example, more liberal attitudes about teenage sexuality have been found to relate to higher levels of sexual risk-taking behavior (L. S. Jemmott & Jemmott, 1990). Several researchers also have documented the finding that adolescent attitudes toward risk-reduction strategies, such as condom use, are associated with their use. Adolescents with more positive attitudes toward condoms tend to report greater use of condoms (e.g., L. S. Jemmott & Jemmott, 1990; Reitman et al., 1996). Similarly, adolescents who report higher levels of religiosity are less likely to engage in sexual intercourse (Bingham & Crockett, 1996; Levinson, Jaccard, & Beamer, 1995). However, religiosity has not been found to reliably predict sexual risk behavior, such as inconsistent condom use.

Self-efficacy, or the belief that an individual has the ability to perform a particular action effectively (Bandura, 1986), has been a central concept in social-cognitive theories of HIV prevention in general (see Herlocher, Hoff, & DeCarlo, 1995, for a review of HIV prevention theories). Several studies have found an association between greater self-efficacy for risk reduction and less risky sexual practices, including fewer sexual partners and more condom use (Overby & Kegeles, 1994; Reitman et al., 1996).

Various indicators of psychosocial or emotional distress (e.g., depressive symptoms, anxiety) have been found to relate to adolescent sexual activity, with higher levels of distress being associated with greater sexual activity (e.g., Harvey & Spigner, 1995; Tubman et al., 1996). Several researchers have found that a history of sexual victimization is associated with sexual risk-taking behaviors. The experience of sexual coercion is related to several indicators of sexual risk, including having sex under the influence of drugs or alcohol and having sex with an unknown partner, as well as to a higher incidence of pregnancy and STDs (Biglan et al., 1995; Roosa, Tein, Reinholtz, & Angelini, 1997).

Substantial evidence has accumulated to support the association between adolescent sexual risk behavior and involvement in other problem behaviors during adolescence. Higher rates of sexual risk behavior have been found among both male and female adolescents who engage in delinquent behavior (Devine, Long, & Forehand, 1993), and adolescents who report higher rates of aggressive or delinquent behavior experience a higher incidence of teenage pregnancy or parenthood (e.g., Scaramella et al., 1998; Stouthamer-Loeber & Wei, 1998).

A number of other studies have documented the relationship between substance use in particular and sexual risk practices. The national YRBS data indicate that high-risk sexual behaviors (e.g., multiple sexual partners, no condom use at last intercourse) were most prevalent among adolescents who had used illicit substances during the past year (Lowry et al., 1994). Others have found that a history of alcohol and/or drug use correlated with inconsistent condom use (e.g., Cooper, Peirce, & Huselid, 1994; Miller et al., 1999; Millstein & Moscicki, 1995; Shrier et al., 1996) and having multiple sexual partners (e.g., Devine et al., 1993; Duncan, Strycker, & Duncan, 1999). Use of alcohol or drugs immediately before or during sexual encounters is also related to decreased condom use (e.g., J. B. Jemmott & Jemmott, 1993; Strunin & Hingson, 1992).

Family Factors

Familial influences on adolescent sexual activity can be divided into two primary categories: family structure and family process. Because the focus of this chapter is on prevention and because structural variables, such as family SES or the absence of one parent, do not lend themselves to behavioral interventions, we review only those findings pertaining to family process variables associated with adolescent sexual risk behavior.

Parenting and the role of parents in the sexual socialization of their children have been widely studied. This research has generally focused on three aspects of parenting: parental monitoring, the quality of the parent-adolescent relationship, and parent-adolescent communication about sex. Greater parental monitoring, or supervision, of adolescents' social activities has been associated with less risky sexual behavior among youth, including less frequent sexual behavior (Romer et al., 1994), fewer sexual partners (e.g., Miller, Forehand, & Kotchick, 2000; Rodgers, 1999), and more consistent use of contraception (e.g., Luster & Small, 1994; Rodgers, 1999). Parental monitoring may also be protective for youth by limiting their involvement in other risk behaviors during adolescence that have been associated with higher sexual risk practices. Indeed, better parental monitoring has been associated with lower levels of problem behavior and drug abuse among adolescents (e.g., Barber, Olsen, & Shagle, 1994; Steinberg, 1987).

However, evidence suggests the relationship between parental monitoring and adolescent sexual risk may be protective only to a certain point. Excessive control by parents that denies adolescents adequate autonomy is associated with higher odds that adolescents would engage in sexual risk-taking behavior (Rodgers, 1999). This finding is consistent with research demonstrating that either too much or too little parental control was associated with increased problem behaviors among African American adolescents (Mason, Cauce, Gonzales, & Hiraga, 1996).

The quality of an adolescent's relationship with his or her parents is another aspect of the family system that appears to affect sexual risk behaviors. Parental support and involvement appears to be related to decreased sexual risk behaviors and reduced risk of pregnancy (e.g., Luster & Small, 1994; Scaramella et al., 1998). Likewise, youth who report positive and supportive communication with their parents (a proxy for parent-adolescent relationship quality) also report having fewer sexual partners and more consistent use of condoms (Miller et al., 2000). However, other studies have not documented such a clear association between parent-adolescent relationships and sexual risk behaviors. Rather, the quality of the parent-adolescent relationship may indirectly affect sexual risk behavior either through its impact on other adolescent behaviors that increase or decrease sexual risk (e.g., substance use, academic performance) or through its effects on the frequency and quality of communication between parents and children about sexuality and sexual risk reduction.

Communication between teens and parents is particularly important for the transmission of information on sexuality, HIV/AIDS, and appropriate risk reduction strategies for adolescents. Family communication about sex and its potential risks has been found to relate to more correct knowledge about sexuality and AIDS among adolescents (e.g., Pick & Palos, 1995; Sigelman, Derenowski, Mullaney, & Siders, 1993). More importantly, parent-adolescent communication about sex is associated with decreased sexual risk-taking behavior among adolescents (e.g., Kotchick, Dorsey, Miller, & Forehand, 1999; Miller, Kotchick, Dorsey, Forehand, & Ham, 1998; Miller et al., 1999). The quality of parent-teen discussions of sexual issues appears to be particularly important in reducing sexual risk. Research has demonstrated that open, receptive, and empathic communication is most effective at reducing sexual risk-taking behavior (e.g., Miller et al., 1999).

In addition to communication quality, the timing of parent-adolescent discussions about sex is critical. Research with high-risk minority adolescents has demonstrated that parent-adolescent discussions about sex are most effective in delaying sexual intercourse or reducing sexual risk-taking behavior when they occur before the first sexual encounter (Miller, Levin, Xu, & Whitaker, 1998). Unfortunately, many parents do not discuss sexuality or sexual risk with their children (e.g., Miller, Kotchick, et al., 1998), and when parents do talk to their children, it is often later rather than sooner.

Extrafamilial Factors

For adolescents who are in the midst of developing their own identities and establishing more complex social networks, the point of reference by which they guide their behavior naturally shifts from the family to the social environment (Forehand & Wierson, 1993). Peers, neighborhoods, and other community factors all relate in important, though poorly understood, ways to adolescent sexual risk behavior.

Because peers become an important source of reinforcement, modeling, and support during adolescence (Forehand & Wierson, 1993), it is not surprising that adolescents whose peers are sexually active are more likely to be sexually active themselves (e.g., Miller et al., 2000; Romer et al., 1994). Additionally, indicators of sexual risk-taking behavior among adolescents' peer groups (e.g., pregnancy, inconsistent condom use) have been shown to relate to increased adolescent sexual risk (Gillmore, Lewis, Lohr, Spencer, & White, 1997; Millstein & Moscicki, 1995). More subjectively, adolescents' perceptions of their peers' behaviors have also been found to relate to sexual risk taking, as several researchers have found that consistent condom use is associated with the perception of condom use among friends (e.g., Romer et al., 1994; Stanton et al., 1994).

Beyond peer sexual behavior, other characteristics of an adolescent's peer group appear to be related to adolescent sexual risk behavior. Research has repeatedly indicated that association with a deviant peer group, such as one that is involved with alcohol and drug use or delinquency, has been related to participation in high-risk sexual practices (e.g., Brewster, 1994; Miller et al., 2000). A prospective study by Scaramella et al. (1998) found that deviant peer affiliations in the 8th grade were significantly related to sexual risk behavior in the 12th grade.

On the broadest level of the extrafamilial system, the neighborhood or community in which the adolescent lives also appears to influence the types of risk behaviors in which he or she may be involved. The community provides myriad levels of social support through schools, jobs, social contacts, and other resources. The community can also serve to hinder an adolescent's development or place the adolescent at greater risk through a lack of future opportunities, insufficient monitoring, or socioeconomic disadvantage or instability. However, these levels of influence are often difficult to characterize and have not been extensively studied in the adolescent sexual risk literature. In the only study identified in this review to focus exclusively on the relationship of sociodemographic variables to sexual risk status, Brewster (1994) found that, among African American adolescent girls, lower SES, increased levels of female employment, and higher divorce rates in the community were all associated with greater sexual risk taking. The degree of social support garnered from extrafamilial sources is also likely to be important, as less social support was related to more frequent engagement in sexual risk behaviors among African American adolescents in one study (St. Lawrence et al., 1994).

In summary, factors at the individual, family, and extrafamilial levels influence whether an adolescent is likely to contract HIV, another STD, or become pregnant as a result of risky sexual behavior. Preventive interventions vary in the extent to which they have addressed factors within each of the three levels. Whereas the earliest generation of HIV/STD/pregnancy prevention programs most often targeted individual level variables and typically only one individual level component (i.e., knowledge), more recently developed programs attempt to address factors at two or even all three levels. Moreover, most successful interventions are informed by theories or models that guide the selection of intervention targets. We begin our discussion of interventions with an overview of the theories and models most often used in the development of the prevention programs.

THEORETICAL UNDERPINNINGS OF PREVENTIVE INTERVENTIONS

Theories are not always explicitly considered in intervention development; however, when they are, four theories or models of behavior change are most commonly used to develop preventive interventions targeting teen sexual behavior:

1. Social learning theory
2. Cognitive behavior theory
3. Social influence or inoculation model
4. Information-motivation-behavioral skills model

Some interventions reviewed later (e.g., Reducing the Risk) combine intervention components based on more than one of these theories, while others (e.g., Becoming a Responsible Teen) are based primarily on one model or theory.

Social learning theory is the conceptual foundation for the majority of effective preventive interventions. According to social learning theory, to implement a protective behavior (e.g., condom use), a teen must know about the protective behavior, believe that he or she will be able to engage in the behavior, believe that the method will be successful, and anticipate a benefit once he or she completes the behavior. In social learning theory, modeling behavior and practicing skills are fundamental to learning new behaviors (Bandura, 1986).

Cognitive behavior theory is also commonly used in the development of preventive interventions. This theory is similar to social learning theory and posits that youth need cognitive and behavioral skills to combat societal pressures toward engaging in risky behavior. These skills help teens effectively negotiate interpersonal encounters (Kirby et al., 1991). Three components of this theory are particularly important: personalizing information about sexual health, skills training in decision-making and/or assertive communication, and generalization of the skills to individual situations.

The *social influence* or *social inoculation model* has been employed in some interventions and primarily addresses the powerful role of peer pressure in the onset of sexual risk behaviors. This model posits that youth engage in behaviors, including risk behaviors, in large part because of societal and peer influences. Through the public health concept of immunization, interventions based on the social inoculation model expose youth to societal or peer messages that promote risky behaviors and encourage these youth to consider the negative influences on their lives and develop skills to combat them (Ellickson, 1984).

The final and more recently construed model, the *information-motivation-behavioral skills (IMB) model* (J. D. Fisher & Fisher, 1992, 2000; W. A. Fisher & Fisher, 1993; W. A. Fisher, Williams, Fisher, & Malloy, 1999), was developed in response to the AIDS epidemic; and interventions relying on IMB have demonstrated efficacy (e.g., Carey et al., 1997). According to IMB, the individuals who are most likely to engage in protective behaviors and maintain their behavior are those who have adequate information about risks and preventive behaviors, are motivated to change their behavior, and have the necessary skills to engage in preventive behavior. In addition to specifying the necessary components for behavior change discussed previously, IMB proposes a process for determining the most appropriate content and format of interventions in a particular community. More specifically, three steps are involved in the creation and implementation of an intervention.

1. Elicitation research (e.g., focus groups, key informant interviews) is conducted with a subgroup of the targeted population to determine strengths and weaknesses with respect to information, behavior, and skills.

2. The results of the elicitation research are used to create and implement empirically targeted interventions for the populations.

3. Independent evaluation research is conducted to determine intervention effects (J. D. Fisher, Fisher, Bryan, & Misovich, 2002).

These theories/models have elements in common. For example, interventions relying on these models almost always begin with an informational component. All models emphasize the importance of skills building and skill generalization. However, the models also differ. For example, the social inoculation model places clear emphasis on the impact of peer pressure. IMB is unique in that it offers an approach for the creation, implementation, and evaluation of an intervention. In summary, one theory or model does not appear to be inherently better than the others; rather, relying on one or more theories when creating and evaluating an intervention is the important factor.

EFFECTIVE PREVENTIVE INTERVENTIONS

Because of the large number of available prevention programs targeting HIV, STD, and teen pregnancy, we employed the following guidelines in determining which programs to include:

1. We included only interventions with empirical evidence of effectiveness as determined either by the CDC (1999) or the National Campaign to Prevent Teen Pregnancy (Kirby, 2001). In addition to including only studies conducted in the United States or Canada that targeted adolescents between the ages of 12 and 18, methodological standards must have been met for the programs to be included in this review. These standards include the use of an experimental or quasi-experimental design, a sample size of at least 100, and measurement of the intervention's impact on sexual or contraceptive behavior, pregnancy, or childbearing outcomes (see Kirby, 2001).

2. We focused only on studies published in the past decade (1992 to 2002) because they represent the most advanced knowledge of proven effective prevention strategies. In addition, we discuss some examples of ongoing intervention studies that show promise based on their reliance on proven strategies and their methodological rigor.

Given the normative data on adolescent sexual behavior, it could be argued that almost one-half of adolescents are at risk for contracting HIV, another STD, or becoming pregnant merely by being sexually active. Additionally, certain subgroups of this population are at greater risk than others because of the individual, family, or extrafamilial factors reviewed previously. Thus, HIV, STD, and pregnancy risk reduction interventions may be either universally applied or targeted to a particular group of at-risk adolescents. Regardless of the intended audience, all of the programs included in our review have many elements in common (e.g., a focus on increasing knowledge and building skills). The most fundamental difference in intervention programs is whether they focus on the sexual antecedents of HIV, STDs, and pregnancy (e.g., inconsistent condom use) or on the nonsexual antecedents (e.g., academic failure, lack of job skills) of these outcomes. The latter category of intervention programs may begin as early as preschool and intervene in multiple domains, sometimes including sexuality education. In contrast, interventions focused on sexual antecedents typically do not occur before middle school and are more specific in their focus on sexual risk behaviors.

We first review interventions focused on altering the sexual antecedents to sexual risk behavior because this is the more commonly employed type of intervention. We then review programs focusing on nonsexual antecedents and include a discussion of the newest generation of prevention programs currently undergoing evaluation. In each of these sections, we discuss study samples and methodology, program format, program content, and program outcome. At the conclusion of each of these two sections, we review the universal, selective, and targeted application of both types of interventions. The information provided in this text is presented in detail sufficient to allow the reader to evaluate methodology, gain an understanding of program components, and ascertain the potential for efficacy. However, details are not adequate to allow replication of a specific intervention.

Interventions Focused on Sexual Antecedents

We located 11 empirically evaluated prevention programs focused specifically on the reduction of risky sexual behavior that met the criteria previously discussed. See Table 11.1 for the program titles and authors of these interventions.

Table 11.1   Preventive Interventions Focused on the Sexual Antecedents of HIV, STD, and Pregnancy

Universal	
Draw the Line/Respect the Line	Coyle, Kirby, Marin, Gomez, & Gregorich (2000)
Reducing the Risk	Hubbard, Geise, & Rainey (1998); Kirby, Barth, Leland, & Fetro (1991)
Safer Choices	Coyle, Basen-Engquist, Kirby, Parcel, Banspach, Collins, et al. (2001)
Get Real About AIDS	Main, Iverson, McGloin, Banspach, Collins, Rugg, et al. (1994)
Selective	
Be Proud/Be Responsible	J. B. Jemmott, Jemmott, & Fong (1998)
AIDS Prevention for Adolescents in School	Walter & Vaughan (1993)
Becoming a Responsible Teen	St. Lawrence, Brasfield, Jefferson, Alleyne, O'Bannon, & Shirley (1995)
Healthy Oakland Teens	Ekstrand, Siegel, Nido, Faigeles, Cummings, Battle, et al. (1996)
Focus on Kids	Stanton, Li, Ricardo, Galbraith, Feigelman, & Kaljee (1996)
Targeted	
Intensive AIDS Education in Jail	Magura, Kang, & Shapiro (1994)
Street Smart	Rotheram-Borus, Koopman, Haignere, & Davies (1991)

The majority of the 11 studies included ethnically and economically diverse samples. If a study sample was not ethnically diverse, it most commonly consisted of only ethnic minority youth. For example, Becoming a Responsible Teen, Focus on Kids, and Be Proud/Be Responsible included only African American participants. When study samples were not economically diverse (e.g., Be Proud/Be Responsible, Healthy Oakland Teens), they consisted only of participants from the lower socioeconomic bracket. The focus on ethnic minority youth from the lower socioeconomic bracket reflects the higher rates of teen pregnancy, HIV, and other STDs occurring among these youth relative to middle-and upper-class Caucasian youth.

The majority of the studies targeted high school-age youth, though two focused on children in middle school (i.e., Draw the Line, Be Proud/Be Responsible). Waiting until youth are in high school to discuss sexual risk is common and reflects the cultural proscriptions against providing comprehensive sexuality education to youth at younger ages. However, it is ideal to intervene with youth about sexual behavior before they begin engaging in it. Thus, some of the newer, though still incomplete, interventions discussed later include younger youth.

Only 5 of the 11 interventions (i.e., Draw the Line, Becoming a Responsible Teen, Be Proud/Be Responsible, Focus on Kids, and Safer Choices) employed an experimental design using random assignment of participants or institutions (e.g., schools) to the treatment or a control condition. The remaining investigations relied on a quasi-experimental design in which participants or institutions were assigned to conditions out of convenience, most often because of practical constraints relating to the location of the schools relative to the study site or the willingness of a school to facilitate intervention implementation. Investigators using a quasi-experimental design attempted to minimize the impact of this weaker strategy by matching participants or schools on demographic characteristics or statistically controlling for differences between groups.

As to program format, all interventions listed in Table 11.1 were implemented via multiple group-based sessions, ranging in number from 4 to 20. The schedule for session implementation varied considerably. Whereas some interventions held sessions weekly during consecutive weeks (e.g., Becoming a Responsible Teen, Reducing the Risk, Focus on Kids), two spread the intervention across multiple years. For example, Draw the Line involved a total of 20 sessions. Five of these sessions were implemented in the sixth grade, eight in the seventh grade, and seven in the eighth grade. In perhaps the most compacted format, the eight one-hour modules that comprise Be Proud/Be Responsible were delivered over two Saturdays. Decisions about the scheduling of sessions depend, at least in part, on practical considerations such as the intervention site. For example, it is more feasible to spread an intervention across multiple years in a school setting than in a community setting. Similarly, if intervening with a transitory sample (e.g., runaway teens, teens living in housing developments), sessions should likely adhere to a more compacted schedule.

When implemented in a school setting, program sessions were most often led by teachers. When intervening in a community setting, representatives from the community setting were trained to lead the group sessions. However, in two studies, peers were also trained to lead groups. In one of these studies (i.e., Be Proud/ Be Responsible), the behavioral outcomes of the participants in groups led by adults were compared to those in peer-led groups. The results of these comparisons indicated that there were no differences between the peer- versus adult-led groups with respect to the program's impact on adolescent sexual behavior (J. B. Jemmott, Jemmott, & Fong, 1998).

All interventions were designed to increase the likelihood of maximum impact by presenting the information in a dynamic and interactive format. For example,

Street Smart, an intervention for runaway youth, included a component where teens created soap opera dramatizations to practice the skills taught in the intervention. Similarly, several interventions (e.g., Reducing the Risk, Becoming a Responsible Teen) used role plays to build skills and self-efficacy. Some interventions (e.g., Be Proud/Be Responsible, Becoming a Responsible Teen, Focus on Kids) included videos and games in the curricula as well. In a unique and potentially powerful attempt to impact youths' behavior, Becoming a Responsible Teen also included a component that involved discussion groups held with HIV-infected youth. This component was included in an attempt to promote accurate perceptions of vulnerability to HIV infection.

The majority of the interventions focused exclusively on the individual factors involved in risky sexual behavior (e.g., knowledge, attitudes, skills), rather than on family or extrafamilial factors. However, a few interventions also targeted change at these systems levels as well. For example, in addition to group-based sessions, Get Real About AIDS attempted to intervene in the students' extrafamilial environment by posting informational posters about sexual risk in the schools. Reducing the Risk contained two homework assignments where students were required to talk to their parents about abstinence and birth control. Safer Choices was unique among these interventions in that these investigators targeted individual variables, familial variables, and extrafamilial variables. Participants received classroom-based intervention sessions focused on knowledge and skills, and the investigators attempted to incorporate parents into the intervention through homework and parent newsletters. Moreover, the investigators also incorporated models of school change and corresponding components targeting change in the school environment. For example, Safer Choices trained students from the schools to be peer educators who would reinforce safer sex messages in the school environment (e.g., at assemblies). Additionally, Safer Choices relied on councils consisting of parents, teachers, students, administrators, and community members to plan and monitor project implementation.

Participants in all interventions received information about the risks of unprotected sex and methods for protecting themselves (e.g., abstinence, condom use). Additionally, all interventions covered skills for delaying intercourse and/or consistently using condoms (e.g., assertive communication). Two intervention programs (i.e., Safer Choices, AIDS Prevention for Adolescents in School) also attempted to change youths' perceptions of the frequency with which their peers were engaging in sexual behavior. These interventions used group discussions about the rate of youth sexual behavior in an attempt to debunk the misperception that "everyone is doing it" (Coyle, Kirby, Marin, Gomez, & Gregorich, 2000).

Values clarification was a part of several of the interventions. Specifically, Focus on Kids, AIDS Prevention for Adolescents in School, Becoming a

Responsible Teen, and Healthy Oakland Teens included a component of the intervention designed to help teens identify their values on sexuality. For example, Becoming a Responsible Teen devoted a discussion session to sexual decisions and values. Subsequent to viewing a video, the participants continued this discussion with an emphasis on support from friends and family around their sex-related personal values.

With respect to behavioral outcomes of the interventions, all programs collected follow-up data (at least three months and typically 12 months) and demonstrated effectiveness at reducing risky behaviors. The outcomes measured have included initiation of sexual behavior for sexually inexperienced youth and, in sexually active youth, condom use, intercourse frequency, and number of partners. All of the 11 interventions addressed here assessed the impact on initiation of sexual behavior, and in four of those studies (Reducing the Risk, Becoming a Responsible Teen, Be Proud/Be Responsible, and Draw the Line), youth in the treatment group were less likely to have initiated sex than those in the control group. In Draw the Line, treatment group males, but not females, delayed sexual onset. Though the remaining seven studies did not demonstrate a positive effect for delay of sexual intercourse, it is important that in no case did an intervention hasten the onset of intercourse. This finding refutes the argument that the discussion of adolescent sexual behavior, its consequences, and means of protection that occur in sex education programs will lead to an increase in adolescent sexual behavior.

All of the studies presented here assessed protective behaviors that can occur after the initiation of sexual behavior, and the findings are mixed. Specifically, all 11 studies assessed the impact of the intervention on condom use. Safer Choices, AIDS Prevention for Adolescents in School, Becoming a Responsible Teen, and Get Real About AIDS evidenced a positive effect with higher rates of condom use in the treatment sample relative to the control participants. Reducing the Risk also had a positive effect on condom use but only for those youth who were sexually inexperienced at baseline, emphasizing the importance of intervening early with youth. Only five studies assessed frequency of intercourse, with only two demonstrating a positive effect for the intervention. More specifically, Be Proud/Be Responsible evidenced less frequent intercourse for those in one of the treatment groups. In the Becoming a Responsible Teen program, males in the treatment group engaged less frequently in intercourse than the no treatment males, but there was no difference between groups for females. Last, four studies assessed number of partners, with one-half showing a positive effect. Becoming a Responsible Teen and Get Real About AIDS treatment participants reported fewer partners at follow-up relative to the control groups.

The behavioral outcomes discussed previously indicate that interventions targeting the sexual antecedents of HIV, STD, and teen pregnancy can be, but are not always, effective. Perhaps the most exciting results offered are that in the majority of these studies, teen protective behaviors persisted at follow-up assessments occurring at least 12 months after the intervention. Additionally, Safer Choices sustained its effect on condom use and number of partners at a 31-month follow-up. These findings are very important because the potential negative effects of risky sexual behaviors loom well beyond the early adolescent years. Thus, interventions must be powerful enough to have an enduring impact.

The majority of the 11 interventions that were focused on the sexual antecedents of HIV, STD, and pregnancy selectively intervened with samples. More specifically, whereas four of the interventions (i.e., Draw the Line, Reducing the Risk, Safer Choices, & Get Real About AIDS) were universally applied to youth not identified to be at particular risk for contracting HIV or another STD or becoming pregnant, the remaining seven interventions were targeted to at-risk youth. Five of the targeted interventions were implemented with youth from the lower socioeconomic bracket, the majority of whom were also ethnic minorities. The remaining two interventions were targeted to youth who had the additional risk factor of being imprisoned (Intensive AIDS Education in Jail) or runaways (Street Smart).

Missing from our review are those prevention programs that exclusively promote abstinence as a method of sexual risk reduction. These popular programs were not included because they did not meet the criteria of having been empirically demonstrated to significantly reduce sexual risk behavior among youth. See Kirby (2001) for more information concerning the effectiveness of abstinence-only interventions.

Interventions Focused on Nonsexual Antecedents

Research indicates that improving females' educational and employment opportunities reduces their pregnancy rates (Kirby, 2001). Additionally, the male and female youth most at risk for HIV and other STDs are those with relatively poor educational and career opportunities (e.g., Airhihenbuwa, DiClemente, Wingood, & Lowe, 1992; Brown, DiClemente, & Park, 1992). Thus, some professionals working with youth have targeted the improvement of educational and career opportunities, rather than or in addition to sexual behavior per se, as the intervention focus. These interventions, known as youth development programs, have aims broader than simply a reduction in youth sexual risk behavior. More specifically, they focus on enhancing factors such as involvement with other adults, attachment to school, employment opportunities, and educational goals (Kirby, 2001).

Four interventions met the methodological and other criteria discussed previously. The program names and investigators of these interventions are presented in Table 11.2. Unlike the interventions focused exclusively on sexual antecedents, the youth development programs are generally more different than they are similar. We discuss these interventions with respect to methodology, program format and content, and outcomes.

All but one of the interventions (i.e., Teen Outreach Program) included primarily youth from the lower socioeconomic bracket. Two of the four interventions targeted ethnic minority youth, and the other two included ethnically diverse youth (i.e., Teen Outreach Program & the Seattle Social Development Program). As with the sex education interventions discussed previously, the youth development projects focus primarily on youth demographically at risk for negative outcomes.

There is a much broader age range represented in the youth development interventions compared to those focused exclusively on sex. Two interventions focused on preschool and/or elementary school-age children (Abecedarian Project & the Seattle Social Development Program), whereas the others focused on high school youth. As expected, the format and content of the programs varied considerably depending on the age of the youth.

All but one of the studies employed a rigorous methodology with an experimental design, involving random assignment of participants or institutions. The exception was the Seattle Social Development Program, which used a quasi-experimental design because of the inability to randomly assign schools to conditions.

As previously mentioned, the format and content of these interventions varied considerably. However, unlike most of the sexually specific interventions, the youth development programs are consistent in their incorporation of all three levels of intervention: the individual, family, and extrafamilial systems.

Table 11.2   Preventive Interventions Focused on the Nonsexual Antecedents of HIV, STD, and Pregnancy

Universal	
Teen Outreach Program	Philliber & Allen (1992) and Allen, Philliber, Herrlin, & Kuperminc (1997)
Targeted	
Abecedarian Project	Campbell (1999)
Seattle Social Development Project	Hawkins, Catalano, Kosterman, Abbott, & Hill (1999)
Carrera Program	Philliber, Kaye, Herrling, & West (2000)

The most distinctly different program was the Abecedarian program, which included a preschool and elementary school component and lasted up to eight years. The preschool component consisted of enriched full-day childcare year round from infancy to kindergarten. The elementary school intervention involved a teacher devoted to the home-school connection (e.g., increasing parental involvement in the child's learning, enhancing parent-school communication).

Of the three other interventions, the Seattle Social Development Project is the most similar to the Abecedarian Program, occurring in schools with an emphasis on the home-school connection. However, the format and content of this intervention was different and included components with teachers, parents, and children. Teachers and parents were taught skills aimed at facilitating the child-school and the child-parent attachment and represent the extrafamilial and family levels, respectively. Children met in small groups to learn social skills.

The other two interventions also included a small group component for youth participants. The Teen Outreach Program was implemented in schools and community settings with a small group focused on values, decision making, communication skills, and parenting. This intervention was a service learning program, and treatment youth participated in an average of 46 hours of service in the school or community.

The last of the four interventions was presented exclusively in a small group format in a community setting and was the only one to include a sexual education component. The Carrera program was implemented for 16 hours each month throughout the high school years and included five components:

1. Family life and sex education
2. Academic assessment and tutoring
3. A career skills and awareness
4. Self-expression through art
5. Athletics

Though different in their methodology, format, and content, each of the four youth development programs had a positive impact on the same outcome. The participants in the treatment groups in all four interventions evidenced lower pregnancy or birth rates than control group participants. For three of the programs, follow-up occurred well after the intervention. The Abecedarian program followed youth to age 21, and the Seattle Social Development Project assessed participants at age 18, whereas the Carrera Program followed up with youth three years after participation. Youth development programs have the potential for long-term impact with respect to unintended pregnancy.

The programs focusing on nonsexual antecedents were less consistent in measurement of sex behavior outcomes other than pregnancy. However, when these behavioral data were collected, the results were positive. Youth in the Carrera and Seattle Social Development programs were less likely to initiate sex, and the latter program also had a positive impact on number of sexual partners. Neither program was reported to impact condom use.

All but one of the four previously discussed interventions were selectively applied. Whereas the Teen Outreach Program was implemented with ethnically and socioeconomically diverse youth, the other three interventions were implemented with youth at greater risk for HIV, STD, or pregnancy as a result of demographic factors (e.g., low SES).

New Generation of Interventions

Several prevention programs are currently being evaluated and appear to offer promise with respect to their impact on youth sexual behavior. These new programs set themselves apart from existing prevention efforts by incorporating families and targeting children younger than those reached by the programs reviewed previously (e.g., CHAMP Family Program; McKay, & Williams, 2002; Parents Matter! Program; Kotchick et al., 2002). For example, the Parents Matter! Program is a group intervention for African American parents of fourth- and fifth-grade students. Parents participating in the treatment groups of this intervention learn about the numerous health and sexual risks facing youth as they transition into adolescence and are taught general parenting skills, such as monitoring and relationship building, that are known to be protective for youth. Following this foundation, the intervention emphasizes the importance of parent-child communication about sexual health and provides training in specific communication skills parents can use to initiate discussions or respond to their children's questions about sexuality (Kotchick et al., 2002).

IMPLICATIONS FOR FUTURE RESEARCH AND PROGRAM DEVELOPMENT

Research concerning adolescent sexual risk behavior has come a long way in the past decade. Much has been learned about the variables that are related to adolescent sexual risk behavior, and effective programs have been developed based on this research literature that provide youth with the knowledge, skills, and resources to manage their transition to sexual adulthood more safely. Based on this research, social and political attention also has been devoted to the larger contextual variables and environmental conditions that appear to promote sexual risk taking by adolescents, and public policies dedicated to empowering youth and their families have been implemented (e.g., Children Now & Kaiser Family Foundation, 1999).

Nevertheless, there is much room to grow in the field of adolescent sexual behavior research and prevention program development. First, more attention must be given to comprehensive models that take into account factors from multiple systems of influence and their combined effects on adolescent sexual risk-taking behavior. Future research should focus more attention on the familial and extrafamilial factors that may contribute to adolescent sexual risk behavior and on programs that successively intervene across multiple contexts. Extrafamilial contexts, such as school and neighborhood conditions, offer particular promise for inclusion as both targets and resources in prevention programs designed to reduce STD infection, pregnancy, and the transmission of HIV among youth.

Second, prevention programs typically start too late. Early intervention efforts that take place before the initiation of sexual activity are the most effective, and with the rates of sexual activity in younger cohorts increasing, it is imperative that prevention specialists reach youth sooner. As demonstrated by the promise shown by the Parents Matter! Program, the family represents a very powerful socializing force in the lives of children and adolescents and one that is more politically amenable to early intervention. Parents are in a unique and powerful position to shape young people's attitudes and behaviors and to socialize them to become sexually healthy adults. They can do this, in part, by providing accurate information about sex and its risks, consequences, and responsibilities and by imparting skills to make responsible decisions about health. However, the strength of parents as interventionists stems from their unique ability to engage their children in dialogues about sexual development and decision-making that occur early and are continuous (i.e., not one-time events), sequential (i.e., building on each other as the child's cognitive, emotional, physical, and social development and experiences change), and time-sensitive (i.e., information is immediately responsive to the child's questions and anticipated needs rather than programmed to a curriculum).

Finally, targets for intervention should include both competencies specific to sexual behavior and more general areas of psychosocial or family functioning. For adolescents, knowledge, attitudes, and sexual self-efficacy represent specific competencies known to be related to reduced sexual risk taking. For parents, specific targets for intervention include knowledge of adolescent sexual behavior, monitoring of dating behavior, and skills to communicate with their adolescent children about sex. However, broader indexes of functioning, such as depression and anxiety, self-esteem, school involvement, and parent-child relationship quality, are all appropriate targets for interventions seeking to promote well-being and reduce sexual risk behavior among adolescents. In this sense, we encourage prevention and intervention efforts that have as their ultimate goal the development of healthy and well-adjusted youth. Risk reduction would be part, but only a part, of such programs, and the result would be teens and families that value and foster sexual health and safety as part of overall well-being.

REFERENCES

Airhihenbuwa, C. O., DiClemente, R. J., Wingood, G. M., & Lowe, A. (1992). Perspective: HIV/AIDS education and prevention among African-Americans: A focus on culture. *AIDS Education and Prevention, 4,* 267–276.

Allen, J. P., Philliber, S., Herrling, S., & Kuperminc, G. (1997). Preventing teen pregnancy and academic failure: Experimental evaluation of a developmentally-based approach. *Child Development, 64,* 729–742.

Baldwin, J. I., Whitely, S., & Baldwin, J. D. (1990). Changing AIDS and fertility-related behavior. The effectiveness of AIDS education. *Journal of Sex Research, 27,* 245–262.

Bandura, A. (1986). *Social foundations of thought and action.* Englewood Cliffs, NJ: Prentice-Hall.

Barber, B. K., Olsen, J. E., & Shagle, S. C. (1994). Associations between parental psychological and behavioral control and youth internalized and externalized behaviors. *Child Development, 65,* 1120–1136.

Biglan, A., Noell, J., Ochs, L., Smolkowski, K., & Metzler, C. (1995). Does sexual coercion play a role in the high-risk sexual behavior of adolescent and young adult women? *Journal of Behavioral Medicine, 18,* 549–568.

Bingham, C. R., & Crockett, L. J. (1996). Longitudinal adjustment patterns of boys and girls experiencing early, middle, and late sexual intercourse. *Developmental Psychology, 32,* 647–658.

Brewster, K. L. (1994). Neighborhood context and the transition to sexual activity among young Black women. *Demography, 31,* 603–614.

Bronfenbrenner, U. (1979). *The ecology of human development.* Cambridge, MA: Harvard University Press.

Bronfenbrenner, U. (1989). Ecological systems theory. *Annals of Child Development, 6,* 187–249.

Brown, L. K., DiClemente, R. J., & Park, T. (1992). Predictors of condom use in sexually active adolescents. *Journal of Adolescent Health, 13,* 651–657.

Campbell, F. A. (1999, April 16). Long term outcomes from the Abecedarian study. In F. A. Campbell (Chair), *How high-quality early childhood programs enhance long-term development: Comparison of findings and models.* Symposium presented at the biennial meeting of the Society for Research in Child Development, Albuquerque, NM.

Carey, M. P., Maisto, S. A., Kalichman, S. C., Forsyth, A. D., Johnson, B. T., & Wright, E. (1997). Enhancing motivation to reduce the risk of HIV infection for economically disadvantaged urban women. *Journal of Consulting and Clinical Psychology, 65,* 531–541.

Centers for Disease Control and Prevention. (1999). *HIV/AIDS Prevention Research Synthesis Project: Compendium of HIV Prevention Interventions with Evidence of Effectiveness.*

Centers for Disease Control and Prevention. (2000). Tracking the hidden epidemics: Trends in STDs in the United States. Retrieved July 15, 2002, from http://www.cdc.gov.

Centers for Disease Control and Prevention. (2001). *HIV/AIDS Surveillance Report Midyear Edition, 13*(1), 5.

Chesney, M. A. (1994). Prevention of HIV and STD infections. *Preventive Medicine, 23,* 655–660.

Children Now & the Kaiser Family Foundation. (1999). Talking with kids about tough issues. Retrieved August 17, 1999, from http://www.talkingwithkids.org.

Cooper, M. L., Peirce, R. S., & Huselid, R. F. (1994). Substance use and sexual risk taking among Black adolescents and White adolescents. *Health Psychology, 13,* 251–262.

Coyle, K. K., Basen-Enquist, K. M., Kirby, D. B., Parcel, G. S., Banspach, S. W., Collins, J. L., et al. (2001). Safer Choices: Long-term impact on a multi-component school-based HIV, STD, and pregnancy prevention program. *Public Health Reports, 116*(1), 82–93.

Coyle, K. K., Kirby, D., Marin, B., Gomez, C., & Gregorich, S. (2000). *Effect of Draw the Line/Respect the Line on sexual behavior in middle schools.* Santa Cruz: ETR Associates.

Devine, D., Long, P., & Forehand, R. (1993). A prospective study of adolescent sexual activity: Description, correlates, and predictors. *Advances in Behaviour Research and Therapy, 15,* 185–209.

Duncan, S. C., Strycker, L. A., & Duncan, T. A. (1999). Exploring associations in developmental trends of adolescent substance use and risky sexual behavior in a high-risk population. *Journal of Behavioral Medicine, 22,* 21–34.

Ekstrand, M. L., Siegel, D. S., Nido, V., Faigeles, B., Cummings, G. A., Battle, R., et al. (1996, July). *Peer-led AIDS prevention delays onset of sexual activity and changes peer norms among urban junior high school students.* Paper presented at the 11th International Conference on AIDS, Vancouver, British Columbia, Canada.

Ellickson, P. (1984). *Designing an effective prevention program* [Rand paper series]. Santa Monica, CA: Rand Corporation.

Fisher, J. D., & Fisher, W. A. (1992). Changing AIDS risk behavior. *Psychological Bulletin, 111,* 455–474.

Fisher, J. D., & Fisher, W. A. (2000). Theoretical approaches to individual level change in HIV risk behavior. In J. Peterson & R. J. DiClemente (Eds.), *HIV prevention handbook* (pp. 3–55). New York: Kluwer Academic/Plenum Press.

Fisher, J. D., Fisher, W. A., Bryan, A., & Misovich, S. J. (2002). Theoretically grounded school-based interventions change HIV risk behavior in inner city youth. *Health Psychology, 2,* 177–186.

Fisher, W. A., & Fisher, J. D., (1993). A general social psychological model for changing AIDS risk behavior. In J. Pryor & G. Reeder (Eds.), *The social psychology of HIV infection* (pp. 127–153). Hillsdale, NJ: Erlbaum.

Fisher, W. A., Williams, S. S., Fisher, J. D., & Malloy, T. E. (1999). Understanding AIDS risk behavior among sexually active urban adolescents: An empirical test of the information-motivation-behavioral skills model. *AIDS and Behavior, 3,* 13–23.

Forehand, R., & Wierson, M. (1993). The role of developmental factors in planning behavioral interventions for children: Disruptive behavior as an example. *Behavior Therapy, 24,* 117–141.

Gillmore, M. R., Lewis, S. M., Lohr, M. J., Spencer, M. S., & White, R. D. (1997). Repeat pregnancies among adolescent mothers. *Journal of Marriage and the Family, 59,* 536–550.

Grunbaum, J., Kann, L., Kinchen, S. A., Williams, B., Ross, J. G., Lowry, R., et al. (2002). Youth risk behavior surveillance—United States, 2001. *MMWR, 51*(SS-04), 1–64.

Hardy, J. B., Astone, N. M., Brooks-Gunn, J., Shapiro, S., & Miller, T. L. (1998). Like mother, like child: Intergenerational patterns of age at first birth and associations with childhood and adolescent characteristics and adult outcomes in the second generation. *Developmental Psychology, 34,* 1220–1232.

Harvey, S. M., & Spigner, C. (1995). Factors associated with sexual behavior among adolescents: A multivariate analysis. *Adolescence, 30,* 253–264.

Hawkins, J. D., Catalano, R. F., Kosterman, R., Abbott, R. D., & Hill, K. G. (1999). Preventing adolescent health-risk behaviors by strengthening protection during childhood. *Archives of Pediatric and Adolescent Medicine, 153,* 226–234.

Henshaw, S. K. (1998). Unintended pregnancy in the United States. *Family Planning Perspectives, 1,* 24–29.

Herlocher, T., Hoff, C., & DeCarlo, P. (1995). *Can theory help in HIV prevention?* HIV Prevention Fact Sheet. University of California, San Francisco.

Hubbard, B. M., Giese, M., II, & Rainey, J. (1998). A replication of Reducing the Risk, a theory-based sexuality curriculum for adolescents. *Journal of School Health, 68,* 243–247.

Jemmott, J. B., & Jemmott, L. S. (1993). Alcohol and drug use during sexual activity: Predicting the HIV-risk-related behaviors of inner-city Black male adolescents. *Journal of Adolescent Research, 8,* 41–57.

Jemmott, J. B., III, Jemmott, L. S., & Fong, G. T. (1998). Abstinence and safer sex: A randomized trial of HIV sexual risk-reduction interventions for young African American adolescents. *Journal of the American Medical Association, 279,* 1529–1536.

Jemmott, L. S., & Jemmott, J. B. (1990). Sexual knowledge, attitudes, and risky sexual behavior among inner-city Black male adolescents. *Journal of Adolescent Research, 5,* 346–369.

Joseph, S. C. (1991). AIDS and adolescence: A challenge to both treatment and prevention. *Journal of Adolescent Health, 12,* 614–618.

Kann, L., Kinchen, S. A., Williams, B., II, Ross, J. G., Lowry, R., Hill, C., et al. (1998). Youth risk behavior surveillance-United States, 1997. *MMWR, 47*(SS-3), 1–89.

Kann, L., Warren, C. W., Harris, W. A., Collins, J. L., Douglas, K. A., Collins, M. E., et al. (1995). Youth risk behavior surveillance—United States, 1993. *MMWR, 44,* 1–57.

Kirby, D. (2001). *Emerging answers: Research findings on programs to reduce teen pregnancy.* Washington, DC: National Campaign to Prevent Teen Pregnancy.

Kirby, D., Barth, R., Leland, N., & Fetro, J. (1991). Reducing the risk: A new curriculum to prevent sexual risk-taking. *Family Planning Perspectives, 23,* 253–263.

Kirby, D., Short, L., Collins, J., Rugg, D., Kolbe, L., Howard, M., et al. (1994). School-based programs to reduce sexual risk behaviors: A review of effectiveness. *Public Health Reports, 109,* 339–360.

Kotchick, B. A., Armistead, L., Forehand, R., Long, N., Miller, K. S., Kelly, A., et al. (2002, November). *The Parents Matter! Program: A preliminary report.* Paper presented at the annual meeting of the Association for the Advancement of Behavior Therapy, Reno, NV.

Kotchick, B. A., Dorsey, S., Miller, K. S., & Forehand, R. (1999). Adolescent sexual risk-taking behavior in single-parent ethnic minority families. *Journal of Family Psychology, 13,* 93–102.

Kotchick, B. A., Shaffer, A., Forehand, R., & Miller, K. S. (2000). Adolescent sexual risk behavior: A multi-system perspective. *Clinical Psychology Review, 21,* 493–519.

Langer, L. M., & Tubman, J. G. (1997). Risky sexual behavior among substance-abusing adolescents: Psychosocial and contextual factors. *American Journal of Orthopsychiatry, 67,* 315–322.

Levinson, R. A., Jaccard, J., & Beamer, L. (1995). Older adolescents' engagement in casual sex: Impact of risk perception and psychosocial motivation. *Journal of Youth and Adolescence, 24,* 349–364.

Lowry, R., Holtzman, D., Truman, B. I., Kann, L., Collins, J. L., & Kolbe, L. J. (1994). Substance use and HIV-related sexual behaviors among U.S. high school students: Are they related? *American Journal of Public Health, 84,* 1116–1120.

Luster, T., & Small, S. A. (1994). Factors associated with sexual risk-taking behaviors among adolescents. *Journal of Marriage and the Family, 56,* 622–632.

Magura, S., Kang, S., & Shapiro, J. L. (1994). Outcomes of intensive AIDS education for male adolescent drug users in jail. *Journal of Adolescent Health, 15,* 457–463.

Main, D. S., Iverson, D. C., McGloin, J., Banspach, S. W., Collins, K., Rugg, D., et al. (1994). Preventing HIV infection among adolescents: Evaluation of a school-based education program. *Preventive Medicine, 23,* 409–417.

Martin, J. A., Hamilton, B. E., Ventura, S. J., Menacher, F., & Park, M. M. (2002). Births. *National Vital Statistics Reports, 50*(5).

Mason, C. A., Cauce, A. M., Gonzales, N., & Hiraga, Y. (1996). Neither too sweet nor too sour: Problem peers, maternal control, and problem behavior in African American adolescents. *Child Development, 67,* 2115–2130.

McKay, M., & Williams, J. (2002, July). *The CHAMPS (Collaborative HIV Prevention and Adolescent Mental Health Project) family program.* Workshop conducted at the annual NIMH conference on the Role of Families in Preventing and Adapting to HIV/AIDS, Miami, FL.

Melchert, T., & Burnett, K. F. (1990). Attitudes, knowledge, and sexual behavior of high-risk adolescents: Implications for counseling and sexuality education. *Journal of Counseling and Development, 68,* 293–298.

Miller, K. S., Forehand, R., & Kotchick, B. A. (1999). Adolescent sexual behavior in two ethnic minority samples: The role of family variables. *Journal of Marriage and the Family, 61,* 85–98.

Miller, K. S., Forehand, R., & Kotchick, B. A. (2000). Adolescent sexual behavior in two ethnic minority groups: A multi-system perspective. *Adolescence, 35,* 313–333.

Miller, K. S., Kotchick, B. A., Dorsey, S., Forehand, R., & Ham, A. Y. (1998). Family communication about sex: What are parents saying and are their adolescents listening? *Family Planning Perspectives, 30,* 218–222, 235.

Miller, K. S., Levin, M. L., Xu, X., & Whitaker, D. J. (1998). Patterns of condom use among adolescents: The impact of maternal-adolescent communication. *American Journal of Public Health, 88,* 1542–1544.

Millstein, S. G., & Moscicki, A. (1995). Sexually-transmitted disease in female adolescents: Effects of psychosocial factors and high risk behaviors. *Journal of Adolescent Health, 17,* 83–90.

National Campaign to Prevent Teen Pregnancy. (2002). Research, resources, and information. Retrieved July 15, 2002, from http://www.teenpregnancy.org.

Orr, D. P., Beiter, M., & Ingersoll, G. (1991). Premature sexual activity as an indicator of psychosocial risk. *Pediatrics, 87,* 141–147.

Overby, K. J., & Kegeles, S. M. (1994). The impact of AIDS on an urban population of high-risk female minority adolescents: Implications for intervention. *Journal of Adolescent Health, 15,* 216–227.

Pendergrast, R. A., DuRant, R. H., & Gaillard, G. L. (1992). Attitudinal and behavioral correlates of condom use in urban adolescent males. *Journal of Adolescent Health, 13,* 133–139.

Philliber, S., & Allen, J. P. (1992). Life options and community service: Teen Outreach Program. In B. C. Miller, J. J. Card, R. L. Paikoff, & J. L. Peterson (Eds.), *Preventing adolescent pregnancy* (pp. 139–155). Newbury Park, CA: Sage.

Philliber, S., Kaye, J. W., Herrling, S., & West, E. (2000). *Preventing teen pregnancy: An evaluation of the Children's Aid Society Carrera Program.* Accord, NY: Philliber Research Associates.

Pick, S., & Palos, P. A. (1995). Impact of the family on the sex lives of adolescents. *Adolescence, 30,* 667–675.

Reitman, D., St. Lawrence, J. S., Jefferson, K. W., Alleyne, E., Brasfield, T. L., & Shirley, A. (1996). Predictors of African American adolescents' condom use and HIV risk behavior. *AIDS Education and Prevention, 8,* 499–515.

Resnick, M. D., Bearman, P. S., Blum, R. W., Bauman, K. R., Harris, K. M., Jones, J., et al. (1997). Protecting adolescents from harm. *Journal of the American Medical Association, 278,* 823–832.

Rodgers, K. B. (1999). Parenting processes related to sexual risk-taking behaviors of adolescent males and females. *Journal of Marriage and the Family, 61,* 99–109.

Romer, D., Black, M., Ricardo, I., Feigelman, S., Kaljee, L., Galbraith, J., et al. (1994). Social influences on the sexual behavior of youth at risk for HIV exposure. *American Journal of Public Health, 84,* 977–985.

Roosa, M. W., Tein, J. Y., Reinholtz, C., & Angelini, P. J. (1997). The relationship of childhood sexual abuse to teenage pregnancy. *Journal of Marriage and the Family, 59,* 119–130.

Rotheram-Borus, M. J., Koopman, C., Haignere, C., & Davies, M. (1991). Reducing HIV sexual risk behaviors among runaway adolescents. *Journal of the American Medical Association, 266,* 1237–1241.

Scaramella, L. V., Conger, R. D., Simons, R. L., & Whitbeck, L. B. (1998). Predicting risk for pregnancy by late adolescence: a social contextual perspective. *Developmental Psychology, 34,* 1233–1245.

Seidman, S. N., & Reider, R. O. (1994). A review of sexual behavior in the United States. *American Journal of Psychiatry, 151,* 330–341.

Shafer, M. A., & Boyer, C. B. (1991). Psychosocial and behavioral factors associated with risk of sexually transmitted diseases, including human immunodeficiency virus, among urban high school students. *Journal of Pediatrics, 119,* 826–833.

Shrier, L. A., Emans, S. J., Woods, E. R., & DuRant, R. H. (1996). The association of sexual risk behaviors and problem drug behaviors in high school students. *Journal of Adolescent Health, 20,* 377–383.

Sigelman, C. K., Derenowski, E. B., Mullaney, H. A., & Siders, A. T. (1993). Parents' contributions to knowledge and attitudes regarding AIDS. *Journal of Pediatric Psychology, 18,* 221–235.

Smith, C. A. (1997). Factors associated with early sexual activity among urban adolescents. *Social Work, 42,* 334–346.

St. Lawrence, J. S., Brasfeld, T. L., Jefferson, K. W., Alleyne, E., O' Bannon, R. E., III, & Shirley, A. (1995). Cognitive-behavioral intervention to reduce African American adolescents' risk for HIV infection. *Journal of Consulting and Clinical Psychology, 63,* 221–237.

St. Lawrence, J. S., Jefferson, K. W., Banks, P. G., Clince, T. R., Alleyne, E., & Brasfield, T. L. (1994). Cognitive-behavioral group intervention to assist substance-dependent adolescents in lowering HIV infection risk. *AIDS Education and Prevention, 6,* 424–435.

Stanton, B., Li, X., Black, M., Ricardo, I., Galbraith, J., Kaljee, L., et al. (1994). Sexual practices and intentions among preadolescent and early adolescent low-income urban African Americans. *Pediatrics, 93,* 966–973.

Stanton, B. F., Li, X., Galbraith, J., Feigelman, S., & Kaljee, L. (1996). Sexually transmitted diseases, human immunodeficiency virus, and pregnancy prevention: Combined contraceptive practices among urban African American early adolescents. *Archives of Pediatrics and Adolescent Medicine, 150,* 17–24.

Steinberg, L. (1987). Familial factors in delinquency: A developmental perspective. *Journal of Adolescent Research, 2,* 255–268.

Stouthamer-Loeber, M., & Wei, E. H. (1998). The precursors of young fatherhood and its effect on delinquency of teenage males. *Journal of Adolescent Health, 22,* 56–65.

Strunin, L., & Hingson, R. (1992). Alcohol, drugs, and adolescent sexual behavior. *International Journal of the Addictions, 27,* 129–146.

Tubman, J. G., Windle, M., & Windle, R. C. (1996). Cumulative sexual intercourse patterns among middle adolescents: Problem behavior precursors and concurrent health risk behaviors. *Journal of Adolescent Health, 18,* 182–191.

Walter, H. J., & Vaughn, R. D. (1993). AIDS risk reduction among a multiethnic sample of urban high school students. *Journal of the American Medical Association, 270,* 725–730.

Zimet, G. D., Bunch, D. B., Anglin, T. M., Lazebnik, R., Williams, P., & Krowchuk, D. P. (1992). Relationship of AIDS-related attitudes to sexual behavior changes in adolescents. *Journal of Adolescent Health, 13,* 493–498.

Chapter 12

TOBACCO USE

JOHN P. ELDER, ESMERALDA M. INIGUEZ, AND SANDRA LARIOS

Tobacco kills. It is unique in this sense because with the possible exception of handguns, it is the only product to do so when used normally. There are no safe alternatives to smoking, and other forms of tobacco such as spit tobacco have also been found to have deleterious health effects. Tobacco use remains the leading preventable cause of death in the United States, resulting in more than 430,000 deaths per year among adults. This equals more than five million years of potential life lost (Centers for Disease Control [CDC], 2002b). The deleterious effects of tobacco use are realized not only in terms of health but in economic indicators as well. The CDC (2002a) reports that tobacco-related diseases produced an annual cost of more than $150 billion in health-related economic losses from 1995 to 1999 including $81.9 billion in mortality-related productivity losses and $75.5 billion in excess medical expenditures in 1998.

Despite overwhelming evidence indicating that the nicotine found in tobacco is addictive and destructive to health, tobacco use among adolescents increased in the 1990s after decreasing in the 1970s and 1980s (U.S. Department of Health and Human Services [USDHHS], 2000a). The importance of these statistics lies in the fact that approximately 90% of adult smokers started smoking before the age of 18 (Myers, 2002). According to the CDC, every day nearly 5,000 young people under the age of 18 try their first cigarette. More than 6.4 million children living today will die prematurely because of a decision they will make as adolescents—the decision to smoke cigarettes. These statistics have prompted an increase in both governmental and nongovernmental efforts to prevent smoking and other tobacco-related behaviors, especially among youth.

Healthy People 2010 (USDHHS, 2000a) is the current prevention agenda for the nation. Healthy People 2010 contains 10 leading health indicators to measure American health over the next 10 years. As a group, these health indicators represent our country's major health concerns, with tobacco use holding the third position (USDHHS, 2000a). By the year 2010, the Surgeon General expects to see a reduction in illness, disability, and deaths related to tobacco use and exposure to secondhand smoke. To achieve this goal, more population-based interventions with an emphasis on prevention of smoking initiation and reduction of exposure to environmental tobacco smoke should be developed and implemented in a culturally appropriate manner (USDHHS, 2000a). In addition to microlevel interventions, macrolevel elements should be taken into account in promoting the changing of social norms and environments that support tobacco use.

Of the 26 tobacco-related objectives proposed by Healthy People 2010, only three have been met. A review of the Healthy People 2010 objectives found a reduction in the rate of lung cancer deaths, a reduction in oral cancer deaths, and an increase in the number of states that have tobacco control plans (USDHHS, 2000a). Sixteen additional objectives evidence favorable progress, including reducing cigarette smoking among adults, which declined in the early part of the 1990s and then leveled off, and reducing children's exposure to secondhand smoke, which also declined because of the reduction in smoking among adults (USDHHS, 2000a). Although some progress has been realized, many objectives are yet to be met, specifically in the area of youth tobacco use. Although Healthy People 2000 data indicate that smoking among adolescents is declining, other surveys show that smoking among youth has increased through 1997 and has remained unchanged since (NCHS, 1999). The enforcement of minors' access to cigarettes and the ability to illegally purchase cigarettes is another important objective. Healthy People 2000 expressed the hope that efforts to purchase cigarettes illegally would succeed less than 20% of the time, but data suggest that only 12 states have met this target (NCHS, 1999).

Although substantial efforts have been made to prevent youth access to tobacco products from retail outlets, a new threat from the Internet has emerged. A 1997 report identified 13 Internet cigarette vendors and found that few had asked or attempted to verify the buyer's age (Forster, Wolfson, Murray, Wagenaar, & Claxton, 1997). Currently, there is no federal law that bans the sale of tobacco products to minors through the Internet. If this trend continues without regulation, in the next five years more than 100 stores could be selling tobacco to minors through the Internet. According to the State Youth Tobacco Surveys, approximately 1% of middle school and 1.4% of high school current smokers reported purchasing their last pack of cigarettes from the Internet (CDC, 2000b). Although the percentage is relatively small, more than eight million teens access the Internet, representing more than half of the U.S. teen population. Researchers report that most Internet cigarette vendors use inadequate procedures for age verification (Ribisl, Kim, & Williams, 2002).

TRENDS AND INCIDENCE

Public health has made great strides in reducing smoking prevalence and preventing the initiation of smoking. In 1963, the per capita consumption of cigarettes was 4,345, falling by half to 2,261 in 1998, the latter figure being the lowest per capita consumption since the 1940s (CDC, 1999a). The CDC noted that there is still great need to decrease the prevalence among young people, which has increased since 1991. Specifically, society still must decrease the morbidity and mortality due to smoking and to ensure that laws meant to protect people from secondhand smoke are enforced (CDC, 1999a). In the latter half of the twentieth century, progress in the fight against tobacco included the following:

- Smoking prevalence among adults 18 years of age and older decreased from 42% in 1965 to 25% in 1997.
- Approximately 1.6 million deaths were postponed because of antitobacco efforts.
- Deaths due to heart disease decreased from 307 per 100,000 in 1950 to 135 per 100,000 in 1996.
- Smoking during commercial flights was prohibited.
- About 12.5% of parents who smoked reported smoking is not allowed in their homes (CDC, 1999b).

The reduction of cigarette smoking that has occurred since the 1960s has been acknowledged as one of the 10 greatest public health achievements of the twentieth century according to the CDC (1999a). Although there has been substantial progress in the prevention of initiation of smoking, tobacco use cessation, decreasing exposure to secondhand smoke, and decreasing the incidence of disease due to smoking, much remains to be done. Past-month smoking prevalence for high school seniors decreased between the late 1970s and the mid-1980s, but smoking rebounded from 28.3% in 1991 to 36.5% in 1997 (CDC, 1999a). Each day, about 3,000 teenagers become daily smokers (CDC, 1996). Of the current cohort of American 18-year-olds, approximately five million will die prematurely as adults because they initiated smoking during their adolescence (CDC, 2000a). The smoking pandemic threatens youth not only in the United States but also around the world. In 2002, a Global Youth Tobacco Survey (GYTS) carried out international comparisons of tobacco use for 13- to 15-year-old students from 75 sites in 43 different countries. This survey showed that 14% of students around the world (ages 13 to 15) currently smoke, 25% of students who smoke tried their first cigarette by the age of 10, and more than two-thirds (68%) of young smokers want to quit (CDC, 2002a). Among U.S. students, 18% smoke cigarettes (compared to a global mean of 14%), 42% were exposed to smoke at home, and 56% of American youth wanted to quit smoking (CDC, 2002a). From all points of view, tobacco control will remain a top public health priority for the foreseeable future.

RISK FACTORS

Smoking initiation and maintenance are influenced by a combination of psychological and social factors, including a poor self-image, low self-esteem, lack of self-efficacy, and insufficient knowledge about the consequences of tobacco use. These factors may contribute to an inability to refuse peer pressure to smoke. If adolescents lack the skill to refuse a cigarette or at least to do so without angering their friends, they will be more likely to succumb to peer pressure to smoke. Insufficient knowledge about tobacco use may partially contribute to initiation; those who are unaware that smoking is harmful or have incorrect knowledge about its addictive capabilities are more likely to accept a cigarette. Subjective norms lead adolescents to believe that tobacco use is more prevalent than is actually the case, in turn making them more likely to initiate smoking. Other psychosocial risk factors include poor academic achievement and low school involvement. Individuals with poor grades and low school involvement are more likely to have low self-esteem and feelings of self-worth, which in turn make them more vulnerable to tobacco and other substance use. Finally, interpersonal skill deficits, specifically, a lack of ability to refuse the offer of a cigarette or other substance from a peer in a socially adept manner, may predict the initiation of smoking, although the literature has been inconsistent in this area (Elder, Sallis, Woodruff, & Wildey, 1993). A combination of these factors must be taken into account when designing interventions to properly address the process of smoking initiation (Elder, Larios, & Iniguez, in press).

Even more salient risks for the onset of smoking among youth are the social and physical environments. Cohen, Scribner, and Farley (2000) propose a *structural model* of environment-behavior relationships consisting of four factors:

1. *Availability* is how accessible a product is to the consumer (e.g., sale of cigarettes over the Internet).

2. *Physical structures* are environmental factors that are likely to encourage a certain behavior to occur (e.g., the use of characters that appeal to youth when advertising cigarettes).

3. *Social structures* are composed of social norms, laws, and policies.

4. *Media and cultural messages* influence favorable and unfavorable attitudes about healthy and at-risk behaviors.

Cohen and her colleagues argue that these four factors represent a blueprint for explaining much of public health risk-related behavior and how to change it (Elder, 2001). The tobacco industry has made sure that their products are widely available, that tobacco is viewed as a positive and rewarding product, that laws and policies are enacted and implemented as slowly and weakly as possible, and that there is ample advertising to reach their targeted populations, thereby indicating that they already have mastered an understanding of these environment-behavior relationships.

Despite the efforts to control the availability of cigarettes, a high percentage of youth in the United States are still able to buy their own (USDHHS, 2000b). Former Surgeon General David Satcher noted some of the successful measures to reduce youth access to tobacco were restricting distribution, regulating mechanisms of sale, enforcing minimum age laws, and providing merchant education and training (USDHHS, 2000b). In the Global Youth Tobacco Survey, 10.6% of students reported that they had received free cigarettes from a tobacco company (CDC, 2002a). Cigarettes are still available in some states through vending machines and the Internet. Public health forces must strive for strict bans on the sale of cigarettes in places frequented by youth and to ensure that vendors are strictly enforcing the age requirement to buy cigarettes.

Social sources for cigarettes and *social structures* in general also play a central role in the onset of smoking. The need to be accepted by peers represents a powerful negative reinforcer for taking up smoking. The GYTS found that 28% of students believed that boys who smoked had more friends (CDC, 2002a). What starts as a need to be accepted by peers may develop into a physiological and psychological addiction later in life and lead to a person's becoming a regular smoker. Thus, an important subtheme within tobacco control interventions is to influence the way tobacco is viewed and make teenagers realize that there are other ways to be accepted by their peers besides smoking cigarettes.

The tobacco industry targets the public with media and cultural messages that associate cigarettes with glamour, sex appeal, and diversion. Although tobacco industry executives vehemently deny that they target children and youth, they have created marketing campaigns where the main characters (exemplified by the infamous Joe Camel by R.J. Reynolds) are extremely and even uniquely appealing to this market segment. Researchers have found that as much as one-third of all experimentation with smoking may be directly attributable to advertising and other promotion (Pierce, Choi, Gilpin, Farkas, & Berry, 1998). Because youth make up the majority of new smokers, tobacco companies try to target specifically this part of the population (USDHHS, 2000b). Although tobacco companies have been restricted in the types of advertisements they can use for their products, public health vigilance remains an ongoing requirement. In 2002, R.J. Reynolds was fined $20 million for targeting California youth in magazines, a direct violation of the 1998 tobacco settlement (Myers, 2002). Despite the industry's promise to stop marketing to youth, they continue both direct and indirect advertisement in convenience stores and other venues and through product placement in movies and at sporting events popular among youth (Myers, 2002). The GYTS found that almost 80% of the students that they interviewed saw tobacco ads at sporting and other events (CDC, 2002a).

PREVENTION STRATEGIES

In the past 15 years, various researchers have attempted to go beyond a simple smoker/nonsmoker dichotomy by categorizing youth with respect to their susceptibility to tobacco use. For example, Kaufman et al. (2002) examined the smoking uptake continuum by defining three categories of youth who in their lifetime have never smoked an entire cigarette and four categories of those who have. In the former group are *never smokers, susceptible never smokers* (i.e., have not smoked but will not commit to staying smoke free), and *experimenters.* The latter three categories include current smokers who have smoked fewer than 100 cigarettes lifetime, regular smokers, and former smokers (no cigarettes in the past 30 days) who either have or have not committed to remaining smoke free. Prevention approaches may be categorized as universal, selective, and indicated in the context of the smoking uptake continuum (National Institute of Drug Abuse [NIDA], 1997). Universal prevention targets entire populations, not all of whom will be at high risk for any given habit or illness. For example, 60% to 70% of youth may never proceed beyond the nonsusceptible or susceptible never-smoker stage. Selective interventions are critical for youth who may be susceptible to beginning tobacco use, who have already experimented, or who have recently quit. Indicated interventions are especially relevant to current and regular smokers, many of whom already would like to quit.

Universal Prevention Strategies: Interpersonal and Mass Media Interventions

As with any approach to prevention, activities targeted at smoking are based on the assumption that the relevant behaviors develop over time. Given the trend toward tobacco use initiation at a younger age, most prevention programs are universal in nature, targeting all adolescents in specific settings, groups, or age cohorts (usually between 12 and 14, but extending to 18). It is at this age that the influence of parents begins to decrease with a concurrent rise in peer influence. Although the source of influence shifts, the functioning of the family, including continued support by parents and communication between parents and adolescents, can serve to reduce the risk of tobacco use in adolescents (Hawkins, Catalano, & Miller, 1992). Much of adolescent risk behavior, such as experimenting with sex and tobacco use, is part of the normal adolescent development process (Baumrind, 1985; Logan, 1991). However, preadolescents are more likely to initiate tobacco use and delinquent behavior if they do not get along with family members, have less affectionate relationships, identify less with their parents, or perceive themselves to be in poor communication with their parents (Stern, Northman, & Van Slyck, 1984).

Adolescent and parent-oriented interventions that develop skills allowing adolescents to combat peer influence, promote parental support of healthy behaviors, and improve decision making and communication have been shown to be effective approaches to preventing tobacco use, at least in the short term. Such approaches can also provide the context for intervening in parental tobacco use (which is associated with use among children).

School-based educational interventions traditionally focus on *information deficit,* or *rational* models (Smedley & Syme, 2000), whereas other *affective education* approaches have emphasized affective responses among youth in attempts to influence beliefs, attitudes, intentions, and subjective norms related to smoking while enhancing self-esteem and clarifying values (Durell & Bukoski, 1984). The former of these two approaches appears to be ineffective, and affective education has a fairly minor impact as well (Lantz et al., 2000).

A third widely used educational intervention evolved somewhat more recently, emphasizing social influence resistance or *social inoculation.* Brief interventions center around social inoculation activities, which through role plays teach refusal skills for resisting prompts to smoke. These role plays are placed in the context of realistic mock situations, in which peers play the part of the friend, sibling, or adult trying to convince the participant to have a smoke. Social inoculation programs have been shown to be somewhat effective in reducing smoking onset (Lantz et al., 2000). School-based interventions are typically led by teachers, older youth (e.g., college students), or same-age peers (Elder, Wildey, et al., 1993). Involving peers in the development and delivery of educational interventions helps the recipient of the intervention to feel more powerful and enhances the possibility of behavior change (Quirk, Godkin, & Schwenzfeier, 1993). Thus, peer-led interventions have often been viewed as being more effective than teacher-led programs (Botvin, 1986; Klepp, Halper, & Perry, 1986); however, training and deploying same-age peers can present significant logistical problems

(Elder, Wildey, et al., 1993). Multiple-year school-based interventions, extending throughout the middle-school years and even into high school (and thereby capturing the adolescent at different developmental stages), may be more effective than single-year interventions (Elder, Wildey, et al., 1993).

The NCI-funded Project SHOUT incorporated the previously discussed components in a three-year intervention (seventh through ninth grades) with high school boosters using college-age facilitators. SHOUT produced a one-third lower tobacco use rate (22% versus 14%) in intervention schools by the end of the ninth grade. However, much of the success of the intervention stemmed from the third-year (ninth grade), home-based component rather than the previous two years' (seventh and eighth grades) curriculum implemented in the school. This differential was thought to be due to the stronger one-to-one relationships established between college-age facilitators and ninth graders through personalized phone calls contrasted to presentations in large classrooms. SHOUT's effects were maintained through the high school years for adolescents who continued to receive the home-based intervention (Eckhardt, Woodruff, & Elder, 1997).

Some studies have shown mass media campaign to be effective in decreasing tobacco use onset and increasing antitobacco attitudes (Popham et al., 1993). However, Flay and colleagues concluded that media programs alone are not effective (Flay, 1985; Flay et al., 1998), but instead are more effectively used in the dissemination of other prevention resources. Other researchers have advocated the use of mass media if accompanied by other potentially powerful interventions such as taxation (Hu, Sung, & Keeler, 1995) or school interventions (Flynn et al., 1997). Media advocacy messages (Wallack & Dorfman, 1992), in which youth are exhorted to be aware of the manipulation that the tobacco industry is trying to realize in promoting smoking to them, may be especially attractive to youth (Goldman & Glantz, 1998).

Recent advertising campaigns have been deployed to counter tobacco advertising and to increase the attention to and attractiveness of the nonsmoking/antitobacco spots. The California and Florida state campaigns emphasize an anti-industry message. Innovative media spots and web sites (such as thetruth.com) encourage youth to become social activists through individual activities such as ripping tobacco ads out of magazines and destroying them and through collective actions such as communicating directly with politicians and the tobacco industry about the exploitation of youth that occurs through the promotion of tobacco use. Ads in Arizona and Massachusetts are more typically oriented toward changing tobacco-related affect, as well as the anticipation of the consequences of smoking. Although these campaigns appear to be important complements to the overall tobacco control effort (e.g., increasing excise taxes, developing and enforcing sales policies), it is difficult to say whether they provide independent contributions to preventing uptake and improving cessation. There have been several studies of mass media-based prevention programs (Bauman, LaPrelle, Brown, Koch, & Padgett, 1991; Bauman et al., 1998; Flay et al., 1995), ranging from videotapes and paid spots to messages delivered in different languages. These studies do not represent all that is known about general health promotion through mass media, but they show how mass media can be helpful in tobacco use prevention and how to make use of communication and behavioral sciences in planning effective media materials (Bettinghaus et al., 1988).

Several authors have spoken to the effectiveness of tobacco advertising in increasing youth curiosity about and attraction to using tobacco products. Specific ad campaigns undertaken by the industry over the past decades have apparently been effective in promoting sales to this market segment. However, the effectiveness of restricting tobacco advertising has yet to be proven. Partial bans appear to be especially ineffective because they allow cigarettes to be promoted via movies, sporting events, and other formats popular among youth (Saffer & Chaloupka, 1999). Recently, the European Union realized a very important step in the fight against tobacco by banning advertisements in magazines and newspapers, on the radio, and via the Internet. Tobacco companies are also prohibited from sponsoring events such as Formula One motor racing. Recommended but not required are bans on billboard advertisements and the use of brands and logos on clothing and other consumer materials. Barring court challenges, member countries are to enact these regulations no later than January 2005 (Meller, 2002).

Selective Prevention: Controlling Tobacco and Promoting Tobacco-Free Environments

Some youth, although not yet smoking themselves, may be at risk for taking up the habit by virtue of encountering readily available tobacco products in their environments. Several approaches for reducing tobacco availability to minors who are susceptive (never smoked) or who have experimented with tobacco products have been described in the literature, including:

- Restricting distribution
- Regulating how cigarettes are sold
- Enforcing minimum age laws (age 18 or 19 in all states)
- Easing the burden of enforcement by allowing civil rather than criminal penalties for illegal sales
- Providing merchant training on the laws and compliance with them

Recent years have witnessed substantial progress in reducing availability of tobacco products. Free samples are no longer distributed to adolescents nor in general to the public. Vending machines, for more than a generation the pusher of choice among adolescent smokers, have been restricted to adult-only establishments or banned altogether.

Three decades ago, adults and even youth were allowed to smoke cigarettes in numerous and varied public places, including on some school grounds. Today, proscriptions on indoor environmental tobacco smoke (ETS) inhibit not only youth but also adult smoking, thereby reducing physical harm to the nonsmoker while communicating to the adolescent the social undesirability of the habit. Other physical structural interventions include the design of vending machines so that they may be electronically locked or require special tokens purchased from the merchant. The elimination of self-service tobacco displays also may reduce sales to minors (Biedell, Furlong, Dunn, & Koegler, 2000).

Research has shown that adolescents are less likely to smoke in settings where tobacco prices are higher, tobacco tax revenues are earmarked for antitobacco activities, there are statutes that strictly limit public smoking, and bans on retailing to youth are strictly enforced (Chaloupka & Pacula, 1998). Price increases may be especially effective at dissuading low-income youth from smoking (Biener, Aseltine, Cohen, & Anderka, 1998). Although youth may continue to spend money on cigarettes, continuing to increase the price may decrease consumption and thus reduce addiction (Elder, 2001).

The primary method for increasing tobacco product prices is through tobacco excise taxes, especially given that cigarette taxes in many of the United States are still low compared to many European and Canadian standards. Tobacco excise taxes are specific state and local government taxes on cigarette products. Until about fifteen years ago, such taxes were seldom seen as a method of tobacco control. However, following the Proposition 99 voter-initiated tax increase in California (Elder et al., 1990), in which excise taxes were increased 25 cents and a sharp reduction in tobacco purchasing was quickly evident, public health officials have increasingly advocated the use of such *sin taxes*. Excise taxes may be especially effective if the revenue is dedicated to additional antitobacco education and policy development.

The Symar Amendment of 1991 mandates that all states in the United States enforce laws that restrict the sale of tobacco to youth, and they must demonstrate success in reducing youth access. By involving adolescents themselves in enforcement, the impact of social structural changes may be enhanced. In numerous states and communities, adolescent sting operations are coordinated by local police, whereby underage youth enter a store, attempt a purchase, and record the vendor's response (i.e., whether he or she asked for identification and refused the sale or proceeded with the illegal sale). The vendor or owner may then be cited for an illegal sale or reinforced for obeying the law. This amendment has lead to a variety of complementary interventions to restrict youth access and enforce existing laws, such as Project TRUST (Wildey et al., 1995). Project TRUST (Teens and Retailers United to Stop Tobacco) employed underage confederates who conducted sting operations for the project in targeted tobacco retail outlets such as convenience stores and gas stations. These teens attempted a purchase of a tobacco product and, if successful, informed the sales clerk that he or she had broken the law by offering to sell the product. Alternatively, they would reinforce other merchants who complied with the law and refused the attempted purchase. This effort apparently was effective in reducing illegal tobacco sales, at least in those particular stores targeted by the intervention. Developing similar interventions through community political bodies, Forster et al. (1998) showed that localities that promulgated new ordinances and policies and ways of enforcing these policies, especially with sales to minors, experienced lower rates of adolescent tobacco use as a result.

DiFranza, Richard, Radecki, and Savageau (2001) modeled the potential cost effectiveness of enforcing a prohibition on the sale of tobacco to minors nationwide. They estimate that there are 543,000 tobacco outlets nationwide, and enforcement of prohibitions on youth sales would cost as much as $190 million per year. Depending on the model, this cost would average anywhere from $44 to $8,200 per year of life saved. Even toward the upper end of this wide range, the per unit of cost such a nationwide enforcement program could eventually save is 10 times as many lives per amount of money compared to mammography or colorectal cancer screening. A simple one-cent nationwide excise tax increase could fully fund such a national enforcement. In contrast to DiFranza et al.'s predicted savings for increased enforcement, Tengs, Osgood, and Chen (2001) estimate that an intensive national school-based antitobacco education effort would cost between $4,900 and $340,000 per quality adjusted life year, depending on program factors and effectiveness.

In spite of success, increased Internet access to tobacco products has probably offset some of this progress in reducing illegal sales. Whatever retail sources of tobacco have been diminished, social sources seem to have made up for less access from the commercial sector (Forster, Klepp, & Jeffrey, 1989; Soldz, Kreiner, Clark, & Krakow, 2001). For example, Matei and McFee (2001) note that it is easier for youth to attain cigarettes than nicotine gum or nicotine replacement therapy product. Adolescents are still going to have ample opportunity to become regular smokers for the foreseeable future.

Indicated Interventions: Working with the Adolescent Experimenter and Early Smoker

Interventions to achieve acceptable cessation rates among adolescents who are already regular or addicted smokers have gained increasing attention over the past few years. Smoking cessation among motivated adolescents enrolled in formal programs may approach those of adults (Sargent, Mott, & Stevens, 1998). The NOT on Tobacco (NOT) Program in Florida (Dino et al., 2001) provides a good example of a promising smoking cessation effort. This American Lung Association program includes ten 50-minute sessions that occur once a week for 10 consecutive weeks. NOT is designed to be delivered in same-gender groups by trained same-gender facilitators. NOT comprises a *total health approach* to smoking cessation, with a focus on:

1. Motivation
2. Smoking history
3. Addiction
4. Consequences of smoking
5. Preparing for quitting
6. Preventing relapse
7. Dealing with ongoing social pressure to smoke
8. Increasing healthy physical activity levels and nutrition change

Covalidated quit rates were nearly twice as high in the NOT group contrasted to a more typical brief intervention approach (this differential, however, was almost totally accounted for by the females in the program).

Adult smokers who receive regular advice from their physicians to quit smoking evidence modest but important improvements in their cessation rates over those who do not receive such advice. Experts have begun to argue that adolescents should receive similar medical advice. Schubiner, Howard, and Hurt (1998) recommended physician participation in promoting adolescent cessation at the same level as used in adult cessation. They also recommend that the office environment and systems support such efforts through chart marking, waiting room literature and signs, and identifying a smoking cessation coordinator. Nurses and other allied health professionals can also complement the advice and follow up on referrals to make sure that teen smokers get the help they need to quit. All health professionals may be briefly trained in motivational interviewing to enhance their ability to conduct appropriate cessation interventions. Pharmacological adjuncts may be important elements of cessation promotion. Nevertheless, evaluations of the methods are few, and quasi-experimental research of the nicotine patch for promoting smoking cessation among adolescents has shown the patch to be ineffective (Backinger & Leischow, 2001).

Regardless of what cessation efforts are undertaken, they should start early. In a clinical study in Finland, 13- to 15-year-old smokers were followed until they reached the age of 28 (Paavola, Vartiainenm, & Ouska, 2001). At that time, two-thirds of the smokers were still smoking, an even higher figure among those who had initially been daily smokers. Lamkin, Davis, and Kamen (1998) reviewed numerous studies on cessation interventions for teens. They indicated that many teen smokers, especially daily users, desire to give up the habit (74% of occasional users and 65% of daily users; Stone & Kristeller, 1992). They conclude by advising health care providers to routinely identify and intervene with all tobacco users at every visit and offer smoking cessation treatment, nicotine replacement therapy, social support and skills training, and follow-up visits or phone calls.

Balch (1998) indicated that additional qualitative research may need to be done to determine more effective cessation rates. Specifically, he found that teen smokers in general had trouble imagining being attracted to a structured program. Group discussions and topics that included issues other than smoking, incentives, and sympathetic adult leaders may contribute to program success, at least in recruiting individual teens.

Stanton and Smith (2002) conducted a review of the literature on fully evaluated smoking cessation programs for teens. Eighteen studies were identified, including quasi-experimental (typically pre- and posttest for a single group) and controlled evaluations of smoking cessation programs. Nine of the 18 published studies were of the quasi-experimental variety, showing varying degrees of promise in researching new techniques for adolescent smoking cessation. Of the nine controlled trials, five appeared to be relatively effective, at least at short-term follow-up. Four of these nine showed little or no relative effectiveness for the experimental intervention groups.

Penalties for Possession and Use

A variety of communities and states have initiated efforts to place penalties on the books for underage individuals carrying or using tobacco products in public. Typically, youth are ticketed or fined for possession or use. Teen smoking courts (Lantz et al., 2000) at both state and local levels are being implemented, in which parents often must appear with their children in response to the youths' breaking tobacco control laws. To date, no evaluation of these efforts has been conducted. A specific effort to enforce the possession law was recently evaluated in Florida. A total of 2,088 randomly selected youth were surveyed as part of a study of tobacco-related law enforcement. This study indicated that possession enforcement as part of an overall tobacco control effort may help youth reduce their tobacco use and may be an important component of overall prevention efforts (Livingood, Woodhouse, Sayre, & Wludyka, 2001).

Strong school policies that proscribe smoking, in place with smoking prevention efforts, may prove effective in lowering school-wide prevalence (Pentz et al., 1989). The restrictions on sale in addition to banning vending machines or exiling them to adult-only venues (e.g., bars) has already shown the effectiveness of structurally-oriented policy changes in reducing overall consumption. Recent efforts have emphasized reduction in self-service displays of tobacco. Additionally, some communities have banned billboard advertisement and other forms of marketing tobacco near school grounds.

Restrictions on Smoking and Advertising

Clean indoor air laws in many states and communities ban smoking inside a building in which others may be exposed or at least banish it to a ventilated smoking room. Studies have shown that such indoor smoking bans can be effective not only in reducing on-site smoking but also in increasing the attractiveness of quitting smoking altogether. Restrictions of smoking in public places can indeed reduce cigarette smoking among young people (Chaloupka, & Wechsler, 1997; Grossman & Chaloupka, 1997).

An evaluation of laws prohibiting self-service tobacco displays was conducted by Hyland and Cummings (2001) in which 270 licensed tobacco-selling retail outlets in upstate New York were surveyed. Three of four merchants believed that existing New York law banning the sale of tobacco products that allows direct access to the product were not difficult to comply with. Only 5% of these retailers reported that they had to spend money to comply with the law. Most of the stores reported no change in tobacco sales after the law took effect; 85% of the retailers thought that elimination of direct access probably reduced the theft of tobacco products. It can be assumed that much of this theft was being carried out by underage youth. Finally, 69% of the retailers indicated that fewer underage youth were trying to purchase cigarettes illegally following the implementation of the law.

SUMMARY

Twenty-five years ago, recognizing the futility of trying to get people to withdraw from an established addiction, especially hard-core smokers, tobacco control programs shifted their attention to universal prevention of first-time or regular smoking. These programs specifically addressed peer pressure to begin smoking and interpersonal skills designed to counteract this pressure. However, the bulkiness (e.g., requiring 10 to 20 classroom hours over two or more school years) and limited effectiveness of many prevention programs have limited their widespread adoption.

Over time, tobacco control experts sought more aggressive and accessible structural changes to promote tobacco control. Mass media spots to counter the tobacco industry image, taken off the airways as part of an American congressional compromise with the industry 30 years ago, once again came into vogue. Not only did these spots aim to encourage prevention and cessation, but also they are used to question the very legitimacy of the tobacco industry and its marketing. Mass media interventions have helped lower smoking initiation in the United States (Biener & Siegel, 2000; Worden et al., 1996). Provocative themes and messages may be especially attractive to adolescents and may boost the preventive power of such spots (Hafstad et al., 1997).

Selective interventions target adolescents who may be more proactively interested in starting smoking by either restricting distribution, regulating how cigarettes are sold, enforcing minimum age laws, allowing civil penalties for illegal sales, and/or providing merchant training about the laws and compliance with them. Finally, indicated programs focus on the experimenter and young smoker, through direct cessation interventions or through penalizing possession and use of cigarettes.

REFERENCES

Aveyard, P., Sherratt, E., Almond, H., Lawrence, T., Lancashire, R., Griffen, C., et al. (2001). The change-in-stage and updated smoking status results from a cluster-randomized trial of smoking prevention and cessation suing the transtheoretical model among British adolescents. *Preventive Medicine, 33,* 313–324.

Backinger, C. L., & Leischow, S. J. (2001). Advancing the science of adolescent tobacco use cessation. *American Journal of Health Behavior, 25*(3), 183–190.

Balch, G. (1998). Exploring perceptions of smoking cessation among high school smokers: Input and feedback from focus groups. *Preventive Medicine, 27*(5, Pt. 3), A55–A63.

Bauman, K. E., Brown, J. D., Bryan, E. S., Fisher, L. A., Padgett, C. A., & Sweeney, J. M. (1998). Three mass media campaigns to prevent adolescent cigarette smoking. *Preventive Medicine, 17*(5), 510–530.

Bauman, K. E., LaPrelle, J., Brown, J. D., Koch, G. G., & Padgett, C. A. (1991). The influence of three mass media campaigns on variables related to adolescent cigarette smoking: Results of a field experiment. *American Journal of Public Health, 81*(1), 597–604.

Baumrind, D. (1985). Familial antecedents of adolescent drug use: A developmental perspective. *National Institute of Drug Abuse: Research Monograph Series, 56,* 13–44.

Bettinghaus, E. P. (1988). Forum: A mass media campaign. *Preventive Medicine, 17,* 503–509.

Biedell, M. P., Furlong, M. J., Dunn, D. M., & Koegler, J. E. (2000). Case study of attempts to enact self-service tobacco display ordinances: A tale of three communities. *Tobacco Control, 9,* 71–77.

Biener, L., Aseltine, R. J., Cohen, B., & Anderka, M. (1998). Reactions of adult and teen smokers to the Massachusetts tobacco tax. *American Journal of Public Health, 88*(9), 1389–1391.

Biener, L., & Siegel, M. (2000). Tobacco marketing and adolescent smoking: More support for a causal inference. *American Journal of Public Health, 90,* 407–411.

Botvin, G. J. (1986). Substance abuse prevention research: Recent developments and future directions. *Journal of School Health, 56*(9), 369–374.

Centers for Disease Control and Prevention. (1996). The Great American Smokeout. *Morbidity and Mortality Weekly Report, 45*(44), 961.

Centers for Disease Control and Prevention. (1999a). Achievements in public health: Tobacco use: United States, 1900–1999. *Morbidity and Mortality Weekly Report, 48*(43), 986–993.

Centers for Disease Control and Prevention. (1999b). Cigarette smoking among adults: United States, 1997. *Morbidity and Mortality Weekly Report, 48*(43), 993.

Centers for Disease Control and Prevention. (2000a). Youth tobacco surveillance: United States, 1998–1999. *Morbidity and Mortality Weekly Report, 49*(SS–10),1–93.

Centers for Disease Control and Prevention. (2000b). Youth tobacco surveillance: United States. *Morbidity and Mortality Weekly Report, 50*(SS–04), 1–84.

Centers for Disease Control and Prevention. (2002a). *Tobacco information and prevention source.* Retrieved October 25, 2002, from http://www.cdc.gov/tobacco/issue .htm.

Centers for Disease Control and Prevention. (2002b, August 28). *Youth tobacco use and exposure is a global problem* [Press release]. Washington, DC: Government Printing Office.

Chaloupka, F. J., & Pacula, R. L. (1998). *Limiting youth access to tobacco: The early impact of the Synar Amendment on youth smoking.* Paper presented at the third biennial Pacific Rim Allied Economic Organizations Conference, Bangkok, Thailand. (Available from F. J. Chaloupka, 361 Wildwood Drive, N., Aurora, IL 60542)

Chaloupka, F. J., & Wechsler, H. (1997). Price, tobacco control policies and smoking among young adults. *Journal of Health Education, 16,* 359–373.

Cohen, D., Scribner, R., & Farley, T. (2000). A structural model of health behavior: A pragmatic approach to explain and influence health behaviors at the population level. *Preventive Medicine, 30,* 146–154.

DiFranza, J. R., Richard, P. M., Radecki, T. E., & Savageau, J. (2001). What is the potential cost-effectiveness of enforcing a prohibition on the sale of tobacco to minors? *Preventive Medicine, 32,* 168–174.

Dino, F., Horn, K., Goldcamp, J., Fernandes, A., Kaleskar, I., & Massey, C. (2001). A 2-year efficacy study of not on tobacco in Florida: An overview of program successes in changing teen smoking behavior. *Preventive Medicine, 33(6),* 600–605.

Durell, J., & Bukoski, W. (1984). Preventing substance abuse: The state of the art public health report. *Public Health Report, 99(1),* 23–31.

Eckhardt, L., Woodruff, S. I., & Elder, J. (1997). Relative effectiveness of continued, lapsed and delayed smoking prevention intervention in senior high school students. *American Journal of Health Promotion, 11(6),* 418–421.

Elder, J. (2001). Preventing smoking in multiethnic communities. *American Journal of Health Behavior, 25(3),* 200–205.

Elder, J., de Moor, C., Young, R., Wildey, M., Molgaard, C., Golbeck, A., et al. (1990). States of adolescent tobacco-use acquisition. *Addictive Behaviors, 15,* 449–454.

Elder, J., Larios, S., & Iniguez, E. M. (in press). Smoking prevention. In N. Anderson (Ed.), *Encyclopedia of behavioral medicine.* Thousand Oaks, CA: Sage.

Elder, J., Sallis, J., Woodruff, S., & Wildey, M. (1993). Tobacco-refusal skills and tobacco use among high-risk adolescents. *Journal of Behavioral Medicine, 16(6),* 629–642.

Elder, J., Wildey, M., de Moor, C., Sallis, J., Eckhardt, L., Edwards, C., et al. (1993). Long term prevention of tobacco use among junior high school students through classroom telephone interventions. *American Journal of Public Health, 83,* 1239–1244.

Flay, B. R. (1985). Psychosocial approaches to smoking prevention: A review of findings. *Health Psychology, 4(5),* 449–488.

Flay, B. R., Brannon, B. R., Johnson, C. A., Hansen, W. B., Ulene, A. L., Whitney-Saltiel, D. A., et al. (1998). The Television, School, and Family Smoking Prevention and Cessation Project: 1. Theoretical basis and program development. *Preventive Medicine, 17(5),* 585–607.

Flay, B. R., Miller, T. Q., Hedeker, D., Siddiqui, O., Britton, C. F., Brannon, B. R., et al. (1995). The Television, School, and Family Smoking Prevention and Cessation Project: VIII. Student outcomes and mediating variables. *Preventive Medicine, 24(1),* 29–40.

Flynn, B. S., Worden, J. K., Secker-Walker, R. H., Pirie, P. L., Badger, G. J., & Carpenter, J. H. (1997). Long-term responses of higher and lower risk youths to smoking preventive interventions. *Preventive Medicine, 26(3),* 389–394.

Forster, J. L., Klepp, K. I., & Jeffrey, R. W. (1989). Sources of cigarettes for tenth graders in two Minnesota cities. *Health Education Research, 4,* 45–50.

Forster, J. L., Murray, D. M., Wolfson, M., Blaine, T. M., Wagenaar, A. C., & Hennrikus, D. J. (1998). The effects of community policies to reduce youth access to tobacco. *American Journal of Public Health, 88(8),* 1193–1198.

Forster, J. L., Wolfson, M., Murray, D. M., Wagenaar, A. C., & Claxton, A. J. (1997). Perceived and measured availability of tobacco to youths in 14 Minnesota communities: The TPOP Study (Tobacco Policy Options for Prevention). *American Journal of Preventive Medicine, 13(3),* 167–174.

Goldman, L. K., & Glantz, S. A. (1998). Evaluation of antismoking advertising campaigns. *Journal of the American Medical Association, 279,* 772–777.

Grossman, M., & Chaloupka, F. J. (1997). Cigarette taxes: The straw to break the camel's back. *Public Health Report, 112,* 290–297.

Hafstad, A., Aaro, L. E., Engeland, A., Andersen, A., Langmark, F., & Stray-Pedersen, B. (1997). Provocative appeals in anti-smoking mass media campaigns in adolescents: The accumulated effect of multiple exposures. *Health Education Research, 12,* 227–236.

Hawkins, J. D., Catalano, R. F., & Miller, J. Y. (1992). Risk and protective factors for alcohol and other drug problems in adolescence and early adulthood: Implications for substance abuse prevention. *Psychological Bulletin, 112*(1), 64–105.

Hu, T. W., Sung, H. Y., & Keeler, T. E. (1995). Reducing cigarette consumption in California: Tobacco taxes vs. an anti-smoking media campaign. *American Journal of Public Health, 85*(9), 1218–1222.

Hyland, A., & Cummings, K. M. (2001). Laws restricting self-service tobacco displays: Will they help? *Preventive Medicine, 33,* 59–60.

Kaufman, N. J., Castrucci, B. C., Mowery, P. D., Gerlack, K. K., Emont, S., & Orleans, T. (2002). Predictors of change on the smoking update continuum among adolescents. *Archive of Pediatric Adolescent Medicine, 156,* 581–587.

Klepp, K. I., Halper, A., & Perry, C. L. (1986). The efficacy of peer leaders in drug abuse prevention. *Journal of School Health, 56,* 407–411.

Lamkin, L., Davis, B., & Kamen, A. (1998). Rationale for tobacco cessation interventions for youth. *Preventive Medicine, 27,* A3–A8.

Lantz, P., Jacobson, P., Warner, J., Wasserman, J., Pollack, H., Berson, J., et al. (2000). Investing in youth tobacco control: A review of smoking prevention and control strategies. *Tobacco Control, 9,* 47–63.

Livingood, W., Woodhouse, C., Sayre, J., & Wludyka, P. (2001). Impact study of tobacco possession law enforcement in Florida. *Health Education and Behavior, 28*(6), 733–748.

Logan, B. D. (1991). Adolescent substance abuse prevention: An overview of the literature. *Family and Community Health, 13*(4), 25–36.

Matei, M. E., & McFee, R. (2001). Youth tobacco use: A multifactorial problem. *Preventive Medicine, 33,* 514–515.

Meller, P. (2002, December 3). Europe outlaws tobacco ads in magazines and newspapers. *New York Times,* A, p. 12.

Myers, M. L. (2002, June 6). *California judge finds R.J. Reynolds guilty of marketing to kids in violation of 1998 settlement agreement* [Press release *Campaign for Tobacco-Free Kids*]. Retrieved October 15, 2002, from http://tobaccofreekids .org/Script/DisplayPressRelease.php3?Display=506.

National Center for Health Statistics. (1999). *Healthy people 2000 review, 1998–1999.* (Library of Congress Catalog Card Number 76-641496). Hyattsville, MD: Public Health Service.

National Institute of Drug Abuse. (1997). *Drug abuse prevention: What works* (NIH Publication No. 97–4110). Rockville, Maryland: Office of Science Policy and Communications, Public Information Branch.

Paavola, M., Vartiainenm, E., & Ouska, P. (2001). Smoking cessation among teenage years and adulthood. *Health Education Research, 16*(1), 49–57.

Pentz, M. A., Brannon, B. R., Charlin, V. L., Barrett, E. J., MacKinnon, D. P., & Flay, B. R. (1989). The power of policy: The relationship of smoking policy to adolescent smoking. *American Journal of Public Health, 79*(7), 857–862.

Pierce, J. P., Choi, W. S., Gilpin, E. A., Farkas, A. J., & Berry, C. (1998). Tobacco industry promotion of cigarettes and adolescent smoking. *Journal of the American Medical Association, 279,* 511–515.

Popham, W. J., Potter, L. D., Bal, D. G., Johnson, M. D., Duerr, J. M., & Quinn, V. (1993). Do anti-smoking media campaigns help smokers quit? *Public Health Report, 108*(4), 510–513.

Quirk, M. E., Godkin, M. A., & Schwenzfeier, E. (1993). Evaluation of two AIDS preventive interventions for inner-city adolescent and young adult women. *American Journal of Preventive Medicine, 9*(1), 21–26.

Ribisl, K. M., Kim, A. E., & Williams, R. S. (2002). Are the practices of Internet cigarette vendors good enough to prevent sales to minors? *American Journal of Public Health, 92*(6), 940–941.

Saffer, H., & Chaloupka, F. J. (1999). *Tobacco advertising, economic theory and international evidence* (Working Paper No. 6958). Washington, DC: National Bureau of Economic Research.

Sargent, J. D., Mott, L. A., & Stevens, M. (1998). Predictors of smoking cessation in adolescents. *Archives of Pediatric Adolescent Medicine, 152,* 388–393.

Schubiner, H., Howard, A., & Hurt, R. (1998). Tobacco cessation and youth: The feasibility of brief office interventions for adolescents. *Preventive Medicine, 27,* A47–A54.

Smedley, B. D., & Syme, S. L. (Eds.). (2000). *Institutes of Medicine Report: Unequal treatment: Promoting health: Intervention strategies from social and behavioral research.* Washington, DC: National Academy Press.

Soldz, S., Kreiner, P., Clark, T. W., & Krakow, M. (2001). Tobacco use among Massachusetts youth: Is tobacco control working? *Preventive Medicine, 33,* 287–295.

Stanton, W., & Smith, K. (2002). A critique of evaluated adolescent smoking cessation programs. *Journal of Adolescence, 25,* 427–438.

Stern, M., Northman, J. E., & Van Slyck, M. R. (1984). Father absence and adolescent "problem behaviors": Alcohol consumption, drug use and sexual activity. *Adolescence, 19*(74), 302–312.

Stone, S. L., & Kristeller, J. L. (1992). Attitudes of adolescents toward smoking cessation. *American Journal of Preventive Medicine, 8*(4), 221–225.

Tengs, T., Osgood, N., & Chen, L. (2001). The cost-effectiveness of intensive national school-based anti-tobacco education: Results from the Tobacco Policy Model. *Preventive Medicine, 33,* 558–570.

U.S. Department of Health and Human Services. (2000a). *Healthy People 2010 Objectives.* Retrieved October 26, 2002, from http://www.healthypeople.gov.

U.S. Department of Health and Human Services. (2000b). *Reducing tobacco use: A report of the Surgeon General.* Atlanta, GA: U.S. Department of Health and Human Services, Centers for Disease Control and Prevention, National Center for Chronic Disease Prevention and Health Promotion, Office on Smoking and Health.

Wallack, L., & Dorfman, L. (1992). Health messages on television commercials. *American Journal of Health Promotion, 6*(3), 190–196.

Wildey, M. B., Woodruff, S. I., Agro, A., Keay, K. D., Kenney, E. M., & Conway, T. L. (1995). Sustained effects of educating retailers to reduce cigarette sales to minors. *Public Health Reports, 110*(5), 625–629.

Worden, J. K., Flynn, B. S., Solomon, L. J., Secker-Walker, R. H., Badger, G. J., & Carpenter, J. H. (1996). Using mass media to prevent cigarette smoking among adolescent girls. *Health Education Quarterly, 23,* 453–468.

Chapter 13

EATING DISORDERS

GAIL McVEY

This chapter provides a review of the incidence, risk factors, and current approaches used in the prevention of eating disorders and disordered eating. Moreover, policy implications and future directions are discussed.

TRENDS AND INCIDENCE

Adolescents' preoccupation with their weight and appearance ranges from periodic monitoring of food intake, to dieting, to clinical eating disorders. The most common types of eating disorders are anorexia nervosa (AN) and bulimia nervosa (BN). *Anorexia nervosa* is defined as a refusal to maintain body weight at or above 85% of what is expected for age and height, an intense fear of gaining weight, body image disturbance whereby individuals fail to recognize the seriousness of their low weight, and amenorrhea (in postmenarcheal females; American Psychiatric Association [APA], 2000). *Bulimia nervosa* involves recurrent episodes of binge eating with an accompanying sense of loss of control over eating during the episode, followed by recurrent compensatory behaviors to prevent weight gain (e.g., self-induced vomiting; misuse of laxatives, diuretics, or other medications; fasting; excessive exercise). An estimate of the lifetime prevalence of AN in young women is 0.6% (Garfinkel et al., 1996) and is in the range of 1% to 3% for BN (Garfinkel et al., 1995). Although eating disorders (particularly AN) usually develop in adolescence, they can also occur well into adulthood and are increasingly seen in young children. The diagnosis of eating disorders is particularly prevalent among adolescent females (Lewinsohn, Striegel-Moore, & Seeley, 2000), and the prevalence is reportedly increasing (Goldman, 1996). Whereas, historically, eating disorders were perceived as afflictions of middle or upper-middle class Caucasian females, today, the demography of eating disorders

275

has expanded to include various socioeconomic backgrounds and racial/ethnic groups (Croll, Neumark-Sztainer, Story, & Ireland, 2002). Furthermore, it has been suggested that males comprise 10% to 15% of the eating disorder population (Carlat, Camargo, & Herzog, 1997), with that percentage rising to 30% in male adolescents (Fosson, Knibbs, Bryant-Waugh, & Lask, 1987). An even larger number of young females, while not meeting the clinical criteria for an eating disorder, have serious subclinical symptoms. For example, studies have shown that 11% to 80% of adolescent females report at least one symptom of an eating disorder (e.g., fasting, skipping meals to lose weight, diet pills, vomiting, bingeing; Jones, Bennett, Olmsted, Lawson, & Rodin, 2001; Mellin, Scully, & Irwin, 1992) whereas others report a high prevalence of dieting (Bost, Vaughn, Washington, Cielinski, & Bradbard, 1998; Button, Sonuga-Barke, Davies, & Thompson, 1996; Devaud, Jeannin, Narring, Ferron, & Michaud, 1998; McVey, Pepler, Davis, Flett, & Abdolell, 2002; Roberts, McGuiness, Bilton, & Maxwell, 1999). Similarly, weight concerns, dieting, and a fear of fatness have been reported in children as young as 9 years of age (for reviews, see Smolak & Levine, 2001, and Ricciardelli & McCabe, 2001). By age 6, children are aware of the societal bias against overweight people (Lerner & Jovanovic, 1990).

Because of untreated clinical eating disorders, young people can experience permanent growth arrestation at the prepubertal stage and develop chronic health problems, such as osteoporosis in their mid-teens (Fisher et al., 1995). Anorexia nervosa is the third most common chronic illness in older female adolescents after obesity and asthma (Fisher et al., 1995; Robb, 2001). Eating disorders are also associated with mood problems, suicidal ideation, and self-harm behaviors and can have a devastating impact on the sufferers and their families (Garfinkel et al., 1995).

Whereas clinical eating disorders can lead to severe health problems, subclinical eating disorders (or disordered eating) and dieting can also be harmful to a girl's physical growth and overall health (Lock, Reisel, & Steiner, 2001). For example, the accelerated growth rate of adolescent girls necessitates increased amounts of energy, calcium, and iron (Levine & Smolak, 1998). As such, food restriction that coincides with the growth spurt of adolescence can lead to rapid weight loss. Dieting has been linked to the rising rates of obesity because it is thought to contribute to unhealthy eating behaviors (e.g., bingeing, consumption of high-fat foods; Gortmaker, Must, Perrin, Sobol, & Dietz, 1993; Polivy & Herman, 1985).

There is also growing evidence that many boys are troubled by their body size (i.e., being underweight or overweight) and that these concerns are correlated with body image dissatisfaction, disordered eating, and attempts at muscle gain (Cohane & Pope, 2001; Croll et al., 2002; McCabe, Ricciardelli, & Finemore,

2002; McCreary & Sasse, 2002; O'Dea & Rawstorne, 2001; Smolak & Levine, 2001). Not surprisingly, health risks associated with disordered eating have been reported in male adolescents (Lock et al., 2001). Finally, it has been reported that adolescents (male and female) who engage in disordered eating are at greater risk for engaging in other general risk-taking behaviors (e.g., substance abuse, risky sexual behaviors; Lock et al., 2001; Shisslak, Crago, Renger, & Clark-Wagner, 1998). Given the severe complications associated with disordered eating and eating disorders, the need for effective primary prevention is critical.

RISK FACTORS

Research has shown that the etiology of eating disorders is multidimensional (personal vulnerability variables including genetic, biological, and personality factors; familial factors; peers and larger social context variables; cultural factors; traumatic events; Garfinkel & Garner, 1982; Striegel-Moore, Silberstein, & Rodin, 1986). These dimensions are often characterized as either potential risk or protective factors for high-risk behaviors. In this context, risk factors are variables that have been shown to prospectively predict disordered eating, whereas protective factors mitigate the adverse effects of those risk factors (Stice, 2001). Effective prevention is then dependent on the identification of specific risk and protective factors that significantly influence the onset of a particular disorder (Cicchetti, 1990; Rutter, 1990). The study of risk and protective factors that are associated with specific periods of development is especially useful so that prevention strategies can be matched accordingly. (For a more complete review of the state of risk factor research for eating disorders, see Shisslak & Crago, 2001, and Stice, 2001.)

Children

Whereas some evidence suggests that eating problems in young children might be linked to early childhood temperament (e.g., negative emotionality, anxiety-depression; Martin et al., 2000; Moorhead et al., 2002) and childhood adversities such as maladaptive parenting behavior, digestive problems, and picky eating (Johnson, Cohen, Kasen, & Brook, 2002; Marchi & Cohen, 1990), the development of body image concerns has received more attention in risk factor research, given its link to disordered eating in later development (Smolak & Levine, 2001). In particular, the role parental factors play in the development of childhood body image concerns has been studied. Research has shown that parental concern or comments about children's weight status (e.g., suggestions to slim down, restrict food intake) have been associated with body image concerns in children (Davison & Birch, 2001; Edmunds & Hill, 1999; Gardner, Stark, Freidman, & Jackson, 2000; Smolak, Levine, & Schermer, 1999). In addition, parents' own body dissatisfaction, body mass index, internalization of the thin ideal, or disordered eating have been linked to children's body image concerns (Stice, Agras, & Hammer, 1999). Overall, the literature suggests that children whose parents transmit messages about the importance of thinness, either through role modeling or direct comments, are more likely to develop concerns with their own weight and shape. In turn, those concerns might be generalized to negative self-evaluations in other areas of competence (Davison & Birch, 2001).

Early Adolescence

The development of eating problems during early adolescence is best understood in the context of the normative stressors associated with this period of development, such as the physical changes associated with puberty (natural increases in weight and body fat), increased desire for peer acceptance, the onset of dating, and changes in academic expectations (Smolak & Levine, 1996). Young adolescent girls become increasingly aware of the sociocultural forces that strongly equate female desirability with appearance and desired appearance with a thin body (Stice, 1994). On their own, each of these stressors is believed to increase girls' preoccupation and possible dissatisfaction with their weight and shape. However, research has shown that girls who experience more than one of these stressors within the same year are more likely to also experience disturbed levels of eating (Levine & Smolak, 1992). The risk for the development of an eating disorder during this stage of development is further intensified if a girl demonstrates certain personality features such as strong perfectionistic tendencies or the endorsement of the thin ideal (Levine & Smolak, 1992). Because of the potential cumulative impact of these normative stressors, the early adolescent transition is thought to be a period of high risk for body image concerns and disordered eating (Smolak & Levine, 2001). In addition, as girls approach adolescence, many experience natural drops in self-esteem and often lose their ability to speak out and voice their opinions (Friedman, 1998; Gilligan, 1982; Piran, 1999; Shisslak & Crago, 1993; Steiner-Adair & Purcell, 1996). Low self-esteem among early adolescent girls has been identified as a risk factor for the later development of disordered eating (Button et al., 1996).

Using longitudinal studies, other variables including early pubertal development, high body mass index (BMI; Graber, Brooks-Gunn, Paikoff, & Warren, 1994; Keel, Fulkerson, & Leon, 1997), body dissatisfaction, weight concerns, depression, weight-related teasing (Cattarin & Thompson, 1994; Killen et al., 1996; Leon, Fulkerson, Perry, Keel, & Klump, 1999), and impulsive behaviors (Pine,

Cohen, Brook, & Coplan, 1997) have been shown to be predictive of disordered eating in adolescent females. Although dieting has been correlated with the later onset of disordered eating, its causal link to clinical eating disorders has been questioned (Stice, 2001). If however, there is a family history of an eating disorder, mood disorder, or alcohol/substance use and if dieting is intensified by certain developmental issues, a causal relationship has been shown (Hsu, 1997).

Additional factors correlated with disordered eating include avoidance or emotion-focused coping (Fryer, Waller, & Kroese, 1997), perfectionism (McVey et al., 2002) perception of being overweight (Ackard & Peterson, 2001), internalization of the thin ideal (Cusumano & Thompson, 2000; Levine, Piran, & Stoddard, 1999; Levine & Smolak, 1998; Levine, Smolak, & Schermer, 1996; Shisslak et al., 1998), pressures from peers to diet (Lieberman, Gauvin, Bukowski, & White, 2001; Lunner et al., 2000; Muir, Wertheim, & Paxton, 1999; Paxton, Schutz, Wertheim, & Muir, 1999; Taylor et al., 1998), sexual harassment (Murnen & Smolak, 2000), and participation in aesthetic or appearance-oriented sports (e.g., dance, gymnastics, cheerleading, baton twirling, swimming, aerobics, figure skating; Davison, Earnest, & Birch, 2002).

Although risk factor research continues to grow, limited information is available on the protective factors associated with disordered eating. Muir et al. (1999) reported that adolescent girls' reasons for not dieting included a conscious resistance to dieting pressures, a belief that dieting is bad, and size acceptance by peers. More recently, one study found that high involvement and unconditional support from fathers, in the face of school-related stress, played a protective role against disordered eating among females attending middle school (McVey et al., 2002). Finally, Croll et al. (2002) reported that positive self-esteem, emotional well-being, school achievement, and family connectedness served as protective factors for disordered eating among male and female adolescents. Findings from these studies are based on correlational research, which does not provide information about the causal effect. Nevertheless, the findings can serve as pilot work to future longitudinal studies in the search for protective factors that can help direct prevention practices.

EFFECTIVE UNIVERSAL PREVENTIVE INTERVENTIONS

Universal prevention involves fostering resilience and reducing risk among non-symptomatic populations. In the short term, prevention programs are expected to increase resiliency and decrease risk factors. In the long term, it is expected that those changes will lead to fewer eating problems and eating disorders. Smolak (1999) suggests that elementary school children are an appropriate audience for this type of prevention because they have not yet experienced the developmental challenges of puberty, which increase their risk for negative body image and disordered eating.

A trend in the primary prevention literature involves adopting health promotion programs designed to promote overall wellness and alter some of the predisposing factors related to disordered eating. This contrasts with the traditional approach of teaching adolescents about the methods of, and the dangers associated with, eating disorders (Moreno & Thelen, 1993; Paxton, 1993; Shisslak, Crago, & Neal, 1990). O'Dea (2000) underscores the need for safe and effective approaches for the prevention of eating problems in children and adolescents, given the potentially adverse effects of health education strategies (Carter, Stewart, Dunn, & Fairburn, 1997; Mann, Nolen-Hoeksema, Huang, & Burgard, 1997). To prevent harm, O'Dea suggests that school-based education programs change their focus from highlighting negative, problem-based issues (e.g., glamorization of eating disorders, suggestive information about weight control techniques, negative language around food messages) to helping young people build self-esteem and enjoy healthy, active lifestyles without developing a fear of food. Thus, universal prevention may address a number of issues, such as self-esteem, media literacy, and nutrition.

Given the link between disordered eating and the internalization of the thin ideal, media literacy training has been identified as an important component to include in universal prevention programs (Levine et al., 1999; Steiner-Adair & Vorenberg, 1999). For example, Smolak, Levine, and Schermer (1998) taught elementary school children about:

1. Ways to critically evaluate the unrealistic images of women portrayed in the media,
2. The genetic influences on body shape and the need to appreciate and accept individual differences in body shape and size, and
3. How to adopt a nondieting approach to eating and exercise.

The authors were the first to publish a controlled prevention study with children as young as 9 and 10 years of age, using cognitive social learning and developmental principles. Over the short term, the program helped to improve students' knowledge about nutrition, the effects of dieting, and the causes of body fat. However, specific behaviors, including eating patterns, exercise patterns, weight reduction attempts, and teasing of fat children were not changed through participation in the curriculum. Despite these findings, the curriculum did positively affect the students' attitudes about overweight people. A two-year follow-up evaluation of this program revealed that the participants were more knowledgeable, used fewer unhealthy weight management techniques, and had higher body esteem compared to controls (Smolak & Levine, 2001). These findings underscore the need to include long-term follow-up evaluations in prevention research because attitudinal or behavioral changes may not be evident shortly after the intervention.

In a community context, Neumark-Sztainer, Sherwood, Coller, and Hannan (2000) examined the effectiveness of a media literacy program with preadolescent girls attending Girl Scouts. The six-session program had a positive influence on the girls' attitudes toward weight-related social norms, their knowledge about their bodies, and media attitudes immediately following the program, but these changes were not maintained at the three-month follow-up. Other prevention programs involving media-literacy components conducted with elementary school children have shown similar promising results over the short term (Kater, Rohwer, & Levine, 2000; Kater, Rohwer, & Londre, 2002).

More recently, programs have focused on self-esteem enhancement strategies given the link between low self-esteem in late childhood and the onset of eating disorder symptoms in later adolescence (Button et al., 1996; Shisslak et al., 1998). O'Dea (2002) suggests that the development of a positive self-image can act as a protective factor against the unrealistic body image ideals portrayed in the media. O'Dea and Abraham (2000) examined the effect of a school-based, self-esteem education program on body image and eating attitudes and behaviors in 11- to 14-year-old males and females. The study emphasized student involvement, a positive sense of self, and the building of general self-esteem over nine weekly lessons. Students' attitudes and behaviors were measured before, immediately following, and 12 months after the program. Immediately following the program, the body satisfaction and eating attitudes or behaviors of the intervention students had significantly improved over those in the control group. These changes were still present at the 12-month follow-up.

Using a similar research design, McVey and colleagues implemented self-esteem enhancement strategies, stress management techniques, peer relational skills, and media literacy lessons with girls in grade 6 (McVey, Davis, Tweed, & Shaw, in press). The six-session program, Every Body Is a Somebody (Seaver, McVey, Fullerton, & Stratton, 1997), was delivered to the students during their regularly scheduled health classes with the goal of teaching life skills to girls before they experienced the stressors that can trigger the onset of body image concerns and dieting. The program was successful in improving body satisfaction, global self-esteem, and eating attitudes and behaviors in the short term, but the gains were not maintained at the 12-month follow-up (McVey et al., in press). McVey, Lieberman, Voorberg, Wardrope, & Blackmore (2003) later examined the delivery of the same life skills program with slightly older female students in middle school (grades 7 and 8), using a peer support-group format. The program was delivered over 10 weekly sessions to small groups of female students during the school lunch hour. Incorporating support groups to help ease the transition into middle school has been proposed given the importance of peer acceptance in early and middle adolescence (Shisslak, Crago, Estes, & Gray, 1996). In addition to teaching girls life skills to help them deal with transitional pressures, the groups can serve as a forum to help girls cope with peer teasing and dieting pressures (Shisslak et al., 1996).

A unique feature of the McVey et al. 2003; study was that the peer support groups were facilitated by trained local public health nurses who routinely offered services to the schools where the groups were held. This permitted sustainability of the groups beyond the scope of the research project. Participation in the peer support group program led to improved body esteem scores and decreases in disordered eating. However, a replication of the study with a group of young adolescent females who exhibited higher disordered eating scores at baseline found that the program was not as effective (McVey, Lieberman, Voorberg, Wardrope, Blackmore, & Tweed, 2003). Because the prevalence of disordered eating is increasing among this age group, universal prevention strategies such as the life skills approach might be better suited for elementary school children, as previously suggested. For middle school students, the content of a peer support group intervention might require strategies that focus more directly on reducing students' existing negative attitudes and behaviors. As discussed in a later section, peer support groups designed for adolescent females in a high-risk setting (i.e., residential ballet school) have been shown to be successful in reducing their disordered eating (Piran, 1999).

Finally, Steiner-Adair and colleagues (2002) evaluated an esteem-building program with seventh-grade girls, Full of Ourselves: Advancing Girl Power, Health, and Leadership. The program, which taught girls a range of coping strategies to resist dieting and the cultural emphasis on weight and shape preoccupation, led to improvements in their knowledge and weight-related body esteem in comparison to controls. A unique feature of the program, which has yet to be evaluated, was the inclusion of a mentoring component to provide participants with leadership opportunities. By coaching the seventh-grade students to be role models for the younger-age students, the intervention has the added potential to raise the self-esteem of young adolescent girls, further protecting them against disordered eating.

An advantage to using the self-esteem approach is that it can have a positive effect on other health-related outcomes (e.g., depression, anxiety, sexual risk taking, substance abuse). Additional prevention programs designed to promote resiliency factors with elementary or middle school students have demonstrated promising results (Baranowski & Hetherington, 2001; Dalle Grave, De Luca, & Campello, 2001; Heinze, Wertheim, & Kashima, 2000; Irving, 2000; Phelps, Sapia, Nathanson, & Nelson, 2000; Stewart, Carter, Drinkwater, Hainsworth, & Fairburn, 2001; Varnado-Sullivan et al., 2001). Nevertheless, there is still a debate over whether universal programs are of greater benefit to high-risk students (Killen et al., 1993; O'Dea & Abraham, 2000; Porter, Morrell, & Moriarty, 1986). (For a comprehensive summary of prevention work in the field of eating disorders, see Levine & Piran, 2001; Piran, Levine, & Steiner-Adair, 1999; Vandereycken & Noordenbos, 1998.)

EFFECTIVE SELECTIVE PREVENTIVE INTERVENTIONS

Unlike universal prevention, selective prevention refers to programs for non-symptomatic individuals who are considered at risk because of person variables or contextual factors (Levine, 2001). Few published studies have reported on the effectiveness of selective prevention programs conducted with children or adolescents. With respect to high-risk settings, Piran (1999) developed and implemented over a 10-year period a prevention program with adolescent females attending a residential ballet school. Ballet dancers experience the regular societal, familial, and individual factors that can put any individual at risk for developing disordered eating. In addition, they are members of an environment that emphasizes the need for a small size or thin shape (Thompson & Sherman, 1993). Those additional pressures appear to be associated with a higher degree of eating disorder symptomatology. As an initial step toward the prevention of disordered eating, peer support groups were designed to help female adolescents find ways to combat the expression of prejudices and inequities in the ballet school. Over time, those efforts led to the development of systemic changes designed to reduce weight and shape preoccupation among the females attending the ballet school (Piran, 1998, 1999). Outcome-based research revealed that the program led to positive qualitative outcomes, such as feelings of empowerment and decreases in disordered eating (Piran, 1999).

Similarly, the competitive sports environment represents a potential high-risk setting for disordered eating because of pressures to attain an ideal body size, shape, or weight for performance reasons in endurance sports such as distance running or for sports that emphasize a specific type of physique (e.g., gymnastics, figure skating, diving; Powers & Johnson, 1999). It is not uncommon for weight loss or body fat reduction to be recommended as potential solutions for athletes not performing well. A controlled outcome-based study is currently underway to examine the effectiveness of a positive body image initiative designed to prevent or reduce disordered eating among females in gymnastic clubs (Buchholz, Mack, & McVey, 2003). The Bodysense program is aimed at teaching health promotion strategies and the dangers associated with dieting to female athletes, parents, and coaches. The research project is being carried out in partnership with national sporting, coaching, physical and health organizations, as well as sport-specific regulating bodies. The hope is that their collaboration will facilitate the development and delivery of the intervention program, while disseminating the findings into practice and policies.

EFFECTIVE INDICATED PREVENTIVE INTERVENTIONS

Whereas universal prevention and selective prevention engage nonsymptomatic individuals, indicated prevention programs seek to identify early signs of maladjustment in symptomatic individuals and to intervene before clinical disorders develop (Durlak & Wells, 1998). It has been argued that early detection and intervention are key indicators of recovery in the treatment of eating disorders. Most programs aimed at high-risk individuals (e.g., body image concerns, depression) have been conducted with females at either the college or upper high school levels and, with one exception (Santonastaso et al., 1999), have shown promising results (Buddeberg-Fischer, Klaghofer, Gnam, & Buddeberg, 1998; Franko, 1998; Kaminski & McNamara, 1996; Springer, Winzelberg, Perkins, & Taylor, 1999; Stice, Mazotti, Weibel, & Agras, 2000; Stice & Ragan, 2002; Stice, Trost, & Chase, 2002). Varnado-Sullivan et al. (2001) indicated prevention as an additional component to their universal prevention program conducted with male and female middle school students. This component consisted of intensive family-based intervention for students exhibiting risk factors for disordered eating (e.g., abnormal eating patterns or elevated levels of body dysphoria combined with depressive symptoms or low appearance esteem and high BMI). Specifically, the family-based program was designed to provide high-risk students and their parents with in-depth information on the topics covered in the universal program and to help families with communication and problem-solving skills as well as ways to improve a negative body image. The program was successful in reducing fear of fatness scores among the female student participants. However, the level of participation in the intensive program was very low. The lack of enthusiasm exhibited by the high-risk students (and their parents) in Varnado-Sullivan et al.'s program has led to the suggestion that incentives may be necessary to entice at-risk youth to attend intervention programs designed to reduce disordered eating (Franko, 2001).

Latzer and Shatz (1999) conducted an uncontrolled evaluation of an indicated prevention program designed for adolescent females living in a kibbutz in northern Israel. Supportive one-on-one counseling was made available at the local health clinic to adolescent females identified as at risk. Services included dietary assessment, medical follow-up, identification of difficulties related to body image, self-acceptance, and coping skills. In addition, an intervention program was designed for parents and other significant adults who were identified as at risk. The indicated prevention program was just one aspect of a three-level community-based intervention carried out with the community at large (e.g., adolescent girls, parents, teachers, health clinic staff, and other adults in the community). For example, health promotion strategies were carried out with students in the school setting, whereas parents and significant others were invited to attend three weekly meetings to learn about the etiology of eating disorders, ways to promote self-esteem and positive body image in children, and the normal developmental tasks of adolescence. Following the multilevel intervention, health professionals working in the clinic reported changes in their attitudes concerning the importance of adopting a nondieting approach to eating. In addition, public awareness about the clinic staff's abilities to provide assistance to those with eating disorders increased. Adolescents became more aware of the negative consequences associated with dieting and visited the clinic less often for weight loss purposes. The number of self-referrals to the clinic for eating-related problems increased, which led to earlier intervention, and the youth were also more likely to seek help from the clinic for other health-related problems.

The school setting is ideal for the delivery of indicated prevention programs because it has the advantage of providing specialized care to students who may otherwise not seek treatment for their eating disorder symptoms. For example, it has been reported that most adolescents with eating disorder symptoms do not seek treatment until it is medically necessary. In addition to being accessible and available in a familiar and nonthreatening environment, a school-based indicated program can reach students before their eating disorder symptoms worsen or motivate them to seek professional treatment. Motivation and readiness to change have been identified as key factors in the successful treatment of adolescent eating disorders (Gusella, Butler, Nichols, & Bird, 2003). Training school support staff to assess and carry out evidence-based indicated prevention programs in the area of eating disorders has been initiated (McVey, Davis, et al., 2003). To date, community-based training has been shown to be successful in raising the confidence and skill levels of school support staff carrying out interventions. Further research is required to evaluate whether indicated programs delivered by school support staff result in changes in adolescents' eating disorder symptoms.

PRACTICE, POLICY IMPLICATIONS, AND FUTURE DIRECTIONS

It has been argued that universal programs should be the central focus of prevention efforts, particularly those emphasizing ecological, empowerment, and activism approaches to the prevention of disordered eating (Levine & Piran, 2001; Levine & Smolak, 2002). To date, most of the prevention programs have been designed to target and measure change almost exclusively on the individual level (female adolescents' disordered eating). The need to develop comprehensive programs that target multiple factors has been underscored (Austin, 2000; Huon, Braganza, Brown, Ritchie, & Roncolato, 1998; Neumark-Sztainer, 1996; O'Dea & Maloney, 2000; Taylor & Altman, 1997). For example, the inclusion of males in prevention has been initiated (Dalle Grave et al., 2001; Kater et al., 2002; O'Dea & Abraham, 2000; Smolak et al., 1998; Varnado-Sullivan et al., 2001) and has potential benefits on several levels. First, the health promotion messages might help to protect against body image concerns and unhealthy eating and physical activity practices among male adolescents. Second, sensitizing male students to the pressures that female students face and instituting school policies to reduce or eliminate harassment and weight and shape teasing might help to create a healthier and more positive environment for female youth. This is especially noteworthy given the research evidence that suggests that boys are more likely than girls to initiate weight-based teasing and harassment of other children (Smolak et al., 1998). The involvement of males in prevention requires an in-depth study of risk and protective factors associated with disordered eating among male children and adolescents. Work in this area is still in its infancy (Cohane & Pope, 2001; O'Dea & Rawstorne, 2001).

The need to incorporate parents, teachers, school support staff, and coaches in school-based interventions is also crucial given their important roles in young people's social environment (Graber, Archibald, & Brooks-Gunn, 1999; Smolak & Levine, 2001). Prevention work with adult role models could highlight awareness-raising to help adults determine what messages they might be sending to youth (e.g., personal attitudes, beliefs, and behaviors concerning weight and shape). Other work should involve training adults on ways to promote positive body image among children, including:

1. The promotion of positive child-rearing practices (Rosenvinge & Borresen, 1999; e.g., ones that teach parents to accept overweight or weight variations in children, when to seek counseling for early feeding problems, to provide support during the time of normal physical and psychological pubertal changes, not to replace food for comfort)
2. The inclusion of all children in sports and physical activities regardless of their weight and shape
3. Ways to help children combat weight and shape teasing

Whatever the strategy, Piran and colleagues argue for a *whole school* approach that involves members of the school system in efforts to change the entire school culture (Levine & Piran, 2001; Piran, 1995, 1996). According to Piran, prevention is required to move from a didactic to a participatory approach, whereby new norms of relating, acceptance, support, and power are developed.

Varnado-Sullivan et al. (2001) were the first to publish a controlled comprehensive outcome-based study that involved male and female adolescents, parents, and teachers. Their two-stage intervention program (universal and selective), the Body Logic Program, led to improvements on measures of food avoidance and fear of fatness among the female participants. However, Varnado-Sullivan and colleagues reported that following the completion of their school-based program, the intervention schools refused to participate in the planned long-term follow-up because of scheduling problems and complaints from parents. Challenges to involving parents and teachers in prevention efforts have been raised elsewhere (Franko, 2001; Levine, 2001; McVey, Davis, & Shaw, 1999; McVey, Tweed, & Blackmore, 2003). For example, McVey et al. (1999) compared the effectiveness of two school-based prevention programs: one involving students only and the other involving students and their parents. Whereas more than 90% of the parents initially agreed to participate in their study, less than 10% showed up for the parent intervention. In a more recent study, McVey and colleagues (McVey, Tweed, et al., 2003) evaluated a comprehensive study aimed at changing aspects of school climate in male and female students in middle school. In this case, the intervention schools were uncooperative when carrying out the teacher-delivered curriculum, despite its being matched to ministry of education's expectations and spread across various course topics (as recommended by Neumark-Sztainer, 1996). In addition, the time period made available to the researchers to train teachers on the curriculum was minimal (McVey, Tweed, et al., 2003). Finally, parental participation in the program was very low, leaving researchers to rely on school newsletters to transfer knowledge about the health promotion curriculum. Other aspects of the program were well received by the intervention schools, however. These included nurse-facilitated peer support groups for female students, group sessions about the negative effects of teasing for male students, play performance and follow-up discussions about the negative effects of teasing, media and peer pressures to diet and gain muscle, and general strategies to influence the school climate (public service announcements, posters).

Smolak, Harris, Levine, and Shisslak (2001) also conducted interviews with teachers to solicit their attitudes and opinions about their potential role in school-based eating disorder prevention work. The findings revealed that most teachers expressed a desire to receive pamphlets on how to recognize and help students who appear to have eating problems, as well as videos to show in the classroom. Teachers also expressed a need to have a resource person who could answer their questions and concerns about students at risk available in each school. Given these barriers, finding ways to engage parents and teachers in prevention efforts is a topic that warrants further study (Franko, 2001; Levine, 2001).

Schools are an important arena for health promotion and prevention efforts. Ideally, preventive intervention would be implemented in a stepped fashion (e.g., elementary through high school), matching the prevention level to the developmental level of students. For example, in kindergarten through grade 4, the focus could be on raising awareness with parents, teachers, and school support staff about their own beliefs and behaviors with respect to dieting and slimness, as well as creating a school climate that fosters child health. Health promotion could be introduced with students beginning in grade 4 and continuing through the end of high school (e.g., booster sessions). The material could be incorporated into the school curriculum across various topics. In addition, peer support groups could be offered to students approaching the high-risk period of early adolescence (grades 5 to 7) to help them combat weight and shape teasing and peer pressures to diet. Given the higher prevalence of disordered eating among high school students, selective or indicated intervention strategies could be implemented with students who exhibit early symptoms of an eating disorder. The support groups and interventions could be facilitated by trained school support personnel or public health nurses with direct referrals to specialized health services in the community.

In addition, schoolwide policies should be implemented to:

1. Sensitize teachers and school support staff about the genetic influences of weight and shape and the normative factors that influence body image and eating behavior (e.g., physical changes in puberty), as well as their own beliefs and behaviors with respect to dieting, self-esteem, slenderness, and weight

2. Reduce or eliminate weight and shape teasing and sexual harassment

3. Discourage starve-a-thons as fundraising techniques

4. Provide opportunities for healthy eating at school (e.g., wide variety of food choices)

5. Discourage lunchroom talk that promotes unhealthy eating

6. Replace fat-caliper testing and group weigh-ins with the promotion of physical activity that includes students of all sizes and shapes

Given the challenges of involving teachers in prevention efforts, it is now crucial to work with governments to incorporate evidence-based practices into the school curriculum. In fact, integrating broad-based prevention strategies in the field of eating disorders with other adolescent health concerns (e.g., substance abuse, depression and anxiety, obesity, diabetes, cardiovascular disease, and some cancers) would be an innovative way to address health concerns of adolescents as well as capitalize on the available resources (e.g., the limited time of teachers). In particular, there is a current debate in the literature about how best to integrate eating disorder and obesity prevention work. For example, current concerns about childhood obesity have increased the focus on the importance of teaching youth about healthy eating and active living. However, advice about what to eat to stay healthy can make girls preoccupied with foods and serve to undermine their own control and confidence about eating. Similarly, advice about physical activity can lead some girls to engage in excessive exercise, particularly if they are going through the early adolescent period of high risk for body image concerns and disordered eating. The development of health promotion programs designed to prevent obesity without promoting weight and shape preoccupation in children requires further collaboration among researchers in both of these fields.

Finally, prevention efforts should extend from the school setting into the community (Latzer & Shatz, 1999). A proposed strategy is to have students, staff, and parents facilitate outreach activities with students from other schools, families, shoppers, media stations, readers of newspapers, radio listeners, and politicians (Neumark-Sztainer, 1996). Best practices in the delivery of prevention strategies to this broader audience are largely unexplored (e.g., community health clinics, parks and recreation, prenatal classes, youth clubs). The use of the Internet to reduce risk factors for eating disorders has shown some promising results and also warrants further study (Celio et al., 2000; Winzelberg et al., 1998; Zabinski et al., 2001). Equally important is the need for the continued development of ethnically sensitive intervention programs (Nichter, Vuckovic, & Parker, 1999) that are based on findings from risk factor research carried out with various ethnic groups (Croll et al., 2002; Pike & Walsh, 1996; Striegel-Moore, 1997; Striegel-Moore & Smolak, 1996). For example, the sample of middle school students who participated in the comprehensive prevention program conducted by McVey, Tweed, et al, 2003 was ethnically diverse. The researchers discovered that some families denied permission for their daughters to participate in one of the program components, namely the nurse-led peer support group entitled Girl Talk, because of the inclusion of puberty in the session topics. The topics that were selected for the Girl Talk groups were based on a resource designed to empower adolescent girls through a life skills approach. The researchers made the wrong assumption that the selected topics would be acceptable to, and interpreted similarly by, all of the female students and their parents.

In conclusion, several recommendations have been made to improve knowledge in the field of eating disorders prevention (Levine & Piran, 2001; Levine & Smolak, 2002). First, researchers conducting outcome-based studies are urged to specify the type of prevention program that is being evaluated (i.e., universal, selective, or indicated) as well as the theoretical model underlying the strategy (e.g., disease-specific model, nonspecific vulnerability-stressor model, relational-empowerment model). Second, researchers are encouraged to select outcome measures that can detect realistic changes brought on by the intervention. For example, programs that focus on modifying predisposing or moderating factors (e.g., self-esteem, size acceptance) might not have any impact on disordered eating behaviors, at least in the short term. However, additional longitudinal research can determine whether improvements in resiliency factors help to protect against the onset of eating disorder symptoms later on. The target audience and expected outcome(s) will vary within each of the prevention categories. Third, there is a need to broaden the measurement of outcome indexes from individual (e.g., students' knowledge, attitudes, and behaviors) to contextual factors (e.g., teachers' awareness about weight and shape issues, school policies around weight and shape teasing and sexual harassment, opportunities for physical activity, and availability of a wide variety of foods in the school) to determine if comprehensive prevention programs result in healthier and more positive environments for youth.

The growth of research in the field of eating disorders prevention over the past few years has led to changes in how prevention is defined, carried out, and measured. The traditional approach of teaching adolescent females about the dangers associated with eating disorders has been replaced with efforts to:

1. Increase the individual resilience of children and young adolescents through the promotion of media literacy, self-esteem enhancement, and life skills (universal prevention)

2. Involve males, parents, teachers, and other significant adults in prevention programs in an effort to create supportive environments for female youth, particularly among those who might be at risk because of their developmental stage (e.g., early adolescent period of high risk for body image and disordered eating) or participation in a high-risk setting (e.g., sports environment or dance school; selective prevention)

3. Increase, where needed, youths' access to more intensive prevention programs to prevent early symptoms from developing into clinical eating disorders (secondary prevention)

The prevention research outlined in this chapter demonstrates some innovative ways to help youth, particularly females, resist societal pressures to pursue thinness. Additional research is required to determine whether these efforts will lead to decreases in the prevalence of eating disorders and disordered eating among youth in our society.

REFERENCES

Ackard, D. M., & Peterson, C. B. (2001). Association between puberty and disordered eating, body image, and other psychological variables. *International Journal of Eating Disorders, 29,* 187–194.

American Psychiatric Association. (2000). *Diagnostic and statistical manual of mental disorders* (4th ed., text rev.). Washington, DC: Author.

Austin, S. B. (2000). Prevention research in eating disorders: Theory and new directions. *Psychological Medicine, 30,* 1249–1262.

Baranowski, M. J., & Hetherington, M. M. (2001). Testing the efficacy of an eating disorder prevention program. *International Journal of Eating Disorders, 29,* 119–124.

Bost, K. K., Vaughn, B. E., Washington, W. N., Cielinski, K. L., & Bradbard, M. R. (1998). Social competence, social support, and attachment: Demarcation of construct domains, measurement, and paths of influence for preschool children attending Head Start. *Child Development, 69*(1), 192–218.

Buchholz, A., Mack, H., & McVey, G. (May, 2003). *Bodysense: A positive body image initiative for young female athletes.* Paper presented at Academy for Eating Disorders' International Conference on Eating Disorders "Athletes" Special Interest Group, Denver, Colorado.

Buddeberg-Fischer, B., Klaghofer, R., Gnam, G., & Buddeberg, C. (1998). Prevention of disturbed eating behavior: A prospective intervention study in 14- to 19-year-old Swiss students. *Acta Psychiatrica Scandinavica, 98,* 146–155.

Button, E. J., Sonuga-Barke, E. J. S., Davies, J., & Thompson, M. (1996). A prospective study of self-esteem in the prediction of eating problems in adolescent schoolgirls: Questionnaire findings. *British Journal of Clinical Psychology, 35,* 193–203.

Carlat, D. J., Camargo, C. A., & Herzog, D. B. (1997). Eating disorders in males. A report on 135 patients. *American Journal of Psychiatry, 154,* 1127–1132.

Carter, J. C., Stewart, D. A., Dunn, V. J., & Fairburn, C. G. (1997). Primary prevention of eating disorders: Might it do more harm than good? *International Journal of Eating Disorders, 22,* 167–172.

Cattarin, J. A., & Thompson, J. K. (1994). A three-year longitudinal study of body image, eating disturbance, and general psychological functioning in adolescent females. *Eating Disorders: Journal of Treatment and Prevention, 2,* 114–125.

Celio, A. A., Winzelberg, A. J., Wilfley, D. E., Eppstein-Herald, D., Springer, E. A., Dev, P., et al. (2000). Reducing risk factors for eating disorders: Comparison of an Internet- and a classroom-delivered psychoeducational program. *Journal of Consulting and Clinical Psychology, 68,* 650–657.

Cicchetti, D. (1990). A historical perspective on the discipline of developmental psychopathology. In J. Rolf, A. S. Masten, D. Cicchetti, K. H. Neuchterlein, & S. Weintraub (Eds.), *Risk and protective factors in the development of psychopathology* (pp. 2–28). Cambridge, England: Cambridge University Press.

Cohane, G. H., & Pope, H. G. (2001). Body image and boys: A review of the literature. *International Journal of Eating Disorders, 29,* 373–379.

Croll, J., Neumark-Sztainer, D., Story, M., & Ireland, M. (2002). Prevalence and risk and protective factors related to disordered eating behaviors among adolescents: Relationship to gender and ethnicity. *Journal of Adolescent Health, 31,* 166–175.

Cusumano, D. L., & Thompson, J. K. (2000). Media influence and body image in 8–11-year-old boys and girls: A preliminary report on the Multidimensional Media Influence Scale. *International Journal of Eating Disorders, 29,* 37–44.

Dalle Grave, R., De Luca, L., & Campello, G. (2001). Middle school primary prevention program for eating disorders: A controlled study with a twelve-month follow-up. *Eating Disorders: Journal of Treatment and Prevention, 9,* 327–337.

Davison, K. K., & Birch, L. L. (2001). Weight status, parent reaction, and self-concept in five-year-old girls. *Pediatrics, 107,* 46–53.

Davison, K. K., Earnest, M. B., & Birch, L. L. (2002). Participation in aesthetic sports and girls' weight concerns at ages 5 and 7 years. *International Journal of Eating Disorders, 31*(3), 312–317.

Devaud, C., Jeannin, A., Narring, F., Ferron, C., & Michaud, P. A. (1998). Eating disorders among female adolescents in Switzerland: Prevalence and association with mental and behavioral disorders. *International Journal of Eating Disorders, 24,* 207–216.

Durlak, J. A., & Wells, A. M. (1998). Evaluation of indicated preventive intervention (secondary prevention) mental health programs for children and adolescents. *American Journal of Community Psychology, 26,* 775–802.

Edmunds, H., & Hill, A. J. (1999). Dieting and the family context of eating in young adolescent children. *International Journal of Eating Disorders, 25,* 435–440.

Fisher, M., Golden, N. H., Katzman, D. K., Kreipe, R. E., Rees, J., Schebendach, J., et al. (1995). Eating disorders in adolescents: A background paper. *Journal of Adolescent Health, 16,* 420–437.

Fosson, A., Knibbs, J., Bryant-Waugh, R., & Lask, B. (1987). Early onset anorexia nervosa. *Archives of Disease in Childhood, 62,* 114–118.

Franko, D. L. (1998). Secondary prevention of eating disorders in college women at risk. *Eating Disorders: Journal of Treatment and Prevention, 6,* 29–40.

Franko, D. L. (2001). Rethinking prevention efforts in eating disorders. *Cognitive and Behavioral Practice, 8,* 265–270.

Friedman, S. S. (1998). Girls in the 90s: A gender-based model for eating disorder prevention. *Patient Education and Counseling, 33,* 217–224.

Fryer, S., Waller, G., & Kroese, B. S. (1997). Stress, coping, and disturbed eating attitudes in teenage girls. *International Journal of Eating Disorders, 22,* 427–436.

Gardner, R. M., Stark, K., Freidman, B. N., & Jackson, N. A. (2000). Predictors of eating disorder scores in children ages 6 through 14: A longitudinal study. *Journal of Psychosomatic Research, 49,* 199–205.

Garfinkel, P. E., & Garner, D. M. (1982). *Anorexia nervosa: A multidimensional perspective.* New York: Brunner/Mazel.

Garfinkel, P. E., Lin, E., Goering, P., Spegg, C., Goldbloom, D. S., Kennedy, S. H., et al. (1995). Bulimia nervosa in a Canadian community sample: Prevalence and comparison of subgroups. *American Journal of Psychiatry, 152,* 1052–1058.

Garfinkel, P. E., Lin, E., Goering, P., Spegg, C., Goldbloom, D. S., Kennedy, S. H., et al. (1996). Should amenorrhea be necessary for the diagnosis of anorexia nervosa? Evidence from a Canadian community sample. *British Journal of Psychiatry, 168*(4), 500–506.

Gilligan, C. (1982). *In a different voice: Psychological theory and women's development.* Cambridge, MA: Harvard University Press.

Goldman, E. L. (1996). Eating disorders are on the rise in preteens and adolescents. *Psychiatry News, 24,* 10.

Gortmaker, S. L., Must, A., Perrin, J. M., Sobol, A. M., & Dietz, W. H. (1993). Social and economic consequences of overweight in adolescence and young adulthood. *New England Journal of Medicine, 329,* 1008–1012.

Graber, J. A., Archibald, A. B., & Brooks-Gunn, J. (1999). The role of parents in the emergence, maintenance, and prevention of eating problems and disorders. In N. Piran, M. P. Levine, & C. Steiner-Adair (Eds.), *Preventing eating disorders: A handbook of interventions and special challenges* (pp. 44–62). Philadelphia: Brunner/Mazel.

Graber, J. A., Brooks-Gunn, J., Paikoff, R. L., & Warren, M. P. (1994). Prediction of eating problems: An 8-year study of adolescent girls. *Developmental Psychology, 30,* 823–834.

Gusella, J., Butler, G., Nichols, L., & Bird, D. (2003). A brief questionnaire to assess readiness to change in adolescents with eating disorders: Its applications to group therapy. *European Eating Disorders Review, 11,* 58–71.

Heinze, V., Wertheim, E. H., & Kashima, Y. (2000). An evaluation of the importance of message source and age of recipient in a primary prevention program for eating disorders. *Eating Disorders: Journal of Treatment and Prevention, 8*(2), 131–145.

Hsu, L. K. G. (1997). Can dieting cause an eating disorder? *Psychological Medicine, 27,* 509–513.

Huon, G. F., Braganza, C., Brown, L. B., Ritchie, J. E., & Roncolato, W. G. (1998). Reflections on prevention in dieting-induced disorders. *International Journal of Eating Disorders, 23,* 455–458.

Irving, L. M. (2000). Promoting size acceptance in elementary school children: The EDAP puppet program. *Eating Disorders: Journal of Treatment and Prevention, 8*(3), 221–232.

Johnson, J. G., Cohen, P., Kasen, S., & Brook, J. S. (2002). Childhood adversities associated with risk for eating disorders or weight problems during adolescence or early adulthood. *American Journal of Psychiatry, 159,* 394–400.

Jones, J. M., Bennett, S., Olmsted, M. P., Lawson, M. L., & Rodin, G. (2001). Disordered eating attitudes and behaviors in teenaged girls: A school-based study. *Canadian Medical Association Journal, 165,* 547–552.

Kaminski, P. L., & McNamara, K. (1996). A treatment for college women at risk for bulimia: A controlled evaluation. *Journal of Counseling and Development, 74*(3), 288–294.

Kater, K. J., Rohwer, J., & Levine, M. P. (2000). An elementary school project for developing healthy body image and reducing risk factors for unhealthy and disordered eating. *Eating Disorders: Journal of Treatment and Prevention, 8,* 3–16.

Kater, K. J., Rohwer, J., & Londre, K. (2002). Evaluation of an upper elementary school program to prevent body image, eating, and weight concerns. *Journal of School Health, 72,* 199–204.

Keel, P. K., Fulkerson, J. A., & Leon, G. R. (1997). Disordered eating precursors in pre- and early adolescent girls and boys. *Journal of Youth and Adolescence, 26,* 203–216.

Killen, J. D., Taylor, C. B., Hammer, L., Litt, I., Wilson, D. M., Rich, T., et al. (1993). An attempt to modify unhealthful eating attitudes and weight regulation practices of young adolescent girls. *International Journal of Eating Disorders, 13,* 369–384.

Killen, J. D., Taylor, C. B., Hayward, C., Haydel, K. F., Wilson, D. M., Hammer, L., et al. (1996). Weight concerns influence the development of eating disorders: A 4-year prospective study. *Journal of Consulting and Clinical Psychology, 64,* 936–940.

Latzer, Y., & Shatz, S. (1999). Comprehensive community prevention of disturbed attitudes to weight control: A three-level intervention program. *Eating Disorders: Journal of Treatment and Prevention, 7*(1), 3–31.

Leon, G. R., Fulkerson, J. A., Perry, C. L., Keel, P. K., & Klump, K. L. (1999). Three to four year prospective evaluation of personality and behavioral risk factors for later disordered eating in adolescent girls and boys. *Journal of Youth and Adolescence, 28,* 181–189.

Lerner, R., & Jovanovic, J. (1990). The role of body image in psychosocial development across the life span: A developmental contextual perspective. In T. Cash & T. Pruzinsky (Eds.), *Body images: Development, deviance, and change* (pp. 110–127). New York: Guilford Press.

Levine, M. P. (2001). Commentary on Varnado-Sullivan et al.'s. (2001). "development and implementation of the Body Logic Program for adolescents: A two-stage prevention program for eating disorders." *Cognitive and Behavioral Practice, 8,* 271–276.

Levine, M. P., & Piran, N. (2001). The prevention of eating disorders: Toward a participatory ecology of knowledge, action, and advocacy. In R. H. Striegel-Moore & L. Smolak (Eds.), *Eating disorders: Innovative directions in research and practice* (pp. 233–253). Washington, DC: American Psychological Association.

Levine, M. P., Piran, N., & Stoddard, C. (1999). Mission more probable: Media literacy, activism and advocacy as primary prevention. In N. Piran, M. P. Levine, & C. Steiner-Adair (Eds.), *Preventing eating disorders: A handbook of interventions and special challenges* (pp. 1–25). Philadelphia: Brunner/Mazel.

Levine, M. P., & Smolak, L. (1992). Toward a model of the developmental psychopathology of eating disorders: The example of early adolescence. In J. H. Crowther, D. L. Tennenbaum, S. E. Hobfoll, & M. A. P. Stephens (Eds.), *The etiology of bulimia nervosa: The individual and familial context* (pp. 59–80). Washington, DC: Hemisphere.

Levine, M. P., & Smolak, L. (1998). The mass media and disordered eating: Implications for primary prevention. In W. Vandereycken & G. Noordenbos (Eds.), *The prevention of eating disorders: Studies in eating disorders: An international series* (pp. 23–56). New York: New York University Press.

Levine, M. P., & Smolak, L. (2002). Ecological and activism approaches to the prevention of body image problems. In T. F. Cash & T. Pruzinsky (Eds.), *Body image:*

A handbook of theory, research, and clinical practice (pp. 497–505). New York: Guilford Press.

Levine, M. P., Smolak, L., & Schermer, F. (1996). Media analysis and resistance by elementary school children in the primary prevention of eating problems. *Eating Disorders: Journal of Treatment and Prevention, 4*(4), 310–322.

Lewinsohn, P. M., Striegel-Moore, R. H., & Seeley, J. R. (2000). Epidemiology and natural course of eating disorders in young women from adolescence to young adulthood. *Journal of the Academy of Child and Adolescent Psychiatry, 39,* 1284–1292.

Lieberman, M., Gauvin, L., Bukowski, W. M., & White, D. R. (2001). Interpersonal influence and disordered eating behaviors in adolescent girls. The role of peer modeling, social reinforcement, and body-related teasing. *Eating Behaviors, 2,* 215–236.

Lock, J., Reisel, B., & Steiner, H. (2001). Associated health risks of adolescents with disordered eating: How different are they from their peers? Results from a high school survey. *Child Psychiatry and Human Development, 31,* 249–265.

Lunner, K., Wertheim, E. H., Thompson, J. K., Paxton, S. J., McDonald, F., & Halvaarson, K. S. (2000). A cross-cultural examination of weight-related teasing, body image, and eating disturbance in Swedish and Australian samples. *International Journal of Eating Disorders, 28*(4), 430–435.

Mann, T., Nolen-Hoeksema, S., Huang, K., & Burgard, D. (1997). Are two interventions worse than none? Joint primary and secondary prevention of eating disorders in college females. *Health Psychology, 16,* 215–225.

Marchi, M., & Cohen, P. (1990). Early childhood eating behaviors and adolescent eating disorders. *Journal of the American Academy of Child and Adolescent Psychiatry, 29,* 112–117.

Martin, G. C., Wertheim, E. H., Prior, M., Smart, D., Sanson, A., & Oberklaid, F. (2000). A longitudinal study of the role of childhood temperament in the later development of eating concerns. *International Journal of Eating Disorders, 27,* 150–162.

McCabe, M. P., Ricciardelli, L. A., & Finemore, J. (2002). The role of puberty, media and popularity with peers on strategies to increase weight, decrease weight and increase muscle tone among adolescent girls and boys. *Journal of Psychosomatic Research, 52,* 145–153.

McCreary, D. R., & Sasse, D. K. (2002). Gender differences in high school students' dieting behavior and their correlates. *International Journal of Men's Health, 1,* 195–213.

McVey, G., Davis, R., & Shaw, B. F. S. (1999, April). *Primary prevention of eating disorders: Preliminary findings of a school-based program for grade 6 girls and their parents.* Poster presented at the biennial meeting of the Society for Research in Child Development, Albuquerque, New Mexico.

McVey, G. L., Davis, R., Kaplan, A., Katzman, D. K., Pinhas, L., Geist, R. et al. (2003). *The development of a provincial network of specialized services: A community based training program for eating disorders.* Manuscript in preparation.

McVey, G. L., Davis, R., Tweed, S., & Shaw, B. (in press). *An evaluation of a school-based program designed to promote positive body image and self-esteem: A replication study.* International Journal of Eating Disorders.

McVey, G. L., Lieberman, M., Voorberg, N., Wardrope, D., & Blackmore, E. (2003). School-based peer support groups: A new approach to the prevention of eating disorders. *Eating Disorders: Journal of Treatment and Prevention, 11*(8), 169–186.

McVey, G. L., Lieberman, M., Voorberg, N., Wardrope, D., Blackmore, E, & Tweed, S. (2003). A replication of a peer support group program designed to reduce disordered eating in middle school students. *Eating Disorders: Journal of Treatment and Prevention, 11*(8), 187–195.

McVey, G. L., Pepler, D., Davis, R., Flett, G. L., & Abdolell, M. (2002). Risk and protective factors associated with disordered eating during early adolescence. *Journal of Early Adolescence, 22,* 75–95.

McVey, G. L., Tweed, S., & Blackmore, E. (2003). *Correlates of body image, dieting and muscle gain in male and female middle school students: Preliminary findings from a comprehensive prevention program.* Manuscript submitted for publication.

Mellin, L. M., Scully, S., & Irwin, C. S. (1992). Prevalence of disordered eating in girls: A survey of middle-class children. *Journal of the American Dietetic Association, 92,* 851–853.

Moorhead, D. J., Stashwick, C. K., Reinherz, H. Z., Gaiconia, R. M., Striegel-Moore, R. M., & Paradis, A. D. (2002). Child and adolescent predictors for eating disorders in a community population of young adult women. *International Journal of Eating Disorders, 33,* 1–9.

Moreno, A. B., & Thelen, M. H. (1993). A preliminary prevention program for eating disorders in a junior high school population. *Journal of Youth and Adolescence, 22,* 109.

Muir, S. L., Wertheim, E. H., & Paxton, S. J. (1999). Adolescent girls' first diets: Triggers and the role of multiple dimensions of self-concept. *Eating Disorders: Journal of Treatment and Prevention, 7,* 259–270.

Murnen, S. K., & Smolak, L. (2000). The experience of sexual harassment among grade-school students: Early socialization of female subordination? *Sex Roles, 43*(1/2), 1–17.

Neumark-Sztainer, D. (1996). School-based programs for preventing eating disorders. *Journal of School Health, 66,* 64–71.

Neumark-Sztainer, D., Sherwood, N. E., Coller, T., & Hannan, P. J. (2000). Primary prevention of disordered eating among preadolescent girls: Feasibility and short-term effect of a community-based intervention. *Journal of the American Dietetic Association, 100,* 1466–1473.

Nichter, M., Vuckovic, N., & Parker, S. (1999). The Looking Good, Feeling Good program: A multiethnic intervention for healthy body image, nutrition, and physical activity. In N. Piran, M. P. Levine, & C. Steiner-Adair (Eds.), *Preventing eating disorders: A handbook of interventions and special challenges* (pp. 175–193). Philadelphia: Brunner/Mazel.

O'Dea, J. A. (2000). School-based interventions to prevent eating problems: First do no harm. *Eating Disorders: Journal of Treatment and Prevention, 8*(2), 123–130.

O'Dea, J. A. (2002). The new self-esteem approach for the prevention of body image and eating problems in children and adolescents. *Healthy Weight Journal, 16,* 89–93.

O'Dea, J. A., & Abraham, S. (2000). Improving the body image, eating attitudes, and behaviors of young male and female adolescents: A new educational approach that focuses on self-esteem. *International Journal of Eating Disorders, 28,* 43–57.

O'Dea, J. A., & Maloney, D. (2000). Preventing eating and body image problems in children and adolescents using the health promoting schools framework. *Journal of School Health, 70,* 18–21.

O'Dea, J. A., & Rawstorne, P. R. (2001). Male adolescents identify their weight gain practices, reasons for desired weight gain, and sources of weight gain information. *Journal of the American Dietetic Association, 101,* 105–107.

Paxton, S. J. (1993). A prevention program for disturbed eating and body dissatisfaction in adolescent girls: A 1 year follow-up. *Health Education Research, 8,* 43–51.

Paxton, S. J., Schutz, H. K., Wertheim, E. H., & Muir, S. L. (1999). Friendship clique and peer influences on body image concerns, dietary restraint, extreme weight-loss behaviors, and binge eating in adolescent girls. *Journal of Abnormal Psychology, 10,* 255–266.

Phelps, L., Sapia, J., Nathanson, D., & Nelson, L. (2000). An empirically supported eating disorder prevention program. *Psychology in the Schools, 37*(5), 443–452.

Pike, K. M., & Walsh, B. T. (1996). Ethnicity and eating disorders: Implications for incidence and treatment. *Psychopharmacology Bulletin, 32,* 265–274.

Pine, D. S., Cohen, P., Brook, J., & Coplan, J. D. (1997). Psychiatric symptoms in adolescence as predictors of obesity in early adulthood: A longitudinal study. *American Journal of Public Health, 87,* 1303–1310.

Piran, N. (1995). Prevention: Can early lessons lead to a delineation of an alternative model? A critical look at prevention with schoolchildren. *Eating Disorders: Journal of Treatment and Prevention, 3,* 28–36.

Piran, N. (1996). The reduction of preoccupation with body weight and shape in schools: A feminist approach. *Eating Disorders: Journal of Treatment and Prevention, 4,* 323–333.

Piran, N. (1998). A participatory approach to the prevention of eating disorders in a school. In G. Noordenbos & W. Vandereycken (Eds.), *Prevention of eating disorders. Studies in eating disorders: An international series* (pp. 173–186). New York: New York University Press.

Piran, N. (1999). Eating disorders: A trial of prevention in a high risk school setting. *Journal of Primary Prevention, 20*(1), 75–90.

Piran, N., Levine, M. P., & Steiner-Adair, C. (1999). *Preventing eating disorders: A handbook of interventions and special challenges.* Philadelphia: Brunner/Mazel.

Polivy, J., & Herman, C. P. (1985). Dieting and binging: A causal analysis. *American Psychologist, 40*(2), 193–201.

Porter, J. E., Morrell, T. L., & Moriarty, D. (1986, July/August). Primary prevention of anorexia nervosa: Evaluation of a pilot project for early and preadolescents. *Canadian Association for Health, Physical Education and Recreation Journal,* 21–26.

Powers, P. S., & Johnson, C. (1999). Small victories: Prevention of eating disorders among athletes. *Eating Disorders, 4,* 364–377.

Ricciardelli, L. A., & McCabe, M. P. (2001). Self-esteem and negative affect as moderators of sociocultural influences on body dissatisfaction, strategies to decrease weight, and strategies to increase muscles among adolescent boys and girls. *Sex Roles, 33,* 189–207.

Robb, A. S. (2001). Eating disorders in children. *Psychiatric Clinics of North America, 24,* 259–270.

Roberts, S. J., McGuiness, P. J., Bilton, R. F., & Maxwell, S. M. (1999). Dieting behavior among 11–15-year-old girls in Merseyside and the North West of England. *Journal of Adolescent Health, 25,* 62–67.

Rosenvinge, J. H., & Borresen, R. (1999). Preventing eating disorders—time to change programs or paradigms? Current update and further recommendations. *European Eating Disorders Review, 7*(1), 5–16.

Rutter, M. (1990). Psychosocial resilience and protective mechanisms. In J. Rolf, A. S. Masten, D. Cicchetti, K. H. Neuchterlein, & S. Weintraub (Eds.), *Risk and protective factors in the development of psychopathology* (pp. 181–214). Cambridge, England: Cambridge University Press.

Santonastaso, P., Zanetti, T., Ferrara, S., Olivotto, M. C., Magnavita, N., & Favaro, A. (1999). A preventive intervention program in adolescent schoolgirls: A longitudinal study. *Psychotherapy and Psychosomatics, 68,* 46–50.

Seaver, A., McVey, G. L., Fullerton, Y., & Stratton, L. (1997). *Every BODY is a somebody: An active learning program to promote healthy body image, positive self-esteem, healthy eating and an active lifestyle for female adolescents.* Brampton, ON: Body Image Coalition of Peel.

Shisslak, C. M., & Crago, M. (1993). Toward a new model for the prevention of eating disorders. In P. Fallon, M. A. Katzman, & S. Wooley (Eds.), *Feminist perspectives on eating disorders* (pp. 419–437). New York: Guilford Press.

Shisslak, C. M., & Crago, M. (2001). Risk and protective factors in the development of eating disorders. In J. K. Thompson & L. Smolak (Eds.), *Body image, eating disorders, and obesity in youth: Assessment, prevention, and treatment* (pp. 103–125). Washington, DC: American Psychological Association.

Shisslak, C. M., Crago, M., Estes, L. S., & Gray, N. (1996). Content and method of developmentally appropriate prevention programs. In L. Smolak, M. P. Levine, & R. H. Striegel-Moore (Eds.), *The developmental psychopathology of eating disorders* (pp. 341–363). Mahwah, NJ: Erlbaum.

Shisslak, C. M., Crago, M., & Neal, M. E. (1990). Prevention of eating disorders among adolescents. *American Journal of Health Promotion, 5,* 100–106.

Shisslak, C. M., Crago, M., Renger, R., & Clark-Wagner, A. (1998). Self-esteem and the prevention of eating disorders. *Eating Disorders: Journal of Treatment and Prevention, 6,* 105–117.

Smolak, L. (1999). Elementary school curricula for the primary prevention of eating problems. In N. Piran, M. P. Levine, & C. Steiner-Adair. *Preventing eating disorders: A handbook of interventions and special challenges* (pp. 85–104). Philadelphia: Brunner/Mazel.

Smolak, L., Harris, B., Levine, M. P., & Shisslak, C. M. (2001). Teachers: The forgotten influence on the success of prevention programs. *Eating Disorders: Journal of Treatment and Prevention, 9,* 261–265.

Smolak, L., & Levine, M. P. (1996). Adolescent transitions and the development of eating problems. In L. Smolak, M. P. Levine, & R. H. Striegel-Moore (Eds.), *The developmental psychopathology of eating disorders: Implications for research, prevention, and treatment* (pp. 207–233). Mahwah, NJ: Erlbaum.

Smolak, L., & Levine, M. P. (2001). A two-year follow-up of a primary prevention program for negative body image and unhealthy weight regulation. *Eating Disorders: Journal of Treatment and Prevention, 9,* 313–325.

Smolak, L., Levine, M. P., & Schermer, F. (1998). A controlled study evaluation of an elementary school primary prevention program for eating problems. *Journal of Psychosomatic Research, 44,* 339–353.

Smolak, L., Levine, M. P., & Schermer, F. (1999). Parental input and weight concerns among elementary school children. *International Journal of Eating Disorders, 25,* 263–271.

Springer, E. A., Winzelberg, A. J., Perkins, R., & Taylor, C. B. (1999). Effects of a body image curriculum for college students on improved body image. *International Journal of Eating Disorders, 26,* 13–20.

Steiner-Adair, C., & Purcell, A. (1996). Approaches to mainstreaming eating disorders prevention. *Eating Disorders: Journal of Treatment and Prevention, 4,* 294–309.

Steiner-Adair, C., Sjostrom, L., Franko, D. L., Pai, S., Tucker, R., Becker, A. E., et al. (2002). Primary prevention of risk factors for eating disorders in adolescent girls: Learning from practice. *International Journal of Eating Disorders, 32*(4), 401–411.

Steiner-Adair, C., & Vorenberg, A. P. (1999). Resisting weightism: Media literacy for elementary-school children. In N. Piran, M. P. Levine, & C. Steiner-Adair. *Preventing eating disorders: A handbook of interventions and special challenges* (pp. 105–121). Philadelphia: Brunner/Mazel.

Stewart, D. A., Carter, J. C., Drinkwater, J., Hainsworth, J., & Fairburn, C. G. (2001). Modification of eating attitudes and behavior in adolescent girls: A controlled study. *International Journal of Eating Disorders, 29*(2), 107–118.

Stice, E. (1994). Review of the evidence for a sociocultural model of bulimia nervosa and an exploration of the mechanisms of action. *Clinical Psychology Review, 14,* 633–661.

Stice, E. (2001). Risk factors for eating pathology: Recent advances and future directions. In R. H. Striegel-Moore & L. Smolak (Eds.), *Eating disorders: Innovative directions in research and practice* (pp. 51–73). Washington, DC: American Psychological Association.

Stice, E., Agras, W. S., & Hammer, L. D. (1999). Risk factors for the emergence of childhood eating disturbances. *International Journal of Eating Disorders, 25,* 375–387.

Stice, E., Mazotti, L., Weibel, D., & Agras, W. S. (2000). Dissonance prevention program decreases thin-ideal internalization, body dissatisfaction, dieting, negative affect, and bulimic symptoms: A preliminary experiment. *International Journal of Eating Disorders, 27,* 206–217.

Stice, E., & Ragan, J. (2002). A preliminary controlled evaluation of an eating disturbance psychoeducational intervention for college students. *International Journal of Eating Disorders, 31,* 159–171.

Striegel-Moore, R. H. (1997). Risk factors for eating disorders. In M. S. Jacobson, J. M. Rees, N. H. Golden, & C. E. Irwin (Eds.), *Adolescent nutritional disorders: Prevention and treatment* (pp. 98–109). New York: New York Academy of Sciences.

Striegel-Moore, R. H., Silberstein, L. R., & Rodin, J. (1986). Toward an understanding of risk factors in bulimia. *American Psychologist, 41,* 246–263.

Striegel-Moore, R. H., & Smolak, L. (1996). The role of race in the development of eating disorders. In L. Smolak, M. P. Levine, & R. H. Striegel-Moore (Eds.), *The developmental psychopathology of eating disorders: Implications for research, prevention, and treatment* (pp. 259–284). Mahwah, NJ: Erlbaum.

Taylor, C. B., & Altman, T. (1997). Priorities in prevention research for eating disorders. *Psychopharmacology Bulletin, 33,* 413–417.

Taylor, C. B., Sharpe, T., Shisslak, C. M., Bryson, S., Estes, L. S., Gray, N., et al. (1998). Factors associated with weight concerns in adolescent girls. *International Journal of Eating Disorders, 34,* 31–42.

Thompson, R. A., & Sherman, R. T. (1993). Reducing the risk of eating disorders in athletics. *Eating Disorders: Journal of Treatment and Prevention, 1,* 65–78.

Vandereycken, W., & Noordenbos, G. (1998). *The prevention of eating disorders.* New York: New York University Press.

Varnado-Sullivan, P. J., Zucker, N., Williamson, D. A., Reas, D., Thaw, J., & Netemeyer, S. B. (2001). Development and implementation of the Body Logic Program for adolescents: A two-stage prevention program for eating disorders. *Cognitive and Behavioral Practice, 8,* 248–259.

Winzelberg, A. J., Taylor, C. B., Sharpe, T., Eldredge, K. L., Dev, P., & Constantinou, P. S. (1998). Evaluation of a computer-mediated eating disorder intervention program. *International Journal of Eating Disorders, 24,* 339–349.

Zabinski, M. F., Wilfley, D. E., Pung, M. A., Winzelberg, A. J., Eldredge, K. L., & Taylor, C. B. (2001). An interactive Internet-based intervention for women at risk of eating disorders: A pilot study. *International Journal of Eating Disorders, 30,* 129–137.

Chapter 14

OBESITY

LOIS ANN WODARSKI AND JOHN S. WODARSKI

THE OBESITY EPIDEMIC

Obesity (including overweight) is the principal public health nutrition problem in the United States, largely because of its ability to increase chronic disease risk and its increasing prevalence among adults and children (Nestle, 2003, p. 39). Properly described by Rippe (1998) as "epidemic" in the United States as well as in other developed countries, obesity has become a public health priority (U.S. Department of Health and Human Services [USDHHS], 2000). Defined as body fatness in excess of an age- and sex-specified standard, obesity is estimated to affect 22.5% of adults, with another 32% considered overweight (Flegal, Caroll, Kuczmarski, & Johnson, 1998). The data for children and adolescents are increasingly alarming. An estimated 13% of children ages 6 to 11 years and 14% of adolescents ages 12 to 19 are overweight according to data from the Youth Risk Behavior Surveillance—United States 1999 (National Center for Health Statistics, 2001). This report noted that from 1988 to 1994, 11% of children and adolescents between the ages of 6 and 19 were considered overweight or obese. This is double the figure for children recorded in 1980 and triple the figure reported for adolescents that same year (National Center for Health Statistics, 2001; Troiano, Flegal, Kuczmarski, Campbell, & Johnson, 1995).

The incidence of obesity varies according to age, gender, race, and ethnicity, although no segment of the population appears to be exempt. Rates of increase are particularly high, however, in African American and Hispanic youth where increases of more than 10 percentage points from 1988 to 1994 and again from 1999 to 2000 have been noted (Strauss & Pollack, 2001).

THE OUTCOMES OF OBESITY

Overweight and obesity, resulting mainly from poor dietary and exercise habits, are linked with coronary heart disease, certain cancers, hypertension, Type 2 diabetes, osteoarthritis, dyslipidemias, and a reduction in life span (American Dietetic Association, 1997). In terms of actual causes of death among the U.S. population in 1990, diet and inadequate physical activity were second only to tobacco use (McGinnis & Foege, 1993). The consequences of childhood or adolescent obesity are particularly severe. Childhood obesity is a disorder that tracks over time, such that obese children are at an increased risk for becoming obese adults (Gortmaker, Dietz, Sobol, & Wehler, 1987; Price, Stunkard, & Ness, 1990; Troiano et al., 1995). Studies suggest that between 70% and 80% of overweight and obese children and adolescents will most likely remain so as adults (Moran, 1999). Being obese in adolescence increases the risk of adult morbidity and mortality more than 50 years later independently of adult obesity status (Epstein, 1995a).

Obesity that develops in childhood or adolescence is more difficult to treat and may cause more severe personality and psychological problems than obesity that develops in adulthood (Klesges, Coates, & Brown, 1983). Emotionally, overweight and obese children are characterized by defective body image development, depression, low self-esteem, and social isolation (Stunkard & Wadden, 1992). In their families, these children are often the focus of parental conflicts, a source of embarrassment, or a sibling scapegoat (Hammar et al., 1972), and among their peers, overweight children are often rated as less attractive, lazier, and not well-liked (Hill & Silver, 1995; Tiggemann & Wilson-Barrett, 1998). Social and economic consequences to overweight individuals include discrimination in obtaining admission to college and/or gaining employment (Puhl & Brownell, 2001). Overweight or obese young adults are less likely to marry (Gortmaker, Must, Perrin, Sobol, & Dietz, 1993).

In addition to the physiological and psychosocial costs of obesity, the economic burden to our society is immense. An estimated $70 billion is the direct cost of obesity in the United States. This represents about 7% of total health care expenditures (Field, Barnoya, & Colditz, 2002). Hospital costs related to childhood obesity have more than tripled in the past 20 years to $127 million annually (Frist, 2002).

THE ETIOLOGY OF CHILD AND ADOLESCENT OBESITY

The etiology and treatment of overweight and obese children and adolescents have received widespread attention, yet little undisputed knowledge has accrued as to cause and cure. It is agreed, however, that overweight and obesity generally, if not always, can be attributed to an imbalance between energy intake and energy output (Lewis et al., 1997; Stock & Rothwell, 1982). When an individual eats more calories (energy in) than he or she burns up (energy out), weight gain results. In spite of the rather simplistic equation that explains the root cause of obesity, numerous factors appear associated with food and exercise habits maladjusted to the energy needs of children and adolescents. These factors include genetic, biological, psychological, environmental, and behavioral (Wadden & Stunkard, 2002). Most likely, genetic differences mediate differential responses to cultural change through the gene-environment interaction (Price, 2002).

GENETICS VERSUS LIFESTYLE

Heredity plays a major role in the development of body size and obesity with certain individuals and groups of individuals having a propensity toward fatness (Price, 2002). For example, variations of up to 200 calories in metabolic energy expenditures have been observed among individuals (Ravussin et al., 1988). However, the fact that obesity rates have skyrocketed from 4% to 30% during the past century suggests that genetic effects are behaviorally mediated, or "genes do not change that quickly" (Stice, 2002, p. 33). Thus, although genetics may play a role, the development of obesity largely depends on individual behavior, and the most plausible explanation for the exponential increase in obesity is "unhealthy lifestyle—we are consuming more calories that is warranted given our sedentary lifestyle" (Stice, 2002, p. 33; Lewis et al., 1997). Those who are obese, in general, eat more and/or exercise less than their nonobese counterparts (Drogas, Redd, & Hill, 1992; Heitmann, Sorensen, & Bengtsson, 1995; Lichtman et al., 1992; Livingstone et al., 1990; Maffeis, Schutz, Zafanello, Piccoli, & Pinelli, 1994; Schoeller et al., 1990). For adolescents, the scale seems to be tilted in the direction of increased sedentary behavior rather than on increased eating. Findings from the Bogalusa Heart Study indicated that children's energy intakes have remained relatively stable over the past 15 years (Nicklas, 1995). Experts suggest that if we change our lifestyle so that there is equilibrium between calorie intake and output, we should be able to dramatically reduce the rates of obesity and the consequent morbidity and mortality (Stice, 2002). This appears to be an especially prudent prescription for our nation's vulnerable youth.

COMPONENTS OF COMPREHENSIVE INTERVENTIONS FOR PREVENTION AND TREATMENT OF OBESITY

The seriousness and complexity of obesity present a difficult task for professionals who wish to prevent the onset in children, especially those considered to be high risk, that is, those with a familial history of obesity. Yet, there are still to be developed effective comprehensive programs to help youths acquire knowledge and behavior requisites to weight control. Given the multifaceted nature of obesity, it stands to reason that interventions for treatment and prevention must be comprehensive, addressing the various dimensions of the problem. Goldfield, Raynor, and Epstein (2002) examined 39 clinic-based and 6 school-based obesity treatment studies. They concluded that the most successful programs are those that incorporate a multidimensional approach, characterized by the inclusion of diet, exercise, and the application of behavior modification principles. They also suggest that the goals for treating childhood obesity are regulating body weight through adequate nutrition for growth and development, thereby allowing natural growth, minimizing loss of lean body mass, and preventing endocrine disturbances, as outlined by Rees (1990), while ensuring that treatments are associated with positive changes in physiological and psychological sequelae of obesity. They propose treatments that modify eating and exercise behaviors, along with the factors that regulate these behaviors, so that new, healthier behaviors persist throughout development. In line with this goal, the comprehensive treatment program should address the behavioral components of diet, exercise, and lifestyle and the social environment of family and peers. Additionally, treatment should include in each component special attention to the cognitive factor of body image, especially as it relates to a realistic ideal weight for the individual.

Behavioral Components

Unhealthy dietary behaviors and inadequate physical activity are behaviors most commonly associated with overweight and obesity. Both have been defined by the National Institutes of Health as "risky behaviors," that is, those that have the potential for some type of loss. These particular risky behaviors frequently are established during the adolescent years and continue to the adult years (National Center for Health Statistics, 2001). Dietary choices and physical activity are learned behaviors and are thus subject to alteration. Although the behaviors are believed to be potentially amenable to a variety of health promotion and prevention efforts, interventions to alter food intake and energy output to achieve weight loss and to maintain the loss have met with limited success (Lawrence, Zittel, Wodarski, & Wodarski, in press).

Diet

Typically, children and adolescents consume diets that are high in calories; high in fat, especially saturated fat; and low in nutrient-dense foods such as whole grains and fruits and vegetables (Subar, Krebs-Smith, Cook, & Kahle, 1998). It has been reported that only 2% of schoolage children meet the Food Guide Pyramid recommendations for the five food groups; thus, they have inadequate intakes of a number of nutrients including calcium, vitamin A, vitamin B6, and iron (U.S. Department of Agriculture [USDA], 1998). In the review of studies by Goldfield et al. (2002) cited previously, no conclusions were drawn about the most effective dietary prescription for children because few, if any, studies have compared the effects of different dietary approaches while holding other aspects of treatment constant. Any dietary prescription, however, must incorporate the principles of good nutrition providing the necessary calories and nutrients essential for growth and development. Furthermore, successful dietary intervention will likely address the issue of nutritionally sound food choices. When food preferences are taken into account, it is more likely that long-term changes in food choices will be achieved. The following recommendations for diet published by the American Heart Association (1996) for all children over the age of 2 and adolescents address these requisites:

1. Adequate nutrition should be achieved by eating a wide variety of foods.
2. Energy (calories) should be adequate to support growth and development and to reach or maintain desirable body weight.
3. The following pattern of nutrient intake is recommended:
   a. Saturated fatty acids—less than 10% of total calories.
   b. Total fat—an average of no more than 30% of total calories.
   c. Dietary cholesterol—less than 300 milligrams per day.

Cautions about Dieting

Overweight or obese children and adolescents represent a unique challenge in dieting or calorie restrictions. Nutritional adjustments must be made to keep calorie intake in line with energy expenditure. In most cases, efforts to reduce weight or to maintain weight while increases in height occur require dietary modifications. Caution must be exercised, however, in efforts to control weight in children and adolescents because a number of undesirable consequences may result from unhealthy weight-loss attempts. Children and adolescents are at risk for adverse nutritional, physical, and psychosocial consequences of excessive dieting (Neumark-Sztainer, Wall, Story, & Perry, 2003). Behaviors such as food restriction, laxative use, and self-induced vomiting are not uncommon and may lead to serious eating disorders such as bulimia nervosa (Marchi & Cohen, 1990; Neumark-Sztainer et al., 2003; Patton, Johnson-Sabine, Wood, Mann, & Wakeling, 1990). Moreover, it has been observed that these unhealthy weight-control behaviors have potential for increasing the risk of obesity in adolescents

(Stice, Cameron, Killen, Hayward, & Taylor, 1999). In terms of psychosocial consequences, children and adolescents can easily come to believe that their worth or lovability is somehow tied to their weight, and the low sense of self-worth may open the door to depression or taking risks of another nature, such as alcohol or drug use, without regard for personal well-being (Neumark-Sztainer, Story, Dixon, & Murray, 1988). In a test of a theoretical model to explain unhealthy weight-control behaviors among a multicultural sample of adolescent girls and boys, Neumark-Sztainer et al. (2003) found that weight-body concerns were a strong correlate of unhealthy weight-control behaviors in both girls and boys. In light of these adverse consequences of dieting, emphasis should be on the development of healthy eating patterns rather than on weight loss per se.

Exercise

At the same time their diets are questionable, our youth are engaging in inadequate physical activity. Physical activity has direct and indirect benefits on health. Exercise is critical to both the prevention and treatment of obesity (Clark, Niaura, King, & Pera, 1996). Increased physical activity results in increased energy expenditure and is important for weight loss and maintenance. Exercise also aids in weight loss by suppressing the appetite and offsets the decline in basal metabolic rate created by dieting (Fletcher et al., 1995). Furthermore, physical activity may reduce body fat and prevent the loss of lean body mass during weight loss (Marks & Rippe, 1996). Physical activity also helps reduce the risk of cardiovascular disease and diabetes and provides benefits beyond those achieved by weight loss alone. In addition to its contribution to energy output, exercise has positive effects on plasma insulin levels, blood pressure, and coronary efficiency (King, Taylor, Haskell, & DeBusk, 1989; Morris, Clayton, Everitt, Semmence, & Burgess, 1990).

It is likely that physically active individuals are less likely to develop obesity during their lives as compared to inactive people (Ching et al., 1996). Good exercise patterns established in adolescence have the added benefit of carry-over to adulthood. The association between participation in a wide variety of adolescent sports and physical activity during adulthood was studied by Tammelin, Nayha, Hills, and Jarvelin (2003). Their evaluation of data from 7,794 males and females of the Northern Finland 1966 birth cohort revealed that participation in sports at least once a week in female adolescents and twice a week among male adolescents was associated with a high level of physical activity in adulthood. Although the differences among the various types of sports were modest, participation in intensive endurance sports, such as cross-country skiing and running, and some sports that require and encourage diversified sports skills, such as track and field and ballgames for males, appeared to be most beneficial with respect to the enhancement of adult physical activity.

Only 27% of adolescents currently engage in the recommended amounts of moderate-intensity physical activity (USDHHS, 2000). Healthy People 2010 emphasizes increasing the proportion of adolescents who engage in physical activity that promotes cardiovascular fitness three or more days a week for a minimum of 20 minutes per occasion (USDHHS, 2000). Additionally, goals for increasing daily school physical education, decreased television viewing, and increased trips made by walking or bicycling to school and elsewhere have been established (USDHHS, 2000).

Engaging in physical activity is particularly important to obese adolescents who have been observed to be significantly less active than their nonobese peers, and even when physically active, they exert themselves less (Epstein, Smith, Vara, & Rodefer, 1991). In their examination of clinic-based and school-based outcomes studies of childhood obesity, Goldfield et al. (2002) found that exercise interventions alone do not appear to have substantial impact on weight change, but exercise combined with diet appears to enhance weight loss and improve long-term maintenance. Less structured, more flexible lifestyle exercise appeared to be more effective than high-intensity aerobic exercise for weight control. Reinforcing children for reducing sedentary activity, in conjunction with the use of a structured eating plan, appeared to be a promising alternative method of increasing physical activity, fitness, and weight loss.

Lifestyle Modification

Environmental forces play a major role in the development of obesity. Americans live in an environment where food is plentiful, energy-dense, and good tasting and where technology has decreased the need for physical activity (Rippe, Crossley, & Ringer, 1998). The prevalence of labor-saving devices such as TV remote controls; garage door openers; automatic dishwashers, clothes washers, and dryers; and ready-to-eat foods and fast-food establishments makes it easier for people to lead less physically active lives (Coulston, 1998). Significant increases in portion sizes of a large number of foods consumed by individuals ages 2 years and over have been reported over the past decade (Smiciklas-Wright, Mitchell, Mickle, Goldman, & Cook, 2003). Nestle (2003) argues convincingly that the increased portion sizes of foods served outside the home have contributed significantly to the increase in calories consumed. She suggests that these increases are both consumer driven and government and industry driven. From the consumer standpoint, it is difficult to pass up a bargain. From the standpoint of government and industry, corporate farming price supports and marketing policies are formulated to bring greater profits through increased consumption of food and the products used to produce, package, and advertise it.

Changes in lifestyles and the environment have brought about significant alterations in children's eating patterns and food choices (Crockett & Sims, 1995). The influence of television and computer games cannot be underestimated. Television viewing has been suggested as a leading cause of the increasing obesity among children in the United States (Gortmaker et al., 1996). Among adolescents 12 to 17 years, the prevalence of obesity was observed to increase by 2% for every hour of television viewed (Dietz & Gortmaker, 1985). Children and adolescents spend an estimated 24 hours per week in the sedentary activity of television watching. Not only does television viewing decrease the time spent in physical activity, but also it is suggested that the correlation with television watching and snacking and consumption of high-fat, high-calorie foods advertised on television exacerbates the problem (Dietz & Gortmaker, 1985). In light of the positive correlations observed between obesity and blood cholesterol with hours of television watched (Stunkard & Wadden, 1992), we have reason for concern. It stands to reason that lifestyle modification is one of the main predictors of success for weight management programs (Coulston, 1998).

Understanding lifestyle changes is pivotal if we are to help today's children establish healthy eating patterns that contribute to the prevention and delay of chronic disease later in life (Nicklas, 1995). Education alone will not necessarily induce individuals to modify their lifestyles. The finding that, in general, overweight and obese children have a reasonably good knowledge of dietary needs and causes of obesity is evidence that knowledge is a necessary but not significant condition for change (Dwyer, Feldman, & Mayer, 1967). Nutrition education, however, is paramount in any behavioral intervention program to enable children to develop sensible attitudes toward food and physical activity as well as to counteract myriad invalid nutritional messages received from those who would capitalize on the vulnerability and plight of the obese.

Lytle and Achterberg (1995) note that the majority of nutrition intervention programs that have resulted in positive behavior change were behaviorally based and theory driven. Behavioral therapies may be employed to promote adoption of dietary and activity adjustments. Specific behavioral strategies included in successful weight loss/maintenance interventions include self-monitoring, recording, and feedback of food intake and physical activity; stress management to use in situations where environmental stimuli are difficult; stimulus control, that is, identifying and overcoming barriers or settings that lead to overeating; problem solving; contingency management; cognitive restructuring to focus on well-being, body image, personal ideal body weight, and healthful behavior patterns; and social support (Coulston, 1998). Dietary intervention attempts, likewise, should include recognition of factors that trigger personal motivation and behavioral change and incorporate a variety of reinforcement techniques. The effective comprehensive intervention program should result in increased knowledge of food and nutrition as it relates to physical appearance and health, inspire interest and motivation within the child or adolescent, provide an accepting environment where learning can take place, and lead ultimately to the application of newly acquired knowledge to improved behavior. Additionally, all effective programs should include a behavioral analysis of discriminative stimuli and consequences for eating. Intervention should focus on changing or removing discriminative stimuli for eating and reinforcement of prosocial changes in individual behavior and cognitive images of body size.

Social Environmental Factors

The improved child outcome when both parents and children are targeted for behavior change suggests that factors common to the shared family environment, including changes in parent-child interactions that encourage and support new eating and exercise habits, are important for success in behavior change (Epstein, Valoski, Wing, & McCurley, 1990, 1994). Neumark-Sztainer et al. (2003) add that because family peer weight norms are strongly correlated with a youth's personal weight-body concerns, prevention and intervention programs must address peer groups as well as family members.

Family Intervention

One of the most important risk factors for the development and maintenance of obesity during childhood is parental obesity, which, through modeling and reinforcement, may facilitate the acquisition of and maintain the eating and exercise behaviors associated with obesity (Johnson & Birch, 1994; Klesges et al., 1983). In their review of interventions, Goldfield et al. (2002) noted that the inclusion of parents in a family-based comprehensive behavioral intervention enhanced short- and long-term weight control. They suggest that a family-based nutrition program that focuses on improved parent and child eating and exercise behaviors would be more effective than a program that focuses only on child eating and exercise behaviors.

Because the most salient environmental factor affecting children's eating patterns is the family (Crockett & Sims, 1995), we must provide parents with the appropriate tools for modeling and reinforcement of healthy eating patterns. With these tools, they will be equipped to provide healthful food choices and facilitate development of sound eating practices that prevent overeating and resulting obesity. It has been observed that parents who attempt to control their child's intake of healthy foods through the use of controlling child-feeding strategies (e.g., restricting intake of unhealthy foods) may inadvertently decrease a child's preference for and intake of the healthy foods (Birch, 1999). In a recent program based on social learning theory, child-focused interactive lessons and skill-building activities were combined with parent-focused lessons on child-feeding strategies to increase fruit intake of children and to reduce parents' use of controlling child-feeding strategies (Gribble, Falciglia, Davis, & Couch, 2003). Results indicated that the program was successful in positively increasing the children's knowledge scores and fruit intake, and there was a significant decrease in the use of controlling child-feeding strategies by parents in the intervention group.

Golan and Weizman (2001) used a family-based approach for management of childhood obesity where change was delivered through the parents as opposed to delivery directly to the obese child. The emphasis was on a healthy lifestyle rather than on weight reduction. The intervention integrated behavioral, social learning, and family system approaches. The authors noted that parental cognitive and behavioral change was fostered by increasing parental nutrition and parenting skills, and environmental change was fostered by restructuring family mealtimes and leisure-time activities and reinforcing appropriate eating cues.

Peer Group Intervention

Effective interventions should address the role of peers in behavioral change and maintenance. Similar to family therapy, peer group therapy based on a behavioral model has been demonstrated to be effective in effecting changes of the fat to fat-free mass ratio, of the body mass index (BMI), and of everyday eating behavior in obese children ages 10 to 14 years. In the study by Lehrke, Becker, and Laessle (2002), obese children treated by either group therapy or with family therapy significantly lowered their BMI, decreased the mass of body fat, and showed a lower overall caloric intake and lower percentage of fat intake.

An added benefit of group treatment of pediatric obesity, as opposed to individual treatment, is the cost effectiveness of the former. Goldfield, Epstein, Kilanowski, Paluch, and Kogut-Bossler (2001) found that group intervention was significantly more cost effective as measured by the magnitude of reductions in BMI and percent overweight per dollar spent for recruitment and treatment.

Studies by Wodarski, Wodarski, & Parris (in press) have established that peer reinforcement is one of the most potent variables in the acquisition, alteration, and maintenance of behavior in children and adolescents. Based on results of a number of studies of child and adolescent preventive health interventions, they suggest an education/behavioral change approach. The intervention of choice combines knowledge gained through results of a substantial number of studies that indicate that peer learning team techniques based on behavioral analysis have great promise in achieving positive effects on many dimensions at the same time. These techniques are known by various names, but they are referred to here as *group reward structures,* because they all involve youth working in cooperative learning teams. In group reward structures, the knowledge and behavior of each group member further group goals. This, in turn, has been shown to increase performance in itself under a variety of circumstances and to increase the frequency of relevant social behaviors.

In summary, the comprehensive intervention program for weight control in children and adolescents should include components oriented both toward food choice and diet composition as well as increasing activity. The program should be family based, providing training to parents in rearranging the environment, modeling healthier behaviors, and using positive reinforcement to support positive changes in eating and exercise behaviors. Likewise, given the important role of peers in effecting and maintaining behavioral change, peer group treatment is the treatment of choice.

The following points summarize key ingredients of the evidence-based weight control interventions cited previously and should guide the development and implementation of prevention and treatment programs for children and adolescents:

1. Adequate biological, physical, and psychosocial assessment should precede any intervention. It is inappropriate to assume that every child or adolescent will respond to the same intervention. Based on the assessment, treatment goals and objectives should be developed to reflect the particular situation of the individual child or adolescent.

2. Appropriate diets should be determined according to the outcomes of the assessment. During the growing years, it is critical that adequate calories and nutrients be provided to allow for growth and development. There must be a balance between energy intake and energy expenditure that will allow for moderate weight loss or maintenance of weight while growth in height continues. Food choices as dictated by personal and cultural preferences, as well as by lifestyle, should be considered. The development of healthy eating patterns that can be continued on a long-term basis should be emphasized while dieting and fads are avoided. Consumption of regular meals and planned snacks should be encouraged along with increased consumption of fruits and vegetables and decreased consumption of foods high in fat and sugar.

3. Exercise goals and mechanisms to increase energy output should be established according to the individual assessment. As with diet, personal preferences and lifestyle must be considered if lifelong patterns are to be established. Simple steps that encourage daily energy output should be emphasized, such as using the stairs versus the elevator or parking the car farther from the building.

4. Principles of behavioral change should be observed. A food intake and exercise diary provides baseline data as well as a mechanism for identifying

environmental cues that trigger unhealthy eating and sedentary behavior. Discriminative stimuli that prompt unhealthy eating or sedentary behavior should be determined and avoided when possible. Reinforcement of weight loss or maintenance and increased physical activity should be included in the intervention. When weight change can be reinforced by activities that increase physical activity, the benefit is double. For example, when an established weight goal is achieved, the reward might be a family outing of bowling, swimming, or horseback riding. Feedback is essential. For example, the ongoing recording of food intake and physical activity in daily diaries provides the data necessary to pinpoint problems, and frequent monitoring of weight by household and/or clinic scales provides information about progress toward goals.

5. Supports for maintenance of change are crucial. Data indicate that few succeed in losing weight, and even fewer succeed in maintaining any losses (Epstein, 1995b). Regular clinic or support group contact is recommended. Buddy systems are one mechanism of providing peer support for behavioral change and maintenance. Family involvement, likewise, helps ensure success.

6. Interventions must include means of preparing for relapse. Setbacks should be expected, and information should be provided on how to deal with temporary lapses. Programs should focus on problem solving, emphasizing the anticipation of problem situations and specification of plans to deal with temptations and obstacles.

7. Inclusion of information on cognitive restructuring is important and enables the adolescent to view behavioral change as *possible* as opposed to *impossible*. Emphasis should be on development of a positive body image with realistic goals for weight change. The focus should be on weight management with the goal of achieving the best weight possible within the context of overall health (American Dietetic Association, 1997).

In addition to these principles of intervention, it is prudent to hear from adolescents themselves and include them in planning for interventions. Neumark-Sztainer and Story (1997) provide suggestions for school-based intervention programs for overweight youth that were derived from asking overweight adolescents for their recommendations. These suggestions, which they infer are applicable to individual and group counseling in clinical settings, include ideas such as involving youth in all stages of program planning and implementation; enlisting persons who have been overweight themselves as group leaders; being sensitive to the social stigma of overweight in recruitment and program planning; providing a supportive and accepting environment for participants, including discussions aimed at improving self-esteem; providing fun activities that include information about foods and nutrition and require plenty of physical activity; emphasizing improvements in self-perceptions and eating and exercise skills and behaviors as well as weight change in program evaluation; and reducing technical barriers to participation such as time, location, and costs.

FOCUS ON PREVENTION

Neumark-Sztainer et al. (2003) stress the importance of prevention strategies in light of the prevalence of unhealthy weight-control behaviors among youth and their potentially serious consequences. Losing weight and keeping it off once an individual has become obese is difficult. Habits established in childhood or during adolescence, such as eating high-fat, nutrient-poor foods and sedentary behavior, tend to be difficult to break during adulthood. For example, Stice (2002) has noted evidence that biological changes occur with a high-fat diet that may make it more difficult to switch to a low-fat diet (e.g., receptor upgrading for the opiate effects of certain high-fat foods). Therefore, emphasis should be placed on efforts promoting a healthy lifestyle that promotes a healthy weight.

Elements of successful prevention efforts have been reviewed by Wodarski and Thyer (1998). They note that the literature provides the rationale for behavioral interventions of sufficient duration, having clear goals and expectations, using small groups, and including families. Elements in the successful prevention efforts they reviewed include:

1. Most successful programs are comprehensive, have multiple components, and are directed at individuals, families, peers, schools, communities, the media, and the workplace. (For suggestions and examples, see Kahn et al., 2002; and Task Force on Community Preventive Services, 2002.)

2. Prevention strategies need to incorporate efforts by the media, through community education to raise public awareness, develop community support, and maintain the momentum of established prevention efforts. (For suggestions and examples, see Kahn et al., 2002; and Task Force on Community Preventive Services, 2002.)

3. Prevention strategies need to be provided in sufficient intensity and duration to achieve desired effects. As to interventions for children, Goldfield et al. (2002) noted that the percentage of overweight generally decreases as duration of treatment increases, within the parameters of 15 months of treatment. Findings suggest that extending the length of treatment as long as 12 to 15 months may enhance outcome.

4. Booster sessions are important in establishing initial progress and maintaining effects over time.

5. Prevention programming should follow a primary prevention model of targeting the large diverse population, but also be adaptable to specific sub-populations (e.g., high-risk adolescents) to address differences in gender, culture or ethnicity, socioeconomic status (SES), and stage of adolescent development (e.g., adolescence or preadolescence).

6. Programs should follow a structured organizational plan to include needs assessments, program reviews, refinement processes, and feedback to and from the community. These objectives should also be time-limited and feasible according to the capabilities of each program and its components.

7. Interventions should consider culturally specific adaptations.

FUTURE DIRECTIONS

Stice (2002) suggests that there are a number of important gaps in our knowledge about the etiology, prevention, and treatment of obesity. He outlines several important components of obesity interventions. First, we need additional factors on the risks for the onset of obesity; for example, are there certain foods that increase risk for weight gain? Second, prevention programs need to consider the shared risk factors for both obesity and eating pathology. Prevention programs should target both of these adverse outcomes. Data currently indicate that (sensible) dieting does not result in eating disorders. In fact, the opposite is true, according to Stice. Rather than increasing the risk for the onset of exacerbation of eating pathology, dieting seems to reduce eating disturbances. Placing people on caloric-deficit diets if they are overweight or on caloric-balance diets if they are not yet overweight decreases binge eating and bulimic pathology.

Significant progress has been made in the treatment of childhood obesity (Epstein, Valoski, Koeske, & Wing, 1986; Epstein et al., 1985) and the demonstration of short- and long-term weight control and associated eating and exercise change (Epstein et al., 1990, 1994). These studies provide a framework for preventing obesity, but there is very little research on the prevention of obesity in children at risk. Obesity in adulthood is refractive to treatment, with few obese adults becoming nonobese and maintaining a healthy weight (Abraham, Collins, & Nordsieck, 1971). In that regard, Epstein, Coleman, and Myers (1996) suggests that additional research is needed to develop programs to prevent adult obesity by treating children who are already obese and, perhaps more importantly, prevent the development of obesity in those children at risk because of parental obesity. Neumark-Sztainer et al. (2003) further add that it is important that we increase our understanding of the etiological processes leading to unhealthy weight-control practices among multicultural and socioeconomically disadvantaged populations, who are at increased risk for obesity.

There are a number of macrolevel areas where social workers can work in reducing overweight and obesity, according to O'Neill (2003). He remarks that the Surgeon General's Call to Action to Prevent and Decrease Overweight and Obesity recommends strong societal action in five areas:

1. Families and communities, with the recommendation to form community coalitions to support development of increased opportunities for leisure time activity and increased availability of low-calorie, nutritious food

2. Schools, with the recommendation to build awareness among teachers and staff about the role of proper nutrition and physical activity to the maintenance of lifelong healthy weight

3. Health care, with the recommendation to look for ways to cover reimbursement as a member benefit of health care services associated with weight management, including nutrition education and physical activity programs

4. Media and communications, with the recommendation to emphasize to media professionals the disproportionate burden of overweight and obesity in low-income and racial and ethnic minority populations and the need for culturally sensitive health messages

5. Worksites, with the recommendation that employers be informed of the return-on-investment data for worksite obesity prevention and treatment strategies

SUMMARY

Obesity is a chronic condition with a complex etiology. Therapeutic intervention must address the multifaceted etiology and include components to address the variables that initiate and maintain the condition. Given the poor prognosis for cure, prevention provides the greatest hope for reducing the number of individuals afflicted.

The future will bring new developments and insights into the causes and cures for obesity. Breakthroughs in pharmacotherapy, genetic manipulation, and surgical procedures occur on a regular basis and offer hope for those struggling to reduce and control their weight. It is unlikely that a magic bullet will provide the remedy suitable to every individual. Much more probable is the likelihood that the effective cure will require a lifelong commitment to a healthy lifestyle that includes disciplined food choices and regular physical activity. This commitment will involve not just the individual but will require a macrolevel effort, involving cooperation among families, communities, business, industry, and government.

REFERENCES

Abraham, S., Collins, G., & Nordsieck, M. (1971). Relationship of childhood weight status to morbidity in adults. *Public Health Records, 85,* 273–284.

American Dietetic Association. (1997). Position of the American Dietetic Association: Weight management. *Journal of the American Dietetic Association, 97*(1), 71–74.

American Heart Association. (1996). *Dietary guidelines for healthy children.* Dallas, TX: American Heart Association.

Birch, L. L. (1999). Development of food preferences. *Annual Review of Nutrition, 19,* 41–62.

Ching, P., Willett, W. C., Rimm, E. B., Colditz, G. A., Gortmaker, S. L., & Stampfer, M. J. (1996). Activity level and risk of overweight in male health professionals. *American Journal of Public Health, 86,* 25–30.

Clark, M. M., Niaura, R., King, T., & Pera, V. (1996). Depression, smoking, activity level, and health status: Pretreatment predictors of attrition in obesity treatment. *Addictive Behaviors, 21*(4), 509–513.

Coulston, A. M. (1998). Obesity as an epidemic: Facing the challenge. *Journal of the American Dietetic Association, 98*(10, Suppl. 2), S6–S8.

Crockett, S. J., & Sims, L. (1995). Environmental influences on children's eating. *Journal of Nutrition Education, 27,* 235–250.

Dietz, W. H., & Gortmaker, S. L. (1985). Do we fatten our children at the television . set? Obesity and television viewing in children and adolescents. *Pediatrics, 75*(5), 807–812.

Drogas, H. J., Redd, G., & Hill, J. O. (1992). Comparison of dietary self-reports with energy expenditure measured using a whole room indirect calorimeter. *Journal of the American Dietetic Association, 92,* 1073–1077.

Dwyer, J. T., Feldman, J. J., & Mayer, J. (1967). Adolescent dieters: Who are they? *American Journal of Clinical Nutrition, 20,* 1045–1050.

Epstein, L. H. (1995a). Application of behavioral economic principles to treatment of childhood obesity. In D. B. Allison & F. X. Pi-Sunyer (Eds.), *Obesity treatment* (pp. 113–119). New York: Plenum Press.

Epstein, L. H. (1995b). Management of obesity in children. In K. D. Brownell & C. G. Fairburn (Eds.), *A comprehensive handbook of eating disorders and obesity* (pp. 516–519). New York: Guilford Press.

Epstein, L. H., Coleman, K. J., & Myers, M. D. (1996). Exercise in treating obesity in children and adolescents. *Medicine and Science in Sports and Exercise, 28,* 428–435.

Epstein, L. H., Smith, J. A., Vara, L. S., & Rodefer, J. S. (1991). Behavioral economic analysis choice in obese children. *Health Psychology, 10,* 311–316.

Epstein, L. H., Valoski, A. M., Koeske, R. O., & Wing, R. R. (1986). Family-based behavioral weight control in obese young children. *Journal of the American Dietetic Association, 86,* 481–484.

Epstein, L. H., Valoski, A. M., Wing, R. R., & McCurley, J. (1990). Ten-year follow-up of behavioral family based treatment for obese children. *Journal of the American Medical Association, 264,* 2519–2523.

Epstein, L. H., Valoski, A. M., Wing, R. R., & McCurley, J. (1994). Ten-year outcomes of behavioral family based treatment for childhood obesity. *Health Psychology, 13,* 373–383.

Epstein, L. H., Wing, R. R., Woodall, K., Penner, B. C., Kress, M. H., & Koeske, R. O. (1985). Effects of family based behavioral treatment on obese 5–8 year old children. *Behavior Therapy, 16,* 205–212.

Field, A. E., Barnoya, J., & Colditz, G. A. (2002). Epidemiology and health and economic consequences of obesity. In T. A. Wadden & A. J. Stunkard (Eds.), *Handbook of obesity treatment* (pp. 3–18). New York: Guilford Press.

Flegal, K. M., Caroll, M. D., Kuczmarski, R. J., & Johnson, C. L. (1998). Overweight and obesity in the United States: Prevalence and trends, 1960–1994. *International Journal of Obesity, 22,* 39–47.

Fletcher, G. F., Balady, G., Froelicher, V. F., Hartley, L. H., Haskell, W. L., & Pollock, M. L. (1995). Exercise standards: A statement for healthcare professionals from the American Heart Association. *Circulation, 91*(2), 596–601.

Frist, B. (2002, September 19). Obesity poses serious health challenge. *Knoxville News Sentinel,* p. B5.

Golan, M., & Weizman, A. (2001). Familial approach to the treatment of childhood obesity: Conceptual model. *Journal of Nutrition Education, 33,* 102–107.

Goldfield, G. S., Epstein, L. H., Kilanowski, C. K., Paluch, R. A., & Kogut-Bossler, B. (2001). Cost-effectiveness of group and mixed family based treatment for childhood obesity. *International Journal of Obesity and Related Metabolic Disorders, 25,* 1843–1849.

Goldfield, G. S., Raynor, H. A., & Epstein, L. H. (2002). Treatment of pediatric obesity. In T. A. Wadden & A. J. Stunkard (Eds.), *Handbook of obesity treatment* (pp. 532–555). New York: Guilford Press.

Gortmaker, S. L., Dietz, W. H., Sobol, A. M., & Wehler, C. A. (1987). Increasing pediatric obesity in the United States. *American Journal of Diseases in Children, 141,* 535–540.

Gortmaker, S. L., Must, A., Perrin, J. M., Sobol, A. M., & Dietz, W. H. (1993). Social and economic consequences of overweight in adolescence and young adulthood. *New England Journal of Medicine, 329,* 1008–1012.

Gortmaker, S. L., Must, A., Sobol, A. M., Peterson, K., Colditz, G. A., & Dietz, W. H. (1996). Television viewing as a cause of increasing obesity among children in the United States, 1986–1990. *Archives of Pediatric Adolescent Medicine, 150,* 356–362.

Gribble, L. S., Falciglia, G., Davis, A. M., & Couch, S. C. (2003). A curriculum based on social learning theory emphasizing fruit exposure and positive parent child-feeding strategies: A pilot study. *Journal of the American Dietetic Association, 103*(1), 100–103.

Hammar, S. L., Campbell, M. M., Campbell, V. A., Moores, N. L., Sareen, C., Gareis, F. J., et al. (1972). An interdisciplinary study of adolescent obesity. *Journal of Pediatrics, 80,* 373–380.

Heitmann, B. L., Sorensen, T. I., & Bengtsson, C. (1995). Dietary fat intake and weight gain in women genetically predisposed for obesity. *American Journal of Clinical Nutrition, 61,* 1213–1217.

Hill, A. J., & Silver, E. K. (1995). Fat, friendless and unhealthy: 9-year-old children's perception of body shape and stereotypes. *International Journal of Obesity, 19,* 423–430.

Johnson, S. L., & Birch, L. L. (1994). Parents' and children's adiposity and eating style. *Pediatrics, 94,* 653–661.

Kahn, E. B., Ramsey, L. T., Brownson, R. C., Heath, G. W., Howze, E. H., Powell, K. E., et al. (2002). The effectiveness of interventions to increase physical activity. *American Journal of Preventive Medicine, 22*(4S), 73–107.

King, A. C., Taylor, C. B., Haskell, W. L., & DeBusk, R. F. (1989). Influence of regular aerobic exercise on psychological health. *Health Psychology, 8,* 305–324.

Klesges, R. C., Coates, T. J., & Brown, G. (1983). Parental influences on children's eating behavior and relative weight. *Journal of Applied Behavioral Analysis, 16,* 371–378.

Lawrence, S. A., Zittel, K. M., Wodarski, L. A., & Wodarski, J. S. (in press). Behavioral health: Treatment and prevention of chronic disease and the implications for social work practice. *Journal of Health and Social Policy.*

Lehrke, S., Becker, S., & Laessle, R. G. (2002). Structured behavioral therapy with obese children: Therapeutic effects in nutrition. *Verhaltenstherapie, 12*(1), 9–16.

Lewis, C. E., Smith, D. E., Wallace, D. D., Williams, O. D., Bild, D. E., & Jacobs, D. R. (1997). Seven-year trends in body weight and associations with lifestyle and behavioral characteristics in Black and White young adults: The CARDIA study. *American Journal of Public Health, 87*(4), 635–642.

Lichtman, S. W., Pisarski, K., Berman, E. R., Prestone, M., Dowling, H., Offenbacher, E., et al. (1992). Discrepancy between self-reported and actual food intake and exercise in obese subjects. *New England Journal of Medicine, 327,* 1893–1898.

Livingstone, M. B. E., Prentice, A. M., Strain, J. J., Coward, W. A., Black, A. E., Barker, M. E., et al. (1990). Accuracy of weighed dietary records in studies of diet and health. *British Medical Journal, 300,* 708–712.

Lytle, L., & Achterberg, C. (1995). Changing the diet of America's children: What works and why? *Journal of Nutrition Education, 27,* 235–250.

Maffeis, C., Schutz, Y., Zafanello, M., Piccoli, R., & Pinelli, L. (1994). Elevated energy expenditure and reduced energy intake in obese prepubertal children: Paradox of poor dietary reliability in obesity. *Journal of Pediatrics, 124,* 348–354.

Marchi, M., & Cohen, P. (1990). Early childhood eating behaviors and adolescent eating disorders. *Journal of the American Academy of Child and Adolescent Psychiatry, 29,* 112–117.

Marks, B. L., & Rippe, J. M. (1996). The importance of fat free mass maintenance in weight loss programs. *Sports Medicine, 5,* 273–281.

McGinnis, J. M., & Foege, W. H. (1993). Actual causes of death in the United States. *Journal of the American Medical Association, 270,* 2201–2212.

Moran, R. (1999). Evaluation and Treatment of Childhood Obesity. *American Family Physician, 59*(4), 861.

Morris, J. N., Clayton, D. G., Everitt, M. G., Semmence, A. M., & Burgess, E. H. (1990). Exercise in leisure time: Coronary attack and death rates. *British Heart Journal, 63,* 325–334.

National Center for Health Statistics. (2001). *Prevalence of overweight among children and adolescents: United States 1999.* Washington, DC: National Center for Health Statistics.

Nestle, M. (2003). Increasing portion sizes in American diets: More calories, more obesity. *Journal of the American Dietetic Association, 103*(1), 39–40.

Neumark-Sztainer, D., & Story, M. (1997). Recommendations from overweight youth regarding school-based weight control programs. *Journal of School Health, 67*(10), 428–433.

Neumark-Sztainer, D., Story, M., Dixon, L. B., & Murray, D. M. (1988). Adolescents engaging in unhealthy weight control behaviors: Are they at risk for other health-compromising behaviors? *American Journal of Public Health, 88,* 952–955.

Neumark-Sztainer, D., Wall, M. M., Story, M., & Perry, C. (2003). Correlates of unhealthy weight-control behaviors among adolescents: Implications for prevention programs. *Health Psychology, 22*(1), 88–98.

Nicklas, T. A. (1995). Dietary studies of children: The Bogalusa Heart Study experience. *Journal of the American Dietetic Association, 95,* 1127–1133.

O'Neill, J. (2003, March 5). Field of overeating offers opportunities. *NASW News,* 27.

Patton, G. C., Johnson-Sabine, E., Wood, K., Mann, A. H., & Wakeling, A. (1990). Abnormal eating attitudes in London schoolgirls: A prospective epidemiological study: Outcome at twelve-month follow-up. *Psychological Medicine, 20,* 383–394.

Price, R. A. (2002). Genetics and common obesities: Background, current status, strategies, and future prospects. In T. A. Wadden & A. J. Stunkard (Eds.), *Handbook of obesity treatment* (pp. 73–94). New York: Guilford Press.

Price, R. A., Stunkard, A. J., & Ness, R. (1990). Childhood onset (age < 10) obesity has high familial risk. *International Journal of Obesity, 14,* 185–195.

Puhl, R., & Brownell, K. D. (2001). Bias, discrimination, and obesity. *Obesity Research, 9,* 788–805.

Ravussin, E., Lillioja, S., Knowler, W. C., Christin, L., Freymond, D., Abbott, W., et al. (1988). Reduced rate of energy expenditure as a risk factor for body-weight gain. *New England Journal of Medicine, 318,* 467–472.

Rees, J. M. (1990). Management of obesity in adolescence. *Medical Clinics of North America, 74,* 1275–1292.

Rippe, J. M. (1998). The obesity epidemic: A mandate for a multidisciplinary approach. *Journal of the American Dietetic Association, 98*(10), S5.

Rippe, J. M., Crossley, S., & Ringer, R. (1998). Obesity as a chronic disease: Modern medical and lifestyle management. *Journal of the American Dietetic Association, 98*(10, Suppl. 2), S9–S15.

Schoeller, D. A. (1990). How accurate is self-reported dietary energy intake? *Nutrition Reviews, 48,* 373–387.

Smiciklas-Wright, H., Mitchell, D. C., Mickle, S. J., Goldman, J. D., & Cook, A. (2003). Foods commonly eaten in the United States, 1989–1991 and 1994–1996: Are portion sizes changing? *Journal of the American Dietetic Association, 103*(1), 41–47.

Stice, E. (2002, March). The neglect of obesity. *Monitor on Psychology, 33.*

Stice, E., Cameron, R. P., Killen, J. D., Hayward, C., & Taylor, C. B. (1999). Naturalistic weight-reduction efforts prospectively predict growth in relative weight and onset of obesity among female adolescents. *Journal of Consulting and Clinical Psychology, 67,* 967–974.

Stock, M., & Rothwell, N. (1982). *Obesity and leanness: Basic aspects.* New York: Wiley.

Strauss, R. D., & Pollack, H. A. (2001). Epidemic increase in childhood obesity. *Journal of the American Medical Association, 286,* 2845–2848.

Stunkard, A. J., & Wadden, T. A. (1992). Psychological aspects of human obesity. In P. Bjorntorp & B. N. Brodoff (Eds.), *Obesity* (pp. 352–360). Philadelphia: Lippincott.

Subar, A. F., Krebs-Smith, S. M., Cook, A., & Kahle, L. L. (1998). Dietary sources of nutrients among, U.S. children, 1989–1991. *Pediatrics, 102,* 913–923.

Tammelin, T., Nayha, S., Hills, A. P., & Jarvelin, M. (2003). Adolescent participation in sports and adult physical activity. *American Journal of Preventive Medicine, 24*(1), 22–29.

Task Force on Community Preventive Services. (2002). Recommendations to increase physical activity in communities. *American Journal of Preventive Medicine, 22*(4S), 67–72.

Tiggemann, M., & Wilson-Barrett, E. (1998). Children's figure ratings: Relationship to self-esteem and negative stereotyping. *International Journal of Eating Disorders, 23,* 83–88.

Troiano, R. P., Flegal, K. M., Kuczmarski, R. J., Campbell, S. M., & Johnson, C. L. (1995). Overweight prevalence and trends for children and adolescents: The National Health and Nutrition Examination Surveys, 1963 to 1991. *Archives of Pediatric Adolescent Medicine, 149,* 1085–1091.

U.S. Department of Agriculture, Agricultural Research Service. (1998). *The 1994–96 Continuing Survey of Food Intakes by Individuals and the 1994–96 Diet and Health Knowledge Survey.* (Available from the National Technical Information Service, Springfield, VA, Accession No. PB98–500457)

U.S. Department of Health and Human Services. (2000). *Healthy People 2010* (Conference edition). Washington, DC: Author.

Wadden, T. A., & Stunkard, A. J. (Eds.). (2002). *Handbook of obesity treatment.* New York: Guilford Press.

Wodarski, J. S., & Thyer, B. (1998). *Handbook of empirical social work* (Vol. 2). New York: Wiley.

Wodarski, J. S., Wodarski, L. A., & Parris, H. (in press). Teams-Games-Tournaments: Four decades of programmatic research. *Journal of Evidence-Based Social Work: Advances in Practice, Programming, Research and Policy.*

PART IV

Preventive Interventions for Children's and Adolescents' Social Problems

Chapter 15

FOSTER CARE DRIFT

SUSAN KLEIN-ROTHSCHILD and ADRIENNE EKAS

Foster care is intended to provide safe, temporary care for children who cannot remain safely with their biological families. Children who have been abused, neglected, or abandoned and have a high risk of future harm if they remain in their family homes are placed in foster care. Many children who have been abused and neglected can remain safely with their families when services or interventions are provided to the families. Children who have been removed from their families are a subset of all maltreated children. (Chapter 18, this volume, on child maltreatment provides further insight into the factors and situations that lead to foster care.)

There is a growing awareness that, too often, the intention that foster care is temporary has been lost. In the 1970s, it became apparent that a significant number of children languished in *temporary* foster care homes for years. The longer children remained in foster care, the greater the likelihood that the children endured multiple placements, multiple transitions, and a lack of permanency. This is often referred to as *foster care drift*. Foster care drift is associated with poorer outcomes for children.

Emotional and legal permanency for every child in foster care is now sought through reunification, adoption, or legal guardianship. For the majority of children, interventions with families can reduce the risk of future harm and children can be safely reunified with their families. For children who cannot return home safely, relatives, foster families, and other families become resources for adoption and legal guardianship. A less desirable permanency alternative is another planned living arrangement without both emotional and legal commitments to children. The goal is a *family for life* for every child.

Prevention of foster care drift would result in timely permanency and improved outcomes for all children in foster care. This chapter focuses on preventing foster care drift for those children who are placed in out-of-home care for their own safety.

TRENDS AND INCIDENCE

There have always been some children who need care outside their own families because of the death of parents, rejection, or other family circumstances. In 1875, the first Society for the Prevention of Cruelty to Children was established in New York City after a young child was treated brutally and was removed from her caregiver. In 1974, the Child Abuse and Prevention Treatment Act added requirements for every state related to the reporting, investigation, and treatment of child maltreatment cases. There has been a long-term trend of substantial growth in child abuse reporting, largely because of greater public awareness, although the proportion of reports that have been substantiated over the years has grown smaller with time (Children's Bureau web site: www.acf.dhhs.gov/programs/cb).

At the same time that reporting and awareness of child maltreatment has increased, there has been an increased understanding of the trauma experienced by children who are removed from their families. Instead of removing children from their families, there has been a renewed effort to strengthen families to safely care for their children. In 1980, the U.S. Congress passed Public Law 96-272, also known as the Adoption Assistance and Child Welfare Act. This law requires that reasonable efforts be made to prevent removal of children from their families, and reasonable efforts must be made to reunite children with their parents. This law focuses on the safety, well-being, and permanency of children. The philosophy changed from "rescuing the child" from the abusing family to "rescue the family for the child." The rates of foster care placements have been influenced by the implementation of the 1980 law, professional practices, and community trends, such as substance abuse.

In the 1970s, more than half a million children were in foster care nationally. This number was reduced with strengthened in-home services, the review and monitoring of cases emphasizing permanency, and the implementation of focused casework and contracts with parents. The numbers of children in foster care began to rise again in the late 1980s. Between the late 1980s and the early 1990s, the federal government estimates that the average monthly number of children in foster care nationwide . . . increased from 280,000 to 429,000 (Zlotnick, 1999). It is estimated that 581,000 children were in foster care on September 30, 1999 (Children's Bureau web site www.acf.dhhs.gov/programs/cb). The average age of the foster care population is about 10 years old. The number of children entering foster care is greater than the number of children exiting care, contributing to an increasing foster care population in this country. Many of the children entering foster care are young children under 1 year of age. Often, these young children enter care because of substance use by their mothers. In the federal fiscal year of 1999, 297,000 children entered foster care while 251,000 exited care. Of the total 581,000 children in foster care, 127,000 were waiting to be adopted.

One of the most concerning descriptors of children in foster care is the race and ethnicity of these children. The number of African American children in foster care in 1999 was larger than the number of children from any other ethnicity group. Adoption and Foster Care Analysis and Reporting System (AFCARS) reports that in 1999, 34% (199,735) of children in foster care were Caucasian, 17% (98,396) were Hispanic, and 39% (223,751) were African American (AFCARS, 2001). In 2000, Caucasian children represented 69% of the child population (under 18 years of age) in the United States, Hispanic children represented 17%, and African American children represented 15% of the total child population in the United States (U.S. Census, 2000). When the percentage of African American children in foster care is compared to the percentage of African American children as a part of the total child population in the United States, the effect of their overrepresentation in the child welfare system is fully appreciated.

As the number of children in foster care has increased, so has the number of children who have experienced foster care drift, unplanned, long-term foster care. One of the most serious concerns of long-term foster care is the high rate of placement disruption, where a move from one caretaker to another is required. "In the 1960s the rate of disruption was found to be between 40% to 50% of all placements in a 5 year period . . . and rates do not appear to have improved much since then" (Minty, 1999). Multiple foster care placements are associated with negative outcomes for youth (Greenblatt & Day, 2000). Youth previously in foster care who had more foster placements while in foster care have an increased likelihood of getting into trouble with the law, being incarcerated, living on the streets or being homeless, having higher rates of pregnancy, and having more violence in a dating relationship (Reilly, in press).

In response to the identified concerns, the Adoption and Safe Families Act of 1997 was passed. This legislation emphasized that safety and well-being of children is paramount and added requirements to address foster care drift and achieve timely permanency for children. The act also created bonuses to states for increasing adoptions and tightened time frames for making permanent placement decisions for children. There are renewed efforts across the country to identify strategies that move children from temporary foster care to permanent families in one or two years.

RISK FACTORS

Risk factors that are associated with foster care drift are being African American and having special needs.

African American Children

Research has shown that African American children enter the foster care system in increased numbers, remain in out-of-home care longer than Caucasian children, receive fewer in-home services, and have an unequal amount of negative experiences (Gould, 1991). The overrepresentation of African American children in the child welfare system that is already overburdened and underfunded increases their risk for foster care drift and other negative outcomes even when there is intervention (Brown & Bailey-Etta, 1997). African American children are half as likely to be reunified with their families as Caucasian children are (Barth, 1997; McMurtry & Lie, 1992; Wells & Guo, 1999). Similarly, African American children are less likely to exit foster care to adoption than are Caucasian children (Barth, Courtney, & Berry, 1994). African American children have decreased permanence and greater risk of foster care drift.

Children with Special Needs

Risk factors for children languishing in foster care include those with special needs. Children with special needs are medically fragile, have emotional and behavioral disturbances, and/or have other disabilities requiring special services. Children with health problems are less likely to be reunified and more likely to return to foster care if reunified (Courtney, 1994, McMurtry & Lie, 1992; Wells & Guo, 1999). These children are also less likely to exit foster care to adoption (McMurtry & Lie, 1992). Children with behavioral problems are more likely to have disrupted placements (Barth, Berry, Yoshiakami, Goodfield, & Carson, 1988; Barth et al., 1986). Children with special needs are more likely to experience less timely permanence and more foster care drift.

EFFECTIVE UNIVERSAL PREVENTIVE INTERVENTIONS

Universal preventive interventions target the general public or whole population group that has not been identified on the basis of individual risk. When considering the prevention of foster care drift, universal preventive interventions are those that are targeted to the general public to maintain the safety of children and prevent the need for foster care placement. Foster care drift is relevant only for children who have been placed in foster care. The need for foster care can be minimized through the prevention of child maltreatment and the prevention of substance abuse.

Preventing Child Maltreatment

The majority of children in foster care are placed there because of child abuse and neglect, which includes all forms of child maltreatment, such as physical abuse, neglect, inadequate supervision, emotional abuse, sexual abuse, and medical neglect. Thomlison suggests that "large-scale universal interventions targeted to the general public and focused on child maltreatment prevention with rigorous research are difficult to identify" (Chapt. 18, this volume). Although there are a number of parenting enhancement, parent support group programs, and sexual abuse prevention or intervention programs, there are major challenges to evaluation because these programs are embedded in other programs and the rigorous examination of these programs is limited. Prevention of child maltreatment has a direct impact on the prevention of the need for foster care, thereby preventing foster care drift.

Preventing Substance Abuse

Just as the prevention of child maltreatment would reduce the need for foster care and foster care drift, the prevention of substance abuse would likely result in a decrease of child maltreatment and foster care placements, thus preventing foster care drift. Substance abuse is cited as a factor in many of the families coming to the attention of child welfare agencies (Administration for Children and Families, 2002; Child Welfare League of America, 1999; Chaffin, Kelleher, & Hollenberg, 1996; Harrington, Dubowitz, Black, & Binder, 1995; Peterson, Gable, & Saldana, 1996). It is estimated that anywhere from 13% to 70% of all child welfare cases involve substance abuse problems (SAMHSA grant references; Magura & Laudet, 1996). In one national study (U.S. Department of Health and Human Services [USDHHS], 1997), substance abuse was the presenting problem in 26% of child neglect cases alone. Alcohol and drug abuse interfere with parents' ability to provide safe care for their children. Chapter 10 in this volume on preventing substance abuse among youth provides general principles and strategies of effective interventions that would also serve as universal preventive interventions for foster care drift.

Preventing Foster Care for Children at Imminent Risk of Out-of-Home Placement

In addition to universal preventive interventions to prevent foster care aimed at the general public, there are universal preventive interventions targeting the whole population of children who are at imminent risk of foster care—children who are not safe in their family homes without intervention. The most closely examined of these interventions is intensive family preservation. Intensive family preservation programs have shown success in preventing out-of-home placement in 40% to 95% of participating families (Fraser, Pecora, & Haapala, 1991; Schuerman, Rzepnicki, & Littell, 1994). Intensive family preservation services vary across the country, yet they share basic elements including:

- The child remains in the family home, and immediate services are provided in the family home.
- Services are short term (usually up to 12 weeks), with frequent family contacts (a minimum of once per week).
- A variety of flexible concrete and clinical services are provided to families.
- There is an emphasis on skill building with families.

EFFECTIVE SELECTIVE PREVENTIVE INTERVENTIONS

Selective preventive interventions target subgroups of the general population who are at higher risk for developing a problem than other members of the broader population. For the purposes of preventing foster care drift, selective preventive interventions target the entire population of children in foster care.

Broad Strategies

As discussed earlier, the intensified effort to prevent foster care drift and limit the time children and youth spend in temporary foster care is a relatively recent initiative. No broad base of research provides clear evidence of interventions that effectively prevent foster care drift. According to the National Resource Center for Foster Care and Permanency Planning at the Hunter College School of Social Work (1999), the following broad strategies reflect best practices to ensure that children and youth have safe and stable, lifelong families:

- Targeted and appropriate efforts to protect safety, achieve permanence, and strengthen families' and children's well-being
- Early intervention and prevention with reasonable efforts to prevent unnecessary out-of-home care when safety can be ensured
- Safety as a paramount concern throughout the life of the case, with aggravated circumstances identified when reasonable efforts to preserve or reunify families may not be required

- Appropriate, least restrictive, out-of-home placements within the family, culture, and community, with comprehensive family and child assessments, written case plans, goal-oriented practice, and concurrent permanency plans encouraged
- Reasonable efforts to reunify families and maintain family connections and continuity in children's relationships when safety can be ensured
- Reasonable efforts to find alternative permanency options outside the child welfare system when children cannot return to parents, through adoption, legal guardianship, or, in special circumstances, another planned, alternative permanent living arrangement
- Filing of the termination of parental rights petition at 15 months after placement when termination is in the best interests of the child and when exceptions do not apply
- Collaborative case activity, which includes partnerships among birth parents, foster parents, agency staff, court and legal staff, and community service providers
- Frequent and quality parent-child visitation
- Timely case reviews, permanency hearings, and decision making about where children will grow up, based on children's sense of time

Kinship Care

Beyond the broad strategies identified previously, selective preventive interventions have been found effective for children who must be placed in out-of-home care for their own safety. Kinship care is such an intervention. Kinship care is placement of a child with a blood relative or fictive family member instead of placement with a stranger or an individual with no particular ties to the family of origin. For children who must be placed outside the home for their own safety, kinship care placements tend to be more stable and longer lasting than nonrelated foster placements (Inglehart, 1994; Scannapieco & Hegar, 2002; Scannapieco & McAlpine, 1997; Wulczyn & Goerge, 1992). The stability offered by kin placements prevents foster care drift for these children. The additional length of time before exit from foster care has been a concern in the child welfare field because although there is stability, many of the kinship placements lack the legal permanency of adoption, guardianship, or parental custody (Testa, 2001). Testa has found that there is likely more potential for legal permanency with relatives than previously believed, but the additional stability of kinship care placement diminishes with lengthier durations of care. These findings reflect that kinship care with timely movement to legal permanency is the best combination as a prevention intervention strategy for foster care drift.

Family Engagement

Few rigorous research studies involving large numbers of children and families provide solid evidence of effective strategies to prevent foster care drift. However, there are specific promising practices related to family engagement. Effective engagement strategies that build active family participation and positive relationships between families and workers are identified as contributing to positive case outcomes (Dawson & Berry, 2002; Petras, Massat, & Essex, 2002).

In the realm of foster care, the vast majority of clients are involuntary. The court and public agencies place children outside their homes to protect those at risk of harm with their families. Parents do not voluntarily seek services, nor do they want them. However, if parents want their children to return to their care, parents are required to participate in services to remedy problems that interfere with safety. Interventions that build family engagement appear particularly promising for involuntary clients.

Family engagement is a strategy that can be incorporated into service structure as well as worker behavior. For instance, the Intensive Family Preservation service model, which includes an immediate response to families and frequent contacts with the family, incorporates the concept of family engagement. Family group conferencing is another intervention strategy that holds promise to promote permanency and prevent foster care drift. In the family group conferencing approach, family members, relatives, and individuals who are part of informal support networks for the family are brought together to make decisions related to the child's safety and permanency. Dawson and Berry (2002) have reviewed the research and found that effective service components that engage families in treatment include:

- Immediate, in-home services
- Flexible, concrete services to families
- Family-focused services that use family strengths, promote decision making based on family needs, and allow for the cooperation of parents and workers in the planning process

A recent study (Potter & Klein-Rothschild, 2002) that examined factors associated with achieving permanency within 12 months of initial out-of-home placement for young children suggests that additional service components contribute to family engagement and success in achieving permanency, including:

- Stability in the relationship between the worker and the family (fewer workers per family)
- Increased visitation offered between parents and their children
- Timely court hearings (less time between hearings)

In addition to service components, specific worker behaviors build a cooperative, mutual relationship that increases family engagement and achievement of treatment goals. The treatment goal that prevents foster care drift is the achievement of a safe, permanent home. Worker behaviors that exemplify the qualities of empathy, trust, and respect appear to be particularly effective at achieving success for involuntary clients (Rooney, 1992). Rooney summarized worker behavior recommendations:

- Make a specific request rather than a vague one.
- Seek overt commitments from clients to comply.
- Provide training in performing the task.
- Supply positive reinforcement of the task.
- Choose tasks that require little discomfort or difficulty.
- Ensure client participation in the selection and design of tasks.

Effective prevention strategies depend on worker skills in addition to program characteristics.

EFFECTIVE INDICATED PREVENTIVE INTERVENTIONS

Indicated preventive interventions are directed at specific populations of children in foster care who are at a particular risk of foster care drift. Children at particular risk include African American children and children with special needs. As with all types and levels of prevention efforts related to foster care drift, there is limited rigorous research to validate effectiveness. Some approaches and practices have been evaluated and show promise for effectiveness. In the area of indicated prevention for youth most at risk of foster care drift, there are growing initiatives focused on foster parents and foster care providers. Because multiple placements with multiple care providers have such potential negative impacts to development of healthy personal relationships and emotional attachments, adding stability to the foster care provider side of the equation provides direct benefits to children and youth, regardless of the length of time they spend in foster care. Stability in foster care is the goal of these foster parent-focused initiatives. These interventions are related to the preparation, training, and support of foster parents to promote stability in placement and timely achievement of permanency.

Foster Parent Preparation, Training, and Support

Foster parent preparation, training, and support are essential components for any foster care program. New specialized training and support components within these programs teach foster parents skills and coping mechanisms to deal with challenges of fostering. A longitudinal study of foster care parents found that two-thirds of the participants had experienced one or more stressful events. These stressful events were most likely to be a breakdown or disruption of a placement or severe family tensions because of a difficult placement (Wilson, Sinclair, & Gibbs, 2000). About 60% of the foster parents who participated in this study had considered giving up fostering at some time in the past. It is interesting that the older the foster child, the more likely the foster family was to experience a stressful event. Special needs children, who are at higher risk for foster care drift, create more stress for foster parents, which increases the likelihood that foster parents will discontinue fostering or ask for the removal of the child. Both circumstances add placement moves for children. Specialized foster parent preparation, training, and support to teach skills in dealing with difficult children, providing realistic expectations, and coping with stressful events minimize placement moves and foster care drift (Redding, Fried, & Britner, 2000).

Foster parent preparation, training, and support interventions are also teaching the importance of keeping foster children connected to their biological parents. "Keeping foster children connected to their biological parents, through visiting and other forms of contact, is essential for reunification because it helps to reestablish and maintain family tie during out-of-home placement" (Sanchirico, & Jablonka, 2000). In a study of 650 foster parents in New York, foster parents who received both specialized training and ongoing support performed significantly more visitation, nonvisitation, and total activities than other foster parents (Sanchirico, & Jablonka, 2000). This promising intervention is particularly important for older children and youth because teenagers who have no contact with biological parents are at greater risk for foster care breakdown (Smith, 1986). Reunification, timely permanency, and placement stability is supported through specialized foster parent training and support.

PRACTICE AND POLICY IMPLICATIONS

Child welfare practice is greatly hampered by the limitations of existing research. More than half a million children and youth are in foster care at any time in this country, and we have little solid evidence about how to prevent foster care drift and provide these children and youth with safety and permanency. This leaves practitioners operating without sufficient information to know what will provide the best outcomes for these children and their families. Rigorous research and evaluation is desperately needed in this area.

This situation is further heightened with the passage of the Adoption and Safe Families Act of 1997. This federal law requires that children achieve permanency and stability, yet it is not clear on the best way of achieving the desired outcomes. With the advent of the new law, many new strategies are emerging. Evaluation of these strategies is needed to determine if they are achieving the desired outcomes.

FUTURE DIRECTIONS

As noted throughout this chapter, there are limited research and few large-scale evaluations of interventions that prevent foster care drift. Kinship care and intensive family preservation services are areas that include evidence-based practice. The area of engagement techniques also supports effectiveness. More research is needed in all areas of preventive practices with foster care children and youth who are at risk of drifting from one home to another without the security and stability of a permanent family.

Some types of intervention and practice appear to be promising practices for high rates of effectiveness at preventing foster care drift. These intervention strategies should be studied in the near term.

Concurrent Planning

One promising intervention is concurrent planning (Katz, 1999). When a child is placed in foster care, a process of assessing the needs and strengths of the child and family ensues so that a plan for services to address barriers to safety can be developed. Each plan includes a permanency goal for the child. The permanency goal may be reunification with a parent, relative care, adoption, guardianship, or another planned living arrangement. Traditional practice dictates that the initial permanency goal for most children is reunification with a parent. In cases where timely reunification is achieved, foster care drift is avoided. However, in families where reunification is not achieved because parents are unwilling or unable to successfully complete a case plan, a subsequent case plan is developed with an alternative permanency goal. Work on the second case plan begins after the first case plan has failed. This process inherently includes long time delays for children who move to a second case plan and alternative forms of permanency. Concurrent planning addresses this time delay.

Concurrent planning involves the development of two permanency goals and associated case plans at the onset. The primary plan, with the permanency goal and associated tasks and services, usually reunification, proceeds as planned. The secondary plan and back-up permanency goal are identified if the first goal is not successful. If the secondary goal is set at the beginning of intervention with a family and steps are taken in concert with the secondary case plan, it takes less time to achieve the secondary permanency goal. It is believed that this practice results in less time in foster care for the child. Research is needed to confirm if concurrent planning is effective at preventing extended lengths of stay in foster care.

Concurrent planning is being implemented in various degrees across the country. In practice, concurrent planning is done differently in different locations. If there is a secondary plan, when does the agency take active steps to implement it? How can practitioners be consistent at providing parents with all available services and opportunities to parent before an adoptive family or alternative caregiver is involved? When should a child who is living in a temporary foster home be placed in a home with parents who will become permanent parents? There are many practice issues that need a research-informed response.

Mental Health Services

Children at most risk for foster care drift include children and youth in out-of-home care who are in need of mental health services. Most children in foster care have experienced traumatic early lives with physical abuse, sexual abuse, neglect, and unmet basic needs. Many of these children are not receiving the mental health services they need at the level needed. Psychological and emotional problems may worsen rather than improve while they are in foster care (Simms, Dubowitz, & Szilagyi, 2000). This may be particularly true for children of color in foster care (Garland et al., 2000). Children and youth with untreated or undertreated mental health needs are frequently difficult to manage and difficult to parent. Biological parents and foster parents who provide care for these children are overwhelmed by their behaviors, and many foster parents request that children with severe emotional and behavioral disturbance be moved from their homes because of their behavior. This behavior makes these children at a higher risk for initial foster care placement, multiple placement moves, and longer foster care placement. Just as substance abuse and child abuse prevention would likely serve to prevent foster care drift, it is likely that mental health services provided at the level of need would reduce foster care drift.

In addition to many unmet mental health needs, there is some controversy about which clinical interventions are most successful with this population. Many foster parents, adoptive parents, and professionals agree that traditional psychotherapy may not be effective with the population of foster care children. Many foster care children have early life experiences that lead to difficulties with attachment and bonding (Bowlby, 1969, 1988). Research on the relationship between mental health treatment and foster care placement is needed to add to our knowledge about interventions that prevent foster care drift.

REFERENCES

Administration for Children and Families Children's Bureau. (2002). *Recent trends affecting child welfare populations and programs.* Available from www.acf.dhhs.gov /programs.

Adoption and Foster Care Analysis and Reporting System. (2001). AFCARS data. Report transmitted by states to the Administration and Families (ACF). Available from www.acf.dhhs.gov/programs.

Barth, R. P. (1997). Effects of age and race on the odds of adoption versus remaining in long-term out-of-home care. *Child Welfare, 76,* 285–308.

Barth, R. P., Berry, M., Yoshiakami, R., Goodfield, R. K., & Carson, M. L. (1988). Predicting adoption disruption. *Social Work, 33*(3), 227–233.

Barth, R. P., Courtney, M., & Berry, M. (1994). Timing is everything: An analysis of the time to adoption and legalization. *Social Work Research, 18*(3), 139–148.

Barth, R. P., Snowden, L. R., Broeck, E. T., Clancy, E., Jordan, C., & Barusch, A. S. (1986). Contributors to reunification or permanent out-of-home care for physically abused children. *Journal of Social Service Research, 9*(2/3), 31–45.

Bowlby, J. (1969). *Attachment and loss: Volume I. Attachment.* New York: Basic Books.

Bowlby, J. (1988). *A secure base: Parent-child attachment and healthy human development.* New York: Basic Books.

Brown, A. W., & Bailey-Etta, B. (1997). An out-of-home care system in crisis: Implications for African American children in the child welfare system. *Child Welfare, 76*(1), 65–84.

Chaffin, M., Kelleher, K., & Hollenberg, J. (1996). Onset of physical abuse and neglect: Psychiatric, substance abuse, and social risk factors from prospective community data. *Child Abuse and Neglect, 20*(3), 191–203.

Child Welfare League of America. (1999, January/February). Family foster care in the next century [Special issue]. *Child Welfare Journal of Policy, Practice and Program.*

Courtney, M. E. (1994). Factors associated with the reunification of foster children with their families. *Social Service Review, 68*(1), 81–108.

Dawson, K., & Berry, M. (2002, March/April). Engaging families in child welfare services: An evidence-based approach to best practice. *Child Welfare, 81*(2), 293–317.

Fraser, M. W., Pecora, P. J., & Haapala, D. A. (1991). *Families in crisis: The impact of intensive family preservation services.* New York: Aldine de Gruyter.

Garland, A., Hough, R., Landsverk, J., McCabve, K., Yeh, M., Ganger, W., et al. (2000). Racial and ethnic variations in mental health care utilization among children in foster care. *Children's Services: Social Policy, Research, and Practice, 3*(3), 133–146.

Gould, K. H. (1991). Limiting damage is not enough: A minority perspective on child welfare. In J. E. Everett, S. S. Chipungu, & B. R. Leashore (Eds.), *Child welfare: An Africentric perspective* (pp. 58–78). New Brunswick, NJ: Rutgers University Press.

Greenblatt, S. B., & Day, P. (2000). *Renewing our commitment to permanency for children: Wingspread conference summary report.* Washington, DC: Child Welfare League of America Press.

Harrington, D., Dubowitz, H., Black, M. M., & Binder, A. (1995). Maternal substance use and neglectful parenting: Relations with children's development. *Journal of Clinical Child Psychology, 24*(3), 258–263.

Inglehart, A. P. (1994). Kinship foster care: Placement, service and outcome issues. *Children and Youth Services Review, 16*(1/2), 107–122.

Katz, L. (1999). Concurrent planning: Benefits and pitfalls. *Child Welfare, 78*(1), 71–87.

Magura, S., & Laudet, A. B. (1996). Parental substance abuse and child maltreatment: Review and implications for intervention. *Children and Youth Services Review, 18*(3), 193–220.

McMurtry, S. L., & Lie, G. L. (1992). Differential exit rates of minority children in foster care. *Social Work Research and Abstracts, 28*(1), 42–48.

Minty, B. (1999). Annotation: Outcomes in long-term foster family care. *Journal of Child Psychology and Psychiatry, 40*(7), 991–999.

National Resource Center for Foster Care and Planning. (1999). *Concurrent planning and permanency planning* [Handout]. New York: Hunter College, School of Social Work.

Peterson, L., Gable, S., & Saldana, L. (1996). Treatment of maternal addiction to prevent child abuse and neglect. *Addictive Behaviors, 21*(6), 789–801.

Petras, D., Massat, C. R., & Essex, E. L. (2002, March/April). Overcoming hopelessness and social isolation: The engage model for working with neglecting families toward permanence. *Child Welfare, 81*(2), 225–248.

Potter, C. C., & Klein-Rothschild, K. (2002, March/April). Getting home on time: Predicting timely permanence for young children. *Child Welfare, 81*(2), 123–150.

Redding, R., Fried, C., & Britner, P. (2000, December). Predictors of placement outcomes in treatment foster care: Implications for foster parent selection and service delivery [Special issue]. *Journal of Child and Family Studies, 9*(4), 425–447.

Reilly, T. (in press). Transition from care: The status and outcomes of youth who have aged out of the foster care system. *Child Welfare.*

Rooney, R. H. (1992). *Strategies for work with involuntary clients.* New York: Columbia University Press.

Sanchirica, A., & Jablonka, K. (2000, June). Keeping foster children connected to their biological parents: The impact of foster parent training and support. *Child and Adolescent Social Work Journal, 17*(3), 185–203.

Scannapieco, M. H., & Hegar, R. (2002, August). Kinship care providers: Designing an array of supportive services. *Child and Adolescent Social Work Journal, 19*(4), 315–327.

Scannapieco, M. H., & McAlpine, C. (1997). Kinships care and foster care: Comparison characteristics and outcomes. *Families and Society, 78*(5), 480–488.

Schuerman, J. S., Rzepnicki, T. L., & Littell, J. H. (1994). *Putting families first.* Hawthorne, NY: Aldine de Gruyter.

Simms, M., Dubowitz, H., & Szilagyi, M. (2000, October). Health care needs of children in the foster care system. *Pediatrics, 106*(4), 909–918.

Smith, P. M. (1986). Evaluation of Kent placements. *Adoption and Fostering, 10,* 29–33.

Testa, M. (2001). Kinship, care and permanency. *Journal of Social Service Research, 28*(1), 25–42.

U.S. Bureau of the Census. (2000). *Population estimates.* Washington, DC: U.S. Government Printing Office.

U.S. Department of Health and Human Services. (1997). *National study of protective, preventive, and reunification services delivered to children and their families.* Washington, DC: Author.

Wells, K., & Guo, S. (1999). Reunification and reentry of foster children. *Children and Youth Services Review, 22*(4), 273–294.

Wilson, K., Sinclair, I., & Gibbs, I. (2000, April). The trouble with foster care: The impact of stressful events on foster care. *British Journal of Social Work, 39*(2), 193–209.

Wulczyn, F. H., & Goerge, R. M. (1992). Foster care in New York and Illinois: The challenge of rapid change. *Social Science Review, 66*(2), 278–294.

Zlotnick, C., Kronstadt, D., & Klee, L. (1999, October). Essential case management services for young children in foster care. *Community Mental Health Journal, 35*(5), 421.

Chapter 16

SCHOOL VIOLENCE

GARY L. BOWEN, JOELLE D. POWERS, MICHAEL E. WOOLLEY, AND
NATASHA K. BOWEN

Our nation's schools should represent havens where all children are safe to grow
and learn. Unfortunately, many schoolchildren in America attend schools where
they feel unsafe. From bullying to school shootings, from the daily victimization
at school to the constantly frightening stories in the national media, children and
their parents or guardians cannot help but be keenly aware of this national crisis.
As a result, an increasing number of school violence prevention programs have
been developed and tested in recent years. The major focus of this chapter is to
delineate prevention programs on a universal, selective, and indicated level that
have demonstrated their efficacy at reducing school violence. We begin with a
review of school violence trends and incidence, followed by a discussion of risk
factors associated with the occurrence of school violence at the student level and
at different ecological levels. The chapter concludes with a discussion of policy
and program implications and future directions.

TRENDS AND INCIDENCE

School violence lacks a widely accepted or precise definition in the empirical
literature, and it often includes a wide range of disruptive and illegal behaviors. We base our chapter on the definition presented by Astor, Vargas, Pitner,
and Meyer (1999): "School violence covers a wide range of intentional or reck-
less behaviors that include physical harm, psychological harm, and property
damage" (p. 140). Our primary focus is on programs targeting the prevention
of violence on school grounds or on the way to school, whether students are the
perpetrators or the victims.

Despite the heavy media coverage of the horrific series of school shootings
in the late 1990s, violent death remains a rare event in our public schools

(Kaufman et al., 2001). During the 1998 to 1999 school year, 2,407 youths between 5 and 19 years old were murdered in America; only 33 of those murders occurred at school. In 1999, students were victims of serious violent crime 476,000 times away from school, compared to 186,000 times at school. Overall, there were 2.5 million crimes reported at schools. However, overall rates of serious violent crime at school declined between 1992 and 1999 (Kaufman et al., 2001).

Cantor and Wright (2002) report that 60% of violence occurs in just 4% of our schools, and they use rates of violence to identify four categories of schools:

1. No crime
2. Isolated crime
3. Moderate crime
4. Violent crime

These researchers found that schools in the *violent crime* category usually targeted their violence-prevention efforts at programs intended to modify the behavior of individual students, whereas the schools in the other three categories tended to put their efforts into prevention instruction.

In an analysis of national survey data gathered from principals (Crosse, Burr, Cantor, Hagen, & Hantman, 2002), middle schools exhibited the highest rates of violence, followed by high schools, and then elementary schools. According to that study, 72% of middle schools reported physical fights between students, compared to 56% of high schools and 11% of elementary schools. Overall, 66% of schools experienced less serious violent crime (e.g., fighting, vandalism, or theft), whereas 10% experienced at least one serious violent crime (e.g., fights with a weapon or robbery).

In addition, Crosse et al. (2002) reported disturbing rates of students and teachers feeling unsafe and being threatened at school. Eighteen percent of students reported having been threatened with a beating, 13% reported having been attacked, and 11% reported having been the victim of a serious violent act. Likewise, 62% of teachers experienced one or more incidents of violent or property crime, such as being threatened by a student, or experienced theft or property damage, although only 3% of teachers actually experienced a serious violent crime.

In light of these statistics, it is unsurprising that many students feel unsafe at school. Our experience over the past 10 years of assessing middle and high school students with the School Success Profile (SSP) suggests that many students are afraid at school or are afraid while going to and from school (G. L. Bowen & Richman, 1993, 1997, 2001). In a nationally representative sample of students, 38% of middle school students and 24% of high school students reported they were "sometimes or often afraid" of being hurt or bothered at school (G. L. Bowen, Bowen, & Richman, 1998). Likewise, 32% of middle school students and 21% of high school students reported they were "sometimes or often afraid" of being hurt or bothered on their way to and from school. These fears seem congruent with student reports of many crime- and violence-related activities being "big problems" at school. Students surveyed report fights among students (28%), stealing (27%), destruction of school property (27%), and student use of alcohol (28%) or illegal drugs (30%; G. L. Bowen et al., 1998).

Thus, it seems that while most of our nation's schools are safe from more serious forms of violence, moderate forms of violence and disruptive behavior remain a pervasive problem in middle and high schools. Additionally, many students feel afraid at school and on their way to or from school. In the next section, we identify risk factors associated with the incidence of school violence in the context of an ecological perspective.

RISK FACTORS

The ecological perspective, as laid out by Richman and Bowen (1997), guides this chapter. An ecological perspective considers the environment within and around the school to prevent violent student behavior in school settings. The ecological environment of students includes the central microsystems of neighborhood, family, school, and peer group (Bronfenbrenner, 1992). Physical safety and freedom from psychological intimidation in each of these environments are prerequisites for positive child and youth development; conversely, the incidence of violence in any of these environments has implications for the level of safety in the others and for the health and development of students.

The ecological perspective also employs the concepts of *risk factors* and *protective factors* in the assessment of students and their environments. Nash and Bowen (2002) associate risk factors with "poor developmental outcomes, or with the failure to attain positive outcomes." On the other hand, they state, "positive developmental outcomes are more likely when protective factors are present at multiple system levels" (p. 248).

We see resilience as the result of the operation of risk and protective factors, both internal and environmental, which impact student developmental outcomes. Although resilience is an individual characteristic, we agree with Richman and Fraser's (2001) assertion that "Resilience is not necessarily based on individual characteristics; it occurs at the nexus of high risk and exceptional resources [protective factors], whether these resources are personal or environmental in nature" (p. 7). School violence-prevention programs should aim to reduce risk, enhance protection, and thereby ultimately build the resilience of individual students and groups of students.

Although our definition of school violence refers primarily to harmful or damaging individual behaviors occurring on school grounds, school violence is a phenomenon also observable at the aggregate school level. Some schools are more violent than others, and the causes of school violence reside both in the ecologies of schools and in the individuals who attend those schools. Therefore, it is not surprising that the literature on school violence in particular, like the literature on youth violence in general, identifies both micro- and macrofactors as correlates and predictors of school violence. The following is a brief review of the risk factors associated with school violence in different ecological domains; special attention is given to school- and community-level factors because they have received less attention as prevention and intervention targets.

Student Characteristics

Several studies have examined the relationship between school violence and factors such as gender, sexual orientation, race/ethnicity, and age (Alexander & Curtis, 1995; N. K. Bowen & Bowen, 1999; Harris & Associates, 1999; Singer & Miller, 1999; Snyder & Sickmund, 1999; Youth Pride, 1997). Boys continue to be the primary offenders and primary victims of school violence (Singer & Miller, 1999; Snyder & Sickmund, 1999). Boys also are most likely to report carrying a weapon to school (Snyder & Sickmund, 1999). Sexual orientation is associated with victimization by school violence (Youth Pride, 1997). Some studies indicate that African Americans are exposed to more school violence than Caucasians (N. K. Bowen & Bowen, 1999). African American and Hispanic youth also may be more likely than youths of other racial or ethnic backgrounds to fight at school or to report that they missed school because they felt unsafe at or on the way to school (Snyder & Sickmund, 1999). Finally, a comprehensive and rigorous review by Hawkins et al. (1998) lists individual-level predictors of youth violence, including early developmental factors, such as pregnancy and birth complications or symptoms of attention deficit/hyperactivity disorder, and later factors such as childhood aggression and dishonesty, favorable attitudes toward violence, and hostility toward police.

Characteristics of Families

Certain family demographics, such as low socioeconomic status or living in a single-parent household, have been associated with school violence (Barton, Coley, & Wenglinsky, 1998; N. K. Bowen & Bowen, 1999; Orpinas & Murray, 1999). Moreover, some parenting behaviors and attitudes, including low monitoring levels, poor parent-child relationships, and favorable parental attitudes toward fighting, are associated with aggressive behaviors that include school violence (Orpinas & Murray, 1999). A review of the broader youth violence literature by Hawkins et al. (1998) identifies additional family factors predicting violent behavior, including parent criminality, inconsistent or ineffective discipline practices, family conflict, life stressors, residential mobility, and disruptions of the parent-child relationship.

Characteristics of Peers

Adolescent exposure to peers engaged in negative behaviors or to peers involved with gangs increases the risk of antisocial behaviors, including violence (Hawkins et al., 1998; Henggeler, Schoenwald, Borduin, Rowland, & Cunningham, 1998). To reduce school violence, therefore, school intervention efforts must assess and target peer systems. Evidence also exists that parental support moderates the impact of negative peer influences on youths' delinquent behavior (Poole & Regoli, 1979); thus, it seems efforts to reduce negative behaviors spurred by peers also need to assess and target families.

Characteristics of Schools

School violence is linked to both structural and climate characteristics of schools. Larger enrollments (G. L. Bowen, Bowen, & Richman, 2000; Cantor & Wright, 2002), higher percentages of minority students (Cantor & Wright, 2002), and the presence of gangs in a school (Barton et al., 1998) are all associated with higher levels of school violence. Barton et al. report that public school eighth graders feel less safe than their counterparts in private schools and that students in schools in the southeastern part of the country feel less safe than those in the northeast. Cantor and Wright's investigation found 36% of violent crime schools were in rural areas, challenging the stereotype that school violence is strictly an urban problem. Findings about the relative violence of middle and high schools remain inconsistent; some studies suggest that middle schools are more violent (Crosse et al., 2002) whereas others find the opposite (N. K. Bowen & Bowen, 1999; Singer & Miller, 1999).

Aspects of the school social environment or climate associated with levels of school violence include expectations for behavior and interaction, teacher-student relationships, disciplinary strategies, and administrative leadership (Alexander & Curtis, 1995; Welsh, 2000; Yogan, 2000). In a study of more than 6,000 Philadelphia middle school students, Welsh examined how numerous measures of school climate, including the clarity and fairness of rules, the respect for students, students' influence on school affairs, and the efforts to plan and implement school improvement, were related to school violence and disorder. The study found that levels of disorder varied in relation to school climate. Specifically, Welsh concluded that characteristics of and expectations about the relationships among children and staff at the school were associated with both perceived levels of safety and with offenses, victimization, and other components of school disorder.

Likewise, in a study using a national dataset, Oesterle, Stoner-Eby, and Elder (2002) found that school climate and individual student characteristics independently impact student perceptions of safety. Students feel safer at school when they feel they are part of the school community, when they feel appreciated by the teachers, and when they attend schools in low crime neighborhoods or schools with fewer students.

Hawkins et al. (1998) indicate that academic failure and a low commitment to school are among the school-related factors generally associated with youth violence. Thus, the extent to which school staff successfully promotes academic achievement and a sense of belonging among students may constitute a school process characteristic associated with lower rates of school violence. Most school climate factors associated with student behavior relate to the relationships and interactions between the youth and the adults in schools, and these are feasible targets for efforts aimed at preventing undesirable behaviors.

Characteristics of Communities

School violence is also related to the characteristics of the neighborhoods or communities in which schools are located and in which students live. For example, schools with inadequate school resources (which are derived from community resources) and schools located in communities with widespread social disadvantage, high residential mobility, or high levels of crime, poverty, and unemployment experience more school violence and victimization (G. L. Bowen & Van Dorn, 2002; N. K. Bowen & Bowen, 1999; Cantor & Wright, 2002; Welsh, 2000). A study of the effects of neighborhood social disorganization and parenting behaviors on adolescents' self-reported school behaviors found a direct relation between the neighborhood characteristics and students' school behaviors (N. K. Bowen, Bowen, & Ware, 2002). The study, which included but did not focus specifically on disruptive and fighting behavior, also discovered neighborhoods exert more effect than family on school outcomes. In their review of the more general youth violence literature, Hawkins et al. (1998) cite poverty and social disorganization, prevalence of drug and crime activity, and exposure to violence and racial prejudice as community-level predictors of youth violence.

Given the effect of neighborhood conditions on youth behavior both within and outside school, it seems interventions aimed at reducing youth violence should assess and target the neighborhood experiences of youth. Promoting social integration among residents and strengthening the social control mechanisms in neighborhoods will likely prevent and reduce violence. Indeed, researchers have concluded that collaboration among schools and community agencies such as law enforcement, juvenile justice, and social services can effectively reduce and prevent school violence (Vera Institute of Justice, 1999).

Understanding that violent behavior at school results from multiple interrelated determinants at different ecological levels is necessary before practitioners can design appropriate and effective prevention strategies. Recognizing such multiple determinants also leads practitioners to consider strategies targeting more than one risk factor and, importantly, to consider factors *outside* an individual violent student.

EFFECTIVE PREVENTIVE INTERVENTIONS

Prevention is a term with multiple definitions in the current literature (Clayton, Ballif-Spanvill, & Hunsaker, 2001). This chapter relies on Gordon's (1983, 1987) risk-benefit perspective and restricts the classification of prevention to three categories: universal prevention, selective prevention, and indicated prevention. Gordon (1983) designed his model as an alternative classification in physical disease prevention. The Substance Abuse and Mental Health Services Administration (SAMHSA, 2000a;2002b) uses the Institute of Medicine's slight variation of Gordon's original definition of prevention to distinguish the level of approach in violence prevention programs. Because the two definitions are used frequently in current literature, we include the Institute of Medicine's definition along with Gordon's as we provide examples of effective school violence prevention programs.

Key Features of Effective Programs

Programs for which empirical evidence of efficacy exists share a number of key features:

1. Each program includes a manual or curriculum that promotes fidelity and consistency in program implementation.
2. The programs all aim to replace negative behaviors with more prosocial behavior, which serves as a protective factor for children.

3. Most of the programs target multiple domains in the child's environment by offering components such as parenting classes, home visits, or mentoring.

4. The majority of the programs target students at an early age and maintain a long-term commitment.

5. Several of the programs work to improve the school climate and culture by providing staff development and training seminars on the programs.

We have chosen to detail only three or four programs in each category of prevention. The programs detailed are intended to serve as examples of effective interventions and to assist school practitioners in matching their students' specific needs with an appropriate prevention program. We found earlier reviews of youth prevention programs by Catalano, Berglund, Ryan, Lonczak, and Hawkins (1998) and by Greenberg, Domitrovich, and Bumbarger (1999) to be highly informative in our discussion of these programs. See Appendix II for School Violence Programs.

Universal Programs

Universal preventive interventions are defined by SAMHSA and the Institute of Medicine as "activities targeted to the general public or a whole population group that has not been identified on the basis of individual risk" (SAMHSA, 2002a). Similarly, Gordon qualifies universal prevention as a "measure that is desirable for everybody" (Gordon, 1983, p. 24). The universal prevention programs detailed in this section are Second Step, Responding in Peaceful and Positive Ways (RIPP), and the Seattle Social Development Project. Promoting Alternative Thinking Strategies (PATHS) is also a universal program, but it is discussed in the multicomponent section because it is often combined with Fast Track, a selective interventions program.

Second Step

The Committee for Children developed Second Step. This school-based social skills program uses a combination of cognitive-behavioral and social learning principles, and it targets students between the ages of 4 and 14. The program's three key skills-building components focus on empathy, impulse control, and anger management (Leff, Power, Manz, Costigan, & Nabors, 2001). The Second Step curriculum is taught by the classroom teacher and includes photographic lesson cards demonstrating scenarios based on the skill-building components to generate discussion and promote skill-building opportunities (Frey, Hirschstein, & Guzzo, 2000; Greenberg et al., 1999). There is also a video-based parent guide to reinforce new skills at home.

Evaluations of the Second Step program show reduced physical aggression in the classroom. One study assessed 790 second- and third-grade students from 49 classrooms in a randomized controlled study (Grossman et al., 1997). After two weeks, posttreatment results showed increased prosocial behavior and decreased physical aggression; a six-month follow-up noted significant reductions in physical aggression in the classroom (Frey et al., 2000).

Responding in Peaceful and Positive Ways

This program, developed by Albert Farrell, targets junior high/middle school students (Farrell, Meyer, & White, 2001). The RIPP program focuses on risk reduction and asset building to decrease violent behavior and to increase prosocial behavior (SAMHSA, 2002b). The program is based on social-cognitive learning theory and promotes the use of nonviolent alternative behavior. The RIPP curriculum includes 25 sessions implemented in the sixth grade and 12 sessions implemented in the seventh and eighth grades. A schoolwide peer-mediation program is implemented along with the classroom curriculum. The curriculum is taught in weekly 45- to 50-minute blocks and uses techniques such as team-building activities, repetition and rehearsal, and role playing to assist with skills attainment and generalization (Greenberg et al., 1999).

There are several unique aspects of the RIPP program. One is the use of an adult role model who teaches the lessons and then functions as the prevention facilitator. Inclusion of a role model is intended to actively demonstrate the skills and attitudes necessary to reach nonviolent problem resolution. Another unique aspect of RIPP is that populations targeted in the past have been primarily urban, African American students (Greenberg et al., 1999).

Research shows RIPP participants required fewer disciplinary actions and fewer in-school suspensions after concluding the program, and this reduction was maintained after 12 months (Farrell et al., 2001). The study sample consisted of 602 sixth-grade students; 50% of the students in the sample were male and 96% were African American. The randomized control study indicated that RIPP participants showed decreased rates of bringing weapons to school, fighting, and in-school suspensions, compared to control groups (Greenberg et al., 1999).

The Seattle Social Development Project

David Hawkins and Richard Catalano started the Seattle Social Development Project (SSDP), which is based on the social-development model. This school- and home-based program targets first- through sixth-grade students and seeks to reduce the childhood risks of drug abuse and delinquency by enhancing protective factors. The program aims to increase pro-social bonds and to strengthen attachments to school, thereby decreasing negative behaviors. The SSDP combines a focus-on-strength teaching practice and a commitment to increased parental effectiveness (Greenberg et al., 1999). Teachers receive cooperative learning and classroom management training while parents receive optional training on topics pertinent to the development and well-being of children, including family management and home learning environments.

Research indicates the SSDP reduced rates of teacher-reported aggression and increased student reports of family communication and family management (Greenberg et al., 1999). One study found that students in the full-intervention groups showed improvements in self-reported achievement and significantly less involvement in school misbehavior than students in control groups (Catalano et al., 1998).

Selective Programs

The Institute of Medicine classifies *selective preventive interventions* as those "activities targeted to individuals or a subgroup of the population whose risk of developing a disorder is significantly higher than average" (SAMHSA, 2002a). According to Gordon (1983), selective prevention is targeted to subgroups of the population with a greater probability of experiencing an undesirable outcome. Under these guidelines, the selective programs highlighted in this section are Families and Schools Together (FAST) and First Steps to Success (FSS). Fast Track is also a selective approach program, but it is detailed in the multicomponent section because it is commonly used in combination with PATHS, a universal program.

Families and Schools Together

Developed by Lynn McDonald, FAST is a school-, home-, and community-based family therapy program. The program targets students between the ages of 4 and 13 who are considered at risk for drug and alcohol abuse, school failure, and juvenile delinquency. Using parent-professional collaborative teams, the FAST program systematically reaches out to entire families and organizes multifamily groups to increase parental involvement with at-risk youth (Bilchik, 1999). Weekly FAST family sessions last 2½ hours and span 8 to 10 weeks, with monthly follow-up sessions for two years. The aim of this group process is to prevent juvenile delinquency and substance abuse by reducing social isolation (SAMHSA, 2002b).

Many of the specific program activities included in the FAST program have been individually evaluated and have proven successful (OJJDP Juvenile Justice Bulletin, 1999). Furthermore, evaluation of the comprehensive FAST program shows an increase in students' positive classroom and home behavior, and positive school outcomes have been shown to continue two years after intervention

(McDonald, Billingham, Conrad, Morgan, & Payton, 1997). For example, the parents of a group of 249 FAST participants were interviewed at two years and at four years postintervention. Completion of a standardized evaluation of functioning and behavior indicated the children's behavior was either maintained or improved (McDonald et al., 1997).

First Steps to Success

Developed by Hill Walker, this program targets kindergarten children at risk of developing antisocial behavior patterns (Walker, Stiller, Severson, Feil, & Golly, 1998). The intervention is based on the assumption that children learn patterns of negative behavior at home that can be indicative of the beginning of a pattern of maladaptive future behaviors (Greenberg et al., 1999). The program's aim is to prevent the development of antisocial behavior in kindergarten students and to teach social skills (Walker et al., 1998).

A two- to three-month program, FSS teaches a system of behavior rather than a particular curriculum; the goal is to initiate an ongoing teaching and parenting approach lasting well beyond the program itself. The program works by screening and identifying high-risk kindergarteners, by intervening in the classroom to reduce aggression and increase social skills, and by working with parents in the home to develop effective parenting skills (Leff et al., 2001; Walker et al., 1998). The program includes a point system and rewards for good behavior, strategies that provide the child with consistent daily feedback. A consultant works with both teachers and parents (Greenberg et al., 1999).

Research has found that FSS participants exhibit more adaptive behavior and less antisocial behavior than control groups (Greenberg et al., 1999). One study randomly assigned 46 students to experimental or wait-list control groups. At one and two years after the intervention ended, teachers rated intervention groups as less aggressive and significantly more adaptive (Walker et al., 1998).

Indicated Programs

Indicated preventive interventions are defined by SAMHSA and the Institute of Medicine as "activities targeted to individuals in high-risk environments identified as having minimal but detectable signs of symptoms foreshadowing a disorder or having biological markers indicating predisposition for disorder but not yet meeting diagnostic levels" (SAMHSA, 2002a). Gordon (1983) defines *indicated prevention* as targeting those who are "found to manifest a risk factor, condition, or abnormality that identifies them, individually, as being at sufficiently high risk to require the preventive intervention" (p. 24). Indicated-level prevention programs detailed in this section include the Anger Coping Program (ACP), Early Risers-Skills for Success (ER), and Multisystemic Family Therapy (MST).

The Anger Coping Program

This program, developed by John Lochman, is founded on a social-cognitive model of anger arousal. The school-based program targets students between the ages of 9 and 12 who are aggressive and disruptive or who display difficulty with anger management. The goal of the intervention is to reduce future conduct disorders, substance abuse, and delinquency (Greenberg et al., 1999). This small-group (four- to six-student) intervention program includes one 45- to 60-minute session per week for 18 weeks (Lochman, Dunn, & Klimes-Dougan, 1993). Lessons implemented by a health professional/school employee focus on self-monitoring, perspective-taking, and social problem-solving skills. The ACP enforces goal-setting and rewards goal attainment. This program has been adapted for boys between 5 and 7 years old, though previously it was used primarily with preadolescent boys between the ages of 8 and 14 (Leff et al., 2001). A parenting component was recently added.

One evaluation of this program used a sample of 76 boys from eight schools; the subjects were between 9 and 12 years old, and 56% were African American. Boys in the treatment groups exhibited lower rates of disruptive and aggressive behavior during classroom observations than boys in the control group, and a seven-month follow-up showed those who had received the intervention exhibited greater on-task behavior (Greenberg et al., 1999). Another evaluation found that groups receiving the ACP, wherein the goal-setting component is monitored and evaluated weekly for each student, had stronger behavioral generalization to the classroom setting (Lochman et al., 1993).

Early Risers: Skills for Success Program

Developed by Gerald August, George Realmuto, and Michael Bloomquist, the ER program is premised on an early starter model of antisocial behavior and targets students between the ages of 6 and 10 who are at risk for developing conduct disorders (August, Realmuto, Hektner, & Bloomquist, 2001). The goal of the program is to enhance the development of positive self-image, along with problem-solving, decision-making, and coping skills. The program includes supplementary reading and math education, along with its focus on general social skills. Special attention is given to aggressive or disruptive behavior. In addition, the program incorporates a family support component that addresses parent-school interaction and stress management (SAMHSA, 2002b).

One study of ER was conducted with 10 intervention schools and 10 control schools. A study two years posttest found academic competence improved in the intervention group, while it declined slightly in control groups. After two years of intervention, students also showed improvement in school behaviors, compared to control groups (August et al., 2001).

Multisystemic Family Therapy

This program, developed by Scott Henggeler, targets adolescents between 12 and 17 (Henggeler & Borduin, 1990). MST is unique among the programs in this chapter in that it is a family-oriented, home-based program rather than primarily school based. The program aims to reduce antisocial behavior, substance abuse, and criminal activity among youths by strengthening parenting skills and the relationships among family members (SAMHSA, 2002b). This multisystemic approach views the adolescent as a participant in interconnected systems. The approach emphasizes the need to intervene in more than one of these systems for a treatment to be effective (Kazdin, 2000).

The MST sessions include approximately 60 hours over a four-month period, with components that focus on empowering parents and identifying strengths and support systems. A substantial amount of research shows that this approach facilitates long-term reductions in juvenile criminal activity (Henggeler, Melton, Brondino, Scherer, & Hanley, 1997). Follow-up studies evaluating the program two to five years after intervention found reductions in emotional and behavioral problems and delinquency and improvements in family functioning, compared to other treatments (Kazdin, 2000).

Multicomponent Programs

Programs that fit into the multicomponent classification combine two or more of Gordon's original categories and involve a combination of prevention-level approaches. Three such programs, detailed in this section, include the Bullying Prevention Program (BPP), the Strengthening Families Program (SFP), and Fast Track (FS), in combination with Promoting Alternative Thinking Strategies (PATHS).

The Bullying Prevention Program

Developed by Dan Olweus, this program is a multicomponent program with universal and selective interventions targeting students between 6 and 15 years old. The program is school based, includes ongoing sessions, and is a structural approach rather than a curriculum. The BPP includes anonymous questionnaires for all students, classroom rules and meetings, and a separate intervention for children and the parents of children identified as bullies or victims (Olweus, Limber, & Mihalic, 1999). The program improves peer relationships and creates a more positive school climate, characterized by positive interest, clear and firm limits, nonhostile negative consequences, and adult role models (Olweus, 1994).

One research study used a sample of 2,500 students in grades 4 through 7 and a selection cohort design (Olweus, 1994). Findings included a reduction in peer-rated estimation of the numbers of bullies in classrooms and in the level of bullying problems. Students also reported increased satisfaction with school life. Furthermore, the study found that the BPP reduced reports of bullying, anti-social behavior, and new victims for more than two years after intervention.

The Strengthening Families Program

Karol Kumpfer developed this program, formerly known as the Iowa Strengthening Families Program (Spoth, Redmond, & Shin, 1998). It is a multicomponent program including universal, selective, and indicated interventions targeting students 6 to 14 years of age. The program is both school and home based and includes 7 to 14 sessions with students and their families. The program uses a cognitive-behavioral approach and aims to delay the onset of adolescent alcohol/substance abuse and destructive-aggressive behavior. As the name indicates, the program works to strengthen relationships within families and to increase the life skills of parents and youths (SAMHSA, 2002b).

One study of the program used a sample of 238 intervention families and 208 control group families. Program participants showed significant positive effects in parenting behaviors, child management, and child affective quality, compared to control participants (Spoth et al., 1998). The SFP has also proven effective in reducing aggressive behavior (Spoth, Redmund, & Shin, 2000).

Fast Track and Promoting Alternative Thinking Strategies

This multicomponent program, developed by the Conduct Problems Prevention Research Group (CPPRG), aims to prevent conduct problems among at-risk children. The program is both school and home based, and it is implemented in the first through sixth grades (CPPRG, 2002). The intervention is based on a developmental theory of conduct disorder and assumes that an interaction of multiple influences leads to negative adolescent outcomes (Greenberg et al., 1999). Fast Track alone is specifically a selective school-based prevention program, but it is commonly combined with the Promoting Alternative Thinking Strategies (PATHS) curriculum, adding a universal approach and creating a multicomponent prevention program.

The FT program specifically targets children who demonstrate poor peer relations and disruptive, aggressive behavior in kindergarten (CPPRG, 1999). The program aims to enhance cognitive, social, and problem-solving skills (Greenberg et al., 1999). It includes components for the parents of identified students, for teachers, for classroom peers, and for the high-risk students themselves. Students in the program receive weekly social-skills group training, engage in guided play sessions with socially skilled peers, and receive academic tutoring in reading (Clayton et al., 2001).

The FT curriculum includes 57 lessons delivered three times per week during first grade (Greenberg et al., 1999). In addition, twenty-two 120-minute parent-training sessions emphasize anger control, effective discipline techniques, and the fostering of academic performance and school participation (Mytton, DiGuiseppi, Gough, Taylor, & Logan, 2002). Finally, the program includes 12 biweekly home visits to reinforce parental problem-solving skills and enhance parental feelings of empowerment and efficacy (Greenberg, Kusche, & Mihalic, 1998).

The PATHS curriculum, created by Mark Greenberg, consists of universal school-based competence promotion lessons focused on strengthening the management of behavior and reactions in social and emotional situations (Greenberg et al., 1998). The program is based on the Affective-Behavioral-Cognitive-Dynamic model of development. The program has also proven effective with students in special education.

Educators and counselors implement the 131-lesson curriculum three times per week for up to five years. Teachers attend a two- to three-day training workshop as well as biweekly meetings with the curriculum consultant to promote consistency (Greenberg et al., 1999). Teachers introduce PATHS into the classroom simultaneously with the initial Fast Track intervention for high-risk students.

Students involved in the PATHS intervention show significant improvements (Greenberg et al., 1999). One study used a sample of 200 first-grade students in regular education (65% Caucasian). At a two-year follow-up, students from the intervention group self-reported significantly lower rates of conduct problems, and teachers reported fewer behavior problems among those students than among students in control groups (Greenberg et al., 1999).

Research also shows that students enrolled in the Fast Track multicomponent program exhibit fewer conduct problems than students in control groups (CPPRG, 1999, 2002). In one study, more than 9,000 kindergarten students were screened at four sites. Of those, 891 were identified as high risk and were randomly assigned to intervention or control groups. A multiyear, multicomponent Fast Track program was implemented. By the time those high-risk students reached third grade, according to CPPRG (2002), 37% of the students in the intervention group were free of conduct problems, compared to 27% of the students in the control group.

IMPLICATIONS AND FUTURE DIRECTIONS

The public outcry about school violence in the context of high-profile school shootings in the late 1990s resulted in a significant increase in public and private funding to improve the safety of students at schools. A number of innovative and effective prevention programs, such as those reviewed here, have been implemented in schools across the nation in an attempt to reduce the incidence and severity of school violence. The programs have designs informed by an explicit theory-of-change model and empirical evidence that support their effectiveness.

The prevention programs reviewed in this chapter all represent current best practice, and they provide an important foundation for reducing school violence. However, many of these programs are rather narrowly targeted toward single correlates of violence and toward a school-based and student-focused orientation. In addition, with the exception of prevention efforts that include parental involvement either as a focus or target of intervention efforts, most programs generally neglect conditions in the larger environment outside school that fuel problem behavior at school.

Though these programs generally fail to address the issue, research into the incidence of school violence suggests the importance of broader social contexts such as neighborhood and community. For example, G. L. Bowen et al. (1998) found a positive and significant correlation between perceived danger at school and perceived danger in the neighborhood. Similarly, G. L. Bowen and Van Dorn (2002) found that male students living in communities with a high violent crime rate reported greater danger at school. Improving student safety at school involves more than increasing conflict resolution skills and providing a more supportive school and home climate; it also involves strengthening the nature of relationships and opportunities that students encounter in the broader community.

An ecological perspective explains student- and school-level outcomes as a function of the multiple systems in which students are embedded. For example, earlier in this chapter, we noted a number of student, family, peer, school, and community risk factors associated with the incidence of school violence. Within such systems, it is important to reduce risks and build protective factors to achieve desired results such as the reduction of school violence.

In addition to the more narrowly focused preventive interventions reviewed in this chapter, we suggest the need for more comprehensive and multifaceted school violence prevention programs focused on building school and community partnerships. Schools cannot solve the problem of school violence alone, and many of the risk factors for school violence reside in the context outside the school building. Effective solutions require a community approach—for instance, a coalition of formal and informal networks sharing responsibility and working together to create a safe learning environment for students (G. L. Bowen, Bowen, Richman, & Woolley, 2002). Student groups are important members of such partnerships. As evidenced in a recent report, *Youth and Violence: Colorado Students Speak Out for a More Civil Society,* by the Families and Work Institute (Galinsky & Salmond, 2002), students have many ideas about how to reduce school violence.

An important focus of such partnerships is to first assess the incidence of school violence and to set performance standards and time lines for achieving desired results. In our work with schools (G. L. Bowen et al., 2002), we ask: "What changes in this community are needed to reduce school violence rates from current to desired levels within the specified time frame?" We assume that the current level of school violence (the status quo) represents the total of everything that is happening in the community to prevent and reduce school violence. Therefore, for school violence rates to change, either more of the same is required, which almost always involves a greater allocation of resources, or something different is required, which may require a reallocation of resources.

In addressing this question, we ask partnerships first to identify potential allies in a successful school violence reduction initiative. Such allies might include police, community agencies, religious/faith organizations, neighbors, teachers, peer groups, or parents. For each ally group, we then ask what this group ought to know, believe, or do to reduce school violence. We pay relatively greater attention to behavior than to knowledge or attitudes, although knowledge and attitudes may be important prerequisites to action. Finally, although we focus first on ally groups other than students, students are nonetheless a focus of attention. In this case, we ask: "What should students know, believe, or do to achieve desired school violence rates?" The extensive literature on school violence frames and informs this discussion.

The result of this process is a comprehensive theory-of-change model that includes both the desired result and the leverage points for achieving the desired result. The partnership identifies the intervention and prevention activities necessary to influence the knowledge, attitudes, and behavior of allies and students (the leverage points). With such information in hand, the partnership designs a plan for implementing such activities, including the allocation of needed resources, and specifies a plan for monitoring and evaluating the overall theory-of-change model. In our experience, this process results in a comprehensive school violence reduction plan, broad-based ownership of the plan, and a means to integrate effective preventive interventions that correspond to targeted leverage points.

This is an exciting time in our efforts to reduce the incidence of school violence; a number of prevention programs have demonstrated efficacy in reducing the incidence of school violence. Although the choice of prevention programs should be based on a careful assessment of student needs and available resources, comprehensive and multifaceted prevention efforts that create community partnerships, address the whole school climate, and provide support services for aggressive students are recommended, in addition to single-focus preventive interventions.

REFERENCES

Alexander, R., & Curtis, C. M. (1995). A critical review of strategies to reduce school violence. *Social Work in Education, 17,* 73–82.

Astor, R. A., Vargas, L. A., Pitner, R. O., & Meyer, H. A. (1999). School violence: Research, theory, and practice. In J. M. Jenson & M. O. Howard (Eds.), *Youth violence: Current research and recent practice innovations* (pp. 139–172). Springfield, VA: Sheridan Books.

August, G. J., Realmuto, G. M., Hektner, J. M., & Bloomquist, M. L. (2001). An integrated components preventive intervention for aggressive elementary school children: The early risers program. *Journal of Consulting and Clinical Psychology, 69*(4), 614–626.

Barton, P. E., Coley, R. J., & Wenglinsky, H. (1998). *Order in the classroom: Violence, discipline, and student achievement* (Policy Information Report). Princeton, NJ: Educational Testing Service, Policy Information Center.

Bowen, G. L., Bowen, N. K., & Richman, J. M. (1998). *Students in peril: Crime and violence in neighborhoods and schools.* Chapel Hill: University of North Carolina, Jordan Institute for Families, School of Social Work.

Bowen, G. L., Bowen, N. K., & Richman, J. M. (2000). School size and middle school students' perceptions of the school environment. *Social Work in Education, 22,* 69–82.

Bowen, G. L., Bowen, N. K., Richman, J. M., & Woolley, M. E. (2002). Reducing school violence: A social capacity framework. In L. A. Rapp-Paglicci, A. R. Roberts, & J. S. Wodarski (Eds.), *Handbook of violence* (pp. 303–325). Hoboken, NJ: Wiley.

Bowen, G. L., & Richman, J. M. (1993). *The School Success Profile.* Chapel Hill: University of North Carolina.

Bowen, G. L., & Richman, J. M. (1997). *The School Success Profile.* Chapel Hill: University of North Carolina.

Bowen, G. L., & Richman, J. M. (2001). *The School Success Profile.* Chapel Hill: University of North Carolina.

Bowen, G. L., & Van Dorn, R. A. (2002). Community violence crime rates and school danger. *Children and Schools, 24,* 90–104.

Bowen, N. K., & Bowen, G. L. (1999). Effects of crime and violence in neighborhoods and schools on the school behavior and performance of adolescents. *Journal of Adolescent Research, 14,* 319–342.

Bowen, N. K., Bowen, G. L., & Ware, W. B. (2002). Neighborhood social disorganization, families, and the educational behavior of adolescents. *Journal of Adolescent Research, 17,* 468–490.

Bronfenbrenner, U. (1992). Ecological systems theory. In R. Vasta (Ed.), *Six theories of child development: Revised formulations and current issues* (pp. 187–248). Philadelphia: Jessica Kingsley.

Cantor, D., & Wright, M. M. (2002). *School crime patterns: A national profile of U.S. public schools using rates of crime reported by police.* Rockville, MD: Westat.

Catalano, R. F., Berglund, M. L., Ryan, J. A. M., Lonczak, H. S., & Hawkins, J. D. (1998). *Positive youth development in the United States: Research findings on evaluations of positive youth development programs.* Washington, DC: U.S. Department of Health and Human Services.

Clayton, C. J., Ballif-Spanvill, B., & Hunsaker, M. D. (2001). Preventing violence and teaching peace: A review of promising and effective anti-violence, conflict-resolution, and peace programs for elementary school children. *Applied and Preventive Psychology, 10,* 1–35.

Conduct Problems Prevention Research Group. (1999). Initial impact of the fast track prevention trial for conduct problems: II. Classroom effects. *Journal of Consulting and Clinical Psychology, 67*(5), 648–657.

Conduct Problems Prevention Research Group. (2002). Evaluation of the first 3 years of the Fast Track prevention trial with children at high risk for adolescent conduct problems. *Journal of Abnormal Child Psychology, 30*(1), 19–35.

Crosse, S., Burr, M., Cantor, D., Hagen, C. A., & Hantman, I. (2002). *Wide scope, questionable quality: Drug and violence prevention efforts in American schools.* Rockville, MD: Westat.

Farrell, A. D., Meyer, A. L., & White, K. S. (2001). Evaluation of Responding in Peaceful and Positive Ways (RIPP): A school-based prevention program for reducing violence among urban adolescents. *Journal of Clinical Child and Adolescent Psychology, 30,* 451–463.

Frey, K., Hirschstein, M., & Guzzo, B. (2000). Second step: Preventing aggression by promoting social competence. *Journal of Emotional and Behavioral Disorders, 8,* 102–113.

Galinsky, E., & Salmond, K. (2002). *Youth and violence: Colorado students speak out for a more civil society.* New York: Families and Work Institute.

Gordon, R. (1983). An operational classification of disease prevention. *Public Health Reports, 98,* 107–109.

Gordon, R. (1987). An operational classification of disease prevention. In J. A. Steinberg & M. M. Silverman (Eds.), *Preventing mental disorders: A research perspective* (pp. 20–26). Rockville, MD: U.S. Department of Health and Human Services.

Greenberg, M. T., Domitrovich, C., & Bumbarger, B. (1999). *Preventing mental disorders in school-age children: A review of the effectiveness of prevention programs.* Available from www.psu.edu/dept/prevention/CMHS.htm.

Greenberg, M. T., Kusche, C. A., & Mihalic, S. F. (1998). *Blueprints for violence prevention, book ten: Promoting alternative thinking strategies (PATHS).* Boulder, CO: Center for the Study and Prevention of Violence.

Grossman, D. C., Neckerman, H. J., Koepsell, T. D., Liu, P. Y., Asher, K. N., Beland, K., et al. (1997). Effectiveness of a violence prevention curriculum among children in elementary school. *Journal of the American Medical Association, 277*(20), 1605–1611.

Harris & Associates. (1999). *The Metropolitan Life survey of the American teacher, 1999: Violence in America's public schools—five years later.* New York: Metropolitan Life Insurance Company.

Hawkins, J. D., Herrenkohl, T., Farrington, D. P., Brewer, D., Catalano, R. F., & Harachi, T. (1998). A review of predictors of youth violence. In R. Loeber & D. P. Farrington (Eds.), *Serious and violent juvenile offenders* (pp. 106–146). Thousand Oaks, CA: Sage.

Henggeler, S. W., & Borduin, C. M. (1990). *Family therapy and beyond: A multisystemic approach to treating the behavior problems of children and adolescents.* Pacific Grove, CA: Brooks/Cole.

Henggeler, S. W., Melton, G., Brondino, M., Scherer, D., & Hanley, J. (1997). Multisystemic therapy with violent and chronic juvenile offenders and their families: The role of treatment fidelity in successful dissemination. *Journal of Consulting and Clinical Psychology, 65,* 821–833.

Henggeler, S. W., Schoenwald, S. K., Borduin, C. M., Rowland, M. D., & Cunningham, P. B. (1998). *Multisystemic treatment of antisocial behavior in children and adolescents.* New York: Guilford Press.

Kaufman, P., Chen, X., Choy, S. P., Peter, K., Ruddy, S. A., Miller, A. K., et al. (2001). *Indicators of school crime and safety, 2001* (NCES 2002–113). Washington, DC: U.S. Departments of Education and Justice.

Kazdin, A. E. (2000). Treatments for aggressive and antisocial children. *Child and Adolescent Psychiatric Clinics of North America, 9,* 841–859.

Leff, S., Power, T., Manz, P., Costigan, T., & Nabors, L. (2001). School-based aggression prevention programs for young children: Current status and implications for violence prevention. *School Psychology Review, 30,* 344–362.

Lochman, J. E., Dunn, S. E., & Klimes-Dougan, B. (1993). An intervention and consultation model from a social-cognitive perspective: A description of the Anger Coping Program. *School Psychology Review, 22,* 456–469.

McDonald, L., Billingham, S., Conrad, T., Morgan, A., & Payton, E. (1997). Families and schools together (FAST): Integrating community development with clinical strategies. *Families in Society: Journal of Contemporary Human Services, 78,* 140–155.

Mytton, J. A., DiGuiseppi, C., Gough, D. A., Taylor, R. S., & Logan, S. (2002). School-based violence prevention programs; systematic review of secondary trials. *Archives of Pediatric and Adolescent medicine, 156,* 752–762.

Nash, J. K., & Bowen, G. L. (2002). Defining and estimating risk and protection: An illustration from the School Success Profile. *Child and Adolescent Social Work Journal, 19,* 247–261.

Oesterle, S., Stoner-Eby, S., & Elder, G. H., Jr. (2002). *The influence of school and student characteristics on perceived school safety.* Chapel Hill: University of North Carolina, Carolina Population Center.

OJJDP Juvenile Justice Bulletin (1999, November). *Families and schools together: Building relationships.* Retrieved August 29, 2002, from http://www.ncjrs.org/html/ojjdp/9911_2/contents.html.

Olweus, D. (1994). Annotation: Bullying at school: Basic facts and effects of a school based intervention program. *Journal of Child Psychology and Psychiatry, 35,* 1171–1190.

Olweus, D., Limber, S., & Mihalic, S. F. (1999). The bullying program. In D. S. Elliott (Series Ed.), *Blueprints for violence prevention.* Boulder: University of Colorado at Boulder, Institute of Behavioral Science, Center for the Study and Prevention of Violence.

Orpinas, P., & Murray, N. (1999). Parental influences on students' aggressive behavior and weapon carrying. *Health and Education Behavior, 26,* 774–788.

Poole, E. D., & Regoli, R. M. (1979). Parental support, delinquent friends, and delinquency: A test of interaction effects. *Journal of Criminal Law and Criminology, 70,* 188–193.

Richman, J. M., & Bowen, G. L. (1997). School failure: An ecological-interactional-developmental perspective. In M. W. Fraser (Ed.), *Risk and resilience in childhood: An ecological perspective* (pp. 95–116). Washington, DC: National Association of Social Workers Press.

Richman, J. M., & Fraser, M. W. (Eds.). (2001). *The context of youth violence: Resilience, risk, and protection.* Westport, CT: Praeger.

Singer, M. I., & Miller, D. B. (1999). Contributors to violent behavior among elementary and middle school children. *Pediatrics, 104,* 878–885.

Snyder, H. N., & Sickmund, M. (1999). *Juvenile offenders and victims: 1999 national report.* Washington, DC: Office of Juvenile Justice and Delinquency Prevention.

Spoth, R., Redmund, C., & Shin, C. (1998). Direct and indirect latent-variable parenting outcomes of two universal family focused preventive interventions: Extending a public health-oriented research base. *Journal of Consulting and Clinical Psychiatry, 66,* 385–399.

Spoth, R., Redmund, C., & Shin, C. (2000). Reducing adolescents' aggressive and hostile behavior. *Archives of Pediatric and Adolescent Medicine, 154,* 1248–1257.

Substance Abuse and Mental Health Services Administration. (2002a). *Institute of Medicine (IOM) classifications.* Retrieved September 30, 2002, from http://modelprograms.samhsa.gov/IOMClass.cfm.

Substance Abuse and Mental Health Services Administration. (2002b). *SAMHSA model programs.* Retrieved September 30, 2002, from http://modelprograms.samhsa.gov/matrix_all.cfm.

Vera Institute of Justice. (1999). *Approaches to school safety in America's largest cities* (Prepared for Lt. Governor's Task Force on School Safety). New York: Author.

Walker, H., Stiller, B., Severson, H., Feil, E., & Golly, A. (1998). First steps to success: Intervening at the point of school entry to prevent antisocial behavior patterns. *Psychology in the Schools, 35*(3), 259–269.

Welsh, W. N. (2000). The effects of school climate on school disorder. *Annals of the American Academy of Political and Social Science, 567,* 88–108.

Yogan, L. J. (2000). School tracking and student violence. *Annals of the American Academy of Political and Social Science, 567,* 108–123.

Youth Pride. (1997). *Creating safe schools for lesbian and gay students: A resource guide for school staff.* [Electronic version]. Retrieved November 5, 2000, from http://members.tripod.com/~twood/guide.html.

Chapter 17

SCHOOL DROPOUT

BETH DOLL AND ROBYN HESS

More than 40 years ago, the National Education Association (NEA) released a forceful report urging the nation to adopt a plan for the study of high school dropouts (Schreiber, Kaplan, & Strom, 1965). On the surface, the United States had successfully transitioned into a more educated society. Rates of high school graduation had steadily risen since the beginning of the century and had exceeded 50% for the first time in 1950. Still, the economic consequences for those who dropped out of school were becoming increasingly dire. The economic status of boys who did not graduate from high school declined relative to their parents, jobs for unskilled laborers were disappearing rapidly, and dropping out of school had become a dividing line that deprived families from the lower classes of the benefits of the booming, postwar economy (Hathaway, Reynolds, & Monachesi, 1969). Researchers had been working to identify the causes of school dropout since 1911, and their attempts intensified with a number of state-sponsored studies conducted in the 1950s. Still, after carefully reviewing the existing research, the NEA concluded that methodological deficiencies made it impossible to reach any national understanding of the reasons that students were dropping out of high school or the policies and practices that could improve school completion rates (Schreiber et al., 1965).

Too little progress has been made in the past 40 years. The shortcomings that precluded any national understanding of school dropouts in the 1960s are the same ones that blocked notable progress toward the 1990s National Education Goal to increase the graduation rate to 90% (Doll & Hess, 2001; U.S. Department of Education, 1990). Then and now, researchers and school districts have found it almost impossible to clearly define a high school dropout. A common but imprecise practice is to designate students as *presumed dropouts* if they stopped attending high school and no other district requested their cumulative file. In some but not all cases, schools also check with nearby schools and districts to verify that the student has not reenrolled elsewhere. When presumed dropouts are identified only when students disappear from high school attendance rolls, large numbers of middle school dropouts are overlooked. Clear conventions have not yet been devised for tracking the school enrollment status of the many adolescents who drop in and out of school or students who leave school without graduating but subsequently earn a GED.

Second, in the 1960s and the 1990s, the overwhelming majority of studies examined correlations between school dropout and fixed risk factors of students such as ethnicity, gender, and social class (e.g., Fernandez, Paulsen, & Hirano-Nakanishi, 1989; Rumberger, 1995). The utility of these studies for intervention is negligible because the characteristics they identify cannot be changed. (As an extreme example, you cannot pull impoverished students into middle class families as a strategy to increase their high school completion rates.) At most, such research can profile a typical prospective dropout for an identification that has minimal accuracy and dubious practical utility.

Third, most efforts to study or intervene with potential high school dropouts have been concentrated in the nation's high schools despite convincing evidence that students' journeys into dropping out of school begin as early as the fourth grade (Barclay, 1966; Barclay & Doll, 2001; Fitzsimmons, Cheever, Leonard, & Macunovich, 1969). Indeed, a significant portion of dropping out students never appear in the high school corridors, where dropout prevention programs are most likely to be delivered.

Fourth, too many efforts have been narrowly focused on providing students with a high school diploma, although dropping out of school is part of a larger syndrome of academic and social failure (Christenson, Sinclair, Lehr, & Godber, 2001). Before leaving school, students who drop out have typically struggled with grade retention, poor academic achievement, and limited social competence, and, after leaving school, they struggle with underemployment, financial difficulties, early parenthood, and social and psychological disturbances (Dryfoos, 1990; Kaplan, Damphousse, & Kaplan, 1994). There is no good reason to believe that the high school diploma alone is sufficient to interrupt these youths' trajectory into social disruption. Instead, efforts need to refocus on the broader goal of school completion and all of the competencies that this entails: mastery of a basic academic curriculum, social competence that allows students to work with others, self-control and the ability to persevere in endeavors, and preparation for productive employment. Changing the vocabulary from *school dropout* to *school completion* is a change in perspective that focuses attention on the skills necessary for students to complete school and lead successful lives.

Still, the complexity of school completion stands in stark and discouraging contrast to the simplicity of much of the empirical research that seeks to explain it, as well as the school and community practices that seek to promote it. In the remainder of this chapter, we describe the identified trends and developmental trajectories into dropping out of school, detail the risk factors that predispose students to leave school before graduating, and review the effective programs and practices that promote school completion. Although emphasis is placed on empirically supported practices and programs, the limited availability of high-quality research in school completion requires that we also discuss some promising practices that have not yet been determined to be effective through careful empirical studies.

TRENDS AND INCIDENCE

It is almost impossible to cite precise statistics describing the percentage of students who fail to graduate from high school. The often-quoted dropout rates are misleading because they mask the compounding of noncompleters across multiple years of school. For example, the National Center for Educational Statistics (NCES) reports a national *event* dropout rate of 4.8% for students who dropped out of grades 10, 11, or 12 between October 1999 and October 2000 (NCES, 2002). This number describes only the rate of dropping out for one year. If this same rate persisted across the entire four years of a high school cohort, 95.2% of students who started their freshman year would progress to be sophomores, 90.6% of the original cohort would then progress to be juniors, 86.3% would progress to be seniors, and 82.1% would graduate from their senior year of high school. Thus, an event dropout rate of 4.8% could compound to a rate of almost 18% across the four years of high school. Event rates also overestimate the number of dropouts because they do not account for students who might reenter school by transferring to another school or otherwise completing a credential (National Research Council, 2001).

As an alternative to event rates, *status dropout rates* describe the percentage of an age group that is not enrolled in school and that has not earned a high school diploma, GED, or other certificate of completion (NCES, 2002). Status dropout rates for the year 2000 are described in Table 17.1. The table shows that almost 11% of 16- to 24-year-olds were out of school without a high school credential in 2000. Males had a slightly higher rate of school dropout than females, and the problem of school dropout was more prevalent in the South and West than in the Northeast or Midwest. Furthermore, a consistent trend in the data that is not reflected in status rates is that young adults from the poorest 20% of families are six times more likely to drop out of school than their peers living in the top 20% of the income distribution (NCES, 2002).

Table 17.1   Status Dropout Rates and School Completion Rates for the Year 2000

Characteristic	Percentage of 16- to 24-year-olds who were dropouts in October 2000	Percentage of 18- to 24-year-olds who were high school completers in October 2000
Total	10.9	86.5
By Gender		
Male	12.0	84.9
Female	9.9	88.1
By Race/Ethnicity		
White, non-Hispanic	6.9	91.8
Black, non-Hispanic	13.1	83.7
Hispanic	27.8	64.1
Asian Pacific Islander	3.8	94.6
By Age		
16 years	3.9	
17 years	7.6	
18 years	11.6	84.0
19 years	13.5	
20–21 years	12.4	86.4
22–24 years		88.1
By Region of the Country		
Northeast	8.5	89.1
Midwest	9.2	88.9
South	12.9	84.4
West	11.3	85.5

Note: From National Center for Educational Statistics (2002). *Dropout rates in the United States: 2000.* Washington, DC: U.S. Department of Education.

Table 17.1 also shows high school completion rates, which count youth within an age group who have received some certificate of high school completion. In 2000, 86.5% of 18- through 24-year-olds were high school completers. The proportion was somewhat lower for Black youth and was strikingly lower for Hispanic youth. Such inequities in the rates of high school completion are one of the most important social dilemmas faced by modern American communities.

The effects of not completing school fall disproportionately on the shoulders of underrepresented groups including the poor, members of ethnic minorities, and those speaking English as a second language (Velez & Saenz, 2001). More importantly, the very high status dropout rate among Hispanic students changed very little between 1972 and 1994 (34.3% and 27.8%, respectively), while during this same period, the gap between dropout rates for African American students and White, non-Hispanic students narrowed considerably (NCES, 2002). Higher dropout rates among recent Hispanic immigrants partially account for the elevated rates. For example, 44% of Hispanic 16- to 24-year-olds who were born outside the United States were not enrolled in school and had not earned a certificate of high school completion, a rate more than double the rates for first- or second-generation Hispanic youth born in this country and approximately six times the rate for non-Hispanic immigrant populations (7.4%).

Both status rates and school completion rates vary considerably depending on the age range that is selected (e.g., 16- to 24-year-olds versus 18- to 24-year-olds), making comparisons difficult unless all schools have used the same criteria. These methods also count individuals who earn GEDs and other certificates as completers, a practice that may mask important inequities. For example, the rate of GED completion has increased sharply for Hispanic and African American youth, creating the appearance of a narrowing gap in school dropout rates. However, wages, hours of work, unemployment experiences, and job tenure are similar for dropouts and GED recipients, leading some to question the utility of GED certificates for noncompleting students (Cameron & Heckman, 1993). To further complicate the status of high school graduates, many states are offering different forms of diplomas to demonstrate differing levels of achievement. For example, Florida now provides six different types of diplomas, and other states have begun to adopt this practice (National Research Council, 2001). Thus, the task of tracking school completion has become even more complicated, and very little is known about the long-term social and economic outcomes for individuals who earn these different types of diplomas.

Each of these data collection methods treats dropping out of school as a singular event when, in fact, it is a long-term process (Christenson et al., 2001; Jimerson, Egelund, Sroufe, & Carlson, 2000). As early as fourth grade, prospective high school dropouts begin to demonstrate a pattern of increased absences, discipline problems, and lower academic achievement (Roderick, 1993). Furthermore, these students often drop out of school temporarily, then return only to drop out again (National Research Council, 2001). Each of these factors points to a pattern of increasing disengagement from schooling.

RISK FACTORS

Researchers carefully differentiate among three kinds of risk factors:

1. Fixed factors that cannot be demonstrated to change
2. Variable factors that change but without apparent or immediate effect on outcomes
3. Causal factors that can be changed and, when they are, improve outcomes (Kraemer et al., 1997)

These categories are of special relevance for dropout prevention practices because large numbers of fixed risk factors have been identified, but relatively few of these inform efforts to improve school completion rates. Moreover, only some of the risk factors for dropping out of high school are characteristics of the students, whereas many others are characteristics of the schools they attend or their families of origin (Christenson et al., 2001). The large number of contextual risk factors suggests that dropping out of school is at least partially a product of school practices that were insufficient to promote the success of all students and of community pressures that fall disproportionately on underprivileged families.

Fixed Factors

Slightly more males than females, more poor students than wealthy students, and more students of color leave school without graduating. These patterns of dropping out shift considerably when interactions among gender, ethnicity, and socioeconomic status (SES) are examined (Fine, 1991). For example, even though students from low SES backgrounds are more likely to drop out than those students from higher SES backgrounds, the effect of low SES on school completion for Hispanic students is relatively small (Fernandez et al., 1989). Although descriptive, fixed characteristics do not inform interventions or identify at-risk populations in large urban schools where most students match these characteristics.

Variable Factors

Research has focused on environmental variables that place a student at risk for not completing school. For example, large school size is positively correlated with decreased attendance, lower grade point averages and standardized test scores, higher dropout rates, and higher crime than smaller schools serving similar children (Klonsky, 1995; Raywid, 1996). Structural practices, such as tracking, have a negative correlation with school completion rates independent of the student's ability level (Baker et al., 2001). Other school-related factors such as high concentrations of low-achieving students and less qualified teachers are also associated with higher dropout rates (National Research Council, 2001).

Causal Factors

The single most powerful predictor of school dropout is repeating a grade. Even after controlling for differences in background, postretention grades, and attendance, Roderick (1994) found that repeating a grade from kindergarten to sixth grade was associated with a significant increase in the likelihood that a student would drop out. In essence, schools that regularly practice retention are contributing to the problem of increased dropout rates (G. A. Hess & Greer, 1987). Related causal risk factors include poor academic achievement, poor peer acceptance, and academic disengagement as evidenced by absences, tardies, chronically uncompleted work, and similar indexes of nonparticipation in class and school activities (Rumberger, 1995). Similarly, limited participation in social activities of schools and limited social acceptance can predict dropping out (Wehlage, Rutter, Smith, Lesko, & Fernandez, 1989).

Less is known about the psychological factors that relate to students' school-leaving decisions. Although researchers have examined students' self-esteem, attitudes toward school, and educational aspirations, there has been only limited success in understanding the individual factors that influence high school completion (Ekstrom, Goertz, Pollack, & Rock, 1986). Students who drop out do not differ from graduates on global self-esteem indexes (Ekstrom et al., 1986). However, ratings of students who subsequently drop out of high school are lower on more specific measures of academic self-competence, perceptions of *self as student* (e.g., smart, ambitious, responsible, helpful to others), and expectations for educational attainment (Catterall, 1998; Ekstrom et al., 1986; Persaud & Madak, 1992).

Dropping out is best viewed as a process that occurs over time and results from a combination of fixed, variable, and causal factors, rather than a single risk event (Dryfoos, 1990; Jimerson et al., 2000). Indeed, many of these risk factors tend to have cumulative effects and to cluster together, as do lower SES and attending a large urban school. As preschoolers, children who subsequently drop out of high school come from homes with poor maternal-child attachment and poor maternal sensitivity to the child (Jimerson et al., 2000). In elementary school, students demonstrate poor academic achievement, lower expectations for school achievement, and higher rates of absence (R. S. Hess & D'Amato, 1996). Chronic academic failure leads to a perception of school as an unwelcoming place (Kaplan, Peck, & Kaplan, 1997). In middle school, low academic achievement, high absenteeism, misbehavior, and moving predict school dropout (Rumberger, 1995). To feel better about themselves, students engage in a variety of noncompliant behaviors, adopt resistant attitudes, and gradually disengage from school, such that dropping out of school becomes more acceptable (Alexander, Entwisle, & Horsey, 1997; Kaplan et al., 1997; Wehlage et al., 1989). Some students, especially minority students, drop out even before they reach high school (Oetting & Beauvais, 1990).

Much of the current dropout research has focused on creating a model that would allow schools to identify those students most at risk for school dropout and provide targeted interventions to this group. Unfortunately, it is not very effective to use individual risk factors as predictors to determine which students should receive intervention. For example, in the School Dropout Demonstration Assistance Program, Gleason and Dynarski (1998) found that even though high absenteeism was a significant predictor of school dropout, it correctly identified high school dropouts only 16% of the time. If this factor were used to identify 60 students who should receive an intervention, only 9 to 10 students would have likely gone on to drop out, and the majority of the students receiving the intervention would have likely graduated regardless. Even when more complex formulas were developed considering up to 40 different risk characteristics, researchers were able to accurately identify only 23% of the middle school students who ultimately dropped out of school and 42% of high school students.

EFFECTIVE INTERVENTIONS

Dropout prevention programs have existed in most school districts since the 1950s. The earliest examples were *continuation schools,* alternative high schools that were established in the 1920s to provide young, working-class immigrants with an opportunity to attend school on a part-time basis while working as unskilled laborers during the day (Kelly, 1996). Continuation schools' original mission was that of vocational education, and federal funding for them was eliminated after Congress passed the Vocational Education Act in 1963 that provided for vocational programs in conventional high schools. However, some continuation schools persisted to provide *adjustment education* as a strategy to meet the special needs of many young people who continued to drop out. Eventually, these came to be known as *alternative schools,* with the explicit mission of providing specialized programs of study for students at high risk of dropping out. Unfortunately, as a stand-alone approach, alternative schools generally are not effective in reducing the incidence of school dropout (Dynarski & Gleason, 1998).

Instead, programs that recognize the complexity and longevity of dropping out of school hold more promise for increasing a community's school completion. Universal prevention programs alter the educational practices for every student in a district in ways that will subsequently increase the rate of school completion. Selective prevention programs are provided to a select group of students who are at increased risk for dropping out of school sometime in the future. Indicated prevention programs are provided to very high-risk students who have already shown the early signs of dropping out of school and are an attempt to reengage them in educational activities to earn their high school diploma. In all three groups, we give special emphasis to those programs that have some empirical evidence of success.

Effective Universal Preventive Interventions

The services of universal prevention programs are available to every student in a school district and are intended to lower a district's overall high school dropout rate. Unlike selective and indicated prevention programs, universal programs are frequently provided at the elementary or middle school level, where the precursors to dropping out of school originate. Research evaluating these programs is longitudinal in nature because the ultimate outcome may be several years displaced from the actual program. In most cases, evidence of the programs' effectiveness is quasi-experimental, based on the comparison of school completion rates across naturally occurring subgroups within a community. The resulting relations between practices and school completion rates are less convincing than carefully controlled experimental studies but are also more meaningful because they emerged from real practices of school districts.

Academic Support/Remediation

Much emphasis has been placed on early interventions to combat academic failure for students who are struggling. Providing opportunities for quality preschool programs before a child enters elementary school can raise the child's readiness for school. For example, a longitudinal study of the Perry Preschool Project showed that just two years of attendance at a high-quality preschool program resulted in a higher graduation rate as well as higher intelligence and fewer placements in special education (Barnett, 1996).

Compensatory programs such as Title I have improved the academic achievement of disadvantaged and nondisadvantaged students who continue to struggle. Similarly, significant academic gains have been demonstrated through the use of Success for All, Reading Recovery, and Bilingual Cooperative Integrated Reading and Composition (Fashola, Slavin, Calderon, & Duran, 2001). It is especially important to provide appropriate academic supports for the growing number of students who are English language learners. When possible, continued formal learning in the native language is preferred because children who are taught to read in their native language and then transitioned to English ultimately become better readers in English than do students taught to read only in English (Garcia, 1991).

Alternatives to Retention

When students do not experience academic success, some school districts use retention as an opportunity for students to catch up. In fact, grade retention increases the risk that students will not complete high school whereas promotion with remediation provides more short-term academic benefits than retention alone, retention with remediation, or promotion alone (Karweit, 1991). In her study of long-term effects of retention, Roderick (1994) promoted three alternatives to retention at the middle and high school levels: nontraditional grouping and grade arrangements, provision of remedial and supplemental instruction, and the use of alternative classrooms and programs. At the middle school level, substituting an extra remedial class for an elective and attending summer school were the most effective strategies for increasing student achievement (MacIver & Epstein, 1991).

Creating Community

Because of the strong connection between negative peer interactions and dropping out of school (Wehlage et al., 1989), intervention programs have targeted the social competence of students by teaching social problem solving (Elias & Clabby, 1992) or forming peer support groups (Wassef, Mason, Collins, O'Boyle, & Ingham, 1996). Frequently, students who become disengaged from school seek out peers like themselves, and their negative peer choices are reinforced when schools routinely track students into low-ability groups (Kubitschek & Hallinan, 1998). Schools can respond by increasing opportunities for extracurricular activities and using grouping strategies that connect students to successful peers.

Involving Parents

Students who drop out report less parental involvement in their education than those who complete school (Ekstrom et al., 1986; Rumberger, Ghatak, Poulos, Ritter, & Dornbusch, 1990). Strategies to promote family involvement are frequently mentioned as promising, but there are no long-term studies that demonstrate that parental involvement leads to higher rates of school completion (Schargel & Smink, 2001). However, parental involvement in children's schooling has been shown to contribute to higher academic achievement (Kohl, Lengua, & McMahon, 2000; Peña, 2000).

Attending to Early Warning Signs

When students begin to disengage from school, they show increased truancy, absences, or challenging behavior problems. In response, schools use tracking systems that accurately record attendance and discipline trends for students and allow school personnel to follow up promptly on absences. One example of a comprehensive tracking system is that used in the Check and Connect program, a selective prevention program that also incorporates strategies for intervention when trends show that students are becoming too disengaged from school (Sinclair, Christenson, Evelo, & Hurley, 1998).

Antisocial and aggressive behavior is a strong and early predictor of dropping out of high school (Cairns, Cairns, & Neckerman, 1989). In response, schools can create comprehensive schoolwide programs that prevent behavioral problems and increase student learning (Nelson, Martella, & Marchand-Martella, 2002). Young adolescents have a heightened sense of fairness, and students are less likely to drop out of schools that are perceived to have fair discipline policies (Rumberger, 1995).

School Reform

During the 1980s and 1990s, as the emphasis on restructuring and reforming schools gained momentum, some policymakers came to see whole school reform as the best strategy for increasing school completion. Dynarski and Gleason (1998) studied five secondary schools that used this strategy and found only negligible effects on school dropout. The findings suggested that the programs that improved related outcomes, such as academic achievement or perception of positive school climate, were those that improved curriculum and instruction through staff development, summer courses, and classroom changes. In schools where restructuring efforts increased student services, neither teacher nor student outcomes improved. Schools in this study had only five years to implement restructuring, and it is possible that their reforms could have improved school completion rates if they had been implemented in the earliest grades, used across academic levels, and maintained over longer time periods.

Effective Selective Preventive Interventions

Selective prevention programs typically operate as smaller programs within comprehensive high schools, middle schools, or community organizations. They enroll students identified as being at high risk of dropping out and address the variables that place students at risk, such as academic achievement, attendance, or peer relationships. In most cases, students spend the majority of their day in the regular school environment and receive the special programming for a small part of their educational program.

Increasing School Engagement

The truancies, behavioral problems, and poor academic achievement associated with school dropout can be viewed as symptoms of a student's disengagement from school (Finn, 1993; Wehlage et al., 1989). Consequently, the Check and Connect program made school engagement of students with disabilities the primary focus of their intervention (Sinclair et al., 1998). The program continuously assessed student engagement in school through regular tracking of tardies, truancies, and behavioral referrals. Through ongoing consultation, the at-risk students were given regular information about the monitoring system, provided with regular feedback about their educational progress, reminded frequently of the importance of staying in school, and helped to solve some of the problems that placed them at risk for dropping out. When tracking records showed that students' engagement in school was faltering, the program added more services, including convening the family and school to problem-solve barriers to school attendance, providing intensive academic instruction, and promoting extracurricular activities of the student. After two years of enrollment in the program, Check and Connect students were found to be more engaged in school and had earned more credit toward graduation than similar students in the control group (Christenson & Carroll, 1999). Results showed that 91% of students in the program were still in school at the end of ninth grade, compared to 70% of students in a control group.

Easing School Transitions

Transitions between elementary and middle and middle and high schools are difficult, especially for students who are at risk for school dropout. The School Transitional Environment Project (STEP) was designed to ease the harmful effects of school transitions to reduce student disengagement and dropout (Felner et al., 1993). STEP used two strategies to facilitate successful transitions. To reduce the demands of the new school, STEP students were provided with smaller learning environments, learned with a small group of other students in the STEP program, and had classes located near the STEP homeroom. To increase student coping, a homeroom teacher served as an advisor and linked the students, their parents, and the school into a partnership to foster school completion. STEP was evaluated each year using a comparison group with the same demographics and pretransition levels of school adjustment (e.g., grades, attendance) as the STEP students. A five-year longitudinal study showed that students in the comparison group had a significantly higher dropout rate than did STEP students. By the end of the first four years, STEP students had a 24% dropout rate as compared to students in the control group who had a dropout rate of 43%. STEP students also demonstrated higher GPAs for the first two years of high school.

Service Learning

Schargel and Smink (2001) suggest that community service activities can be a promising addition to dropout prevention programs. When meaningful community service experiences can be connected to academic and personal supports, the experiences can simultaneously address the poor academic skills, peer difficulties, and lack of belonging that characterize students who drop out. The Coca-Cola Valued Youth Program (VYP) has used community service activities with demonstrated success in reducing school dropout among Latino students who speak English as their second language (Fashola & Slavin, 1998). The program recruited secondary students who were limited English proficient and at risk of dropping out of school and paid them to be tutors for elementary students. The paid tutors attended special classes, participated in field trips, were introduced to role models, and received recognition for their efforts. They were supported by an enriched curriculum, were taught effective tutoring strategies, and had their own academic progress closely monitored. The program also formed home-school partnerships to increase the level of support available to students in the program. The main evaluation of this program was carried out in four San Antonio, Texas, schools (Fashola & Slavin, 1998). After two years, students in the comparison group had a dropout rate of 12% whereas only 1% of those in VYP had dropped out. Additionally, VYP students achieved higher reading grades and showed significant gains in self-concept and school satisfaction relative to similar peers who were not in the program.

Effective Indicated Preventive Interventions

Prospects for reengaging students are not great once they are overage for their grades and have established longstanding patterns of self-doubt and alienation from academic goals (Alexander et al., 1997). Many recovery programs are predicated on substitution of a GED for a high school diploma, but some studies found that the outcomes for students who obtain GEDs without earning additional credentials are no better than for those who drop out of school without earning a GED (Cameron & Heckman, 1993). Alternatively, studies suggest that a GED may lead to more opportunities for additional job training and, when this occurs, benefits do accrue to those who have higher skills (Murname, Willett, & Boudett, 1995; Murname, Willett, & Tyler, 1999).

Successful indicated prevention programs are intensive, comprehensive efforts that are personalized, connect students to an attainable future, give students opportunities to work while in school, provide academic assistance, and give students high-status roles in the school (Fashola & Slavin, 1998). When life events pull students out of conventional high school programs, flexible scheduling or programming alternatives in the regular school (i.e., reduced day, credit for work, childcare programs) can help students through transitions. At the very least, students should be informed that they are welcome to come back to school and should be told who to contact to initiate their return.

High-Intensity Programming in the School

One promising example of an intensive support program was the Achievement for Latinos through Academic Success (ALAS) program (Rumberger & Larson, 1994). This program provided comprehensive support for the highest risk Latino youth. Participating students received the program for three years while enrolled in middle school (grades 7, 8, 9). Each ALAS student was assigned an advocate who worked directly with the student and also fostered and coordinated efforts of the school, family, and community to keep the student in school.

The ALAS program incorporated four strategies:

1. Social problem-solving training for students
2. Frequent teacher feedback to students and parents as well as intensive monitoring of attendance and class work
3. Links to community resources and training in school participation for families
4. Support for the delivery of appropriate, multiagency services to Latino families in the community

Students were randomly assigned to ALAS or to a no-treatment control group, and their school enrollment was carefully monitored throughout the program. As long as the program continued, the outcomes for ALAS students were remarkable. By the end of the ninth grade, 100% of the ALAS students were still in school compared to 83% of control students, and 79% of the ALAS students were on track to graduate in four years compared to 47% of the control group. At the end of the 10th grade, one year after the intervention ceased, 91% of the ALAS students were still in school compared to 69% of the control students. Unfortunately, the long-term outcomes were discouraging when only 34% of ALAS students and 26% of control students graduated after four years of high school (Rumberger & Larson, 1994). The authors suggest that the intervention might have been more successful if the support had continued throughout the high school years.

Alternative Schools

When conventional school settings seem inappropriate for students, alternative schools are offered as a method for obtaining a high school diploma.

Unfortunately, attendance at alternative schools generally does not result in lower dropout rates or increased learning (Dynarski & Gleason, 1998). Kelly's (1996) qualitative examination of three alternative schools showed that alternative schools are at risk for becoming second-chance programs that are also second rate. Students were frequently pressed to transfer to the alternative schools despite their own misgivings or those of their parents. Once there, insensitive policies around tardiness and preparation sometimes accelerated the rates of dropping out. Students who were most disengaged were sometimes encouraged to leave so that spaces could open up for more committed students. Finally, students complained that the alternative schools' more limited academic preparation constrained their careers and educational choices in the future. Transferring to the alternative school was a tacit admission of failure and, for many students, represented one more benchmark on their trajectory into leaving school.

Dynarski and Gleason (1998) found that alternative middle schools could be effective in promoting school completion when they featured smaller class size, occurred in more personalized settings, and focused on teaching and learning. Students who attended these schools showed higher rates of grade promotion and lower dropout rates than their matched peers who did not attend these alternative middle schools. One program in this study, Project ACCEL (Accelerating the Learning of At-Risk Student), was designed to allow previously retained students to rejoin their peers at the appropriate grade level through the provision of concentrated academic instruction. Project ACCEL sought to compress two years of middle school learning into one year with intensive training for teachers and strengthened parental involvement, community partnerships, and counseling services. Initial results were encouraging when students in the first cohort showed a dropout rate that was 19% lower than that of the control group. However, for the second cohort, the dropout rate was only 2% lower, an insignificant difference. Because both cohorts received identical programs of services, these results suggest that the program's effects are inconsistent, although promising (Dynarski, Gleason, Rangarajan, & Wood, 1998).

Dropout Retrieval Programs

Seattle's Middle College High School represented one of a small number of programs designed for dropout retrieval. The program was housed on a community college campus and was open to students who were not enrolled in high school. Applicants typically had failed at least two grade levels, had a history of poor school attendance, and many felt "too old" to attend regular high school (Houston, Byers, & Danner, 1992). An evaluation of the program found that Middle College students who had fewer than four academic risk factors were less likely to drop out and more likely to receive their high school diploma whereas similar students in the control group were more likely to receive GEDs (Dynarski et al., 1998). However, there was no difference in school completion rates for students with four or more risk factors. Across all students, 31% of the Middle College students completed high school after three years compared to 23% of the control group, but the difference was not statistically significant.

PRACTICE AND POLICY IMPLICATIONS

The size of the school dropout problem varies dramatically from one school district to another, depending on societal factors such as the proportion of poverty in the community, its ethnic and linguistic composition, and the geographic location of the school district. However, the severity of the dropout problem is universal across all states, all races, all languages, and all social classes: Students who do not complete high school are at very high risk to be underemployed in low-paying and uninteresting jobs that limit their economic security and that of their families and children. Given these high stakes, it is critically important that every community support locally appropriate school completion programs and policies. The responsibility for retaining students in school must stretch across grades and recognize that students' journeys into dropping out begin while they are infants, are evident in elementary school, intensify in middle school, and reach crisis proportions in high schools. Consequently, cross-grade collaborative teams should be responsible for defining the nature and extent of the dropout problem in the community and proposing culturally sensitive solutions that are compatible with the local values and expectations for schooling.

School completion is as much a community responsibility as it is a school responsibility, and the policies and practices that foster school completion cannot be exclusively educational. In the Jimerson et al. (2000) study, the quality of caretaking during infancy was a powerful predictor of school completion 18 years later. Their longitudinal study showed that when communities lack essential support services for disadvantaged families, they are predisposing disadvantaged children to higher rates of school failure. Consequently, communities must be encouraged to play their essential role in developing and providing programs that foster children's developmental success.

Defining the nature and extent of any community's dropout problem is impossible unless local school districts maintain accurate records of absences, school dropouts, and students who transition to alternative settings. As a solution, the NCES has proposed a common definition of *dropping out* and uniform conventions for keeping dropout statistics. These guidelines include counting students as dropouts who were enrolled in the previous year but are not enrolled by October 1 of the current year and who have not graduated from high school or completed a state- or district-approved educational program. Certain exclusionary clauses are also applied, including a statement that the student has not transferred, is not excused due to illness or suspension, and has not died. Unfortunately, only 22 states have adopted the NCES conventions (Schargel & Smink, 2001).

It is imperative that schools discontinue policies that are correlated with high rates of dropping out of high school. Punitive or insensitive policies for disciplinary suspensions, expulsions, or truancy may address schools' short-term need for a cooperative student body, but they have the paradoxical effect of pushing out students who are already at high risk for not completing school. Communities will carry the heavy burden of underemployment and economic dependence until school completion becomes a priority and increased incentives are provided for practices that *hold in* rather than *push out* students at the highest risk.

FUTURE DIRECTIONS

Future research must address the nation's urgent need for selective and indicated school completion programs whose effectiveness has been empirically tested in well-designed studies. Useful studies compare program participants with a control group, follow program participants across several years and through their scheduled graduation dates, and thoroughly examine school-leaving decisions with both quantitative and qualitative measures. Research needs to compare the benefits of competing programs for students; compare the relative benefit of providing programs at elementary, middle, and high school levels; and analyze benefits relative to the programs' financial and human costs. Those programs that are empirically supported must be easily accessible so that school and communities can find the tools to promote school completion in comprehensive and effective ways.

A special emphasis must be placed on understanding how to raise the school completion rates of immigrant, language minority students, and especially of Hispanic students. The country cannot afford to wait through two generations of acculturation until immigrant school completion rates rise of their own accord. In the current century, equitable access to the social and financial benefits of American citizenship is more closely linked to school completion than it has been during prior waves of immigration. Equity problems will not be solved by GED programs alone, but require that all groups have similar access to a high-quality high school education.

The utility of the GED requires further scrutiny. Conflicting research suggests that the GED alone does not lead to better employment opportunities or recognition for students, but the GED in combination with additional educational programs can provide students with a ticket into more secure futures. Additional research is required to ensure that GED-leading programs do not become broken promises for students that only perpetuate the inequities that already exist.

Finally, more attention should be paid to those students whose demographic characteristics place them at very high risk for dropping out of school, but who complete school nonetheless. The characteristics of students who are successful despite the odds could highlight the essential supports that act as protective factors for school completion. Once these protective factors are identified, planned programs can work to reinstate these supports in communities where they are missing and raise students' likelihood of success. Programs based on protective factors have the potential to be strength-based interventions that support school completion without labeling, tracking, and segregating those very populations that need support.

REFERENCES

Alexander, K. L., Entwisle, D. R., & Horsey, C. S. (1997). From first grade forward: Early foundations of high school dropout. *Sociology of Education, 70,* 87–107.

Baker, J. A., Derrer, R. D., Davis, S. M., Dinklage-Travis, H. E., Linder, D. S., & Nicholson, M. D. (2001). The flip side of the coin: Understanding schools' contribution to dropout and completion. *School Psychology Quarterly, 16,* 406–426.

Barclay, J. R. (1966). Sociometric choices and teacher ratings as predictors of school dropouts. *Journal of School Psychology, 4,* 40–44.

Barclay, J. R., & Doll, B. (2001). Early prospective studies of the high school dropout. *School Psychology Quarterly, 16,* 357–369.

Barnett, W. S. (1996). *Lives in the balance: Age-27 benefit-cost analysis of the High/Scope Perry Preschool Program* (Monographs of the High/Scope Educational Research Foundation No. 11). Ypsilanti, MI: High/Scope Press.

Cairns, R. B., Cairns, B. D., & Neckerman, H. J. (1989). Early school dropout: Configurations and determinants. *Child Development, 60,* 1437–1452.

Cameron, S. V., & Heckman, J. L. (1993). The nonequivalence of high school equivalents. *Journal of Labor Economics, 1,* 1–47.

Catterall, J. (1998). Risk and resilience in student transitions to high school. *American Journal of Education, 106,* 302–333.

Christenson, S. L., & Carroll, E. B. (1999). Strengthening the family school partnership through check and connect. In E. Frydenberg (Ed.), *Learning to cope: Developing as a person in complex societies* (pp. 248–273). New York: Oxford University Press.

Christenson, S. L., Sinclair, M. F., Lehr, C. A., & Godber, Y. (2001). Promoting successful school completion: Critical conceptual and methodological guidelines. *School Psychology Quarterly, 16,* 468–484.

Doll, B., & Hess, R. S. (2001). Through a new lens: Contemporary psychological perspectives on school completion and dropping out of high school. *School Psychology Quarterly, 16,* 351–356.

Dryfoos, J. G. (1990). *Adolescents at risk: Prevalence and prevention.* New York: Oxford University Press.

Dynarski, M., & Gleason, P. (1998). *How can we help? What we have learned from evaluations of federal dropout-prevention programs.* Princeton, NJ: Mathematica Policy Research. Available from http://www.mathematica-mpr.com/PDFs/dod-syn.pdf.

Dynarski, M., Gleason, P., Rangarajan, A., & Wood, R. (1998). *Impacts of dropout prevention programs: Final report.* Princeton, NJ: Mathematica Policy Research. Available from http://www.mathematica-mpr.com/PDFs/dod-fr.pdf.

Ekstrom, R. B., Goertz, M. E., Pollack, J. M., & Rock, D. A. (1986). Who drops out of high school and why? Findings from a national study. *Teachers College Record, 87,* 356–373.

Elias, M. J., & Clabby, J. F. (1992). *Building social problem-solving skills: Guidelines from a school-based program.* San Francisco: Jossey-Bass.

Fashola, O. S., & Slavin, R. E. (1998). Effective program prevention and college attendance programs for students placed at risk. *Journal for the Education of Students Placed at Risk, 3,* 159–183.

Fashola, O. S., Slavin, R. E., Calderon, M., & Duran, R. (2001). Effective programs for Latino students in elementary and middle schools. In R. E. Slavin & M. Calderon (Eds.), *Effective programs for Latino students* (pp. 67–100). Mahwah, NJ: Erlbaum.

Felner, R. D., Brand, S., Adan, A. M., Mulhall, P. F., Flowers, N., Sartain, B., et al. (1993). Restructuring the ecology of the school as an approach to prevention during school transitions: Longitudinal follow-ups and extensions of the School Transitional Environment Project (STEP). *Prevention in Human Services, 10,* 103–136.

Fernandez, R. M., Paulsen, R., & Hirano-Nakanishi, M. (1989). Dropping out among Hispanic youth. *Social Science Research, 18,* 21–52.

Fine, M. (1991). *Framing dropouts: Notes on the politics of an urban public high school.* Albany: State University of New York Press.

Finn, J. D. (1993). *School engagement and student at risk.* Washington, DC: National Center for Education Statistics.

Fitzsimmons, S. J., Cheever, J., Leonard, E., & Macunovich, D. (1969). School failures: Now and tomorrow. *Developmental Psychology, 1,* 134–146.

Garcia, E. E. (1991). Bilingualism, second language acquisition, and the education of Chicano language minority students. In R. R. Valencia (Ed.), *Chicano school failure and success: Research and policy agendas for the 1990s* (pp. 93–118). New York: Falmer Press.

Gleason, P., & Dynarski, M. (1998). *Do we know whom to serve? Issues in using risk factors to identify dropouts.* Princeton, NJ: Mathematica Policy Research. Available from http://www.mathematica-mpr.com/PDFs/dod-risk.pdf.

Hathaway, S. R., Reynolds, P. C., & Monachesi, E. D. (1969). Follow-up of the later careers and lives of 1,000 boys who dropped out of high school. *Journal of Consulting and Clinical Psychology, 33,* 370–380.

Hess, G. A., & Greer, J. L. (1987). *Bending the twig: The elementary years and dropout rates in the Chicago public schools.* Chicago: Chicago Panel on Public School Policy and Finance. (ERIC Document Reproduction Service No. ED287951)

Hess, R. S., & D'Amato, R. C. (1996). High school completion among Mexican American children: Individual and familial risk factors. *School Psychology Quarterly, 11,* 353–368.

Houston, A. V., Byers, S. M., & Danner, D. (1992). A successful alternative to traditional education: Seattle Middle College High School at Seattle Central Community College. *Journal of Negro Education, 61,* 463–470.

Jimerson, S., Egelund, B., Sroufe, L. A., & Carlson, B. (2000). A prospective, longitudinal study of high school dropouts: Examining multiple predictors across development. *Journal of School Psychology, 38,* 525–549.

Kaplan, D. S., Damphousse, K. R., & Kaplan, H. B. (1994). Mental health implications of not graduating from high school. *Journal of Experimental Education, 62,* 105–123.

Kaplan, D. S., Peck, B. M., & Kaplan, H. B. (1997). Decomposing the academic failure-dropout relationship: A longitudinal analysis. *Journal of Educational Research, 90,* 331–343.

Karweit, N. L. (1991). *Repeating a grade: Time to grow or denial of opportunity* (Report No. 16). Baltimore: Johns Hopkins University, Center for Research on Effective School for Disadvantaged Students.

Kelly, D. M. (1996). "Choosing" the alternative: Conflicting missions and constrained choice in a drop out prevention program. In D. Kelly & J. Gaskell (Eds.), *Debating dropouts: Critical policy and research perspectives on school leaving* (pp. 101–122). New York: Teachers College Press.

Klonsky, M. (1995). *Small schools: The numbers tell a story. A review of the research and current experiences.* Chicago: University of Chicago. (ERIC Document Reproduction Service No. ED386517)

Kohl, G. O., Lengua, L. J., & McMahon, R. J. (2000). Parent involvement in school: Conceptualizing multiple dimensions and their relations with family and demographic risk factors. *Journal of School Psychology, 38,* 501–523.

Kraemer, H. C., Kazdin, A. E., Offord, D. R., Kessler, R. C., Jensen, P. S., & Kupfer, D. J. (1997). Coming to terms with the terms of risk. *Archives of General Psychiatry, 54,* 337–343.

Kubitschek, W. N., & Hallinan, M. T. (1998). Tracking and students' friendships. *Social Psychology Quarterly, 61,* 1–15.

MacIver, D. J., & Epstein, J. L. (1991). Responsive practices in the middle grades: Teacher teams, advisory groups, remedial instruction, and school transition programs. *American Journal of Education, 99,* 587–622.

Murname, R. J., Willett, J. B., & Boudett, K. (1995). Do high school dropouts benefit from obtaining a GED? *Educational Evaluation and Policy Analysis, 17,* 133–147.

Murname, R. J., Willett, J. B., & Tyler, J. (1999). Who benefits from obtaining a GED? Evidence from high school and beyond. *Review of Economics and Statistics, 82,* 23–37.

National Center for Educational Statistics. (2002). *Dropout rates in the United States: 2000.* Washington, DC: U.S. Department of Education.

National Research Council. (2001). *Understanding dropouts: Statistics, strategies, and high-stakes testing.* Washington, DC: National Academy Press.

Nelson, J. R., Martella, R. M., & Marchand-Martella, N. (2002). Maximizing student learning: The effects of a comprehensive school-based program for preventing problem behaviors. *Journal of Emotional and Behavioral Disorders, 10,* 136–148.

Oetting, E. R., & Beauvais, F. (1990). Adolescent drug use: Findings of national and local surveys. *Journal of Consulting and Clinical Psychology, 58,* 385–394.

Peña, D. C. (2000). Parent involvement: Influencing factors and implications. *Journal of Educational Research, 94,* 42–54.

Persaud, D., & Madak, P. R. (1992). Graduates and dropouts: Comparing perceptions of self, family, and school supports. *Alberta Journal of Educational Research, 38,* 235–250.

Raywid, M. A. (1996). *Taking stock: The movement to create mini-schools, schools-within-schools, and separate small schools.* Madison, WI: Center on Organization and Restructuring of Schools. (ERIC Document Reproduction Service No. ED393958)

Roderick, M. (1993). *The path to dropping out: Evidence for intervention.* Westport, CT: Auburn House.

Roderick, M. (1994). Grade retention and school dropout: Investigating the association. *Journal of Educational Research, 31,* 729–757.

Rumberger, R. W. (1995). Dropping out of middle school: A multilevel analysis of students and schools. *American Educational Research Journal, 32,* 583–625.

Rumberger, R. W., Ghatak, R., Poulos, G., Ritter, D. L., & Dornbusch, S. M. (1990). Family influences on dropout behavior in one California high school. *Sociology of Education, 63,* 283–299.

Rumberger, R. W., & Larson, K. A. (1994). Keeping high-risk Chicano students in school: Lessons from a Los Angeles middle school dropout prevention program. In R. J. Rossi (Ed.), *Schools and students at risk: Context and framework for positive change* (pp. 141–162). New York: Teachers College Press.

Schargel, F. P., & Smink, J. (2001). *Strategies to help solve our school dropout problem.* Larchmont, NY: Eye on Education.

Schreiber, D., Kaplan, B. A., & Strom, R. D. (1965). *Dropout studies: Design and conduct.* Washington, DC: National Education Association.

Sinclair, M. F., Christenson, S. L., Hurley, C., & Evelo, D. (1998). Dropout prevention for high-risk youth with disabilities: Efficacy of a sustained school engagement procedure. *Exceptional Children, 65,* 7–21.

U.S. Department of Education. (1990). *National goals for education* (Publication No. 455-B-2). Washington, DC: U.S. Government Printing Office.

Velez, W., & Saenz, R. (2001). Toward a comprehensive model of the school leaving process among Latinos. *School Psychology Quarterly, 16,* 445–467.

Wassef, A., Mason, G., Collins, M. L., O'Boyle, M., & Ingham, D. (1996). In search of effective programs to address students' emotional distress and behavioral problems: Part III. Student assessment of school-based support groups. *Adolescence, 31,* 1–16.

Wehlage, G. G., Rutter, R. A., Smith, G. A., Lesko, N., & Fernandez, R. R. (1989). *Reducing the risk: Schools as communities of support.* New York: Falmer Press.

Chapter 18

CHILD MALTREATMENT

BARBARA THOMLISON

Child abuse and neglect is a serious public health problem, and the need to identify and apply preventive interventions is urgent. Although the incidence rate of child abuse is 10 times higher than all forms of cancer, child maltreatment is not viewed by policymakers as seriously as other health epidemics; consequently, it receives significantly less attention and economic recognition at all levels (Sadler, Chadwick, & Hensler, 1999). There has been considerable progress in prevention science over recent decades that benefits children and families; however, more research is needed to extend and further refine effective intervention strategies. Based on a growing understanding of the consequences of maltreatment and the risk and protective factors associated with child abuse and neglect, a set of prevention approaches that work are identified (Thomlison, 2004). Implemented during early childhood, these family-centered and multi-component strategies improve the health-related behaviors of maltreated children and parental caretaking practices of targeted populations. Family factors play a central role in child maltreatment, as well as a protective role in the child's developmental outcome. Data show that interventions targeted at the earliest signs of risk factors benefit parenting practices and, when parenting practices improve, child outcomes improve.

This chapter summarizes findings from well-established programs of research that exemplify both the progress and current approaches to child maltreatment using universal, selective, and indicated preventive interventions. The selected exemplary program interventions impacted child maltreatment problems in a positive way. Each of the interventions:

1. Are based on published findings from studies that employed either a representative community sample or a clinical sample with an appropriate control group,

2. Clearly defined the type of maltreatment targeted by the intervention, and
3. Described the intervention in adequate detail to permit replication.

In some cases, a treatment manual is available. With perhaps the exception of the Nurse-Family Partnership (Olds, 2002) program, which is grounded in epidemiology and theories of development and has produced enduring and replicated effects, none of the programs are in a position to provide larger scale intervention implementation for the greater public health impact. To the extent possible, the studies are organized by the guidelines proposed by the Institute of Medicine (Mrazek & Haggerty, 1994) using three categories:

1. *Universal preventive interventions* target the general public or an entire population of interest (e.g., childhood immunizations, media-based parenting information campaign).

2. *Selective preventive interventions* target subgroups of the general population who are at higher risk for developing a problem than other members of the broader population (e.g., folic acid for women of child-bearing age, information and advice for specific parenting of child's behavior or development concerns).

3. *Indicated preventive interventions* target individuals who have detectable signs or symptoms of difficulty, but not longstanding serious problems or full-blown clinical disorders (e.g., parent education and skills training for children with multiple behavior problems or aggressive behavior or learning delays).

This chapter presents the trends and incidence of maltreatment, summarizes the risk and protective factors, summarizes the intervention studies, and presents the policy and practice implications.

TRENDS AND INCIDENCE

After increasing in the early 1990s, the estimated number of children who were victims of abuse and neglect declined from one million in 1994 to an estimated 879,000 in 2000. Neglect consistently accounts for most (62.8%) of the substantiated cases of maltreatment; 19.3% were physically abused and 10.1% were sexually abused; and combinations of neglect, abuse, and additional types of maltreatment account for the remaining 7.8%. Most children, however, suffered from more than one form of maltreatment (U.S. Department of Health and Human Services [USDHHS], 2001).

Victims

The rate of substantiated victimization declined from 15.3 per 1,000 children in the child population in 1993 to 13.8 per 1,000 children in 1997, further declined through 1999 to 11.8 per 1,000 children, and then increased to 12.2 per 1,000 children in 2000 (USDHHS, 2001). Rates were similar for male and female victims—11.2 and 12.8 per 1,000 children, respectively, except for sexual abuse where the rate for victims was 1.7 per 1,000 female children compared to 0.4 per 1,000 male children. In 1999, the victimization rate for child neglect (including medical neglect) was 6.9 per 1,000 children; for physical abuse, the rate was 2.5 children per 1,000; and the rate for sexual abuse was 1.3 per 1,000 children (p. 22). More than half of all victims were White (50.6%), a quarter (24.7%) were African American, and a sixth (14.2%) were Hispanic. Children who had been victimized in a prior year were more than three times as likely to experience recurrence compared to children without a history of victimization.

Perpetrators

Women were responsible for 59.9% of all physical abuse incidences, and parents committed the majority of all abuse types (USDHHS, 2001). Children placed in foster care were 20% more likely to experience abuse and neglect than children who remained with their families.

Fatalities

Child deaths are the most reliable indicator of the level of child maltreatment in a population, and changes in the child death rate between 1993 and 2000 have slightly increased. Three or more children die each day from maltreatment, and rates are highest for the youngest children (ages 0 to 6), who comprise 86% of these deaths (USDHHS, 2001). In addition, 43% of all child maltreatment-related fatalities occurred during the first year of life; these fatalities are more often associated with neglect. Fatalities from maltreatment in 1993 resulted in a rate of 1.62 per 100,000 children (Sedlak & Broadhurst, 1996), and in 2000, 1,200 children died from child maltreatment, yielding an increasing maltreatment fatality rate of 1.71 per 100,000 children (USDHHS, 2001, p. 42). Approximately 2.7% of child fatalities occurred in foster care.

Poverty

Impoverished families continue to be overrepresented in the child maltreatment statistics. Children from families with annual incomes below $15,000 as compared to children from families with annual incomes above $30,000 per year were more than 22 times likely to be injured from maltreatment (Sedlak & Broadhurst, 1996). Children from the lowest income families were 18 times more likely to be sexually abused and almost 56 times more likely to be educationally neglected (Sedlak & Broadhurst, 1996). Experts suggest that race, culture, and ethnicity are not directly related to rates of child maltreatment (Korbin, 1994, p. 195); however, racism and other discriminatory experiences may exacerbate risk factors for abuse and neglect (Chaffin, Kelleher, & Hollenberg, 1996; Kendall-Tackett & Eckenrode, 1996; Schumacher, Smith Slep, & Heyman, 2001).

CONCEPTUAL UNDERPINNINGS

Recognition of the constructs and conceptual underpinnings of child maltreatment is important to implementing interventions. Two key constructs or areas provide the foundation of the interventions: the definition of child maltreatment and developmental psychopathology for identifying specific child maltreatment risk and protective factors linked to development of psychopathology in children (Rutter, 2000).

Definition of Maltreatment

The major types of abuse identified in the literature are physical abuse, neglect, inadequate supervision, emotional/verbal abuse, sexual abuse, as well as educational and medical neglect. Increasing attention has focused on related risky parental behaviors and specific forms of maltreatment such as shaken baby syndrome, child exposure to parental violence, sibling abuse, and Munchausen syndrome by proxy; similarly, the literature indicates these situations involve complex discrete processes (USDHHS, 2001). Across countries and cultures, definitions of maltreatment vary, and the criteria for substantiation of maltreatment are often open to interpretation and public debate, complicated by the fact that many children are victims of multiple forms of abuse and neglect.

There are no consensus definitions to identify child maltreatment. Although the *Diagnostic and Statistical Manual of Mental Disorders* (*DSM-IV*, American Psychiatric Association [APA], 1994) provides a diagnostic V code (V61.21) for physical abuse of child, sexual abuse of child, and neglect, there is no diagnostic code for emotional abuse. Studies of conceptual definitions of maltreatment (Korbin, Coulton, Lindstrom-Ufuti, & Spilsbury, 2000; Portwood, 1999) determined that although there are some differences in legal definitions, neighborhood populations, professionals, and scholars assume a shared definitional catalogue of abuse and neglect behaviors and adopt a working definitional consensus as those acts of commission or omission by parents or responsible caregivers that result in or pose substantial risk of injury or harm to a child (Korbin et al., 2000; Portwood, 1999). Other sources provide fully developed discussions of the definition of maltreatment (see Coulton, Korbin, Su, & Chow, 1995; Korbin, 1994; Korbin, Coulton et al., 2000).

Risk and Protective Factors

Research from developmental etiology identifies specific child maltreatment risk and protective factors linked to child outcomes. *Biopsychosocial risk and protective factors* refers to the range of individual, parent, family, and environmental factors that interact to influence the onset, development, and maintenance of child maltreatment behaviors within the context of various life settings (Hansen, Sedlar, & Warner-Rogers, 1999; Mrazek & Haggerty, 1994; Rutter, 2000; Thomlison, 1997). It is a complex and dynamic set of processes, not an individual trait or characteristic. A risk factor is an influence associated with an increased vulnerability for a negative developmental outcome. Some risk factors are causally related to negative outcomes, whereas others simply represent correlates, sometimes called markers, of potential negative outcomes. Risk factors often occur together or cluster to produce heightened susceptibility for maltreatment and, as the number of risk factors increases, the cumulation exerts an increasingly strong influence on children. Fraser, Kirby, and Smokowski (2004, p. 21) state "The concept of risk is continually being refined. It is widely agreed that different types of risk exist, including individual and contextual risks plus stressful life events. Understanding risk is further complicated by related concepts, such as cumulative risk, risk chains, and risk mechanisms. What is clear is that risk is probabilistic, meaning that children exposed to risk factors are more likely to experience negative outcomes. It is equally certain that some children who are exposed to a high level of risk manage to overcome the odds (Rutter, 2001; Werner & Smith, 1992). They are resilient."

Protective factors are recognized as personal attributes and environmental assets and as both internal and external resources that modify risk. Table 18.1 shows specific risk and protective factors associated with maltreatment by source or system level from a review of research. (For a review of the risk and protective factors, see Thomlison, 2004, and for an excellent discussion of risk and resilience concepts and processes, see Fraser et al., 2004.)

The goal of the intervention is to reduce the effect of the targeted risk factors (Fraser & Galinsky, 1997). Risk factors provide *points of entry* for the assessment process, as well as focus, to maximize treatment effectiveness. Whereas

Table 18.1   Risk and Protective Factors for Child Maltreatment

Individual Child Risk and Protective Factors

Risk Factors	Protective Factors
Poor infant attachment to mother	Outgoing or easy temperament
Poor child health/medical disorder	Affectionate
Developmental difficulties	Positive or secure attachment to mother
Premature birth or complications	Active and alert
Difficult temperament, behavior, and mood	Good nutrition and health care
Cognitive impairment	Quality consistent child care
Low intellect	Low distress
	Advanced self-help skills
Child Competencies	
Lack of a positive and healthy adult model	*Child Competencies*
Early educational failure	Developmentally competent
Negative peer role models	Educational achievement
Poor adult supervision	Normal/above-average intelligence and
Poor problem-solving skills	language skills
	High sociability
	High cognitive functioning
	Self-efficacy/perception of competence
	High self-esteem
	Gets along with both children and adults
	Competent problem-solving skills
	Sense of belonging and security
	Gets along with adults and children
	Has external sources of support

Parent and Family Risk and Protective Factors

Risk Factors	Protective Factors
Parent Life and Stress	*Parent Life and Stress*
Inadequate housing	Supervision, routines, and rituals
Inadequate material resources	Family and marital harmony
Prolonged economic distress	Family cohesiveness
Employment stress or unemployment	Positive and caring family interactions
Rapid and stressful life changes	Economic security
Single parent	Employment consistency
High levels of conflict or violence	
Threats of separation/divorce	*Parent Competencies*
Large number of children	Available in times of stress
	History of good parenting
Parent Disorder	Psychological well-being of parents
Parent with substance abuse	Competence in roles and responsibilities
Parent with mental disorder/depression	Satisfaction in parenting role
Parent with antisocial behavior	High self-esteem
Poor reasoning and problem-solving skills	Provides positive adult model
Unrealistic expectations	Provides supervision of child
Poor emotional control	

Table 18.1   *Continued*

Parent and Family Risk and Protective Factors	
Risk Factors	Protective Factors
Parent Disorder (Continued)	*Family Social Support*
Low warmth	Emotional closeness with family and friends
Low nurturing skills	Good social skills
High criticism	Social support network of family and friends
Use of harsh, inconsistent discipline	Positive marital support
Family Social Support	
Excessive reliance on others	
Isolation	
Lack of support from others	
Marital/relationship discord	
Parent Experiences	
Distorted perception of history of care	
Lack of emotional closeness with child	
Limited positive family interactions	

Community and Environmental Risk and Protective Factors	
Risk Factors	Protective Factors
Social Cultural Environment	*Social Cultural Environment*
Inaccessible or unaffordable health and child care	Many positive adult and peer role models
High levels of neighborhood crime/violence	Stable and cohesive neighborhood
Reduced or negative neighboring interactions	Strong informal networks of social support
Social disintegration or disorganization	Access to health, education, and support services
Social intolerance or discrimination	Safe community
Socially impoverished community	Good schools and teachers
Exposure to environmental toxins	

Source: From "Child Maltreatment: A Risk and Protective Factors Perspective" (pp. 26–27), by B. Thomlison, in *Risk and Resilience in Childhood: An Ecological Perspective* (2nd ed.), by M. W. Fraser (Ed.), 2003, Washington, DC: NASW Press. Reprinted with permission.

many children exposed to maltreatment show no obvious clinical dysfunction on standardized tests, some may indicate considerable variability in severity of clinical dysfunction, and others are symptom free as is often true in sexual abuse (Kolko, 1992). The term *risk* reflects this uncertainty; therefore, it is not possible to affect all risk conditions at the same time, and, consequently, interventions target the most readily modifiable risk conditions at the same time as strengthening protective factors. As shown in Table 18.1, risk factors overlap and vary in influence, but the goal of intervention efforts is to reduce the effect of the specifically targeted risk factors, noting that intervention strategies do not affect all risk conditions (Fraser & Galinsky, 1997).

To prevent the initial occurrence of maltreatment or to prevent future reabuse, interventions should be configured to intervene as early as modifiable risk factors can be clearly identified. To the extent that they are malleable, risk factors are addressed using developmentally appropriate, culturally sensitive multilevel intervention approaches. (For a more complete discussion of the theoretical constructs and processes of risk and resilience development, see Fraser, 2003; Fraser & Galinsky, 1997; and Fraser et al., 2004.) Interventions identified in this chapter distinguish abuse-specific interventions and apply this ecological-developmental framework using the risk and protective factor perspective. Too few attempts are made to prevent child maltreatment, even though family-focused selective and indicated preventive interventions implemented during early childhood show promising results. A family focused preventive approach is a philosophy, not a method of intervention, where the family strengths and protective factors are identified and developed in partnership with the family and then used to solve child and family problems.

UNIVERSAL PREVENTIVE INTERVENTIONS

Large-scale universal interventions targeted to the general public and focused on child maltreatment prevention with rigorous research are difficult to identify. Although many good family support and parenting skills programs exist and rigorous intervention outcome research studies have demonstrated success in reducing or curtailing parent-child problem behaviors and enhancing parental social and emotional competencies for lowering the risk for adverse mental health outcomes, none are scaled to large populations or embedded in nationwide service programs (Hawkins et al., 1992; Mrazek & Haggerty, 1994; Olds, 2002; Spoth, Kavanagh, & Dishion, 2002). Science-driven practice is available, but there are major challenging tasks that make offering universal interventions in child maltreatment difficult, particularly through the existing service systems and policies.

Research of parenting enhancement and parent support programs coordinated through information campaigns using print and electronic media and other health promotion strategies to raise awareness of parenting issues and normalize participation in parenting programs are available. Such programs need to be embedded in policy and other service systems to raise awareness of resources and participation (Sanders, Turner, & Markie-Dadds, 2002). Health research on changing health risk behaviors among the population suggests these approaches are effective, but both policy and political support are required for responsive implementation.

Promising program leads exist for sexual abuse preventive interventions. For example, the Who Do You Tell? Child Sexual Abuse Education Program was designed to teach elementary school-age children basic concepts to prevent and protect themselves from sexual assault. The program is designed for grades K through 2, grades 3 and 4, and grades 5 and 6, each with developmentally specific curriculum. The program has had an impact on level of knowledge about sexual abuse, but there is no evidence it reduced the number of children exposed to or experiencing sexual abuse (Tutty, 1997, 2000). Future research on sexual abuse preventive intervention recommends expanding the abuse-specific concepts taught to children to include teaching skills to communicate and approach trusted adults with uncomfortable experiences (Tutty, 2000). The development, evaluation, and dissemination of preventive intervention strategies that could move beyond clinical trials to address the broader ecological and organizational context need to be examined more thoroughly. Researchers and practitioners need to advocate for evidence-based prevention initiatives that can influence funding priorities.

SELECTIVE PREVENTIVE INTERVENTIONS

Selective interventions target only those individuals or families at the highest risk as members of at-risk subgroups. Interventions at this system level are longer in length, and often involve parent and child and attempt to reduce empirically established risk factors such as psychosocial environmental risk factors. Empirically based programs in this category follow.

The Incredible Years Training Series

This program is a series of three comprehensive, multilevel, and developmentally based curriculums for parents, teachers, and children. The series is implemented as a selective and indicated program (Webster-Stratton, 1990, 1998a, 1998b, 2000, 2001).

Program Target Population

Children ages 2 to 8 at risk for and/or presenting conduct problems defined as aggression, defiance, oppositional, and impulsive behaviors are the target population. In addition, the intervention focus is high-risk children in Head Start settings and elementary children (up to grade 3) as an indicated intervention for problem behaviors, often exacerbated by transitional points in development such as starting school.

Risk Factors Addressed

Multiple risk factors related to conduct-disordered behaviors, across settings, are targeted. Problem behaviors that place children at risk include aggressive behavior, social skill deficits, and achievement difficulties such as early reading problems. Interventions aim to promote emotional and social competence so that children are ready to learn and to achieve success in school. The goal is to prevent, reduce, and treat behavior and emotional problems in young children in the environment of the child—at home and school.

Program Summary

The Incredible Years Training series has been field-tested in six randomized trials in various settings with Head Start and other diverse and low-income families over the past 18 years (Sanders et al., 2002; Webster-Stratton, 2001). Translated into several languages, this manualized parenting skills program for both parents and teachers uses trained facilitators, videotapes with 250 vignettes to stimulate group discussion and problem-solving behavior, and home visiting to focus on managing common child problems. Cognitive and social learning interventions are used to teach parents and teachers about positive, nonviolent discipline methods and supportive parenting approaches to promote children's self-confidence, prosocial behaviors, and academic success.

There are three components to the curriculum: (1) BASIC, (2) ADVANCE, and (3) SCHOOL. The core program, BASIC, the prevention component, is the parent training program targeting parents of high-risk children and/or those displaying behavior problems. The BASIC program includes promoting positive play, clear limit setting, helping children learn, using praise and encouragement, providing incentives to motivate children, and handling misbehavior. There are two versions of the BASIC program: one for parents of young children 2 to 7 years and one for parents of school-age children 5 to 12 years. The second component, the ADVANCE parent-training program, is for families with children 4 to 10 years. This is an indicated intervention supplement to the BASIC training addressing other family risk factors such as depression, marital discord, poor coping skills, poor anger management, and lack of support. The EDUCATION or SCHOOL parenting program supplements either the early childhood or school-age BASIC program by focusing on ways to advance children's academic competence as well as promoting strong connections between home and school. Parents are taught strategies to strengthen their children's reading and academic skills, increase parent and teacher positive communication, and develop routines for homework and collaborative relationships with the school.

The teacher training program has been evaluated in two independent, randomized control studies with Head Start teachers, as well as with teachers of students in kindergarten through third grade. Skills addressed include classroom management skills such as effective use of teacher attention, praise, and encouragement; use of incentives for difficult behavior problems; proactive teaching strategies; managing inappropriate classroom behavior, as well as developing positive relationships with students; and teaching empathy, social skills, and problem solving in the classroom (Webster-Stratton, 1998a, 1998b, 2001).

Program Outcomes

Six randomized control group studies (Webster-Stratton & Hammond, 1997; Webster-Stratton & Taylor, 2001) of the parenting series indicated significant increases in parental positive affect such as praise and reduced use of criticism and negative comments. Further, there were increases in improved limit setting, decreased use of spanking and harsh discipline, and increased monitoring of children. Positive family communication and problem solving also occurred. Two randomized control studies of the child training series indicated significant improvement in social skills, positive conflict management with peers, decreased aggression, and improved academic skills. Reductions in conduct problems at school and home occurred. Two randomized control group studies of the teacher training series indicated significant increase in teacher use of praise and encouragement and reduced use of criticism and harsh discipline. Increased use of positive interactions with peers, teachers, and others and school readiness and engagement with school activities were significant (Webster-Stratton & Taylor, 2001). Results indicate that children's problem behaviors decrease while social competence and academic engagement are increased. Finally, combining parent and child training was more effective than parent training alone. Both were superior to a control condition.

Webster-Stratton (personal communication, 2001) indicates that child maltreatment occurred or was a risk factor for many of the families and children in the studies. Increasing evidence from parenting and family support outcome studies (Sanders et al., 2002; Webster-Stratton & Taylor, 2001) indicates that low school performance and conduct disorders are related, and both are related to the same child and family risk factors for maltreatment discussed earlier in this chapter. Finally, it is not entirely clear whether the Incredible Years Training Series prevents child maltreatment, but it improves parenting skills and reduces children's aggression with peers and teachers and decreases conduct problems at home and in school settings—factors that place children at high risk of maltreatment (Thomlison, 2004).

The Nurse-Family Partnership

This comprehensive program is a family-centered, home-based intervention focused on maternal and child health and development (previously named Nurse Home Visitor Program; Olds, 2002; Olds et al., 1997).

Program Target Population

The Nurse-Family Partnership program has been implemented as a selective intervention program targeted to low-income, first-time young mothers and their babies through prenatal and infancy and continuing through the child's second birthday.

Risk Factors Addressed

Risk factors addressed include geographical areas with high poverty and maltreatment rates, maternal and prenatal health behaviors, parental caretaking, family management practices, and economic deprivation.

Program Summary

The Nurse-Family Partnership program provides counseling, family planning, parenting education, nutrition, and substance abuse information. Careful attention is paid to following protocols to ensure that nurses implement the program with fidelity although they can adapt the home visit guidelines to each family's strengths and needs. Nurses receive extensive training and technical assistance throughout the two years. The family receives weekly visits during the first month of enrollment, every other week throughout a woman's pregnancy, weekly visits for the first six weeks postpartum, and every other week thereafter through the child's 21st month. In the final three months, they visit monthly until the child reaches age 2. Service targets the caregiver-child relationship process with teaching mother-child attachment or relational behaviors, consistent feeding and child care, infant-toddler stimulation, and home management (Carnegie Task Force on Meeting the Needs of Young Children, 1994; Olds, 2002).

Program Outcomes

Since 1977, the program has undergone three field studies (Olds, 2002) with two studies conducted as large-scale randomized controlled trials with different populations in different environmental contexts. The young women came from a wide range of backgrounds: 45% were Hispanic, 34% were White, 16% were African American, 4% were Native American, and 1% were Asian. Outcomes from the two randomized trials and a 15-year follow-up showed that participants had a 43% reduction in subsequent pregnancies, 83% increase in the rates of labor force participation by the child's first birthday than the control group, and 80% fewer verified cases of child abuse and neglect than their counterparts in the control groups through the child's second year. There were 32% fewer visits to the emergency department, a difference that was explained by a 56% reduction in visits for injuries and ingestions compared to the control group. Nurse-visited mothers had significantly fewer beliefs about child-rearing that were associated with child abuse and neglect (such as lack of empathy, belief in physical punishment, unrealistic expectations of infants) than the control group. Nurses were more likely than paraprofessionals to retain contact with the mother and complete the program through the second year of the child's life. Many other beneficial functional and economic effects of the program were found in the studies (Olds, 2002). The program benefits are greatest for families at greatest risk (Guterman & Embry, 2004; Olds, 2002).

Selected 15-year evaluation findings found children of the mothers in the treatment group had sustained benefits over the children in the control group, including significantly fewer arrests, convictions, violations of probation, and less alcohol use (Olds et al., 1999, 2002; Olds et al., 1997). Findings suggest that, to prevent child maltreatment, comprehensive home-based interventions that both monitor parents and provide support and skills training need to be introduced early during pregnancy and followed with regular and intense services in the postpartum period (Kendall-Tackett & Eckenrode, 1996; Kitzman, 1997; Olds & Kitzman, 1993; Olds et al., 1997, 1999). A cost benefit analysis through the 15-year follow-up found that for high-risk families, there is an overall savings of more than four times the cost of the program ($24,694; Olds, 2002). The program is most effective for first-time mothers who exhibited multiple risk factors. The program is currently being replicated in more than 20 states.

INDICATED PREVENTIVE INTERVENTIONS

Indicated preventive programs are designed to address the multiple risk factors in individual families identified with problems. These preventive programs are more intrusive, provide longer interventions and can involve multiple components. These are strategies and programs, which have been shown through substantial research and evaluation to be effective at preventing and/or delaying problems and risk factors.

Resilient Peer Training Intervention

This indicated school-based intervention enhances the social competence of maltreated preschool children (Fantuzzo, Sutton-Smith, Atkins, & Meyers, 1996; Fantuzzo, Weiss, & Coolahan, 1998).

Program Target Population

The program targets vulnerable, low-income, maltreated preschool children and families in high-risk urban environments. Interventions are provided in therapeutic day care of Head Start classrooms.

Risk Factors Addressed

Social interactional skills are targeted in physically abused and neglected preschool children who are at higher than average risk for maladaptive social functioning to improve social and emotional competence.

Program Summary

The focus of the program is to promote early positive peer relationships among high-risk preschoolers and families who experienced physical abuse and neglect. Resilient peers are identified; teachers and parent volunteers enhance the development of social and emotional competencies of the children. Children engage in 20 play sessions of activities over an eight-week period. In therapeutic preschool or Head Start classroom environments, parent helpers at the beginning of each session orient a resilient peer to the play area activities and identify successful play encounters with the withdrawn, maltreated, and poorly functioning child. Intervention techniques include following simple instructions, pictorial prompts, task analyses, modeling, rehearsal, role playing, feedback, token economies, behavioral contracting, and positive reinforcement to teach new skills.

Program Outcomes

Using an experimental design to study the effectiveness of resilient peer training for 46 children, this study found significant improvements in positive peer interaction, decreases in social isolation, and trends toward reducing aggression in maltreated children at treatment completion and at two-month follow-up when compared to a randomly assigned control group (Corcoran, 2000a, 2000b, 2000c; Fantuzzo et al., 1998; Webster-Stratton & Taylor, 2001). The play interventions compared the effects of adult and peer social initiation for withdrawn neglected children and physically abused children. All children responded more positively to peer-initiated interactions, which resulted in significant increase in positive social behaviors across various home and school settings. Physically aggressive abused children showed a preference for the adults and initiated play with them more frequently. Positive peer interventions promoted prosocial behavior, positive self-concepts, and cognitive development in maltreated and neglected children.

Homebuilders

Homebuilders (English, 1999; Fraser, Nelson, & Rivard, 1997; Fraser, Pecora, & Haapala, 1991; Kinney, Haapala, & Booth, 1991) is a home-based, family-centered crisis intervention and parent education program designed to improve the functioning of families and prevent the unnecessary placement of children out of their homes to state care (Staudt & Drake, 2002).

Program Target Population

Families whose children are at risk for out-of-home placement into foster care, group care, or other psychiatric or correctional institution and whose children may be at subsequent risk for the onset of mental disorders because of their behavior problems and/or maltreatment are the target population.

Risk Factors Addressed

Designed to prevent out-of-home placement and reduce the risk for child maltreatment, service targets parent skills and other factors parents need to take care of their children at home.

Program Summary

Homebuilders is one of several intensive family preservation service models (Tracy, Haapala, Kinney, & Pecora, 1991). The goal of the Homebuilders program is to help families of troubled children remain at home by offering time-limited— as brief as four to six weeks in duration—and intensive services. Using a blend of clinical and material services, the caseworker is available for face-to-face contact 8 to 10 hours per week and 24 hours a day during the contact period by telephone. Case management and service coordination are the primary methods of delivering service focused on the risk factors. Service varies significantly but often focuses on parenting skills, anger management, and the family crisis. A family systems theory approach, behavioral management techniques, and concrete services directed to the family's needs are used to protect children, improve parent and family functioning, maintain the child in the family home, and moderate the impact of abuse and neglect. Treatment components are primarily cognitive-behavioral and matched to identified problem areas.

Program Outcomes

Research studies (Corcoran, 2000c; Fraser et al., 1997; Lindsey, Martin, & Doh, 2002; Staudt & Drake, 2002) observed that the multiservice approaches of

Homebuilders appeared beneficial in improving parent-child relationships and family functioning compared to control group families. Additionally, using meta-analytic methods, Corcoran (2000c) reported modest, but statistically significant, differences in rates of postservice maltreatment referrals for the Homebuilders in-home services group (21.3%) compared to a standard child protective services group (28.5%). Services in the short term reduced risk of out-of-home placement, stabilized families in crisis, and developed family competencies and supports. Findings using home-based family preservation services in juvenile justice programs are positive whereas the studies of the effectiveness of in-home family preservation approaches in child welfare population are mixed, suggesting that for younger children, intervention needs to focus on specific child maltreatment risk factors and that services of greater duration may be needed (for a review, see Fraser et al., 1997). Evaluations of families completing Homebuilders programs indicated fewer children (6%) compared to control families (16.5%) entered out-of-home placement and the families had improved their social support networks, reduced family conflict, and strengthened family bonding. At follow-up 12 months after service, placement rates were 42.7% for the treatment group and 56.7% for the control group. Although these rates suggest that the service is effective in the short term with less impressive results in the long term (Mrazek & Haggerty, 1994), Fraser et al. (1997) suggest it is premature to make conclusions other than that family preservation services are equivocal. Researchers (Fraser et al., 1997; Littell & Schuerman, 2002) recommend future studies to obtain more specific information about the characteristics and problems of families and to develop guidelines to match families and services. Families receiving Homebuilders' intervention are often receiving other services and continue to need more service after the Homebuilders program is complete. For example, interventions need to be consistent with knowledge of child maltreatment risk factors, including poverty and domestic violence, which are serious risk factors for a host of other problems, and then matched to needs of the family (Staudt & Drake, 2002).

Early Intervention Foster Care

Early Intervention Foster Care (EIFC) is an intense and comprehensive treatment program for seriously maltreated children and their families in a community context of special foster care placement (Fisher & Chamberlain, 2000; Fisher, Ellis, & Chamberlain, 1999).

Program Target Population

Young abused and neglected children (3 to 7 years) in protective services custody, their parents, and foster parents are the target population.

Risk Factors Addressed

Early Intervention Foster Care addresses biological and foster parenting practices to reduce the cognitive, social, emotional, and developmental delays associated with child maltreatment and to improve parenting techniques.

Program Summary

Abused and neglected children in need of protective custody are placed with foster treatment parents in special foster family-based homes. The treatment foster parents receive intensive and extensive parent management training and supervision. A manualized, extensively researched, parent management training (PMT) model is used, and trained helpers take on a consulting role to the child's parents and foster parents. A working alliance with the child's family that is supportive and constructive is developed before introducing parent-training techniques. As the parent learns particular skills—first in office-based treatment sessions, then in the home—practice of skills occurs. Supervised visits with the child at the treatment center begin, and visits are lengthened with eventual transition to the family home. Treatment of the child occurs simultaneously in the treatment foster care home. Interventions with the child focus on the development of emotional regulation capabilities, and, as needed, other consequences of maltreatment such as social skills competence and behavioral change are addressed. Treatment foster parents receive extensive support through daily telephone contacts, guidelines and protocols for tracking the child's behavior and progress, and attending weekly support groups. Techniques found to be effective in changing child behaviors and social and emotional competence include intense and close supervision of children, the use of contracts and rewards for prosocial behaviors, behavioral reinforcement, time out, and limit setting (Chamberlain & Reid, 1991; Patterson, Reid, & Dishion, 1992). The same parent management techniques are taught to parents, who begin to practice the skills during child visits. Services are delivered by a multidisciplinary team, which may include parents, teachers, foster parents, family therapists, and others necessary for the treatment of the child and family. The therapist remains in contact with the family up to three months after the child is reunified.

Program Outcomes

Pilot study results compared 30 substantiated maltreated children in protective custody in three different parenting environments: specialized foster care, regular foster care, and a comparison community sample. In Early Intervention Foster Care, the specialized treatment foster parents showed higher levels of consistent discipline, had greater and consistent monitoring of the child's whereabouts, and provided positive reinforcement methods superior to regular foster care parents or the community comparison group of children. Children in regular foster care were more similar to the community comparison group. Outcome analyses revealed a positive impact of the specialized foster parents' parenting strategies on the child. Emotional regulation and responses to stress (impacted by maltreatment) improved in the EIFC group of children as early as three weeks of treatment and continued throughout the 12-week treatment. This research suggests the possibility of bringing about physiological changes related to emotion regulation through an environmental intervention as assessed in the study.

Addressing some of the limitations of the pilot study, such as small sample size and sufficient follow-up period, a new longitudinal study with 180 maltreated children is currently in progress. Preliminary evidence suggests that EIFC may be an effective approach to the treatment of seriously maltreated children in a community context while appearing to hold promise for reducing the cognitive, social, emotional, and developmental delays associated with child maltreatment. Moreover, the program appears to promote the development of stable, safe foster and home placements (Fisher & Chamberlain, 2000; Fisher et al., 1999; Meadowcroft, Thomlison, & Chamberlain, 1994).

Parent-Child Education Program for Physically Abusive Parents

Parent-Child Education is an in-home or clinic-based parenting enhancement intervention to establish positive parent-child interactions and supportive child-rearing methods (Wolfe, 1987, 1994, 2001; Wolfe, Edwards, Manion, & Koverola, 1988; Wolfe & Sandler, 1981).

Program Target Population

Parents who use power-assertive methods, such as verbal and physical abuse, that can turn into maltreatment, and their preschool children are targeted.

Risk Factors Addressed

Parent-child relationships and child behavior and cognitive skill development are the risk factors addressed.

Program Summary

The goals of Parent-Child Education for physically abusive parents is to strengthen the parent-child relationship process, improve parental ability to cope with stress, and teach parents effective child-rearing methods based on practical applications of social learning principles. Education and guidance are provided in a flexible format and responsive to the needs of the family and children on a weekly basis for 4 to 12 months with follow-up, which may occur up to two years. Three intervention components to the program are:

1. Teaching parents methods for enhancing parental sensitivity to the child's social and emotional needs

2. Teaching parents how to set reasonable expectations for children's social, emotional, and behavioral development

3. Teaching parents anger control and effective discipline strategies

Procedures such as modeling, practice, rehearsal, and feedback (verbal and video-taped) are provided to promote skill enhancement—to teach the use of nonviolent discipline methods, self-control, and ways to access community resources.

Program Outcomes

The intervention was evaluated in three studies (Wolfe, Sandler, & Kaufman, 1981; Wolfe et al., 1988, 1992). The control group received parenting information only from the protection agency, and the treatment group received the same information plus behavioral parent support training. At the end of one year, the parent-training group was associated with reductions in child problems and improved child management skills, and none of the treated families had been reported or suspected of abuse at one-year follow-up (Lyons, 1998; Wolfe, 1987, 1994). Subsequent maltreatment rates were not reported for the control group (Wolfe, 1987, 1994). Outcome results have indicted that parent training is effective in reducing negative parent and child behaviors, although questions remain whether it is an effective intervention for child neglect.

Multisystemic Family Treatment

Multisystemic Family Treatment (MST) is a comprehensive family therapy treatment approach that targets child behavior problems in the family and the systemic context of families (Henggeler, Schoenwald, Borduin, Rowland, & Cunningham, 1998).

Program Target Population

The population target group is school-age maltreated children and their parents, who had been investigated for abuse or neglect.

Risk Factors Addressed

Poor anger management, substance abuse, and limited parenting skills, including child monitoring, are the risk factors the intervention addresses.

Program Summary

Behavior is viewed as multidetermined; therefore, multisystemic interventions focus on various system levels (e.g., family, peer, school, community) to address the problem behaviors and the interactions that influence or maintain problems. Present-focused and action-orienting interventions that have empirical support are used to target risk factors (e.g., cognitive-behavioral techniques for anger management and parenting). MST is an intensive, in-home, family-based treatment originally designed to improve antisocial behavior of juvenile offenders and their families. MST interventions use reframing, joining, and tasks aimed at restructuring the family system to improve interactions and functioning. In addition, parent education, information about parent-child expectations, marital therapy, advocacy, coaching, and emotional support are delivered in the home or other settings such as the school or community. Youth and their families are expected to learn how to function more effectively in their natural environment if they are to sustain improvements after treatment concludes. Service lasts four to six months and involves several hours of contact per week. Treatment manuals or protocol descriptions are required in addition to the essential use of well-trained master-level therapists who receive extensive supervision.

Program Outcomes

Originally developed to address antisocial youth behavior, MST shows highly promising results for other serious problems. Eight randomized clinical trials with youth and their families, most in field settings, have been published (Henggeler, Melton, Brondino, Scherer, & Hanley, 1997; Henggeler et al., 1999), and, in comparison with control groups, MST has consistently demonstrated improved parenting practices, family relations, and family functioning; improved school attendance; decreased drug use; 25% to 70% decrease in long-term rates of rearrest; and 47% to 64% decrease in long-term rates of days in out-of-home placements. To date, there is only one randomized study with 43 families comparing the effectiveness of MST to parent training with abusive and neglectful families on individual functioning, family relations, and stress/social support (Brunk, Henggeler, & Whelan, 1987).

Both treatment groups showed decreased parental psychiatric symptoms, reduction in stress, and an improvement in individual and identified family problems. Multisystemic Family Treatment was superior to parent training for improving parent-child interactions associated with maltreatment. Parents receiving MST showed greater progress in controlling their child's behavior, maltreated children showed less passive compliance, and neglecting parents became more responsive to their children. Parent training was superior to MST on one measure of change—decreased social isolation and improved social support, which is likely attributed to the group context of parent training.

Although parent training is an effective treatment for many parent-child problems (Gershater-Molko, Lutzker, & Sherman, 2002), multisystemic intervention may provide the flexibility maltreating families need and provide it in their own homes. Finally, this study did not report follow-up period and rates of maltreatment for the control group as well as the MST group (Brunk et al., 1987). Findings suggest that MST may also be useful in working with abusive families, but it is important to replicate the studies, separate the abuse and neglect families, and report maltreatment rates in follow-up. Multisystemic Family Treatment is currently being tested specially with physically abusive families in a randomized trial (Saunders, Berliner, & Hanson, 2001).

Family Connections Intervention

Family Connections is a community based family focused and early intervention approach to child neglect prevention. The program promotes the safety and well-being of children and families by identifying and developing formal and informal supports to meet each family member's individual needs building on their strengths (http://www.family.umaryland.edu, contact D. DePanfilis; U.S. Department of Health and Human Services, 2003).

Program Target Population

Family Connections targets at-risk families with children ages 5 to 11 years who are considered at risk of child abuse and neglect but have no child protection services involvement.

Risk Factors Addressed

Risk factors addressed included parent-child relationships, parental depression, and child behavioral problems. Family Connections addresses risk factors by reducing family conflict, reducing social isolation, and reducing caregiver mental and physical health problems.

Program Summary

The Family Connections intervention builds on principles from what is known about what works with high-risk families: community outreach, family assessment, and customized interventions. There are three essential elements to service: emergency assistance, family assessment, and social support.

Program Outcomes

The intervention was evaluated using an experimental pre- and post-design with a comparison group of families who received a shorter period of services (U.S. Department of Health and Human Services, 2003; www.calib .com/nccanch/prevention/emerging/report.pdf). There were two intervention groups: three months of services compared to nine months of service and random assignment to intervention groups. There were 26 outcome measures used and the sample size was 1,154 caregivers and 473 children. The findings suggest the Family Connections can: increase the protective factors for child neglect; decrease the risk factors for child neglect and reduce the incidents of child abuse and neglect; and increase child safety and well-being (http://www .family.umaryland.edu).

Project 12 Ways

Project 12 Ways is a comprehensive multicomponent intervention for families of neglected children to enhance environments and social supports (Gershater-Molko & Lutzker, 1999; Gershater-Molko, Lutzker, & Wesch, 2002; Lutzker, Bigelow, Doctor, & Kessler, 1998).

Program Target Population

This program targets parents and children of substantiated child neglect to improve behavioral problems and developmental delays of children by improving child-care and parenting practices.

Risk Factors Addressed

Child-care needs and parent-child interaction are addressed through parenting enhancement interventions.

Program Summary

Project 12 Ways is a multifaceted intervention with the goal of improving three elements—child health, home safety, and parent-child interactions—for complex and difficult families with substantiated neglect. Using a practical and direct teaching approach, Planned Activities Training (PAT), parents learn to structure activities and child-care skills. Interventions include parent-child training, stress reduction, self-control, social support, health and nutrition information, and job placement (Lutzker & Rice, 1984). Marital counseling, financial planning, home health, and similar concerns are addressed using paraprofessionals, such as neighbors, child-care practitioners, and volunteers, to provide help in the home based on the needs of parents and children.

Program Outcomes

In a quasi-experimental (without random assignment) evaluation of Project 12 Ways, 352 neglectful families received 12 Ways treatment and 358 neglectful families received routine services. At one-year follow-up, families from Project 12 Ways were less likely to be reported for child abuse or neglect (21.3%) than comparison families (28.5%) as noted in the Child Abuse Registry (Lutzker & Rice, 1987). Project 12 Ways reports success at improving several aspects of family environmental conditions associated with child neglect.

Social Support Network Intervention

Social Support Network Intervention aims to reduce social isolation for families of neglect (Gaudin, Wodarski, Arkinson, & Avery, 1990/1991; Lutzker et al., 1998; Webster-Stratton, 1998a, 1998b).

Program Target Population

Families of neglect are the target population.

Risk Factors Addressed

Social isolation is the key risk factor addressed.

Program Summary

The program goal is to increase the level of informal social support for families with the intent of improving personal and social resources for parenting. Strengthening parental and family support networks is thought to reduce stress and isolation, while increasing control over the environment and providing resources for dealing with children's behavior problems (Bronfenbrenner, 1986; Clark & Clarke, 1996; Garbarino & Kostelny, 1992, 1994; Gaudin et al., 1990/1991).

Program Outcomes

Gaudin et al. (1990/1991) randomly assigned a culturally diverse sample of substantiated families of children with neglect from child protective service caseloads to either services as usual (36 families) or to a multicomponent intervention group (52 families). The multicomponent intervention consisted of family support networking, a mutual aid group, social skills training, and assistance from volunteers and neighbors. Interventions ranged in duration from 10 weeks to 23 months of services. The intensive social network interventions were successful in strengthening the informal networks and improving parenting adequacy at 6- and 12-month follow-up. Nearly 60% of the treatment families had their cases closed, and 80% of families who received more than nine months of treatment improved significantly on measures of parenting adequacy. Subsequent neglect is not reported in the study, and there is limited information about the efficacy of social network interventions in general. Nevertheless, there are currently few empirical studies with this population despite the documented consequences of long-term neglect on children's cognitive, social, developmental, and psychological development.

Trauma-Focused Cognitive-Behavioral Therapy

Trauma-Focused Cognitive-Behavioral Therapy is an abuse-informed therapy to treat negative emotional and behavioral responses and correct maladaptive beliefs and attributions related to abusive sexual experiences while providing support and skills to nonoffending parents to respond positively to their child (Cohen & Mannarino, 1993, 1997; Deblinger, Steer, & Lippmann, 1999).

Program Target Population

Sexually abused children experiencing abuse trauma symptoms and their parents are targeted.

Risk Factors Addressed

Abuse trauma symptoms are the target and include negative emotional and behavioral responses, irrational or maladaptive beliefs and attributions of the child, and parental emotional distress.

Program Summary

Targeted to child and parent, this cognitive abuse-informed intervention consists of six components:

1. Education about sexual abuse
2. Facilitation of the abuse-related feelings
3. Identifying and correcting distorted or maladaptive cognitions
4. Teaching anxiety management skills
5. Teaching self-protection skills
6. Interventions directed at managing problematic behaviors associated with abuse

Cognitive-behavioral interventions for the child focus on the conditioned emotional associations to memories and reminders of the abuse, distorted cognitions about the event(s), and negative attributions about self, others, and the world (Cohen & Mannarino, 1997). Nonoffending parents are taught:

1. To be supportive,

2. To reduce their own stress, and

3. Cognitive-behavioral strategies to manage the child's reactions.

Individual, family, and group sessions over 12 to 16 weeks are conducted in office and school settings.

Educational and cognitive strategies for the child and parent include psychoeducation about child abuse and typical reactions; safety skills and health sexuality; gradual exposure techniques including verbal, written, and/or symbolic recounting of the abusive event; cognitive reframing of inaccurate attributions about the cause of, responsibility for, and results of the abusive experience; stress management techniques such as muscle relaxation exercises; and thought stopping. Parents engage in a parallel process and then in conjoint sessions with the child. In addition, parents receive coping and parenting skills training to improve their communication and interactions with their children, thereby reducing children's behavioral and emotional difficulties.

Program Outcomes

At posttreatment, improvements of sexually abused children's externalizing behavior improved (56% were in the normal range compared with 22% of those in the comparison group), and depression and posttraumatic stress disorder (PTSD) decreased; these improvements were maintained over a two-year followup. Parenting practices also maintained effectiveness over the two-year followup (Deblinger et al., 1999), indicating strong support for the long-term effectiveness of cognitive-behavioral interventions for sexually abused children. The maintenance of treatment gains over two years is particularly meaningful given the often chronic and recurring issues associated with PTSD and sexual abuse symptoms. A treatment manual is available (Deblinger & Heflin, 1996). There is some evidence that programs that offer support to parents and children simultaneously are more beneficial than a focus on either the child or parent. Cognitive-behavioral therapy receives strong empirical support for intervention with sexually abused children and their parents (Cohen & Mannarino, 1997; Deblinger et al., 1999).

PRACTICE AND POLICY IMPLICATIONS

Treatment efficacy studies have identified useful interventions for reducing and preventing recurring child maltreatment during early childhood. Interventions using family-centered approaches for enhancing caregiving practices and targeting skills and behaviors, particularly in the parent-child communications that benefit ongoing social and cognitive development of the child, are most effective. However, from a research perspective, no treatment is fully validated, and there are inevitable questions raised about these interventions and the population characteristics that may make the treatment more or less effective than others. All interventions related to child maltreatment must first ensure the safety of the child, including those in out-of-home placements, and address child health for development as well as education to improve child outcomes. Practice initiatives derived from research studies, therefore, should be monitored carefully, to the extent possible, to ensure that at-risk children do not face further harm. Some of the practice lessons learned from these studies follow.

Timing of Interventions

There is strong evidence that many child and family risk factors must be addressed early and immediately using high-quality preventive efforts and family approaches to improve parenting practices and the family environment. The timing of the reduction of risk factors may be the most critical factor addressed by these programs. If the number of protective factors can be increased in the child and family, resilience is likely to be increased and further risk avoided.

The Setting

Home-based interventions have been demonstrated to meet diverse needs of maltreating families and families at risk of maltreating, especially where interventions incorporated a combination of behavioral interventions targeting multiple factors, including family support. Further, services can effectively be provided to maltreated children in child-care settings but must combine both parent group activities and parent involvement. Effective interventions focus also on parents' and teachers' strengths (not deficits) and are sensitive to low-income and culturally diverse families. In-home services that target and support skill-based parenting practices during home visits contribute to the quality of the parent-child relationship and may act as a protective strategy to enhance high-risk children's academic needs so they are successful in school, as well as in their social and emotional lives (Stormshak, Kaminski, & Goodman, 2002).

Abuse-Specific Interventions

Interventions with maltreated children are most successful when the sequelae of abuse are specifically targeted (Macdonald, 2001). Some behavior problems are common among maltreated children, although they can have other etiologies. Behavior problems are present in about one-third of sexually abused children, and physically abused children often exhibit aggression and anger control problems (Saunders et al., 2001). To address these common problems, interventions that focus on parent skills and training are supported—teaching cognitive, behavioral, and affective competencies, especially when tailored to the family's needs and cultural values (Daro & Cohn-Donnelly, 2002). Family involvement is essential and perhaps the single most important social-environmental influence on children's behaviors. Family-focused strategies appear to be more effective than either child-focused or parent-focused approaches. Child-only approaches, not combined with parenting or family approaches, may negatively affect family functioning. The next most promising strategies involve creating collaborative efforts with parents, teachers, and others in the community. Interventions must target the abuse-specific risk factors if they are to be effective, enhance protection, and promote resilience (Fraser & Galinsky, 1997).

FUTURE DIRECTIONS AND CHALLENGES

Interventions identified here are not an exhaustive list and, as a group, these interventions should be regarded with caution until there is substantial and well-established evidence of potential efficacy. In addition, few evaluations of intervention strategies have assessed the implementation of programs, that is, whether the programs were carried out correctly. This factor is important because, if programs are not implemented as designed, program designers and practitioners cannot know whether the program intended is really the program that was implemented and evaluated. On the whole, there is a shortage of data-driven treatment strategies to improve the effects of child maltreatment (American Psychological Association, 1995; Saunders et al., 2001).

Although the outcome studies presented here suggest that maltreated children can benefit from a range of interventions, few studies have provided long-term results to make definitive conclusions with perhaps the exception of the Nurse-Family Partnership Program (Olds, 2002) and Cognitive-Behavior Therapy for Sexual Abuse (Cohen & Mannarino, 1996; Deblinger, Steer, & Lippmann, 1999). Most intervention programs for the treatment of abuse and neglect focus on treating parents; few offer direct therapeutic interventions to children. Questions need to be asked about the efficacy of the many parenting enhancement programs in communities where parents are referred for interventions. The interventions identified here are model programs, and it may be that community-based parenting programs are not as intensive and systematically delivered as those identified here. Interventions vary in length, and short-term inventions may produce time-limited benefits as found in reviews of effectiveness of preventive programs for mental disorders in school-age children (Greenberg, Domitrovich, & Bumbarger, 2001).

Child maltreatment researchers may benefit from research findings in other areas. For example, early childhood literature may contribute to understanding the maltreatment process. More work needs to focus on the enhancement of parent-child relationships during the preschool years, which appears to act as one of the more important factors in protecting children from maltreatment and in creating resilience in children who have been victimized. The developmental psychopathology research literature is also fruitful. Although a caring adult remains critical as a child reaches school age, other processes become important in shaping the child, giving the child a positive sense of worth, and creating a resilient developmental pathway. Identifying effective interventions for very young children and their families may moderate risk in the early years, but there is a need to understand family and social relationships for school-age and adolescent children who are maltreated. The link between internal and external familial supports and school and social relationships is not well understood in terms of the processes that influence resilience to maltreatment.

Finally, there is great need for studies to use randomized trials that compare routine child welfare services to new models of service. Child welfare agencies have been reluctant to engage in rigorous research, and they have rarely had resources to fund early intervention. But the outcomes of existing services are sufficiently poor in some—not all—states, so routine services should not be regarded as a standard for ethical practice (Lindsey et al., 2002). The research reviewed here suggests that much can and should be done, and it may be unethical to fail to engage in developing and testing new services. This research is suggestive at best, and follow-up data are lacking. Where promising findings exist, there is a need to disentangle the elements of programs that may be more or less effective. Problems such as poverty, substance abuse, and maternal depression remain significant risk factors for child maltreatment, particularly neglect, and no intervention studies address these in the context of child welfare services. Little research attention is given to neglect. Optimally, addressing these challenges will build on a series of intervention efforts that can be directed to one of the most serious public health problems. The types of interventions represented in these studies can advance the preventive efforts of child maltreatment so that eventually large-scale implementation efforts to targeted risk populations can contribute to an inventory of preventive interventions and greater public health impact.

REFERENCES

American Psychiatric Association. (1994). *Diagnostic and statistical manual of mental disorders* (4th ed.). Washington, DC: Author.

American Psychological Association. (1995). Training in and dissemination of empirically validated psychological treatments: Report and recommendations. *The Clinical Psychologist, 48*(1), 3–23.

Bronfenbrenner, U. (1986). Ecology of the family as a context for human development research perspectives. *Developmental Psychology, 22,* 723–742.

Brunk, M., Henggeler, S. W., & Whelan, J. P. (1987). A comparison of multisystemic therapy and parent training in the brief treatment of child abuse and neglect. *Journal of Consulting and Clinical Psychology, 55,* 311–318.

Carnegie Task Force on Meeting the Needs of Young Children. (1994). *Starting points: Meeting the needs of our youngest children.* New York: Carnegie Corporation of New York.

Chaffin, M., Kelleher, K., & Hollenberg, J. (1996). Onset of physical abuse and neglect: Psychiatric, substance abuse, and social risk factors from prospective community data. *Child Abuse and Neglect, 20*(3), 191–203.

Chamberlain, P., & Reid, J. B. (1991). Using a specialized foster care treatment model for children and adolescents leaving the state mental hospital. *Journal of Community Psychology, 19,* 266–276.

Clark, H. B., & Clarke, R. T. (1996). Research on the wraparound process and individualized services for children with multisystem needs. *Journal of Child and Family Studies, 5,* 1–5.

Cohen, J. A., & Mannarino, A. P. (1993). A treatment model for sexually abused preschoolers. *Journal of Interpersonal Violence, 8,* 115–131.

Cohen, J. A., & Mannarino, A. P. (1997). A treatment study of sexually abused preschool children: Outcome during a one year follow-up. *Journal of the Academy of Child and Adolescent Psychiatry, 36*(9), 1228–1235.

Corcoran, J. (2000a). Family treatment with child abuse and neglect. In J. Corcoran (Ed.), *Evidence-based social work practice with families* (pp. 3–75). New York: Springer.

Corcoran, J. (2000b). Family interventions with child physical abuse and neglect: A critical review. *Children and Youth Services Review, 22,* 563–591.

Corcoran, J. (2000c). Family treatment with child maltreatment using family preservation approaches. In J. Corcoran (Ed.), *Evidence-based social work practice with families* (pp. 76–123). New York: Springer.

Coulton, C. J., Korbin, J. E., Su, M., & Chow, J. (1995). Community level factors and child maltreatment rates. *Child Development, 66,* 1262–1276.

Daro, D., & Cohn-Donnelly, A. (2002). Charting the waves of prevention: two steps forward, one step back. *Child Abuse & Neglect, 26,* 731–742.

Deblinger, E., & Heflin, A. H. (1996). *Treating sexually abused children and their nonoffending parents.* Thousand Oaks, CA: Sage.

Deblinger, E., Steer, R., & Lippmann, J. (1999). Two-year follow-up study of cognitive behavioral therapy for sexually abused children suffering posttraumatic stress symptoms. *Child Abuse & Neglect, 23*(12), 1371–1378.

English, D. (1999). *Family preservation services and intensive family preservation services evaluation progress report.* Office of Children's Administration Research, State of Washington.

Fantuzzo, J., Sutton-Smith, B., Atkins, M., & Meyers, R. (1996). Community-based resilient peer treatment of withdrawn maltreated preschool children. *Journal of Clinical and Consulting Psychology, 64,* 1377–1368.

Fantuzzo, J., Weiss, A., & Coolahan, K. (1998). Community-based partnership-directed research: Actualizing community strengths to treat victims of physical abuse and neglect. In R. J. Lutzker (Ed.), *Child abuse: A handbook of theory, research, and treatment* (pp. 1213–1238). New York: Pergamon Press.

Fisher, P. A., & Chamberlain, P. (2000). Multidimensional treatment foster care: A program for intensive parenting, family support, and skill building. *Journal of Emotional and behavioral Disorders, 8*(3), 155–164.

Fisher, P. A., Ellis, B. H., & Chamberlain, P. (1999). Early intervention foster care; a model for preventing risk in young children who have been maltreated. *Children's Services: Social Policy, Research, and Practice, 2*(3), 159–182.

Fraser, M. W. (Ed.). (2003). *Risk and resilience in childhood: An ecological perspective* (2nd ed.). Washington, DC: National Association of Social Workers Press.

Fraser, M. W., & Galinsky, M. J. (1997). Toward a resilience-based model of practice. In M. W. Fraser (Ed.), *Risk and resilience in childhood. An ecological perspective* (pp. 265–275). Washington, DC: National Association of Social Workers Press.

Fraser, M. W., Kirby, L. D., & Smokowski, P. R. (2004). Risk and resilience in childhood. In M. W. Fraser (Ed.), *Risk and resilience in childhood. An ecological perspective* (2nd ed., pp. 13–16). Washington, DC: National Association of Social Workers Press.

Fraser, M. W., Nelson, K. E., & Rivard, J. C. (1997). Effectiveness of family preservation services. *Social Work Research, 21,* 138–153.

Fraser, M. W., Pecora, P. J., & Haapala, D. A. (1991). *Families in crisis: The impact of intensive family preservation services.* New York: Aldine de Gruyter.

Garbarino, J., & Kostelny, K. (1992). Child maltreatment as a community problem. *Child Abuse and Neglect, 16,* 455–464.

Gaudin, J. M., Wodarski, J. S., Arkinson, M. K., & Avery, L. S. (1990/1991). Remedying child neglect: Effectiveness of social network interventions. *Journal of Applied Social Science, 15,* 97–123.

Gershater-Molko, R. M., & Lutzker, J. (1999). Child neglect. In R. T. Ammerman & M. Hersen (Eds.), *Assessment of family violence. A clinical and legal sourcebook* (2nd ed., pp. 157–183). New York: Wiley.

Gershater-Molko, R. M., Lutzker, J., & Sherman, J. (2002). Intervention in child neglect: An applied behavioral perspective. *Aggression and Violent Behavior, 7,* 103–124.

Gershater-Molko, R. M., Lutzker, J., & Wesch, D. (2002). Using recidivism data to evaluate Project Safecare: Teaching bonding, safety, and health care skills to parents. *Child Maltreatment, 7,* 277–285.

Greenberg, M. T., Domitrovich, C., & Bumbarger, B. (2001). Effectiveness of prevention programs for mental disorders in school-age children. In C. Newman, C. Liberton, K. Kutash, & R. M. Friedman (Eds.), *The 13th annual Research Conference Proceedings, A System of Care for Children's Mental Health: Expanding the research base* (pp. 179–181). Tampa: University of South Florida, The Louis de la Parte Florida Mental Health Institute, Research and Training Center for Children's Mental Health.

Guterman, N. B., & Embry, R. A. (2004). Prevention and treatment strategies targeting physical child abuse and neglect. In P. Allen-Meares & M. Fraser (Eds.), *Intervention with children and adolescents: An interdisciplinary perspective* (pp. 130–158).

Hansen, D. J., Sedlar, G., & Warner-Rogers, J. E. (1999). In R. T. Ammerman & M. Hersen (Eds.), *Assessment of family violence. A clinical and legal sourcebook* (2nd ed., pp. 127–156). New York: Wiley.

Hawkins, J. D., Catalano, R. F., Morrison, D. M., O'Donnell, J., Abbott, R. D., & Day, L. E. (1992). The Seattle Social Development Project: Effects of the first four years on protective factors and problem behaviors. In J. McCord & R. E. Tremblay (Eds.), *Preventing antisocial behavior* (pp. 139–161). New York: Guilford Press.

Henggeler, S. W., Melton, G., Brondino, M., Scherer, D., & Hanley, J. (1997). Multisystemic therapy with violent and chronic juvenile offenders and their families: The role of treatment fidelity in successful dissemination. *Journal of Consulting and Clinical Psychology, 65,* 821–833.

Henggeler, S. W., Rowland, M. D., Randall, J., Ward, D., Pickrel, S., Cunningham, P. B., et al. (1999). Home-based multisystemic therapy as an alternative to the hospitalization of youths in psychiatric crisis: Clinical outcomes. *Journal of the American Academy of Child and Adolescent Psychiatry, 38,* 1331–1339.

Henggeler, S. W., Schoenwald, S. K., Borduin, C. M., Rowland, M. D., & Cunningham, P. B. (1998). *Multisystemic treatment of antisocial behavior in children and adolescents.* New York: Guilford Press.

Kendall-Tackett, K., & Eckenrode, J. (1996). The effects of neglect on academic achievement and disciplinary problems: A developmental perspective. *Child Abuse and Neglect, 20,* 161–171.

Kinney, J. M., Haapala, D., & Booth, C. L. (1991). *Keeping families together: The Homebuilders model.* New York: Aldine de Gruyter.

Kitzman, H. (1997). Effects of prenatal and infancy home visitation by nurses on pregnancy outcomes, childhood injuries, and repeated childbearing: A randomized controlled trial. *Journal of the American Medical Association, 278,* 644–652.

Kolko, D. (1992). Characteristics of child victims of physical violence: Research findings and clinical implications. *Journal of Interpersonal Violence, 7*(2), 244–276.

Korbin, J. (1994). Sociocultural factors in child maltreatment. In Melton, G. B., & Barry, F. D. (Eds.), *Protecting children from abuse and neglect. Foundations for a new national strategy* (pp. 182–223). New York: Guilford Press.

Korbin, J., Coulton, C., Lindstrom-Ufuti, H., & Spilsbury, J. (2000). Neighborhood views on the definition and etiology of child maltreatment. *Child Abuse & Neglect, 24,* 1509–1527.

Lindsey, D., Martin, S. K., & Doh, J. (2002). The failure of intensive casework services to reduce foster care placements; an examination of family preservation studies. *Children and Youth Services Review, 24,* 743–775.

Littell, J. H., & Schuerman, J. R. (2002). What works best for whom? A closer look at intensive family preservation services. *Children and Youth Services Review, 224,* 673–699.

Lutzker, J. R., Bigelow, K. M., Doctor, R. M., & Kessler, M. L. (1998). Safety, health care, and bonding, within an ecobehavioral approach to treating and preventing child abuse and neglect. *Journal of Family Violence, 13,* 163–185.

Lutzker, J. R., & Rice, J. M. (1984). Project 12 Ways: Measuring outcome of a large in-home service for treatment and prevention of child abuse and neglect. *Child Abuse and Neglect, 8*(4), 519–524.

Lutzker, J. R., & Rice, J. M. (1987). Using recidivism data to evaluate Project 12 Ways: An ecobehavioral approach to the treatment and prevention of child abuse and neglect. *Journal of Family Violence, 2,* 283–290.

Lyons, P. (1998). Child maltreatment. In J. S. Wodarski & B. A. Thyer (Eds.), *Handbook of empirical practice: Social problems and practice issues* (Vol. 2, pp. 33–53). New York: Wiley.

Macdonald, G. (2001). *Effective interventions for child abuse and neglect: An evidence-based approach to planning and evaluating interventions.* New York: Wiley.

Meadowcroft, P., Thomlison, B., & Chamberlain, P. (1994). Treatment foster care services: A research agenda for child welfare [Special issue]. *Child Welfare, 73*(5), 565–581.

Mrazek, P. J., & Haggerty, R. J. (Eds.). (1994). *Reducing risks for mental disorders. Frontiers for preventive intervention research.* Washington, DC: National Academy Press.

Olds, D. L. (2002). Prenatal and infancy home visiting by nurses: From randomized trials to community replication. *Prevention Science. (3)*2, 153–172.

Olds, D. L., Eckenrode, J. J., Henderson, C. R., Kitzman, H. J., Powers, J., Cole, R., et al. (1997). Long-term effects of home visitation on maternal life course and child abuse and neglect: Fifteen-year follow-up of a randomized trial. *Journal of the American Medical Association, 278,* 637–643.

Olds, D. L., Henderson, C. R., Kitzman, H. J., Eckenrode, J. J., Cole, R. E., & Tatelbaum, R. C. (1999). Prenatal and infancy home visitation by nurses: Recent findings. *The Future of Children, 9,* 44–65.

Olds, D. L., & Kitzman, H. J. (1993). Review of research on home visits for pregnant women and parents of young children. *The Future of Children* (Center for the Future of Children), *3,* 53–92.

Patterson, G. R., Reid, J. B., & Dishion, T. J. (1992). *A social learning approach: IV. Antisocial boys.* Eugene, OR: Castalia.

Portwood, S. (1999). Coming to terms with a consensual definition of child maltreatment. *Child Maltreatment, 4,* 56–68.

Rutter, M. (2000). Resilience reconsidered: Conceptual considerations, empirical findings, and policy implications. In J. P. Shonkoff & S. J. Meisels (Eds.), *Handbook of early childhood intervention* (2nd ed., pp. 651–683). New York: Cambridge University Press.

Sadler, B. L., Chadwick, D. L., & Hensler, D. J. (1999). The summary chapter—The national call to action: Moving ahead. *Child Abuse & Neglect, 23,* 1011–1018.

Sanders, M. R., Turner, K. M., & Markie-Dadds, C. (2002). The development and dissemination of the Triple P-Positive Parenting Program: A multilevel, evidence-based system of parenting and family support. *Prevention Science, 3*(3), 173–189.

Saunders, B. E., Berliner, L., & Hanson, R. F. (2001, July 30). *Guidelines for the psychosocial treatment of intrafamilial child physical and sexual abuse* (Final draft report). Charleston, SC: Authors.

Schumacher, J. A., Smith Slep, A. M., & Heyman, R. E. (2001). Risk factors for child neglect. *Aggression and Violent Behavior, 6,* 231–254.

Sedlak, A. J., & Broadhurst, D. D. (1996). *Third national incidence study of child abuse and neglect: Final report.* Washington, DC: U.S. Department of Health and Human Services.

Spoth, R. L., Kavanagh, K. A., & Dishion, T. J. (2002). Family-centered preventive intervention science: Toward benefits to larger populations of children, youth, and families. *Prevention Science, 3*(3), 145–152.

Staudt, M., & Drake, B. (2002). Research on services to preserve maltreating families. *Children and Youth Services Review, 24,* 645–652.

Stormshak, E. A., Kaminski, R. A., & Goodman, M. R. (2002). Enhancing the parenting skills of Head Start families during the transition to kindergarten. *Prevention Science, 3*(3), 223–233.

Thomlison, B. (1997). Risk and protective factors in child maltreatment. In M. W. Fraser (Ed.), *Risk and resilience in childhood: An ecological perspective* (pp. 50–72). Washington DC: National Association of Social Workers Press.

Thomlison, B. (2004). Child maltreatment: A risk and protective factor perspective. In M. W. Fraser (Ed.), *Risk and resilience in childhood: An ecological perspective* (2nd ed., pp. 89–131). Washington, DC: National Association of Social Workers Press.

Tracy, E. M., Haapala, D. A., Kinney, J., & Pecora, P. J. (Eds.). (1991). *Intensive Family Preservation Services: An instructional sourcebook.* Cleveland, OH: Case Western Reserve University, Mandel School of Applied Social Sciences.

Tutty, L. M. (1997). Child sexual abuse prevention programs: Evaluating "Who Do You Tell." *Child Abuse and Neglect, 21,* 869–881.

Tutty, L. M. (2002). What children learn from sexual abuse prevention programs: Difficult concepts and developmental issues. *Research on Social Work Practice, 10,* 275–300.

U.S. Department of Health and Human Services, Administration for Children and Families. (2003). Emerging practices in the prevention of child abuse and neglect. Washington, DC: US Government Printing Office.

U.S. Department of Health and Human Services. (2001). *Child maltreatment 1999.* Washington, DC: U.S. Government Printing Office, Administration on Children, Youth, and Families.

Webster-Stratton, C. (1990). Long-term follow-up with young conduct problem children: From preschool to grade school. *Journal of Clinical Child Psychology, 19*(2), 144–149.

Webster-Stratton, C. (1998a). Parent training with low-income families: Promoting parental engagement through a collaborative approach. In J. R. Lutzker (Ed.), *Handbook of child abuse research and treatment* (pp. 183–211). New York: Plenum Press.

Webster-Stratton, C. (1998b). Preventing conduct problems in Head Start children: Strengthening parenting competencies. *Journal of Consulting and Clinical Psychology, 66*(5), 715–730.

Webster-Stratton, C. (2000). *The Incredible Years Training Series* [Juvenile Justice Bulletin]. Washington, DC: Office of Juvenile Justice and Delinquency Prevention.

Webster-Stratton, C. (2001, July 26–28). *Prevention and treatment for young children with conduct problems: The Incredible Years Training Series.* Paper presented at the second biennial Niagara Conference on Evidence-Based Treatments for Childhood and Adolescent Mental Health Problems, Niagara-on-the-Lake, Ontario, Canada.

Webster-Stratton, C., & Hammond, M. (1997). Treating children with early onset conduct problems: Comparison of child and parent training interventions. *Journal of Consulting and Clinical Psychology, 65*(1), 93–109.

Webster-Stratton, C., & Taylor, T. (2001). Nipping early risk factors in the bud: Preventing substance abuse, delinquency, and violence in adolescence through interventions targeted at young children (0–8 years). *Prevention Science, 2*(3), 165–192.

Wolfe, D. A. (1987). *Child abuse: Implications for child development and psychopathology.* Newbury Park, CA: Sage.

Wolfe, D. A. (1994). The role of intervention and treatment services in the prevention of child abuse and neglect. In G. B. Melton & F. D. Barry (Eds.), *Protecting children from abuse and neglect: Foundations for a new national strategy* (pp. 224–304). New York: Guilford Press.

Wolfe, D. A. (2001, July). *Interventions for physically abused children and adolescents.* Paper presented at the second biennial Niagara Conference on Evidence-Based Treatments for Childhood and Adolescent Mental Health Problems, Niagara-on-the-Lake, Ontario, Canada.

Wolfe, D. A., Edwards, B., Manion, I., & Koverola, C. (1988). Early intervention for parents at-risk for child abuse and neglect: A preliminary investigation. *Journal of Consulting and Clinical Psychology, 56,* 40–47.

Wolfe, D. A., & Sandler, J. (1981). Training abusive parents in effective child management. *Behavior Modification, 5,* 320–335.

Wolfe, D. A., Sandler, J., & Kaufman, K. (1981). A competency-based parent training program for child abusers. *Journal of Consulting and Clinical Psychology, 49,* 633–640.

Wolfe, D. A., St. Lawrence, J., Graves, K., Brehony, K., Bradlyn, A., & Kelly, J. A. (1982). Intensive behavioral parent training for a child abusive mother. *Behavior Therapy, 13,* 438–451.

Chapter 19

DATING VIOLENCE

GRETCHEN E. ELY

Adolescents are involved in serious and sexual dating relationships, often resulting in negative consequences for self and society (Miller, Christopherson, & King, 1993). Serious physical injuries frequently occur as a result of adolescent dating violence perpetration (Carlson, 1987; Simons, Lin, & Gordon, 1998; Williams & Martinez, 1999). Sexual dating behaviors typically begin in the teen years, and adolescent involvement in sexual behavior is frequently coerced (Miller et al., 1993). Sexually transmitted diseases continue to spread among the adolescent population, and approximately one million adolescents per year become pregnant (Gulotta, Adams, & Montemayor, 1993). Acquaintance rape is alarmingly frequent in the U.S. adolescent population (Miller et al., 1993), and adolescent relationships emulate the violence found in other segments of our society. Some experts have estimated that up to 60% of teens have experienced some type of violence in a dating relationship. These patterns of violence during adolescence take an economic and social toll on our society. Thus, it is vital to gain a strong scientific understanding of the problem of adolescent dating violence so that it may be effectively prevented.

INCIDENCE

Adolescent romantic relationships are often idealized or thought of as carefree or innocent (Henton, Cate, Koval, Lloyd, & Christopher, 1983; Makepeace, 1981). However, medical doctors estimate that 10% of intentional injuries to adolescents are the result of dating violence (Sege, Stigol, Perry, Goldstein, & Spivak, 1996). Early dating violence studies suggested that adolescent dating relationships were often based on and sustained by acts of aggression such as pushing and shoving (Carlson, 1987; Cate, Henton, Koval, Christopher, & Lloyd, 1982;

Henton et al., 1983; Makepeace, 1981). The Centers for Disease Control's 1997 Youth Risk Behavior Survey (1998) revealed that students in grades 9 to 12 engaged in 115 physical fights per 100 adolescents during the 12 months preceding the survey. In a follow-up study of this population, it was found that 1.8% of the males and 4.2% of the females reported that their last physical altercation was with a dating partner (Krieter et al., 1999). Other research results reported higher incidence rates. Experts found that between 32% and 60% of females reported that they had been victims of dating violence, and around 40% to 50% of boys and girls reported perpetration of dating violence (Bergman, 1992; Foshee, 1996; Jezl, Molidor, & Wright, 1996; Molidor & Tolman, 1998; Watson, Cascardi, Avery-Leaf, & O'Leary, 2001).

RISK FACTORS

Risk factors are those characteristics, variables, or hazards that, if present for a given adolescent, make it more likely that a particular adolescent, rather than someone selected from the general population, will be a victim or perpetrator of dating violence (Werner & Smith, 1992). Using this model, risk groups can be identified on the basis of biological, psychological, or social risk factors that are known to be associated with the onset of adolescent dating violence. Once identified, individuals or subgroups of the population who are at risk can be targeted with appropriate preventive interventions. An examination of a significant body of dating violence literature reveals that adolescent dating violence risk factors tend to occur in these domains: personal/individual, family, societal, and related to gender differences. These domains incorporate both the genetic and environmental factors that may influence adolescent risk for involvement in dating violence.

Personal/Individual Risk Factors

The following individual risk factors were reported in the research literature as associated with adolescent involvement in dating violence:

- Jealousy
- Need for power
- Need for control
- Disagreements about sex and sexual activity
- Higher number of suicide attempts
- Greater number of sexual partners

- Riding in a car with someone consuming alcohol
- Injection of illegal drugs
- Alcohol use before last sexual encounter
- Alcohol or marijuana use in general
- Unplanned pregnancies
- Forced sexual contact
- Inhalant use
- General sexual activity
- Number of times getting someone pregnant
- Frequency of dating experiences
- Thoughts of watching out for others' well-being
- Number of times threatened with physical violence in the last 12 months
- Early onset of drug use (Bergman, 1992; Carlson, 1987; Chase, Treboux, & O'Leary, 2002; Krieter et al., 1999; Molidor & Tolman, 1998; Reuterman & Burcky, 1989; Williams & Martinez, 1999)

Violence to induce sexual activity is reported most frequently in the literature examined for this chapter. Violence as a result of sexual advances, as a result of jealousy, and during alcohol and drug use were also frequently reported risk factors associated with dating violence in this literature.

Dysfunctional conflict approaches, personal aggressiveness, and tendency toward aggressive acts have been associated with male propensity to use dating violence as a tactic. Billingham and Sack (1986) indicate that dating violence should be viewed as a breakdown in conflict resolution rather than a phenomenon in and of itself. Researchers reported that dysfunctional conflict negotiation approaches, which include being disagreeable, being insulting, and using inflammatory language, are associated with increased likelihood of involvement in dating violence (Bird, Stith, & Schladale, 1991; Riggs & O'Leary, 1996).

Because studies of adolescents in this area are limited, it is important to call attention to Ryan (1995), who conducted three studies designed to examine the presence of battering personalities in courtship-violent men and found that previous use of threats, verbal abuse, and aggression were most predictive of the use of courtship violence. Later, Ryan (1998) reported that aggressiveness in one category such as verbal aggression was associated with higher levels of other types of aggression, such as sexual or physical aggression toward a dating partner. His results support those of another study that found that aggression in one category was related to aggression in another category (Riggs & Caufield, 1997).

If problems resulting from inappropriately managed aggression and conflict lead to dating violence, it might be primarily prevented through healthy handling of conflict and aggression before dysfunctional problem-solving strategies emerge. Future research efforts need to evaluate conflict resolution training programs beginning in elementary school. This approach to teaching early conflict resolution could lessen all types of adolescent violence, including adolescent dating violence.

Perceived beneficial outcomes have been associated with the use of dating violence in boys (M. O'Keefe, 1998; Williams & Martinez, 1999). Adolescents who were involved in dating violence were reportedly more accepting of it; respondents who reported being involved in premarital violence also reported more positive attitudes toward marital violence (Foshee, Bauman, & Fletcher, 1999; Henton et al., 1983). Other experts reported that the need to gain control in a dating relationship and dissatisfaction with relationship power predicted physical and psychological dating abuse (Ronfeldt, Kimerling, & Arias, 1998). M. O'Keefe (1998) found that girls were more likely to be violent to a dating partner when they believed that female-to-male violence was acceptable and male-to-female violence was not acceptable. Bethke and DeJoy (1993) reported that relationship status affected the acceptability of violence and affected which actions (such as ending the relationship) following a violent episode are viewed as acceptable. Another study demonstrated that reactions to receipt of violence were most strongly correlated with the expressed use of dating violence, followed by high levels of the attitude of romantic jealousy, which was also highly correlated with verbal aggression (Bookwala, Frieze, Smith, & Ryan, 1992). Foshee et al. (1999) found that adolescents who were perpetrators of dating violence were more accepting of the use of dating violence than adolescents who were not perpetrators.

Riggs and Caufield (1997) indicate that violent men were significantly more likely than nonviolent men to report believing that violence would result in the winning of an intimate argument. In addition, they found that, as compared to violent men's beliefs, nonviolent men were more likely to believe that the use of violence would bring about a permanent end to the relationship.

The length of the dating relationship and number of dating experiences may affect the likelihood of involvement in violence for adolescents. Some experts report that up to 35% of violence occurred in short-term relationships of less than six months (Bergman, 1992; Roscoe & Callahan, 1985), as compared to 6% of violence that occurred in relationships of two years or more (Roscoe & Callahan, 1985). Another expert suggested that longer relationships have an increased likelihood of violence (M. O'Keefe, 1997). Reuterman and Burcky (1989) found that adolescents who experienced dating violence reported a higher number of dating experiences. Alarmingly, teens tend to minimize or rationalize even severe abuse in more serious relationships (Becky & Farren, 1997). Miller et al. (1993) warn that adolescents who begin dating by age 14 have higher chances of engaging in more frequent intercourse with more partners. They report that younger age of onset of intercourse may lead to a greater number of sexual partners and a greater individual risk of negative consequences, such as dating violence, associated with dating relationships.

The age an adolescent begins dating may affect his or her likelihood of becoming involved in dating violence. Experts indicate that dating violence frequently begins in early to mid-adolescence because most students start dating between 14 and 16 years (Bethke & DeJoy, 1993; Krieter et al., 1999; Sigelman, Berry, & Wiles, 1984; Wekerle & Wolfe, 1999). These results are consistent with an earlier study that found that as many as 12.1% of adolescents reported dating violence by age 15 (Henton et al., 1983). Burcky, Reuterman, and Kopsky (1988) reported that 28.5% of female dating violence victims were between the ages of 12 and 13 years, 40% were between 14 and 15 years, 28.5% were between 16 and 17 years, and 2.3% were age 18 or over; 35% of the partners of girls in their study were over age 18 years. Conversely, Reuterman and Burcky (1989) also examined age of onset of dating violence yet found no statistically significant relationship between rates of dating violence and the age when dating began.

N. K. O'Keefe, Brockopp, and Chew (1986) report that ongoing violence in dating relationships destroys adolescents' self-esteem. Low self-esteem has been found to be a predictor of involvement in dating violence in other studies (Ackard & Neumark-Sztainer, 2002; Burke, Stets, & Pirog-Good, 1988; M. O'Keefe, 1998; Sharpe & Taylor, 1999; Stets & Pirog-Good, 1987). It is also reported that involvement in dating violence causes diminishment in self-esteem (Kasian & Painter, 1992). Conversely, self-esteem has also been found to be unrelated to involvement in dating violence (Bird et al., 1991; Makepeace, 1981). Because of inconsistent findings involving self-esteem and dating violence, researchers need to include measures of self-esteem in future studies to be able to draw some stronger conclusions about the relationships between these two variables.

Mental health disorders, such as antisocial personality disorder, may play a role in adolescent dating violence involvement, although this relationship has not been explored at length (Williams & Martinez, 1999). Involvement in delinquent behavior as a child has been shown to increase the likelihood of involvement in delinquent behavior, such as dating violence, as an adolescent (Andrews, Foster, Capaldi, & Hops, 2000; Giordano, Millhollin, Cernovich, Pugh, & Rudolph, 1999).

In a recent study of more than 81,000 teens in grades 9 and 12, Ackard and Neumark-Sztainer (2002) report that dating violence is associated with higher rates of eating disorders in girls and boys, including skipping meals, binge eating, fasting, taking laxatives, and taking diet pills. This study is significant because of the large sample size and is helpful in making a case for the extreme prevalence of dating violence in adolescents.

Family-Related Risk Factors

With some adolescents, dating violence may be a continuation of violence in the family of origin, because adolescents who grew up exposed to violence in the home may be desensitized to it (Williams & Martinez, 1999). Experience with violence in the family of origin may increase adolescent involvement in violent dating relationships and/or model how to interact violently in intimate relationships (Carlson, 1987; Foshee et al., 1999; Gwartney-Gibbs, Stockard, & Bohmer, 1987; N. K. O'Keefe et al., 1986; Simons, Lin, & Gordon, 1998; Smith & Williams, 1992). Roscoe and Callahan (1985) found that 59% of adolescents who reported involvement in dating violence also reported violent treatment in their families of origin. M. O'Keefe (1998) found evidence that high school students who witnessed violence in the family of origin were more likely to be involved in dating violence either as victims or perpetrators, although not all of the students from violent backgrounds were violent with dating partners. Riggs and O'Leary (1996) found that dating aggression was associated with exposure to violence in the family of origin for female college students but not for males. Negative family of origin communication was also shown to predict couple physical aggression in one study (Andrews et al., 2000). Some studies have failed to find that parental violence is a factor in teen dating violence (Riggs & O'Leary, 1996; Sigelman et al., 1984; Simons et al., 1998).

Harsh corporal punishment in the family of origin has also been associated with dating violence in adolescents (Foshee et al., 1999; Gershoff, 2002; O'Leary et al., 1989; Simons et al., 1998; Straus & Smith, 1990). Reuterman and Burcky (1989) found that adolescents who had experienced dating violence were more likely than others to report that their parents had used various forms of violence as a means of disciplining them. Harsh discipline from a father was particularly predictive of involvement in dating violence, and those involved in dating violence were less likely than others to report close relationships with their fathers. They also found that being hit by a mother was not associated with the perpetration of dating violence for females, but was associated for males. In another study, being hit by a father was positively associated with dating violence for either gender (Foshee et al., 1999).

Some authors suggest that previous experiences of child abuse/maltreatment may contribute to adolescent involvement in dating violence (M. O'Keefe, 1998;

Wekerle & Wolfe, 1999). Parent-child violence has been shown as one predictor of the use of courtship violence with females but not with males (Tontodonato & Crew, 1992). Wolfe, Wekerle, Reitzel-Jaffe, and Lefebvre (1998) reported that youths who are maltreated before age 12 have significantly more verbal and physical conflicts with dating partners than nonmaltreated youths in their sample of more than three hundred 15-year-olds. Other researchers have discovered consistent findings (Marshall & Rose, 1988; Riggs, O'Leary, & Breslin, 1990). Simons et al. (1998) examined criminology literature and concluded that adolescent dating violence may be a manifestation of antisocial tendencies that develop in childhood, often as a result of antisocial parents with ineffective parenting strategies. The results of their three-year longitudinal survey of parents and adolescents in three counties provided strong evidence in support of their hypothesis. Other experts have found evidence that unskilled parenting and family instability mediated the development of antisocial behavior, such as adolescent dating violence (Capaldi & Clarke, 1998; Wekerle & Wolfe, 1999). Recent study results indicate that, compared to females not involved in dating violence, females involved in dating violence perceived their parents to be less involved, less open, less mutual with decision making, and less likely to monitor their whereabouts and well-being (Chase et al., 2002). Unskilled parenting practices have elsewhere been associated with the intergenerational transmission of partner aggression (Capaldi & Clark, 1998).

Research suggests that divorce in the family of origin may contribute to use of dating violence in adolescence. Billingham and Notebaert (1993) revealed that students in their study who came from a divorced family reported higher scores of violent behavior on the Violence subscale; they also reported higher scores for their dating partners on both the Violence subscale and the Verbal Aggression scale.

Societal Risk Factors

Adolescents are often exposed to violence in their schools and communities (Krieter et al., 1999), which appears to play a role in dating violence involvement (Bergman, 1992; M. O'Keefe, 1998; Williams & Martinez, 1999), particularly when coupled with the stressor of violence in the family of origin (M. O'Keefe, 1998). Malik, Sorenson, and Aneshensel (1997) found in their study of more than 700 high school students that weapon ownership, coupled with injuries resulting from community violence, were associated with higher rates of student involvement in dating violence. They concluded that, for high school students, being exposed to violence in one context, such as the community of origin, appears to have crossover effects related to victimization and perpetration in another context, such as involvement in dating violence. Previous involvement in dating violence has recently been found to be predictive of future dating violence in males (Chase et al., 2002). Girls who grow up in neighborhoods where more female-on-female fighting takes place were found to be more prone toward other delinquent acts, such as participation in and acceptance of dating violence (Giordano et al., 1999). Teen violence in one context again appears to be associated with the use of violence in other contexts.

M. O'Keefe (1998) found that male adolescent involvement in dating violence was mediated by lower socioeconomic status. This supports the findings of a later study that suggested that women reared in economically depressed areas might be more prone to engage in dating violence (Giordano et al., 1999). Other experts found that subjects who experienced dating violence were more likely to live in rural areas (Reuterman & Burcky, 1989). Perhaps the economic stressors often associated with poor rural/urban living conditions are somehow associated with higher rates of dating violence.

The social construction of gender (Andersen, 2000) essentially promotes and contributes to the high rates of dating violence that have been reported. Many of the gender messages in our society promote and model romantic love in the context of controlling and violent behavior (Andersen, 2000). Jealousy that turns violent is portrayed in the media frequently. Teens may misperceive these media portrayals as real messages about love relationships. Research suggests that pop culture appears to encourage dating violence in adolescents (Bergman, 1992). Teens are often exposed to music and media that perpetuate the use of violence against women as acceptable and sometimes expected. Engagement in hostile talk about women with male peers has been associated with male involvement in dating aggression toward female partners (Capaldi, Dishion, Stoolmiller, & Yoerger, 2001; Sharpe & Taylor, 1999). Results reported from 60 African American boys and girls ranging in age from 11 to 16 years suggest significant acceptance of violence against women present in the adolescents who were exposed to rap music videos depicting male-on-female violence (Johnson, Adams, Ashburn, & Reed, 1995).

Risk Factors Related to Gender Differences

Gender has been described as a significant risk factor for involvement in and/or injury from adolescent dating violence (Ely, Dulmus, & Wodarski, 2002). Girls and boys even differ in their reported perceptions of what causes dating violence episodes. Riggs (1993) found that boys most often reported that problems with the girlfriend's parents, her friends, her involvement with other boys, lack of love, and poor sexual relations led them to use dating violence as a relationship tactic. Girls in this study reported personal problems with parents, boyfriend's alcohol/drug use, and verbal dating fights as problems they were concerned would initiate dating violence. Riggs also found that the correlation between dating aggression and conflict was higher for females, suggesting that female aggression in response to a potential conflict more often results in a violent conflict, which may be expressed as violence in the dating relationship. Another study examined the motivation of student perpetrators and victims to participate in dating violence (Follingstad, Wright, Lloyd, & Sebastian, 1991). Researchers found that girls perceived that dating violence was perpetrated against them so that boys could gain control over their actions. Boys reported that dating violence was perpetrated against them because girls were extremely emotionally hurt and angry. In this same study, the motivators for use of dating violence also differed. Boys reported using violence in retaliation for being hit first or in response to feelings of jealousy, whereas girls reported using violence because they were emotionally hurt and angry. This same study examined the perceived effects of dating violence. Girls perceived that boys would think that female-to-male violence was acceptable. Girls also thought that if they used mild violence on boys, it would result in making boys feel guilty for whatever they had done to emotionally hurt them. Boys thought that male-on-female violence caused fear, depression, and anxiety in girls (Follingstad et al., 1991).

Compared to female adults, male adults report viewing restrictive and coercive behavior as less controlling than it actually is (Ehrensaft & Vivian, 1999). The strongest predictor of dating violence for women in one study was the receipt of violence from the male, which indicates that violence expressed by females may often be in the form of self-defense (Bookwala et al., 1992). Earlier data collected from victims of domestic abuse support the idea of female self-defense strategies (Saunders, 1986). Harned (2001) found that females were not more likely than men to use dating violence as a self-defense strategy.

Gender is a profoundly significant risk factor determining whether injury will occur because of involvement in dating violence. This is significant from a prevention and intervention perspective because research results differ by gender and intervention outcomes depend on gender. By adapting research projects and interventions to meet the unique needs of each gender, professionals could more effectively diminish the problem.

PREVENTIVE INTERVENTIONS

Certainly, adolescent dating violence is a social issue that must be addressed through a preventive intervention approach. Teens themselves recommend that preventive interventions take place before dating begins (Jaffe & Reitzel, 1990).

Barker (1995) defines prevention as: "Actions taken by social workers and others to minimize and eliminate those social . . . conditions known to cause or contribute to physical and emotional illness and sometimes economic problems" (p. 292). Preventive interventions may be divided into categories depending on what type of population is targeted: universal, selective, and indicated (Gordon, 1987). In applying these categories to the prevention of adolescent dating violence, *universal* preventive interventions are defined as interventions targeted and applied to the general adolescent or preadolescent population or to a whole group of children/adolescents that have not yet been identified on the basis of individual risk for involvement in dating violence. *Selective* preventive interventions are interventions targeted toward individual adolescents/children or toward a subgroup of the adolescent/youth population who are at high risk for involvement in adolescent dating violence. *Indicated (targeted)* preventive interventions are interventions targeted to high-risk adolescents who may not have yet experienced dating violence, but who are manifesting minimal but detectable signs related to such. Preventive intervention research is still a relatively young field that holds particular challenges for research on adolescents. Limited knowledge and inconsistent findings about the causes and development of adolescent dating violence constrain professional ability to fully engage in preventive intervention efforts. Furthermore, there is an obvious absence of published, empirically sound program evaluations that examine the effectiveness of existing dating violence prevention programs. Although the numbers are relatively small, some excellent illustrations of program evaluations of preventive interventions specifically related to adolescent dating violence are available (Avery-Leaf et al., 1997; Foshee et al., 1998; Hilton et al., 1998; Jaffe et al., 1992; LaVoie et al., 1995; MacGowan, 1997; Pacifici, Stoolmiller & Nelson, 2001; Weisz & Black, 2001).

Effective Universal Preventive Interventions

Universal prevention programs are important because such programs educate and inform individuals about the existence of and potential harm associated with certain social problems. Many adolescent prevention programs are administered in school settings because school is the most logical place to access youth in a large group where interventions can be administered before students are faced with dealing with the targeted problem. Universal, school-based prevention programs typically address issues related to health, sexual education, abuse, and drug and alcohol use. For example, some states and/or school districts implement mandatory sexual education programs aimed at pregnancy prevention at certain grade levels, whereas others require that drug education programs be instituted at certain intervals to discourage drug use and drunk driving.

Along these lines, a limited number of programs designed to address dating violence and sexual coercion in one area or school system do exist. These programs are primarily administered at the middle or high school level, and the adolescents who participate in the programs have often already begun to have dating experiences.

The following programs are examples of universal dating violence prevention programs in the United States and Canada that were found to be effective in published program evaluations within the last five years. (See Appendix II for a complete list of dating violence programs from all years that were found in the empirical dating violence literature examined for this chapter.)

Prevention Program for Teenagers on Sexual Coercion

Pacifici, Stoolmiller, and Nelson (2001) examined a program designed to improve adolescent attitudes underlying coercive sexual dating behavior. The participants consisted of all students enrolled in health education classes in two suburban high schools in the Pacific Midwest. Participants were 10th graders and almost evenly distributed by gender.

Six experienced health education teachers administered a detailed multimedia curriculum, titled *Dating and Sexual Responsibility,* during health class that was designed to help students examine individual and social attitudes underlying coercive sexual dating behavior and to teach them communication skills aimed at preventing or dealing with unwanted sexual dating advances. The curriculum was organized in three 80-minute instruction sections with one additional section to participate in and evaluate a virtual date scenario. This curriculum was participatory and included videos, role plays, and discussion formats. Parts of the curriculum were divided into sections on coercion; beliefs, attitudes, and expectations; and refusals and responses.

To evaluate the effectiveness of this prevention program, student pre- and posttest questionnaires were administered using an interactive computer program developed by Northwest Media, Inc. (1998). This innovative testing approach promoted student interaction with the pre- and posttesting procedure and allowed the data to be entered with a mouse instead of a keyboard. Lab computers were networked, and data was recorded instream and sent to a central database on a network server to be evaluated.

The results of this study indicate that this innovative and interactive dating violence prevention program was effective in reducing high school student acceptance of sexual coercion. Benefits were apparent only for students who were identified to be at greatest risk at pretest. Students at or above the prescore mean on coercive attitudes reportedly benefited from the intervention, whereas those below the pretest coercive score mean reportedly did not benefit from the intervention. Female adolescents were generally less tolerant of sexual coercion at baseline as compared to males. However, beneficial outcomes at posttest were similar across gender lines.

Sexual Assault and Dating Violence Prevention Program for Urban Youths

To address the need for dating violence prevention in middle schools, Weisz and Black (2001) examined a dating violence and sexual assault program for urban middle school students. In conjunction with the local Rape Crises Center, researchers administered a 12-session, after-school program to African American youths in a university-affiliated charter middle school as part of their required after-school curriculum. Each program session lasted 1 hour and 30 minutes. Participants in this program were separated by gender, which was a good way to address the gender differences presented in previous empirical dating violence literature. The group facilitators used activities developed by the Nebraska Domestic Violence Sexual Assault Coalition (1995) to target attitudes, knowledge, and behavior and to implement the program goals of increasing knowledge about the causes of dating violence, increasing knowledge of community resources, decreasing tolerance of sexual assault/dating violence, and increasing knowledge of how to prevent and react to dating violence.

The curriculum was developed for use with middle school students and was considered culturally appropriate for the group. Groups engaged in discussions, modeling, experiential exercises, and role plays. Role play was described as the most useful activity among these group tools because students reportedly responded most positively to this technique.

Evaluation results suggest that this program was effective at improving attitudes and increasing knowledge related to dating violence and that such effects were maintained at six-month follow-up. As to gender, follow-up findings do not indicate any gender differences in changes in knowledge after program participation. However, gender differences were found in attitude change immediately after program implementation.

Dating Violence Program in Ontario

The goal of the Ontario program was to provide a controlled and consistent dating violence intervention in one school region, designed to increase students' knowledge of practical information about risk factors for violence, provide information about the law as to assault and sexual assault, and provide information about how to get help for interpersonal violence (Hilton, Harris, Rice, Krans, & Varigne, 1998). The authors also noted that they would look for backlash effects that had been found in another antiviolence attitude change study (Winkel & DeKleuver, 1997). Participants in this intervention were from four high schools, with enrollment ranging from 400 to 1,200 students, in a mixed urban/rural region of Ontario, Canada. The one-time intervention was offered to all grade 11 students in these schools. Students were presented a dating violence program via various activities including large assemblies and workshop discussions.

The half-day antiviolence seminar from this study showed promising results related to violence prevention without the expected backlash effect. There was some evidence that small workshops produced more desired changes than large assemblies. However, students who most needed the intervention were the least likely to attend. Results indicated that victims and perpetrators who attended the intervention reported learning no more or less compared to students who were not former victims or perpetrators.

Dating Aggression Pilot Program in Long Island, New York

The goals of the Long Island dating aggression project were to deliver an intervention that treats dating aggression as a multidetermined phenomenon; is sensitive to gender inequities, while providing a didactic, skills-based approach focused on changing attitudes and enhancing skills; and recognizes that males and females may be both perpetrators and victims (Avery-Leaf, Cascardi, O'Leary, & Cano, 1997). To achieve these goals, the program had the following objectives:

1. Promote equity in dating relationships via demonstrating how gender inequity fosters violence
2. Challenge attitudes toward violence as a means of resolving conflict
3. Identify constructive communication skills
4. Increase support resources for victims seeking help
5. Cover help-seeking for all those involved in aggressive relationships
6. Show alternatives to violent dating relationships

The dating aggression program was administered to 193 students in junior- and senior-level health education classes in a Long Island, New York, high school.

Pre- and postevaluation assessments indicated that this type of short dating violence curriculum can be an effective tool at changing adolescent attitudes that promote the acceptance of dating violence. Treatment group participants reported a reduction in attitudes justifying dating aggression when compared to control group participants.

Teen Dating Violence Program of Dade County, Florida

The goal of the Dade County intervention was to help students recognize dating violence, understand its causes, and make decisions to avoid or end abusive relationships (MacGowan, 1997). The participants in this preventive intervention were all sixth- to eighth-grade students in a Dade County, Florida, middle school.

The program consists of five 1-hour sessions that were implemented over a five-day period. The program was presented by five trained teachers and included activities surrounding teacher-student discussions and experiential activities. This curriculum was developed by Domestic Violence Intervention Services of Oklahoma (Krazier & Larson, 1993; MacGowan, 1997) to teach students to recognize, understand, and make decisions about dating violence. Evidence from this evaluation suggests that this dating violence program did significantly contribute to increased posttest knowledge, attitudes, and preparedness for dealing with dating violence.

Boys' attitudes did not improve as much as girls' on issues of physical and sexual violence. This finding suggests that boys are still more prone to interpreting dating violent acts as acceptable, even after a preventive intervention demonstrates otherwise (MacGowan, 1997).

The previously discussed programs were all shown to be effective and, therefore, promising. Yet, it is still difficult to determine whether such programs maintain the demonstrated beneficial changes over the long term. Programs offered one time at one grade level may improve reported attitudes, knowledge, and behaviors, but follow-up studies that take place more than six months after program completion are still rare. Dating violence information needs to be elevated to a primary concern in all schools. Regularly occurring dating violence workshops appear to be an important missing step in the current approach to dating violence reduction. All students of dating age need to be continually exposed to dating violence prevention programs to demonstrate that dating violence is an important concern for adolescents.

Furthermore, most dating violence prevention is taking place too late for primary prevention to occur. Of these featured effective universal dating violence prevention programs, all are administered in middle and high schools, times when students may have already begun to have dating relationships, because many students, especially females, have reported dating at age 12 and younger. Universal, age-appropriate dating violence prevention programs need to begin in kindergarten and continue at regular intervals and take place through college.

Effective Selective and Indicated Preventive Interventions

Selective preventive interventions are important because they are designed to prevent individuals or subgroups who are at high risk of becoming involved in a specific social problem and the associated negative effects. Selective program interventions for adolescents often take place in school systems and at other points of contact for social services. For example, some community centers serving economically disadvantaged youths offer specialized athletic programs, such as late-night basketball for urban males who are highly at risk for involvement in violence. This type of selective prevention intervention is intended to engage such youths in positive, legal activities that build self-esteem and provide socially acceptable alternatives to destructive behavior, thus attempting to thwart involvement in destructive behavior.

As to dating violence, no selective prevention programs were evaluated in the literature examined for this chapter. This demonstrates the need for selective dating violence prevention efforts to be developed and empirically tested for the benefit of students who, based on the empirical data available on dating violence to date, are at highest risk for becoming involved in dating violence.

For example, researchers indicate that students with lower grade point averages, students following less advanced academic programs, and students who have been suspended or expelled from school were more likely to become involved in dating violence compared to students who had no history of academic problems (Bergman, 1992; Reuterman & Burcky, 1989). Based on this information, it would make sense to focus on developing selective dating violence prevention interventions in school systems for students who have school attendance problems and/or who demonstrate failing grades and/or a decline in academic engagement.

Evaluations of indicated adolescent dating violence programs are also absent from the dating violence literature examined for this chapter. Based on Gordon's (1987) model, indicated adolescent dating violence interventions could be described as interventions aimed at high-risk adolescents who do not meet the entire criteria for involvement in dating violence, but who are experiencing some of the risk factors.

For example, certain family issues, including involvement with harsh corporal punishment and/or abuse in the family of origin, have been associated with involvement in dating violence as a teen. One practical place to target dating violence interventions is with children and adolescents whose families are involved in the child protective system. Part of the intervention process for troubled families could include indicated psychosocial program interventions that educate children in areas such as sexual education and dating violence. Such programs could be offered in alternative settings, such as local libraries, health clinics, or school systems. Children and adolescents could be referred to these programs by child protective caseworkers as part of a family intervention strategy. Wolfe and Jaffe (1999) recommend that indicated interventions be implemented through home visit programs to high-risk families who are referred to child protective services.

As previously discussed, involvement in one type of violence puts adolescents at risk for involvement in other kinds of violence. Based on this knowledge, it seems logical to assume that adolescents who appear in juvenile court for violent offenses would be highly at risk for involvement in dating violence. Many adolescent offenders have likely already been involved in dating violence. Therefore, dating violence interventions should be required for violent offenders and should be developed to appropriately address the age of the offender as well as the seriousness of the current violent offense. For first time offenders who are not incarcerated, referrals to indicated psychosocial dating violence prevention programs in the alternative community setting could be made by the court system and/or parole officers. For incarcerated youths, antiviolence interventions that include a dating violence component would be an important part of a rehabilitation program. More work to develop such programs must be done.

In the school system, adolescents who are identified as involved in or previously involved in violent dating relationships need to be targeted for prevention interventions in addition to any universal program that is already present. Such interventions could be done in small group form with a qualified school social worker and would be developed to end violence and to prevent its reoccurrence.

IMPLICATIONS FOR PRACTICE AND POLICY

Society is still a long way from knowing the most effective practice approaches for dealing with adolescent dating violence. It seems clear that society must provide some interventions for this problem. Professionals who deal with the effects of violence on adolescents are just beginning to understand some of the risk factors and outcomes associated with adolescent involvement in dating violence through the extensive body of empirical literature that has been emerging for over two decades. However, the research on program effectiveness is still murky at best. Dating violence programs are offered in a limited number of school districts and often begin after dating violent behavior has already occurred in the target population. Few of these programs have been empirically evaluated for effectiveness. Those programs that have been evaluated demonstrate positive results. But for how long? The evaluation literature still lacks long-term studies that evaluate the effects of dating violence programs much more than six months postintervention.

Furthermore, what type of program works best? Evaluation results indicate that using interactive activities and incorporating technology might be good ways to reach children with anti-dating-violence messages, but no conclusions have been drawn as to which combination of activities works best to effectively address this complex issue.

In addition, what types of programs do we need? Should practitioners focus on short half-day assemblies or once-a-week sessions that continue for several months? How often should these interventions be offered to both maintain positive results and advance age-appropriate messages at the most beneficial time of child and adolescent development?

Although exact rates of the problem have not been determined, research indicates that adolescent dating violence occurs frequently and warrants public concern. Practice efforts must be allocated toward this problem. Various levels of program development, implementation, and testing must occur. Efforts must be made to make empirically valuable programs universally available. Additional program efforts must also be targeted toward adolescents most at risk of harm from involvement in dating violence. Professionals working with children and adolescents must begin to acknowledge what a tremendous problem interpersonal violence is within the school system. Interdisciplinary efforts must be made to decrease the use of and tolerance for violence in dating relationships. Adolescents must be taught to rethink their approaches to dating and to improve their help-seeking behaviors and knowledge of their rights (Hilton et al., 1998). It would also be important to consider how such interventions can be made more attractive to higher risk students. Perhaps such antiviolence interventions should be required and, therefore, offered repeatedly until each student has had a chance to attend when an intervention is presented.

Practitioners must also develop and implement programs that focus on educating school personnel about the high rates and serious nature of adolescent dating violence. Adolescents are involved in dating relationships that start earlier and are more sexual and committed than relationships of previous generations (Dryfoos, 1990). Significant adults and school personnel may be slow to accept the serious nature and potential hazards of these relationships, as evidenced by the lack of policy and program development that addresses the problem in the school system. Comprehensive dating violence prevention programs should have components that focus on educating teachers, parents, and other individuals about how to recognize, prevent, address, and end dating violence with the students in their school systems.

Social policy must be reformed to include funding for universal psychosocial education programs that address issues of violence, including dating violence. In the United States, the focus of social policy must shift to prevention if we are to address the rampant youth violence in our society. Secondary schools must implement policies to protect students from dating violence, especially in light of findings suggesting that 43% of students in one study reported that acts of dating violence were perpetrated against them on school campus (Molidor & Tolman, 1998).

FUTURE DIRECTIONS

A comprehensive prevention strategy based on zero tolerance for dating and domestic violence, which is strongly supported by the public and backed by scientific research and evaluation, is essential if we want to eliminate the problem of adolescent dating violence (Wolfe & Jaffe, 1999).

Repeated, significant gender differences demonstrated in the literature are troubling in light of evidence that males inflict the most serious harm during violent episodes. It may be necessary to focus program development efforts on anti-dating-violence interventions that are specifically targeted toward boys or that separate boys and girls into different groups so that their specific issues may be dealt with at length. Perhaps interventions for males could focus on changing male gender-appropriate attitudes (i.e., altering male notions that they are owed sexual favors from females), whereas programs for girls could focus on changing female gender-appropriate attitudes (i.e., that girls deserve violent treatment or that violent treatment is an expression of love). Targeting both perpetrators and victims for treatment, peer counseling, and support groups may be the most appropriate approach for students already involved in violent dating relationships (LaVoie, Vezina, Piche, & Boivin, 1995).

Prevention efforts must also focus on making existing resources accessible to underage dating violence victims because many conventional domestic violence resources are not available for teens (Molidor & Tolman, 1998; Wekerle & Wolfe, 1999). Adolescents are likely to encounter both real and imagined obstacles to accessing services (Williams & Martinez, 1999), which is why professional efforts must focus on how best to make victim services easy to use, easy to get, and highly confidential no matter the age of the victim.

Adolescent dating violence is so common in our society that every clinician who practices with adolescents needs to screen for the problem (Adams, 1997). Thus, professionals must also concentrate on developing and using empirically valid dating violence assessment instruments.

Adolescent dating violence is a real problem in American culture that must be addressed by the professionals who deal with adolescents in everyday settings. Adolescents need to be informed about dating violence and taught ways to effectively deal with it on their own. The long-term effects of dating violence on adolescent development are still unclear. What is clear is that adolescents suffer when they are involved in abusive relationships that are supposed to be based on love. It is time to start considering adolescent relationships, and the violence that often accompanies them, as a serious public health problem.

REFERENCES

Ackard, D. N., & Neumark-Sztainer, D. (2002). Date violence and date rape among adolescents: Associations with disordered eating behaviors. *Child Abuse and Neglect, 26,* 455–473.

Adams, J. A. (1997). Sexual abuse and adolescents. *Pediatric Annals, 26,* 299–304.

Andersen, M. L. (2000). *Thinking about women: Sociological perspectives on sex and gender.* Needham Heights, MA: Allyn & Bacon.

Andrews, J. A., Foster, S. L., Capaldi, D. M., & Hops, H. (2000). Adolescent and family predictors of physical aggression, communication and satisfaction in young adult couples: A prospective analysis. *Journal of Consulting and Clinical Psychology, 62,* 195–208.

Avery-Leaf, S., Cascardi, M., O'Leary, K. D., & Cano, A. (1997). Efficacy of a dating violence prevention program on attitudes justifying aggression. *Journal of Adolescent Health, 21,* 11–17.

Barker, R. L. (1995). *The social work dictionary* (3rd ed.). Washington, DC: National Association of Social Workers Press.

Becky, D., & Farren, P. M. (1997). Teaching students how to understand and avoid abusive relationships. *School Counselor, 44,* 303–308.

Bergman, L. (1992). Dating violence among high school students. *Social Work, 37,* 21–27.

Bethke, T., & DeJoy, D. (1993). An experimental study of factors influencing the acceptability of dating violence. *Journal of Interpersonal Violence, 8,* 36–51.

Billingham, R. E., & Notebaert, N. L. (1993). Divorce and dating violence revisited: Multivariate analyses using Straus's conflict tactics subscores. *Psychological Reports, 73,* 679–684.

Billingham, R. E., & Sack, A. R. (1986). Courtship violence and the interactive status of the relationship. *Journal of Adolescent Research, 1,* 305–325.

Bird, G. W., Stith, S. M., & Schladale, J. (1991). Psychological resources, coping strategies, and negotiation styles as discriminators of violence in dating relationships. *Family Relations, 40,* 45–50.

Bookwala, J., Frieze, L. H., Smith, C., & Ryan, K. (1992). Predictors of dating violence: A multivariate analysis. *Violence and Victims, 7,* 297–311.

Burke, P. J., Stets, J. E., & Pirog-Good, M. A. (1988). Gender identity, self-esteem, and physical and sexual abuse in dating relationships. *Social Psychology Quarterly, 15,* 272–285.

Burcky, W., Reuterman, N., & Kopsky, S. (1988). Dating violence among high school students. *School Counselor, 35,* 353–358.

Capaldi, D. M., & Clark, S. (1998). Prospective family predictors of aggression toward female partners for at-risk young men. *Developmental Psychology, 34,* 1175–1188.

Capaldi, D. M., Dishion, T. J., Stoolmiller, M., & Yoerger, K. (2001). Aggression toward female partners by at-risk young men: The contribution of male adolescent friendships. *Developmental Psychology, 37,* 61–73.

Carlson, B. E. (1987). Dating violence: A research review and comparison with spouse abuse. *Social Casework, 68,* 16–23.

Cate, R., Henton, J., Koval, J., Christopher, F. S., & Lloyd, S. (1982). Premarital abuse: A social psychological perspective. *Journal of Family Issues, 3,* 79–90.

Centers for Disease Control and Prevention. (1998). Youth Risk Behavior Surveillance, United States, 1997. *Morbidity and Mortality Weekly report CDC Surveillance Summary, 47,* 1998.

Chase, K. A., Treboux, D., & O'Leary, K. D. (2002). Characteristics of adolescents' dating violence. *Journal of Interpersonal Violence, 1,* 33–49.

Dryfoos, J. G. (1990). *Adolescents at risk.* New York: Oxford University Press.

Ehrensaft, M. K., & Vivian, D. (1999). Is partner violence related to appraisals of coercive control by a partner? *Journal of Family Violence, 14,* 251–266.

Ely, G. E., Dulmus, C. N., & Wodarski, J. S. (2002). Adolescent dating violence. In L. Rapp-Paglicci, A. Roberts, & J. Wodarski (Eds.), *Handbook of violence* (pp. 34–53). Hoboken, NJ: Wiley.

Follingstad, D. R., Wright, S., Lloyd, S., & Sebastian, J. A. (1991). Sex differences in motivations and effects in dating violence. *Family Relations, 40,* 51–57.

Foshee, V. A. (1996). Gender differences in adolescent dating abuse prevalence, types and injuries. *Health Education Research, 11,* 275–286.

Foshee, V. A., Bauman, K. E., Arragia, X. B., Helms, R. W., Koch, G. G., & Linder, G. F. (1998). An evaluation of safe dates, an adolescent dating violence prevention program. *Journal of Public Health, 88,* 45–50.

Foshee, V. A., Bauman, K. E., & Fletcher, L. G. (1999). Family violence and the perpetration of adolescent dating violence: Examining social learning and social control processes. *Journal of Marriage and the Family, 61,* 331–342.

Gershoff, E. T. (2002). Corporal punishment and associated child behaviors and experiences: A meta-analytic and theoretical review. *Psychological Bulletin, 4,* 539–579.

Giordano, P. C., Millhollin, T. J., Cernovich, S. A., Pugh, M. D., & Rudolph, J. L. (1999). Delinquency, identity and women's involvement in relationship violence. *Criminology, 37,* 17–29.

Gordon, R. (1987). An operational classification of disease prevention. In J. A. Steinberg & M. M. Silverman (Eds.), *Preventing mental disorders: A research perspective* (pp. 20–26). Rockville, MD: U.S. Department of Health and Human Services.

Gullotta, T. P., Adams, G. R., & Montemayor, R. (Eds.). (1993). *Adolescent sexuality* (introduction). Newbury Park, CA: Sage.

Gwartney-Gibbs, P. A., Stockard, J., & Bohmer, S. (1987). Learning courtship aggression: The influence of parents, peers and personal experiences. *Family Relations, 36,* 276–282.

Harned, M. S. (2001). Abused women or abused men? An examination of the context and outcomes of dating violence. *Violence and Victims, 16,* 269–285.

Henton, J., Cate, R., Koval, J., Lloyd, S., & Christopher, S. (1983). Romance and violence in dating relationships. *Journal of Family Issues, 4,* 467–482.

Hilton, N. Z., Harris, G. T., Rice, M. E., Krans, T. S., & Varigne, S. E. (1998). Antiviolence education in high schools: Implementation and evaluation. *Journal of Interpersonal Violence, 13,* 726–742.

Jaffe, P., & Reitzel, D. (1990). Adolescents' views on how to reduce family violence. In R. Roesch, D. G. Dutton, & V. F. Sacco (Eds.), *Family violence: Perspectives on treatment, research and policy* (pp. 51–66). Burnaby, British Columbia, Canada: Simon Frasier University.

Jaffe, P. G., Sudermann, M., Reitzel, D., & Killop, S. M. (1992). An evaluation of a secondary school prevention program on violence in intimate relationships. *Violence and Victims, 7,* 129–146.

Jezl, D. R., Molidor, C. E., & Wright, T. L. (1996). Physical, sexual and psychological abuse in high school dating relationships: Prevalence rates and self-esteem issues. *Child and Adolescent Social Work Journal, 13,* 69–87.

Johnson, J. D., Adams, M. S., Ashburn, L., & Reed, W. (1995). Differential gender effects of exposure to rap music on African American adolescents' acceptance of teen dating violence. *Sex Roles, 33,* 597–605.

Kasian, M., & Painter, S. L. (1992). Frequency and severity of psychological abuse in a dating population. *Journal of Interpersonal Violence, 7,* 350–364.

Krazier, S., & Larson, C. L. (1993). *Dating violence: Intervention and prevention for teenagers.* Tulsa: University of Oklahoma, College of Continuing Education, National Resource Center for Youth Services.

Krieter, S. R., Krowchuk, D. P., Woods, C. R., Sinal, S. H., Lawless, M. R., & DuRant, R. H. (1999). Gender differences in risk behaviors among adolescents who experience date fighting. *Pediatrics, 104,* 1286–1298.

LaVoie, F., Vezina, L., Piche, C., & Boivin, M. (1995). Evaluation of a prevention program for violence in teen dating relationships. *Journal of Interpersonal Violence, 10,* 516–524.

MacGowan, M. J. (1997). An evaluation of a dating violence program for middle school students. *Violence and Victims, 12,* 223–235.

Makepeace, J. M. (1981). Courtship violence among college students. *Family Relations, 30,* 97–102.

Malik, S., Sorenson, S. B., & Aneshensel, C. S. (1997). Community and dating violence among adolescents: Perpetration and victimization. *Journal of Adolescent Health, 21,* 291–302.

Marshall, L. L., & Rose, P. (1988). Family of origin and courtship violence. *Journal of Counseling and Development, 66,* 414–418.

Miller, B. C., Christopherson, C. R., & King, P. K. (1993). Sexual behavior in adolescents. In T. P. Gullotta, G. R. Adams, & R. Montemayor (Eds.), *Adolescent sexuality* (pp. 55–76). Newbury Park, CA: Sage.

Molidor, C., & Tolman, R. M. (1998). Gender and contextual factors in adolescent dating violence. *Violence Against Women, 4,* 180–194.

Nebraska Domestic Violence Sexual Assault Coalition. (1995). *Reaching and teaching teens to stop violence*. Lincoln, NE: Author.

Northwest Media, Inc. (1998). *Dating and Sexual Responsibility Curriculum* (computer program, video and teacher's guide). Eugene, OR: Author.

O'Keefe, M. (1997). Predictors of dating violence among high school students. *Journal of Interpersonal Violence, 12,* 546–569.

O'Keefe, M. (1998). Factors mediating the link between witnessing interparental violence and dating violence. *Journal of Family Violence, 13,* 39–57.

O'Keefe, N. K., Brockopp, K., & Chew, E. (1986). Teen dating violence. *Social Work, 46,* 3–8.

O'Leary, K. D., Barling, J., Arias, I., Rosenbaum, A., Malone, J., & Tyree, A. (1989). Prevalence and stability of physical aggression between spouses: A longitudinal analysis. *Journal of Consulting and Clinical Psychology, 57,* 263–268.

Pacifici, C., Stoolmiller, M., & Nelson, C. (2001). Evaluating a program for teenagers on sexual coercion: A differential effectiveness approach. *Journal of Consulting and Clinical Psychology, 69,* 552–559.

Reuterman, N. A., & Burcky, W. D. (1989). Dating violence in high schools: A profile of the victim. *Psychology, 26,* 1–9.

Riggs, D. S. (1993). Relationship problems and dating aggression. *Journal of Interpersonal Violence, 8*(1), 18–35.

Riggs, D. S., & Caufield, M. B. (1997). Expected consequences of male violence against their female dating partners. *Journal of Interpersonal Violence, 12,* 229–240.

Riggs, D. S., & O'Leary, K. D. (1996). Aggression between heterosexual dating partners: An examination of a causal model of courtship aggression. *Journal of Interpersonal Violence, 11,* 519–540.

Riggs, D. S., O'Leary, K. D., & Breslin, F. C. (1990). Multiple correlates of physical aggression in dating couples. *Journal of Interpersonal Violence, 5,* 61–73.

Ronfeldt, H. M., Kimerling, R., & Arias, I. (1998). Satisfaction with relationship power and the perpetration of dating violence. *Journal of Marriage and the Family, 60,* 70–79.

Roscoe, B., & Callahan, J. (1985). Adolescents' self-reports of violence in families and dating relationships. *Adolescence, 20,* 545–553.

Ryan, K. M. (1995). Do courtship-violent men have characteristics associated with a "battering personality?" *Journal of Family Violence, 10,* 99–120.

Ryan, K. M. (1998). The relationship between courtship violence and sexual aggression in college students. *Journal of Family Violence, 13,* 377–394.

Saunders, D. G. (1986). When battered women use violence: Husband abuse or self-defense? *Violence and Victims, 1,* 47–60.

Sege, R., Stigol, L. C., Perry, C., Goldstein, R., & Spivak, H. (1996). Intentional injury surveillance in a primary care pediatric setting. *Archives of Pediatric and Adolescent Medicine, 150,* 277–283.

Sharpe, D., & Taylor, J. K. (1999). An examination of variables from a social-developmental model to explain physical and psychological dating violence. *Canadian Journal of Behavioral Science, 31,* 165–175.

Sigelman, C. K., Berry, C. J., & Wiles, K. A. (1984). Violence in college students dating relationships. *Journal of Applied Social Psychology, 5,* 530–548.

Simons, R. L., Lin, K. H., & Gordon, L. C. (1998). Socialization in the family of origin and male dating violence: A prospective study. *Journal of Marriage and the Family, 60,* 467–478.

Smith, J. P., & Williams, J. G. (1992). From abusive household to dating violence. *Journal of Family Violence, 7,* 153–165.

Stets, J. E., & Pirog-Good, M. A. (1987). Violence in dating relationships. *Social Psychology Quarterly, 50,* 237–246.

Straus, M. A., & Smith, C. (1990). Family patterns and primary prevention of family violence. In M. A. Straus & R. J. Gelles (Eds.), *Physical violence in American families* (pp. 507–528). New Brunswick, NJ: Transaction.

Tontodonato, P., & Crew, B. K. (1992). Dating violence, social learning theory and gender: A multivariate analysis. *Violence and Victims, 7,* 3–14.

Watson, J. M., Cascardi, M., Avery-Leaf, S., & O'Leary, K. D. (2001). High school students' responses to dating aggression. *Violence and Victims, 16,* 339–348.

Weisz, A. N., & Black, B. M. (2001). Evaluating a sexual assault and dating violence prevention program for urban youths. *Social Work Research, 25,* 89–106.

Wekerle, C., & Wolfe, D. A. (1999). Dating violence in mid-adolescence: Theory, significance and emerging prevention issues. *Clinical Psychology Review, 19,* 435–456.

Werner, E. E., & Smith, R. S. (1992). *Overcoming the odds: High risk children from birth to adulthood.* Ithaca, NY: Cornell University Press.

Williams, S. E., & Martinez, E. (1999). Psychiatric assessment of victims of adolescent dating violence in a primary care clinic. *Clinical Child Psychology and Psychiatry, 4,* 427–439.

Winkel, F. W., & DeKleuver, E. (1997). Communication aimed at changing cognitions about sexual intimidation: Comparing the impact of a perpetrator-focused versus a victim-focused persuasive strategy. *Journal of Interpersonal Violence, 12,* 513–529.

Wolfe, D. A., & Jaffe, P. G. (1999). Emerging strategies in the prevention of domestic violence. *Future of Children, 9,* 133–144.

Wolfe, D. A., Wekerle, C., Reitzel-Jaffe, D., & Lefebvre, L. (1998). Factors associated with abusive relationships among maltreated and nonmaltreated youth. *Development and Psychopathology, 10,* 61–85.

PART V

Conclusion

Chapter 20

THE FUTURE OF PREVENTION

LISA A. RAPP-PAGLICCI AND CATHERINE N. DULMUS

Prevention of children's and adolescents' problems has recently emerged as an important and compelling area of study. Researchers and practitioners alike have begun to recognize the vast benefits and tremendous potential in germinating prevention protocols. As described in these chapters, some problems have well-developed and researched prevention protocols, whereas other problems such as dating violence, child maltreatment, unresolved grief, foster care drift, birth defects, and chemical exposure lag seriously behind. This concluding chapter explicates the current challenges, recommendations, and future of prevention interventions for children and adolescents.

CHALLENGES AND RECOMMENDATIONS

Despite the advances in prevention research, there are still issues that need to be further addressed or improved to obtain the greatest possible benefits from prevention programs and protocols. The following are recommendations from the chapter authors or experts as to prevention interventions:

1. Although effective prevention programs have been developed, tested, and are available, ineffective programs are still being funded and implemented. One example is the DARE program, which continues to be used though few, if any, studies have found it effective. Educational programs with no skill base have been found to change knowledge but are generally considered ineffective because they fail to change the actual behaviors of youth. If researchers are to garner support and funding for prevention research, these programs need to be discontinued. In the least, they are ineffective, but at most, they are unethical and potentially

harmful. They also dilute the strength of viable prevention programs by proliferating the belief that prevention does not work.

2. Prevention programs found to be effective in research studies are not accurately replicated and, therefore, are shown to be ineffective outside the studies. The fidelity of replicated programs must be closely assessed and accuracy ensured; otherwise, time and money are being wasted. Programs must be carried out precisely by using manuals and specific step-by-step instructions and should not be modified until research studies have indicated that the modifications result in continued effectiveness.

3. Child and adolescent problems may be universal, but they differ with respect to location and subpopulation. For example, school violence type, duration, severity, and so on differs from location to location. Therefore, before implementing school violence prevention programs, local data must be obtained or a thorough assessment must be completed to identify the appropriate types and targets of prevention. Local data can also identify the specific risk and protective factors for that area. Until this pertinent information is gathered, the appropriate prevention program will not be identified. This matching of problem and prevention protocol is essential for effective outcomes.

4. Researchers have repeatedly found that prevention protocols that involve collaboration among multiple agencies tend to be the most effective. This is not surprising because interventions that integrate and coordinate services among multiple agencies have also been found to be more effective. Prevention programs will be more potent if partnering agencies can avoid duplication, gaps, and redundancy.

5. Prevention programs that address multiple levels of intervention have also been found to be most effective. In other words, protocols that are comprehensive and address macroneeds as well as microneeds of clients are more influential. For example, a program that provides concrete services (food, housing) as well as socioemotional assistance (skills) will be far more effective than one that provides only socioemotional assistance. This approach fits with our understanding of intervention research that encourages problems to be addressed in a multifaceted approach.

6. Prevention research needs to become more specific. Research studies should begin to identify the types of prevention programs (universal, selective, indicated) that work best with each subgroup (males, females, ethnic groups, children, adolescents, etc.). For instance, what type of protocol benefits Black males under age 12? Further questions such as where prevention programs should be delivered and who is most effective in delivering them also need to be answered. Are adults or peers more valued and respected? Finally, the intensity and duration of prevention programs need further research. Do programs really need 16 weeks or is 12 weeks sufficient? Costs/benefits and effectiveness need to be considered.

7. More longitudinal studies need to be conducted to assess how effective these programs are later on as youth age. Many programs have been posttested only a year after the program was completed and do not tell researchers about the long-term benefits. Furthermore, booster sessions need to be considered as relatively efficient methods of ensuring that achievements from the program continue after the program has finished. Booster sessions can refresh information learned and present more age-appropriate material for the developing youth. For example, effective drug refusal skills for a 10-year-old may no longer be adequate for peer pressure exacted on a 14-year-old. Booster sessions can address this concern. Math and English aren't learned in just one year; why would drug refusal skills be any different?

8. Many prevention programs are only partially successful because they begin too late. Intervening after a problem has begun and sometimes waiting until it is severe have been our pattern and continue to be our modus operandi. Gordon's model of true prevention requires us to change our theoretical emphasis. Prevention has the best outcome for all youth, and all disciplines need to begin to refocus efforts toward prevention.

9. Because intervention, rather than prevention, is still emphasized, funding is scarce and more difficult to obtain for prevention programs and studies. Prevention is a risk. It costs money before a problem begins, and funding agencies have a difficult time accepting this risk. However, until more funding becomes available, prevention studies will be limited and, consequently, prevention programs will remain infrequent and deficient. The federal government needs to begin providing more grant opportunities for prevention researchers.

10. The Internet has begun to offer many opportunities in the area of child and adolescent social problems. It provides scientific and educational material for parents and professionals, and interventions are often conducted by professionals and paraprofessionals online. Perhaps prevention programs can use the flexibility and influence of the World Wide Web, too. Universal prevention programs would easily conform to this format. Parents, teachers, counselors, social workers, physicians, and so on could direct youth to web pages of information, groups could practice skills offered on web pages, and so on. Creative prevention researchers and practitioners need to begin using this tool to advance prevention ideology and practice.

FUTURE DIRECTIONS

The chapter authors have delineated many challenges and recommendations for the future of prevention research. The future of prevention is full of promise in forestalling devastating social, emotional, and health problems facing children and adolescents. It is imperative that a commitment to true prevention using Gordon's model be a priority. Too often in the name of prevention, programs and monies are targeted to intervening and rehabilitating problems once they present themselves. Researchers must develop and test preventive interventions that address risk and protective factors. Once such interventions are developed and have empirical evidence to their effectiveness, practitioners should incorporate such into their practice. Furthermore, policymakers must make prevention a priority and find necessary funding to implement prevention strategies with empirical evidence and stop funding programs known to be ineffective. An evidence-based approach to prevention is not only essential, but also ethically sound. This book provides practitioners, policymakers, and researchers a compilation of the current status of knowledge related to the prevention of a number of emotional, health, and social problems facing youth today. The future of prevention depends on the further development of this empirical knowledge base, subsequent dissemination of research findings, and funding priority for prevention interventions in the community.

Appendix I

DIRECTORY OF EXEMPLARY PROGRAMS

Baltimore Mastery Learning
(formerly Good Behavior Game and
Mastery Learning Interventions)
Sheppard G. Kellam
American Institutes for Research
1000 Thomas Jefferson Street, NW PRC,
Suite 400
Washington, DC 20007
(202) 944-5418
E-mail: skellam@air.org
Web site: http://www.bpp.jhu.edu

Child Development Project
Denise Wood
Developmental Studies Center
200 Embareadero, Suite 305
Oakland, CA 94606-5300
(800) 666-7270, ext. 239
E-mail: info@devstu.org
Web site: www.devstu.org

Dare to Be You
Jan Miller-Heyl
Colorado State University
Cooperative Extension
215 N. Linden, Suite E
Cortez, CO 81321
(970) 565-3606
E-mail: darecort@coop.ext.colostate.edu

Fast Track
Kenneth Dodge
Center for Child and Family Policy
Duke University
P.O. Box 90264
Durham, NC 27708-90264
(919) 613-7319
E-mail: Dodge@duke.edu
Web site: http://www.fasttrackproject.org
/default.htm

The Incredible Years
Lisa St. George
Parenting Clinic
University of Washington
1411 8th Avenue West
Seattle, WA 98119
Seattle area phone: (206) 285-7565
Toll Free Phone: (888) 506-3562
E-mail: incredibleyears@seanet.com
Web site: www.incredibleyears.com

**Linking the Interests of Families
    and Teachers**
Rebecca Fetrow
Oregon Social Learning Center
160 E. 4th Avenue
Eugene, OR 97401
(541) 485-2711
Web site: http://www.oslc.org/dprojframe
    .html

Nurse-Family Partnership
(formerly Nurse Home Visitation Program)
Matthew Buhr-Vogl
National Center for Children, Families
    and Communities
4200 E. 9th Avenue
P.O. Box C288-13
Denver, CO 80218
(303) 315-0896
E-mail: matt.buhr-vogl@uchsc.edu

Seattle Social Development Project
Chris Abbott
Social Development Research Group
University of Washington
9725 3rd Avenue NE, Suite 401
Seattle, WA 98115-2024
(206) 685-5208
E-mail: chabbott@u.washington.edu
Web site: http://depts.washington.edu
    /ssdp/

Appendix II

SCHOOL VIOLENCE PROGRAMS

Universal Programs	Web Sites
Second Step	www.cfchildren.org
Responding in Peaceful and Positive Ways (RIPP)	ameyer@vcu.edu (Dr. Aleta Meyer)
Seattle Social Development Project	www.channing-bete.com

Selective Programs	Web Sites
Families and Schools Together (FAST)	www.wcer.wisc.edu/FAST
First Steps to Success	www.sopriswest.com/swstore/findresults.asp
Positive Alternative Thinking Strategies (PATHS)	www.prevention.psu.edu/PATHS

Indicated Programs	Web Sites
Anger Coping Program	jlochman@gp.as.ua.edu
Early Risers: Skills for Success	Augus001@umn.edu (Dr. G. August)
Multisystemic Family Therapy (MST)	www.mstservices.com

Multicomponent Programs	Web Sites
Bullying Prevention Program	www.colorado.edu/csvp/blueprints/model/BPPmaterials.html
Strengthening Families Program	www.projectfamily.isbr.iastate.edu (project information)
	www.extension.iastate.edu/sf (web site for parents and youth)
Fast Track	www.fasttrackproject.org

Appendix III

DATING VIOLENCE PROGRAM EVALUATIONS

Citation	Program Goals	Participants	Purpose of Evaluation	Results
P. G. Jaffe, M. Sudermann, D. Reitzel, and S. M. Killip, 1992, "An Evaluation of a Secondary School Primary Prevention Program on Violence in Intimate Relationships," *Violence and Victims, 7,* pp. 126–146.	–Reach total school community w/message. –Increase knowledge about violence against women. –Address sexist attitudes. –Increase knowledge of warning signs. –Expand definition of abuse. –Provide information to community. –Develop antiviolence commitments in community.	Students in four London, Ontario high schools	Test positive effects of program in knowledge of violence against women, attitudes about dating violence, and intentions about dating violence.	–Overall positive. –Changes in knowledge and behavior on 22 of 48 items at posttest. –Negative changes on 8 items for boys.
F. LaVoie, L. Vezina, C. Piche, and M. Boivin, 1995, "Evaluation of a Prevention Program for Violence in Teen Dating Relationships," *Journal of Interpersonal Violence, 10,* pp. 516–524.	*Short-term program:* –Show students their control in dating process. –Teach them to identify and denounce control. *Long-term program:* –Establish dating partner rights. –Teach how to apply those rights to dating situation. –Teach that partners are responsible for mutual respect.	10th grade students in large Quebec City high school	–Measure short-term outcomes. –Compare effectiveness of short and long term. –Assess effects on boys compared to girls. –Assess effects on students who hold how much negative knowledge coming in.	–Significant differences in pre- and posttest scores. –Both programs improved attitudes. –Short-term yielded greatest improvements.

S. Avery-Leaf, M. Cascardi, K. D. O'Leary, and A. Cano, 1997, "Efficacy of a Dating Violence Prevention Program on Attitudes Justifying Aggression," *Journal of Adolescent Health, 21*, pp. 11–17.

Deliver an intervention that:

—Treats dating violence as multidetermined phenomenor.

—Is sensitive to gender inequity.

—Changes attitudes.

—Enhances skills.

—Recognizes that both genders may perpetrate.

Objectives to achieve goals:

—Promote equity in dating.

—Challenge attitudes toward violence.

—Identify constructive communication skills.

—Support victim resources.

—Teach help-seeking.

—Show alternatives to violence.

193 students in junior/senior level health classes in Long Island, New York

Do an evaluation with psychometrically sound instruments.

No significant changes in rates of aggression, victimization, and injury between treatment and control. More girls report being aggressive in last year. Significant pre- to postprogram scores found in treatment group on aggression attitudes.

M. J. MacGowan, 1997, "An Evaluation of a Dating Violence Prevention Program for Middle School Students," *Violence and Victims, 12*, pp. 223–235.

Help students recognize and understand violence and its causes. Help them understand violence and make decisions to end and avoid abuse.

All 6th- to 8th-grade students in a Dade County, Florida, middle school—440 students ages 11 to 16 years.

Test these hypotheses as compared to control: Treatment group will score higher on composite measure at posttest, treatment group composite scores will be higher at posttest, girls in treatment group will have higher scores compared to boys.

Treatment group scores were significantly higher than control group at posttest. Advanced students scored better than regular students. Male advanced made highest gains. Overall significant positive results for treatment groups compared to control. First two hypotheses were supported; third was not.

(*continued*)

Citation	Program Goals	Participants	Purpose of Evaluation	Results
V. A. Foshee, K. E. Baumann, X. B. Arrigia, and others, 1998, "An Evaluation of Safe Dates, an Adolescent Dating Violence Prevention Program." *American Journal of Public Health*, 88, pp. 45–50.	Primary and secondary prevention of dating violence through school and community-based activities.	8th- to 9th-grade students in 14 North Carolina public schools	Assess effectiveness of Safe Dates on the primary and secondary prevention of dating violence, assess effects of program on theoretically based mediating variables, and assess if program prevents dating violence.	Overall, students in treatment group reported less psychological abuse and less current perpetration than students in the control group.
N. Z. Hilton, G. T. Harris, M. E. Rice, T. S. Krans, and S. E. Vavigne, 1998, "Antiviolence Education in High Schools," *Journal of Interpersonal Violence*, 13, pp. 726–742.	Provide a controlled/consistent dating violence intervention in a school region, designed to increase knowledge of risk factors, provide information about the law, provide information for help-seeking, and look for backlash effects.	All grade 11 students in 4 high schools	Determine if knowledge increased and if attitudes positively changed. Hypothesized that program would result in backlash and positive changes would not be maintained.	Overall, promising results were found related to violence prevention without the expected backlash effect.
C. Pacifici, M. Stoolmiller, and C. Nelson, 2001, "Evaluating a Prevention Program for Teenagers on Sexual Coercion: A Differential Approach," *Journal of Clinical Psychology*, 69, pp. 552–559.	Change sexual attitudes about coercive sexual behavior and improve communication skills aimed at preventing or dealing with unwanted sexual advances.	458 high school students	Assess changes in sexual attitudes using sexual attitudes scales.	Students in the treatment group with initial coercive attitude scores at or above the mean benefited significantly more than students who had the same range of scores in the control group.
A. N. Weisz and B. Black, 2001, "Evaluating a Sexual Assault and Dating Program for Urban Youths," *Social Work Research*, 25, pp. 89–106.	–Increase knowledge about the extent and causes of dating violence, including knowledge of resources. –Increase intolerance of sexual assault and dating violence. –Increase appropriate prevention behavior	250 urban 7th graders in a charter middle school	Test the knowledge and attitudes of an intervention and comparison group.	The intervention group's scores improved significantly at follow-up while the control group reported no change.

Author Index

Subject Index ————————————————